A PANORAMA OF CHRISTIAN HYMNODY

Related books published by GIA Publications, Inc.

An English-Speaking Hymnal Guide
  Erik Routley
  Edited and Expanded by Peter W. Cutts

Let the People Sing: Hymn Tunes in Perspective
  Paul Westermeyer

G-6475

A Panorama of Christian Hymnody

Erik Routley

Edited and Expanded by
Paul A. Richardson

With a Foreword by Alan Luff

GIA Publications, Inc.
Chicago

GIA Publications, Inc.
7404 South Mason Avenue
Chicago, IL 60638
www.giamusic.com

© 2005, 1979 GIA Publications, Inc.

Printed in the United States of America
ISBN: 1-57999-352-4

First edition published 1979 by Liturgical Press, Collegeville, MN

Library of Congress Cataloging-in-Publication Data

Routley, Erik.
  A panorama of Christian hymnody / by Erik Routley.-- [2nd ed.] / edited and expanded by Paul A. Richardson.
    p. cm.
  Includes bibliographical references (p.   ) and indexes.
  ISBN 1-57999-352-4 (hardcover)
  1. Hymns, English. 2. Hymns, English--History and criticism. I. Richardson, Paul Akers, 1951- II. Title.
  BV459 .R75
  264'.23'09--dc22
                              2005040005

In Memoriam

Nathaniel Micklem, D.D.

preacher, teacher, scholar, wit

who guided my feet into this path

Table of Contents

Foreword:
A Personal Introduction

Those who worked with Erik Routley are now an aging group. After all, Erik would now be 87 had he lived. I worked alongside him with some awe and a certain amount of trembling. Not that he was not always delightful and inspiring company to be with, but he was formidable. I was drawn into the Dunblane Music Consultation when it was well established and had already published *Dunblane Praises 1*. Indeed, it was that publication that drew me to write to Erik, and to his replying by inviting me to attend. I was on the staff of Manchester Cathedral at the time, and he would address me with a certain mock deference as "Mr. Precentor." My sole claim to fame may eventually be that at one of the meetings of the consultation my humming and singing in the room next to his led Erik to give up writing a hymn tune to turn to write the words, which appeared as possibly the finest hymn of its kind in our generation—"All who love and serve your city," almost our first truly urban hymn.

It was Erik in his turn who, when the invited speaker on Welsh hymnody for the 1969 conference of the Hymn Society unexpectedly died, suggested that I, newly moved to North Wales, should be invited to take his place. At the meeting, after my paper, the treasurer, John Wilson, bore down on me and more or less insisted on my joining the society. The rest, as they say, is history, since I was soon on the committee, then to serving as secretary, chairman, and now as, I hope, the useful odd-job man, and vice executive president. A pleasure of my early years as secretary was to have regular dealings with Erik in his capacity as editor of the Society's *Bulletin*.

When we were working at Dunblane we, of course, had no idea that the "hymn explosion" would soon be upon us. Good new hymns are always treasured, but we became aware that Erik was squirreling away some promising new texts for a venture not connected with Dunblane. He had had conversations with the people at the new Coventry Cathedral, with the idea of editing a hymnbook for them that would be as new and exciting as their building. It was a mark of their ecumenical outlook that they turned to the Congregationalist Erik to mastermind this. Sadly, it came to nothing. On the other hand, by the beginning of the 1970s, when the book would have appeared, things were moving so fast in the world of hymnody that more than one hymnbook came to be quite out-of-date between its final editorial work and its appearance for use. Perhaps Erik was saved from this indignity.

Again, with the help of hindsight, it can seem astonishing that we at Dunblane had so little knowledge and so little perspective on what was going on more widely in the field of hymnody. For example, I remember that the name Albert Bayly came up. I had never heard of him, and Erik and Peter Cutts told me no more than that he was an older Congregationalist who had written a few quite interesting hymns. We account him now the first of the moderns, with a complete edition of his hymns at last available. In the 1960s we ought to have been making his groundbreaking hymns better known.

On my side I was reporting nothing from Manchester, although under my very nose the beginning of the Jubilate Hymns group was coming into being. It must have been in 1966 or 1967 that I was sharing a platform with Michael Baughen, at that time vicar of Holy Trinity Platt Fields, which is the Anglican Evangelical pastorate for the students of the university. He was telling Sunday school teachers of the Manchester diocese about his new book, *Youth Praise* (1966), while I was hoping to interest them in the Gelineau Psalms. He invited me to see *Youth Praise* in its native surroundings, and I for once escaped my Sunday evening duties in the cathedral to go to his vicarage, which was crammed with students, and where the singing was from *Youth Praise*, with the inevitable guitar accompaniment. We sang, I think, mainly Michael Baughen's own pieces. When I took the book away I was mainly impressed by the translations of sturdy popular pieces from the German, which I have never heard sung. What I missed both on that first evening, and when I looked through the book at leisure, was that at number 3 stands Timothy Dudley-Smith's "Tell out, my soul, the greatness of the Lord"; that there are two other texts by him; and that at number 10 is Michael Saward's "Christ triumphant, ever reigning," which, like Timothy's version of the *Magnificat*, has since traveled the world. I was probably looking more at the music than the words, and both are set to rather dull tunes by Michael Baughen. There soon followed *Youth Praise 2*, which contained more texts by Timothy Dudley-Smith, including another favorite, "Lord, for the years your love has kept and guided," which, in fairness it must be said, is still sung to a rather better Michael Baughen tune. The Anglican group that was working on the *Anglican Hymn Book* (1965) knew about Timothy Dudley-Smith and published three of his texts. In that book "Tell out my soul" was set to a distinguished but difficult tune by William Llewelyn—"takeoff" had not yet occurred. But in Dunblane we knew nothing of all this.

On the Congregationalist side, how could it be that both Erik and Peter seemed to be unaware of Fred Kaan, who was at the Pilgrim Church in Plymouth from 1963 until 1968, and on leaving there produced *Pilgrim Praise*, his collection of the hymns written Saturday by Saturday over those years to fulfill the needs of his preaching and the deficiencies of the hymn book? In a hymn-book committee less than ten years later, so Sam Young tells us, Erik had marked every one of those texts as deserving attention.

Erik knew that the *Hymns Ancient and Modern* folk were looking to produce a supplement to their book of 1950. He was quite convinced that they ("poor dears" he would call them) had hardly anything to go in it. We heard nothing from him about the Methodist supplement on which work

was going on in parallel, and for which Fred Pratt Green was writing his first texts—again, unknown to us in Dunblane—and where three of Fred Kaan's texts would appear. That appeared in 1969 as *Hymns and Songs*. In the same year, the proprietors of *Hymns Ancient and Modern* produced *100 Hymns for Today*, with five hymns from Kaan and one from Fred Pratt Green, and the hymn explosion was upon us. For the Anglicans the presiding genius (in both senses of the word) was Cyril Taylor. He had somehow inherited that gift of successive generations of editors of *Hymns Ancient and Modern* of wedding a tune to words. Some time later I was given a firsthand reminiscence of the meetings of the tunes committee of the Methodist *Hymns and Psalms* (1983), where discussion would range to and fro on the choice of a tune for a particular text, with Cyril sitting silent. He would then name a tune, and that was that; the committee would see that he was (again) right. He was certainly right when in 1969 he put WOODLANDS to "Tell out, my soul." To that tune it has gone round the world, however many other tunes have been composed to it since. Michael Saward had to wait a few more years for John Barnard to write his majestic GUITING POWER for "Christ triumphant." I suspect that Saward's words would never have gone so far without it. But from Dunblane, that was all in the future.

In the event the two final booklets from Dunblane, *New Songs for the Church*, books 1 and 2, which we had so much hoped would enliven the churches' repertory and fire debate about congregational song, were eclipsed by the two hymn-book supplements. We had contributed to the debate, particularly with *Dunblane Praises 1* and 2, but hardly at all to the repertory. We had not been as alone as we had thought.

Another authoritative voice on the *Hymns and Songs* committee was that of John Wilson. Most of those who could look on Erik on equal terms are no longer with us. John was certainly one. Erik would often be introduced as "the greatest hymnologist of our time," and he would equally often demur, saying that that accolade belonged to the English scholar John Wilson. When Erik moved to America, he and John began an almost weekly correspondence, largely on matters hymnological. John valued this hugely, and when Erik died, besides the personal loss, it was a great sadness to him that this exchange of letters had now come to an end. (Does this correspondence still exist somewhere, perhaps only in fragmented form? An edited version of even part of it, containing as it did the meeting of the two best minds in hymnody of their period, would be worth having.)

Erik respected John for his meticulous scholarship. This was not always Erik's best side. He had a phenomenal memory; he knew, for example, the numbers of the hymns in any number of books. But he could forget things as well, while assuming that the whole was in his grasp, and certainly details could go wrong. What John respected him for, and what made the original *Panorama* so valuable, were his broad vision and his huge enthusiasm for what hymns have been and what they can be in the life of the church and of the individual Christian. This is clear in that series of books published in the 1950s. Being confined to the house for a few months in 2003 gave me the chance to look at these again and to use two of them, *I'll Praise My Maker* (1951) and *Hymns and the Faith* (1955), as material for my daily meditation. I had not read them right through before. But *Hymns and Human Life* (1952) was my first book of hymnology, a present from a wise pastor and counselor who clearly intuited in what direction I might go, and *The Music of Christian Hymnody* (1957) opened my eyes to a line of study that I had not dreamed of.

Both these possibilities—the use of the hymn texts as prayer and the opening of minds to the study of hymnody—remain behind this new edition of *Panorama*, as of the companion volumes. Besides these important uses, the book did much, and will do more in this enlarged edition, to purify the stream of hymnody. For the currency of hymnody

has always been at risk of being debased. The quantity of hymns that has been written is huge. Some of them rise to the surface and become such as no hymn-book editor can ignore, even if it is thought necessary to amend and "improve" them— a process that can be traced with some of the hymns in *Panorama*. Some remarkably bad hymns cling on in popular use because hymns are so very powerful and the hymn that helps and moves at a particular time in our lives can stay with us for ever (and as I write this I wonder whether I really may mean "for ever," as we sing with the angels, or whatever it is that we do in heaven). But hymns can teach falsehoods and arouse false expectations. This can be seen in the simplest form perhaps in F. W. Faber's great hymn "Souls of men! why will ye scatter," where he promises:

> If our love were but more simple,
> we should take him at his word;
> and our lives would be all sunshine,
> in the sweetness of our Lord.

I think that many saintly souls would beg to differ, since that is not the way God has dealt with them. Another weakness is that many hymns do not take seriously St. Paul's words that "we walk by faith and not by sight." Whether we call this "the dark night of the soul" or no, this is the experience that is common and proper to most Christians, and hymns that lead us to expect otherwise are wrong, even though it is most certainly the role of the hymn to encourage and to point to the underlying truth and glory that is behind the quieter experience of our daily pilgrimage.

In his last book, *Christian Hymns Observed* (1982), Routley provided, in an astonishing sweep of commentary, an overview of where we have come from and where we were in the 1980s. Little has changed. His analysis of the situation in the popular hymn culture in his chapter "The Crisis of Denial" is fierce. While at the beginning of the chapter he has the aphorism "Christian eschatology insists that no mortal who says 'only the best is good enough' ever gets the last word" (pp. 83–84), later in the chapter he speaks of the "sinfully undemanding" hymnody with which so many congregations are being fed. Much of this is again the hymnody that people like to hear instead of the truth about God and about ourselves, which is the real territory of the hymn.

In Britain, at least, the sales of books that offer this kind of fare greatly exceed that of the mainline hymn books. To counter this we need to do whatever will bring our people to engage their minds more in what happens in worship. The original *Panorama* was an important tool in this, bringing as it did in its original version its author's intellectual rigor and warmth to the study of hymns. He was a special person at a rather special time, and who he was and where he came from lent its own particular flavor to the work. Now, a generation later, with the worth of his approach clearly validated, there is need of revision and expansion. Routley, always one to encourage the work of others, would delight to see his work given greater depth and breadth. These are precisely the qualities that this splendid new edition adds to the study of what is at the same time the most influential and the best-loved element in our common praise.

Alan Luff
Cardiff, Wales

Preface to the Second Edition

To be invited to take up the work of Erik Routley is a great honor—and one not accepted lightly. He once wrote that hymns are "delightful and dangerous things"; following in his footsteps is likewise inspiring and intimidating. I met Routley only once, but my knowledge of, appreciation for, and perspective on hymns and their use have been significantly shaped by his writing. In this I am hardly alone, for his influence on generations of scholars, writers, and editors has been immense.

In his introduction to the first edition, Routley established three purposes for this *Panorama*: to sustain "the godly and sensible pleasure of reading hymns"; to support the teaching of hymnology; and to stimulate the editors of hymnals. While in the intervening years other writers have greatly enriched the resources that might enable all these noble aims, Routley's own approach remains of such value as to prompt its extension in a new edition, still directed toward these goals.

Though I have adopted much of Routley's purpose and approach, I cannot claim to have duplicated his perspective, for our surveys have taken place in different places and times. Routley wrote *Panorama* after he had come to teach hymnology in the United States, and he expressed gratitude for the opportunity to invest himself in that work. Not surprisingly, however, he wrote from a British perspective—though certainly with an awareness of and insatiable curiosity about hymnody everywhere. As an American living in the early years of the twenty-first century, I have written from my own distinctive background and for an audience whose experience of congregational song is different from that of the first edition's readers. We are heirs to what has gone before, but what we encounter in worship and study has been greatly expanded by many of the same forces that have caused the often-noted shrinkage of our world. The danger of our situation is the potential loss of the intellectual and devotional heritage recounted by Routley.

In the survey of any field, distance is a critical influence on perspective. The closer a writer is to the material, the less accurate judgments are likely to be, for trends are difficult to gauge at close range, and no individual's estimate can substitute for the wisdom of the whole church at worship. For example, only one of the hymns for children in chapter 22 achieved broad use, and none of the others would likely be seen now as "significant." In selecting examples for chapter 23, considering material with which he was intimately acquainted, Routley chose thirty-four texts, nine of which were used widely enough at the time of his writing to be included in the companion volume, *An English-Speaking Hymnal Guide*. Seventeen—exactly half—now qualify according to these same principles as applied in Peter Cutts's revision of that book. Of course, what was in favor has changed with the passing of time, and these groups, though overlapping, are not congruent.

The first edition of this work, published in 1979, traced the development of hymnody as used in the English-speaking church through 1975, encompassing the first phases of what has come to be known as the "hymn explosion." This edition adds four chapters to extend the collection of texts and accompanying narrative through 2000. That these chapters are large is a reflection of the extensive developments in hymn writing during this quarter century. That is, of course, the principal reason for a new edition.

These new chapters take their trajectory from that established by Routley in their geographical grouping, but they do so without making the distinctions of type that he employed. There are no separate sections of hymns by women, for children, or in folk style. One of the changes in hymn writing, use, and appreciation over this quarter century has been the blurring of categories. Maintaining separate treatments would have required setting separate standards, which not only has inherent difficulties but is complicated by what we have learned from congregational song in other parts of the world. To the extent that different styles still exist, it must be noted that some accomplished hymnists have written across their boundaries. This phenomenon can be observed even before considering idioms—African, Asian, Taizé, commercial/pop—that eschew literary expansiveness, but that often have power through the combination of simplicity, repetition, and improvisation, and that cannot be fairly represented on the printed page.

"Folk" style, as Routley identified it, has largely been merged, musically, with popular/commercial elements and now includes some liturgical texts. Many topics and concerns that were once the province of such hymnody because they were considered to be beyond the bounds of liturgical song are now extensively addressed by "mainstream" writers, while folk/pop/commercial congregational song has become, in many cases and in its own way, textually traditional and often trite. In the mainstream, there is greater inclusion of ballads or narrative texts reflecting the interests of preachers, teachers, and worshipers in "story," both biblical and personal. Just as theology has given greater attention to narrative forms, hymns have adopted varied approaches to draw worshipers into the biblical story.

A few texts have been added to the chapters from the first edition. Some illustrate recent trends in translation, while others demonstrate the continuing efforts of recent writers to deal with changing views about language in worship. In many instances in which stanzas were omitted in the first edition, complete versions of texts have been supplied. In the new chapters, there has been a bit of reaching back for significant texts that, for whatever reason, Routley did not include.

This revision has deleted a few elements that made the first edition useful in its own time, but that would, if retained, immediately date this new version. Gone are the brief bibliographies that accompanied a few chapters, the index to hymnals, and the biographical appendix. In compensation for this last omission, full names and dates of birth and death have been added to the index of authors and translators. (The excitement of discovering writers in non-Western cultures has sometimes been matched by the frustration of attempts to locate even basic biographical information about them.) Cross-references to the new edition of *An English-Speaking Hymnal Guide* are made in the Index of First Lines of Hymns rather than in the body of the text.

Some aspects of style, such as spelling, punctuation, and abbreviation, have been altered to reflect contemporary practice in the United States. A few details of content have been revised to incorporate recent scholarship or to correct typographical errors. Full names of individuals are provided at their first appearance in a chapter. A more significant change regards the display of the texts themselves and of the information that accompanies them. Each item is now identified by a unique number and/or letter. "Revised" is used to indicate changes by an author; "altered" indicates emendation by another hand. For each item under copyright, the owner is identified following the text; detailed information is provided in the List of Copyright Holders.

A more substantial matter, that of the titles appearing about the texts, has also been addressed—though imperfectly. In the first edition, some of these headings were from the authors; some were from secondary sources (including topical labels supplied by Julian's *Dictionary*); and some were created by Routley. Where it could be determined that the hymn writer provided a particular title, it is presented. Where it could be verified that the author used no title, the incipit is employed as a heading. Where there was no clear evidence for making a change, the title from the first edition is left in place.

There has been no desire in any of this editing to alter Routley's insights, his opinions, or the memorable cadences of his writing. Thus, even where my opinion might differ (as in chapter 19), I have refrained from expressing a competing or even complementary view.

I am grateful to many persons who have contributed in various ways to this project. First among these are the hymn writers and translators whose work, in service to the church, has made this new edition desirable and necessary. A large number of them have been gracious in responding to questions about dates, editions, and other matters.

Close behind are those writers of hymnal companions, handbooks, and reference works who have traced details and verified stories to promote greater understanding of what we sing. Outstanding among these, in their published scholarship and in their personal assistance, have been Raymond Glover (*The Hymnal 1982 Companion*), David Goodall (*Companion to Rejoice and Sing* and its on-line *Enchiridion*), Alan Luff (*HymnQuest*), Marilyn Kay Stulken (*Hymnal Companion to the Lutheran Book of Worship* and, with Cathy Salika, *Hymnal Companion to Worship—Third Edition*), and Carlton Young (*Companion to the United Methodist Hymnal*).

Numerous other scholars and publishers have responded generously to questions in their areas of expertise. These include John Ambrose, George Black, Melva Costen, Carl Daw, Hedda Durnbaugh, Colin Gibson, Michael Hawn, Donald Hustad, I-to Loh, Loretta Manzara, Graham Maule, John Murray, David Schaap, George Shorney, Dieter Trautwein, and Nancy Wicklund.

Four friends contributed their linguistic skills to review texts in languages other than English. In addition to his other consultation, the late George Black examined the French texts; Harry and Margaret Eskew, the German hymns; and Randy Todd, those in Latin.

Brandi Stanton, a hymnology student at Samford University, invested numerous hours in entering the texts in the added chapters. The staff of Samford University's Davis Library—particularly those handling interlibrary loans—have been of great assistance in securing resources. Dean Milburn Price has provided unflagging encouragement.

I am indebted to Peter Cutts, revisor of *An English-Speaking Hymnal Guide*, and Paul Westermeyer, author of *Let the People Sing: Hymn Tunes in Perspective* (the successor to Routley's *Music of Christian Hymns*), for sharing their work and their wisdom.

I am particularly grateful to Bob Batastini, who provided this opportunity to learn about and contribute to the discipline of hymnology—for which we share a passion. He had the vision for this undertaking, the desire that it be done well, the patience to enable this to be possible, and, at every point, a positive word. His colleagues at GIA have been dauntless in bringing this complex work to fruition. Neil Borgstrom's careful editing and insightful questioning have enabled the work of authors, translators, and editors to be presented with integrity. Tim Redmon and Michael Boschert have traced copyrights and secured permissions. The skills of Robert M. Sacha and Paul Burrucker, in book design and layout, respectively, are everywhere in evidence. Innumerable details have been handled by editorial assistants Cathy Kennerk, Vicki Krstansky, and Clarence Reiels.

Many authors, agents, and publishers have granted permission for the reproduction of material under their copyright so that this volume could provide a more complete account of recent hymnody. I am grateful for their generosity and hope that their kindness will be rewarded by widespread interest in this new material.

I would be remiss if I did not acknowledge my debt to Erik Routley for writing numerous works, including *Panorama*. The hours spent reading, rereading, and editing this book have been a marvelous education and have truly provided the "godly and sensible pleasure" he intended.

Finally, I express deepest thanks to my wife, Susan, and my children, Robert and Rachel. They have granted long hours away from being partner and parent, while continually expressing interest in and support for this project, knowing that my love for the discipline does not diminish my love for my family. In gratitude, I dedicate my work to them.

Paul A. Richardson
Samford University
Birmingham, Alabama

Preface to the First Edition

This book has a threefold purpose; and it is right to say that two, at least, of these purposes were aroused in my mind by the privilege I have recently been granted, of teaching the study of hymns in two institutions in America.

The first purpose of the book is to provide pleasure, a pleasure which I discover to be now wholly hidden from those friends in America whom I admire and love so much as to wish to share it with them. That is the godly and sensible pleasure of *reading* hymns. I do not mean reading them communally in church, which strikes me as a miserable substitute for that cheerful song which is now the delight of all Christian communions. I mean reading them in solitude, reading them as lyric poetry. When one does this, their crudities and roughness, which any literary critic must observe, which the best lover of hymns must admit, and which some Christians (among them my revered C. S. Lewis) have openly despised, become softened by the associations of communal song which these texts must inevitably carry. There will be a tune in the reader's mind; if there is not, he is likely, especially in America, to have a music copy about the house. But when I remember how in my own youth, say thirty years back, men and women in so many branches of the church in England, my home country, would read their hymnals as eagerly and regularly as they read their Bibles, and would, if whipped off to hospital, reach for the hymn book as well as the Bible, I simply grieve to think that this particular pleasure and religious nourishment is withheld from so many or ignored by so many in these later days.

The reason for that in my own country is simple laziness. In America it is less blameworthy, at least in the innocent reader. It is now the custom in America to print all hymnals with the texts interlined between the music staves. The advantages of this are the certain one of saving paper (it is indeed more economical) and the dubious one of making hymns easier to sing; in respect of which I am bound to say that in the ordinary congregation I have not detected any greater readiness in America than in my own country to sing unfamiliar tunes, which is what makes me think that second advantage doubtful. Being, however, resigned to the inevitable continuance of a practice which makes it impossible to read the text as it should be read, I thought it right here to provide an anthology of hymn texts set out, for the most part, in the manner in which their authors wrote them. Then, I thought, my reader can have the best of both worlds: a full music edition for worship, or for musical pleasure at home, and this book for his more intimate meditation.

Now I am aware, and what I said above implies, that a hymn without its tune is incomplete. And just as it is unwise to use literature above a certain level of greatness as the libretto of an opera (as Sir Donald Tovey once pointed out), so there is a level beyond which literature cannot rise if it is to be good hymnody. The most obvious restraint on poetic inspiration and technique is the need, in a hymn, to use regular stresses, which gives its text, in the reading, a sing-song monotony which no master of poetry would tolerate in his verse for a moment. Indeed, it is a very clear necessity in the writing of large-scale poetry that the rhythm should be injected with surprise and vitality precisely by the conflict between the regular meter which is the framework and the more natural flow of the words which are disciplined but, in a true poet's hands, never constricted by that framework. Similarly, in great poetry the sense of a sentence will not end with the end of a line; it is, indeed, important that it should not always do so. In a hymn, it must. A "run-on" from line to line, especially where there is an important natural break in the music, provides discomfort in singing. (On this matter see further the note on hymn 45 in chapter 4).

Probably it is less necessary to warn the reader against being too impatient with the "in-group" language, mythology, and thought-forms of

Evangelical hymnody. It is perfectly true that during one period (that between Watts and Bridges) a certain vocabulary was understood to have significance for author and reader who were connected by the language of the Bible. The pervasive "blood," the Wesleyan "interest," the whole complex of atonement theology which could be conveyed to pious singers by the use of certain cue words is part of a system towards which a modern reader must exercise imaginative forbearance, especially when he has not a tune to carry him through these rough places. But it is worth persevering.

Another pleasure the reader may perhaps receive with gratitude (that is my hope) is that of being able now and then to let an author talk himself out. Our usual conventions make it necessary to limit the length of hymns to something between twelve and, at the most, forty lines. Modern hymn writers know this and write accordingly. Not so always the classical writers, whose ecstasy and energy might carry them much farther. It is interesting to notice that Isaac Watts very rarely goes beyond the demands of reasonable prudence, though in one hymn, which we have included here, he does run to seventy-two lines; and, given the right amount of goodwill, would any reader really wish it shorter, however legitimate the demand of a singer would be? Is there not some satisfaction in being able to see the whole delectable autobiographical length of Addison's "Gratitude" (47), or in being able to relax into the expansive joy of Nicolai's *Wie schön leuchtet* (188A)? To follow Charles Wesley through the eighty-four agonized, yet in the end triumphant, lines of "Wrestling Jacob" (62), even though a perfectly good 24-line hymn in congregational use can be made out of it, is something of a privilege, especially if one has one's Bible open at Genesis 32. In a few cases the restoration of an original text bespeaks a powerful, even indignant, conviction in your editor; for I do regard it as something of a crime to omit, as hymnals so often do, the fourth

stanza of "When I survey the wondrous cross"; and I equally think it no bad thing for any who are familiar with "Our God, our help in ages past"(44) in the significantly emasculated version beginning "O God . . ." to read the whole of that section of Watts' Psalm 90, and feel again the overpowering solemnity of that sometimes overused piece; or, in another mood, to enjoy the picturesque stanzas of "Jesus shall reign" (43) that are now never sung (even if my American friends think Watts somewhat insular in confining his picture of western civilization to Europe).

My second purpose in furnishing this book has also something to do with America. In this blessed land, the subject of hymnology is taught. (It is not, in the length and breadth of Britain, unless perhaps it appears on the occasional Scottish curriculum). My gratitude to the USA owes much to its having permitted me to teach the subject here. Now this is very difficult if the only textbook you have is the hymnal of the denomination favored by the teaching institution. It's not likely that the seminary chapel will have more than one, or at most two, books. It will surely be handy for an instructor and his or her pupils to have, within the covers of a single volume, a conspectus of the literature of hymnody. Reference can always be made to the standard hymnals, and of course, such references will have to be made in respect of tunes. And (copyright materials excepted) there is always the friendly Xerox machine to provide copies of any noncopyright material you need that I have omitted.

But it is with that in mind that I have arranged the material in the form you will find. When the book is used for other purposes, its indexes will help the reader to handle it as he wishes; but for teaching purposes, one needs to survey the story of hymnody from the viewpoint on which twentieth-century Americans or Britishers inevitably stand. Hymnody of our kind begins with Luther, is submerged under metrical psalmody, and emerges again with Watts. The peculiar glories of seventeenth-century poetry were very largely unknown to English-speaking hymn singers before Robert Bridges and Percy Dearmer brought them to our notice at the beginning of the twentieth century. So George Herbert comes later than he would appear in an ordinary poetry anthology. Similarly, hymns from the Latin and from the German flooded into the English books in the later nineteenth century, ancient though many of them are; and therefore (excepting Luther, who must clearly have his place right at the beginning) that is where you find them here. In my own teaching, anyhow, that is the line I take. Anybody can take a different one and use this book equally well.

The third person I have my eye on is the hymnal editor. I have observed a tendency lately among editors to receive into any newly projected hymnal a text and tune as what we may call a package deal; or, to use a more elegant metaphor, to regard marriages between texts and tunes as made in heaven and indissoluble. Whether I am acting on the principle that hymnody moves in a permissive society, or whether on the higher principle that there is no marrying or giving in marriage in heaven, I leave it to a psychoanalyst to determine; but I know for sure that some marriages between texts and tunes, though of long standing, are calamitous (the most scandalous of all being that commonly honored in America in respect of "When I survey the wondrous cross"). I think editors may well be assisted, if they do not care to examine books of English provenance that use a different printing format, by having a collection of texts to study; this assistance may come through their being able simply to judge the words without having to disentangle them from a music stave, or through their being the more readily able to find better tunes for those ineptly paired at present, or by having a more complete text to select from than the standard hymnals provide.

I do have to say, however, that this book should not be regarded as a pedantically faithful presentation of original spellings and punctuations. Most of the time there is no advantage in being

anything else; but for one thing, I wish my devotional reader to have a text that he or she can easily read, and therefore I have, with one or two exceptions, modernized the spelling; for another, the use of capitals in such authors as Watts is, to a modern eye, distracting, and I have usually followed modern customs there (but not in the reprinting of his very first hymn, which I thought we might see exactly as he wrote it); for a third, I happen to think that the old custom of beginning every line of poetry with a capital is, for these purposes, over ponderous, and that it has the special disadvantage of making it difficult to see when, as occasionally happens, the syntax runs through the end of a stanza, as it does at stanzas 4–5 of "Jesus shall reign" (43). For ease of reading, I have followed a uniform system except in those few places where for a special reason I reproduced an older style.

In respect of the two greatest sources, any editor or interested reader will find punctilious exactitude wholly satisfied in Dr. Selma Bishop's great work on *Isaac Watts: Hymns and Spiritual Songs*, and in F. W. Baker's no less important study, *Representative Verse of Charles Wesley*. But in any case an editor will go as near as he can to the original before deciding what emendations will be prudent. In two cases I have refused to reproduce the original; that is where the word "bowels" is so often written by the classicals for "mercies" and where "worms" represents "creatures of no importance." Nobody now is going to feel underprivileged in being deprived of a few words which have become grotesque in ways which their original users could not have foreseen. Any editor who wishes to restore these is welcome, but not with help from me.

One final word. This, of course, is not a hymnal. It is a "panorama of hymnody." No reader will be so ill-advised as to think that I include here all the hymns I love best, or that I approve, for public worship, of everything I have put in. That is far from being the case. A panorama will include some disagreeable sights, the world being what it is. No reader will find here everything he hoped for, any more than I do. I could easily have included forty great pieces of Watts, and as many of Wesley, and it is gratifying to have to admit that I could have found many more pieces from the period 1965–1975 than I have found room for. However, I do claim that a tolerable degree of justice has been achieved for all legitimate forms of hymnody (at least for all that can be transcribed without music and still make sense).

Having thus assigned my book to the categories of *uti* and *frui* (of usefulness and enjoyment) I leave it in the hope that it may appear on some bedside tables, and on some academic desks, and perhaps do something towards recovering for the hymn writer that long-lost claim to be, in a humble form, a man of letters.

Erik Routley
Princeton, New Jersey

Chapter 1:
Martin Luther and the
Anabaptists (1–6)

Hymnody as it is now understood throughout Christendom began with Martin Luther—or so it is convenient to say. That statement must at once be qualified by an historical maxim which is irrefutable in whatever field one chooses to apply it. This is that whenever popular belief ascribes the inception of some great movement to any given person, that person will always be found to be not the first, not often even the second, to express the ideas, affect the style, or long for the achievement which is attributed to the famous "Founder." The Reformation itself we regard as owed to Luther; but how many persons, groups, and movements looked in that direction, without succeeding in making it a continent-wide operation, for two hundred years before Luther, as tradition has it, nailed up his Theses? English hymnody, we shall later observe, regards its founder as Isaac Watts. Thirty years before his time, the Baptist Benjamin Keach was writing freely-composed hymns, though nobody now sings them. The Oxford Movement we say was founded by John Keble, and we judge its greatest mind to have been John Henry Newman. But a look at the content of Keble's hymns, all written before the Movement started, and at the developing thought in a few small groups before it became a movement, even a look at the thought of John Wesley in his earliest days of ministry, will indicate not only that this movement had roots in a remoter past, but that many of the suppositions we entertain about it need to be modified if we take into account the earlier utterances of its own leading figures, especially the hymns of Keble. The renaissance of English church music, especially of hymnody, we properly attribute to Percy Dearmer and Ralph Vaughan Williams in *The English Hymnal* of 1906; but the things they there said with such emphasis and success had already been said by George Ratcliffe Woodward in his early carol collections from 1894 onwards and by Robert Bridges in his *Yattendon Hymnal* of 1899. What it is necessary to say of any "founder" is that he, influenced by certain obscurer and more local figures and movements, or responding to needs already made known at that lower level, made an achievement of what before his time was a dream, or an eccentricity, or a hope. It was so with Luther and hymnody.

What we mean when we ascribe this historical role to Luther is that it was he who successfully propagated the idea that the communal singing of Christian songs could be an integral part of public worship. People had plenty of religious songs before his time; but not at the Mass, not at the center of worship, and not songs known all over Europe. The story of the carols, the *Laudi spirituali*, and the songs of pre-Reformation dissenting groups is a story of what happened outside the church, or far from the church's liturgical center, and mostly also of what happened locally. It is quite different from the story that begins with Luther.

It will be familiar to any reader that there was a medieval hymnody, a great store of Latin texts (to which at a later stage we shall attend), many of which in translation are familiar to the English-speaking world. But these were for the monastic choirs to sing, not for the congregation; and the style of music to which they were set (plainsong) was kept very carefully clear of secular associations and influences.

Not but what Luther's hymnody was influenced by these medieval songs; often he rewrote a plainsong tune in a style which he reckoned ordinary people could easily sing, and, as we see with our 1, more than once he recast a medieval text to transform it into material suitable for a congregation to use as a song of its faith.

The best source for the study of Luther's own hymns is volume 53 of the Augsburg edition of Luther's *Works*, where all thirty-seven of them, texts and music, are set out (the texts in the translation of George Macdonald). The very first hymn there given, *"Ein neues Lied,"* provides a great surprise and establishes a great principle. The surprise is in its content, for it is a pugnacious song celebrating the deaths of two early Reformation martyrs and trouncing their detractors. It is a polemical ballad of the most red-blooded kind, very little like the dogmatic style which we usually associate with Luther. The principle established is in his using for the tune a melody based on the form of the troubadour and Minnesinger songs, the court music, or, you might almost say, "classical music" of his time. The idea that Luther used "popular tunes," insofar as it is put about to give credibility to the modern use of vulgar music, should at once be disposed of. The sources of the Luther tunes are either the monastic plainsong or the kind of music the aristocracy enjoyed.

It is difficult to resist the theory—though it has never been officially sanctioned by scholars—that Luther's hymn writing began with a quite overt imitation of these aristocratic ballads, and that, as it were, finding he had a gift for this kind of thing, he then turned to what one is obliged to call more serious writing; at least, to matters of more enduring importance. Our 1 through 4 give a reasonable conspectus of his various styles: the adapted and developed medieval sequence at 1; the metricized and Christianized psalm at 2 (which reminds us that psalmody was the almost invariable Christian praise at the Mass during the Middle Ages); the domestic Christmas carol at 3; and the famous battle song at 4. These show Luther's versatility in providing people with Christian songs. Dogma and drama are unusually combined in his forceful texts. Notice how in 1 the drama in the old sequence (the conversation with Mary) is replaced by the spiritual drama of the Eucharist, and how, on the other hand, the pivotal and arresting phrase "*Mors et vita duello conflixere mirando*" is gratefully retained. Note also how New Testament Scriptures are used to illuminate Psalm 130 in 2 in a manner almost foreshadowing Isaac Watts. Contrast these immensities with the homeliness of 3, written for his own family with a

child playing the part of the angel, the other children joining in the heavenly chorus, and everybody singing the final doxology. In any company, of course, 4 is unique. Taking its opening lines from Psalm 46, it summons the Reformed world to arms against the oppressions of those Establishment figures who were mustering all their forces to stop what had by this date (about 1528) become a menace they could no longer ignore. Everybody now sings this song as a hymn of spiritual confidence, including modern Catholics; but its original meaning is quite unquestionable. Still, it has inspired so many fine translators that it has now gone quite beyond Luther's control.

A great hymn writer tends to stifle the next generation. Charles Wesley did so almost completely, and there is hardly a Methodist hymn of any importance to be found before 1900. (Watts, that other pioneer, did not have this effect; others at once, and successfully, imitated and developed his style. We cannot here stop to ask why this was, but it is an interesting and important point of difference between him and the Wesleys.) By the same token, there is not much text-writing in the Lutheran church for a generation after Luther's death. We shall not come back to the Lutherans until we reach 188.

But that other stream of the Reformation, the radical Anabaptists, produced a style of hymnody with which only Luther's very first hymn has much in common. Anabaptist hymnody mostly has not turned out to be exportable; those most faithful to this tradition today are the conservative branches of the Mennonites in the USA, among whom the *Ausbund*, last revised in 1622, is still in use. This is a collection of hymns in German, many of which are historical songs recounting the heroic witness of vintage Anabaptists under persecution, and it is nothing out of the way for one of these to run as far as twenty stanzas. One or two exceed thirty. Anabaptism, in the sixteenth century, was a faith which Luther neither understood nor wanted to understand; his special facility in making converts from the upper reaches of society was the opposite of their homespun, common-man approach. And their ballads were just such songs as would appeal to groups of people who proudly claimed, as did Paul writing to Corinth, that their ranks number "not many wise men after the flesh, not many mighty, not many noble" which was really a claim that Luther could never have made. Our 5 is a short selection made for the American *Mennonite Hymnal* (1969) from a 27-stanza original and has the characteristic "vintage" Anabaptist emphasis on personal suffering and sacrifice. The first official *Ausbund* appeared in 1583, and this was 11 in that book. Our 6, which is translated complete and is unusually brief, is 131 in that book, being part of a supplement added in 1622. Its translator is the eminent English Baptist historian Dr. Ernest Payne, and this is the only Anabaptist hymn known to Britishers. Some idea of the expansive manner of most Anabaptist hymns will be gathered from the fact that the present edition of the *Ausbund*, including the 1622 additions, uses 812 pages to print 140 pieces (texts only).

It will be the end of the sixteenth century, and our chapter 13, before we can again take up the tale of mainstream German hymnody.

I

A Song of Praise, "Christ ist erstanden," Improved

A.

Christ lag in Todesbanden,
    für unsre Sünd gegeben,
der ist wieder erstanden
    und hat uns bracht das Leben.
Des wir sollen fröhlich sein,
Gott loben and dankbar sein
    und singen Halleluja,
        Halleluja.

Den Tod neimand zwingen konnt
    bei allen Menschenkindern;
das macht' alles unsre Sünd,
    kein Unschuld war zu finden.
Davon kam der Tod so bald
und nahm über uns Gewalt,
    heilt uns in sein'm Reich gefangen.
        Halleluja.

Jesus Christus, Gottes Sohn,
    an unser Statt ist kommen
und hat die Sünd abgetan,
    damit dem Tod genommen
all sein Recht und sein Gewalt;
da bleibt nichts denn Tods Gestalt,
    den Stachel hat er verloren.
        Halleluja.

Es war ein wunderlich Krieg,
    da Tod und Leben rungen;
das Leben behielt den Sieg,
    es hat den Tod verschlungen.
Die Schrift hat verkündet das,
wie ein Tod den andern fraß,
    ein Spott aus dem Tod ist worden.
        Halleluja.

Hier ist das recht Osterlamm,
    davon wir sollen leben,
das ist an des Kreuzes Stamm
    in heißer Lieb gegeben.
Des Blut zeichnet unsre Tür,
das hält der Glaub dem Tod für,
    der Würger kann uns nicht rühren.
        Halleluja.

So feiern wir das hoh Fest
    mit Herzensfreud und Wonne,
das uns der Herr scheinen läßt.
    Er ist selber die Sonne,
der durch seiner Gnaden Glanz
erleucht' unsre Herzen ganz;
    der Sünden Nacht ist vergangen.
        Halleluja.

Wir essen und leben wohl,
    zum süßen Brot geladen;
der alte Sauerteig nicht soll
    sein bei dem Wort der Gnaden.
Christus will die Kost uns sein
und speisen die Seel allein;
    der Glaub will keins andern leben.
        Halleluja.

Martin Luther
based on *"Christ ist erstanden,"* which is, in turn,
based on *"Victimae paschali laudes"*
Enchiridion, 1524

B.

Christ Jesus lay in death's strong bands
    for our offenses given;
but now at God's right hand he stands
    and brings us light from heaven.
Wherefore let us joyful be
and sing to God right thankfully
    loud songs of Hallelujah!
        Hallelujah!

No son of man could conquer death,
    such mischief sin had wrought us,
for innocence dwelt not on earth,
    and therefore death had brought us
into thraldom from of old
and ever grew more strong and bold
    and kept us in his bondage.
        Hallelujah!

But Jesus Christ, God's only Son,
    to our low state descended.
The cause of death he has undone,
    his power forever ended.
Ruined all his right and claim
and left him nothing but the name,
    his sting is lost forever.
        Hallelujah!

It was a strange and dreadful strife
    when life and death contended;
the victory remained with life,
    the reign of death was ended;
stripped of power, no more he reigns,
an empty form alone remains;
    his sting is lost for ever.
        Hallelujah!

Here the true Paschal Lamb we see,
    whom God so freely gave us;
he died on the accursed tree—
    so strong his love!—to save us.
See, his blood doth mark our door;
faith points to it, death passes o'er,
    and Satan cannot harm us.
        Hallelujah!

So let us keep the festival
    whereto the Lord invites us;
Christ is himself the joy of all,
    the sun that warms and lights us;
by his grace he doth impart
eternal sunshine to the heart;
    the night of sin is ended.
        Hallelujah!

Then let us feast this Easter day
 on the true Bread of heaven.
The word of grace hath purged away
 the old and wicked leaven.   (1 Cor. 5:6–8)
Christ alone our souls will feed,
he is our meat and drink indeed,
 faith lives upon no other.
  Hallelujah!

translated, Richard Massie, 1854, altered
Martin Luther's *Spiritual Songs*, 1854
The usual form of the text, comprising stanzas 1, 4, 6, and 7,
was prepared for *Church Hymns*, 1871.

C. Easter sequence

Victimae paschali laudes
immolent Christiani.

Agnus redemit oves;
Christus innocens Patri
reconciliavit peccatores.

Mors et vita duello
conflixere mirando;
dux vitae mortuus regnat vivus.

"Dic nobis, Maria,
quid vidisti in via?"

"Sepulchrum Christi viventis,
et gloriam vidi resurgentis;

angelicos testes,
sudarium et vestes.

Surrexit Christus, spes mea,
praecedet suos in Galilaeam."

Credendum est magis soli
Mariae veraci,
quam Judaeorum turbae fallaci.

Scimus Christum surrexisse
ex mortuis vere.
Tu nobis, victor Rex, miserere.

attributed to Wipo of Burgandy

D.

Christians, to the Paschal Victim
offer your thankful praises!

A Lamb the sheep redeemeth:
Christ, who only is sinless,
reconcileth sinners to the Father;

death and life have contended
in that combat stupendous:
The Prince of Life, who died, reigns immortal.

Speak, Mary, declaring
what thou sawest wayfaring:

"The tomb of Christ, who is living,
the glory of Jesu's resurrection:

Bright angels attesting,
the shroud and napkin resting.

Yea, Christ my hope is arisen:
To Galilee he goes before you."

Happy they who bear the witness
Mary's word believing
above the tales of Jewry deceiving.

Christ indeed from death is risen,
our new life obtaining.
Have mercy, victor King, ever reigning!

composite translation, *The English Hymnal*, 1906
based on *Antiphoner and Grail*, 1880

2
Psalm 130

A.

Aus tiefer Not schrei ich zu dir,
    Herr Gott, erhör mein Rufen.
Dein gnädig Ohren kehr zu mir
    und meiner Bitt sie öffen;
denn so du willst das sehen an,
was Sünd und Unrecht ist getan,
    wer kann, Herr, vor dir bleiben?

Bei dir gilt nichts denn Gnad und Gunst,
    die Sünde zu vergeben;
es ist doch unser Tun umsonst
    auch in dem besten Leben.
Vor dir niemand sich rühmen kann,
des muß dich fürchten jedermann
    und deiner Gnade leben.

Darum auf Gott will hoffen ich,
    auf mein Verdienst nicht bauen;
auf ihn mein Herz soll laßen sich
    und seiner Güte trauen,
die mir zusagt sein wertes Wort;
das ist mein Trost und treuer Hort,
    des will ich allzeit harren.

Und ob es währt bis in die Nacht
    und wieder an den Morgen,
doch soll mein Herz an Gottes Macht
    verzweifeln nicht noch sorgen.
So tu Israel rechter Art,
der aus dem Geist erzeuget ward,
    und seines Gotts erharre.

Ob bei uns ist der Sünden viel,
    bei Gott ist viel mehr Gnade;
sein Hand zu helfen hat kein Ziel,
    wie groß auch sei der Schade.
Er ist allein der gute Hirt,
der Israel erlösen wird
    aus seinen Sünden allen.

Martin Luther, 1523
Geystliche gesangk Buchleyn, 1524
a 4-stanza version had appeared in *Etlich Christlich Lider*, 1524

B.

From depths of woe I raise to thee
    the voice of lamentation;
Lord, turn a gracious ear to me
    and hear my supplication.
If thou shouldst be extreme to mark
each secret sin and misdeed dark,
    O who could stand before thee?

To wash away the crimson stain,
    grace, grace alone availeth;
our works, alas! are all in vain;
    in much the best life faileth:
no man can glory in thy sight,
all must alike confess thy might
    and live alone by mercy.

Therefore my trust is in the Lord,
    and not in mine own merit;
on him my soul shall rest: his word
    upholds my fainting spirit:
his promised mercy is my fort,
my comfort and my sweet support;
    I wait for it with patience.

What though I wait the livelong night,
 and till the dawn appeareth,
my heart still trusteth in his might;
 it doubteth not nor feareth:
so let the Israelite in heart,
born of the Spirit, do his part   (John 1:47)
 and wait till God appeareth.

Although our sin is great indeed,
 God's mercies far exceed it;
his hand can give the help we need,
 however much we need it:
he is the Shepherd of the sheep
who Israel doth guard and keep,   (Ps. 80:1)
 and shall from sin redeem him.

translated, Richard Massie
Martin Luther's Spiritual Songs, 1854

C.

Out of the depths I cry to you;
 O Father, hear me calling.
Incline your ear to my distress
 in spite of my rebelling.
Do not regard my sinful deeds.
Send me the grace my spirit needs;
 without it I am nothing.

All things you send are full of grace;
 you crown our lives with favor.
All our good works are done in vain
 without our Lord and Savior.
We praise the God who gives us faith
and saves us from the grip of death;
 our lives are in his keeping.

It is in God that we shall hope,
 and not in our own merit.
We rest our fears in his good Word
 and trust his Holy Spirit.
His promise keeps us strong and sure;
we trust the holy signature
 inscribed upon our temples.

My soul is waiting for the Lord
 as one who longs for morning;
no watcher waits with greater hope
 than I for his returning.
I hope as Israel in the Lord;
he sends redemption through his Word.
 We praise him for his mercy.

translated, Gracia Grindal, 1975
Lutheran Book of Worship, 1978
© 1978, Augsburg Fortress Press

3
The Angel's Song

A.

(Angel)
Vom Himmel hoch da komm ich her,
ich bring euch gute neue Mär;
der guten Mär bring ich so viel,
davon ich sing'n und sagen will.

Euch ist ein Kindlein heut geborn
von einer Jungfrau auserkorn,
ein Kindelein so zart und fein,
das soll eur Freud und Wonne sein.

Es ist der Herr Christ, unser Gott,
der will euch führn aus aller Not,
er will eur Heiland selber sein,
von allen Sünden machen rein.

Er bringt euch alle Seligkeit,
die Gott der Vater hat bereit',
daß ihr mit uns im Himmelreich
sollt leben nun und ewiglich.

So merket nun das Zeichen recht:
die Krippen, Windelein so schlecht,
da findet ihr das Kind gelegt,
das alle Welt erhält und trägt.

(Children)
Des laßt uns alle fröhlich sein
und mit den Hirten gehn hinein,
zu sehn, was Gott uns hat beschert,
mit seinem lieben Sohn verehrt.

Merk auf, mein Herz, und sieh dorthin;
was liegt doch in dem Krippelein?
Wes ist das schöne Kindelein?
Es ist das liebe Jesulein.

Sie mir willkommen, edler Gast!
Den Sünder nicht verschmähet hast
und kommst ins Elend her zu mir;
wie soll ich immer danken dir?

Ach Herr, du Schöpfer aller Ding,
wie bist du worden so gering,
daß du da liegst auf dürrem Gras,
davon ein Rind und Esel aß!

Und wär die Welt vielmal so weit,
von Edelstein und Gold bereit',
so wär sie doch dir viel zu klein,
zu sein ein enges Wiegelein.

Der Sammet und die Seiden dein
das ist grob Heu und Windelein,
darauf du König groß und reich
herprangst, als wärs dein Himmelreich.

Das hat also gefallen dir,
die Wahrheit anzuzeigen mir,
wie aller Welt Macht, Ehr und Gut
vor dir nichts gilt, nichts hilft, noch tut.

Ach mein herzliebes Jesulein,
mach dir ein rein sanft Bettelein,
zu ruhen in meins Herzens Schrein,
daß ich nimmer vergesse dein.

Davon ich allzeit fröhlich sei,
zu springen, singen immer frei
das rechte Susaninne schön,
mit Herzenslust den süssen Ton.

(All)
Lob, Ehr sei Gott im höchsten Thron,
der uns schenkt seinen eingen Sohn.
Des freuen sich der Engel Schar'
und singen uns solch neues Jahr.

Martin Luther, 1534
Joseph Klug's *Geistliche Lieder*, 1535

B.

(Angel)
From heaven high I come to earth.
I bring you tidings of great mirth.
This mirth is such a wondrous thing
that I must tell you all and sing.

A little child for you this morn
has from a chosen Maid been born;
a little child, so tender, sweet,
that you should skip upon your feet.

He is the Christ, our God indeed,
who saves you all in every need.
He will himself your Savior be,
from all wrongdoing make you free.

He brings you every one to bliss.
The Heavenly Father sees to this.
You shall be here with us on high.
Here shall you live and never die.

Look now, you children, at the sign,
a manger cradle far from fine,
a tiny baby you will see.
Upholder of the world is he.

(Children)
How glad we'll be if this is so!
With all the angels let us go
to see what God for us has done
in sending us his own dear Son.

Look, look, my heart, and let me peek.
Whom in the manger do you seek?
Who is that lovely little one?
The baby Jesus, God's own Son.

Be welcome, Lord, be now our guest.
By you poor sinners have been blessed.
In nakedness and cold you lie.
How can I thank you—how can I?

O Lord, who made and molded all,
how did you come to be so small
that you could lie upon dry grass,
the fodder of the ox and ass?

And if the world were twice as wide,
with gold and precious jewels inside,
still such a cradle would not do
to hold a babe as great as you.

The velvet and the silken ruff,
for these the hay is good enough,
Here lies a prince and Lord of all,
a king within an ass's stall.

You wanted so to make me know
that you had let all great things go.
You had a palace in the sky;
you left it there for such as I.

O dear Lord Jesus, for your head
now will I make the softest bed.
The chamber where this bed shall be
is in my heart, inside of me.

Now I can play the whole day long.
I'll dance, and sing for you a song,
a soft and soothing lullaby,
so sweet that you will never cry.

(All)
To God who sent his only Son
be glory, laud, and honor done.
Let all the choir of heaven rejoice,
the new ring in with heart and voice.

translated, Roland H. Bainton, 1948
The Martin Luther Christmas Book, 1948
© 1948, Westminster Press

4

Psalm 46. God Is Our Refuge and Strength

A.

Ein feste Burg ist unser Gott,
    ein gute Wehr und Waffen.
Er hilft uns frei aus aller Not,
    die uns jetzt hat betroffen.
        Der alt böse Feind
        mit Ernst ers jetzt meint;
        groß Macht und viel List
        sein grausam Rüstung ist,
auf Erd ist nicht seinsgleichen.

Mit unsrer Macht ist nichts getan,
    wir sind gar bald verloren;
es streit' für uns der rechte Mann,
    den Gott hat selbst erkoren.
        Fragst du, wer der ist?
        Er heißt Jesus Christ,
        der Herr Zebaoth,
        und ist kein andrer Gott,
das Feld muß er behalten.

Und wenn die Welt voll Teufel wär
    und wollt uns gar verschlingen,
so fürchten wir uns nicht so sehr,
    es soll uns doch gelingen.
        Der Fürst dieser Welt,
        wie saur er sich stellt,
        tut er uns doch nicht;
        das macht, er ist gericht'.
    Ein Wörtlein kann ihn fällen.

Das Wort sie sollen lassen stahn
    und kein' Dank dazu haben;
er ist bei uns wohl auf dem Plan
    mit seinem Geist und Gaben.
        Nehmen sie den Leib,
        Gut, Ehr, Kind und Weib;
        laß fahren dahin,
        sie habens kein' Gewinn,
    das Reich muß uns doch bleiben.

Martin Luther, 1528
Joseph Klug's *Geistliche Lieder*, 1529

And though this world, with devils filled,
    should threaten to undo us,
we will not fear, for God hath willed
    his truth to triumph through us.
        The prince of darkness grim,
        we tremble not for him;
        his rage we can endure,
        for lo, his doom is sure;
    one little word shall fell him.

That word above all earthly powers,
    no thanks to them, abideth;
the Spirit and the gifts are ours
    through him who with us sideth.
        Let goods and kindred go,
        this mortal life also;
        the body they may kill;
        God's truth abideth still,
    his kingdom is for ever.

translated, Frederick H. Hedge
Gems of German Verse, 1852
See also the translation by Thomas Carlyle at 330.

B.

A mighty fortress is our God,
    a bulwark never failing;
our helper he amid the flood
    of mortal ills prevailing.
        For still our ancient foe
        doth seek to work us woe;
        his craft and power are great,
        and armed with cruel hate
    on earth is not his equal.

Did we in our own strength confide
    our striving would be losing,
were not the right Man on our side,
    the Man of God's own choosing.
        Dost ask who that may be?
        Christ Jesus, it is he;
        Lord Sabaoth his name,
        from age to age the same,
    and he must win the battle.

5
Ein schön Lied von Jörg Wagner, zu Mönchen verbrandt, Ann. 1527

A.

Wer Christo jetzt will folgen nach
muss achte nichte der Welt schmach,
    das Kreutz er auch muss tragen.
Kein ander Weg in Himmel geht,
    hör ich von jugend sagen.

Also thät Jörg der Wagner auch,
gen Himmel fuhr er in dem Rauch,
    durchs Kreutz ward er bewähret,
gleich wie man thut dem klaren Gold,
    von hertzen ers begehret.

Der Falkenthorn ward ihm zu theil,
es galt ihm seiner Seelen Hehl,
        er acht kein's Menschen trauren,
cr acht auch nicht sein kleine Kind,
        noch seiner Ehlichen Frauen.

Wiewohl sie ihm nich warn nunmehr,
und er gern ben ihn'n blieben wär,
        hat Liebs und Leids gelitten,
kein Arbeit an seim Lieb gespart,
        nach frommer Ehleut Sitten:

Gleichwohl er sie verlaffen muss,
es war ihm kein geringe Buss,
        dass er von ihn'n musst schehden.
Kein Fürst mit seinem Fürstentum,
        hätts ihm mögen erleiden.

[stanzas 6–27 omitted]

anonymous
Ausbund, 1564

B.

Who now would follow Christ in life
must scorn the world's insult and strife,
        and bear the cross each day.
For this alone leads to the throne;
        Christ is the only way.

Christ's servants follow him to death,   (1 Pet. 1:7)
and give their body, life, and breath
        on cross and rack and pyre.
As gold is tried and purified
        they stand the test of fire.

Renouncing all, they choose the cross,
and, claiming it, count all as loss,
        e'en husband, child, and wife.
Forsaking gain, forgetting pain,
        they enter into life.

translated, David Augsburger, 1962, revised, 1983
Hymnal: A Worship Book, 1982
© 1969, 1983, David Augsburger
The translation condenses the first five stanzas of the original and
applies the saga of Jörg Wagner to all martyrs.

6
Ein geistlich Lied

A.

O Gott Vater wir loben dich,
        und deine Güte preisen:
dass du uns O Herr so gnädiglich,
        an uns neun hast beweisen,
und hast und Herr zusammen g'führt
uns zu ermahnen durch dein Wort,
        gib uns Genad zu diesem.

Öffne den Mund Herr deiner Knecht
        gib ihn Weissheit darneben,
dass er dein Wort mög sprechen recht,
        was dient zum frommen Leben,
und nützlich ist zu deinem Preiss,
gib uns Hunger nach solcher Speiss,
        dass ist unser Begehren.

Gib unserm Hertzen auch Verstand,
        Erleuchtung hie auf Erden
dass dein Wort in uns werd bekandt
        dass wir fromm mögen werden,
und leben in Gerechtigkcit,
achten auf dein Wort allezeit,
        so bleibt man unbctrogen.

Dein O Herr ist das Reich allein,
    und auch die Macht zusammen,
wir loben dich in der Gemein
    und danken deinem Namen,
und bitten dich aus Hertzen grund,
wollst ben uns senn zu dieser Stund,
    durch Jesum Christum, amen.

Leonaerdt Clock, ca. 1590
Ausbund, 1622

As with our brethren here we meet,
    thy grace alone can feed us,
as here we gather at thy feet
    we pray that thou wilt feed us.
The power is thine, O Lord divine,
the kingdom and the rule are thine.
    May Jesus Christ still lead us!

translated, Ernest A. Payne, 1956
The Baptist Hymn Book, 1962
© 1956, Ernest A. Payne

B.

Our Father God, thy name we praise,
    to thee our hymns addressing,
and joyfully our voices raise,
    thy faithfulness confessing.
Assembled by thy grace, O Lord,
we seek fresh guidance from thy Word:
    now grant anew thy blessing.

Touch, Lord, the lips that speak for thee,
    set words of truth before us,
that we may grow in constancy,
    the light of wisdom o'er us.
Give us this day our daily bread;
may hungry souls again be fed;
    may heavenly food restore us.

Lord, make thy pilgrim people wise,
    the gospel message knowing,
that we may walk with lightened eyes
    in grace and goodness growing.
The righteous must thy precepts heed;
thy Word alone supplies their need,
    from heaven their succor flowing.

Chapter 2:
Metrical Psalmody and Hymnody, 1549–1700 (7–31)

The only way in which Lutheran hymnody (so far as texts go) impinged on English culture in the sixteenth century was through the translations of the English Thomas Coverdale and the Scottish Wedderburn brothers, John and Robert. Coverdale's version of "*Christ ist erstanden*" can occasionally be found in carol books (*University Carol Book*, 183, for example), and his version of a fragment of our 3 also appears here and there. The Wedderburns are chiefly famous now for having introduced a Scottish version of "*In dulci jubilo*" on which modern English versions are based. But this translated material did not turn out to be the foundation of English hymnody.

It was the influence of Calvin, not that of Luther, that was decisive in the shaping of both the English and the Scottish Reformed churches. In our field the effect of that influence was to restrict congregational song quite firmly to psalmody. And although there was much interaction in the musical field (for that which you can hear, you cannot shut out as you can that which you can see; we were not born with earflaps), there was an impassable frontier between the psalm style and the hymn style. For metrical psalmody in its English form is not hymnody based on the psalms; it is the very words of the English version of the psalter rearranged, so far as is possible, into metrical form for singing. Calvin himself, having encountered Clément Marot, the French court poet who was amusing the French court in the 1530s with metrical psalmody for purely secular and recreational purposes, decided that this style was what would be appropriate to the Reformed church as he envisaged it; and in Marot, and even more in his friend Théodore de Bèze, who carried on the work, he was as fortunate as he was in the incomparable musician Louis Bourgeois, who set these new metrical psalms to music. The French metrical psalms, then, are a passable sort of literature. The French Psalter, when completed in

1562, had 125 meters (and 110 tunes) for its 150 psalms, many of the meters wayward, expansive, and beautiful.

As luck would have it, an English psalm style was developing at the same time through the work of Thomas Sternhold (1500–1549), who, as Groom of the Royal Wardrobe, sought to entertain and educate the young King Edward VI (who was ten when he became king in 1547) by arranging the psalter in the style of the English and Scottish ballads, using their meter. Sternhold at his death left thirty-seven of these done into meter; and perhaps nothing would have come of this had it not been for the flight of so many English Protestant divines to Geneva in 1553 when King Edward's successor, Queen Mary, came to the throne and at once reacted violently towards the old Catholic faith.

Anyone entering the great church at Geneva in 1553 would have found a psalter of eighty-three psalms (the 1551 edition) in use, and could hardly fail to be impressed with the sonorous simplicity of the French psalms and their music. From the first it was clear to the exiles from Scotland and England that metrical psalmody could be a most appropriate vehicle for public praise. But there were difficulties. It was found, naturally enough, that hardly any Genevan tune would fit an English psalm unless the psalm were retranslated in the Genevan meter. Ingenious devices for adapting the Genevan style of tune to the English meters took a while to work out; the first attempts were less successful than some historians claim. But the conflict remained between a literary desire to write poetry, which the fine Genevan meters looked like encouraging, and the pious desire to keep as close as possible to the language of the newly translated Book of Psalms.

By 1562 the whole English Psalter had been done into ballad meter. It contained a handful of concessions to the Genevan style, of which the best known are the OLD HUNDREDTH and the OLD 124TH (thus called because they are versions of psalms in this 1562 collection which fairly soon became known as the "Old Version"). These indeed were the only psalms not in ballad meter that became popular at once—although there are a dozen others in Genevan meters which though constantly reprinted we may guess remained largely unused.

The style of 1562 is illustrated in 9B and 9C, and 10. "Sternhold and Hopkins" (which is another name for this Old Version, taken from its two chief authors) is now scarcely sung at all; only Psalm 18 (10) has been taken seriously by modern editors. It's a fine, long psalm of fifty verses and contains a number of couplets which, carefully selected, make a good hymn. But the theologically-minded reader may well pause to reflect on how those Calvinists who so rigorously confined public praise to psalmody assimilated the spiritual complacency of old King David in the Third Part as here quoted.

One other thing must be noted about this historic and now embalmed 1562 collection. That is its title, which is worth quoting.

The Whole Booke
of Psalmes, collected into Eng-
lysh metre by T. Starnhold I. Hopkins
& others: conferred with the Ebrue,
with apt Notes to synge the with
al, Faithfully perused and alow-
ed according to thordre appointed in the Quenes maie-
sties Iniunctions.
Very mete to be vsed of all sortes of people priuately for
their solace & comfort: laying apart all vngodly
Songes and Ballades, which tende only to the
norishing of vyce, and corrupting of youth

The "Iniunctions" of 1559 had indeed very cautiously provided for the singing of "a Hymn" (a term which by common consent was interpreted as a "metrical psalm or canticle") at public worship in the Church of England; but the promoters of this collection especially commend it for private use in the home. And indeed it was such private use

which provided the largest market for copies of this psalter and which encouraged the making of truly English music for it.

Now, so far as official edict went, this remained the official book of praise throughout the Church of England for 134 years, without any authorized competitors. Scotland produced its own psalter, a parallel but quite independent version, sharing only a few of the "Geneva-type" versions, including Psalms 100 and 124 (8D). This appeared first in 1564 (an example of its contents is at 11), and it lasted ninety-six years. Its final revision came in 1650 and produced the Scottish Psalter, which is known in the Church of Scotland and all Presbyterian communions affiliated with it to this day. This, whose contents are too well known to need much quotation (see 12–14), was made by a committee of the Westminster Assembly, which reviewed all the most reasonable private efforts that had been made in intervening years to improve the original, including some that were made for Dissenting congregations. And it will be noted especially here how the primary need to keep as close as possible to the words of the King James Bible overcame any impulse to write what flows naturally as poetry; with the result, so familiar, of syntactical inversions like "He makes me down to lie," and "God keep for ever will." In the final Scottish version every psalm appears in Common Meter, but some have alternative versions (like, again, Psalms 100 and 124); and one or two English compositions are slipped in among these.

But it is only quite recently that the Scottish Psalter has made any impact at all on hymn singing outside the Scottish-centered Presbyterian churches. "The Lord's my Shepherd" (9E) would now be regarded as a universally popular hymn: but this development is almost entirely the work of the twentieth century. The English Methodists have used it since 1876; the Congregationalists took it in 1916; the Baptists waited until 1933, and, as for the Church of England, the first widely used hymnal to take it was the *Anglican Hymn Book* of 1965, if we do not count the ecumenical *BBC Hymn Book* (1951) and a much more obscure book, *Church Hymnal for the Christian Year* (1917). There is little doubt that the sudden rise to popularity of the tune CRIMOND, used at the wedding of Princess Elizabeth (now Queen Elizabeth II) in November 1947 did much to make widely known a psalm which, though venerable, had till then served a minority constituency.

The English metrical psalter was officially revised in 1696 by Nahum Tate, the Poet Laureate, and Nicholas Brady, being known thereafter as "Tate and Brady" or the "New Version." This version was a good deal smoother than the former, and two fragments from it, Psalms 34 and 42, have been received into the general repertory (15 and 16). This did not replace the Old Version; that version was still being printed in the mid-nineteenth century, having run through well over three hundred editions. The New Version actually had more success in the USA, where in the eighteenth century it was very widely used, particularly by Episcopalians.

Very little was permitted to public praise beyond the psalter, but in the Old Version there was an appendix containing some additional matter. This consisted of the metrical *"Veni Creator"* (found also in the *Book of Common Prayer*, 1549); the Gospel canticles (*"Benedictus," "Magnificat," "Nunc dimittis"*); the Lord's Prayer; the Ten Commandments, followed by a "prayer" (Long Meter, no doubt to carry the Genevan "Commandments" tune thus adapted); the Athanasian Creed; the Lamentation of a Sinner (17); a second Lamentation in Long Meter; a hymn, "Preserve us, Lord, by thy dear word," founded on an older hymn by Luther and using his tune; and three Glorias. The first (C.M.) "Lamentation" was retained until quite recently in the general repertory, judicious selections and revisions usually overtaking it; so it stands as the oldest original English hymn in continuous and authorized use.

The Scottish Psalters of 1564 and 1650 had no such appendix; the large appendix of "paraphrases"

came later, in 1781, and is dealt with in its proper place (96–102). But the New Version did indeed have a *Supplement*. To be exact, it had two: one textual, and one musical, the musical one of 1708 being an important musical source (it contains the tune now well known to "Our God, our help in ages past," as well as several other important first appearances). The textual supplement was somewhat expanded, containing, besides the material above (sometimes conservatively revised), the *"Te Deum"*; a second (L.M.) *"Veni Creator"* (not that at 160 which was in the 1662 Prayer Book alongside the 1549 version); the Apostles' Creed; a second (L.M.) Lord's Prayer; "The Song of the Angels" (22); two Easter hymns; two hymns from the Book of Revelation; a postcommunion thanksgiving hymn; the *"Benedicite;"* and "A Hymn on the Divine Use of Musick" (21) of which more in a moment. The Athanasian Creed and "Preserve us, Lord" were dropped.

As has been hinted, private psalters were not uncommon in the seventeenth century; some of them were designed simply for domestic use, others for use by those congregations which braved the hazards of dissenting from the Church of England. (This was illegal and punishable in the England of those days.) Several psalters, including especially those of Francis Rous and Zachary Boyd, were consulted in the revision of the Scottish Psalter, but none seem to have been used by Tate and Brady, who made a fresh start in their revision. Henry Ainsworth's psalter of 1612 was in the hands of the Pilgrim Fathers when they arrived in America in 1620, though it cannot be regarded as literature of any merit, and the attempt to bring back the long and complicated Genevan tunes, quite unsuccessful in England, was impeded even among the sturdy pioneers by the awkward diction of Ainsworth's psalter. The most distinguished author of a complete metrical psalter was King James VI of Scotland, who by then had become King James I of England (the book was not printed until 1631 when he had been dead six years); but his metrical schemes made it impossible for it to be substituted in either country for what was in use, an example (which is as literary work very favorably comparable with other versions) is at 328. George Sandys's *Psalms* of 1637, not a complete version, are of interest chiefly in having generated some tunes by the leading English composer of the day (Henry Lawes: see 28). The versions of Phineas Fletcher and of Sir Philip Sidney and his sister Mary, Countess of Pembroke (who probably wrote our 26), were, of course, far better literature and not intended in any sense for ecclesiastical use. Notice how Fletcher (27) brings the New Testament in at the end, almost in the style of the later Isaac Watts.

Ex hypothesi, there was no hymn writing, at least officially, beyond the psalter supplements we mentioned. George Wither, however, did produce in 1623 *Hymns and Songs of the Church*, and fell foul of the law for doing so without the necessary license (which he could never have obtained anyhow), spending a while in prison for his pains. This has some splendidly crusty lyric in it (see 23); and an added distinction was the appendix of tunes by Orlando Gibbons (1583–1625), the last of England's great madrigalists. Wither later put together *The Hallelujah* (1641) in which were several psalm versions.

One of the most interesting of all the later psalters is that of John Playford, second edition 1677; for this contains certain hymns not before found in psalters. One of these was the John Cosin "*Veni Creator*" (160C); another was 21, "On the Divine Use of Musick" (which had been in the 1671 edition); two others (18 and 19) are from a Roman Catholic source. Roman Catholicism was officially taboo in England since 1558 and was subject to the same interdicts and penalties as nonconformity; but the known sympathy of Charles II (1660–1685) with the Catholics caused some easement of their difficulties during his reign, and in 1668 a book of hymns appeared edited by John Austin, who drew much on the work of the

very great mystical poet Richard Crashaw. The two above-mentioned found their way into Playford, one being a translation from a Latin office hymn (see also 139). A hymn by Austin from that source, not in Playford, is also given as 20.

Thomas Ken's very famous trio (the third is not now in use) at 29 were written for a school, Winchester College, which was in some respects outside the jurisdiction of the hierarchy; and the visionary John Mason, in his *Songs of Praise*, 1694, produced some astonishing literature (30, 31) which, however, was hardly sung at all before the twentieth-century editors discovered him.

If then one excepts the versifications of Prayer Book canticles and scriptural passages especially associated with the liturgy, and of the creeds, there is, stretching it as far as we can, a repertory of hardly a dozen hymns available to seventeenth-century churchgoers. The Catholic hymnody, such as it was, soon returned "underground," and apart from the Baptist Benjamin Keach, none of whose work survives now although he wrote a good deal between about 1673 and 1691, even the nonconformists have nothing to say. The understanding of this makes a proper preparation for the explosion of evangelical hymnody in the following century.

7
Psalm 100

A.

Vous qui la terre habitez,
chantez tout haut à Dieu, chantez:
servez à Dieu joyeusement,
venez devant lui gaiement.

Sachez qu'il est le Souverain,
qui sans nous, nous fit de la main,
nous, dis-je son vrai peuple acquis,
et le troupeau de son pasquis.

Entrez ès portes d'icelui,
louez-le et célébrez chez lui,
par tout son honneur avancez:
et son tres-saint Nom benissez.

Car il est Dieu plein de bonté,
et dure sa benignité
à jamais: voire du Tres-haut
la vérité jamais ne faut.

Théodore of Bèze
Pseaumes de David mis en rime française (Genevan Psalter), 1551

B. Jubilate Deo

All people that on earth do dwell,
sing to the Lord with chereful voyce;
him serve with feare, his praise forthe tell,
come ye before him and reioyce.

The Lord, ye knowe, is God in dede,
without our ayde, he did us make;
We are his folke; he doth us fede,
and for his shepe he doeth us take.

Oh entre then his gates with prayse,
approche with ioye his courtes vnto.
Praise, laude and blesse his name always
for it is semely so to do.

For why? the Lord our God is good:
his mercie is for euer sure:
his trueh at all tymes firmely stood,
and shall from age to age indure.

William Kethe, 1559/1560
Foure Score and Seven Psalmes of David in English Mitre, 1561
Presented with original spelling (which varies through the
early printings).

8
Psalm 124

A.

Or peut bien dire Israël maintenant,
si le Seigneur pour nous n'eust point esté,
si le Seigneur nôtre droit n'eust porté,
quand tout le monde à grand fureur venant
pour nous meurtri dessus nous s'est jeté,

déjà fuissons vifs devorez par eux,
veu la fureur ardente des pervers:
déjà fuissons sous les eaux à l'envois;
et tout ainsi qu'un flot impetueux
nous eussent tous abusmez et couverts.

Par dessus nous leurs gros et forts torrens
eussent déjà passé et repassé.
Loué soit Dieu, lequel n'a point laissé
le peuple sien tomber entre leurs dents
pour le manger, comme ils avoient pensé.

Comme l'oiscau du filé de defait
de l'oiseleur, nous sommes échapez,
rompant le laqs qui nous eust attrapez:
voilà comment le grand Dieu qui a fait
et terre et ciel, nous a dévelopez.

Théodore of Bèze
Pseaumes de David mis en rime française (Genevan Psalter), 1551

B. Nisi quia Dom

Now Israel	may say, and that truly,
if that the Lord	had not our cause maintained,
if that the Lord	had not our right sustained,
when all the world	against us furiously
made their uproars	and said we should all die;

then long ago	they had devoured us all
and swallowed quick	for aught that we could deem.
Such was their rage	as we might well esteem.
And as the floods	with mighty force do fall,
so had they now	our lives ev'n brought to thrall.

The raging streams	most proud in roaring noise,
had long ago	o'erwhelmed us in the deep:
But loved be God	which doth us safely keep
from bloody teeth,	and their most cruel voice,
which as a prey	to eat us would rejoice.

Even as a bird	out of the fowlers grin
escapeth away	right so it fareth with us;
broke are their nets	and we have escaped thus.
God that made heaven	and earth is our help then;
his name hath saved	us from these wicked men.

William Whittingham
Sternhold and Hopkins's *The Whole Booke of Psalmes*, 1562
The display is as in early editions, with the long lines divided at the natural caesura,
where the unskilled singer would take breath.

C.

Now Israel
may say, and that truly,
if that the Lord
had not our cause maintained;
if that the Lord
had not our right sustained,
when cruel men
against us furiously
rose up in wrath
to make of us their prey;

then certainly
they had devoured us all,
   and swallowed quick,
for ought that we could deem;
   such was their rage,
as we might well esteem;
   and, as fierce floods
before them all things drown,
   so had they brought
our soul to death quite down.

The raging streams,
with their proud swelling waves,
   had then our soul
o'erwhelmed in the deep.
   But blest be God,
who doth us safely keep,
   and hath not given
us for a living prey
   unto their teeth
and bloody cruelty.

Even as a bird
out of the fowler's snare
   escapes away,
so is our soul set free:
   Broke are their nets,
and thus escaped we.
   Therefore our help
is in the Lord's great name,
   who heaven and earth
by his great power did frame.

as revised in *The Psalms of David in Meeter* (Scottish Psalter), 1650

9
Psalm 23

A.

Mon Dieu me paist sous sa puissance haute,
c'est mon berger, de rien je n'aurai faute.
   En toict bien seur, joignat les beaux herbages,
   coucher me fait, me mene aux clairs rivages,
traitte ma vie en douceur tres humaine,
et pour son Nom par droits sentiers me mene.

Si seurement, que quand au val viendroye
d'ombre de mort rien de mal ne craindroye:
   car avec moi tu es à chacune heure,
   plus ta houlette et conduite m'asseure.
Tu enrichis de vivres necessaires
ma table aux yeux de tous mes adversaires.

Tu oincts mon chef d'huiles et senteurs bonnes,
et jusqu'aux bords pleine tasse me donnes:
   voire et ferras que cette faveur tuenne
   tent que vivrai compagnie me tienne:
si que toujours de faire ai esperance
en la maison du Seigneur demeurance.

Clément Marot [?]
La forme des prières et chantz ecclesiastiqves (Strasbourg), 1545

B.

My Shepherd is the living Lord, nothing therefore I need;
in pastures fair, with waters calm, he sets me forth to feed.
He did convert and glad my soul and brought my mind in frame;
to walk in paths of righteousness, for his most holy name.

Yea, though I walk in vale of death, yet will I fear no ill;
thy rod, thy staff doth comfort me, and thou art with me still.
And in the presence of my foes my table thou shalt spread;
thou shalt (O Lord) fill full my cup, and eke anoint my head.

Through all my life thy favor is so frankly showed to me;
that in thy house for evermore my dwelling place shall be.

Thomas Sternhold
Sternhold and Hopkins's *The Whole Booke of Psalmes*, 1562
The display is as in early editions, with the long lines divided at the natural caesura, where
the unskilled singer would take breath.

C. Dominus Regit Me

The Lord is only my support and he that doth me feed;
how can I then lack anything whereof I stand in need?
In pastures green he leadeth me where I do safely lie;
and after leads me to the streams which run most pleasantly.

And when I find myself near lost, then doth he me home take
conducting me in his right paths even for his own name's sake.
And though I were even at death's door, yet would I fear no ill;
for both thy rod and shepherd's crook afford me comfort still.

Thou hast my table richly spread in presence of my foe;
thou hast my head with balm refreshed, my cup doth overflow.
And finally while breath doth last, thy grace shall me defend;
and in the house of God will I my life for ever spend.

William Whittingham
Sternhold and Hopkins's *The Whole Booke of Psalmes*, 1562
The display is as in early editions, with the long lines divided at the natural caesura, where the
unskilled singer would take breath.

D.

The Lord is only my support,
 and he that doth me feed;
how can I then lack anything
 whereof I stand in need?
He doth me fold in coats most safe,
 the tender grass fast by;
and after driv'th me to the streams
 which run most pleasantly.

And when I feel myself near lost,
 then doth he me home take;
conducting me in his right paths
 even for his own name's sake.
And though I were even at death's door,
 yet would I fear none ill;
for by thy rod and shepherd's crook
 I am comforted still.

Thou hast my table richly decked
 in despite of my foe;
thou hast my head with balm refreshed,
 my cup doth overflow.
And finally, while breath doth last,
 thy grace shall me defend;
and in the house of God will I
 my life for ever spend.

as altered in
The Whole Psalmes of David in English Meter (Scottish Psalter), 1564

E.

The Lord's my shepherd: I'll not want.
 He makes me down to lie
in pastures green; he leadeth me
 the quiet waters by.
My soul he doth restore again;
 and me to walk doth make
within the paths of righteousness,
 ev'n for his own name's sake.

Yea, though I walk in death's dark vale,
 yet will I fear none ill;
for thou art with me, and thy rod
 and staff me comfort still.
My table thou hast furnished
 in presence of my foes;
my head thou dost with oil anoint,
 and my cup overflows.

Goodness and mercy all my life
 shall surely follow me;
and in God's house for evermore
 my dwelling place shall be.

The Psalms of David in Meeter (Scottish Psalter), 1650

F. The 23rd Psalm

The God of love my shepherd is,
 and he that doth me feed;
while he is mine and I am his,
 what can I want or need?

He leads me to the tender grass
 where I both feed and rest;
then to the streams that gently pass;
 in both I have the best.

Or if I stray, he doth convert
 and bring my mind in frame;
and all this not for my desert,
 but for his holy name.

Yea, in death's shady black abode
 well may I walk, not fear;
for thou art with me; and thy rod
 to guide, thy staff to bear.

Nay, thou dost make me sit and dine,
 ev'n in my enemies sight;
my head with oil, my cup with wine,
 runs over day and night.

Surely thy sweet and wondrous love
    shall measure all my days;
and as it never shall remove,
    so neither shall my praise.

George Herbert
The Temple, 1633

10
from Psalm 18

The First Part

O God, my strength and fortitude,   of force I must love thee:
thou art my castle and defense   in my necessity.

My God, my rock, in whom I trust,   the worker of my wealth;
my refuge, buckler, and my shield,   the horn of all my health.

When I sing laud unto the Lord,   most worthy to be served,
then from my foes I am right sure   that I shall be preserved.

The pangs of death did compass me,   and bound me everywhere;
the flowing waves of wickedness   did put me in great fear.

The sly and subtle snares of hell   were round about me set;
and for my life there was prepared   a deadly trapping net.

I was beset with pain and grief,   did pray to God for grace:
And he forthwith did hear my plaint   out of his holy place.

Such is his power that in his wrath   he made the earth to quake;
yea, the foundation of the mount   of Basan for to shake.

And from his nostrils went a smoke,   when kindled was his ire,
and from his mouth went burning coals   of hot consuming fire.

The Lord descended from above,   and bowed the heavens high;
and underneath his feet he cast   the darkness of the sky.

On cherubs and on cherubims   full royally he rode;
and on the wings of mighty winds   came flying all abroad.

[*The Second Part*, stanzas 11–20, omitted]

The Third Part

But evermore I have respect	to his law and decree;
His statutes and commandments I	cast not away from me.

But pure, and clean, and uncorrupt	appeared before his face;
and did refrain from wickedness,	and sin in any case.

The Lord therefore will me reward,	as I have done aright;
and to the cleanness of my hands	appearing in his sight,

for, Lord, with him that holy is	wilt thou be holy too;
and with the good and virtuous men,	right virtuously wilt do.

And to the loving and elect	thy love wilt thou reserve;
and thou wilt use the wicked men	as wicked men deserve.

For thou dost save the simple folk	in trouble when they lie;
and dost bring down the countenance	of them that look full high.

The Lord will light my candle so	that it shall shine full bright;
the Lord my God will make also	my darkness to be light.

For by thy help an host of men	discomfit, Lord, I shall;
by thee I scale and overleap	the strength of any wall.

Unspotted are the ways of God,	his word is purely tried;
he is a sure defense to such	as in his faith abide.

For who is God except the Lord?	for other there is none;
or else who is omnipotent,	saving our God alone.

[*The Fourth Part* and *Fifth Part*, stanzas 31–48, omitted]

Thomas Sternhold
Sternhold and Hopkins's *The Whole Booke of Psalmes*, 1562
The display is as in early editions, with the long lines divided at the natural caesura, where the
unskilled singer would take breath.

11

Magnificat

My soul doth magnify the Lord,   my spirit evermore
rejoiceth in the Lord my God,   who is my Savior.

And that because he did regard   and had respect unto
the low estate of his handmaid   and let the mighty go.

For now behold all nations and   the generations all,
from this time forth for evermore   shall me right blessed call.

Because he hath me magnified,   who is the Lord of might;
whose name be ever sanctified,   and praised day and night.

For with his mercy and his grace   all men he doth inflame;
throughout the generations   that fear his holy name.

He showed strength with his mighty arm   and made the proud to start;
with all imaginations that   were in their wicked heart.

He hath put down the mighty ones   from their supernal seat;
and did exalt the meek in heart,   even from their low estate.

The hungry he replenished   with all things that were good;
and through his power he made the rich   oft times to want their food.

And calling to remembrance his   great mercy very well,
hath holpen up most graciously   his servant Israel.

According to his promise made   to Abraham before,
and to his seed successively   to stand for evermore.

The Whole Psalmes of David in English Meter (Scottish Psalter), 1564
The Psalms of David in Meeter (Scottish Psalter), 1650
The display is as in early editions, with the long lines divided at the natural caesura, where the
unskilled singer would take breath.

12

Psalm 145, verses 1–6

O Lord, thou art my God and King,
 undoubtedly, I will thee praise;
I will extol and blessings sing
 unto thine holy name always.

From day to day I will thee bless
 and laud thy name world without end;
for great is God, most worthy praise,
 whose greatness none may comprehend.

Race shall thy works praise unto race;
 and so declare thy power, O Lord.
The glorious beauty of thy grace,
 and wondrous works, will I record.

And all men shall the power (O God)
 of all thy fearful acts declare;
and I to publish all abroad
 thy greatness at no time will spare.

John Craig
The Psalms of David in Meeter (Scottish Psalter), 1564

13

Psalm 24

The earth belongs unto the Lord,
 and all that it contains;
the world that is inhabited,
 and all that there remains.

For the foundations thereof
 he on the seas did lay,
and he hath it established
 upon the floods to stay.

Who is the man that shall ascend
 into the hill of God?
or who within his holy place
 shall have a firm abode?

Whose hands are clean, whose heart is pure,
 and unto vanity
who hath not lifted up his soul,
 nor sworn deceitfully.

He from th' Eternal shall receive
 the blessing him upon,
and righteousness, even from the God
 of his salvation.

This is the generation
 that after him enquire,
O Jacob, who do seek thy face
 with their whole heart's desire.

Ye gates, lift up your heads on high;
 ye doors, that last for aye,
be lifted up, that so the King
 of glory enter may.

But who of glory is the King?
 The mighty Lord is this;
even that same Lord, that great in might
 and strong in battle is.

Ye gates, lift up your heads; ye doors,
 doors that do last for aye,
be lifted up, that so the King
 of glory enter may.

But who is he that is the King
 of glory? Who is this?
The Lord of hosts, and none but he,
 the King of glory is.

The Psalms of David in Meeter (Scottish Psalter), 1650

14
Psalm 116

I love the Lord, because my voice
    and prayers he did hear.
I, while I live, will call on him,
    who bowed to me his ear.

Of death the cords and sorrows did
    about me compass round;
the pains of hell took hold on me.
    I grief and trouble found.

Upon the name of God the Lord
    then did I call, and say,
"Deliver thou my soul, O Lord,
    I do thee humbly pray."

God merciful and righteous is,
    yea, gracious is our Lord.
God saves the meek; I was brought low,
    he did me help afford.

O thou my soul, do thou return
    unto thy quiet rest;
for largely, lo, the Lord to thee
    his bounty hath expressed.

For my distressed soul from death
    delivered was by thee;
thou didst my mourning eyes from tears,
    my feet from falling, free.

I in the land of those that live
    will walk the Lord before.
I did believe, therefore I spake;
    I was afflicted sore.

I said, when I was in my haste,
    that all men liars be.
What shall I render to the Lord
    for all his gifts to me?

I'll of salvation take the cup,
    on God's name will I call;
I'll pay my vows now to the Lord
    before his people all.

Dear in God's sight is his saints' death,
    thy servant, Lord, am I;
thy servant sure, thine handmaid's son:
    my bands thou didst untie.

Thank-offerings I to thee will give,
    and on God's name will call.
I'll pay my vows now to the Lord
    before his people all;

within the courts of God's own house,
    within the midst of thee,
O city of Jerusalem,
    praise to the Lord give ye.

The Psalms of David in Meeter (Scottish Psalter), 1650

15
Psalm 42

As pants the hart for cooling streams
    when heated in the chase;
so longs my soul, O God, for thee
    and thy refreshing grace.

For thee, my God, the living God,
    my thirsty soul doth pine;
O when shall I behold thy face,
    thou Majesty Divine?

Tears are my constant food, while thus
    insulting foes upbraid,
"Deluded wretch, where's now thy God,
    and where thy promised aid?"

I sigh when recollecting thought
    those happy days present,
when I with troops of pious friends
    thy temple did frequent;

when I advanced with songs of praise
    my solemn vows to pay;
and led the joyful sacred throng
    that kept the festal day.

Why restless, why cast down, my soul?
    Trust God, and he'll employ
his aid for thee, convert these sighs
    to thankful hymns of joy.

My soul's cast down, O God, but thinks
    on thee and Sion still;
from Jordan's bank, from Hermon's heights,
    and Missar's humbler hill.

One trouble calls another on
    and, bursting o'er my head,
fall spouting down, till round my soul
    a roaring deluge spread.

But when thy presence, Lord of life,
    has once dispelled this storm,
to thee I'll midnight anthems sing,
    and midnight vows perform.

God of my strength, how long shall I,
    like one forgotten, mourn?
forlorn, forsaken, and exposed
    to my oppressor's scorn.

My heart is pierced, as with a sword,
    whilst thus my foes upbraid,
"Vain boaster, where is now thy God?
    and where his promised aid?"

Why restless, why cast down, my soul?
    hope still, and thou shalt sing
the praise of him who is thy God,
    thy health and safety's spring.

Tate and Brady's *A New Version of the Psalms of David*, 1696

16
Psalm 34

Through all the changing scenes of life,
    in trouble and in joy,
the praises of my God shall still
    my heart and tongue employ.

Of his deliverance I will boast,
    till all that are distressed
from my example comfort take,
    and charm their griefs to rest.

O magnify the Lord with me;
    with me exalt his name:
distressed, to him I sought, he heard,
    and to my rescue came.

The drooping hearts were soon refreshed,
    who looked to him for aid;
desired success in every face
    a cheerful air displayed.

"Behold (say they), the supplicant
    whom Providence relieved;
the man so dangerously beset,
    so wondrously retrieved."

His angel hosts encamp around
    the dwellings of the just;
deliverance he affords to all
    who in his succor trust.

O taste th' experience of his love,
    the trial will decide
how blest they are, and only they,
    who in his truth confide.

Fear him, ye saints, and ye will then
    have nothing else to fear;
fear him, make you his service yours,
    he'll make your wants his care.

While hungry rapine fails with prey,
    young lions to provide,
all those that meekly fear the Lord
    shall have their wants supplied.

Approach, ye piously disposed,
    and my instruction hear;
I'll teach you the true discipline
    of his religious fear.

Let him who length of days desires,
    and prosperous days would see,
from slander's venom keep his tongue,
    his lips from falsehood free.

The crooked paths of vice decline,
    and virtue's ways pursue;
establish peace where 'tis begun;
    and where 'tis lost, renew.

The Lord from heaven beholds the just
    with favorable eyes;
and when distressed, his gracious ear
    is open to their cries.

But turn his wrathful look on those
    whom mercy can't reclaim,
to cut them off, and raze from earth
    their hated race and name.

Deliverance to his saints he gives,
    when his relief they crave;
still nigh to heal the broken heart,
    and contrite spirit save.

The wicked oft, but still in vain,
    against the just conspire;
for under their affliction's weight
    he keeps their bones entire.

The wicked, from their wickedness,
    their ruin shall derive;
while them, their malice, and their names
    the righteous shall survive.

The Lord redeems his servants' souls,
    who on his truth depend;
to them and their posterity,
    his blessings shall descend.

Tate and Brady's *A New Version of the Psalms of David*, 1696
This psalm was divided into two parts, the second beginning with
stanza 10. In modern use, various selections have been made, the most
of common of which includes stanzas 1–3 and 7–9.

17

The Lamentation of a Sinner

O Lord, turn not away thy face,
    from him that lieth prostrate;
lamenting sore his sinful life
    before thy mercy gate;
which gate thou openest wide to those
    that do lament their sin;
shut not that gate against me, Lord,
    but let me enter in.

And call me not to mine account
    how I have lived here;
for then I know right well, O Lord,
    how vile I shall appear.
I need not to confess my life,
    I am sure thou canst tell;
what I have been, and what I am
    I know thou knowest it well.

O Lord, thou knowest what things be past,
 and eke the things that be;
thou knowest also what is to come;
 nothing is hid from thee.
Before the heavens and earth were made,
 thou knewest what things were then;
as all things else that have been since
 among the sons of men.

And can the things that I have done
 be hidden from thee then?
Nay, nay, though knowest them all, O Lord,
 where they were done, and when.
Wherefore with tears I come to thee,
 to beg and to entreat:
even as the child that hath done evil,
 and feareth to be beat.

So come I to thy mercy gate,
 where mercy doth abound;
requiring mercy for my sins,
 to heal my deadly wound.
O Lord, I need not to repeat
 what I do beg or crave;
thou knowest, O Lord, before I ask
 the thing that I would have.

Mercy, good Lord, mercy I ask,
 this is the total sum;
for mercy, Lord, is all my suit,
 Lord, let thy mercy come.

John Marckant
John Day's edition of *The Whole Booke of Psalmes*
(Sternhold & Hopkins), 1562

18
For Sunday at Matins

Behold, we come, dear Lord, to thee,
 and bow before thy throne;
we come to offer on our knee
 our vows to thee alone.

Whate'er we have, whate'er we are
 thy bounty freely gave;
thou dost us here in mercy spare,
 and wilt hereafter save.

But O, can all our store afford
 no better gifts for thee?
Thus we confess thy riches, Lord,
 and thus our poverty.

'Tis not our tongue or knee can pay
 the mighty debt we owe;
far more we should than we can say,
 far lower we should bow.

Come then, my soul, bring all thy powers,
 and grieve thou hast no more;
bring every day thy choicest hours,
 and thy great God adore.

But above all, prepare thy heart
 on this his own blest day,
in its sweet task to bear thy part
 and sing, and love, and pray.

John Austin
Devotions in the Antient Way of Offices, 1668

19
A Morning Hymn
Latin: Iam lucis orto sidere

Now that the Daystar doth arise,
beg we of God with humble cries
all hurtful things to keep away,
while we devoutly spend the day;

our tongues to guide, so that no strife
may breed disquiet in all our life;
to shut and close the wandering eye,
lest it doth let in vanity;

to keep the heart most pure and free
from fond and troubled fantasy;
to tame proud flesh, while we deny 't
a too full cup and wanton diet;

that when the daylight shall go out,
time bringing on the night about,
we may, by leaving worldly ways,
neglect no time our God to praise.

anonymous, Medieval Latin
translated, Richard Crashaw and John Austin, 1668
Devotions in the Antient Way of Offices, 1668
See also the original at 139A
and the translation by John Mason Neale at 139B.

20
For Monday at Lauds

Hark, my soul, how everything
strives to serve our bounteous King;
each a double tribute pays,
sings its part, and then obeys.

Nature's chief and sweetest choir
him with cheerful notes admire;
chanting every day their lauds,
while the grove their song applauds.

Though their voices lower be,
streams have too their melody;
night and day they warbling run,
never pause, but still sing on.

All the flowers that gild the spring
hither their still music bring;
if heaven bless them, thankful, they
smell more sweet, and look more gay.

Only we can scarce afford
this short office to our Lord;
we, on whom this bounty flows,
all things gives, and nothing owes.

Wake for shame, my sluggish heart,
wake, and gladly sing thy part;
learn of birds, and springs, and flowers
how to use thy nobler powers.

Call whole nature to thine aid;
since 'twas he whole nature made;
join in one eternal song,
who to one God all belong.

Live for ever, glorious Lord!
live by all thy works adored,
One in Three, and Three in One,
thrice we bow to thee alone.

John Austin
Devotions in the Antient Way of Offices, 1668

21
On the Divine Use of Musick

We sing to thee, whose wisdom formed
    the curious organ of the ear;
and thou, who gav'st us voices, Lord,
    our grateful songs in kindness hear.

We'll joy in God, who is the spring
    of lawful joy and harmless mirth:
whose boundless love is fitly called
    the harmony of heaven and earth.

Those praises, dearest Lord, aloud
    our humblest sonnets shall rehearse;
which rightly tuned, are rightly styled
    the music of the universe.

And whilst we sing we'll consecrate
    that too too much profaned art,
by offering up with every tongue
    in every song a flaming heart.

We'll hallow pleasure, and redeem
    from vulgar use our precious voice;
those lips which wantonly have sung
    shall serve our turn for nobler joys.

Thus we will imitate on earth,
    poor mortals still, the heavenly choirs;
and with high notes, above the clouds
    we'll send with words more raised desires.

And that above we may be sure,
    when we come there our part to know;
whilst we live here, at home and church
    we'll practice singing oft below.

Glory and praise be given most
    to Father, Son, and Holy Ghost:
Hallelujah, hallelujah,
    hallelujah, hallelujah.

anonymous
John Playford's The Whole Book of Psalms, 1677

22

Song of the Angels: The Nativity of Our Blessed Savior. Luke 2:8–15

While shepherds watched their flocks by night,
    all seated on the ground,
the angel of the Lord came down
    and glory shone around.

"Fear not," said he, (for mighty dread
    had seized their troubled mind),
"glad tidings of great joy I bring
    to you and all mankind."

"To you, in David's town this day
    is born, of David's line
the Savior, who is Christ the Lord,
    and this shall be the sign:

"The heavenly Babe you there shall find
    to human view displayed,
all meanly wrapped in swathing bands,
    and in a manger laid."

Thus spake the seraph, and forthwith
    appeared a shining throng
of angels, praising God, and thus
    addressed their joyful song:

"All glory be to God on high,
    and to the earth be peace;
good will henceforth, from heaven to men
    begin, and never cease."

Nahum Tate
A Supplement to the New Version of the Psalms, 1708

23

Ascension Day

To God with heart and cheerful voice
    a triumph song we sing;
and with true thankful hearts rejoice
    in our almighty King;
yea, to his glory we record
    (who were but dust and clay)
what honor he did us afford
    on his ascending day.

The human nature, which of late   (Ps. 8)
    beneath the angels was,
now raised from that meaner state
    above them hath a place.
And at man's feet all creatures bow
    which through the whole world be,
for at God's right hand throned now
    in glory sitteth he.

Our Lord and Brother, who hath on
    such flesh as this we wear,
before us into heaven is gone,
    to get us places there.
Captivity was captived then,
    and he doth from above
send ghostly presents down to men
    for tokens of his love.

Each door and everlasting gate   (Ps. 24:7)
    to him hath lifted been;
and in a glorious wise thereat
    our King is entered in.
Whom if to follow we regard,
    with ease we safely may,
for he hath all the means prepared,
    and made an open way.   (Heb. 10:20)

Then follow, follow on apace,
    and let us not forego
our Captain, till we win the place
    that he hath scaled unto;
and for his honor, let our voice
    a shout so hearty make,
the heavens may at our mirth rejoice,
    and earth and hell may shake.

George Wither
Hymns and Songs of the Church, 1623

24
Psalm 148

The Lord of heaven confess,
    on high his glory raise.
Him let all angels bless,
    him all his armies praise.
      Him glorify
          sun, moon, and stars;
        ye higher spheres,
    and cloudy sky.

From God your beings are,
    him therefore famous make;
you all created were,
    when he the word but spake.
      And from that place,
        where fixed you be
        by his decree
    you cannot pass.

Praise God from earth below,
    ye dragons and all deeps:
Fire, hail, clouds, wind, and snow,
    whom in command he keeps.
      Praise ye his name,
        hills great and small,
        trees low and tall;
    beasts wild and tame;

all things that creep or fly.
    Ye kings, ye vulgar throng,
all princes mean or high;
    both men and virgins young,
      ev'n young and old
        exalt his name;
        for much his fame
    should be extolled.

O let God's name be praised
    above both earth and sky;
for he his saints hath raised
    and set their horn on high;
      ev'n those that be
        of Israel's race,
        near to his grace,
    the Lord praise ye.

George Wither
Psalms of David, 1632
The Psalms of David in Meeter (Scottish Psalter), 1650

25
A General Invitation to Praise God

Come, oh, come in pious lays,
sound we God Almighty's praise;
hither bring in one consent
heart, and voice, and instrument.
Music add of every kind;
sound the trump, the cornet wind;
strike the viol, touch the lute;
let no tongue or string be mute;
    nor a creature dumb be found
    that hath either voice or sound.

Let those things which do not live
in still music praises give;
lowly pipe, ye worms that creep,
on the earth, or in the deep:
loud aloft your voices strain,
beasts and monsters of the main:
birds, your warbling treble sing;
clouds, your peals of thunder ring:
    sun and moon, exalted higher,
    and bright stars, augment this choir.

Come, ye sons of human race,
in this chorus take a place;
and amid the mortal throng,
be you masters of the song.
Angels, and supernal powers,
be the noblest tenor yours;
let, in praise of God, the sound
run a never-ending round;
    that our song of praise may be
    everlasting, as is he.

From earth's vast and hollow womb,
music's deepest bass may come;
seas and floods, from shore to shore,
shall their countertenors roar.
To this consort, when we sing,
whistling winds your descant bring;
that our song may overclimb
all the bounds of place and time,
    and ascend from sphere to sphere
    to the great Almighty's ear.

So from heaven, on earth he shall
let his gracious blessings fall;
and this huge wide orb we see
shall one choir, one temple be;
where, in such a praise, full tone
we shall sing what he hath done,
that the cursed fiends below
shall thereat impatient grow.
    Then, oh, come, in pious lays,
    sound we God Almighty's praise.

George Wither
The Hallelujah, or Britain's Second Remembrancer, 1641

26
Psalm 139

O Lord, in me there lieth nought
    but to thy search revealed lies;
        for when I sit
        thou markest it;
    no less thou notest when I rise;
yea, closest closet of my thought
    hath open windows to thine eyes.

Thou walkest with me when I walk;
    when to my bed for rest I go
        I find thee there
        and everywhere;
    not youngest thought in me doth grow,
no, not one word I cast to talk
    but, yet unuttered, thou dost know.

If forth I march, thou goest before;
    if back I turn, thou comest behind;
        so forth nor back
        thy guard I lack
    nay, on me too thy hand I find.
Well I thy wisdom may adore,
    but never reach with earthy mind.

To shun thy notice, leave thine eye,
    Oh! whither might I take my way?
        To starry sphere?
        Thy throne is there.
    To dead men's undelightsome stay?
There is thy walk, and there to lie
    unknown in vain I should assay.

O sun, whom light nor flight can match,
    suppose thy rightful frightful wings
        thou lend to me,
        and I could flee
    so far as thee the evening brings,
even led to west he would me catch,
    nor should I lurk with western things.

Do thou thy best, O secret night,
    in sable veil to cover me,
        thy sable veil
        shall vainly fail;
    with day unmasked my night shall be;
for night is day, and darkness light,
    O Father of all lights, to thee.

Each inmost piece in me is thine;
    while yet I in my mother dwelt,
        all that me clad
        from thee I had;
    thou in my frame hast strangely dealt.
Needs in my praise thy work must shine
    so inly them my thoughts have felt.

Thou, how my back was beamwise laid
    and raftering of my ribs, dost know;
        know'st every point
        of bone and joint,
    how to this whole these parts did grow,
in brave embroidery fair arrayed,
    though wrought in shop both dark and low.

Nay fashionless, ere form I took,
    thy all and more beholding eye
        my shapeless shape
        could not escape;
    all these time framed successively
ere one had being, in the book
    of thy foresight enrolled did lie.

My God, how I these studies prize,
    that do thy hidden workings show!
        Whose sum is such
        no sum so much,
    nay, summed as sand the sumless grow.
I lie to sleep, from sleep I rise,
    yet still in thought with thee I go.

My God, if thou but one wouldst kill,
    then straight would leave me further chase
        this cursed brood
        inured to blood,
    whose graceless taunts at thy disgrace
have aimed oft; and hating still
    would with proud lies thy truth outface.

Hate not I them, who thee do hate?
    Thine, Lord, I will the censure be.
        Detest I not
        the cankered knot
    whom I against thee banded see?
O Lord, thou knowest in highest rate
    I hate them all as foes to me.

Search me, my God, and prove my heart;
    examine me, and try my thought;
        and mark in me
        if aught there be
that hath with cause their anger wrought.
If not (as not) my life's each part,
    Lord, safely guide from danger brought.

Mary Sidney Herbert, Countess of Pembroke
The Psalmes of David . . . Begun by the Noble and Learned Gent, Sir
Philip Sidney, Knt., and Finished by the Right Honorable the Countess of
Pembroke, His Sister [no date; between 1603 and 1621]

27
Psalm 130

From the deeps of grief and fear,
    O Lord, to thee my soul repairs;
from thy heaven bow down thine ear;
    let thy mercy meet my prayers.
        O if thou mark'st
           what's done amiss,
        What soul so pure
           can see thy bliss?

But with thee sweet mercy stands,
    sealing pardons, working fear;
wait, my soul, wait on his hands;
    wait, mine eye, O wait, mine ear;
        If he his eye
           or tongue affords,
        watch all his looks,
           catch all his words.

As a watchman waits for day,
    and looks for light, and looks again;
when the night grows old and grey,
    to be relieved he calls amain;
        so look, so wait,
           so long, mine eyes,
        to see my Lord,
           my Sun, arise.

Wait, ye saints, wait on your Lord;
    for from his tongue sweet mercy flows;
wait on his cross, wait on his word;
    upon that tree redemption grows.
        He will redeem
           his Israel
        from sin and wrath,
           from death and hell.

Phineas Fletcher
The Purple Island, 1613

28
Psalm 8

Lord, how illustrious is thy name,
whose power both heaven and earth proclaim!
Thy glory thou hast set on high
above the marble-arched sky.

The wonders of thy power thou hast
in mouths of babes and sucklings placed,
that so thou might'st thy foes confound,
and who in malice most abound.

When I pure heaven, thy fabric, see,
the moon and stars disposed by thee;
O what is man, or his frail race,
that thou should'st such a shadow grace!

Next to thy angels most renowned,
with majesty and glory crowned,
the king of all thy creatures made,
that all beneath his feet hast laid;

all that on dales or mountains feed,
that shady woods or deserts breed;
what in the airy regions glide,
or through the rolling ocean slide.

George Sandys
A Paraphrase upon the Divine Poems, 1638

29
Morning, Evening, and Midnight Hymns

A. Morning

Awake, my soul, and with the sun
thy daily stage of duty run,
shake off dull sloth, and joyful rise
to pay thy morning sacrifice.

Thy precious time misspent, redeem,
each present day thy last esteem,
Improve thy talent with due care,
for the Great Day thyself prepare.

[stanza 3 omitted]

By influence of the Light divine,
let thy own light to others shine.
Reflect all heaven's propitious ways
in ardent love, and cheerful praise.

Wake, and lift up thyself, my heart,
and with the angels bear thy part,
who all night long unwearied sing
high praise to the eternal King.

[stanzas 6–8 omitted]

All praise to thee who safe hast kept
and hast refreshed me whilst I slept.
Grant, Lord, when I from death shall wake
I may of endless light partake.

[stanza 10 omitted]

Heaven is, dear Lord, where e'er thou art,
O never then from me depart;
for to my soul 'tis hell to be
but for one moment void of thee.

Lord, I my vows to thee renew,
disperse my sins like morning dew.
Guard my first springs of thought and will
and with thyself my Spirit fill.

Direct, control, suggest this day
all I design, or do, or say,
that all my powers with all their might
in thy sole glory may unite.

B. Evening

All praise to thee, my God, this night
for all the blessings of the light.
Keep me, O keep me, King of kings,
beneath thine own almighty wings.

Forgive me, Lord, for thy dear Son
the ill that I this day have done;
that with the world, myself, and thee
I, ere I sleep, at peace may be.

Teach me to live that I may dread
the grave as little as my bed;
to die, that this vile body may
rise glorious at the awful day.

Oh! may my soul on thee repose
and with sweet sleep mine eyelids close,
sleep that may me more vig'rous make
to serve my God when I awake.

When in the night I sleepless lie,
my soul with heavenly thoughts supply;
let no ill dreams disturb my rest,
no powers of darkness me molest.

[stanzas 6–9 omitted]

O may my Guardian while I sleep
close to my bed his vigils keep,
his love angelical instill,
stop all the avenues of ill.

[stanza 11 omitted]

C. Midnight

My God, now I from sleep awake,
the sole possession of me take.
From midnight terrors me secure,
and guard my heart from thoughts impure.

Blessed angels! while we silent lie,
you hallelujahs sing on high,
you joyful hymn the ever-Blessed
before the throne, and never rest.

I with your choir celestial join
in offering up a hymn divine;
with you in heaven I hope to dwell,
and bid the night and world farewell.

[stanzas 4 and 5 omitted]

O may I always ready stand
with my lamp burning in my hand;
may I in sight of heaven rejoice
when e'er I hear the Bridegroom's voice.

[stanzas 7–12 omitted]

D. Doxology

Praise God from whom all blessings flow,
praise him, all creatures here below;
praise him above, ye heavenly host,
praise Father, Son, and Holy Ghost.

Thomas Ken
A Manual of Prayers, 1695, revised, 1709
Complete texts from both editions are found in John Julian's
Dictionary of Hymnology.

30
A General Song of Praise to Almighty God

How shall I sing that Majesty
    which angels do admire!
Let dust in dust and ashes lie,
    sing, sing, ye heavenly choir.
Thousands of thousands stand around
    thy throne, O God most high;
ten thousand times ten thousand sound
    thy praise; but who am I?

Thy brightness unto them appears
    whilst I thy footsteps trace;
a sound of God comes to my ears,
    but they behold thy face.
They sing, because thou art their Sun;
    Lord, send a beam on me;
for where heaven is but once begun,
    there hallelujahs be.

Enlighten with faith's light my heart,
    enflame it with love's fire,
then shall I sing and bear a part
    with that celestial choir.
I shall, I fear, be dark and cold,
    with all my fire and light;
yet when thou dost accept their gold,
    Lord, treasure up my mite.   (Luke 21:1)

How great a being, Lord, is thine,
    which doth all beings keep.
Thy knowledge is the only line
    to sound so vast a deep.
Thou art a sea without a shore,
    a sun without a sphere;
thy time is now and evermore,
    thy place is everywhere.

[stanzas 5–12 omitted]

John Mason
Spiritual Songs, or, Songs of Praise, 1694

37

31
A Song of Praise for the Lord's Day

My Lord, my Love, was crucified,
    he all the pains did bear;
but in the sweetness of his rest
    he makes his servants share.

How sweetly rest thy saints above,
    which in thy bosom lie!
The church below doth rest in hope
    of that felicity.

Thou, Lord, who daily feedst thy sheep,
    mak'st them a weekly feast;
thy flocks meet in their several folds
    upon this day of rest.

Welcome and dear unto my soul
    are these sweet feasts of love;
but what a sabbath shall I keep
    when I shall rest above!

I bless thy wise and wondrous love
    which binds us to be free;
which makes us leave our earthly snares
    that we may come to thee.

I come, I wait, I hear, I pray:
    thy footsteps, Lord, I trace:
I sing to think this is the way
    unto my Savior's face.

These are my preparation days,
    and when my soul is dressed,
these sabbaths shall deliver me
    to mine eternal rest.

John Mason
Spiritual Songs, or, Songs of Praise, 1683

Chapter 3:
Isaac Watts (32–44)

Isaac Watts needs little introduction here, though he repays the closest study that anyone can afford to give him. The son of an elder of an Independent (Congregational) church in Southampton, born in 1674, precociously literate and learned, finally becoming a minister of a church of that communion in London, Watts is the liberator of hymnody in English. He cannot, as we have seen, be called positively its inventor; but, according to the principle mentioned in chapter 1, he was its first successful practitioner. There are four sources for his work: *Horae Lyricae*, 1705 (which contains not only hymns but some poetry in other forms); *Hymns and Spiritual Songs*, 1707; *Divine and Moral Songs*, 1715 (a very small collection divided into "Divine Songs" and "Moral Songs," both for children); and *The Psalms of David Imitated in the Language of the New Testament*, 1719. Pieces from all four collections are still in common use, but it is the second and fourth which contain his best-known hymns. Only one now in common use comes from any other source: this is "Am I a soldier of the cross?" for which see the *Hymnal Guide*.

Watts's hymns were the consequence of his dissatisfaction with the metrical psalters. He had reason to be discontented with their literature, but far more he was unhappy that Christians were not allowed to sing, apart from the meager allowance provided in the psalter supplements, about Christian doctrine. The accepted story is that in about 1690, at the age of sixteen, he mentioned to his father that the hymnody in church was dull and profitless, and on his father's replying, "Then write something better," he promptly did, and our 32 was the result.

This text should be studied with care. In it is the germ of all the 700-odd pieces he subsequently wrote. One notices that it is in the psalm meter; and all his hymns were written in psalm meters, so that known psalm tunes could carry them. It is, secondly, founded on a lyric passage in Revelation, a passage to which he often later returned, and is indeed so close a paraphrase of that passage that it was admitted in 1781 to the Scottish Paraphrases (see chapter 8). But thirdly, the final stanza gives the hymn an existential quality which is really the principle of the hymn's liberation. In that stanza the congregation is no longer reciting the biblical words but making its own prayer, and this is what finally unlocks the secret of hymnody.

Watts's style is close to that of the metrical psalters, but of course, being no longer bound by the necessity of packing in the words of the Authorized Version of the Bible, he does not need to strain his sentence structure and can write more freely. He still uses rhyme and rhyme is, here and in the psalters, a most necessary aid to memory when hymns are being "lined out," that is, sung by dictation and not from a book. Like so many other practical necessities in hymns (a musical parallel is the "gathering note" in the old psalm tunes), what here begins as a conventional necessity becomes an integral part of the poetry in skilled hands, so that it remained with us until very recently as, in all but a few unusual meters, a hymnic necessity.

It has to be admitted, as soon as you read Watts in any quantity, that he could descend to bathos. It is out of place to include his more risible examples in the quoted texts, but one of his finest pieces, "Begin, my tongue, some heavenly theme," contains a stanza which can hardly be printed now:

> He said, *Let the wide Heav'n be spread*,
>   And Heaven was stretched abroad;
> "Abrah'm, *I'll be thy God*," He said,
>   and he was *Abrah'm's God*.

But the incongruity of that is the consequence not of a failure on his part to write properly but on a shifting of taste and custom in the use of words and phrases. The effect of "worms" and "bowels" (see Preface to the First Edition, p. xix) is nowadays always absurd, but it was not so to him nor to his people.

It is the quality of free and uninhibited writing which produces so often that epigrammatic style that is always the mark of the great hymn writer. The memorable phrase, packing immense amounts into a few simple words, is what makes a hymn live. The last stanza of "When I survey," or the third of "Nature with open volume," two of his supreme moments, are examples to any hymn writer. The zest of mind which produces such fine religious conceits as the third stanza of 40 is what we first find in Watts, and what after him we look for in any writer worth considering.

His *Hymns*, 1707, are in three books: the first, hymns closely paraphrasing Scripture; the second (more fertile in material acceptable to modern editors), "spiritual songs" of freer range; and the third, communion hymns. All this, as well as the material in the 1705 book, was completed before he was thirty-three years old. In reading him, one wants to suspend a facile modern resistance to the diction and rhythm of the eighteenth century and to enjoy the positive gifts of this extraordinary writer.

This section contains nothing from *Divine and Moral Songs*; one hymn from there is at 296 (see chapter 16). But the *Psalms* produce two of his very best known pieces (43 and 44).

The *Psalms* are, in a way, a more dramatic gesture even than the *Hymns*, for, as he expressed it himself in a famous preface which well repays the trouble of finding and reading it, Watts here endeavors "to make David speak like a Christian." References to strictly Old Testament places, people, and events are often replaced with Christian references, so that, in the famous example (43), "Jesus shall reign" translates "His kingdom shall endure from sea to sea," the Hebrew priest-king being replaced by Christ himself. "Israel" often becomes "the church," or, in other contexts, "Britain" (a reference that now always has to be altered). Watts's

psalter is not quite complete; it omits a few psalms, though to compensate this Watts frequently translates a psalm in two or even three versions, throwing the emphasis in different directions or employing different meters. Example 44 shows the original text of his second version, part 1, of Psalm 90.

Watts is represented always by a few hymns in modern hymnals. The most generous selection in a recent hymnal is that in *Congregational Praise* (1951), which gives forty-five of his hymns. American hymnals rarely come near that figure; the *Worshipbook* (1972), for example, presents ten of his texts, in only one case avoiding abridgment, expansion, or alteration. This is quite normal nowadays.

32

A New Song to the Lamb That Was Slain. Revelation 5:6, 8, 9, 10, 12

This, Isaac Watts's first hymn, is displayed with the original spelling, punctuation, and capitalization.

Behold the Glories of the Lamb
    Amidst his Father's Throne:
Prepare new Honours for his Name,
    And Songs before unknown.

Let Elders worship at his Feet,
    The Church adore around,
With Vials full of Odours sweet,
    And Harps of sweeter sound.

Those are the Prayers of the Saints,
    And these the Hymns they raise,—
Jesus is kind to our Complaints,
    He loves to hear our Praise.

Eternal Father, who shall look
    Into thy Secret Will?
Who but the Son should take that Book,
    And open every Seal?   (Rev. 5:2)

He shall fulfil thy great Decrees,
    The Son deserves it well;
Lo! in his Hand the Sov'reign Keys
    Of Heav'n, and Death, and Hell!

Now to the Lamb that once was slain
    Be endless Blessings paid;
Salvation, Glory, Joy, remain
    Forever on thy Head.

Thou hast redeem'd our Souls with Blood,
    Hast set the Pris'ners free,
Hast made us Kings and Priests to God,
    And we shall reign with Thee.

The Worlds of Nature and of Grace
    Are put beneath thy Pow'r;
Then shorten these delaying Days
    And bring the promis'd Hour.

Isaac Watts, ca. 1690
Hymns and Spiritual Songs, 1707, I, 1

33

God Exalted above All Praise

Eternal Power! whose high abode
becomes the grandeur of a God;
infinite lengths beyond the bounds
where stars revolve their little rounds.

The lowest step about thy seat
rises too high for Gabriel's feet:
in vain the tall archangel tries
to reach thy height with wondering eyes.

Thy dazzling beauties while he sings,
he hides his face behind his wings;
and ranks of shining thrones around
fall worshiping, and spread the ground.

Lord, what shall earth and ashes do?
We would adore our Maker too;
from sin and dust to thee we cry,
the Great, the Holy, and the High!

Earth from afar has heard thy fame,
and worms have learnt to lisp thy name;
but, O, the glories of thy mind
leave all our soaring thoughts behind.

God is in heaven and men below;
be short, our tunes; our words be few;
a sacred reverence checks our songs,
and praise sits silent on our tongues.

Isaac Watts
Horae Lyricae, 1705, Book I

34

The Offices of Christ.
From Several Scriptures

Join all the glorious names
    of wisdom, love, and power,
that ever mortals knew,
    that angels ever bore:
All are too mean to speak his worth,
too mean to set my Savior forth.   (John 4:47)

But O what gentle terms,
    what condescending ways
doth our Redeemer use
    to teach his heavenly grace!
Mine eyes with joy and wonder see
what forms of love he bears for me.

Arrayed in mortal flesh
    he like an Angel stands,   (Dan. 6:22)
and holds the promises
    and pardons in his hands,
commissioned from his Father's throne
to make his grace to mortals known.

Great Prophet of my God,   (Acts 3:22)
    my tongue would bless thy name;
by thee the joyful news
    of our salvation came;
the joyful news of sins forgiven,
of hell subdued, and peace with heaven.

Be thou my Counselor,   (Isa. 9:6)
    my Pattern, and my Guide; (John 13–15; Isa. 55:4)
and through this desert land
    still keep me by thy side.
O let my feet ne'er run astray,
nor rove, nor seek the crooked way.

I love my Shepherd's voice,   (Ps. 23)
    his watchful eyes shall keep
my wandering soul among   (John 10:1–10)
    the thousands of his sheep: (Matt. 18)
he feeds his flock, he calls their names,
his bosom bears the tender lambs.

To this dear Surety's hand   (Gen. 43:9)
    will I commit my cause;
he answers and fulfills
    his Father's broken laws.
Behold my soul at freedom set!
My Surety paid the dreadful debt.

Jesus, my great High Priest   (Heb. 5:10)
    offered his blood and died;
my guilty conscience seeks
    no Sacrifice beside.
His powerful blood did once atone;
and now it pleads before the throne.

My Advocate appears   (1 John 2:1)
    for my defense on high,
The Father bows his ear,
    and lays his thunder by.
Not all that hell or sin can say
shall turn his heart, his love away.

My dear Almighty Lord,   (1 Tim 6:15)
    my Conqueror and my King, (Rev. 6:2; Acts 17:7)
Thy scepter, and thy sword,
    thy reigning grace, I sing.
Thine is the power; behold I sit
in willing bonds before thy feet.

Now let my soul arise,
    and tread the Tempter down;
my Captain leads me forth   (Heb. 2:10)
    to conquest and a crown.
A feeble saint shall win the day,
Though death and hell obstruct the way.

Should all the hosts of death
    and powers of hell unknown
put their most dreadful forms
    of rage and mischief on;
I shall be safe, for Christ displays   (Rev. 11:15)
superior power and guardian grace.

Isaac Watts
Hymns and Spiritual Songs, 1707, I, 150

35
A Prospect of Heaven Makes Death Easy

There is a land of pure delight,
    where saints immortal reign;
infinite day excludes the night,
    and pleasures banish pain.

There everlasting spring abides,
    and never withering flowers;
death like a narrow sea divides
    this heavenly land from ours.

Sweet fields beyond the swelling floor
    stand dressed in living green;
so to the Jews old Canaan stood,
    while Jordan rolled between.

But timorous mortals start and shrink
    to cross this narrow sea,
and linger shivering on the brink,
    and fear to launch away.

O could we make our doubts remove,
    these gloomy doubts that rise,
and see the Canaan that we love
    with unbeclouded eyes;

could we but climb where Moses stood,
    and view the landscape o'er,
not Jordan's stream, nor death's cold flood
    should fright us from the shore.

Isaac Watts
Hymns and Spiritual Songs, 1707, II, 66

36
The Christian Race. Isaiah 40:28–31

Awake, our souls, (away our fears,
    let every trembling thought be gone)
awake, and run the heavenly race,
    and put a cheerful courage on.

True, 'tis a strait and thorny road,
    and mortal spirits tire and faint,
but they forget the mighty God
    that feeds the strength of every saint:

thee, mighty God, whose matchless power
    is ever new and ever young,
and firm endures, while endless years
    their everlasting circles run.

From thee, the overflowing spring,
    our souls shall drink a fresh supply,
while such as trust their native strength
    shall melt away and droop and die.

Swift as an eagle cuts the air
    we'll mount aloft to thine abode,
on wings of love our souls shall fly,
    nor tire amidst the heavenly road.

Isaac Watts
Hymns and Spiritual Songs, 1707, I, 48

37
The Examples of Christ and the Saints

Give me the wings of faith, to rise
    within the veil, and see
the saints above, how great their joys,
    how bright their glories be.

Once they were mourning here below
    and wet their couch with tears;   (Ps. 6:6)
they wrestled hard, as we do now,
    with sins, and doubts, and fears.

I ask them whence their victory came,
    they, with united breath,
ascribe their conquest to the Lamb,
    their triumph to his death.

They marked the footsteps that he trod,
    (his zeal inspired their breast)
and following the incarnate God
    possess the promised rest.

Our glorious Leader claims our praise
    for his own pattern given,
while the long cloud of witnesses
    shows the same path to heaven.

Isaac Watts
Hymns and Spiritual Songs, 1707, II, 140

38
Crucifixion to the World by the Cross of Christ. Galatians 6:14

When I survey the wondrous cross
    where the young Prince of Glory died,
my richest gain I count but loss,
    and pour contempt on all my pride.

Forbid it, Lord, that I should boast
    save in the death of Christ my God;
all the vain things that charm me most,
    I sacrifice them to his blood.

See from his head, his hands, his feet,
    sorrow and love flow mingled down;
did e'er such love and sorrow meet,
    or thorns compose so rich a crown?

His dying crimson, like a robe,
    spreads o'er his body on the tree;
then am I dead to all the globe,
    and all the globe is dead to me.

Were the whole realm of nature mine,
    that were a present far too small;
love so amazing, so divine,
    demands my soul, my life, my all.

Isaac Watts
Hymns and Spiritual Songs, 1707, III, 7
In all editions after the first, Watts revised line 1:2 to
"on which the Prince of glory died."

39
Christ Crucified, the Wisdom and Power of God

Nature with open volume stands
    to spread her Maker's praise abroad
and every labor of his hands
    shows something worthy of a God.

But in the grace that rescued man
    his brightest form of glory shines;
here on the cross 'tis fairest drawn
    in precious blood and crimson lines.

Here his whole name appears complete,
    nor wit can guess, nor reason prove
which of the letters best is writ,
    the power, the wisdom, or the love.

Here I behold his inmost heart,
    where grace and vengeance strangely join,
piercing his Son with sharpest smart
    to make the purchased pleasures mine.

O the sweet wonders of that cross,
    where God the Savior loved and died!
Her noblest life my spirit draws
    from his dear wounds, and bleeding side.

I would forever speak his name
    in sounds to mortal ears unknown,
with angels join to praise the Lamb,
    and worship at his Father's throne.

Isaac Watts
Hymns and Spiritual Songs, 1707, III, 10

40
Incomparable Food; or, The Flesh and Blood of Christ

    We sing th' amazing deeds
      that grace divine performs;
th' eternal God comes down and bleeds
      to nourish dying worms.

    This soul-reviving wine,
      Dear Savior, is thy blood;
we thank that sacred flesh of thine
      for this immortal food.

The banquet that we eat
is made of heavenly things;
earth hath no dainties half so sweet
as our Redeemer brings.

In vain had Adam sought
and searched his garden round;
for there was no such blessed fruit
in all that happy ground.

Th' angelic host above
can never taste this food,
they feast upon their Maker's love,
but not a Savior's blood.

On us th' Almighty Lord
bestows this matchless grace,
and meets us smiling at his board,
with pleasure in his face.

Come, all ye drooping saints,
and banquet with the King,
the wine will drown your sad complaints,
and tune your voice to sing—

Salvation to the name
of our adored Christ!
Through the wide earth his grace proclaim,
and glory in the high'st.

Isaac Watts
Hymns and Spiritual Songs, 1707, III, 17
Watts placed brackets around the first two stanzas,
suggesting their potential omission, which is commonly done.

41

Glorying in the Cross; or, Not Ashamed of Christ Crucified

At thy command, our dearest Lord,
here we attend thy dying feast;
thy blood like wine adorns thy board,
and thine own flesh feeds every guest.

Our faith adores thy bleeding love,
and trusts for life in one that died;
we hope for heavenly crowns above
from a Redeemer crucified.

Let the vain world pronounce it shame,
and fling their scandals on the cause;
we come to boast our Savior's name,
and make our triumphs in his cross.

With joy we tell the scoffing age
he that was dead has left his tomb,
he lives above their utmost rage
and we are waiting till he come.

Isaac Watts
Hymns and Spiritual Songs, 1707, III, 19

42

God Our Shepherd. Psalm 23

My Shepherd will supply my need,
Jehovah is his name;
in pastures green he makes me feed
beside the living stream.

He brings my wandering spirit back
when I forsake his ways;
and leads me, for his mercy's sake,
in paths of truth and grace.

When I walk through the shades of death,
thy presence is my stay;
a word of thy supporting breath
drives all my fears away.

Thy hand, in sight of all my foes,
doth still my table spread;
my cup with blessings overflows,
thine oil anoints my head.

The sure provisions of my God
    attend me all my days;
O may thy house be mine abode,
    and all my work be praise!

There would I find a settled rest,
    (while others go and come)
no more a stranger or a guest,
    but like a child at home.

Isaac Watts
*The Psalms of David Imitated
in the Language of the New Testament*, 1719

43

Christ's Kingdom among the Gentiles.
Psalm 72. Part 2.

Jesus shall reign where'er the sun
does his successive journeys run;
his kingdom stretch from shore to shore,
till moons shall wax and wane no more.

Behold the islands with their kings,
and Europe her best tribute brings;
from north to south the princes meet
to pay their homage at his feet.

There Persia glorious to behold,
there India stands in eastern gold;
and barbarous nations at his word
submit and bow and own their Lord.

For him shall endless prayer be made,
and praises throng to crown his head;
his name like sweet perfume shall rise
with every morning sacrifice;

people and realms of every tongue
dwell on his love with sweetest song;
and infant voices shall proclaim
their early blessings on his name.

Blessings abound where'er he reigns,
the prisoner leaps to lose his chains,
the weary find eternal rest,
and all the sons of want are blest.

Where he displays his healing power
death and the curse are known no more;
in him the tribes of Adam boast
more blessings than their father lost.

Let every creature rise and bring
peculiar honors to our King;
angels descend with songs again,
and earth repeat the long Amen.

Isaac Watts
*The Psalms of David Imitated
in the Language of the New Testament*, 1719
The semicolon at the end of line 4:4, indicating that this and the
following stanza are one continuous sentence, is not in any of the
editions of Watts's hymns but is a wholly acceptable conjecture first
offered by the English classical scholar Robert L. Arrowsmith and
incorporated in the text in *Hymns for Church and School*, 1964, 123.

44

Man Frail, and God Eternal.
Psalm 90:1–5. Part 1.

Our God, our help in ages past,
    our hope for years to come,
our shelter from the stormy blast,
    and our eternal home.

Under the shadow of thy throne
    thy saints have dwelt secure;
sufficient is thine arm alone,
    and our defense is sure.

Before the hills in order stood,
    or earth received her frame,
from everlasting thou art God,
    to endless years the same.

Thy Word commands our flesh to dust,
    "Return, ye sons of men":
All nations rose from earth at first,
    and turn to earth again.

A thousand ages in thy sight
    are like an evening gone;
short as the watch that ends the night
    before the rising sun.

The busy tribes of flesh and blood,
    with all their lives and cares,
are carried downwards by the flood
    and lost in following years.

Time, like an ever-rolling stream
    bears all its sons away;
they fly, forgotten as a dream
    dies at the opening day.

Like flowery fields the nations stand
    pleased with the morning light;
the flowers beneath the Mower's hand
    lie withering e'er 'tis night.

Our God, our help in ages past,
    our hope for years to come,
be thou our guard while troubles last,
    and our eternal home.

Isaac Watts
*The Psalms of David Imitated
in the Language of the New Testament*, 1719

Chapter 4:
After Watts and before the Wesleys (45–52)

"After" and "before" are not so much chronological as stylistic terms here. The group of hymns that follows includes some that were written before Watts had finished and some written after Charles Wesley had begun; but the importance of this interim period between the two great hymnic explosions can hardly be overstated.

In it the current is flowing two ways. In 45–49 we see the source of a new style; in 50–52, three pieces by Philip Doddridge, we have the work of a devoted disciple of Watts.

The two fragments of Alexander Pope's *The Messiah* (45) should be studied closely. The whole poem of 108 lines should, if possible, be consulted. (It is 227 in the *Oxford Book of Christian Verse*.) It first appeared in *The Spectator*, whose founding editor was Joseph Addison, on May 12, 1712. Pope was by that time the leading poet of British life, and he was about to bring to its highest perfection a style of writing which is always primarily associated with his name: the didactic and philosophical poem in heroic couplets (rhymed decasyllables). In the *Essay on Man*, his masterpiece, Pope showed how this meter could express in poetic terms a long argument and drive it home with that quality for which it proved to be particularly suited—wit. Pope at his best evokes a quite different kind of smile from that which the lyric poets of the seventeenth century produce. He builds on Dryden rather than on Milton, whose blank verse, using the same metrical line, has a totally different effect.

What I think has not been hitherto pointed out is the effect, to Pope as unexpected as it was unintended, that this had on hymnody. While the heroic couplet is not in any sense a natural meter for hymnody (the few hymns that exist in rhymed tens do not sound at all like Pope's couplets), there is one thing that they do have in common with the hymn style, and that is that, quite unlike the blank verse of Milton and Shakespeare, they depend for their effect on the coincidence of the sentence with the end of a couplet. The "run-on" is essential to the rhythm of blank verse; it is rare in heroic couplets. In our short extract there is only one place, line 102, where the sense runs over the end of a couplet, and that is in fact the only place in the whole poem where it does so. Similarly, and for obvious practical reasons, the "run-on" is always regarded as exceptional in hymn writing.

Now, it cannot escape the most casual eye that in section A of 45 there are several phrases that are familiar to hymn singers. The whole poem is a catena of paraphrases from the Old Testament prophets; but, what is more remarkable is the very clear announcement that lines 29, 37, 39–40 are the source of stanzas 1 and 4 of Doddridge's "Hark the glad sound" (52), and that lines 38 and 43–44 are the source of stanza 5 of Wesley's "O for a thousand tongues" (60). (A much later American hymn, 373, quotes line 37.)

When we add the much better-known fact that the first line of "Love divine" (66) is imitated from Dryden, and that the last is taken verbatim from the fourth line of Addison's "Gratitude" (47), we know what Charles Wesley read in his youth, and what kind of literature inspired his forms of expression. In the less-known Wesley hymns there is much use of classical allusion, and, in his poetry, plenty of picturesque admixture of classical proper names of the kind familiar in Milton and in Pope (and seen in line 100 of our second extract at 45).

This piece, we repeat, appeared in Addison's *The Spectator* in May 1712. In several Saturday issues in July, August, and September of the same year, Addison included hymns of his own which were written in imitation and in admiration of Isaac Watts, whose *Hymns* had appeared five years earlier. Of the five that Addison wrote, three (46–48) are in very wide use still, and all are to be found in current hymnals. (*The English Hymnal* contains all five, at 92, 297, 491, 511, 542, only 511 being abridged.) Three are in Watts's Common Meter; the other two use six- and eight-line stanzas of eight syllables, and both these (46, 48) are psalm paraphrases. His hymns are, however, as characteristically an Anglican layman's work of the period as Watts's are the work of a dissenting Calvinist minister. They sacrifice (if that is the word you want to use) Watts's fervor for a smoothness and urbanity of diction that Watts never rose to and never particularly aimed at. They are more palatable than much of Watts to people who value good literature, less so to those who value the in-group intensity of religious diction. Men of letters have often expressed special admiration of 48, and the compilers of the Scottish Paraphrases of 1781, severe enough in all conscience in their dogmatic standards, included our 47 (in full) and 48, with "When rising from the bed of death" as three of the five hymns they permitted to be appended to their scriptural paraphrases; the other two are by Watts.

"Christians, awake" (49) is worth reading in its entirety alongside the Pope fragments. Pope's poem was not "discovered" as hymn material until the first American Episcopal *Hymnal* of 1826 included a cento that uses lines 85–86, 97–98, 87–94, and 105–108, the only alteration being the reduction of the final line by two syllables. John Byrom's poem, his Christmas present to his daughter in 1749, was sung, as tradition has it, the very next year by the choir of the church that he attended in Manchester, and it was made into a regular hymn by Thomas Cotterill in 1819. Here again we see the attractions of the "heroic couplet" as a vehicle of hymnody. We would give much to know just what selection of lines was sung on that Christmas in 1750 when the magnificent tune was first heard.

Philip Doddridge (50–52) was an industrious hymn writer, almost all of whose work first saw the light of publication after his death. He wrote his hymns at different times to illustrate his preaching, being a minister of the same communion as Watts.

His work is, on the whole, cavalierly treated by modern hymnals and the best-known hymn attributed to him, "O God of Bethel" (96) contains very little of his original work. In this, at least for the first four stanzas, and in 101, the Scottish revisers on the whole improved him; but they were interested in that part of his work which stayed closest to the letter of Scripture. This he frequently did, as in 52, which in its full version is a very uneven piece of work, and makes a far better hymn if every other stanza is left out. But when he is writing more freely he is often very eloquent, and though they are far from well known, 50 and 51 may well be his finest pieces: 50 showing an unusually compressed and poised style that certainly owes a good deal to the Augustans (whose leader was this same Pope); and 51, besides being positively the first hymn on the social applications of the Gospel ever to be written (if we discount Watts's not infrequent effusions on the Popish Plot), is also a beautiful example of disciplined rhetorical power. Other work of his in the current hymnals is always worth looking at, though it does not often rise quite to this standard.

The one other well-known hymn of the "interim" period, which again owes much to Watts but shows something of the new literary freedom, is Simon Browne's "Come, gracious Spirit"; as now sung, however, this text is much altered from the original and is an improvement on it.

45
The Messiah

A. Lines 29–46:

Hark! a glad sound the lonely desert cheers;
prepare the way! a God, a God appears: 30
A God, a God! the vocal trills reply,
the rocks proclaim th' approaching Deity.
Lo, earth receives him from the bending skies!
Sink down, ye mountains, and ye valleys, rise,
with heads declined, ye cedars homage pay;   35
be smooth, ye rocks, ye rapid floods, give way!
The Savior comes! by ancient bards foretold:
Hear him, ye deaf, and all ye blind, behold!
He from thick films shall purge the visual ray,
and on the sightless eyeball pour the day: 40
'Tis he th' obstructed paths of sound shall clear,
and bid new music charm th' unfolding ear:
The dumb shall sing, the lame his crutch forego,
and leap exulting like the bounding roe.
No sigh, no murmur the wide world shall hear,   45
from every face he wipes off every tear.

B. Lines 85–108:

Rise, crowned with light, imperial Salem, rise!   85
Exalt thy towery head, and lift thy eyes!
See, a long race thy spacious courts adorn;
see future sons, and daughters yet unborn,
in crowding ranks on every side arise,
demanding life, impatient for the skies!   90
See barbarous nations at thy gates attend,
walk in thy light, and in thy temple bend;
see thy bright altars thronged with prostrate kings,
and heaped with products of Sabaean springs!
For thee Idumé's spicy forests blow,   95
and seeds of gold in Ophir's mountains glow.
See heaven its sparkling portals wide display,
and break upon thee in a flood of day!
No more the rising sun shall gild the morn,
nor evening Cynthia fill her silver horn;   100
but lost, dissolved in thy superior rays
one tide of glory, one unclouded blaze
o'erflow thy courts: the light himself shall shine
revealed, and God's eternal day be thine!
The seas shall waste, the skies in smoke decay,   105
rocks fall to dust, and mountains melt away;
but fixed his word, his saving power remains—
Thy realm for ever lasts, thy own Messiah reigns!

Alexander Pope
The Messiah, 1712

46
Psalm 23:1–4

The Lord my pasture shall prepare,
and feed me with a shepherd's care;
his presence shall my wants supply,
and guard me with a watchful eye;
my noonday walks he shall attend,
and all my midnight hours defend.

When in the sultry glebe I faint,
or on the thirsty mountain pant,
to fertile vales and dewy meads
my weary wandering steps he leads,
where peaceful rivers, soft and slow,
amid the verdant landscape flow.

Though in the paths of death I tread,
with gloomy horrors overspread,
my steadfast heart shall fear no ill,
for thou, O Lord, art with me still;
thy friendly crook shall give me aid,
and guide me through the dreadful shade.

Though in a bare and rugged way
through devious lonely wilds I stray,
thy bounty shall my pains beguile;
the barren wilderness shall smile,
with sudden greens and herbage crowned,
and streams shall murmur all around.

Joseph Addison
The Spectator, July 26, 1712

47
Gratitude

When all thy mercies, O my God!
    my rising soul surveys,
transported with the view, I'm lost
    in wonder, love, and praise.

O how shall words, with equal warmth,
    the gratitude declare
that glows within my ravished heart!
    but thou canst read it there.

Thy providence my life sustained,
    and all my wants redressed,
when in the silent womb I lay
    and hung upon the breast.

To all my weak complaints and cries
    thy mercy lent an ear,
ere yet my feeble thoughts had learned
    to form themselves in prayer.

Unnumbered comforts to my soul
    thy tender care bestowed,
before my infant heart conceived
    from whom those comforts flowed.

When in the slippery paths of youth
    with heedless steps I ran;
thine arm, unseen, conveyed me safe,
    and led me up to man.

Through hidden dangers, toils, and deaths,
    it gently cleared my way;
and through the pleasing snares of vice,
    more to be feared than they.

When worn with sickness, oft hast thou
    with health renewed my face;
and when in sins and sorrows sunk,
    revived my soul with grace.

Thy bounteous hand with worldly bliss
    hath made my cup run o'er;
and in a kind and faithful friend,
    hath doubled all my store.

Ten thousand thousand precious gifts
    my daily thanks employ;
nor is the least a cheerful heart,
    that tastes these gifts with joy.

Through every period of my life
    thy goodness I'll proclaim;
and after death, in distant worlds,
    resume the glorious theme.

When nature fails, and day and night
    divide thy works no more,
my ever grateful heart, O Lord,
    thy mercy shall adore.

Through all eternity to thee
    a joyful song I'll raise;
for, oh! eternity's too short
    to utter all thy praise.

Joseph Addison
The Spectator, August 9, 1712
Note the similarity between stanza 7 and Newton's "Amazing grace."

48
Psalm 19:1–6

The spacious firmament on high,
with all the blue ethereal sky,
and spangled heavens, a shining frame,
their great Original proclaim.
Th' unwearied sun from day to day
does his Creator's power display;
and publishes to every land
the work of an Almighty hand.

Soon as the evening shades prevail,
the moon takes up the wondrous tale,
and, nightly to the listening earth
repeats the story of her birth;
while all the stars that round her burn,
and all the planets in their turn
confirm the tidings as they roll
and spread the truth from pole to pole.

What though in solemn silence all
move round the dark terrestrial ball?
What though no real voice, no sound,
amidst their radiant orbs be found?
In reason's ear they all rejoice,
and utter forth a glorious voice;
for ever singing, as they shine,
"The hand that made us is divine."

Joseph Addison
The Spectator, August 23, 1712

49
A. Christmas Day for Dolly

Christians, awake, salute the happy morn
whereon the Savior of the world was born.
Rise to adore the Mystery of Love
which hosts of angels chanted from above;
with them the joyful tidings first begun
of God incarnate and the Virgin's Son.
Then to the watchful shepherds it was told,
who heard th' angelic herald's voice—Behold!
I bring good tidings of a Savior's birth
to you and all the nations upon earth.
This day hath God fulfilled his promised Word,
this day is born a Savior, Christ the Lord.
In David's city, shepherds, ye shall find
the long-foretold Redeemer of mankind
wrapped up in swaddling cloths, be this the sign,
a cratch contains the holy Babe divine.

He spake, and straightway the celestial choir
in hymns of joy unknown before conspire
the praises of redeeming Love they sung
and heaven's whole orb with hallelujahs rung.
God's highest glory was their anthem still,
peace upon earth, and mutual good will.
To Bethlehem straight th' enlightened shepherds ran
to see the wonder God had wrought for man.
*They saw their Savior as the angel said,
*the swaddled Infant in the manger laid.
*Joseph and Mary a distressed pair
*guard the sole Object of th' Almighty's care;
*to human eyes none present but they two
*where heaven was pointing its concentered view.
Amazed the wondrous story they proclaim,
the first apostles of his Infant fame.
But Mary kept and pondered in her heart
the heavenly vision which the swains impart.
They to their flocks and praising God return
with hearts no doubt that did within them burn.

Let us like these good shepherds then employ
our grateful voices to proclaim the joy.
Like Mary let us ponder in our mind
God's wondrous love in saving lost mankind,
artless and watchful as these favored swains,
while virgin meekness in the heart remains.
Trace we the Babe who has retrieved our loss
from his poor manger to his bitter cross.
Follow we him who has our cause maintained
and man's first heavenly state shall be regained.
Then may we hope, th' angelic thrones among,
to sing, redeemed, a glad triumphal song.
He that was born upon this joyful day
around us all his glory shall display;
saved by his love, incessant we shall sing
of angels and of angel-men the King.

John Byrom, 1749
By the time that the posthumous volume of Byrom's *Miscellaneous Poems* was issued, 1773, the lines marked with asterisks had been condensed to reduce the poem from 52 to 48 lines. Other word changes were made as well.

B. Arranged as a hymn

Christians, awake, salute the happy morn
whereon the Savior of the world was born;
rise to adore the mystery of love,
which hosts of angels chanted from above;
with them the joyful tidings first begun
of God incarnate and the virgin's son.

Then to the watchful shepherds it was told,
who heard th' angelic herald's voice, "Behold,
I bring good tidings of a Savior's birth
to you and all the nations of the earth;
this day hath God fulfilled his promised word,
this day is born a Savior, Christ the Lord."

He spake; and straightway the celestial choir
in hymns of joy, unknown before, conspire.
The praises of redeeming love they sang,
and heaven's whole orb with alleluias rang;
God's highest glory was their anthem still,
peace upon earth, and unto men goodwill.

To Bethlehem straight th' enlightened shepherds ran
to see the wonder God had wrought for man;
then to their flocks, still praising God, return,
and their glad hearts with holy rapture burn;
amazed, the wondrous tidings they proclaim,
the first apostles of his infant fame.

Like Mary, let us ponder in our mind
God's wondrous love in saving lost mankind;
trace we the babe, who hath retrieved our loss,
from his poor manger to his bitter cross;
tread in his steps, assisted by his grace,
till man's first heavenly state again takes place.

Then may we hope, th' angelic hosts among,
to sing, redeemed, a glad triumphal song;
he that was born upon this joyful day
around us all his glory shall display;
saved by his love, incessant we shall sing
eternal praises to heaven's almighty king.

altered by James Montgomery, 1819
Thomas Cotterill's *Poems and Hymns for Public and Private Use* (8th edition), 1819

50
Ebenezer, or God's Helping Hand Reviewed and Acknowledged. I Samuel 7:12

My helper God! I bless his name;
the same his power, his grace the same.
The tokens of his friendly care
open, and crown, and close the year.

I 'midst ten thousand dangers stand
supported by his guardian hand;
and see, when I survey my ways,
ten thousand monuments of praise.

Thus far his arm has led me on;
thus far I make his mercy known;
and, while I tread this desert land,
new mercies shall new songs demand.

My grateful soul, on Jordan's shore
shall raise one sacred pillar more:
then bear, in his bright courts above
inscriptions of immortal love.

Philip Doddridge
Hymns Founded on Various Texts in the Holy Scriptures, 1755, 23

51
Relieving Christ in His Poor Saints. Matthew 25:40

Jesus, my Lord, how rich thy grace!
    thy bounties how complete!
How shall I count the matchless sum?
    or pay the mighty debt?

High on a throne of radiant light
    dost thou exalted shine;
what can my poverty bestow
    when all the worlds are thine?

But thou hast brethren here below,
    the partners of thy grace,
and wilt confess their humble names
    before thy Father's face.

In them thou may'st be clothed, and fed,
    and visited, and cheered,
and in their accents of distress
    my Savior's voice is heard.

Thy face with reverence and with love
    I in thy poor would see;
O let me rather beg my bread
    than hold it back from thee.

Philip Doddridge
Hymns Founded on Various Texts in the Holy Scriptures, 1755, 188

52
Christ's Message. Luke 4:18, 19

Hark, the glad sound! the Savior comes,
    the Savior promised long!
let every heart prepare a throne,
    and every voice a song.

On him the Spirit largely poured
    exerts its sacred fire:
wisdom and might, and zeal and love
    his holy breast inspire.

He comes the prisoners to release
    in Satan's bondage held;
the gates of brass before him burst,
    the iron fetters yield.

He comes from the thick films of vice
    to clear the mental ray,
and on the eyeballs of the blind
    to pour celestial day.

He comes the broken heart to bind,
    the bleeding soul to cure,
and with the treasures of his grace
    to enrich the humble poor.

His silver trumpets publish loud
    the jub'lee of the Lord;   (Lev. 25)
our debts are all remitted now,
    our heritage restored.

Our glad hosannas, Prince of peace,
     thy welcome shall proclaim,
and heaven's eternal arches ring
     with thy beloved name!

Philip Doddridge
Hymns Founded on Various Texts in the Holy Scriptures, 1755, 203

Chapter 5:
Charles Wesley and His Family (53–72)

This part of our story must begin with John, Charles Wesley's even more celebrated elder brother. John was a hymnologist and a translator but not, it is usually thought, a hymn writer. (We must admit that the ascription of all translations to John and all original hymns to Charles is nowhere supported in anything they themselves said or wrote; but it is an educated guess which there is no serious reason for disturbing.) One of the many distinctions enjoyed by Charles is the preparation of the first hymnal published in America—the Charlestown hymnal of 1737 which he compiled in the course of his unfortunate and ill-starred mission to Georgia. This event took place before what he refers to as his "conversion" (May 24, 1738); but the hymnal is not without interest. It contains, for the first time, a hymn by his father (53) and one by his elder brother (54), which show something of the style of Isaac Watts; and this collection also has for the first time "Before Jehovah's awful throne," rewritten in its first stanza by John Wesley from Watts's Psalm 100. Naturally, there is nothing here by Charles Wesley, who seems not to have begun hymn writing until after his own "conversion," three days before John's, so Isaac Watts is inevitably the chief contributor. But there are several others by Charles's father and brother, and six hymns made out of poems by George Herbert (for whom see chapter 20).

John's contact with the German Pietists, especially the Moravians as newly gathered under their great leader Zinzendorf, inspired him to learn German, and to make a number of translations not always in the meters of the originals, but showing a command of language which introduces a quite new note into hymnody and which he shared with his more prolific brother (see 55, 56, 195C, 202C).

But once Charles got under way in his 1739 collection, he began a hymnic output which is unmatched anywhere in the literature for volume, variety, and distinction of style. The truth about the volume cannot be more precisely stated than as it is put by Frank Baker, who finds that he wrote 8,989 religious poems. Not all qualify as hymns, but it is usually said that something over 6,000 do. Charles lived fifty years from the year of his conversion, so this total works out at 3.4 poems per week, assuming him to have died in the act of writing. If a skeptic says that it would be difficult to avoid writing badly in such an output, and if a kinder critic murmurs that it must have been impossible to avoid repetition, the only honest answer is that it is still remarkable how many indispensable hymns everybody now admits him to have written, and what a high standard of doctrine, eloquence, and lyricism he reaches in so many of them. Not that he is an unhonored prophet. The English *Methodist Hymn Book* of 1904 contained 980 hymns, of which 440 are his; its 1933 successor, almost exactly the same length, could not cut him down below 243. Many hymnals of all denominations contain twenty.

Watts was an Independent. Wesley was a priest of the Church of England. In any of those hymnals which have a theological rather than liturgical arrangement you tend to find Watts near the beginning, Wesley coming into his own in the seasons of the Church's year and, of course, in hymns of Christian experience. Watts was the hymn writer primarily of the glory of God as a good Calvinist heart apprehended it. Wesley was the celebrator of Christ and of the Holy Spirit. In *Congregational Praise* (which I choose because of its theological arrangement) Watts has 14 entries before Wesley's first, and 21 before Wesley's third, while in the second half of the book Wesley has 26 to Watts's 10.

Charles Wesley's two overriding passions were the celebration of the church's year, stemming from his faithfulness to his prayer book, and (that to which he gave even freer rein) hymns exalting the glory of Christ and the bliss of conversion. He is the first and, surely for all time, the greatest evangelical hymn writer. Not infrequently he is didactic, but he is hardly ever anything but ecstatic. Such a pressure of devotion needed the discipline of doctrine, and this we find in him to a degree that is the measure of his outstanding preeminence among evangelicals. The simplest and most "popular" of his hymns (like "Hark the herald," or its original, for which see 59) abound in scriptural echoes and allusions; the profoundest abound equally (see 58). His treatment of Scripture is the poet's as much as the preacher's; for most of the time he uses Scripture to illuminate itself, often providing a mosaic of quotations which produce a new and magnificent pattern, as in "Love divine," 66. The direct paraphrasing of Scripture he hardly attempts before 1762, in which year he produced a small collection of hymns, mostly short and all exquisite, which are largely paraphrases of Matthew Henry's *Commentary* (1700)—see 69–71. The majestic "Come, O thou Traveler" (62) is not really so to be thought of; it is rather a meditation on a mystery. In its full length it is moving, though hardly singable; and yet in the four-stanza selection still to be found in hymnals that have not wholly lost their consciences it becomes an utterance of perfect clarity and trenchant communicativeness. His writing for children may be seen at 72 and 297.

Wesley used over eighty meters compared with Watts's handful. Some are most entertaining and lighthearted (like that of 68), others grave and measured, like the six-eights (8.8.8.8.8.8.) of which he was especially fond. The gate that Watts had opened Wesley joyously entered; and the field that Watts sowed he reaped, literally, a hundred-fold. If one considers these two as two mountain ranges, then perhaps Watts can boast the highest peak. Wesley, it may be fair to say, never quite reached the height of "When I survey" and "Nature with open volume"; but the average level of Wesley is probably higher, considered as literature. Watts could occasionally come down to

a thump of bathos; Wesley sometimes flounders. But between them they ensured, the one in his quiet London congregation, the other anywhere from the tin mines of Cornwall to the coal pits of Newcastle, that the Christian faith should never be without songs for its full expression.

It is just possible, however, that Watts scores over Wesley in one respect. Perhaps, over two centuries after their hymns were written, Watts uses less "in-group" language; perhaps at his best he is more public, easier to offer to Christians whose faith is not learned or intense. Wesley is much more for those who have traveled far. You come to "When I survey" long before you come to "Eternal beam of light divine" (57) which is perhaps the hymn of Wesley's that can be most fairly compared with Watts's masterpieces. Yes, you find Wesley near the end of the road, and yet, as the reader will see, I have, as a disciple of Watts's own communion, had to close my anthology not with a Wesley but with a Watts—whose last two lines say what Wesley never quite said and perhaps never really was likely to say.

53

On the Crucifixion

Behold the Savior of mankind
    nailed to the shameful tree!
How vast the love that him inclined
    to bleed and die for thee!

Hark how he groans! while nature shakes,
    and earth's strong pillars bend!
The temple's veil in sunder breaks,
    the solid marbles yield.

'Tis done! the precious ransom's paid!
    "Receive my soul," he cries;
see where he bows his sacred head!
    He bows his head and dies.

But soon he'll break death's envious chain
    and in full glory shine.
O Lamb of God, was ever pain,
    was ever love like thinc!

Samuel Wesley, Sr., ca. 1709
as in *A Collection of Psalms and Hymns* by John Wesley, Charlestown
[Charleston], South Carolina, 1737, which omitted stanzas 2 and 6 of
the original:

Though far unequal our low praise
    to thy vast sufferings prove,
O Lamb of God, thus all our days,
    thus will we grieve and love.

Thy loss our ruin did repair;
    death by thy death is slain;
thou wilt at length exalt us where
    thou dost in glory reign.

54
Hymn to God the Father

Hail, Father, whose creating call
    unnumbered worlds attend;
Jehovah, comprehending all,
    whom none can comprehend!

In light unsearchable enthroned
    which angels dimly see;
the fountain of the God-head owned
    and foremost of the Three.

From thee through an eternal now
    the Son, thine offering, flowed;
an everlasting Father thou,
    as everlasting God.

Nor quite displayed to worlds above,
    nor quite on earth concealed:
by wondrous, unexhausted love
    to mortal men revealed:

supreme and all-sufficient God,
    when nature shall expire
and worlds created by thy nod
    shall perish by thy fire.

Thy name, Jehovah, be adored
    by creatures without end,
whom none but thy essential Word
    and Spirit comprehend.

Samuel Wesley, Jr.
A Collection of Psalms and Hymns, 1737

55
From the German,
"Verborgne, Gottsliebe du"

Thou hidden love of God, whose height,
    whose depth unfathomed, no man knows;
I see from far thy beauteous light,
    inly I sigh for thy repose:
my heart is pained, nor can it be
at rest, till it finds rest in thee.

Thy secret voice invites me still
    the sweetness of thy yoke to prove;
and fain I would; but though my will
    be fixed, yet wide my passions rove;
yet hindrances strew all the way—
I aim at thee, yet from thee stray.

'Tis mercy all, that thou hast brought
    my mind to seek her peace in thee!
Yet while I seek, but find thee not,
    no peace my wandering soul shall see:
O when shall all my wanderings end,
and all my steps to thee-ward tend?

Is there a thing beneath the sun,
    that strives with thee my heart to share?
Ah, tear it thence, that thou alone
    may'st reign, unrivaled Monarch there;
from earthly loves I must be free
ere I can find repose in thee.

O hide this self from me, that I
    no more, but Christ may in me live!   (Gal. 2:20)
My vile affections crucify,
    nor let one darling lust survive.
In all things nothing may I see,
nothing desire or seek, but thee.

O Love, thy sovereign aid impart,
    to save me from low-thoughted care!
Chase this self-will through all my heart,
    through all its latent mazes there,
make me thy duteous child that I
ceaseless may "Abba, Father" cry.   (Rom. 8:15–16)

Ah, no! ne'er will I backward turn:
    thine wholly, thine alone I am!
Thrice happy he who views with scorn
    earth's toys, for thee his constant flame!
O help, that I may never move
from the blest footsteps of thy love!

Each moment draw my heart away
    from earth, that lowly waits thy call;
speak to my inmost soul, and say,
    "I am thy love, thy God, thy all!"
To feel thy power, to hear thy voice,
to taste thy love, is all my choice.

> translated, John Wesley, 1736
> *Psalms and Hymns*, 1738
> from stanzas 1–3 and 6–10 of original ten
> by Gerhardt Tersteegen, 1729

56

The Believer's Triumph. From the German.

Jesu, thy blood and righteousness
my beauty are, my glorious dress;   (Isa. 61:10)
'midst flaming worlds, in these arrayed,
with joy shall I lift up my head.

Bold shall I stand in that great day;
for who ought to my charge shall lay?   (Rom. 8:33)
Fully absolved through these I am,
from sin and fear, from guilt and shame.

The holy, meek, unspotted Lamb
who from the Father's bosom came,
who died for me, ev'n me to atone,
now for my Lord and God I own.   (John 20:28)

Lord, I believe thy precious blood,   (Lev. 16:2)
which at the mercy seat of God   (Heb. 9:4, 13–14)
for ever doth for sinners plead,
for me, ev'n for my soul was shed.

Lord, I believe, were sinners more
than sands upon the ocean shore,
thou hast for all a ransom paid,
for all a full atonement made.

When from the dust of earth I rise
to claim my mansion in the skies,   (John 14:2)
ev'n then shall this be all my plea,
Jesus hath lived, hath died, for me.

Thus Abraham, the friend of God,   (Rom. 4:3)
thus all heaven's armies bought with blood,
Savior of sinners thee proclaim—
sinners, of whom the chief I am.   (1 Tim. 1:15)

Jesu, be endless praise to thee,
whose boundless mercy hath for me—
for me, and all thy hands have made—
an everlasting ransom paid.

Ah, give to all, Almighty Lord,
with power to speak thy gracious word,
that all who to thy wounds will flee
may find eternal life in thee.

Thou God of power, thou God of love,
let the whole world thy mercy prove!
Now let thy word o'er all prevail!
Now take the spoils of death and hell.

O let the dead hear now thy voice!
Now bid thy banished ones rejoice;
their beauty this, their glorious dress,
Jesu, thy blood and righteousness.

translated, John Wesley
Hymns and Sacred Poems, 1740
as revised in *A Collection of Hymns*, 1780
from *"Christi Blut und Gerechtigkeit"* by Nicholas Ludwig von
Zinzendorf, 1739
The original contains 24 stanzas.

57
In Affliction

Eternal beam of light divine,
    Fountain of unexhausted love,
in whom the Father's glories shine   (Heb. 1:3)
    through earth beneath and heaven above;

Jesu, the weary wanderer's rest,
    give me thine easy yoke to bear,   (Matt. 11:30)
with steadfast patience arm my breast,   (1 Tim. 6:11)
    with spotless love and holy fear.

Thankful I take the cup from thee,
    prepared and mingled by thy skill;
though bitter to the taste it be,
    powerful the wounded soul to heal.   (Matt. 20:23)

Be thou, O Rock of Ages, nigh;
    so shall each murmuring thought be gone,
and grief, and fear, and care shall fly
    as clouds before the midday sun.

Speak to my warring passions, "Peace!"
    Say to my trembling heart, "Be still!"   (Mark 4:39)
Thy power my strength and fortress is,
    for all things serve thy sovereign will.

O death, where is thy sting? Where now
    thy boasted victory, O grave?   (1 Cor. 15:55)
Who shall contend with God? Or who
    can hurt, whom God delights to save?

Charles Wesley
Hymns and Sacred Poems, 1739

58
Free Grace

And can it be, that I should gain
    an interest in the Savior's blood?
Died he for me, who caused his pain?
    for me? Who him to death pursued.
Amazing love! How can it be
that thou, my God, shouldst die for me?

'Tis mystery all: the immortal dies!
    Who can explore his strange design?
In vain the first-born seraph tries
    to sound the depths of love divine.   (1 Pet. 1:12)
'Tis mercy all! Let earth adore!
Let angel minds enquire no more.

He left his Father's throne above
    (so free, so infinite his grace!),
emptied himself of all but love,   (Phil. 2:8)
    and bled for Adam's helpless race:
'Tis mercy all, immense and free,
for, O my God! it found out me!

Long my imprisoned spirit lay
 fast bound in sin and nature's night.
Thine eye diffused a quickening ray;
 I woke; the dungeon flamed with light.
My chains fell off, my heart was free, (Acts 16:25–6)
I rose, went forth, and followed thee.

Still the small inward voice I hear,
 that whispers all my sins forgiven;
still the atoning blood is near,
 that quenched the wrath of hostile heaven.
I feel the life his wounds impart; (Eph. 2:13–14)
I feel my Savior in my heart.

No condemnation now I dread, (Rom. 8:1)
 Jesus, and all in him, is mine.
Alive in him, my living head,
 and clothed in righteousness divine,
bold I approach the eternal throne (Heb. 4:16)
and claim the crown, through Christ my own!

Charles Wesley, 1738
Hymns & Sacred Poems, 1739

59

Hymn for Christmas Day

Hark how all the welkin rings! (Luke 8:15)
"Glory to the King of kings,
peace on earth and mercy mild,
God and sinners reconciled."

Joyful, all ye nations, rise,
join the triumph of the skies;
universal nature say:
"Christ the Lord is born today."

Christ by highest heaven adored,
Christ, the everlasting Lord,
late in time behold him come, (Gal. 4:4)
offspring of a Virgin's womb.

Veiled in flesh the Godhead see,
hail the incarnate Deity!
Pleased as man with men to appear,
Jesus! Our Immanuel here!

Hail the heavenly Prince of Peace! (Isa. 9:7)
Hail the Sun of Righteousness! (Mal. 4:2)
Light and life to all he brings,
risen with healing in his wings.

Mild he lays his glory by, (Phil. 2:8)
born that man no more may die,
born to raise the sons of earth,
born to give them second birth. (John 3:5)

Come, Desire of nations, come, (Hag. 2:7)
fix in us thy humble home;
rise, the woman's conquering seed,
bruise in us the serpent's head. (Gen. 3:15)

Now display thy saving power,
ruined nature now restore,
now in mystic union join
thine to ours, and ours to thine.

Adam's likeness, Lord, efface; (Rom. 6:6)
stamp thy image in its place; (Heb. 1:3)
second Adam from above, (1 Cor. 15:45)
reinstate us in thy love.

Let us thee, though lost, regain,
thee, the life, the inner man; (Eph. 3:16)
O! to all thyself impart,
formed in each believing heart.

Charles Wesley, 1739
Hymns & Sacred Poems, 1739
The usual version omits the final four stanzas and adopts the 10-line
stanza that first appeared among the "additional hymns" in the 1792
edition of Tate and Brady's *A New Version of the Psalms*.

The first two lines were revised in George Whitefield's *A Collection of Hymns for Social Worship*, 1753, as:

Hark! the herald angels sing
glory to the newborn King,

Lines 2:3–4 were altered in Martin Madan's *Collection of Psalms and Hymns*, 1760, as:

With the angelic hosts proclaim:
Christ is born in Bethlehem.

The now-common version of lines 4:3–4 appeared in *Select Portions of Psalms from Various Translations, and Hymns from Various Authors*, 1810:

Pleased as man with man to dwell,
Jesus, our Emmanuel.

60

For the Anniversary Day of One's Conversion

Glory to God, and praise and love
    be ever, ever given;
by saints below, and saints above,
    the church in earth and heaven.

On this glad day the glorious Sun
    of Righteousness arose, (Mal. 4:2)
on my benighted soul he shone,
    and filled it with repose.

Sudden expired the legal strife,
    'twas then I ceased to grieve;
my second, real, living life
    I then began to live.

Then with my heart I first believed,
    believed with faith divine,
power with the Holy Ghost received
    to call the Savior mine.   (Acts 10:38)

I felt my Lord's atoning blood
    close to my soul applied;
me, me, he loved—the Son of God!
    for me, for me he died!

I found, and owned his promise true,
    ascertained of my part,
my pardon passed in heaven I knew
    when written on my heart.

O for a thousand tongues to sing
    my dear Redeemer's praise!
The glories of my God and King,
    the triumphs of his grace.

My gracious Master, and my God,
    assist me to proclaim,
to spread through all the earth abroad
    the honors of thy name.

Jesus, the name that charms our fears,
    that bids our sorrows cease—
'tis music in the sinner's ears,
    'tis life and health and peace!

He breaks the power of canceled sin;
    he sets the prisoner free;
his blood can make the foulest clean
    his blood availed for me.

He speaks, and listening to his voice
    new life the dead receive,
the mournful, broken hearts rejoice,
    the humble poor believe.

Hear him, ye deaf, his praise, ye dumb,
    your loosened tongues employ;
ye blind, behold your Savior come,
    and leap, ye lame, for joy!

Look unto him, ye nations, own
    your God, ye fallen race;
Look, and be saved through faith alone,
    be justified by grace!

See all your sins on Jesus laid:
    the Lamb of God was slain,
his soul was once an offering made
    for every soul of man.

Harlots, and publicans, and thieves,
    in holy triumph join!
Saved is the sinner that believes
    from crimes as great as mine.

Murderers, and all ye hellish crew,
    ye sons of lust and pride,
believe the Savior died for you;
    for me the Savior died.

Awake from guilty nature's sleep,   (Eph. 5:15)
    and Christ shall give you light,
cast all your sins into the deep,
    and wash the Ethiop white.   (Jer. 13:23)

With me, your Chief, you then shall know,
    shall feel your sins forgiven;   (1 Tim. 1:15)
anticipate your heaven below
    and own, that love is heaven.

Charles Wesley, May 21, 1739
Hymns and Sacred Poems, 1740
The stanzas set to the left margin are those presented as the first text
in *A Collection of Hymns for the People Called Methodists*, 1780.

61
A Morning Hymn

Christ, whose glory fills the skies,
    Christ, the true, the only Light,
Sun of Righteousness, arise,   (Mal. 4:2)
    triumph o'er the shades of night:
Dayspring from on high, be near: (Luke 1:78)
Daystar, in my heart appear.

Dark and cheerless is the morn
    unaccompanied by thee.
Joyless is the day's return,
    till thy mercy's beams I see;
till they inward light impart,
glad my eyes, and warm my heart.

Visit then this soul of mine,
    pierce the gloom of sin, and grief,
fill me, radiancy divine,
    scatter all my unbelief,
more and more thyself display,
shining to the perfect day.   (Prov. 4:18)

Charles Wesley
Hymns and Sacred Poems, 1740

62
Wrestling Jacob

Come, O thou Traveler unknown,   (Gen. 32:24–31)
    whom still I hold, but cannot see;
my company before is gone,
    and I am left alone with thee;
with thee all night I mean to stay
and wrestle till the break of day.

I need not tell thee who I am,
    my misery, or sin declare;
thyself hast called me by my name,
    look on thy hands, and read it there.   (Isa. 49:16)
But who, I ask thee, who art thou?
Tell me thy name, and tell me now.

In vain thou strugglest to get free;
    I never will unloose my hold;
art thou the Man that died for me?
    the secret of thy love unfold;
wrestling I will not let thee go
till I thy name, thy nature know.

Wilt thou not yet to me reveal
    thy new, unutterable name?
Tell me, I still beseech thee, tell,
    to know it now resolved I am;
wrestling I will not let thee go
till I thy name, thy nature know.

'Tis all in vain to hold thy tongue,
    or touch the hollow of my thigh;   (Gen. 32:25)
though every sinew be unstrung,
    out of my arms thou shalt not fly;
wrestling I will not let thee go
till I thy name, thy nature know.

What though my shrinking flesh complain,
    and murmur to contend so long?
I rise superior to my pain;
    when I am weak, then I am strong.   (2 Cor. 12:10)
And when my all of strength shall fail
I shall with the God-Man prevail.

My strength is gone, my nature dies,
    I sink beneath thy mighty hand,
faint to revive, and fall to rise;
    I fall, and yet by faith I stand;
I stand, and will not let thee go
till I thy name, thy nature know.

Yield to me now, for I am weak;
    but confident in self-despair:
Speak to my heart, in blessings speak,
    be conquered by my instant prayer.
Speak or thou never hence shalt move,
and tell me if thy name is Love.

'Tis Love! 'Tis Love! thou diedst for me,
    I hear thy whisper in my heart.
The morning breaks, the shadows flee,
    pure universal love thou art.
To me, to all, thy mercies move,
thy nature, and thy name, is Love.

My prayer hath power with God; the grace
    unspeakable I now receive;
through faith I see thee face to face,
    I see thee face to face, and live!
In vain I have not wept and strove;
thy nature, and thy name, is Love.

I know thee, Savior, who thou art,
    Jesus, the feeble sinner's friend;
nor wilt thou with the night depart,
    but stay, and love me to the end;
thy mercies never shall remove;
thy nature, and thy name, is Love.

The Sun of Righteousness on me
    hath rose with healing in his wings,   (Mal. 4:2)
withered my nature's strength; from thee
    my soul its life and succor brings;
my help is all laid up above,   (Col. 1:5)
thy nature, and thy name, is Love.

Contented now upon my thigh
    I halt, till life's short journey end;
all helplessness, all weakness, I
    on thee alone for strength depend,
nor have I power, from thee to move;
thy nature, and thy name, is Love.

Lame as I am, I take the prey,
    hell, earth, and sin with ease o'ercome;
I leap for joy, pursue my way,
    and as a bounding hart fly home,
through all eternity to prove
thy nature, and thy name, is Love.

Charles Wesley, 1742
Hymns and Sacred Poems, 1742
The original wording of 9:5 was "to me, to all, thy bowels move."
The usual hymnal selection includes stanzas 1, 2, 8, and 9.

63
God with Us

Let earth and heaven combine,
    angels and men agree
to praise in songs divine
    th' incarnate Deity,
our God contracted to a span,
incomprehensibly made man.

He laid his glory by,   (Phil. 2:5)
    he wrapped him in our clay,
unmarked by human eye
    the latent Godhead lay:
infant of days he here became,
and bore the loved Immanuel's name.

See in that Infant's face
    the depths of Deity,
and labor, while ye gaze
    to sound the mystery;
in vain: ye angels gaze no more,   (1 Pet. 1:12)
but fall, and silently adore.

Unsearchable the love
    that hath the Savior brought,
the grace is far above
    or men or angels' thought;
suffice for us that God, we know,
our God, is manifest below.

He deigns in flesh to appear,
    widest extremes to join,
to bring our vileness near,
    and make us all-divine;
and we the life of God shall know,
for God is manifest below.

Made perfect first in love,   (1 John 4:17)
    and sanctified by grace,
we shall from earth remove
    and see his glorious face;
his love shall then be fully showed,
and man shall then be lost in God.

Charles Wesley
Nativity Hymns, 1745

64
Victim Divine

Victim Divine, thy grace we claim
    while thus thy precious death we shew,
once offered up a spotless Lamb
    in thy great temple here below,
thou didst for all mankind atone,
and standest now before the throne.   (Heb. 10:22)

Thou standest in the holiest place,
    as now for guilty sinners slain,
thy blood of sprinkling speaks, and prays   (Heb. 12:34)
    all-prevalent for helpless man;
thy blood is still our ransom found,
and spreads salvation all around.

The smoke of thine atonement here   (Matt. 27:51)
    darkened the sun and rent the veil,   (Heb. 10:20)
made the new way to heaven appear,
    and showed the great Invisible:
well pleased in thee our God looked down, (Mark 1:11)
and called his rebels to a crown.

He still respects thy sacrifice,
    its savor sweet doth always please,
the offering smokes through earth and skies,
    diffusing life and joy and peace;
to these thy lower courts it comes
and fills them with divine perfumes.

We need not now go up to heaven   (Rom. 10:6)
    to bring the long-sought Savior down;
thou art to all already given;
    thou dost ev'n now thy banquet crown.
To every faithful soul appear
and show thy real presence here.

Charles Wesley
Hymns on the Lord's Supper, 1745

65
Desiring to Love

O Love divine, how sweet thou art!
When shall I find my longing heart
   all taken up by thee?
I thirst, I faint, and die, to prove
the greatness of redeeming love,
   the love of Christ to me.

Stronger his love than death or hell;   (Song 8:6)
its riches are unsearchable,   (Rom. 11:33)
   the first-born sons of light
desire in vain its depth to see;
they cannot reach the Mystery,
   the length, the breadth, and height.   (Eph. 3:18–19)

God only knows the love of God.
O that it now were shed abroad
   in this poor stony heart!   (Ezek. 36:26)
For love I sigh, for love I pine:
this only portion, Lord, be mine,
   be mine this better part.   (Luke 10:41)

O that I could for ever sit
with Mary, at the Master's feet!
   Be this my happy choice!
My only care, delight and bliss,
my joy, my heaven on earth, be this,
   to hear the bridegroom's voice.   (Mark 2:19)

O that with humbled Peter I
could weep, believe, and thrice reply,   (John 21:15)
   my faithfulness to prove!
Thou know'st, for all to thee is known,
thou know'st, O Lord, and thou alone,
   thou know'st, that thee I love.

O that I could, with favored John,
recline my weary head upon   (John 13:23)
   the dear Redeemer's breast!
from care, and sin, and sorrow free,
give me, O Lord, to find in thee
   my everlasting rest.

The only Love do I require,
nothing on earth beneath desire,
   nothing in heaven above;   (Ps. 73:25)
let earth, and heaven, and all things go,
give me thy only love to know,
   give me thy only love.

Charles Wesley
Hymns on the Great Festivals and Other Occasions, 1746

66
Jesus, Show Us Thy Salvation

Love divine, all loves excelling,
   Joy of heaven, to earth come down,
fix in us thy humble dwelling,
   all thy faithful mercies crown;
Jesu, thou art all compassion,
   pure, unbounded love thou art;
visit us with thy salvation!   (Ps. 106:4)
   Enter every trembling heart.

Come, almighty to deliver,
   let us all thy life receive,
suddenly return, and never,   (Mal. 3:1)
   never more thy temples leave.
Thee we would be always blessing,
   serve thee as thy hosts above,
pray, and praise thee without ceasing,
   glory in thy perfect love.

Finish then thy new creation,   (2 Cor. 5:17)
   pure and spotless let us be;   (Eph. 5:27)
let us see thy great salvation
   perfectly restored in thee;
changed from glory into glory,   (2 Cor. 3:18)
   till in heaven we see thy face,   (1 Cor. 13:12)
till we cast our crowns before thee,   (Rev. 4:10)
   lost in wonder, love, and praise.

Charles Wesley, 1747
Hymns for Those That Seek and Those That Have
Redemption in the Blood of Jesus Christ, 1747

As in *A Collection of Hymns for the People Called Methodists*, 1780, which omitted the original second stanza:

Breathe, O breathe thy loving Spirit
    into every troubled breast!
Let us all in thee inherit;
    let us find that second rest.
Take away our power of sinning;
    Alpha and Omega be;
end of faith, as its beginning,
    set our hearts at liberty.

67
Before Work

Forth in thy name, O Lord, I go,
    my daily labor to pursue,
thee, only thee, resolved to know
    in all I think, or speak, or do.

The task thy wisdom hath assigned
    O let me cheerfully fulfill;
in all my works thy presence find,
    and prove thine acceptable will.   (Rom. 12:2)

Preserve me from my calling's snare,
    and hide my simple heart above,   (Col. 3:2)
above the thorns of choking care,   (Matt. 13:22)
    the gilded baits of worldly love.   (1 John 2:16)

Thee may I set at my right hand
    whose eyes my inmost substance see,   (Ps. 139:2)
and labor on at thy command,
    and offer all my works to thee.

Give me to bear thy easy yoke,   (Matt. 11:30)
    and every moment watch and pray,   (Matt. 26:41)
and still to things eternal look,
    and hasten to thy glorious day;   (Phil. 1:6)

for thee delightfully employ
    whate'er thy bounteous grace hath given,
and run my course with even joy,
    and closely walk with thee to heaven.   (Gen. 5:22)

Charles Wesley, 1749
Hymns and Sacred Poems, 1749

68
For New Year's Day

Come, let us anew
    our journey pursue,
    roll round with the year,
and never stand still till the Master appear;
    his adorable will
    let us gladly fulfill,
    and our talents improve
by the patience of hope and the labor of love.

Our life is a dream,
    our time as a stream
    glides swiftly away,
and the fugitive moment refuses to stay,
    the arrow is flown,
    the moment is gone,
    the millennial year
rushes on to our view, and Eternity's here!

O that each in the day
    of his coming may say,
    "I have fought my way through;   (2 Tim. 4:7)
I have finished the work thou didst give me to do."
    O that each from his Lord
    may receive the glad word,
    "Well and faithfully done!   (Matt. 25:21)
Enter into my joy, and sit down on my throne!"

Charles Wesley
Hymns for New Year's Day, 1750

69

Captain of Israel's Host, and Guide

Captain of Israel's host, and guide
    of all who seek that land above,
beneath thy shadow we abide,
    the cloud of thy protecting love;
our strength thy grace, our rule thy word,
our end, the glory of the Lord.

By thine unerring spirit led,
    we shall not in the desert stray,
the light of man's direction need,
    or miss our providential way;
as far from danger as from fear
while Love, almighty Love, is near.

Charles Wesley
Short Hymns on Select Passages of Scripture, 1762
based on Matthew Henry's *Commentary*, 1700, Exodus 13:21:

They needed not to fear missing their way who were
thus led, or being lost who were thus directed. . . .
They who make the glory of God their end, and the
Word of God their rule, the Spirit of God the guide
of their affections, and the providence of God the
guide of their affairs, may be confident that "the Lord
goes before them."

70

Lord, in the Strength of Grace

Lord, in the strength of grace
    with a glad heart and free
myself, my residue of days
    I consecrate to thee;
    thy ransomed servant, I
    restore to thee thine own,
and from this moment live, or die
    to serve my God alone.

Charles Wesley
Short Hymns on Select Passages of Scripture, 1762

based on Matthew Henry's *Commentary*, 1700, 2 Chronicles 29:5:

The filling of our hands with the service of God
intimates that we must serve him only, serve him
liberally, and serve him in the strength of grace
derived from him.

71

A Charge to Keep I Have

A charge to keep I have,
    a God to glorify,
a never-dying soul to save
    and fit it for the sky;
    to serve the present age,
    my calling to fulfill:
O may it all my powers engage
    to do my Master's will.

Arm me with jealous care
    as in thy sight to live,
and O! thy servant, Lord, prepare
    a strict account to give.
    Help me to watch and pray,
    and on thyself rely,
assured, if I my trust betray,
    I shall for ever die.

Charles Wesley
Short Hymns on Select Passages of Scripture, 1762
based on Matthew Henry's *Commentary*, 1700, Leviticus 8:35:

We have every one of us a charge to keep, an eternal
God to glorify, an immortal soul to provide for,
needful duty to be done, our generation to serve; and
it must be our daily care to keep this charge, for it is
the charge of the Lord our Master, who will shortly
call us to account about it, and it is at our utmost
peril if we neglect it. Keep it, "that ye die not"; it is
death, eternal death, to betray the truth we are
charged with.

In modern use the last couplet, as altered in *Hymns Ancient and
Modern*, 1904, usually reads:

and let me ne'er my trust betray,
    but press to realms on high.

72

For the Lord's Day

Come, let us with our Lord arise,   (Col. 1:3)
our Lord, who made both earth and skies,
who died to save the world he made,
and rose triumphant from the dead;
he rose, the Prince of life and peace,
and stamped the day for ever his.

This is the day the Lord hath made,   (Ps. 118:24)
that all may see his power displayed,
may feel his resurrection's power,   (Phil. 3:10)
and rise again, to fall no more,
in perfect righteousness renewed,
and filled with all the life of God.

Then let us render him his own,
with solemn prayer approach the throne,
with meekness hear the gospel word,
with thanks his dying love record,
our joyful hearts and voices raise
and fill his courts with songs of praise.

Honor and praise to Jesus pay
throughout his consecrated day,
be in all Jesu's praise employed,
nor leave a single moment void,
with utmost care the time improve,
and only breathe his praise and love.

Charles Wesley
Hymns for Children, 1763

Chapter 6:
The Early Evangelicals, 1740–1780 (73–84)

It was natural enough that the hymnody of the Wesleys should generate, during their long lifetime, much imitation. They had completed the liberation; others entered into their labors without ·much delay.

Charles Wesley had published two books containing many of his best-known and finest hymns when John Cennick, one of John Wesley's first lay preachers (but an unstable character who soon left him) began to publish. Cennick's gifts were those of a miniaturist, as 74 and 75 show. Number 74 has the best kind of modest economy of expression; 75, and its companion, "Ere I sleep," have a special charm because of their meter, which later Charles Wesley used but which Cennick seems to have discovered first. "Children of the heavenly King," in many books still, is another piece which with judicious editorial pruning has had deserved success. Beyond these there is not much in Cennick that we need to recover today.

The massive "Yigdal," 73, is a different story. Here is Thomas Olivers, the London cobbler, drinking deep of the Wesleyan love of Scripture (all the scriptural allusions here included are his) and transforming the old Jewish hymn of praise (yigdal is from a root meaning "greatness") into an ecstatic and apocalyptic Christian song; some of its lines are now too rough for normal use, but its generous length leaves at least five stanzas which remain indispensable.

To the same period belongs what is so surprisingly the only Welsh hymn which in translation has found a place in popular affection, 76. It is not easy to say why Offa's Dyke [the boundary between Wales and England, so called for the ditch and earthen wall constructed in the eighth century] has proved so impassable. The English have a liking for Welsh tunes, though their taste is not always what would please a true Welsh connoisseur, but the hymnody of the Welsh evangelicals who were aroused by the missions of Whitefield and his followers has remained in Wales, and one has to read a Welsh hymnal to see their texts. This one, translated jointly by the Welsh author and his brother, has all the grandeur that a true affection for Scripture could give it.

The Baptists in Britain have been surprisingly backward in the production of hymns acceptable outside their immediate circle. They were not without their writers, and they could rise to excellence, as 77 and 83 indicate. Number 77 has again the modesty and naturalness we find in Cennick at his best; 83, which is worth looking at in both its original and its later versions, is on the grand scale, and it has been a wise instinct that has moved modern editors to make it more manageable by removing the refrain and altering a few rough phrases. The same author's "Come, thou Fount of every blessing" is perhaps more famous, but in its original form less singable, and in edited forms is usually too far from the original to appear here; its most practicable and at the same time authentic form is probably that at 442 in *Congregational Praise*.

The appearance of Augustus Toplady's two texts here sufficiently demonstrates the way in which hymnody ignores the frontiers set up by religious dispute, for Toplady's fanatical hatred of John Wesley is one of the best-known facts in church history. Toplady, the Vicar of Broadhembury in East Devon, is best known as the author of a hymn (80) which is now less sung than formerly but which in its day has had countless admirers. It is certainly the only hymn of his which was ever in wide use without abridgment; but 79 is not only a practicable fragment of a longer and uneven original, but is indeed, thus pruned, a hymn in the very best Calvinist tradition. "Inspirer and hearer of prayer," cut down usually to two stanzas as "A Sovereign Protector I have," provides another very fine devotional piece. "Object of my first desire," after an unpromising start, contains many excellent lines. Toplady's brief life of 38 years falls wholly within not merely the lives but the writing lives of the Wesleys. He is the most famous example of the kind of tortured spirit which contributed so much to the praise and devotion of eighteenth-century Evangelicals and Calvinists. Joseph Hart ("Come, Holy Spirit, come") is such another, and of course Robert Robinson (83) was of this kind in his youth.

Three anonymous hymns, 78, 81, and 82, represent perhaps a more sober and less ambitious strain in hymnody, though they all come from the Evangelical tradition. The Easter hymn at 78 settled down to its present form in one of the many music books of this tradition which bridged the gap between the decorous psalm-singing tradition and that of the new hymnody by providing for the metrical psalms a new kind of flexible and expressive tune, and adding a modest number of doctrinal hymns, somewhat in the style of the 1708 *Supplement to the New Version* (chapter 2). It is originally based on a Latin text, *"Surrexit Christus hodie,"* but in this form, now well known, departs some distance from it. The other two, 81 and 82, are the two best-known examples (and in their brevity and sobriety of diction they are very good indeed) of the hymnody generated by the great charity-houses founded in the midcentury by Evangelicals inspired by the social passion of the Wesleys. The Foundling Hospital, an orphanage in London, was not only the most famous of these, but it amounted, in its propagation of children's choral singing, almost to a nonconformist cathedral foundation. Many fine tunes first appeared in the hymnals of this institution and of the Magdalen Hospital, a comparable house for "fallen women," and it is always worth noting that the original association of 82 was undoubtedly with Haydn's tune AUSTRIA, and it is at least a respectable opinion that the two should never have been separated in later hymnals. (It is surprising that in Britain only the *Methodist Hymn Book* and *Hymns Ancient and Modern*, among standard hymnals, preserve this association.)

The section closes with the great hymn "All hail the power," whose celebration of the visions of the Book of Revelation can be described only as heraldic in its boldness. This text, first appearing in its full form in 1780, has often suffered alteration, most of which is quite needless. It generated two great tunes, MILES LANE in England and CORONATION in America, within a very short time of its composition, each of which is its composer's only well-known composition, and each of which in its own way admirably reflects the soaring spirit of the text.

73
A Hymn to the God of Abraham

This hymn is displayed with the original spelling, punctuation, and capitalization.

In Three Parts: adapted to a celebrated Air sung by the Priest, Signior Leoni, &c, at the Jews' Synagogue, in London

Part the First

The God of *Abrah'm* praise	(Exod. 3:6)
Who reigns enthron'd above;	
Antient of Everlasting Days,	(Dan. 7:22)
and GOD of Love;	(2 Cor. 13:11)
JEHOVAH, GREAT I AM	(Exod. 6:3, 3:14)
By earth and heav'n confest;	(Rev. 4:8–11)
I bow and bless the sacred Name	
For ever bless'd.	(Rom. 1:25)

The God of *Abrah'm* praise,	
At whose supreme command	(Gen. 12:1)
From earth I rise—and seek the joys	
At his right hand:	
I all on earth forsake,	(Gen. 12:4)
Its wisdom, fame and power;	
And him my only portion make,	(Gen. 15:1)
My Shield and Tower.	(Ps. 18:2)

The God of *Abrah'm* praise,

Whose all-sufficient grace   (Gen. 17:1)

Shall guide me all my happy days   (Gen. 28:15)

In all my ways:

He calls a worm his friend!   (James 2:23)

He calls himself my GOD!   (Exod. 3:6)

And he shall save me to the end   (1 Pet. 1:5)

Thro' JESU'S blood.

He by Himself hath sworn,   (Gen. 22:16–17)

I on his oath depend,   (Rom. 4:20–1)

I shall on eagle's wings up-borne,   (Exod. 19:4)

To heaven ascend;

I shall behold his face,   (John 17:24)

I shall his power adore,   (Exod. 15:2)

And sing the wonders of his grace   (Ps. 145:1; 146:2)

For evermore.

Part the Second

Tho' nature's strength decay   (Gen. 15:4, 6; Rom. 4:19)

And earth and hell withstand,   (Exod. 5:2)

To *Canaan's* bounds I urge my way,   (Exod. 14:15)

At his command:

The wat'ry deep I pass,   (Exod. 14:22)

With JESUS in my view;   (Exod. 13:21)

And thro' the howling wilderness   (Exod. 13:18)

My way pursue.

The goodly land I see,   (Exod. 3:8)

With peace and plenty bless'd;   (Deut. 8:7–9)

A land of sacred liberty,   (Lev. 25:42)

And endless rest.   (Exod. 33:14)

There milk and honey flow,   (Exod. 3:8)

And oil and wine abound   (Deut. 32:13–14)

And trees of life for ever grow,   (Isa. 61:3)

With Mercy crown'd.

There dwells the LORD our KING,   (Gen. 14:18; Heb. 7:1–2)

THE LORD OUR RIGHTEOUSNESS   (Jer. 33:16)

(Triumphant o'er the world and sin)   (Eph. 4:8; Phil. 2:9–11)

The Prince of Peace: (Isa. 9:6)

On Sion's sacred height,   (Ps. 50:2)

His kingdom still maintains;

And glorious with his saints in light   (Isa. 24:23)

For ever reigns.

He keeps his own secure,   (Ps. 12:7)

He guards them by his side,

Arrays in garments, white and pure   (Rev. 4:4; 19:7–8)

His spotless bride;   (Eph. 5:27)

With streams of sacred bliss   (Rev. 7:17; 22:1)

With groves of living joys—

With all the fruits of Paradise   (Rev. 2:7; 22:2)

He still supplies.

Part the Third

Before the great THREE-ONE   (Rev. 7:9–10)

They all exulting stand;

And tell the wonders he hath done

Thro' all their land:

The list'ning spheres attend,   (Rev. 7:11–12)

And swell the growing fame;

And sing, in songs which never end

The wondrous NAME.

The God who reigns on high,   (Rev. 4:8)

The great arch-angels sing,

And * "Holy, Holy, Holy," cry,

"ALMIGHTY KING!

Who Was, and Is, the same;

And evermore shall be;

JEHOVAH—FATHER—GREAT I AM!

We worship Thee."

*"Sing the following parts of this verse *slow* and *solemn*" (T. O.)

Before the SAVIOUR'S face   (Rev. 5:8–10; 15:24)
The ransom'd nations bow;
O'erwhelmed at his almighty grace,
For ever new:
He shews his prints of Love—   (John 20:27)
They kindle—to a flame!
And sound thro' all the worlds above
The slaughter'd LAMB.

The whole triumphant host,   (Rev. 5:13; 19:1–7)
Give thanks to God on high;
"Hail, FATHER, SON and HOLY-GHOST,"
They ever cry:
Hail, *Abraham's* GOD—and *mine!* (Ps. 89:26; John 20:17, 28)
(I join the heav'nly lays)   (Ps. 103:1-5)
All Might and Majesty are thine
And endless Praise.   (Rev. 4:11; 5:12; 7:10, 12)

Thomas Olivers, probably written in London between 1763 and 1770
included in John Wesley's *Pocket Hymn Book*, 1785
The Scripture references are by Olivers.

74
Divine Protection

Be with me, Lord, where'er I go;
teach me what thou wouldst have me do;
suggest whate'er I think or say;
direct me in the narrow way.

Prevent me, lest I harbor pride,
lest I in my own strength confide;
show me my weakness, let me see
I have my power, my all, from thee.

Assist and teach me how to pray;
incline my nature to obey;
what thou abhorrest let me flee,
and only love what pleases thee.

John Cennick
Sacred Hymns for the Children of God in the Days of Their Pilgrimage, 1741

75
Morning Hymn

Rise, my soul, adore thy Maker!
Angels praise,
join thy lays;
with them be partaker.

Father, Lord of every spirit,
in thy light
lead me right,
through my Savior's merit.

Never cast me from thy presence
till my soul
shall be full
of thy blessed essence.

O my Jesus, God almighty,
pray for me
till I see
thee in Salem's city.

Holy Ghost, by Jesus given,
be my guide,
lest my pride
shut me out of heaven.

Thou by night wast my Protector:
with me stay
all the day
ever my Director.

Holy, Holy, Holy Giver
of all good,
life and food,
reign, adored for ever!

John Cennick
Sacred Hymns for the Children of God in the Days of Their Pilgrimage, 1741

76

A Prayer for Strength to Go through the Wilderness of the World

A.

Arglwydd, arwain trwy'r anialwch
    fi bererin gwael ei wedd,
nad oes ynof nerth na bywyd,
    fel yn gorwedd yn y bedd:
        Hollalluog   (Exod. 16:4)
Ydyw'r Un a'm cwyd i'r lan

Myfi grwydrais hir flynyddau,
    ac heb weled codi'r wawr,
anobeithiais heb dy allu
    dd'od o'r anial dir yn awr;
        dere dy Hunan,
dyna'r pryd y dof i maes.

Rho'r golofn dan y nos i'm harwain,
    a rho'r golofn niwl y dydd,
dal fi pan b'wy'n teithio' mannau
    geirwon yn y ffordd y sydd;
        rho i mi fanna,
fel na b'wyf i lwfrhau.

Agor y ffnonau melus   (Exod. 17:6)
    sydd yn tarddu o'r graig i maes;
'r hyd yr anial mawr canlyned   (Exod. 40:38)
    afon iechydwriaeth gras:
        Rho i mi hyny;
dim i mi ond dy fwynhau.   (Gen. 15:1)

Pan b'wy'n myned trwy'r Iorddonen,
    angeu creulon yn ei rym
ti est trwyddi gynt dy Hunan,
    p'am yr ofnai bellach ddim?
        Buddugoliaeth,
gwna i mi waeddi yn y llif.

Mi ymddiriedaf yn dy allu,   (Jos. 4:16)
    mawr yw'r gwaith a wnest erioed,
tu ge'st angeu, ti ge'st uffern,
    ti ge'st Satan tan dy droed;
        Pen Calfaria,
nac aed hwnnw byth o'm cof.

William Williams
Yy Mor o Wydr, 1762

B. Praying for Strength

Guide me, O thou great Jehovah,
    pilgrim through this barren land;
I am weak, but thou art mighty;
    hold me with thy powerful hand:
        Bread of heaven,   (Exod 16:4)
feed me till I want no more.

Open now the crystal fountain   (Exod. 17:6)
    whence the healing stream doth flow
let the fiery cloudy pillar   (Exod. 40:38)
    guide me all my journey through.
        Strong deliverer,
be thou still my strength and shield.   (Gen. 15:1)

When I tread the verge of Jordan   (Jos. 4:16)
    bid my anxious fears subside,
Death of death, and hell's destruction,
    land me safe on Canaan's side;
        songs of praises
I will ever give to thee.

Musing on my habitation,
    musing on my heavenly home,
fills my soul with holy longings:
    Come, my Jesus, quickly come;
        vanity is all I see;
Lord, I long to be with thee!

Peter Williams, stanza 1; William Williams, stanzas 2, 3, and 4
Hymns on Various Subjects, 1772
The English version, with its distinctive title, is more a new hymn
than a translation. Note that line 4:5 is longer than the corresponding
line of the other stanzas.

C. A new translation

Lead me, God, across the desert
    this poor pilgrim, still a slave;
having neither life nor vigor,
    lost already in the grave:
      Mighty Savior,
you can raise me from the dead!

Let the fiery pillar lead me
    on by night; the cloud by day.
Hold me in your hands securely,
    as I travel life's rough way.
      Send me manna,
so that I may not despair.

Open the sweet wells of water
    from the rock's unyielding face;
through life's desert let me follow
    your clear stream of saving grace.
      Grant this favor,
till I share your full delight.

Though I cross the river Jordan,
    by death's fearsome power dismayed;
you have come this way before me:
    Why, then, should I be afraid?
      Through the torrent,
I will shout your victory!

I will trust your grace, my Savior;
    praise the conquest you have won:
You have trampled hell and Satan;
    all death's powers have been undone!
      Hill of Calvary:
May it never leave my mind.

translated, Alan Gaunt, 1988
after a literal translation by John Richards, 1984
Hymn Texts of Alan Gaunt, 1991
© 1991, Stainer & Bell Ltd.

77
Joining the Church

Witness, ye men and angels, now,
    before the Lord we speak;
to him we make our solemn vow,
    a vow we dare not break:

that long as life itself shall last
    ourselves to Christ we yield;
nor from his cause will we depart,
    or ever quit the field.

We trust not in our native strength,
    but on his grace rely,
that, with returning wants, the Lord
    will all our need supply.

O guide our doubtful feet aright,
    and keep us in thy ways:
and while we turn our vows to prayers,
    turn thou our prayers to praise.

Benjamin Beddome
Hymns Adapted to Public Worship or Family Devotion, 1817

78
Easter Hymn

Jesus Christ is risen today,
    Alleluia!
our triumphant holy day,
    Alleluia!
who did once upon the cross,
    Alleluia!
suffer to redeem our loss.
    Alleluia!

Hymns of praise then let us sing,
    Alleluia!
unto Christ, our heavenly King,
    Alleluia!
who endured the cross and grave,
    Alleluia!
sinners to redeem and save.
    Alleluia!

But the pains that he endured,
    Alleluia!
our salvation have procured,
    Alleluia!
Now above the sky he's King;
    Alleluia!
where the angels ever sing.
    Alleluia!

anonymous

This was, perhaps, translated from *"Enstanden ist der heilig Christ,"* in Johann Leisentrit's *Geistliche Lieder und Psalmen*, 1567, though there are other German versions as early as 1478, which are, in turn, based on the Latin text *"Surrexit Christus, hodie,"* ca. 14th century.
The Compleat Psalmodist, 1749
lines 1:1 and 1:3 from *Lyra Davidica*, 1708
line 1:5 from *Supplement* to Tate and Brady's
A New Version of the Psalms of David, 1816

79

Weak Believers Encouraged

When we in darkness walk,
    nor feel the heavenly flame,
then is the time to trust our God,
    and rest upon his name.

Soon shall our doubts and fears
    subside at his control!
His loving-kindness shall break through
    the midnight of the soul.

Wait till the shadows flee,
    wait thine appointed hour;
wait till the bridegroom of thy soul
    reveals his love with power.

His grace will to the end
    stronger and brighter shine;
nor present things, nor things to come   (Rom. 8:37)
    shall quench the spark divine.

Blest is the man, O God,
    that stays himself on thee!
who wait for thy salvation, Lord,
    shall thy salvation see.

Augustus Montague Toplady
Gospel Magazine, February 1772
These are stanzas 4a, 4b, 7a, 2a, and 8b of the original text, which contained eight 8-line stanzas and began "Your harps, ye trembling saints, / down from the willows take."

80

A Living and Dying Prayer for the Holiest Believer in the World

Rock of Ages, cleft for me,   (Isa. 26:4; Zech. 14:4)
let me hide myself in thee!
Let the water and the blood,
from thy riven side which flowed,   (John 19:34; 1 John 5:6)
be of sin the double cure;
cleanse me from its guilt and power.

Not the labors of my hands
can fulfill thy law's demands,
could my soul no respite know,
could my tears forever flow,
all for sin could not atone:
thou must save, and thou alone!

Nothing in my hand I bring;
simply to thy cross I cling;
naked, come to thee for dress;
helpless, look to thee for grace;
foul, I to the fountain fly:
Wash me, Savior, or I die!   (Ps. 51:7)

Whilst I draw this fleeting breath—
when my eye-strings break in death—
when I soar through tracts unknown—
see thee on thy judgment throne—
Rock of ages, cleft for me,
let me hide myself in thee!

> Augustus Montague Toplady
> *The Gospel Magazine*, March 1776, lines 1:1–2 and 3:5–6 having
> appeared in the October 1775 issue
> Line 4:2 was altered to "when my eyelids close in death"
> by T. S. Cotterill in A *Selection of Psalms and Hymns*, 1815.

81
Spirit of Mercy, Truth, and Love

Spirit of mercy, truth, and love,
send thy blest influence from above,
and still from age to age convey
the wonders of this sacred day.

In every clime, in every tongue
be God's eternal praises sung;
through all the listening earth be taught
the acts our great Redeemer wrought.

Unfailing comfort, heavenly guide,
over thy favored church preside;
still may mankind thy blessings prove,
Spirit of mercy, truth, and love.

> anonymous
> *Psalms, Hymns, & Anthems* (Foundling Hospital Collection), 1774

82
Psalm 148

Praise the Lord! ye heavens, adore him;
    praise him, angels in the height;
sun and moon, rejoice before him,
    praise him, all ye stars of light:
praise the Lord, for he hath spoken,
    worlds his mighty voice obeyed;
laws, which never shall be broken
    for their guidance hath he made.

Praise the Lord! for he is glorious;
    never shall his promise fail;
God hath made his saints victorious,
    sin and death shall not prevail.
Praise the God of our salvation;
    hosts on high, his power proclaim;
heaven and earth, and all creation
    laud and magnify his name!

> anonymous
> *Hymns for Foundling Apprentices, Attending Divine Service to Return
> Thanks*, a leaflet pasted into *Psalms, Hymns, & Anthems*
> (Foundling Hospital Collection), 1796

83
Praise to the Redeemer, for Christmas

A. Original

Mighty God! while angels bless thee,
    may an infant lisp thy name?
Lord of men, as well as angels,
    thou art every creature's theme.

        Hallelujah, hallelujah,
        hallelujah, amen.

Lord of every land and nation,
    Ancient of eternal days!
sounded through the wide creation
    be thy just and lawful praise:

For the grandeur of thy nature,
  grand beyond a seraph's thought;
for created works of power,
  works with skill and kindness wrought:

For thy providence, that governs
  through thine empire's wide domain;
wings an angel, guides a sparrow,
  blessed be thy gentle reign.

But thy rich, thy free redemption,
  dark through brightness all along:
thought is poor, and poor expression,
  who dare sing that awful song?

Brightness of the Father's glory,
  shall thy praise unuttered lie?
Fly, my tongue, such guilty silence!
  sing the Lord who came to die.

Did archangels sing thy coming?
  Did the shepherds learn their lays?
Shame would cover me ungrateful
  should my tongue refuse to praise.

From the highest throne of glory
  to the cross of deepest woe;
all to ransom guilty captives:
  flow, my praise, for ever flow.

Go, return, immortal Savior!
  Leave thy footstool, claim thy throne;
thence return, and reign for ever,
  be the kingdom all thine own.

Robert Robinson, 1774
Joseph Middleton's *Hymns*, 1793

B. The same, in modern use

Mighty God, while angels bless thee,
  may a mortal sing thy name?
Lord of men as well as angels,
  thou art every creature's theme;
Lord of every land and nation,
  Ancient of eternal days,
sounded through the wide creation
  be thy just and endless praise.

For the grandeur of thy nature—
  grand beyond a seraph's thought—
for the wonders of creation,
  works with skill and kindness wrought,
for thy providence that governs
  through thine empire's wide domain,
wings an angel, guides a sparrow,
  blessed be thy gentle reign.

But thy rich, thy free redemption,
  dark through brightness all along—
thought is poor, and poor expression—
  who dare sing that wondrous song?
Brightness of the Father's glory,
  shall thy praise unuttered lie?
Break, my tongue, such guilty silence;
  sing the Lord who came to die.

From the highest throne of glory
  to the cross of deepest woe,
all to ransom guilty captives!
  Flow my praise, for ever flow!
Go, return, immortal Savior,
  leave thy footstool, claim thy throne;
thence return, and reign for ever;
  be the kingdom all thine own!

rearrangement of stanzas, with omission of stanza 7, R. W. Dale
English Hymn Book, 1879
here as in *Congregational Praise*, 1951, which restores a few words
amended by Dale

84

On the Resurrection: The Lord Is King

All hail! the power of Jesu's name;
    let angels prostrate fall;
bring forth the royal diadem
    to crown him Lord of all.

Let highborn seraphs tune the lyre,
    and, as they tune it, fall
before his face who tunes their choir,
    and crown him Lord of all.

Crown him, ye morning stars of light,   (Job 38:7)
    who fixed this floating ball;
now hail the strength of Israel's might,
    and crown him Lord of all.

Crown him, ye martyrs of your God,
    who from his altar call;   (Rev. 6:9)
extol the stem of Jesse's rod   (Isa. 11:1)
    and crown him Lord of all.

Ye seed of Israel's chosen race,
    ye ransomed of the fall,
hail him who saves you by his grace,
    and crown him Lord of all.

Hail him, ye heirs of David's line,
    whom David Lord did call;   (Ps. 110:1)
the God incarnate, Man divine,
    and crown him Lord of all.

Sinners! whose love can ne'er forget
    the wormwood and the gall,   (Lam. 3:19)
go, spread your trophies at his feet,
    and crown him Lord of all.

Let every tribe and every tongue
    that bound creation's call,
now shout in universal song
    the crowned Lord of all.

Edward Perronet
The Gospel Magazine, April 1780
This text has been altered by many editors. The most influential
revision was made by John Rippon in *A Selection of Hymns from the
Best Authors*, 1787. Rippon's version, which assigns a heading to each
stanza, may be seen in John Julian's *Dictionary of Hymnology* or in the
Companion to The Hymnal 1982.

Chapter 7:
The Olney Hymn Book, 1779
(85–95)

Evangelicalism, it must be understood, was not the same as nonconformity; it never has been, and the Wesleys and Toplady, among those we have already encountered, were Anglican priests. But even the Wesleys could not hope to touch the whole of so widespread an institution as the Anglican church, and there were plenty of places where hymnody was quite unknown, so far as it was not contained within the metrical psalters. Such a place was Olney, the Buckinghamshire village (now part of the late twentieth-century new city of Milton Keynes) where John Newton was perpetual curate, and William Cowper a prominent layman. The book of *Olney Hymns* was put together in a very short time by these two men as a means of widening and deepening the religious life of those rustics, and no single book, not even the collections of Watts and the Wesleys, has been, as a collection, more influential on the course of hymnody.

The story of Newton and Cowper has been told often enough not to need repetition here. The briefest biography of Newton must contain the information that he ran away to sea, joined the merchant navy, deserted, and was brought back and punished, and that he rose to the command of a ship engaged in the infamous slave trade. His conversion was the result partly of the faithfulness of his fiancée, Mary Catlett, and partly of reading St. Thomas à Kempis. But he found great difficulty in getting any bishop to ordain him when he sought orders, and until he was fifty-seven found nothing more distinguished than this perpetual curacy (a now defunct order in the Church of England which in effect meant the burden of parish work without the usual sources of clerical emolument) in the heart of the British countryside. Only in 1782 did he receive a rectory, and this was in the City of London and a position of some distinction (St. Mary Woolnoth, near the Bank of England and almost next door to the Mansion House).

Cowper (he is pronounced Cooper), the first man of letters to become a major hymn writer and one of the very small handful who ever did, was of course the only man in the parish on Newton's intellectual level. He was naturally Newton's closest friend, but for other reasons his most difficult and demanding parishioner, for Cowper was a pathological depressive, haunted by a sense of guilt and failure, whose mind became gradually more and more clouded until in his last decade he was to all intents and purposes insane. Newton made use of him, as much for his friend's good as for anyone else's, about the parish, and the most effective way in which he did so was to enlist his help in compiling a hymn book. In the end Cowper's contribution was 68 hymns, and Newton's 280. Even if it ever was Newton's intention to let Cowper write the whole book, they probably labored on it together, and certainly Newton's lyric gift, so different from Cowper's, is one which the church would have been the poorer for missing.

Newton wears his heart on his sleeve: he is direct, candid, and uncomplicated. As literature perhaps his work cannot be expected to match Cowper's, but the five in our selection show him at his best. "How sweet the name," 85, still one of the best known of all hymns, is as tender as any medieval mystic's devotion and as open and durable as Watts; perhaps stanza 4 is rightly omitted in modern books, but who would wish to spare, or to alter, any more of it? Number 86 is as scripturally ingenious as anything in Wesley. In 87 we have the honest teacher instructing his flock, and in the monumental 88, the old sailor recalling the hazards of his early career; the picturesque crudity of its language here is all scriptural, and worth wrestling with. The song is still a great experience if it is sung to the old psalm tune, OLD 104TH. For sheer simplicity based on a profound New Testament text, 89 is as good as anything he wrote; for the rest, consult your hymnal, and if it is an educated one, it will have more good texts to add to these.

It was an inspired providence that brought together in one book the energy and zest of Newton and the gentle, withdrawn talent of Cowper. "O for a closer walk" is one of Cowper's best known (90), and at once we detect the hesitating and wistful spirit that produced it. The terse and simple lines of "Hark, my soul," 92, interweaving scriptural thoughts very much in Newton's style, combine with a typically tender interpretation of the text "lovest thou me?" to make a hymn worthy of a finer tune than the one which is so often set to it that the text is in danger of being suffocated out of the repertory. Number 93 is, in the Newton style again, didactic and thoughtful, the work of a compassionate teacher who has patience with the believer's difficulties. Numbers 94 and 95 express Christian faith and hope in contrasting styles, the one dark, the other (almost uniquely in Cowper), bright and buoyant.

These all speak for themselves. It is 91 that needs special treatment. It is the most difficult case in all hymnodic criticism. In its original version, with the opening, "There is a fountain filled with blood drawn from Emmanuel's veins," it has secured the affection of many devoted disciples and earned the execration of as many people who find it crudely revolting. Often in this collection we preserve a crude text (as we do in 88) because it is worth inviting a reader to suspend his frown or his instinct to reject it in order that a true message may come through which if it were altered would be smothered. It is not so here. The passage behind this opening stanza is this, in the King James Version of Zechariah 13:1:

> In that day there shall be a fountain opened
> to the house of David and the inhabitants
> of Jerusalem for sin and for uncleanness.

Cowper's intention is to identify this, through an accepted course of typology, with the blood of Christ shed on the cross. Were it not that a later English poet whose gifts I should not place much below Cowper's has produced an amendment that reflects the original Scripture more faithfully (in the words "for sin") and that introduces the majesty and pathos of the Atonement with no less sureness and without the graceless literalism into which the usually sensitive Cowper was betrayed, I could not pursue this argument, though I should still have included the hymn.

But my reasons go beyond this. For one thing, this amendment is at present wholly unknown to editors, and therefore nowadays the hymn appears only in those collections which do not make much allowance for the antipathetic reaction I have mentioned; for another, when the hymn is printed it often ends at stanza 5, or, much worse, is further abridged and presented with a spurious chorus (and, to crown it all, a shockingly complacent and jaunty tune), so that contemporary associations with it are further corrupted. Among recent books in England and America, only *The English Hymnal* prints the full text, and this, of course, in its original form. It is inexcusable also, by omitting the last eight lines, to make the hymn more depressing than Cowper meant it to be, or, by treating it as some hymnals do, to make it more casual and commonplace than Cowper could ever have conceived it to be. As we have it here it is something which no serious reader can lightly dismiss.

85

The Name of Jesus

How sweet the name of Jesus sounds   (Song 1:3)
    in a believer's ear!
It soothes his sorrows, heals his wounds,
    and drives away his fear.

It makes the wounded spirit whole,
    and calms the troubled breast;
'tis manna to the hungry soul,
    and to the weary rest.

Dear name! the rock on which I build,
    my shield and hiding place;
my never-failing treasury, filled
    with boundless stores of grace.

By thee my prayers acceptance gain,
    although with sin defiled;
Satan accuses me in vain,
    and I am owned a child.

Jesus! my Shepherd, Husband, Friend,
    my Prophet, Priest, and King,
my Lord, my life, my way, my end,
    accept the praise I bring.

Weak is the effort of my heart,
    and cold my warmest thought;
but when I see thee as thou art,
    I'll praise thee as I ought.

Till then I would thy love proclaim
    with every fleeting breath:
and may the music of thy name
    refresh my soul in death.

John Newton
Olney Hymns, 1779, I, 57

86
Zion, or The City of God.
Isaiah 33:20–21

Glorious things of thee are spoken,
    Zion, city of our God!   (Ps. 87:3)
He, whose word cannot be broken
    formed thee for his own abode:
On the Rock of Ages founded   (Isa. 26:4)
    what can shake thy sure repose?
With salvation's walls surrounded,   (Isa. 60:18)
    thou may'st smile at all thy foes.

See! the streams of living waters,   (Ezek. 47:1)
    springing from eternal love,
well supply thy sons and daughters   (Ps. 46:4)
    and all fear of want remove:
who can faint while such a river   (Rev. 22:1)
    ever flows their thirst to assuage?
Grace, which, like the Lord, the giver,
    never fails from age to age.

Round each habitation hovering,
    see the cloud and fire appear
for a glory and a covering,
    showing that the Lord is near.
Thus deriving from their banner
    light by night and shade by day,
safe they feed upon the manna
    which he gives them when they pray.

Blest inhabitants of Zion,
    washed in the Redeemer's blood!
Jesus, whom their hopes rely on,
    makes them kings and priests to God.   (Rev. 1:5–6)
'Tis his love his people raises
    over self to reign as king,
and, as priests, his solemn praises
    each for a thank-offering brings.

Savior, if of Zion's city
    I through grace a member am,   (Ps. 87:6)
let the world deride or pity,
    I will glory in thy name:
fading is the worldling's pleasure—
    all his boasted pomp and show;
solid joys and lasting treasure
    none but Zion's children know.

John Newton
Olney Hymns, 1779, I, 60

87

The Creatures in the Lord's Hands

The water stood like walls of brass
to let the sons of Israel pass,   (Exod. 14:21)
and from the rock in rivers burst   (Exod. 17:6)
at Moses' prayer, to quench their thirst.

The fire, restrained by God's commands,
could only burn his people's bands;   (Dan. 3:27)
too faint, when he was with them there
to singe their garments or their hair.

At Daniel's feet the lions lay   (Dan. 6:22)
like harmless lambs, nor touched their prey:
and ravens, which on carrion fed
procured Elijah flesh and bread.   (1 Kings 17:6)

Thus creatures only can fulfill
their great Creator's holy will;
and when his servants need their aid,
his purposes must be obeyed.

So, if his blessing he refuse,
their power to help they quickly lose;
sure as on creatures we depend,
our hopes in disappointment end.

Then let us trust the Lord alone,
and creature-confidence disown;
nor if they threaten need we fear,
they cannot hurt if he be near.

If instruments of pain they prove,
still they are guided by his love;
as lancets by the surgeon's skill
which wound to cure, and not to kill.

John Newton
Olney Hymns, 1779, II, 97

88

I Will Trust and Not Be Afraid

Begone, unbelief,
    my Savior is near,
and for my relief
    will surely appear:
by prayer let me wrestle   (Gen. 32:24)
    and he will perform;   (Phil. 1:6)
with Christ in the vessel   (Mark 4:38)
    I smile at the storm.

Though dark be my way,
    since he is my guide
'tis mine to obey,   (Deut. 29:29)
    'tis his to provide.   (Matt. 6:31)
Though cisterns be broken   (Jer. 2:13)
    and creatures all fail,
the word he hath spoken
    will surely prevail.

His love in time past
    forbids me to think
he'll leave me at last
    in trouble to sink.   (Matt. 14:31)
Each sweet Ebenezer   (1 Sam. 7:12)
    I had in review
confirms his good pleasure
    to help me quite through.

Determined to save,
    he watched o'er my path
when, Satan's blind slave,
    I sported with death;
and can he have taught me
    to trust in his name,
and thus far have brought me
    to put me to shame?

Why should I complain
of want or distress?
Temptation or pain?
he told me no less:
The heirs of salvation,
I know from his word,
through much tribulation
must follow their Lord.   (Mark 8:34)

How bitter that cup
no heart can conceive,
which he drank quite up
that sinners might live.   (Mark 14:36)
His way was much rougher
and darker than mine;
did Jesus thus suffer,
and shall I repine?

Since all that I meet
shall work for my good,   (Rom. 8:18)
the bitter is sweet,
the med'cine is food;
though painful at present,
'twill cease before long,
and then, O! how pleasant
the conqueror's song!

John Newton
Olney Hymns, 1779, III, 37

89
Perseverance

Rejoice, believer, in the Lord,
who makes your cause his own;
the hope that's built upon his word
can ne'er be overthrown.

Though many foes beset your road,
and feeble is your arm,
your life is hid with Christ in God   (Col. 3:3)
beyond the reach of harm.

Weak as you are, you shall not faint,
or fainting, shall not die;
Jesus, the strength of every saint
will aid you from on high.

Though sometimes unperceived by sense,
faith sees him always near,
a guide, a glory, a defense;
then what have you to fear?

As surely as he overcame
and triumphed once for you;
so surely you that love his name
shall in him triumph too.   (Rom. 8:39)

John Newton
Olney Hymns, 1779, III, 84

90
Walking with God. Genesis 5:24

O for a closer walk with God,
a calm and heavenly frame,
a light to shine upon the road
that leads me to the Lamb!

Where is the blessedness I knew
when first I saw the Lord?
Where is the soul-refreshing view
of Jesus and his word?

What peaceful hours I once enjoyed!
how sweet their memory still!
But they have left an aching void
the world can never fill.

Return, O holy Dove, return,
sweet messenger of rest;   (Gen. 8:11)
I hate the sins that made thee mourn   (Eph. 4:30)
and drove thee from my breast.

The dearest idol I have known,
    whate'er that idol be,
help me to tear it from thy throne,
    and worship only thee.

So shall my walk be close with God,
    calm and serene my frame;
so purer light shall mark the road
    that leads me to the Lamb.

William Cowper, ca. 1771
Olney Hymns, 1779, I, 3

91

Praise for the Fountain Opened.
Zechariah 13:1

There springs a fountain, where for sin
    Immanuel was slain;
and sinners who are washed therein
    are cleansed from every stain.

The dying thief rejoiced to see   (Luke 23:43)
    that fountain in his day;
and there have I, as vile as he,
    washed all my sins away.

Thy resurrection and thy blood
    shall never lose their power
till all the ransomed church of God
    be saved, to sin no more.

E'er since by faith I saw the stream
    thy flowing wounds supply,
redeeming love has been my theme
    and shall be, till I die.

Then in a nobler, sweeter song
    I'll sing thy power to save—
when this poor lisping, stammering tongue
    lies silent in the grave.

Lord, I believe thou hast prepared
    (unworthy though I be),
for me a blood-bought free reward,
    a golden harp for me!

'Tis strung, and tuned for endless years,
    and formed by power divine
to sound in God the Father's ears
    no other name but thine.

William Cowper, ca. 1771
Olney Hymns, 1779, I, 79
stanzas 1 and 3 altered by Nathaniel Micklem
© Nathaniel Micklem

Cowper's stanzas 1 and 3 read:

There is a fountain filled with blood
    drawn from Emmanuel's veins;
and sinners plunged beneath that flood
    lose all their guilty stains.

Dear dying Lamb, I saw the stream
    thy flowing wounds supply,
redeeming love has been my theme,
    and shall be till I die.

92

Lovest Thou Me? John 21:16

Hark, my soul, it is the Lord;
'tis thy Savior, hear his word;
Jesus speaks, and speaks to thee:
"Say, poor sinner, lov'st thou me?"

"I delivered thee when bound,
and, when bleeding, healed thy wound—
sought thee wandering, set thee right   (Matt. 18:12)
turned thy darkness into light.   (Eph. 5:14)

"Can a woman's tender care
cease toward the child she bare?   (Isa. 49:15)
Yes, she may forgetful be,
yet will I remember thee.

"Mine is an unchanging love,
higher than the heights above,
deeper than the depths beneath,
free and faithful, strong as death.   (Song 8:6)

"Thou shalt see my glory soon,   (Luke 23:43)
when the work of grace is done—
partner of my throne shalt be;
say, poor sinner, lov'st thou me?"

Lord, it is my chief complaint
that my love is weak and faint;
yet I love thee and adore,
O for grace to love thee more!

> William Cowper, ca. 1768
> *Olney Hymns*, 1779, I, 118

93

Exhortation to Prayer

What various hindrances we meet
in coming to the mercy seat!
Yet who that knows the worth of prayer
but wishes to be often there?

Prayer makes the darkened cloud withdraw,
          (Exod. 19:18, 20)
prayer climbs the ladder Jacob saw,   (Gen. 28:12)
gives exercise to faith and love,
brings every blessing from above.

Restraining prayer, we cease to fight:
prayer makes the Christian's armor bright: (Eph. 6:18)
and Satan trembles when he sees
the weakest saint upon his knees.

While Moses stood with arms spread wide
          (Exod. 17:8–12)
success was found on Israel's side;
but when through weariness they failed,
that moment Amalek prevailed.

Have you no words? Ah, think again:
words flow apace when you complain,
and fill your fellow creature's ear
with the sad tale of all your care.

Were half the breath thus vainly spent
to heaven in supplication sent,
your cheerful song would oftener be,
"Hear what the Lord has done for me."   (Ps. 66:16)

> William Cowper
> *Olney Hymns*, 1779, II, 60

94

Light Shining out of Darkness. John 13:7

God moves in a mysterious way
    his wonders to perform;
he plants his footsteps in the sea,   (Ps. 77:19)
    and rides upon the storm.

Deep in unfathomable mines   (Rom. 11:30)
    of never-failing skill
he treasures up his bright designs
    and works his sovereign will.

Ye fearful saints, fresh courage take—
    the clouds ye so much dread
are big with mercy, and shall break
    in blessings on your head.

Judge not the Lord by feeble sense,
    but trust him for his grace:
behind a frowning providence
    he hides a smiling face.

His purposes will ripen fast,
    unfolding every hour;
the bud may have a bitter taste,
    but sweet will be the flower.

Blind unbelief is sure to err,
    and scan his work in vain;
God is his own interpreter
    and he will make it plain.

William Cowper, ca. 1773
Olney Hymns, 1779, III, 15

95

Joy and Peace in Believing

Sometimes a light surprises
    the Christian while he sings;
it is the Lord, who rises
    with healing in his wings.   (Mal. 4:2)
When comforts are declining,
    he grants the soul again
a season of clear shining   (2 Sam. 23:4)
    to cheer it after rain.

In holy contemplation
    we sweetly then pursue
the theme of God's salvation,
    and find it ever new: (Lam. 3:26)
set free from present sorrow,
    we cheerfully can say,
"E'en let the unknown morrow
    bring with it what it may."   (Matt. 6:34)

It can bring with it nothing
    but he will bear us through;
who gives the lilies clothing   (Matt. 6:28)
    will clothe his people too;
beneath the spreading heavens
    no creature but is fed;
and he who feeds the ravens
    will give his children bread.

Though vine nor fig tree neither   (Hab. 3:17–18)
    their wonted fruit should bear,
though all the field should wither,
    nor flocks nor herd be there:
yet God the same abiding,
    his praise shall tune my voice;
for while in him confiding,
    I cannot but rejoice.

William Cowper
Olney Hymns, 1779, III, 48

Chapter 8:
The Scottish Paraphrases
(96–102)

Scotland has its own way of performing Christian praise, and it is hardly too much to say that even the legitimizing of hymnody in Scotland in the mid-nineteenth century hardly disturbed this settled habit between the publication of the first psalter in 1564 and that of the third edition of *The Church Hymnary* in 1973.

For a Scot, the metrical psalms in the 1650 version are the center of all praise. In this he is like a medieval Catholic, for whom hymnody was always secondary to psalmody. And until the year 1781 nothing but psalmody was permitted in any part of the Church of Scotland. (Certain of the most conservative Scottish communions still preserve this rule.) But it was perhaps inevitable that a Watts-like protest against the singer's being confined to the Old Testament for his praise should be heard sooner or later. It was heard in the General Assembly of 1741. By resolution of that Assembly certain men were deputed to draw up a short collection of paraphrases of Scripture passages in psalm-meter which should then be submitted, as are all resolutions of that Assembly, to the Presbyteries for their judgment. A collection of forty-five pieces was presented to the Assembly in 1745 and duly copied and distributed to the Presbyteries. It appears (from Douglas Maclagan's account) that it proved impossible to bring the Assembly to a decision, because, for one reason and another, many Presbyteries withheld their replies, the excuse being that the times were disturbed (they were indeed; 1745 was not the best of all years in which to initiate a project of this sort in Scotland). By 1751, though some work of revision had been done on the recommendation of the Assembly, the project was officially laid aside.

The matter was reactivated some twenty-five years later, and this time came to a successful conclusion. Working on the 1745 and 1751 drafts, and adding more from other sources, the committee brought in, and the Assembly accepted, a collection of sixty-seven pieces. Of these, thirty-two were taken from the Old Testament and thirty-five from the New. Every piece was scrutinized by the new committee, and the result of their work is a homogeneous collection which looks as if it were all written by one hand. In fact a number of the paraphrases come from the works of the few writers in the Calvinist tradition available to be drawn on. Clearly nothing in the Wesleyan style would do, but twenty-three pieces are altered from Isaac Watts; two or three more are based on his work but depart very widely from it; five are based on hymns by Philip Doddridge; nine are untraceable; the rest are by ministers who contributed to the earlier or the later collection, or by members of the editorial committee, of whom the best known are John Logan and William Cameron.

Virtually nothing passed unaltered through the editorial committee's hands; "Paraphrase 64" is the only one, according to Maclagan, that suffered no alteration through the editions of 1745, 1751, and 1781 (and it is not a particularly meritable piece). The very famous Doddridge paraphrase (96) was greatly improved, as to its first four stanzas, by the paraphrasers, though their fifth introduced a legalistic note which while not contradicted in the Scripture at that point comes uneasily to Christians. Even Nahum Tate's "While shepherds" (our 22) was altered in a few details.

The ruthlessness of this revision produced one awkward controversy which has never been satisfactorily cleared up. We are content to attribute our 97 and 100 to Michael Bruce, the young poet who died at 21; but Logan claimed them as his, and indeed he certainly worked on them before they were finally published. As to "Paraphrase 18" (97) it has to be said that a version like it was in the 1745 book (before Bruce was born), and Bruce can only have revised it; but "Paraphrase 58" (100) may indeed be Bruce's work, even if again it was gone over by Logan. It is the only paraphrase in anything but Common Meter, and is an alternative to "Paraphrase 57" on the same passage. Those who wish to go into the matter will need to chase it through many pages of contemporary and later dispute.

This collection, anyhow, was the hymn book of the Church of Scotland for nearly a century after its publication, and many pieces from it have found their way into later and non-Scottish collections. This must be credited to the revisers, who certainly did their work very faithfully. Among Scots the collection is second only to the Psalms. I may say that so great is the gap between the psalms and paraphrases on one hand and the hymns on the other even to this day, that I heard an elder of a famous church in Edinburgh say, of a certain paraphrase which appeared also in the hymn book, that he disapproved of its being announced by the minister as hymn 365 and preferred, with weighty emphasis, that it be always known as "Paraphrase 18." The separate psalter, with paraphrases, was discarded officially only in 1973 when a new hymnal appeared which included selected psalms and paraphrases among the hymns. My elder is not on record as having commented on the fact that Psalm 23 is now hymn 387.

The traditional pairing of shorter stanzas for singing to a longer tune is indicated below.

96
Paraphrase 2. Genesis 28:20–22

O God of Bethel! by whose hand
    thy people still are fed;
who through this weary pilgrimage
    hast all our fathers led;

our vows, our prayers, we now present
    before thy throne of grace:
God of our fathers! be the God
    of their succeeding race.

•   •   •

Through each perplexing path of life
    our wandering footsteps guide;
give us each day our daily bread
    and raiment fit provide.

O spread thy covering wings around
    till all our wanderings cease,
and at our Father's loved abode
    our souls arrive in peace.

•   •   •

Such blessings from thy gracious hand
    our humble prayers implore;
and thou shalt be our chosen God,
    and portion evermore.

probably by John Logan
Translations and Paraphrases, in Verse, of
Several Passages of Sacred Scripture, 1781
altered from a text with the same first line by Philip Doddridge
Hymns Founded on Various Texts in Holy Scriptures, 1755

97
Paraphrase 18. Isaiah 2:2–6

Behold! the mountain of the Lord
    in latter days shall rise
on mountain tops above the hills,
    and draw the wondering eyes.

To this the joyful nations round,
    all tribes and tongues shall flow;
Up to the hill of God, they'll say,
    and to his house we'll go.

•   •   •

The beam that shines from Sion's hill
    shall lighten every land;
the King who reigns in Salem's towers
    shall all the world command.

Among the nations he shall judge;
    his judgments truth shall guide;
his scepter shall protect the just,
    and quell the sinner's pride.

• • •

No strife shall rage, nor hostile feuds
    disturb those peaceful years;
to ploughshares men shall beat their swords,
    to pruning hooks their spears.

No longer hosts encount'ring hosts
    shall crowds of slain deplore;
they hang the trumpet in the hall
    and study war no more.

• • •

Come then, O house of Jacob! come
    to worship at his shrine;
and, walking in the light of God,
    with holy beauties shine.

probably by Michael Bruce, 1751
Translations and Paraphrases, in Verse, of
Several Passages of Sacred Scripture, 1781
based on an anonymous text beginning
"In latter days the mount of God,"
in the 1745 draft of *Translations and Paraphrases*

98
Paraphrase 19. Isaiah 9:2–7

The race that long in darkness pined
    have seen a glorious light;
the people dwell in day, who dwelt
    in death's surrounding night.

To hail thy rise, thou better Sun!
    the gath'ring nations come,
joyous, as when the reapers bear
    the harvest treasures home.

• • •

For thou our burden hast removed,
    and quelled th' oppressor's sway;
quick as the slaughtered squadrons fell
    in Midian's evil day.

To us a Child of hope is born,
    to us a Son is given;
him shall the tribes of earth obey,
    him, all the hosts of heaven.

• • •

His name shall be the Prince of Peace,
    for evermore adored,
the Wonderful, the Counselor,
    the great and mighty Lord.

His power increasing still shall spread,
    his reign no end shall know;
justice shall guard his throne above,
    and peace abound below.

John Morison
Translations and Paraphrases, in Verse, of
Several Passages of Sacred Scripture, 1781

99
Paraphrase 30. Hosea 6:1–4

Come, let us to the Lord our God
    with contrite hearts return;
our God is gracious, nor will leave
    the desolate to mourn.

His voice commands the tempest forth,
    and stills the stormy wave;
and though his arm be strong to smite,
    'tis also strong to save.

* * *

Long hath the night of sorrow reigned,
 the dawn shall bring us light;
God shall appear, and we shall rise
 with gladness in his sight.

Our hearts, if God we seek to know,
 shall know him, and rejoice;
his coming like the morn shall be,
 like morning songs his voice.

* * *

As dew upon the tender herb,
 diffusing fragrance round;
as showers that usher in the spring,
 and cheer the thirsty ground;

so shall his presence bless our souls,
 and shed a joyful light;
that hallowed morn shall chase away
 the sorrows of the night.

John Morison
Translations and Paraphrases, in Verse, of
Several Passages of Sacred Scripture, 1781

* * *

Though now ascended up on high,
he bends on earth a brother's eye;
partaker of the human name,
he knows the frailty of our frame.

Our fellow-suff'rer yet retains
a fellow-feeling of our pains;
and still remembers in the skies
his tears, his agonies, and cries.

* * *

In every pang that rends the heart
the Man of Sorrows has a part;
he sympathizes with our grief,
and to the suff'rer sends relief.

With boldness therefore at the throne,
let us make all our sorrows known;
and ask the aid of heavenly power
to help us in the evil hour.

Michael Bruce, c. 1765
Translations and Paraphrases, in Verse, of
Several Passages of Sacred Scripture, 1781

100
Paraphrase 58. Hebrews 4:14–16

Where high the heavenly temple stands,
the house of God not made with hands,
a great High Priest our nature wears;
the guardian of mankind appears.

He who for men their surety stood,
and poured on earth his precious blood,
pursues in heaven his mighty plan,
the Savior, and the friend of man.

101
Paraphrase 60. Hebrews 13:20–21

A. Original

Father of peace, and God of love,
 we own thy power to save;
that power by which our Shepherd rose
 victorious o'er the grave.

We triumph in that Shepherd's name,
 still watchful for our good;
who brought th' eternal covenant down,
 and sealed it with his blood.

So may thy Spirit seal my soul,
    and mold it to thy will;
that my fond heart no more may stray,
    but keep thy cov'nant still.

Still may we gain superior strength
    and press with vigor on,
till full perfection crown our hopes
    and fix us near thy throne.

Philip Doddridge
Hymns Founded on Various Texts in the Holy Scriptures, 1755

B. Revision

Father of peace, and God of love!
    we own thy power to save,
that power by which our Shepherd rose
    victorious o'er the grave.

Him from the dead thou brought'st again,
    when, by his sacred blood,
confirmed and sealed for evermore
    th' eternal covenant stood.

· · ·

O may thy Spirit seal our souls
    and mold them to thy will,
that our weak hearts no more may stray,
    but keep thy precepts still;

that to perfection's sacred height
    we nearer still may rise,
and all we think, and all we do,
    be pleasing in thine eyes.

probably by William Cameron
*Translations and Paraphrases, in Verse, of
Several Passages of Sacred Scripture,* 1781
based on Doddridge, as altered in the 1751 draft of *Translations and
Paraphrases,* where the text began "Behold the amazing gift"

102
Paraphrase 63. I John 3:1–4

Behold, th' amazing gift of love
    the Father hath bestowed
on us, the sinful sons of men,
    to call us sons of God!

Concealed as yet this honor lies,
    by this dark world unknown,
a world that knew not when he came,
    ev'n God's eternal Son.

· · ·

High is the rank we now possess;
    but higher we shall rise;
though what we shall hereafter be
    is hid from mortal eyes.

Our souls, we know, when he appears,
    shall bear his image bright;
for all his glory, full disclosed,
    shall open to our sight.

· · ·

A hope so great, and so divine,
    may trials well endure;
and purge the soul from sense and sin,
    as Christ himself is pure.

probably by William Cameron
*Translations and Paraphrases, in Verse,
of Several Passages of Sacred Scripture,* 1781
based on an anonymous text in the 1745 draft of *Translations and
Paraphrases;* based, in turn, on a text beginning
"Behold what wonderous grace," by Isaac Watts,
Hymns and Spiritual Songs, 1707

Chapter 9:
From Evangelical to Romantic
(103–129)

"The Romantic" has as many colors as the rainbow, but for our purposes it may broadly be described as including emphases on the personal rather than the public, the distant rather than the easily tractable, the adventurous rather than the cautious, the imaginative rather than the rational. If we speak so (and William Blake would, aside from his hatred of anything so clear cut, mostly have approved), then it is clear that the romantic has affinities with the Evangelical, and is always suspected by the Calvinistic culture.

There is much about the Wesleyan enterprise that is Romantic: the sheer adventure of it; all that traveling; the exposure of evangelists to danger; the pursuit of a far-off but always visible goal; and the free rein given to personal expressions of religion. Wesley does not suspect Nature quite as deeply as a faithful Calvinist must.

Therefore the Romantic strain in hymnody issues very naturally from the Evangelical, even when it is best seen in the work of people who hardly described themselves technically as Evangelicals. In the section 103–129, we see exactly how this works out.

Numbers 103–105 are Evangelical. Thomas Haweis's moving little poem on the words of the penitent thief is intensely personal in a manner worthy of Wesley himself. The two magnificent dogmatic utterances of Thomas Kelly are Evangelical, in the sense of urging a total commitment to the mystery of the cross, and Calvinistic, in their resurrection background. (Kelly, an Irish judge and a Protestant, wrote an enormous number of hymns; we can forgive him all the doggerel in the vast majority of his hymns for these two perfect pieces).

But with 106 comes a change. Number 106 is the work of a vicar, John Marriott, who was more or less a contemporary of Jane Austen and therefore of the alarming clerics that appear in her novels: an absentee incumbent who lived in Torquay while leaving his midlands parish in the hands of a curate. But it is, first and last, a missionary hymn, and so are the much greater examples of James Montgomery that immediately follow (107–109).

Now, the missionary explosion of 1792–1810 is Romanticism coming to life in English religion. It is, of course, evangelism, but it is also remote, adventurous, and perilous. Missionaries really were eaten by cannibals. It was a sharing of experience, not an extension of a system. The very existence of the London Missionary Society, founded in 1795, and its famous peroration in its constitution, which averred that its purpose was not the imposition of any church system (it was at first a wholly nondenominational mission) but to spread "the glorious Gospel of the Blessed God," is Romanticism at its best.

Should it have been said before this that Romanticism is not in any known sense a pejorative word? It is so used by people who have certain theories about organs, and it is used with a special tone of contempt by certain theologians, but I do not so use it here. All the captivating enthusiasms, all the endearing weaknesses, of the Protestant missionary enterprise of this time was Romantic, and perhaps the fact that some other missions promoted from elsewhere have in our own time come to stickier ends has something to do with an inhibition which suffocated true romance in the hearts and minds of their promoters. That is material for somebody else's PhD.

At any rate, James Montgomery, the greatest of English lay hymn writers, focuses this argument in the shape of his life and the cast of his missionary hymns. Here was a young-middle-aged radical, a journalist working for a radical editor who was sent to prison for his political opinions, taking over the paper when the editor disappeared and promoting every philanthropic and humanitarian cause he could reach—a romantic political writer to his finger tips. Our 107 was evoked by news of a special victory in the South Seas. Was there ever a more Romantic (still in the best sense) interpretation of Psalm 72 than 108? Compare it with 43! The sense of distance, of the trajectory of preaching, is nowhere more vividly expressed than in 109. The specially personal and devotional note so sanely and unaffectedly sounded in 110–113 is equally of the Romantic tradition. Romance is not irrational, though it is impatient of pedantry; what better shows that than these beautifully wrought devotional pieces? Montgomery wrote probably three hundred hymns, often dashing them off for special occasions (109 was written for a local missionary celebration in Leeds) and revising them later at leisure. Many others, of which one can say just what we have said of these, are scattered over the hymnals.

"Romantic" is also a proper description of 114, if one recalls its author's background. This author, John Bowring, was a diplomat, businessman, and traveler; the sight of the charred iron cross that was all that remained of the burnt-out cathedral on the island of Macao inspired the hymn. And it is very proper that we are able to include in 115 some lines of Sir Walter Scott, the father of all Romantic novelists in English literature. This is, by design, a Christian's prayer for the conversion of the Jews and is not now seen in hymnals (1927 was the date of the last to include it).

I have insisted that romanticism is not to be regarded as contemptible; but it is fair to point out that it can be perverted. When it is corrupt it becomes loathsome enough. The most obvious perversions of it are the habit of being preoccupied with what is distant at the expense of what is immediately present; Charles Dickens sufficiently disposed of the corrupt "missionary" mentality in his devastating character sketches of Mrs. Jellyby and Mrs. Pardiggle in *Bleak House*, women who, in their pursuit of benefit for people far away, neglected and abused their own families. The Romantic can be irrational, anarchic, egotistical, and impossible to communicate with. It can escape from present duties

in contemplation of imaginary ones. And, of course, it can always dispense itself from the duty of being corrected by new evidence. That happened to many missionary hymns of the less meritable kind and to much devotional poetry as well.

But we have to say that there was more than a touch of the Romantic about the Oxford Movement itself. The historical judgments of some of those who wished to bring the Middle Ages back were as shaky as Sir Walter Scott's; the zeal with which they sought to reconstruct the system of Office Hymns could blind them to the occasional anachronism and even bathos produced by the less inspired of the texts they translated.

That their hymn writers (in chapters 11 and 14) were not worse than they were was undoubtedly to the credit of the writers featured in 116–129. Bishop Reginald Heber (not a bishop when he wrote his hymns) showed a warmth and grace which at this moment were badly needed. "Holy, holy, holy" (116) is more impressionistic than theological; it proved, once John Bacchus Dykes had given it a tune, too easy to sing and has suffered badly from the batterings of incompetent hymn-choosers. But it was Tennyson's favorite hymn, and one can see why. Number 117 is equally impressionistic, but (almost fatally) attractive. Number 118 is a communion hymn, but hardly a eucharistic one. Number 119 is a tender, naturalistic meditation. This is very different from what the Calvinists prescribed. Nothing became Heber so much as his inclusion in his collection of one hymn that was not his, 120, which is surely the finest lyric written in the whole of the nineteenth century.

And John Keble, one of the Oxford Movement's architects, is, as a hymn writer, a pure Romantic. He collected his hymns in *The Christian Year* when he was thirty-five, and the collection became a best-seller which paid for the reconstruction of his country parish church. Many of the "hymns" are really extended poetic meditations, and the fragments now in common use are much better understood when read in the context of their surrounding verses. Number 123 happens to be a hymn well known in a grossly distorted version which uses two of its verses and two platitudinous rhymes by another writer. In its original form it has an immense sense of distance, the more effective because of its restricted meter. And as for 124, this is Romantic in its interest in created nature and its contented contemplation of it as it is.

"O worship the King," in its full text a splendid piece of writing, is as romantic an interpretation of Psalm 104, which lends itself especially to such treatment, as 108 was of Psalm 72. And the much-loved Henry F. Lyte, though scriptural and evangelical in his emphases, always writes good literature and is rarely deserted by an exquisite lyric gift. Perhaps the centrally "Romantic" hymn of all hymns is the intensely personal yet, as it has proved, wholly universal hymn, "Abide with me" (128), which again can be read most profitably in its full version.

As a tailpiece we include 129, one of the handful of hymns left by the young priest Joseph Anstice. His others are actually more overtly Romantic than this one, but what he might have become had he lived longer, as a hymn writer with a touch of Watts about him illuminated by the lyric gifts of the Romantics, is a question which 129 poses forcefully.

This small section, covering a short but important age, indicates how a group of writers demonstrated, just in time, that "the system" need not suffocate literature. Had they not done so, the Oxford Movement might have been a good deal more stuffy than it was.

103

Remember Me. Luke 23:39

Thou, from whom all goodness flows,
    I lift my heart to thee;
in all my sorrows, conflicts, woes,
    Dear Lord, "Remember me!"

While on my poor distressed heart
    my sins lie heavily,
my pardon speak, new peace impart,
    in love "Remember me!"

Temptations sore obstruct my way,
    to shake my faith in thee;
O give me strength, Lord, as my day;
    for good "Remember me!"

Distressed with pain, disease, and grief,
    this feeble body see;
grant patience, rest, and kind relief,
    hear! and "Remember me!"

When in desertion's dismal night
    thy face I cannot see;
then, Lord, arise with glorious light,
    and still "Remember me!"

If on my face for thy dear name
    shame and reproaches be,
all hail, reproach, and welcome, shame,
    if thou "Remember me!"

The hour is near, consigned to death
    I wait thy just decree;
Savior, with my last parting breath,
    I'll cry, "Remember me!"

Thomas Haweis
Carmina Christo, 1792

104

God Forbid That I Should Glory, Save in the Cross. Galatians 6:14

We sing the praise of him who died,
    of him who died upon the cross;
the sinner's hope let men deride,
    for this we count the world but loss.   (Gal. 6:14)

97

Inscribed upon the cross we see
    in shining letters, "God is love";
he bears our sins upon the tree;   (Mark 15:26)
    he brings us mercy from above.   (1 Pet. 2:24)

The cross! it takes our guilt away;
    it holds the fainting spirit up;
it cheers with hope the gloomy day,
    and sweetens every bitter cup.

It makes the coward spirit brave,
    and nerves the feeble arm for fight;
it takes its terror from the grave,
    and gilds the bed of death with light;

the balm of life, the cure of woe,
    the measure and the pledge of love,
'tis all that sinners want below;
    'tis all that angels know above.

Thomas Kelly
Hymns; Not Before Published, 1815

In *Hymns on Various Passages of Scripture* (6th ed.), 1826, Kelly revised the last two lines to:

the sinner's refuge here below,
    the angels' theme in heaven above.

105

Christ Perfect through Sufferings. Hebrews 2:10

The head that once was crowned with thorns
    is crowned with glory now:
a royal diadem adorns
    the mighty Victor's brow.

The highest place that heaven affords
    is his, is his by right,
the King of kings and Lord of lords,   (Rev. 19:16)
    and heaven's eternal light;

the joy of all who dwell above,
    the joy of all below,
to whom he manifests his love,
    and grants his name to know.

To them the cross, with all its shame,
    with all its grace, is given:
their name an everlasting name,
    their joy the joy of heaven.   (Luke 10:20)

They suffer with their Lord below,   (2 Tim. 2:12)
    they reign with him above,
their profit and their joy to know
    the mystery of his love.

The cross he bore is life and health,
    though shame and death to him;
his people's hope, his people's wealth,
    their everlasting theme.

Thomas Kelly
Hymns on Various Passages of Scripture (5th ed.), 1820

106

Missionary Hymn

Thou, whose almighty word
chaos and darkness heard,
    and took their flight;
hear us, we humbly pray;
and where the gospel's day
sheds not its glorious ray,
    let there be light!   (Gen. 1:3)

Thou, who didst come to bring
on thy redeeming wing
    healing and sight,
health to the sick in mind,
sight to the inly blind,
Oh, now to all mankind
    let there be light!

Spirit of truth and love,
life-giving, holy Dove,
    speed forth thy flight!
Move on the waters' face,
bearing the lamp of grace,
and in earth's darkest place
    let there be light!

Holy and blessed Three,
glorious Trinity,
    Wisdom, Love, Might!
Boundless as ocean's tide,
rolling in fullest pride,
through the earth, far and wide
    let there be light!

John Marriott, 1813
The Evangelical Magazine and Missionary Chronicle, June 1825
altered for *Hymns Ancient and Modern*, 1869

107

The Lord God Omnipotent Reigneth

Hark! the song of jubilee,
    loud as mighty thunders' roar,
or the fullness of the sea
    when it breaks upon the shore:
Alleluia! for the Lord
    God omnipotent shall reign;
Alleluia! let the word
    echo round the earth and main.

Alleluia! hark the sound,
    from the depths unto the skies,
wakes above, beneath, around
    all creation's harmonies;
see Jehovah's banner furled,
    sheathed his sword; he speaks—'tis done,
and the kingdoms of this world   (Rev. 11:15)
    are the kingdoms of his Son.

He shall reign from pole to pole
    with illimitable sway;
he shall reign when like a scroll   (Rev. 6:14)
    yonder heavens are passed away;
then the end; beneath his rod   (1 Cor. 15:24)
    man's last enemy shall fall;
Alleluia! Christ in God,
    God in Christ, is all in all.   (Col. 3:11)

James Montgomery, 1818
Evangelical Magazine, April 1818
revised by Montgomery in *Original Hymns*, 1853

108

The Reign of Christ. Psalm 72

Hail to the Lord's Anointed!
    Great David's greater Son;
Hail, in the time appointed,
    his reign on earth begun!
He comes to break oppression,
    to set the captive free,
to take away transgression,
    and rule in equity.

He comes in succor speedy
    to those who suffer wrong;
to help the poor and needy,
    and bid the weak be strong;
to give them songs for sighing,
    their darkness turn to light,
whose souls, condemned and dying
    were precious in his sight.

By such shall he be feared
    while sun and moon endure;
beloved, obeyed, revered;
    for he shall judge the poor
through changing generations,
    with justice, mercy, truth,
while stars maintain their stations,
    or moons renew their youth.

He shall come down like showers
    upon the fruitful earth,
and love, joy, hope, like flowers
    spring in his path to birth:
before him on the mountains,
    shall Peace, the herald, go;
and righteousness, in fountains
    from hill to valley flow.

Arabia's desert ranger
    to him shall bow the knee,
the Ethiopian stranger
    his glory come to see:
with offerings of devotion,
    ships from the isles shall meet,
to pour the wealth of ocean
    in tribute at his feet.

Kings shall bow down before him,
    and gold and silver bring;
all nations shall adore him,
    his praise all people sing:
for he shall have dominion
    o'er river, sea, and shore,
far as the eagle's pinion
    or dove's light wing can soar.

For him shall prayer unceasing
    and daily vows ascend;
his kingdom still increasing,
    a kingdom without end:
the mountain dews shall nourish
    a seed in weakness sown,
whose fruit shall spread and flourish,
    and shake like Lebanon.

O'er every foe victorious,
    he on his throne shall rest,
from age to age more glorious,
    all-blessing and all-blest;
the tide of time shall never
    his covenant remove;
his name shall stand for ever;
    that name to us is Love.

James Montgomery, 1821
Evangelical Magazine, May 1822
revised by Montgomery in *Original Hymns*, 1853

109
The Spirit Accompanying the Word of God

O Spirit of the living God,
    in all thy plenitude of grace,
where'er the foot of man hath trod,
    descend on our apostate race.

Give tongues of fire and hearts of love
    to preach the reconciling word;
give power and unction from above
    whene'er the joyful sound is heard.

Be darkness at thy coming, light:
    confusion, order in thy path;
souls without strength inspire with might;
    bid mercy triumph over wrath.

O Spirit of the Lord, prepare
    all the round earth her God to meet;
breathe thou abroad like morning air
    till hearts of stone begin to beat.

Baptize the nations; far and nigh
    the triumphs of the cross record:
the name of Jesus glorify,
    till every kingdom call him Lord.

God from eternity hath willed
    all flesh shall his salvation see:
so be the Father's love fulfilled,
    the Savior's sufferings crowned through thee.

James Montgomery, 1823
The Evangelical Magazine, August 1823
revised by Montgomery in *The Christian Psalmist*, 1825

Give these—and then thy will be done;
    thus strengthened with all might,
we by thy Spirit and thy Son
    shall pray, and pray aright.

James Montgomery, 1818
Thomas Cotterill's *A Selection of Psalms and Hymns* (8th ed), 1819
revised by Montgomery in *The Christian Psalmist*, 1825

110
Lord, Teach Us to Pray

Lord, teach us how to pray aright   (Luke 11:1)
    with reverence and with fear;
though dust and ashes in thy sight
    wc may, we must draw near.

We perish if we cease from prayer;
    O grant us power to pray;
and when to meet thee we prepare,
    Lord, meet us by the way.

God of all grace, we come to thee
    with broken, contrite hearts;   (Ps. 51:17)
give, what thine eye delights to see,
    truth in the inward parts.   (Ps. 51:6)

Give deep humility, the sense
    of godly sorrow give;
a strong desiring confidence
    to hear thy voice and live;

faith in the only sacrifice
    that can for sin atone;
to cast our hopes, to fix our eyes,
    on Christ, on Christ alone;

patience to watch, and wait, and weep
    though mercy long delay;
courage, our fainting souls to keep
    and trust thee, though thou slay.   (Job 13:15)

111
The Skill of Prayer

Prayer is the soul's sincere desire,
    uttered or unexpressed;
the motion of a hidden fire
    that trembles in the breast.

Prayer is the burden of a sigh,
    the falling of a tear,
the upward glancing of an eye
    when none but God is near.

Prayer is the simplest form of speech
    that infant lips can try;
prayer the sublimest strains that reach
    the Majesty on high.

Prayer is the contrite sinner's voice,
    returning from his ways,
while angels in their songs rejoice
    and cry, "Behold, he prays!"

Prayer is the Christian's vital breath,
    the Christian's native air,
his watchword at the gates of death:
    he enters heaven with prayer.

The saints in prayer appear as one
    in word and deed and mind,
while with the Father and the Son
    sweet fellowship they find.

Nor prayer is made by man alone;
    the Holy Spirit pleads,
and Jesus on the eternal throne
    for sinners intercedes.

O thou, by whom we come to God,
    the Life, the Truth, the Way,   (John 14:6)
the path of prayer thyself hast trod:
    Lord, teach us how to pray.   (Luke 11:1)

James Montgomery, 1818
Thomas Cotterill's *A Selection of Psalms and Hymns* (8th ed.), 1819
revised by Montgomery in *Original Hymns*, 1853

112
Psalm 63

O God, thou art my God alone,
    early to thee my soul shall cry,
a pilgrim in a land unknown,
    a thirsty land whose springs are dry.

O that it were as it hath been
    when, praying in the holy place,
thy power and glory I have seen,
    and marked the footsteps of thy grace!

Yea, through this rough and thorny maze
    I follow hard on thee, my God;
thine hand unseen upholds my ways;
    I safely tread where thou hast trod.

Thee, in the watches of the night,
    when I remember on my bed,
thy presence makes the darkness light;
    thy guardian wings are round my head.

Better than life itself thy love,
    dearer than all beside to me;
for whom have I in heaven above,
    or what on earth, compared with thee?   (Ps. 73:24)

Praise with my heart, my mind, my voice,
    for all thy mercy I will give;
my soul shall still in God rejoice;
    my tongue shall bless thee while I live.

James Montgomery
Songs of Zion, 1822

113
The Family Table

Be known to us in breaking bread,   (Luke 24:35)
    but do not then depart;
Savior, abide with us, and spread
    thy table in our heart.

There sup with us in love divine,
    thy body and thy blood,
that living bread, that heavenly wine
    be our immortal food.

James Montgomery
The Christian Psalmist, 1825

114
Glorying in the Cross. Galatians 6:14

In the cross of Christ I glory,
    towering o'er the wrecks of time;
all the light of sacred story
    gathers round its head sublime.

When the woes of life o'ertake me,
    hopes deceive and fears annoy,
never shall the cross forsake me:
    Lo! it glows with peace and joy.

When the sun of bliss is beaming
    light and love upon my way,
from the cross the radiance streaming
    adds more luster to the day.

Bane and blessing, pain and pleasure,
    by the cross are sanctified;
peace is there which knows no measure,
    joys that through all time abide.

In the cross of Christ I glory,
    towering o'er the wrecks of time;
all the light of sacred story
    gathers round its head sublime.

John Bowring
Hymns, 1825

115
The Song of Rebecca

When Israel, of the Lord beloved,
    out of the land of bondage came,
her fathers' God before her moved,
    an awful guide, in smoke and flame. (Exod. 40:38)
By day, along the astonished lands
    the cloudy pillar glided slow;
by night, Arabia's crimsoned sands
    returned the fiery column's glow.

There rose the choral hymn of praise,
    and trump and timbrel answered keen, (Exod. 15:1)
and Zion's daughters poured their lays,
    with priest's and warrior's voice between.
No portents now our foes amaze;
    forsaken Israel wanders lone;
their fathers would not know thy ways,
    and thou hast left them to their own.

But, present still, though now unseen,
    when brightly shines the prosperous day
be thoughts of thee a cloudy screen
    to temper the deceitful ray.
And O, when stoops on Judah's path
    in shade and storm the frequent night,
be thou, long-suffering, slow to wrath,
    a burning and a shining light!

Our harps we lift by Babel's streams,
    the tyrant's jest, the Gentile's scorn;
no censer round our altar beams,
    and mute our timbrel, trump, and horn.
But thou has said, the blood of goat,
    the flesh of rams, I will not prize;
a contrite heart, an humble thought,
    are mine accepted sacrifice.

Walter Scott
Ivanhoe, 1819
first as a hymn in *Hymns Adapted for the Worship of God*, 1833
This poem appears at the beginning of chapter 39 of the novel, with
this preface:

It was in the twilight of the day when her trial, if it could
be called such, had taken place, that a low knock was heard
at the door of Rebecca's prison-chamber. It disturbed not
the inmate, who was then engaged in the evening prayer
recommended by her religion, and which concluded with a
hymn we have ventured thus to translate into English.

116
Trinity Sunday

Holy, holy, holy! Lord God Almighty!
Early in the morning our song shall rise to thee;
    Holy, holy, holy! merciful and mighty,
God in three Persons, blessed Trinity!

Holy, holy, holy! all the saints adore thee,
casting down their golden crowns around the glassy
                                                                sea,
    cherubim and seraphim falling down before thee,
who wert and art, and evermore shalt be.

Holy, holy, holy! though the darkness hide thee,
though the eye of sinful man thy glory may not see,
    only thou art holy, there is none beside thee
perfect in power, in love and purity.

Holy, holy, holy! Lord God Almighty!
All thy works shall praise thy name in earth and
>> sky and sea;
>> Holy, holy, holy! merciful and mighty!
God in three Persons, blessed Trinity.

Reginald Heber
A Selection of Psalms and Hymns for the Parish Church of Banbury, 1826

117
Epiphany

Brightest and best of the sons of the morning,
>> dawn on our darkness, and lend us thine aid,
star of the east, the horizon adorning,
>> guide where our infant Redeemer is laid!

Cold on his cradle the dewdrops are shining,
>> low lies his head with the beasts of the stall;
angels adore him, in slumber reclining,
>> Maker, and Monarch, and Savior of all.

Say, shall we yield him, in costly devotion,
>> odors of Edom and offerings divine;
gems of the mountain, and pearls of the ocean,
>> myrrh from the forest, or gold from the mine?

Vainly we offer each ample oblation,
>> vainly with gifts would his favor secure;
richer by far is the heart's adoration,
>> dearer to God are the prayers of the poor.

Reginald Heber
The Christian Observer, November 1811

118
Before the Sacrament

Bread of the world, in mercy broken,
>> wine of the soul, in mercy shed,
by whom the words of life were spoken,
>> and in whose death our sins are dead:

Look on the heart by sorrow broken,
>> look on the tears by sinners shed,
and be thy feast to us the token
>> that by thy grace our souls are fed.

Reginald Heber
*Hymns, Written and Adapted to the Weekly
Church Service of the Year*, 1827

119
Fourth Sunday after Trinity

I praised the earth, in beauty seen
with garlands gay of various green;
I praised the sea, whose ample field
shone glorious as a silver shield;
and earth and ocean seemed to say,
"Our beauties are but for a day!"

I praised the sun, whose chariot rolled
on wheels of amber and of gold;
I praise the moon, whose softer eye
gleamed sweetly through the summer sky!
And moon and sun in answer said,
"Our days of light are numbered."

O God! O good beyond compare!
If thus thy meaner works are fair!
If thus thy bounties gild the span
of ruined earth and sinful man,
how glorious must the mansion be
where thy redeemed shall dwell with thee!

Reginald Heber
*Hymns, Written and Adapted to the Weekly
Church Service of the Year*, 1827

120
Palm Sunday

Ride on! ride on in majesty!
Hark, all the tribes "Hosanna!" cry;
thine humble beast pursues his road
with palms and scattered garments strowed.

Ride on! ride on in majesty!
In lowly pomp ride on to die;
O Christ, thy triumphs now begin
o'er captive death and conquered sin.

Ride on! ride on in majesty!
the winged squadrons of the sky
look down with sad and wondering eyes
to see the approaching sacrifice.

Ride on! ride on in majesty!
Thy last and fiercest strife is nigh;
the Father on his sapphire throne
expects his own anointed Son.

Ride on! ride on in majesty!
In lowly pomp ride on to die;
bow thy meek head to mortal pain,
then take, O God, thy power, and reign.

Henry Hart Milman
Hymns, Written and Adapted to the Weekly
Church Service of the Year, 1827

121

Morning. His compassions fail not. They are new every morning. Lamentations 2:22–23

Hues of the rich unfolding morn,
that, ere the glorious sun be born,
by some soft touch invisible
around his path are taught to swell;

thou rustling breeze so fresh and gay,
that dancest forth at opening day,
and brushing by with joyous wing,
wak'nsest each little leaf to sing;

ye fragrant clouds of dewy steam,
by which deep grove and tangled stream
pay, for soft rains in season given,
their tribute to the genial heaven—

why waste your treasures of delight
upon our thankless, joyful sight;
who day by day to sin awake,
seldom of heaven and you partake?

Oh! timely happy, timely wise,
hearts that with rising morn arise!
Eyes that the beam celestial view
which evermore makes all things new!   (Rev. 21:5)

New every morning is the love   (Lam. 3:26)
our wakening and uprising prove;
through sleep and darkness safely brought,
restored to life, and power, and thought.

New mercies, each returning day,
hover around us while we pray;
new perils past, new sins forgiven,
new thoughts of God, new hopes of heaven.

If on our daily course our mind
be set to hallow all we find,
New treasures still, of countless price,
God will provide for sacrifice.   (Gen. 22:8)

Old friends, old scenes, will lovelier be,
as more of heaven in each we see;
some softening gleam of love and prayer
shall dawn on every cross and care.

As for some dear familiar strain
untired we ask, and ask again,
ever, in its melodious strore,
finding a spell unheard before;

such is the bliss of souls serene,
when they have sworn, and steadfast mean,
couring the cost, in all t' espy
their God, in all themselves deny.

O could we learn that sacrifice,
what lights would all around us rise!
How would our hearts with wisdom talk
along life's dullest, dreariest walk.

We need not bid, for cloistered cell,
our neighbor and our work farewell,
nor strive to wind ourselves too high
for sinful man beneath the sky:

The trivial round, the common task
would furnish all we ought to ask;
room to deny ourselves; a road
to bring us, daily, nearer God.

Seek we no more; content with these,
let present rapture, comfort, ease,
as heaven shall bid them, come and go—
the secret, this, of rest below.

Only, O Lord, in thy dear love
fit us for perfect rest above;
and help us, this and every day,
to live more nearly as we pray.

John Keble, 1822
The Christian Year, 1827

122

Evening. Abide with us: for it is evening, and the day is far spent. Luke 24:29

'Tis gone, that bright and orbed blaze,
fast fading from our wistful gaze;
yon mantling cloud has hid from sight
the last faint pulse of quivering light.

In darkness and in weariness
the traveler on his way must press,
no gleam to watch on tree or tower,
whiling away the lonesome hour.

Sun of my soul! thou Savior dear,
it is not night if thou be near:
Oh! may no earthborn cloud arise
to hide thee from thy servant's eyes.

When round thy wondrous works below
my searching rapturous glance I throw,
tracing out wisdom, power, and love,
in earth or sky, in stream or grove;

or by the light thy words disclose
watch time's full river as it flows,
scanning thy gracious Providence,
where not too deep for mortal sense—

when with dear friends sweet talk I hold,
and all the flowers of life unfold;
let not my heart within me burn   (Luke 24:32)
except in all I thee discern.

When the soft dews of kindly sleep
my wearied eyelids gently steep,
be my last thought, how sweet to rest
forever on my Savior's breast.

Abide with me from morn till eve,
for without thee I cannot live;
abide with me when night is nigh,
for without thee I dare not die.

Thou framer of the light and dark,
steer through the tempest thine own ark;
amid the howling winter sea,
we are in port if we have thee.   (John 6:31)

The rulers of this Christian land,
'twixt thee and us ordained to stand—
guide thou their course, O Lord, aright;
let all do all as in thy sight.

Oh! by thine own sad burden, borne
so meekly up the hill of scorn,
teach thou thy priests their daily cross
to bear as thine, nor count it loss!

If some poor wandering child of thine
have spurned, today, the voice divine,
now, Lord, the gracious work begin;
let him no more lie down in sin.

Watch by the sick; enrich the poor
with blessings from thy boundless store;
be every mourner's sleep tonight
like infant's slumbers, pure and light.

Come near and bless us when we wake,
ere through the world our way we take;
till in the ocean of thy love
we lose ourselves in heaven above.

John Keble, 1820
The Christian Year, 1827
The usual selection of stanzas varies, but typically begins with stanza 3.
Compare line 4:3 to Watts's text at 39.

123

The Purification. Blessed are the pure in heart: for they shall see God. Matthew 5:8

Blessed are the pure in heart,
for they shall see our God,
the secret of the Lord is theirs,
their soul is Christ's abode.

Might mortal thought presume
to guess an angel's lay,
such are the notes that echo through
the courts of heaven today.

Such the triumphal hymns
on Sion's Prince that wait,
in high procession passing on
towards his temple gate.

Give ear, ye kings—bow down,
ye rulers of the earth—
this, this is he; your Priest by grace,
your God and King by birth.

No pomp of earthly guards
attends with sword and spear,
and, all-defying, dauntless look
their monarch's way to clear;

yet there are more with him
than all that are with you—
the armies of the highest heaven,
all righteous, good, and true.

Spotless their robes and pure,
dipped in the sea of light,
that hides the unapproached shine
from men's and angels' sight.

His throne, thy bosom blest,
O Mother undefiled—
that throne, if aught beneath the skies
beseems the sinless child.

Lost in high thoughts, "whose son
the wondrous Babe might prove,"
her guileless husband walks beside,
bearing the hallowed dove;   (Luke 2:24)

meet emblem of his vow,
who, on this happy day,
his dove-like soul—best sacrifice
did on God's altar lay.

But who is he, by years
bowed, but erect in heart,
whose prayers are struggling with his tears?
"Lord, let me now depart.   (Luke 2:29)

"Now hath thy servant seen
thy saving health, O Lord;
'tis time that I depart in peace,
according to thy word."

Yet swells the pomp; one more   (Luke 2:36)
comes forth to bless her God:
full fourscore years, meek widow, she
her heavenward way hath trod.

She who to earthly joys
so long had given farewell,
now sees, unlooked for, heaven on earth,
Christ in his Israel.

Wide open from that hour
   the temple gates are set,
and still the saints rejoicing there
   the holy Child have met.

Now count his train today,
   and who may meet him, learn:
Him childlike sires, meek maidens find,
   where pride can nought discern.

Still to the lowly soul
   he doth himself impart,
and for his cradle and his throne
   chooseth the pure in heart.

John Keble, 1819
The Christian Year, 1827

124

Septuagesima Sunday. The invisible things of him from the creation of the world are clearly seen, being understood by the things that are made. Romans 1:20

There is a book, who runs may read,   (Hab. 2:2)
   which heavenly truth imparts,
and all the lore its scholars need,
   pure eyes and Christian hearts.

The works of God above, below,
   within us and around,
are pages in that book, to show
   how God himself is found.

The glorious sky embracing all
   is like the Maker's love,
wherewith encompassed, great and small
   in peace and order move.

The moon above, the church below,
   a wondrous race they run,
but all their radiance, all their glow
   each borrows of its Sun.

The Savior lends the light and heat
   that crowns his holy hill;
the saints, like stars, around his seat
   perform their courses still.   (Dan. 12:3)

The saints above are stars in heaven—
   what are the saints on earth?
Like trees they stand, whom God has given,   (Isa. 60:21)
   our Eden's happy birth.

Faith is their fixed unswerving root,
   hope their unfading flower,
fair deeds of charity their fruit,
   the glory of their bower.

The dew of heaven is like the grace,   (Ps. 68:9)
   it steals in silence down;
but where it lights, the favored place
   by richest fruits is known.

One Name above all glorious names
   with its ten thousand tongues
the everlasting sea proclaims
   echoing angelic songs.

The raging fire, the roaring wind,   (Heb. 12:29)
   thy boundless power display;
but in the gentler breeze we find
   thy Spirit's viewless way.   (John 3:8)

Two worlds are ours: 'Tis only sin
   forbids us to descry
the mystic heaven and earth within,
   plain as the sea and sky.

Thou, who hast given me eyes to see
   and love this sight so fair,
give me a heart to find out thee,
   and read thee everywhere.

John Keble, 1819
The Christian Year, 1827

125
Psalm 104

O worship the King,
    all glorious above,
O gratefully sing
    his power and his love;
our Shield and Defender,
    the Ancient of Days,
pavilioned in splendor
    and girded with praise.

O tell of his might,
    O sing of his grace,
whose robe is the light,
    whose canopy, space.
His chariots of wrath
    the deep thunderclouds form,
and dark is his path
    on the wings of the storm.

This earth, with its store
    of wonders untold,
Almighty, thy power
    hath founded of old;
hath stablished it fast
    by a changeless decree,
and round it hath cast
    like a mantle, the sea.

Thy bountiful care
    what tongue can recite?
It breathes in the air,
    it shines in the light;
it streams from the hills,
    it descends to the plain
and sweetly distills
    in the dew and the rain.

Frail children of dust,
    and feeble as frail,
in thee do we trust,
    nor find thee to fail;
thy mercies, how tender,
    how firm to the end,
our Maker, Defender,
    Redeemer, and Friend.

O measureless might,
    ineffable love,
while angels delight
    to hymn thee above,
thy humbler creation,
    though feeble their lays,
with true adoration
    shall lisp to thy praise.

Robert Grant
Christian Psalmody, 1833
as in *The Hymnal Companion to the Book of Common Prayer*, 1876

126
Psalm 103

Praise, my soul, the King of heaven;
    to his feet thy tribute bring!
Ransomed, healed, restored, forgiven,
    who like me his praise should sing?
        Praise him! Praise him!
    Praise the everlasting King!

Praise him for his grace and favor
    to our fathers in distress!
Praise him, still the same for ever,
    slow to chide, and swift to bless!
        Praise him! Praise him!
    Glorious in his faithfulness!

Father-like, he tends and spares us;
    well our feeble frame he knows.
In his hands he gently bears us,
    rescues us from all our foes.
        Praise him! Praise him!
    Widely as his mercy flows.

Frail as summer's flower we flourish;
    blows the wind, and it is gone.
But, while mortals rise and perish,
    God endures unchanging on.
        Praise him! Praise him!
    Praise the high eternal One!

Angels, help us to adore him;
    ye behold him face to face:
sun and moon, bow down before him;
    dwellers all in time and space.
        Praise him! Praise him!
    Praise with us the God of grace!

Henry Francis Lyte
The Spirit of the Psalms, 1834

127

My Beloved Is Mine, and I Am His

The author adds to his title "Imitated from Quarles," referring to a poem by Francis Quarles (1592–1644) beginning "Ev'n like two little bank-dividing brooks." The imitation consists in the use of the phrase that ends each stanza.

Long did I toil, and knew no earthly rest;
    far did I rove, and found no certain home:
at last I sought them in his sheltering breast,
    who opes his arms, and bids the weary come. (Matt. 11:28)
With him I found a home, a rest divine;
and I since then am his, and he is mine.

Yes, he is mine! and nought of earthly things,
    not all the charms of pleasure, wealth, or power,
the fame of heroes, or the pomp of kings,
    could tempt me to forego his love an hour.
Go, worthless world, I cry, with all that's thine!
Go! I my Savior's am, and he is mine.

The good I have is from his stores supplied:
    the ill is only what he deems the best.
He for my Friend, I'm rich with nought beside;
    and poor without him, though of all possessed.
Changes may come—I take, or I resign,
content, while I am his, and he is mine.

Whate'er may change, in him no change is seen,
    a glorious Sun, that wanes not, nor declines:
above the clouds and storms he walks serene,
    and on his people's inward darkness shines.
All may depart—I fret not, nor repine,
while I my Savior's am, and he is mine.

He stays me falling; lifts me up when down;
    reclaims me wandering; guards from every foe;
plants on my worthless brow the victor's crown,
    which in return before his feet I throw,
grieved that I cannot better grace his shrine,
who deigns to own me his, as he is mine.

While here, alas! I knew but half his love,
    but half discern him, and but half adore;
but when I meet him in the realms above,
    I hope to love him better, praise him more,
and feel, and tell, amid the choir divine,
how fully I am his, and he is mine.

Henry Francis Lyte
Poems, Chiefly Religious, 1833

128

Abide with Us, for It Is toward Evening.
Luke 24:29

Abide with me! Fast falls the eventide;
the darkness thickens. Lord, with me abide.
When other helpers fail, and comforts flee,
Help of the helpless, O abide with me!

Swift to its close ebbs out life's little day;
earth's joys grow dim, its glories pass away;
change and decay in all around I see.
O thou who changest not, abide with me!

Not a brief glance I beg, a passing word;
but as thou dwell'st with thy disciples, Lord,
familiar, condescending, patient, free—
come, not to sojourn, but abide with me.

Come not in terrors, as the King of kings;
but kind and good, with healing in thy wings,
tears for all woes, a heart for every plea—
come, Friend of sinners, and abide with me.

Thou on my head in early youth didst smile;
and though rebellious and perverse meanwhile,
thou hast not left me, oft as I left thee.
On to the close, O Lord, abide with me!

I need thy presence every passing hour.
What but thy grace can foil the Tempter's power?
Who like thyself my guide and stay can be?
Through cloud and sunshine, O, abide with me.

I fear no foe with thee at hand to bless;
ills have no weight, and tears no bitterness.
Where is death's sting? Where, grave, thy victory? (1 Cor. 15:55)
I triumph still, if thou abide with me.

Hold thou thy cross before my closing eyes,
speak through the gloom, and point me to the skies;
heaven's morning breaks, and earth's vain shadows
flee!
In life, in death, O Lord, abide with me!

Henry Francis Lyte, 1847
Remains, 1850

129

The Heedless World

When came in flesh the incarnate Word,
the heedless world slept on,
and only simple shepherds heard
that God had sent his Son.

When comes the Savior at the last,
from east to west shall shine
the awful pomp, and earth aghast
shall tremble at the sign.

Then shall the pure of heart be blest;
as mild he comes to them,
as when upon the Virgin's breast
he lay at Bethlehem:

As mild to meek-eyed love and faith,
only more strong to save;
strengthened by having bowed to death,
by having burst the grave.

Lord, who could dare see thee descend
in state, unless he knew
thou art the sorrowing sinner's friend,
the gracious and the true?

Dwell in our hearts, O Savior blest;
so shall thine advent's dawn
'twixt us and thee, our bosom-guest,
be but the veil withdrawn.

Joseph Anstice
Hymns, 1836

Chapter 10:
Early Nineteenth-Century Dissent (130–136)

The first third of the nineteenth century produces very little hymnody from the dissenting denominations who had shot their bolt in the previous age. Methodists saw no need to add to what John Wesley had collected for them in 1780: a book of about five hundred hymns, most of which were his or his brother's. Baptists were similarly content with the work of their eighteenth-century writers, who mostly seemed to write what lasted a generation or two and then began to get tired. Samuel Medley and John Ryland were their best writers, but for the most part they were happy with Watts. Presbyterians of the non-Scottish kind had been troubled by dissensions which produced the Unitarian connection, reducing orthodox Presbyterianism to a small though elite body which, in pursuit of orthodoxy, was content with the metrical psalter.

It might have been so with the Congregationalists, who were in the direct line of succession from Isaac Watts, had it not been for an historical accident. During the eighteenth century, Congregational churches were self-governing bodies which, although their one constitutional document, the Savoy Declaration, 1658, explicitly warned them against it, tended to be isolationist. Evangelical pressures caused them, from about 1787 onwards, to group themselves in local "Unions" by counties, and the same pressures eventually resulted in their forming themselves into a national "Union" in 1831. (As a total group they were called "The Congregational Union" from then until 1966, and "The Congregational Church" from 1966 until they became in 1972 part of the United Reformed Church in England and Wales.) The formation of this national body, whose Assembly met first in 1832, was the occasion for the commissioning of a national hymnal, which appeared as *The Congregational Hymn Book* in 1836. As it

happened, this released a small but important stream of new hymnody. Its general editor, Josiah Conder, happened to be a very gifted hymn writer.

Conder's work appears in 133–136, and it is very interesting in the way it reacts to the romantic hymnody of the Anglicans whom we have just been discussing. It is clearly founded on the style of Watts; 133 and, even more, 136 have the festive and theologically ecstatic touch of Watts, and Watts would have been proud of either. Perhaps in the tiny but perfect 134 there is a touch of Wesley. But 135 is a versification (one of several Conder made) of a Prayer Book collect. All this, and a study of other hymns he wrote, places Conder as a dogmatic Calvinist with a cultural "finish" which the earlier Calvinists did not aspire to. He is not naturalistic, not personal, not experimental; he adds the only kind of hymnody that a Calvinist body could find acceptable at that time. It is interesting that the Baptists formed themselves into a Union in 1813, but their first general hymnal did not appear until 1858, *Psalms and Hymns*, and in it they did not produce a figure comparable to Conder. The first Congregational hymnal was, of course, mostly Watts, and the later edition of 1855 contained nearly 300 hymns by him; but the fact that hymn writing was never quite extinguished in Watts's own communion must be credited largely to the special genius of Conder.

Two other hymns by Congregationalists appear in this section. Andrew Reed's "Spirit divine" (131) was written for a united evangelical Good Friday service. (That small point indicates the objectivity with which people of that kind placed theology above the customs of the church's year; there is every possible theological reason for invoking the Holy Spirit on Good Friday when one remembers what is written in John 14:16.) But Thomas Binney's superb "Eternal Light" (130), as a purely romantic hymn of the best sort, the Dissenting answer to "Abide with me," did not find a place in official Congregational hymnals until 1859, and perhaps this was because by that time

Binney had become so famous a leader in that church. Here indeed is the romantic "distance," the spiritual adventure, the mystical speculation, and the work of a man who was an artist through and through. (Binney's single-handed efforts to introduce poetry and order and beauty into Congregational worship were responsible for whatever resistance to philistinism that communion managed to raise in the nineteenth century; see our reference to him when we come to T. T. Lynch in chapter 14.)

The Society of Friends, as might be expected, produces few hymns, because the English form of that culture does not sing at worship. Most Quaker hymns come from nineteenth-century America or twentieth-century Britain. Bernard Barton's very neat and orthodox meditation on Psalm 119:89 (132) deserves a place in any book and is probably the earliest Quaker hymn to remain in the repertory, although, naturally, it was not used by Quakers in his time.

130
The Eternal Light

Eternal Light! Eternal Light!
    how pure the soul must be,
when, placed within thy searching sight,
it shrinks not, but with calm delight
    can live, and look on thee.

The spirits that surround thy throne
    may bear the burning bliss;
but that is surely theirs alone,
since they have never, never known
    a fallen world like this.

O how shall I, whose native sphere
    is dark, whose mind is dim,
before th' Ineffable appear,
and on my naked spirit bear
    the uncreated beam?

There is a way for man to rise
    to that sublime abode;
an offering and a sacrifice,
a Holy Spirit's energies,
    an Advocate with God.

There, these prepare us for the sight
    of holiness above
the sons of ignorance and night
may dwell in the eternal light
    through the eternal love!

Thomas Binney, ca. 1826
The New Congregational Hymn Book, 1855

131
Hymn to the Spirit

Spirit divine, attend our prayers,
    and make this house thy home;
descend with all thy gracious powers,
    O come, great Spirit, come!

Come as the light—to us reveal
    our emptiness and woe;
and lead us in the paths of life
    where all the righteous go.

Come as the fire—and purge our hearts
    like sacrificial flame;
let our whole soul an offering be
    to our Redeemer's name.

Come as the dew, and sweetly bless
    this consecrated hour;
may barrenness rejoice to own
    thy fertilizing power.

Come as the dove—and spread thy wings,
    the wings of peaceful love;
and let thy church on earth become
    blest as the church above.

Come as the wind—with rushing sound
    and Pentecostal grace;
that all of woman born may see
    the glory of thy face.

Spirit divine, attend our prayers,
    make a lost world thy home;
descend with all thy gracious powers,
    O come, great Spirit, come!

Andrew Reed
Evangelical Magazine, June 1829

132
Lamp of Our Feet. Psalm 119:105

Lamp of our feet, whereby we trace
    our path when wont to stray;
stream from the fount of heavenly grace;
    brook by the traveler's way;

bread of our souls, whereon we feed,
    true manna from on high;
our guide and chart, wherein we read
    of realms beyond the sky;

pillar of fire through watches dark,
    or radiant cloud by day;
when waves would whelm our tossing bark,
    our anchor and our stay;

Word of the ever-living God,
    will of his glorious Son,
without thee how could earth be trod,
    or heaven itself be won?

Lord, grant that we aright may learn
    the wisdom it imparts,
and to its heavenly teaching turn
    with simple, childlike hearts.

Bernard Barton
The Reliquary, 1836
as modified for *The New Congregational Hymn Book*, 1855,
from the original eleven stanzas

133
Alleluia! for the Lord God Omnipotent Reigneth

The Lord is King; lift up thy voice,   (Ps. 99:1)
O earth, and all ye heavens rejoice.
From world to world the joy shall ring:
the Lord omnipotent is King.

The Lord is King; who then shall dare
resist his will, distrust his care,
or murmur at his wise decrees,
or doubt his royal promises?

The Lord is King; child of the dust,
the Judge of all the earth is just: (Gen. 18:25)
holy and true are all his ways;
let every creature speak his praise.

He reigns! ye saints, exalt your strains:
your God is King, your Father reigns;
and he is at the Father's side,
the Man of Love, the Crucified.   (Heb. 1:3)

Come, make your wants, your burdens known
    (Heb. 4:16)
he will present them at the throne;
and angel bands are waiting there
his messages of love to bear.   (John 1:51)

Oh! when his wisdom can mistake,
his might decay, his love forsake,
then may his children cease to sing,
"The Lord omnipotent is King."

Alike pervaded by his eye
all parts of his dominion lie,
this world of ours, and worlds unseen,
and thin the boundary between.

One Lord, one empire, all secures,
he reigns—and life and death are yours. (1 Cor. 3:16)
Through earth and heaven one song shall ring:
"The Lord omnipotent is King."

Josiah Conder
The Star in the East, with Other Poems, 1824

134
For the Eucharist. John 6:51–54; 15:1

Bread of heaven! on thee I feed,
for thy flesh is meat indeed. (John 6:35)
Ever may my soul be fed
with this true and living bread;
day by day with strength supplied
through the life of him who died.

Vine of heaven! thy blood supplies
this blest cup of sacrifice.
'Tis thy wounds my healing give;
to thy cross I look, and live.
Thou my life! O let me be
rooted, grafted, built on thee. (Eph. 3:17)

Josiah Conder
The Star in the East, with Other Poems, 1824

135
Church Meetings

Head of the church, our risen Lord!
who by thy Spirit dost preside
o'er the whole body; by whose word
they all are ruled and sanctified:

Our prayers and intercessions hear
for all thy family at large,
that each, in his appointed sphere,
his proper service may discharge;

so, through the grace derived from thee,
in whom all fullness dwells above,
may thy whole church united be
and edify itself in love.

Josiah Conder
The Congregational Hymn Book, 1836

136
Praise to Christ

Thou art the everlasting Word,
 the Father's only Son;
God manifestly seen and heard,
 and heaven's beloved One:

> Worthy, O Lamb of God, art thou
> that every knee to thee should bow.

In thee, most perfectly expressed
 the Father's glories shine;
of the full deity possessed,
 eternally divine:

True image of the infinite, (Heb. 1:2)
 whose essence is concealed,
brightness of uncreated light,
 the heart of God revealed:

But the high mysteries of thy name
 an angel's grasp transcend:
the Father only—glorious claim—
 the Son can comprehend: (Luke 10:22)

Yet loving thee, on whom his love
 ineffable doth rest,
thy glorious worshipers above
 as one with thee, are blest:

Throughout the universe of bliss,
 the center thou, and Sun,
the eternal theme of praise is this
 to heaven's beloved One:

Josiah Conder
The Congregational Hymn Book, 1836

Chapter 11:
Hymns from Latin Sources
(137–176)

Latin hymnody has had so great an influence on English-speaking hymnody that it must be approached here from both ends. It appears so late in the course of this work because it did not make any notable impact on English hymn singing until the mid-nineteenth century. But although Martin Luther gave hymnody a "new start," there is a sense in which Latin hymnody is the source of all the rest.

Office Hymns

Latin hymnody begins with St. Ambrose, bishop of Milan (340–397). The Christian Church had received from the Emperor Constantine in 313 a legitimacy which it had never before had, and therefore it began only then to develop its public ministry. But already in the fourth century the Church was divided linguistically into the Greek-speaking half (in the East) and the Latin-speaking half (in the West); the metropolis of the Greek-speaking half was Byzantium (Constantinople), and that of the Latin-speaking half, Rome. The two halves of the church preserved always an uneasy détente until they finally separated in 1054 into what are still known as the Eastern Orthodox and the Roman Catholic communions. It seems as if the earliest hymnody of the Christian Church was certainly in Greek (see 177), but the earliest public hymnody (so to call it) was in Latin. The preeminence of the Latin-speaking Church in the matter of discipline and organization is obviously connected with the fact that both halves of the church began their lives within the Roman empire.

Ambrose's hymnody is referred to more than once by his devoted friend and disciple, St. Augustine of Hippo. Exactly what its purpose was is not as easy to determine as one might expect.

There is, on the one hand, the "*Te Deum laudamus*," a prose composition which was at one time attributed to him but is now thought to have been composed a little later. On the other hand there is quite certainly our 137, "*Deus Creator omnium*," which Augustine knew and quoted more than once.

Now, looking at that text, what does its purpose appear to have been? Why, it has two very clear subjects. The first is the personal discipline of the Christian community, and the second is the praise of God the Trinity in the final stanza (which is the oldest Latin doxology). Further, it is clearly a hymn to be sung at the close of the day. One theory of its origin is that it, and others like it, were composed by Ambrose for the comfort of Christians who were upholding the Faith during the Arian controversy (A.D. 325–381). That controversy produced situations close to civil war in many places; the nearest thing to it in modern times is the situation in Ireland from 1916 onwards. And the point of dispute was the relation between the first two Persons of the Trinity; the end-products included the so-called Nicene Creed, and the patristic formulations of the Nature of Christ. Possibly hymns of this kind, with their affirmations of Trinitarian belief in their doxologies, were another such product; and if, as some say, the Arians, finally judged unorthodox, invented the custom of setting their beliefs to music and singing them in defiance of the Christians from whom they separated themselves, it is plausible to believe that a gifted Christian writer like Ambrose would be moved to provide something for his own people to sing. If, further, the custom was to sing after the day's disputes and fightings had died down, this would explain the evening references.

But whether or not that is true, it is more important, and historically safer, to notice the other aspect of this text. This suggests a company of Christians living together under discipline. Such companies were indeed forming themselves just at this time. The great question whether Christianity was only for spiritual athletes, or whether the athletes were to be regarded as having a special role among a much larger company of "ordinary" Christians, is as old as the days of St. Paul. But for all sorts of reasons a movement began in the fourth century which ran an uninterrupted course, disputed by nobody, until at least the thirteenth century, based on the principle that while all souls in Christendom were regarded as the Church's charge, in every community it was necessary for there to be a company of specially committed souls who engaged in contemplation, prayer, and liturgy, and who, to all intents, did the ordinary people's praying for them.

These communities developed into those medieval monasteries which gathered to themselves not only a special Christian ministry but a monopoly of learning and culture. The only people who could read and write were members of these communities; they preserved the literature of Christianity and indeed became, through their monopoly, the censors of literature. What they did not write down did not get preserved, for from one age to another very different ideas of what it was proper for a Christian lay brother to transcribe and edit prevailed.

Inevitably then, the worship of God was controlled and fashioned in these communities. Mass was celebrated regularly, and on high days the laity would attend, though normally they would not in any modern sense participate. Ancillary services were gradually devised to punctuate the round of work and contemplation in which the monks were primarily engaged.

These services were known as "offices" (duties), and they were performed solely by the members of the religious community. It was for these that the whole system of Office Hymns in the early Middle Ages was set up. And broadly speaking the period during which Office Hymns were written divides itself into the early, running perhaps two hundred years after Ambrose's time, and the middle, running from about 600 to about

1100. The later period is that in which other forms of hymnody principally flourished.

By about 1200 at the latest, all these communities had their Office books and breviaries in which hymns of this sort were written. When one remembers that the church served by this hymnody reached from Sicily to Northumbria, it is not surprising that variations are found from one place to another; scholarly analyses of all this are readily available, and we need not pause here to go into them. The English-speaking versions of Latin hymnody are mostly based on the selections used at Sarum (Salisbury), with occasional additions from York.

Clearly, however, it did not all happen at once. Our 138 is a good example of a very early hymn in the style of Ambrose, though not his own, and 139–144 can be taken closely with it. These five form the series of hymns composed probably in the early period to go with the domestic Offices of the monasteries; 139–143 refer respectively to services held at 6 and 9 A.M. and at 6 and (about) 9 P.M.; 144 is for matins, a service held in the small hours before dawn. ("*Nocte surgentes*" [Getting up in the middle of the night] expresses this exactly; Percy Dearmer's very good English version, for fairly obvious reasons, suppresses that particular point and turns it into a hymn to be sung after daybreak.)

The subject matter of all these hymns, apart from their doxologies, is still domestic and personal. (It may be noted that doxologies soon became adjustable units, so that one used different forms at different seasons; that would explain why John Mason Neale does not reflect the changed doxology in the text of 143.) The morning suggests challenge; the evening, death. There are all manner of devices of the devil peculiar to the successive times of day against which the Christian prays to be defended. Indeed, the whole business looks to a modern Protestant Christian somewhat gloomy, and introverted. But two things have to be remembered: One is that the separateness and sanctity of the monastic life was a tough assignment and was believed to deliver substantial spiritual rewards, but at a high price; the other is that the objective praise of God was provided by the Psalter, and hymns were still regarded as very much an appendix to the Psalms, which contained for these people the strong meat of Christian praise. The two things the Psalms do not mention are the monastic life and the doctrine of the Trinity. These the hymns provided, and they were not expected to provide more.

But as time went on it was natural for hymnody to develop a more didactic and imaginative style. Touches of typology and scriptural adventure appear in the series for the days of the week (see, for example, *The English Hymnal*, 51–62), and in 145–150 in our series there is a handful of distinguished seasonal hymns that make the most of their opportunities. Note the scriptural richness of 145, with its references to four very diverse examples of the efficacy of prayer and fasting before our Lord's ministry. Number 146 is especially rich at the beginning with its references to the Exodus, the white robes of baptismal candidates on Easter Eve, the altar as symbol of the cross, and Christ's final triumph as a fulfillment of Scripture. Here at last we have real New Testament hymnody, real competition with the Psalter. Number 148 tells the Easter story in simpler and more strictly narrative terms. Number 149, by Ambrose, was found useful as soon as celebrations of seasonal and festive offices became the rule; 150 expresses the heraldry of Michaelmas; and 147, a very early hymn on the Trinity, is a good deal more than a formal doxology.

It will be noticed that two meters only are used for these hymns. One is the octosyllabic meter, which generated the English Long Meter and which was exclusively used by St. Ambrose and his direct imitators. Rhyme is not used in the earlier examples of this meter; it is fitfully and inconsistently used a little later. The other meter is Sapphic, as in 144, 147, and 150; this, unlike octosyllables, was a classical Latin meter. If Pope Gregory I is the author of 144, he probably introduced it to hymnody. Rhyme never appears in this meter, and it is one of the few traditional hymn meters which when used in English can with perfect naturalness dispense with rhyme.

Sequences

Numbers 151–153, with which 1C can be taken, are examples of "sequence," which is a quite different form of medieval hymnody. It originates with the setting of words to the musical flourishes that had grown up as glosses on the music of the *Alleluia*, which is a liturgical unit in the Mass. The earliest we know of is 151, which is in prose and is not seasonal. The Easter Sequence (1C) is not much later and is also in prose, though it is a little more regular and rhythmical. Numbers 152 and 153, a good deal later, are in verse and show how the sequence, as it were, dropped off the Alleluia altogether and became a separate unit with its own tune. These, together with 10, 22, 172, and 253 in *The English Hymnal*, show also how sequences came to be associated with especially festive occasions. The genesis of sequences, indeed, exposes the tension so much felt in the medieval church at all stages between the impulse to extend music, especially on festivals, beyond what the texts required, and the more austere principle that suspected any music that was not adequately supported by words. Sequences developed for all the major festivals, and their later manifestations show a very high level of lyric artistry, as in the way every third line throughout 152 follows the same rhyme independently of the other rhyming couplets (beautifully reflected in Neale's translation), and as in the tender diction and profound thought of the "*Dies irae*" (153). Later medieval liturgies always found a place for these fine compositions.

Medieval Latin Lyrics

But many familiar hymns from the Latin are translated from poems which fall altogether outside the liturgical system, even though much later they found a place in it. Our 164, a difficult case, cannot quite be so described; but the rest in the series 154–167 are the work of poets who, even when they wrote in hymnlike meters, did not necessarily expect their material to be sung in church.

Christian Latin lyric begins in the fourth century, and Prudentius (154, 155) was one of a circle of poets who had a special ministry to perform. There is always a danger that Christianity will part company with high culture. In that troubled time the danger was very great, and it was very much increased by the influence of Julian the Apostate, emperor 361–363, who, in the course of a reign of only six hundred days, managed to have more influence on the society of his time than anybody except Constantine had had for the previous two hundred years. That influence was wholly anti-Christian and procultural; he made much of the legend, often before put about by Christianity's opponents, that the faith was fundamentally philistine, and could not hope to compete with true learning, philosophy, and poetry. As had happened before, and as until recently one could count on happening since, the effect on the Christians was to stimulate their best philosophical and poetic minds; Prudentius was one of these. Number 154 is part of a longer poem in the Ambrosian style, no doubt written in imitation of Ambrose, but 155 introduced for the first time a new meter, and is a selection of verses from a long poem in defense of the faith designed to show that being a Christian did not prevent one's being either a poet or a reasoner. Most of it is less lyrical than the part which has now become so famous.

It should at once be noted that although many of these pieces now have tunes that are thought of as inseparable from them, the tunes were always set to them later than the time of their composition;

the tune to 155, for example, appears first in the twelfth century.

Venantius Fortunatus (156), a younger contemporary of Justinian, living long after the fall of the Roman Empire, is perhaps the greatest of all the early lyricists. "*Pange lingua,*" a panorama of the creedal facts of Christ's life with its great peroration on the cross, is very nearly untranslatable, and we have called in a team of translators to make our composite version. The other piece, its companion in octosyllables, "*Vexilla regis,*" has defeated every known translator so far, which is the only reason we omit it here. (See *The English Hymnal,* 1906 and 1933, 94 for Neale's orthodox translation and the Canadian *Hymn Book,* 1971, 445 for a very good, though incomplete, rendering by J. W. Grant.) We are here in a very different literary world from that of the Office Hymns.

The earliest known British hymn, 157, has much in common with the middle-period Office hymns for festal occasions; and the excellent and mystical "*Urbs beata*" (158) builds on the foundation of Fortunatus. (The note given with the hymn is important for its understanding.)

"All glory, laud, and honor" (159) is a popular rendering of a piece in the most famous of the classical lyric meters—Elegiacs. Fortunatus had used this meter for his "*Salve festa dies*" (see *The English Hymnal* 624, 628, etc.). It was brought to its height in secular poetry by Ovid. This and 160 are the two Latin lyrics, apart from Office Hymns, that seem to have survived from the depths of the so-called Dark Ages.

"*Veni Creator*" (160) is another hymn that looks like an Office Hymn, but is not; it is a devotional prayer to the Holy Spirit which has by long tradition been especially associated with ordinations. More about this when we deal with the translations.

Peter Abelard (161, see also 549) was, as is well known, the most acute philosopher of his time, but he was also a supreme poet. He wrote these and several other hymns for the House of the

Paraclete, of which Heloise became abbess. Here is another new meter, unexampled in Christian Latin literature, complete with a fully worked out rhyme scheme.

The incredible "*Hora novissima*" (162) was originally a satirical poem of 2,966 lines mostly devoted to the corruptions and social evils of church and state in medieval Europe. The part that Neale translated is that which contrasts the delights of heaven with these unpleasantnesses. Here again we have a unique Latin meter, all-dactylic hexameters, which only a poet of quite unusual dexterity could have attempted. This, of course, was never intended to be sung and never was used as a hymn until Neale translated it.

No more was the equally celebrated 163 (implausibly attributed to the abbot who became prosecuting counsel when Abelard was indicted for heresy) designed for singing; it was a 42-stanza meditation on the love of Christ in the Ambrosian style, with an intermittent rhyme scheme that is not carried through the whole poem.

That brings us to 164 and 165. Number 164 was composed by St. Thomas Aquinas at the invitation of the reigning pope, about 1263, for the new Office of Corpus Christi and looks like one of the first hymns written in this fashion "to order"; two others accompanied it, the "*Verbum supernum*" (*The English Hymnal*, 330) and "*Lauda, Sion*" (*The English Hymnal*, 317), the second of which is roughly in the form of a metrical sequence. Number 165 is still attributed to St. Thomas by hymnal editors, but it has been shown by the British scholar F. J. E. Raby not to have been his. The three authentic hymns all begin with a first line already familiar in medieval worship. Number 164 shares its first line with 156; it rehearses the actual story of the Last Supper in language that makes an extended interpretative note necessary at the hymn. Number 165 is simpler and, unlike the three by St. Thomas, highly personal. The reference to the Pelican in stanza 6 recalls the ancient belief that the pelican feeds her young with her own blood.

Another medieval devotion of great poetic beauty is "*Stabat Mater*," 166, of which some stanzas are well known in English. It will be seen how rhyme is now firmly established. (St. Thomas uses it; Fortunatus, in the hymn whose first line he echoes, did not.)

Almost at the end of the Middle Ages, St. Thomas à Kempis wrote a good deal of poetry which was fairly soon found to make good hymnody, and 167 is the best known and finest example of that.

Later Latin Lyrics

Hymnody in the Roman Catholic church did not stop with the Middle Ages. For a while it died down. The Council of Trent incepted the Counter Reformation with a thorough overhaul of liturgical procedures and a revision of hymn texts which eventually produced the Roman Breviary, in which the various usages that had become current in different places during the late Middle Ages were organized into a single system. While this went on, and for a time afterwards, no new hymnody was called for. Our 168, which comes from the very turn of the Middle Ages, is a narrative carol that had no liturgical place then or later, agreeable though it has proved to be for modern singers.

But there was a great deal of tune writing, especially in Germany, where a considerable stream of hymnals appeared in the last century. One of these produced the now universally loved tune LASST UNS ERFREUEN, "All creatures of our God and King." Number 169 is a text that was slipped into one of these hymnals.

France, in the next generation or two, was the scene of a considerable liturgical revival in the course of which many new Latin texts were written, especially by Jean Baptiste de Santeüil (170–171) and Charles Coffin (173–174). Indeed a glance over this handful of hymns, 169–176, indicates that there was a certain amount of activity all over Europe. Number 176 comes from Portugal. But it was in France that the greatest activity seems to have taken place, and this included the adaptation and composition of a whole series of new metric tunes to provide music for people for whom the obligatory plainsong of the Counter Reformation was proving too demanding. The subject matter of these new hymns varied considerably, taking in all the mannerisms of the old medieval hymnody without usually adding much to them. The old domestic "in group" Office Hymn is reflected in 174, the seasonal Office Hymn in 170–171, the devotional lyric in 176.

Numbers 172 and 175, now among the twenty most-used hymns in all Christendom, are especially popular products of this revival. "Veni Immanuel" is a versification of part of the late medieval devotion called the "Great O's of Advent" or the "O Antiphons" (for an English text see The English Hymnal, 734), never quite complete and a popular rather than liturgical piece in that it clearly intends all the stanzas to be sung consecutively, whereas the "Great O's" were designed to be said one sentence at a time on each of the eight days before Christmas. "Adeste fideles," its original text being stanzas 1–2 and 7–8 of the version we have here, is, almost certainly, the composition of an English music copyist who spent most of his life at Douay in France, right in the heart of the liturgical revival. It is, as it is now given, one of the few hymns written by three identifiable hands.

The Translators

The impulse to translate Latin hymns came from the Oxford Movement, one of whose aims was the revival of medieval liturgies and values. That movement is dated from 1833, and it is clear at once that the translators lost no time in beginning their work. One of the first shots to be fired must have been Isaac Williams's eloquent translation at 170B, which was in The British Magazine in 1836 before

being included in his large collection of Hymns Translated from the Paris Breviary, 1839. The other translators of this first generation represented in our collection were John Chandler, 1806–1876 (Hymns of the Primitive Church, 1837); Edward Caswall, 1814–1887 (Lyra Catholica, 1849); and John Mason Neale, 1818–1866. John Henry Newman (440–442), one of the movement's leaders, produced a number of translations of which we do not here have an example; another leader, John Keble, wrote all his hymns before the movement began (see 121–124 and 177A).

The chief problem before a translator, as we shall see again when we come to the German hymns, is in the tension between the demands of faithful transcription and those of his own poetic imagination. It will be noticed that Williams, Caswall, and Chandler have no scruples about altering the meter of the original. Williams, in our example (170B), uses an old English meter; so does Chandler in 171B, and so does Caswall in 154B and 163B. Their object then was to make the old Latin look like an English hymn; Williams certainly allows his expansive meter to give him scope for plenty of vivid writing. The problem is made much more difficult when a translator tries so to translate that the original tune—if there is one ascertainable—can be sung to the English version, that is, to keep the original meter. Now it has often been said of Neale, and of those who amended or imitated him, that their translations read stiffly and creakily in places, and we have to admit that Neale is the father of the pedantic "translator's English" that has brought the Office Hymns and saints-day hymns into disrepute among many. It has to be remembered, of course, that Neale must have worked incredibly fast. To produce the contents of The Hymnal Noted, 1851, 2nd ed. 1854, (our chief source for his versions from Latin), together with nearly everything else he translated from Latin, well before his fortieth year, he must have worked at high pressure. There were also original hymns and carols in his collection by then; only the Greek originals seem to have occupied him later. But the truth is, as anyone can see, that it is when he can choose his meter that his poetic instinct is allowed the needful freedom. We find this especially in "*Hora novissima*" (162), which has verse after verse of ecstatic and resounding beauty. In two other well-known cases in our book he abandons the original meter: in 159B, "All glory, laud, and honor," though here he did indeed make another translation in elegiacs so that the plainsong tune could be used (it is a poorish piece compared with the justly popular version we know); and in "*O quanta, qualia*," 161, which had no "proper tune" and where he felt free to give up the ferocious challenge of reproducing Abelard's continuous rhyming dactyls. (His translation is everywhere accessible, "O what their joy and their glory must be"; we have substituted Ronald Knox's because it is rather closer to the original meter.)

But Neale must be honored as an industrious worker who not infrequently produced a fine version and who set an example upon which others improved (whose later versions we often substitute for his), but which, without the initial challenge of his imperfections, they might never have used as an occasion for developing their gifts.

One other translator whose neglect of original meters paid dividends in good writing was James Russell Woodford. It is very unusual to see an original in Long Meter reduced in meter so drastically as he reduces that of 173; but his six-syllable lines achieve a quite remarkable spaciousness. His translation of part of 165 we thought too well known to need a place here, since it is incomplete; but it makes a very good English hymn, and with a little cheating actually goes to the tune associated with the original. (See *The English Hymnal*, 331.)

Only one American translator of Latin texts finds a place in this section—that very fine writer, Ray Palmer (163D, 169C). He keeps the meter of 163, but abandons that of 169; in both cases he produces very good literature indeed.

For the rest, we refer the reader to the *Hymnal Guide* for information about the more modern translators we have pressed into service, noting only that at 174B we have an unusual piece in a translation by a twentieth-century English Presbyterian of the seventeenth-century text by Charles Coffin. Leslie Bunn has not only translated it, but translated it with surpassing grace, and since this is his only extant contribution to hymnody (he was one of the most learned hymnologists of his age), we are glad to pay tribute to him here.

Office Hymns

137
Deus Creator Omnium

The original of this hymn by St. Ambrose is quoted twice by St. Augustine, once in *De Musica*, ca. 389, as an example of meter, and again in his *Confessions*, ca. 410, where he tells how it comforted him on the evening of the day of his mother's funeral. It can be regarded as the text which inspired the creation of the later system of Office Hymns, and therefore, in the translation provided by *The English Hymnal*, stands first in this section.

A.

Deus creator omnium,
polique rector vestiens
diem decoro lumine,
noctem soporis gratia.

Artus solutos ut quies,
reddat laboris usui,
mentesque fessas allevet
luctusque solvat anxios,

grates peracto iam die,
et noctis exortu preces,
votis reos ut adiuves,
hymnum canentes solvimus.

Te cordis ima concinant,
te vox canora concrepet,
te diligat castus amor,
te mens adoret sobria:

Ut cum profundo clauserit
diem caligo noctium,
fides tenebras nesciat
et nox fide reluceat.

Dormire mentem ne sinas,
dormire culpa noverit,
castis fides refrigerans
somni vaporem temperet.

Exuta sensu lubrico
te cordis ima somnient,
nec hostis invidi dolo
pavor quietos suscitet.

Christum rogemus et Patrem,
Christi Patrisque Spiritum,
unum potens per onmia,
fove precantes, Trinitas.

Ambrose of Milan

Thee let the secret heart acclaim,
thee let our tuneful voices name,
round thee our chaste affections cling,
thee sober reason own as King;

that when black darkness closes day,
and shadows thicken round our way,
faith may no darkness know, and night
from faith's clear beam may borrow light.

Rest not, my heaven-born mind and will;
rest, all ye thoughts and deeds of ill;
may faith its watch unwearied keep,
and cool the dreaming warmth of sleep.

From cheats of sense, Lord, keep me free,
and let my heart's depth dream of thee;
let not my envious foe draw near,
to break my rest with any fear.

Pray we the Father and the Son,
and Holy Ghost: O Three in One,
blest Trinity, whom all obey,
guard thou thy sheep by night and day.

translated, Charles Bigg
The English Hymnal, 1906

B.

Creator of the earth and sky,
ruling the firmament on high,
clothing the day with robes of light,
blessing with gracious sleep the night,

that rest may comfort weary men
and brace to useful toil again,
and soothe awhile the harassed mind,
and sorrow's heavy load unbind;

day sinks; we thank thee for thy gift;
night comes; and once again we lift
our prayer and vows and hymns, that we
against all ills may shielded be.

138
Christe Qui Lux Es et Dies

A.

Christe qui lux es et dies,
noctis tenebras detegis,
lucisque lumen crederis
lumen beatum praedicans;

precamur, sancte Domine,
defende nos in hac nocte;
sit nobis in te requies,
quietam noctem tribue.

Oculi somnum capiant,
cor ad te semper vigilet,
dextera tua protegat
famulos qui te diligunt.

Defensor noster aspice,
insidiantes reprime;
guberna tuos famulos,
quos sanguine mercatus es.

Memento nostri, Domine,
in gravi isto corpore,
qui es defensor animae,
adesto nobis, Domine.

Deo Patri sit gloria,
eiusque soli Filio,
cum Spiritu Paraclito,
et nunc et in perpetuum.

anonymous, early period

This, written in imitation of St. Ambrose's style, and certainly earlier than 532, when it is first referred to, became one of the most widely used of all Office Hymns when the system was brought into use in the middle period. It is also the text of several motets by well-known Tudor composers.

B.

O Christ, who art the Light and Day,
thou drivest darksome night away!
We know thee as the Light of light,
illuminating mortal sight.

All-holy Lord, we pray to thee,
keep us tonight from danger free;
grant us, dear Lord, in thee to rest,
so be our sleep in quiet blest.

And while the eyes soft slumber take,
still be the heart to thee awake;
be thy right hand upheld above
thy servants resting in thy love.

Yea, our Defender, be thou nigh
to bid the powers of darkness fly;
keep us from sin, and guide for good
thy servants purchased by thy blood.

Remember us, dear Lord, we pray,
while in this mortal flesh we stay;
'tis thou who dost the soul defend—
be present with us to the end.

Blest Three in One and One in Three,
Almighty God, we pray to thee
that thou wouldst now vouchsafe to bless
our fast with fruits of righteousness.

translated, William John Copeland
Hymns of the Week, 1848

Hymns of the Little Hours (139–144)

139
Prime

A.

Iam lucis orto sidere,
Deum precemur supplices,
ut in diurnis actibus,
nos servet a nocentibus.

Linguam refraenans temperet
ne litis horror insonet;
visum fovendo contegat
ne vanitates hauriat.

Sint pura cordis intima,
absistat et vecordia
carnis terat superbiam
potus cibique parcitas.

Ut cum dies abscesserit
noctemque sors reduxerit
mundi per abstinentiam
ipsi canamus gloriam.

Deo Patri sit gloria
eiusque soli Filio
cum Spiritu Paraclito,
nunc et per omne saeculum.

anonymous, early period

B.

Now that the daylight fills the sky
we lift our hearts to God on high,
that he, in all we do or say,
would keep us free from harm today,

would guard our hearts and tongues from strife,
from anger's din would hide our life,
from all ill sights would turn our eyes,
would close our ears from vanities,

would keep our inmost conscience pure,
our souls from folly would secure,
would bid us check the pride of sense
with due and holy abstinence.

So we, when this new day is gone,
and night in turn is drawing on,
with conscience by the world unstained
shall praise his name for victory gained.

All laud to God the Father be;
all laud, eternal Son, to thee;
all laud, as is for ever meet
to God the Holy Paraclete.

translated, John Mason Neale

The Hymnal Noted, 1851

See also the translation by Richard Crashaw and John Austin at 19.

140
Terce

A.

Nunc sancte nobis Spiritus,
unum Patri cum Filio,
dignare promptus ingeri
nostro refusus pectori.

Os, lingua, mens, sensus, vigor,
confessionem personent;
flammescat igne caritas,
accendat ardor proximos.

Praesta, Pater piissime,
Patrique compar Unice,
cum Spiritu Paraclito,
regnans per onme saeculum.

anonymous, early period

B.

Come, Holy Ghost, with God the Son,
and God the Father, ever one;
shed forth thy grace within our breast,
and dwell with us, a ready guest.

By every power, by heart and tongue,
by act and deed, thy praise be sung;
inflame with perfect love each sense,
that others' souls may kindle thence.

O Father, that we ask be done
through Jesus Christ, thine only Son,
who with the Holy Ghost and thee
shall live and reign eternally.

translated, John Mason Neale

The Hymnal Noted, 1851

141
Sext

A.

Rector potens, verax Deus,
qui temperas rerum vices,
splendore mane instruis,
et ignibus meridiem.

Extingue flammas litium,
aufer calorem noxium,
confer salutem corporum
verumque pacem cordium.

Praesta, Pater piissime,
Patrique compar Unice,
cum Spiritu Paraclito,
regnans per onme saeculum.

anonymous, early period

B.

O God of truth, O Lord of might,
who orderest time and change aright,
and send'st the early morning ray,
and light'st the glow of perfect day;

extinguish thou each sinful fire,
and banish every ill desire;
and while thou keep'st the body whole,
shed forth thy peace upon the soul.

O Father, that we ask be done
through Jesus Christ, thine only Son,
who with the Holy Ghost and thee
shall live and reign eternally.

translated, John Mason Neale
The Hymnal Noted, 1851

142
None

A.

Rerum Deus tenax vigor,
immotus in te permanens,
lucis diurnae tempora
successibus determinans;

largire clarum vespere,
quo vita nusquam decidat,
sed praemium mortis sacrae
perennis instet gloria.

Praesta, Pater piissime,
Patrique compar Unice,
cum Spiritu Paraclito,
regnans per omne saeculum.

anonymous, early period

B.

O God, creation's secret force,
thyself unmoved, all motion's source,
who from the morn till evening's ray
through all its changes guid'st the day,

grant us, when this short life is past,
the glorious evening that shall last:
that by a holy death attained
eternal glory may be gained.

O Father, that we ask be done
through Jesus Christ, thine only Son,
who with the Holy Ghost and thee
shall live and reign eternally.

translated, John Mason Neale
The Hymnal Noted, 1851

143
Compline

A.

Te lucis ante terminum,
rerum creator, poscimus,
ut pro tua clementia
sis praesul et custodia.

Procul recedant somnia
et noctium phantasmata;
hostemque nostrum comprime,
ne polluantur corpora.

Praesta, Pater omnipotens,
per Jesum Christum Dominum,
qui tecum in perpetuum
regnat cum Sancto Spiritu.

anonymous, early period

B.

Before the ending of the day,
Creator of the world, we pray
that with thy wonted favor, thou
wouldst be our guard and keeper now.

From all ill dreams defend our eyes,
from nightly fears and fantasies;
tread under foot our ghostly foe
that no pollution we may know.

O Father, that we ask be done
through Jesus Christ thine only Son,
who with the Holy Ghost and thee
shall live and reign eternally.

translated, John Mason Neale
The Hymnal Noted, 1851
See the preceding narrative, p. 118, regarding the final stanza.

144
Matins

A.

Nocte surgentes vigilemus omnes,
semper in psalmis meditemur, atque
viribus totis Domino canamus
    dulciter hymnos;

ut pio regi pariter canentes
cum suis sanctis mereamur aulam
ingredi coeli, simul et beatam
    ducere vitam.

Praestet hoc nobis Deitas beata
Patris et Nati pariterque sancti
Spiritus, cuius reboatur omni
    gloria mundo.

Gregory I [?]

B.

Father, we praise thee, now the night is over,
active and watchful, stand we all before thee;
singing, we offer prayer and meditation:
    thus we adore thee.

Monarch of all things, fit us for thy mansions;
banish our weakness, health and wholeness sending;
bring us to heaven, where thy saints united
    joy without ending.

All holy Father, Son, and equal Spirit,
Trinity blessed, send us thy salvation;
thine is the glory, gleaming and resounding
    through all creation.

translated, Percy Dearmer
The English Hymnal, 1906

145
Lent

A.

Clarum decus ieiunii
monstratur orbi caelitus;
quod Christus auctor omnium
cibis dicavit abstinens.

Hoc Moyses carus Deo   (Exod. 19:14, 19)
legisque lator factus est;
hoc Heliam per aera   (1 Kgs. 19:5–6)
curru levavit igneo.   (2 Kgs. 2:11)

Hinc Daniel mysteria   (Dan. 6:16–28)
victor leonum viderat;
per hoc amicus intimus   (John 3:29)
sponsi Johannes claruit.

Haec nos sequi dona, Deus,
exempla parsimoniae;
tu robur auge mentium
dans spiritale gaudium.

Praesta, Pater, per Filium,
praesta per almum Spiritum,
cum his per aevum triplici
unus Deus cognomine.

> anonymous, middle period, possibly of English origin

B.

The glory of these forty days
we celebrate with songs of praise;
for Christ, by whom all things were made,
himself has fasted and has prayed.

Alone and fasting Moses saw
the loving God who gave the Law;
and to Elijah, fasting, came
the steeds and chariots of flame.

So Daniel trained his mystic sight,
delivered from the lion's might;
and John, the Bridegroom's friend, became
the herald of Messiah's name.

Then grant us, Lord, like them to be
full oft in fast and prayer with thee;
our spirits strengthen with thy grace,
and give us joy to see thy face.

Father and Son and Spirit blest,
to thee be every prayer addressed,
who art in threefold name adored
from age to age, the only Lord.

> translated, Maurice F. Bell
> *The English Hymnal*, 1906

146
Easter

A.

Ad coenam Agni providi,
et stolis albis candidi,
post transitum maris rubri
Christo canamus principi.

Cuius corpus sanctissimum
in ara crucis torridum,
cruore eius roseo
gustando vivimus Deo.

Protecti Paschae vespero
a devastante angelo,
erepti de durissimo
Pharaonis imperio.

Iam pascha nostrum Christus est,
qui immolatus Agnus est;
sinceritatis azyma
caro eius oblata est.

O vere dignis hostia,
per quam fracta sunt Tartara,
redempta plebs captivata
reddita vitae praemia.

Cum surgit Christus tumulo,
victor redit de barathro,
tyrannum trudens vinculo
et reserans paradisum.

Gloria tibi, Domine,
qui surrexisti a mortuis,
cum Patre et sancto Spiritu
in sempiterna saecula.

anonymous, middle period

B.

The Lamb's high banquet we await,
in snow-white robes of royal state;
and now, the Red Sea's channel past,
to Christ our Prince we sing at last.

Upon the altar of the cross
his body hath redeemed our loss;
and tasting of his roseate blood,
our life is hid with him in God.

That Paschal Eve God's arm was bared,
the devastating angel spared;
by strength of hand our hosts went free
from Pharaoh's ruthless tyranny.

Now Christ our Paschal Lamb is slain,
the Lamb of God that knows no stain,
the true oblation offered here,
our own unleavened bread sincere.

O thou, from whom hell's monarch flies,
O great, O very sacrifice,
thy captive people are set free,
and endless life restored in thee.

For Christ, arising from the dead,
from conquered hell victorious sped;
and thrust the tyrant down to chains,
and paradise for man regains.

To thee who, dead, again dost live,
all glory, Lord, thy people give;
all glory, as is ever meet,
to Father and to Paraclete.

translated, John Mason Neale
The Hymnal Noted, 1851

147
To the Trinity

A.

O Pater sancte, mitis atque pie,
O Jesu Christe, Fili venerande
paracliteque Spiritus o alme,
    Deus aeterne,

Trinitas sancte unitasque firma,
Deitas vera, bonitas immensa,
lux angelorum, salus orphanorum,
    spesque cunctorum,

serviunt tibi cuncta quae creasti;
te tuae cunctae laudant creaturae;
nos quoque tibi psallimus devoti;
    tu nos exaudi.

Gloria tibi, omnipotens Deus,
trinus et unus, magnus et excelsus;
te decet hymnus, honor, laus, et decus   (Ps. 65:1)
    nunc et in aevum.

anonymous, middle period

B.

Father most holy, merciful, and loving,
Jesu, Redeemer, ever to be worshiped,
life-giving Spirit, Comforter most gracious,
    God everlasting;

three in a wondrous Unity unbroken,
one perfect Godhead, love that never faileth,
light of the angels, succor of the needy,
    hope of all living;

all thy creation serveth its Creator,
thee every creature praiseth without ceasing;
we too would sing thee psalms of true devotion:
    hear, we beseech thee.

Lord God almighty, unto thee be glory,
one in three Persons, over all exalted;
thine, as is meet, be honor, praise, and blessing
    now and for ever.

translated, Alfred E. Alston
Hymns Ancient and Modern, 1904

148
Easter Song

A.

Aurora lucis rutilat,
caelum laudibus intonat,
mundus exultans iubilat,
gemens infernus ululat.

Cum rex ille fortissimus
mortis confractis viribus,
pede conculcans tartara,
solvit catena miseros.

Ille, qui clausus lapide
custoditur cum milite,
triumphans pompa nobili
victor surgit de funere.

Solutis iam gemitibus
et inferni doloribus,
quia "Surrexit Dominus"
resplendens clamat angelus.

Tristes erant apostoli
de nece sui Domini,
quem poena mortis crudeli
saevi damnarunt impii.

Sermone blando angelus
praedixit mulieribus:
"In Galilaea Dominus
videndus est quantocius."

Illae dum pergunt concite
apostolis hoc dicere,
videntes eum vivere
osculantur pedes Dei.

Quo agnito, discipuli
in Galilaeam propere
pergunt, videre faciem
desideratam Domini.

Claro paschali gaudio
sol mundo nitet radio
cum Christum iam apostoli
visu cernunt corporeo.

Ostensa sibi vulnera
in Christi carne fulgida
resurrexisse Dominum
voce fatentur publica.

Rex Christe clementissime,
tu corda nostra posside,
ut tibi laudes debitas
reddamus omni tempore.

Quaesumus, auctor omnium,
in hoc paschali gaudio
ab omni mortis impetu
tuum defende populum.

Gloria tibi, Domine
que surrexisti a mortuis,
cum Patre et sancto Spiritu
in sempiterna saecula.

anonymous, early period

B.

Light's glittering morn bedecks the sky,
heaven thunders forth its victor cry;
the glad earth shouts its triumph high,
and groaning hell makes wild reply.

While he, the King of glorious might,
treads down death's strength in death's despite,
and trampling hell by victor's right,
brings forth his sleeping saints to light.

Fast barred beneath the stone of late
in watch and ward where soldiers wait,
now shining in triumphant state,
he rises victor from death's gate.

Hell's pains are loosed, and tears are fled;
captivity is captive led;
the angel, crowned with light, hath said,
"The Lord is risen from the dead."

Th' apostles' hearts were full of pain,
for their dear Lord so lately slain;
that Lord his servants' wicked train
with bitter scorn had dared arraign.

With gentle voice the angel gave
the women tidings at the grave:
"Forthwith your Master shall ye see;
he goes before to Galilee."

And while with fear and joy they pressed
to tell these tidings to the rest,
their Lord, their living Lord, they meet,
and see his form, and kiss his feet.

Th' eleven, when they hear, with speed
to Galilee forthwith proceed;
that there they may behold once more
their Lord's dear face, as oft before.

In this our bright and paschal day
the sun shines out with purer ray:
when Christ, to earthly sight made plain,
the glad apostles see again.

The wounds, the riven wounds he shows
in that his flesh with light that glows,
with public voice both far and nigh
the Lord's arising testify.

O Christ, the King who lov'st to bless,
do thou our hearts and souls possess;
to thee our praise that we may pay
to whom our laud is due, for aye.

We pray thee, King with glory decked,
in this our paschal joy, protect
from all that death would fain affect
thy ransomed flock, thine own elect.

To thee who, dead, again dost live,
all glory, Lord, thy people give:
all glory, as is ever meet,
to Father and to Paraclete.

translated, John Mason Neale
The Hymnal Noted, 1851

In early liturgies the hymn was divided either in two parts, the first
ending at stanza 5, or in three, the first ending at stanza 4, the second
at stanza 8. In either case the two doxology stanzas were sung after
any separated part. The hymn "That Easter day with joy was bright,"
very well known in the United States, is the revision of the last five
stanzas of this hymn made in *Hymns Ancient and Modern*, 1861.
Neale's original, although less smooth than the revision, is given here
to show how, in stanzas 1–6, he preserves a 4-line rhyme, which the
Latin author abandoned after stanza 1.

149
For Apostles

A.

Aeterna Christi munera
apostolorum gloriam
laudes ferentes debitas
laetis canamus mentibus;

ecclesiarum principes,
belli triumphales duces,
caelestis aulae milites
et vera mundi lumina.

Devota sanctorum fides,
invicta spes credentium,
perfecta Christi caritas
mundi triumphat principem.

In his paterna gloria,
in his voluntas Spiritus,
exultat in his Filio;
coelum repletur gaudio.

Te nunc, redemptor, quae sumus,
ut martyrum consortio
iungas precantes servulos
in sempiterna saecula.

Ambrose of Milan
Roman Breviary text

B.

Th' eternal gifts of Christ the King,
th' apostles' glorious deeds, we sing;
and while due hymns of praise we pay,
our thankful hearts cast grief away.

The church in these her princes boasts,
these victor chiefs of warrior hosts,
the soldiers of the heavenly hall,
the lights that rose on earth for all.

'Twas thus the yearning faith of saints,
th' unconquered hope that never faints,
the love of Christ that knows not shame,
the prince of this world overcame.

In these the Father's glory shone,
in these the will of God the Son,
in these exults the Holy Ghost,
through these rejoice the heavenly host.

Redeemer, hear us of thy love,
that, with the glorious band above,
hereafter, of thine endless grace
thy servants also may have place.

translated, John Mason Neale
The Hymnal Noted, 1851

150
Saint Michael and All Angels

A.

Christe, sanctorum decus angelorum,
gentis humanae sator et redemptor,
caelitum nobis tribuas beatas
    scandere sedes.

Angelus pacis Michael in sedes
caelitus nostras veniat, serenae
auctor ut pacis lacrimosa in orcum
    belle releget.

Angelus fortis Gabriel, ut hostes
pellet antiquos et amica caelo,
quae triumphator statuit per orbem,
    templa revisat.

Angelus nostrae medicus salutis
adsit e caelo Raphael, ut omnes
sanet aegrotos dubiosque vitae
    dirigat actus.

Virgo dux pacis genetrixque lucis
et sacer nobis chorus angelorum
semper assistat, simul et micantis
    regia coeli.

Praestat hoc nobis Deitas beata
Patris, ac Nati, pariterque sancte
Spiritus, cuius resonat per omnem
    gloria mundum.

attributed to Rabanus Maurus
Roman Breviary, 1632
The original poem, probably not by Rabanus Maurus, has only two
lines in common with the revision published in the 1632 breviary.
Translators have made different choices in
selecting from the two versions.

B.

Christ, the fair glory of the holy angels,
thou who hast made us, thou who o'er us rulest,
grant of thy mercy unto us thy servants
    steps up to heaven.

Send thy archangel, Michael, to our succor;
peacemaker blessed, may he banish from us
striving and hatred, so that for the peaceful
    all things may prosper.

Send thy archangel, Gabriel, the mighty;
herald of heaven, may he from us mortals
spurn the old serpent, watching o'er the temples
    where thou art worshiped.

Send thy archangel, Raphael, the restorer
of the misguided ways of men who wander,
who at thy bidding strengthens soul and body
    with thine anointing.

May the blest Mother of our God and Savior,
may the assembly of the saints in glory,
may the celestial companies of angels
    ever assist us.

Father almighty, Son, and Holy Spirit,
God ever blessed, be thou our preserver;
thine is the glory which the angels worship,
    veiling their faces.

translated, Athelstan Riley
The English Hymnal, 1906

Sequences

151
The Alleluiatic Sequence

A.

Cantemus cuncti melodum nunc "Alleluia"
in laudibus aeterni regis
haec plebs resultet, "Alleluia!"

hoc denique caelestes chori
cantant in altum, "Alleluia!"

hoc beatorum per prata paradisiata
psallat concentus "Alleluia!"

quin et astrorum micantia luminaria
iubilent altum "Alleluia!"

nubium cursus, ventorum volatus,
fulgurum coruscatio
et tonitruum sonitus
dulce consonent simul "Alleluia!"

fluctus et undae,
imber et procellae,
tempestas et serenitas,
cauma, gelu, nix, pruinae,
saltus, remora, pangant "Alleluia!"

hinc variae volucres creatorem
laudibus concinite cum "Alleluia!"

ast illinc respondeant voces altae
diversarum bestiarum, "Alleluia!"

Istinc montium celsi vertices sonent "Alleluia!"
illinc vallium profunditates saltent "Alleluia!"

tu quoque maris iubilans abysse, dic "Alleluia!"
nec non terrarum molis immensitates, "Alleluia!"

nunc omne genus humanum laudans exultet
                                  "Alleluia!"
et creatori grates frequentans consonet "Alleluia!"

hoc denique nomen audire iugitur delectatur
                                  "Alleluia!"
hoc etiam carmen caeleste comprobat ipse Christus
                                  "Alleluia!"

nunc vos o socii cantate laetantes "Alleluia!"
et vos pueruli respondete semper "Alleluia!"

nunc omnes canite simul Alleluia Domino
Alleluia Christo,
Pneumatique Alleluia

laus Trinitati aeternae,
Alleluia! Alleluia! Alleluia!
Alleluia! Alleluia! Alleluia!

attributed to Notker (Balbulus)

B.

The strain upraise of joy and praise, "Alleluia!"
to the glory of our King
let the ransomed people sing, "Alleluia!"

And the choirs that dwell on high
shall re-echo through the sky, "Alleluia!"

they through the fields of paradise that roam,
the blessed ones, repeat through that bright home,
                                  "Alleluia!"

the planets glittering on their heavenly way,
the shining constellations join and say, "Alleluia!"

Ye clouds that onward sweep,
ye winds on pinions light,
ye thunders, echoing loud and deep,
ye lightnings wildly bright
in sweet consent unite your "Alleluia!"

Ye floods and ocean billows!
Ye storms and winter snow!
Ye days of cloudless beauty,
Hoar frost and summer glow!
Ye groves that wave in spring
and glorious forests, sing, "Alleluia!"

First let the birds, with painted plumage gay,
exalt their great Creator's praise and say, "Alleluia!"

Then let the beasts of earth, with varying strain
join in creation's hymn, and cry again, "Alleluia!"

Here let the mountains thunder forth sonorous,
                                  "Alleluia!"
there, let the valleys sing in gentler chorus,
                                  "Alleluia!"

Thou jubilant abyss of ocean cry, "Alleluia!"
ye tracts of earth and continents reply, "Alleluia!"

To God who all creation made,
the frequent hymn be duly paid. "Alleluia!"

This is the strain, the eternal strain,
the Lord of all things loves: "Alleluia!"

This is the song, the heavenly song,
that Christ himself approves: "Alleluia!"

Wherefore we sing, both heart and voice awaking,
                                  "Alleluia!"
and children's voices echo, answer making,
                                  "Alleluia!"

Now from all men be outpoured
alleluia to the Lord;
with alleluia evermore
the Son and Spirit we adore.

Praise be done to the Three in One,
Alleluia! Alleluia! Alleluia! Alleluia!

translated, John Mason Neale
The Hymnal Noted, 1851

152
The Golden Sequence

A.

Veni, sancte Spiritus
et emitte caelitus
    lucis tuae radium;
veni, pater pauperum;
veni, dator munerum;
    veni, lumen cordium,

consolator optime,
dulcis hospes animae,
    dulce refrigerium,
in labore requies,
in aestu temperies,
    in fletu solacium.

O lux beatissima,
reple cordis intima
    tuorum fidelium;
sine tuo numine
nihil est in homine,
    nihil est innoxium.

Lava quod est sordidum,
riga quod est aridum,
    rege quod est devium,
fove quod est languidum,
flecte quod est rigidum
    sana quod est saucium.

Da tuis fidelibus
in te confidentibus
    sacrum septenarium;
da virtutis meritum,
da salutis exitum,
    da perenne gaudium.

attributed to Stephen Langton [and others]

B.

Come, thou holy Paraclete,
and from thy celestial seat
    send thy light and brilliancy;
Father of the poor, draw near;
giver of all gifts, be here;
    come, the soul's true radiancy.

Come, of comforters the best,
of the soul the sweetest guest—
    come in toil refreshingly;
thou in labor rest most sweet,
thou art shadow from the heat,
    comfort in adversity.

O thou Light, most pure and blest,
shine within the inmost breast
    of thy faithful company.
Where thou art not, man hath nought;
every holy deed and thought
    comes from thy divinity.

What is soiled, make thou pure;
what is wounded, work its cure;
    straighten what goes erringly.
what is frozen, warmly tend,
what is rigid, gently bend,
    what is parched, fructify.

Fill thy faithful, who confide
in thy power to guard and guide,
    with thy sevenfold mystery.
Here thy grace and virtue send;
grant salvation to the end,
    and in heaven felicity.

translated, John Mason Neale
The Hymnal Noted, 1851

153
Dies Irae

A.

Dies irae, dies illa!
solvet saeclum in favilla,
teste David cum Sibylla.

Quantus tremor est futurus,
quando iudex est venturus,
cuncta stricte discussurus!

Tuba mirum spargens sonum
per sepulcra regionum
coget omnes ante thronum.

Mors stupebit et natura,
cum resurget creatura
iudicanti responsura.

Liber scriptus proferetur,
in quo totum continetur,
unde mundus iudicetur.

Iudex ergo cum sedebit,
quidquid latet, apparebit:
nil inultum remanebit.

Quid sum miser tunc dicturus,
quem patronum rogaturus,
cum vix iustus sit securus?

Rex tremendae maiestatis,
qui salvandos salvas gratis,
salva me, fons pietatis!

Recordare, Jesu pie,
quod sum causa tuae viae;
ne me perdas illa die!

Quaerens me, sedisti lassus
redemisti, crucem passus:
tantus labor non sit cassus.

Iuste Iudex ultionis,
donum fac remissionis
ante diem rationis.

Ingemisco tanquam reus,
culpa rubet vultus meus;
supplicanti parce, Deus!

Qui Mariam absolvisti
et latronem exaudisti,
mihi quoque spem dedisti.

Preces meae non sunt dignae;
sed tu bonus fac benigne
ne perenni cremer igne!

Inter oves locum praesta,
et ab haedis me sequestra,
statuens in parte dextra.

Confutatis maledictis,
flammis acribus addictis,
voca me cum benedictis!

Oro supplex et acclinis;
cor contritum quasi cinis;
gere curam mei finis.

Lacrymosa dies illa,
quae resurget ex favilla
iudicandus homo reus,
huic ergo parce deus.
    Pie Jesu Domine,
    dona eis requiem.

attributed to Thomas of Celano

B.

Day of wrath and doom impending,
David's word with Sibyl's blending!
heaven and earth in ashes ending!

O what fear man's bosom rendeth,
when from heaven the Judge descendeth,
on whose sentence all dependeth!

Wondrous sound the trumpet flingeth,
through earth's sepulchers it ringeth;
all before the throne it bringeth.

Death is struck, and nature quaking,
all creation is awaking,
to its Judge an answer making.

Lo, the book exactly worded,
wherein all hath been recorded;
thence shall judgment be awarded.

When the Judge his seat attaineth,
and each hidden deed arraigneth,
nothing unavenged remaineth.

What shall I, frail man, be pleading?
who for me be interceding,
when the just are mercy needing?

King of majesty tremendous,
who dost free salvation send us,
Fount of pity then befriend us!

Think, kind Jesu!—my salvation
caused thy wondrous incarnation;
leave me not to reprobation.

Faint and weary thou hast sought me,
on the cross of suffering bought me;
shall such grace be vainly brought me?

Righteous Judge, for sin's pollution,
ere that day of retribution
grant thy gift of absolution.

Guilty, now I pour my moaning,
all my shame with anguish owning;
spare, O God, thy suppliant groaning!

Through the sinful woman shriven,
through the dying thief forgiven,
thou to me a hope hast given.

Worthless are my prayers and sighing,
yet, good Lord, in grace complying,
rescue me from fires undying.

With thy sheep a place provide me,
from the goats afar divide me,
to thy right hand do thou guide me.

When the wicked are confounded,
doomed to shame and woe unbounded,
call me with thy saints surrounded.

Low I kneel, with heart submission;
see like ashes my contrition!
help me in my last condition.

Ah! that day of tears and mourning!
from the dust of earth returning
man for judgment must prepare him;
spare, O God, in mercy spare him!
    Lord all-pitying, Jesu blest,
    grant them thine eternal rest.

translated, William J. Irons, 1848
Introits, and Hymns for Advent, 1849
stanza 1 altered for The English Hymnal, 1906

The Latin poem *"Dies irae"* by Thomas of Celano, friend and biographer of St. Francis of Assisi, consisted of the seventeen 3-line stanzas ending *"gere curam mei finis"* and was designed as a personal meditation on death and the Judgment. When it came into liturgical use, the six lines at the end, which break the rhyme scheme, were added. The poem now takes its place in the history of hymnody partly because of the sonorous and dramatic beauty of some, though perhaps not all, of its Latin lines and partly because it has inspired so many poets and musicians of later times. Its liturgical use was in its being the one Christian hymn sung at the Requiem Mass; therefore in musical settings of the Mass it took a central place. Moreover, its plainsong melody opens with a phrase that several composers, notably Berlioz and Rachmaninoff, have woven into secular compositions.

It has to be admitted that the only English translation in the original meter (that given above) cannot be rated higher than a brave attempt to translate the original; it makes it possible to sing the original plainsong in English, but it misses too many of the overtones of the Latin to be called a classic version. Recognizing this, we add here a prose translation, the first five sections of which (each corresponding to six lines of the original) are taken from *Hymns for Church and School*, 1964, and the rest of which is added here to complete the poem.

C.

1. That Day, the Day of Wrath, will dissolve the world into ashes, as David and the Sibyl testify. What a trembling will there be, when the Judge will come, who will sternly examine all things!

2. The trumpet will scatter a wonderful sound through the tombs of all parts of the world; it will compel all men before the throne. Death and nature will be astonished into silence when creation arises to answer him who judges.

3. The written book will be produced in which is contained the whole record from which the world will be judged. Therefore when the judge makes his review, whatever is hidden will come to light; nothing will remain unavenged.

4. What am I then to say, in my wretchedness? Whom shall I call on as my defending counsel, seeing that the righteous man is scarcely safe? King of aweful majesty, who dost freely save those who are to be saved, save me, thou fount of pity!

5. Remember, kind Jesus, that I am the cause of thy journey: do not destroy me on that day. Thou didst sit in weariness when searching for me; thou didst redeem me by enduring the Cross. Let not all that labor be in vain.

6. Righteous judge to whom vengeance belongs, give thy pardon before the day of reckoning comes. My guilt makes me cry out; my blame makes me blush. Hear my prayer, O God, and spare me.

7. Thou didst pardon Mary; thou didst hear the thief's prayer, and in this thou hast given me hope. My prayers are not fit to be heard; but thou wilt be kind, and not let me burn in eternal fire.

8. Give me a place with the sheep: separate me from the goats; put me at thy right hand. When the wicked are doomed in shame to the fires of bitterness, call my name with those who are blessed.

9. Humbly, prostrate, I pray: my heart is ground to ashes by penitence; look upon my fate with mercy.

10. Oh, what a day of tears and lamentation, when man, waiting for judgment, rises from earth's ashes: spare him in that day! Kind Lord Jesus, give them rest!

translated, Erik Routley

Medieval Latin Lyrics

154
The City of Bethlehem

A.

O sola magnarum urbium
major Bethlem, cui contigit
ducem salutis caelitus
incorporatum gignere:

quem stella, quae solis rotam
vincit decore ac lumine,
venisse terris nuntiat
cum carne terrestri Deum.

Videre postquam illum magi,
eoa promunt munera,
stratique votis offerunt
thus, myrrham, et aurum regium.

Regem Deumque annuntiant
thesaurus et fragrans odor
thuris Sabaei, ac myrrheus
pulvis sepulcrum praedocet.

Jesu, tibi sit gloria
qui apparuisti hodie,
cum Patre et sancto Spiritu
in sempiterna saecula.

Marcus Aurelius Clemens Prudentius
Cathemerinon, ca. 405

B.

Bethlehem, of noblest cities
    none can once with thee compare;
thou alone the Lord from heaven
    didst for us incarnate bear.

Fairer than the sun at morning
    was the star that told his birth;
to the lands their God announcing,
    his beneath a form of earth.

By its lambent beauty guided
    see the eastern kings appear;
see them bend, their gifts to offer,
    gifts of incense, gold, and myrrh.

Solemn things of mystic meaning:
    incense doth the God disclose,
gold a royal child proclaimeth,
    myrrh a future tomb foreshows.

Holy Jesu, in thy brightness
    to the Gentile world displayed,
with the Father and the Spirit
    endless praise to thee be paid.

translated, Edward Caswall
Lyra Catholica, 1849

155
Corde Natus

A.

Corde natus ex Parentis
    ante mundi exordium
A et Ω cognominatus,
    ipse fons et clausula
omnium quae sunt, fuerunt,
    quaeque post futura sunt,
        saeculorum saeculis.

Ipse iussit, et creata,
    dixit ipse, et facta sunt,   (Ps. 33:9)
terra, caelum, fossa, ponti,
    trina rerum machina,
quaeque in his vigent sub alto
    solis et lunae globo,
        saeculorum saeculis.

Corporis formam caduci,
    membra morti obnoxia
induit, ne gens periret
    primoplasti ex germine,
merserat quam lex profundo
    noxialis tartaro,
        saeculorum saeculis.

O beatus ortus ille,
    virgo cum puerpera
edidit nostram salutem
    foeta sancto Spiritus,
et puer, Redemptor orbis
    os sacratum protulit,
        saeculorum saeculis.

Psallat altitudo coeli,
    psallant omnes angeli,
quidquid est virtutis usquam
    psallat in laudam Dei;
nulla linguarum silescat,
    vox et omnis consonet,
        saeculorum saeculis.

Ecce, quem vates vetustis
    concinebant saeculis,
quem prophetarum fideles
    paginae spoponderant,
emicat promissus olim;
    cuncta collaudent eum
        saeculorum saeculis.

Macte iudex mortuorum,
    macte rex viventium,
dexter in Parentis arce
    qui cluis virtutibus,
omnium venturus inde
    iustus ultor criminum,
        saeculorum saeculis.

Te senes et te iuventus,
    parvulorum te chorus,
turba matrum virginumque,
    simplices puellulae
voce concordes pudicis
    perstrepant concentibus,
        saeculorum saeculis.

Tibi, Christe, sit cum Patre,
    hagioque Pneumate,
hymnus, decus, laus perennis,
    gratiarum actio,
honor, virtus, victoria,
    regnum aeternaliter,
        saeculorum saeculis.

> Marcus Aurelius Clemens Prudentius
> *Cathemerinon*, ca. 405
> The single-line refrain is an addition to the original text.

B.

Of the Father's heart begotten,
    ere the world from chaos rose,
he is Alpha: from that Fountain
    all that is and hath been flows;
he is Omega, of all things
    yet to come the mystic Close,
        evermore and evermore.

By his word was all created;   (Ps. 33:9)
    he commanded and 'twas done
earth and sky and boundless ocean,
    universe of three in one,
all that sees the moon's soft radiance,
    all that breathes beneath the sun,
        evermore and evermore.

He assumed this mortal body,
    frail and feeble, doomed to die,
that the race from dust created
    might not perish utterly,
which the dreadful law had sentenced
    in the depths of hell to lie,
        evermore and evermore.

O how blest that wondrous birthday,
    when the Maid the curse retrieved,
brought to birth mankind's salvation
    by the Holy Ghost conceived;
and the Babe, the world's Redeemer
    in her loving arms received,
        evermore and evermore.

This is he, whom seer and sibyl
    sang in ages long gone by;
this is he of old revealed
    in the page of prophecy;
lo! he comes, the promised Savior;
    let the world his praises cry
        evermore and evermore!

Sing, ye heights of heaven, his praises;
    angels and archangels, sing!
Wheresoe'er ye be, ye faithful,
    let your joyous anthems ring,
every tongue his name confessing,
    countless voices answering,
        evermore and evermore.

Hail! thou Judge of souls departed;
    hail, of all the living King!
On the Father's right hand throned,
    through his courts thy praises ring,
till at last for all offenses
    righteous judgment thou shalt bring,
        evermore and evermore.

Now let old and young uniting
    chant to thee harmonious lays,
maid and matron hymn thy glory,
    infant lips their anthem raise,
boys and girls together singing
    with pure heart their song of praise,
        evermore and evermore.

Christ, to thee with God the Father
    and O Holy Ghost, to thee,
hymn and chant and high thanksgiving
    and unwearied praises be,
honor, glory, and dominion,
    and eternal victory,
        evermore and evermore.

stanzas 1–8 translated, Roby Furley Davis, 1905
The English Hymnal, 1906
based on John Mason Neale
The Hymnal Noted, 1851
The translation inverts the order of stanzas 5 and 6.
Stanza 9 was altered by Henry W. Baker for
Hymns Ancient and Modern, 1861.

156
Veneration of the Cross

A.

Pange, lingua, gloriosi
    lauream certaminis,
et super crucis trophaeo
    dic triumphum nobilem,
qualiter redemptor orbis
    immolatus vicerit.

De parentis protoplasti
    fraude factor condolens,
quando pomi noxialis
    in necem morsu ruit,
ipse lignum tunc notavit,
    damna ligni ut solveret.

Hoc opus nostrae salutis
    ordo depoposcerat,
multiformis proditoris
    ars ut artem falleret,
et medelam ferret inde
    hostis unde laeserat.

Quando venit ergo sacri
    plenitudo temporis,
missus est ab arce Patris
    natus, orbis conditor,
atque ventre virginali
    carne factus prodiit.

Vagit infans inter arcta
    conditus praesepia,
membra pannis involuta
    virgo mater alligat,
et Dei manus pedesque
    stricta cingit fascia.

Lustra sex qui iam peregit
    tempus implens corporis,
sponte libera redemptor
    passioni deditus,
Agnus in crucis levatur
    immolandus stipite.

Felle potus ecce languet
    spina, clavi, lancea;
mite corpus .perforarunt;
    unda manat et cruror.
Terra, pontus, astra, mundus
    quo lavantur flumine.

Crux fidelis, inter omnes
    arbor una nobilis,
nulla silva talem profert
    fronde, flore, germine,
dulce lignum, dulce clavos
    dulce pondus sustinet.

Flecte ramos, arbor alta,
    tensa laxa viscera,
et rigor lentescat ille,
    quem dedit nativitas,
ut superni membra regis
    tende miti stipite.

Sola digna tu fuisti
    ferre pretium victimam,
atque portum praeparare
    arca mundo naufrago,
quam sacer cruor perunxit
    fusus Agni corpore.

Gloria et honor Deo
    usquequo altissimo,
una Patri, Filioque,
    inclito Paraclito,
cuius honor et potestas
    in aeterna saecula.

Venatius Honorius Fortunatus

B.

Sing, my tongue, how glorious battle
    glorious victory became;
and above the cross, his trophy,
    tell the triumph and the fame;
tell how he, the earth's Redeemer,
    by his death for man o'ercame.

God in pity saw men fallen,
    shamed and sunk in misery,
when he fell on death by tasting
    fruit of the forbidden tree;
then another tree was chosen
    which the world from death should free.

Thus the scheme of our salvation
    was of old in order laid,
that the manifold deceiver's
    art by art might be outweighed,
and the lure the foe put forward
    into means of healing made.

Therefore when th' appointed fullness
    of the holy time was come,
he was sent, who maketh all things,
    forth from God's eternal home;
thus he came to earth, incarnate,
    offspring of a maiden's womb.

Laid within a narrow manger,
    uttering but an infant sound,
while the Virgin-Mother fastens
    swaddling clothes his limbs around,
in the tightly girded linen
    God's own hands and feet are bound.

Thirty years fulfilled among us,
    perfect life in low estate—
born for this, and self surrendered,
    to his passion dedicate,
on the cross the Lamb is lifted
    for his people immolate.

His the nails, the spear, the spitting,
    reed and vinegar and gall;
from his patient body pierced
    blood and water streaming fall:
earth and sky and stars and mankind
    by that stream are cleansed all.

Faithful cross, above all other,
    one and only noble tree!
None in foliage, none in blossom,
    none in fruit thy peer may be;
sweetest wood and sweetest iron,
    sweetest weight is hung on thee.

Bend thy boughs, O tree of glory!
    thy relaxing sinews bend;
for a while the ancient rigor
    that thy birth bestowed, suspend;
and the King of heavenly beauty
    on thy bosom gently tend.

Thou alone wast counted worthy
    this world's ransom to uphold;
for a shipwrecked race preparing
    harbor, like the ark of old;
with the sacred blood anointed
    from the smitten Lamb that rolled.

To the Trinity be glory,
    everlasting, as is meet;
equal to the Father, equal
    to the Son, and Paraclete:
Trinal Unity, whose praises
    all created things repeat.

composite translation: stanza 1 by William Mair and Arthur Wellesley Wotherspoon in *Scottish Mission Hymnal*, 1912; stanzas 2, 3, 4, 6, and 7 by Percy Dearmer, in *The English Hymnal*, 1906; stanza 5 by the compilers of *Hymns Ancient and Modern*, 1904. The last four stanzas are by John Mason Neale in *Medieval Hymns and Sequences*, 1851, upon whose translation all the others are based.

157
Ascension

A.

Hymnum canamus gloriae,
hymni novi nunc personent;
Christus novo cum tramite   (Heb. 10:20)
ad Patris ascendit thronum.

Apostoli tunc mystico   (Acts 1:1–11)
in monte stantes Chrismatis
cum matre clara virgine
Jesu videbant gloriam.

Quos alloquentes angeli,
"quid astra stantes cernitis?
Salvator hic est," inquiunt,
"Jesus triumpho nobili."

Sicque venturum asserunt
quemadmodum hunc viderunt
summa polorum culmina
scandere Jesus splendida.

Da nobis illuc sedula
devotione tendere
quo te sedere cum Patre
in arce regni credimus.

Tu esto nostrum gaudium
qui es futurus praemium,   (Gen. 12:1)
sit nostra in te gloria
per cuncta semper saecula.

Gloria tibi, Domine,
qui scandis supra sidera,
cum Patre et sancto Spiritu
in sempiterna saecula.

Bede of Jarrow

B.

Sing we triumphant hymns of praise,
new hymns to heaven exulting raise,
Christ, by a road before untrod,
ascendeth to the throne of God.

The holy apostolic band
upon the Mount of Olives stand,
and with the Virgin-mother see
Jesus' resplendent majesty.

To whom the angels, drawing nigh,
"Why stand and gaze upon the sky?
This is the Savior," thus they say,
"This is his noble triumph day!"

"Again shall ye behold him—so
as ye today have seen him go;
in glorious pomp ascending high,
up to the portals of the sky."

O grant us thitherward to tend,
and with unwearied hearts ascend
toward thy kingdom's throne, where thou,
as is our faith, art seated now.

Be thou our joy and thou our guard,
who art to be our great reward:
our glory and our boast in thee
for ever and for ever be!

All glory, Lord, to thee we pay,
ascending o'er the stars today:
all glory, as is ever meet,
to Father and to Paraclete.

> translated, Benjamin Webb and John Mason Neale
> *The Hymnal Noted*, 1854

158

The Heavenly City as a
Figure of the Earthly Church

A.

Urbs beata Jerusalem,
    dicta pacis visio,
quae construitur in caelis
    vivis ex lapidibus   (1 Pet. 2:5)
et angelis coronata
    ut sponsata comite,   (Rev. 21:1ff)

nova veniens e caelo,
    nuptiali thalamo
praeparata, ut sponsata
    copuletur Domino;
plateae et muri eius
    ex auro purissimo.

Portae nitent margaritis,
    adytis patentibus,
et virtute meritorum
    illuc introducitur
omnis qui pro Christi nomen
    hic in mundo premitur.

Tunsionibus, pressuris
    expoliti lapides,
suisque aptantur locis
    per manum artificis;
disponuntur permansuri
    sacris aedificiis.

Angularis fundamentum
    lapis Christus missus est   (1 Pet. 2:6)
qui compage parietis
    in utroque nectitur,
quem Sion sancte suscepit,
    in quo credens permanet.

Omnis illa Deo sacra
    et dilecta civitas,
plena modulis in laude
    et canore iubilo,
trinum Deum unicumque
    cum favore praedicat.

Hoc in templo, summe Deus,
    exoratus adveni,
et clementi bonitate
    precum vota suscipe;
largam benedictionem
    hic infunde iugiter.

Hic promereantur omnes
    petita acquirere,
et adepta possidere
    cum sanctis perenniter,
paradisum introire
    translati in requiem.

Gloria et honor Deo
    usquequo altissimo,
una Patri Filioque
    inclito Paraclito,
cui laus est et potestas
    per aeterna saecula.

anonymous, middle period

B.

Blessed city, heavenly Salem,
    vision dear of peace and love,
who, of living stones upbuilded,
    art the joy of heaven above,
and, with angel cohorts circled,
    as a bride to earth dost move—

From celestial realms descending,
    ready for the nuptial bed,
to his presence, decked with jewels,
    by her Lord shall she be led;
all her streets, and all her bulwarks
    of pure gold are fashioned.

Bright with pearls her portal glitters;
    it is open evermore;
and by virtue of his merits,
    thither faithful souls may soar,
who for Christ's dear name in this world
    pain and tribulation bore.

Many a blow and biting sculpture
    polished well those stones elect,
in their places now compacted
    by the heavenly Architect,
who therewith hath willed for ever
    that his palace should be decked.

Christ is made the sure foundation
    and the precious cornerstone,
who, the twofold walls surmounting
    binds them closely into one;
holy Sion's help for ever
    and her confidence alone.

All that dedicated city
    dearly loved by God on high,
in exultant jubilation
    pours perpetual melody:
God the One and God the Trinal
    singing everlastingly.

To this temple, where we call thee,
    come, O Lord of hosts, today;
with thy wonted lovingkindness
    hear thy people as they pray;
and thy fullest benediction
    shed within its walls for aye.

Here vouchsafe to all thy servants
    what they supplicate to gain;
here to have and hold for ever
    those good things their prayers obtain;
and hereafter in thy glory
    with thy blessed ones to reign.

Laud and honor to the Father,
    laud and honor to the Son;
laud and honor to the Spirit;
    ever three and ever one:
consubstantial, co-eternal,
    while unending ages run.

translated, John Mason Neale
The Hymnal Noted, 1851

The division of this hymn at stanza 4 goes back to medieval liturgical custom. Those who cheerfully sing part II of the English translation, with or without the opening verse, hardly know from what deep waters of mythological metaphor they have been delivered. Three basic ideas run in uneasy counterpoint in part I: (a) the "marriage" of the heavenly Jerusalem and the victorious Christ, from Revelation 21; (b) the physical process of building and planning a city; and (c) the notion of Christ as the cornerstone and his members as "living stones," from 1 Peter 2. Usually, as soon as one metaphor looks like it is becoming unmanageable, the poet shifts to another; but in stanza 4 the blows of hammers and nicks of chisels are metaphorical: They represent the refining tribulations through which the Divine Architect causes his saints (his "living stones") to pass on the way to perfection. All this prefaces the prayer of the church militant, which comes in the second part and which is more familiar.

159
Palm Sunday

A.

Gloria laus et honor tibi sit Rex Christe redemptor;
cui puerile decus prompsit hosanna pium.

Israel es tu rex Davidis et inclyta proles,
nomine qui in Domini, rex benedicte, venis.

Coetus in excelsis te laudat caelicus omnis,
et mortalis homo, et cuncta creata simul.

Plebs Hebraea tibi cum palmis obvia venit;
cum prece, voto hymnis, adsumus ecce tibi.

Hi tibi passuro solvebant munia laudis,
nos tibi regnanti pangimus ecce melos.

Hi placuere tibi, placeat devotio nostra:
rex pie, rex clemens cui bone cuncta placent.

> Theodulph of Orléans, ca. 821
> This is a selection from the original text of seventy-eight lines.

B.

All glory, laud, and honor
    to thee, Redeemer, King,
to whom the lips of children
    made sweet hosannas ring.

Thou art the King of Israel,
    thou David's royal Son,
who in the Lord's name comest,
    thou King and blessed One.

The company of angels
    are praising thee on high;
and mortal men and all things
    created make reply.

The people of the Hebrews
    with palms before thee went;
our praise and prayer and anthems
    before thee we present.

In hastening to thy passion,
    they raised their hymns of praise;
in reigning 'midst thy glory,
    our melody we raise.

Thou didst accept their praises:
    accept the prayers we bring,
who in all good delightest,
    thou good and gracious King!

> translated, John Mason Neale
> The Hymnal Noted, 1854
> stanza 1 altered for Hymns Ancient and Modern, 1861

160
Veni Creator Spiritus

A.

Veni, Creator Spiritus,
mentes tuorum visita,
imple superna gratia
quae tu creasti pectora.

Qui diceris Paraclitus,
altissimi, donum Dei,
fons vivus, ignis, caritas,
et spiritalis unctio.

Tu septiformis munere,
digitus Dei dexterae
tu rite promisso Patrum,
sermone ditans guttura.

Accende lumen sensibus,
infunde amorem cordibus,
infirma nostri corporis
virtute firmans perpeti.

Hostem repellas longius,
pacemque dones protinus;
ductore sic te praevio
vitemus omne noxium.

Per te sciamus da Patrem,
noscamus atque Filium,
teque utriusque Spiritum
credamus omni tempore.

attributed to Rabanus Maurus

B.

Come, O Creator Spirit, come,
and make within our hearts thy home;
to us thy grace celestial give,
who of thy breathing move and live.

O Comforter, that name is thine,
of God most high the gift divine;
the well of life, the fire of love,
our souls' anointing from above.

Thou dost appear in seven-fold dower
the sign of God's almighty power;
the Father's promise, making rich
with saving truth our earthly speech.

Our senses with thy light inflame,
our hearts to heavenly love reclaim;
our bodies' poor infirmity
with strength perpetual fortify.

Our earthly foes afar repel,
grant us henceforth in peace to dwell;
and so to us, with thee for guide,
no ill shall come, no harm betide.

May we by thee the Father learn,
and know the Son, and thee discern,
who art of both; and thus adore
in perfect faith for evermore.

translated, Robert Bridges
The Yattendon Hymnal, 1899

This, probably the most celebrated of Latin hymns in English-speaking use, is translated above by one poet laureate; below we give the more familiar translation (less accurate) by a bishop of Durham and the highly wrought version by another laureate.

C.

Come, Holy Ghost, our souls inspire,
and lighten with celestial fire;
thou the anointing Spirit art,
who dost thy sevenfold gifts impart.

Thy blessed unction from above
is comfort, life, and fire of love;
enable with perpetual light
the dullness of our blinded sight.

Anoint and cheer our soiled face
with the abundance of thy grace:
keep far our foes, give peace at home;
where thou art guide no ill can come.

Teach us to know the Father, Son,
and thee, of both, to be but One;
that through the ages all along
this may be our endless song:

Praise to thy eternal merit,
Father, Son, and Holy Spirit.

translated, John Cosin
Collection of Private Devotions in the Practice of the Ancient Church, 1627

D.

Creator Spirit, by whose aid
the world's foundations first were laid,
come, visit every pious mind;
come, pour thy joys on human kind;
from sin and sorrow set us free,
and make thy temples worthy thee.

O Source of uncreated light,
the Father's promised Paraclete,
thrice-holy fount, thrice-holy fire,
our hearts with heavenly love inspire;
come, and thy sacred unction bring
to sanctify us while we sing.

Plenteous of grace, descend from high
rich in thy seven-fold energy;
thou strength of his almighty hand
whose power does heaven and earth command;
proceeding Spirit, our defense,
who dost thy gift of tongues dispense,
and crown'st thy gift with eloquence!

Refine and purge our earthly parts;
but oh, inflame and fire our hearts!
Make us eternal truths receive,
and practice all that we believe;
give us thyself, that we may see
the Father and the Son by thee.

Immortal honor, endless fame,
attend the almighty Father's name;
the Savior Son be glorified,
who for lost man's redemption died;
and equal adoration be,
eternal Paraclete, to thee.

translated, John Dryden
Examen Poeticum, 1693
When this appears in hymnals, line 3:4, or
the whole stanza, is normally dropped.

161
O Quanta, Qualia

A.

O quanta, qualia sunt illa sabbata
quae semper celebrat superna curia;
quae fessis requies, quae merces fortibus,
cum erit omnia Deus in omnibus!

Vere Jerusalem est illa civitas,
cuius pax iugis est summa iucunditas,
ubi non praevenit rem desiderium,
nec desiderio minus est praemium.

Quis Rex, quae curia, quale palatium,
quae pax, quae requies, quod illud gaudium,
huius participes exponent gloriam,
si, quantum sentiunt possint exprimere.

Nostrum est interim mentem erigere,
et totis patriam votis appetere,
et ad Jerusalem a Babylonia
post longa regredi tandem exilia.

Illic molestiis finitis omnibus
securi cantica Sion cantibimus,
et iuges gratiae de donis gratiae
beata referet plebs tibi, Domine.

Illic ex sabbato succedit sabbatum,
perpes laetitia sabbatizantium,
nec ineffabiles cessabunt iubili
quos decantabimus et nos et angeli.

Perenni Domino perpes sit gloria,
ex quo sunt, per quem sunt, in quo sunt omnia;
ex quo sunt, Pater est; per quem sunt, Filius,
in quo sunt, Patris et Filii Spiritus.

Peter Abelard
Hymnarius Paraclitensis, ca. 1135

Wondrous that King, and his lieges who reign there,
wondrous the peace and the joy they attain there;
could they but tell of that rapture, who feel it!
Had we but ears, or they words to reveal it!

Yet in the meanwhile our eyes thither turn we;
home of our hearts, for thy loveliness yearn we:
long though this Babylon's exile detaineth,
yonder we press, where a city remaineth.

Free from all cares that on earth can annoy us,
Sion's sweet anthems shall wholly employ us,
grateful at last for those infinite graces
time nor eternity ever effaces.

Holidays still one another o'ertaking
give them fresh joy of their holiday-making;
still of that chorus the echoes are ringing.
Angels and men join together in singing.

Praise to the Godhead unceasingly give we,
of whom, in whom, and by whom ever live we,
God all-creating and God all-sustaining,
God in three Persons eternally reigning.

translated, Ronald A. Knox, 1940
The Westminster Hymnal, 1941
© Continuum International Publishing Group, Ltd.

B.

Oh, what high holiday, past our declaring,
safe in his palace God's courtiers are sharing,
rest after pilgrimage, spoil after fighting!
God, all in all, is their crown and requiting.

Truly Jerusalem's townsmen we call them—
peace everlasting doth fold and enthral them;
never they crave, but the boon hath been granted,
never that boon leaves their hope disenchanted.

162
Hora Novissima

In *Medieval Hymns and Sequences*, 1851, John Mason Neale translated selected lines from the first of the three books into which Bernard's long Latin text is divided. He followed the order previously employed by Richard Chenevix Trench, who had reordered 96 lines in his *Sacred Latin Poetry*, 1849. Neale subsequently translated a larger selection of 218 nonconsecutive lines in *The Rhythm of Bernard de Morlaix*, 1858. As Neale wrote in the preface to this work, "My own translation is so free, as to be little more than an imitation." He went on to suggest that "There would be no difficulty in forming several hymns, by way of cento, from the following verses: suitable to any Saint's day, to the season of Advent, or to an ordinary Sunday." Various combinations of Neale's lines have been grouped to form hymns of manageable length. Four of the more common configurations are shown below, following the lines of the Latin to which they correspond. The numbers to the right of the Latin lines indicate their position in Bernard's original.

A. Hora Novissima

Hora novissima, tempora pessima sunt, vigilemus!   1
Ecce minaciter, imminet arbiter ille supremus: 2
imminet, imminet, ut mala terminet, aequa coronet,   3
recta remuneret, anxia liberet, aethera donet.   4
Curre, vir optime, lubrica reprime, praefer honesta,   101
fletibus angere, flendo merebere coelica festa   102
luce replebere jam sine vespere, jam sine luna: 103
lux nova, lux ea, lux erit aurea, lux erit una.   104
Patria spendida, terraque florida, libera spinis,   113
danda fidelibus est ibi civibus, hic peregrinis.   114
tunc erit omnibus inspicientibus ora tonantis   115
summa potentia, plena scientia, pax rata sanctis.   116
O sacra potio, sacra refectio, visio pacis,   133
mentis et unctio, nullaque mentio ventris edacis!   134
Hac homo nititur, ambulat, utitur, ergo fruetur;   135
pax rata, pax ea, spe modo, postea re, capietur.   136

B. The World Is Very Evil

The world is very evil;
    the times are waxing late:
Be sober and keep vigil;
    the Judge is at the gate:
the Judge that comes in mercy,
    the Judge that comes with might
to terminate the evil,
    to diadem the right.

Arise, arise, good Christian,
    let right to wrong succeed;
let penitential sorrow
    to heavenly gladness lead;
to the light that has no evening,
    that knows no moon nor sun,
the light so new and golden,
    the light that is but one.

The home of fadeless splendor,
    of flowers that bear no thorn,
where they shall dwell as children
    who here as exiles mourn.
Midst power that knows no limit,
    where wisdom free from bound,
the beatific vision
    shall glad the saints around.

O happy, holy portion,
    reflection for the blest;
true vision of true beauty,
    sweet cure of all distressed!
Strive, man, to win that glory;
    toil, man, to gain that light;
send hope before to grasp it,
    till hope be lost in sight.

C. Hic Breve Vivitur

Hic breve vivitur, hic breve plangitur, hic breve
           fletur;   167
non breve vivere, non breve plangere retribuetur.   168
O retributio! stat brevis actio, vita perennis;   169
o retributio! coelica mansio stat luce plenis.   170
Sunt modo proelia, postmodo praemia. Qualia?
           Plena: 183
plena refectio, nullaque passio, nullaque poena.   184
Spe modo vivitur, et Syon angitur a Babylone;   185
nunc tribulatio; tunc recreatio, sceptra, coronae.   186
Qui modo creditur, ipse videbitur, atque scietur;   191
ipse videntibus atque scientibus attribuetur.   192
Mane videbitur, umbra fugabitur, ordo patebit;   227
mane nitens erit, et bona qui gerit, ille nitebit.   228
Nunc tibi tristia; tunc tibi gaudia; gaudia quanta?   179
Vox nequit edere, lumina cernere, tangere planta.   180
Pars mea, rex meus, in proprio Deus ipse decore   231
visus amabitur, atque videbitur auctor in ore.   232
Tunc Jacob Israel, et Lia tunc Rahel efficietur;   233
tunc Syon atria pulchraque patria perficietur.   234

D. Brief Life Is Here Our Portion

Brief life is here our portion;
    brief sorrow, short-lived care;
the life that knows no ending,
    the tearless life, is there.
O happy retribution!
    short toil, eternal rest;
for mortals and for sinners
    a mansion with the blest!

And now we fight the battle,
    but then shall wear the crown
of full and everlasting
    and passionless renown:
And now we watch and struggle,
    and now we live in hope,
and Sion, in her anguish
    with Babylon must cope:

But he whom now we trust in
    shall then be seen and known,
and they who know and see him
    shall have him for their own.
Beheld, when morn shall waken,
    and shadows shall decay,
and each true-hearted servant
    shall shine as doth the day.

Yes! God my King and portion,
    in fullness of his grace,
we then shall see for ever,
    and worship face to face.
Then all the halls of Sion
    for aye shall be complete;
and, in the land of beauty,
    all things of beauty meet.

In Neale's translation, the following four lines come
between lines 4 and 5 of the last stanza above:

Then Jacob into Israel,
    from earthlier self estranged,
and Leah into Rachel
    for ever shall be changed.

E. O Bona Patria

O bona patria, lumina sobria te speculantur: 235
ad tua nomina, sobria lumina collacrymantur: 236
est tua mentio pectoris unctio, cura doloris, 237
concipientibus aethera mentibus ignis amoris. 238
Tu locus unicus, illeque coelicus es paradisus: 239
non ibi lacryma, sed placidissima gaudia, risus. 240
Lux tua, mors crucis, atque caro ducis est crucifixi: 245
laus, benedictio, conjubilatio personat ipsi. 246
Est tibi consita laurus, et insita cedrus hysopo 241
sunt radiantia jaspide moenia, clara pyropo. 242
Hinc tibi sardius, inde topazius, hinc amethystus 243
est tua fabrica concio coelica, gemmaque Christus. 244
Tu sine littore, tu sine tempore, fons, modo rivus; 251
dulce bonis sapis, estque tibi lapis undique vivus. 252
est tibi laurea, dos datur aurea, sponsa decora, 255
primaque principis oscula suscipis, inspicis ora. 256

F. For Thee, O Dear Dear Country

For thee, O dear dear country!
    mine eyes their vigils keep;
for very love, beholding
    thy happy name, they weep:
The mention of thy glory
    is unction to the breast,
and medicine in sickness,
    and love and life and rest.

O one, O onely mansion!
    O Paradise of joy!
Where tears are ever banished,
    and smiles have no alloy;
the Cross is all thy splendor,
    the Crucified thy praise;
his laud and benediction
    thy ransomed people raise.

With jaspers glow thy bulwarks;
    thy streets with emeralds blaze;
the sardius and the topaz
    unite in thee their rays:
Thine ageless walls are bonded
    with amethyst unpriced:
Thy saints build up its fabric,
    and the cornerstone is Christ.

Thou hast no shore, fair ocean!
    Thou hast no time, bright day!
Dear fountain of refreshment
    to pilgrims far away!
Upon the Rock of ages
    they raise thy holy tower:
thine is the victor's laurel,
    and thine the golden dower.

G. Urbs Syon Aurea

Urbs Syon aurea, patria lactea, cive decora,	269
omne cor obruis, omnibus obstruis et cor et ora.	270
Nescio, nescio, quae jubilatio, lux tibi qualis,	271
quam socialia gaudia, gloria quam specialis.	272
Stant Syon atria conjubilantia, martyre plena,	275
cive micantia, principe stantia, luce serena.	276
Est tibi pascua mitibus afflua, praestita sanctis;	277
regis ibi thronus, agminis et sonus est epulantis.	278
Gens duce splendida, concio candida, vestibus albis,	279
sunt sine fletibus in Syon aedibus, aedibus almis.	280
O bona patria, num tua gaudia teque videbo?	369
O bona patria, num tua praemia plena tenebo?	370
Dic mihi, flagito; verbaque reddito, dicque—Videbis:	371
spem solidam gero: remne tenes ero? Dic—Retinebis.	372
Plaude cinis meus, est tua pars Deus: ejus es, et sis:	373
Plaude cinis meus, est tua pars Deus: ejus es, et sis.	374

H. Jerusalem the Golden

Jerusalem the golden,
    with milk and honey blest,
beneath thy contemplation
    sink heart and voice oppressed:
I know not, oh, I know not,
    what social joys are there;
what radiancy of glory,
    what bliss beyond compare!

They stand, those halls of Sion,
    conjubilant with song,
and bright with many an angel,
    and all the martyr throng;
the Prince is ever in them;
    the daylight is serene;
the pastures of the blessed
    are decked in glorious sheen.

There is the throne of David—
    and there, from care released,
the song of them that triumph,
    the shout of them that feast;
and they who, with their Leader,
    have conquered in the fight,
for ever and for ever
    are clad in robes of white.

O sweet and blessed country,
    shall I ever see thy face?
O sweet and blessed country,
    shall I ever win thy grace?
Exult, O dust and ashes,
    the Lord shall be thy part:
his only his for ever
    thou shalt be, and thou art.

Bernard of Cluny
De Contemptu Mundi, ca. 1140
translated, John Mason Neale
*The Rhythm of Bernard de Morlaix, Monk of Cluny,
on the Celestial Country*, 1858

In the introduction to the seventh edition, 1865, of his translation, Neale commended the use, with any of the various excerpts, of the following doxology produced by the editors of *Hymns Ancient and Modern*:

In mercy, Jesu, bring us
    to that dear land of rest
where thou art, with the Father
    and Spirit, ever blest.

In addition to its use with lines from Neale, this doxology is sometimes preceded by four other lines from the editors of *Hymns Ancient and Modern*, which resemble, but do not duplicate, Neale's translation.

O sweet and blessed country,
    the home of God's elect!
O sweet and blessed country
    that eager hearts expect!

163
Dulcis Jesu Memoria

A.

Dulcis Jesu memoria,
dans vera cordis gaudia:
sed super mel et omnia
dulcis eius praesentia.

Nil canitur suavius,
auditur nil iucundius,
nil cogitatur dulcius,
quam Jesus Dei Filius.

Jesu, spes paenitentibus,
quem pius es petentibus,
quam bonus te quaerentibus!
Sed quid invenientibus?

Nec lingua potest dicere,
nec littera exprimere;
expertus potest credere
quid sit Jesum diligere.

Tu esto nostrum gaudium,
qui es futurus praemium;
sit nostra in te gloria
per cuncta semper saecula.

Jesu, rex admirabilis
et triumphator nobilis,
dulcedo ineffabilis,
totus desiderabilis.

Quando cor nostrum visitas,
tunc lucet ei veritas,
mundi vilescit vanitas,
et intus fervet caritas.

Te nostra, Jesu, vox sonet,
nostri te mores exprimant,
te corda nostra diligant
et nunc et in perpetuum.

Mane nobiscum, Domine,
et nos illustra lumine;
pulsa mentis caligine,
mundum reple dulcedine.

Jesu, flos matris virginis,
favus mirae dulcedinis,
laus, honor tibi numinis,
regnum beatitudinis.

uncertainly attributed to Bernard of Clairvaux,
but perhaps by an anonymous English author
The common first line of this text is "Jesu dulcis memoria." *In various*
writings, Routley expressed a preference for the form given above.

B.

Jesu, the very thought of thee
    with sweetness fills my breast;
but sweeter far thy face to see,
    and in thy presence rest.

No voice can sing, no heart can frame,
    nor can the memory find
a sweeter sound than Jesus' name,
    the Savior of mankind.

O hope of every contrite heart,
    O joy of all the meek,
to those who ask, how kind thou art,
    how good to those who seek!

But what to those who find? Ah, this
    nor tongue nor pen can show;
the love of Jesus, what it is,
    none but his loved ones know.

Jesus, our only joy be thou,
    as thou our prize wilt be;
in thee be all our glory now
    and through eternity.

O Jesu, King most wonderful,
    thou Conqueror renowned,
thou sweetness most ineffable
    in whom all joys are found!

When once thou visitest the heart,
    then truth begins to shine,
then earthly vanities depart,
    then kindles love divine.

Thee, Jesu, may our voices bless,
    thee may we love alone,
and ever in our lives express
    the image of thine own.

Abide with us, and let thy light
    shine, Lord, on every heart,
dispel the darkness of our night,
    and joy to all impart.

Jesus, our love and joy, to thee,
    the Virgin's holy Son,
all might and praise and glory be
    while endless ages run.

translated, Edward Caswall
Lyra Catholica, 1849

C. Jesu Dulcedo Cordium

Jesu, dulcedo cordium.
fons vitae, lumen mentium,
excedis omne gaudium
et omne desiderium.

Jesu, spes paenitentibus,
quam pius es petentibus,
quam bonus te quaerentibus!
sed quid invenientibus?

Qui te gustant, esuriunt;
qui bibunt, adhuc sitiunt;
desiderare nesciunt
nisi Jesum quem cupiunt.

Quocunque loco fuero
mecum Jesum desidero,
quam laetus cum invenero,
quam felix cum tenuero!

Mane nobiscum, Domine,
nos tuo replens lumine;
pulse noctis caligine,
mundum reple dulcedine.

uncertainly attributed to Bernard of Clairvaux,
but perhaps by an anonymous English author

D.

Jesu! thou joy of loving hearts!
    thou fount of life, thou light of men!
from the best bliss that earth imparts
    we turn unfilled to thee again.

Thy truth unchanged hath ever stood,
    thou savest those that on thee call;
to them that seek thee, thou art good;
    to them that find thee, all in all.

We taste thee, O thou living Bread,
    and long to feast upon thee still;
we drink of thee, the Fountainhead,
    and thirst our souls from thee to fill.

Our restless spirits yearn for thee,
    where'er our changeful lot is cast,
glad when thy gracious smile we see,
    blest when our faith can hold thee fast.

O Jesus, ever with us stay,
    make all our moments calm and bright;
chase the dark nights of sin away,
    shed o'er the world thy holy light.

> paraphrased, Ray Palmer
> *The Sabbath Hymn Book*, 1858
> based on Latin stanzas appearing in Herman A. Daniel's
> *Thesaurus Hymnologicus*, 1841–1855
> This translation, using another selection from the forty-two stanzas of
> the original poem, comes from America. Although American
> hymnody is dealt with at a later stage, it seems reasonable to include it
> here. It is one of the best known and finest of American hymns.

164
Saint Thomas's Hymn of the Eucharist

A.

Pange, lingua, gloriosi
    corporis mysterium,
sanguinisque pretiosi
    quem in mundi pretium
fructus ventris generosi
    rex effudit gentium.

Nobis datus, nobis natus
    ex intacta virgine,
et in mundo conversatus,
    sparso verbi semine,
sui moras incolatus
    miro clausit ordine.

In supremae nocte coenae
    recumbens cum fratribus,
observata lege plene
    cibis in legalibus,
cibum turbae duodenae
    se dat suis manibus.

Verbum caro, panem verum
    verbo carnem efficit,
fitque sanguis Christi merum,
    et, si sensus deficit,
ad firmandum cor sincerum
    sola fides sufficit.

Tantum ergo sacramentum
    veneremur cernui,
et antiquum documentum
    novo cedat ritui;
praestet fides supplementum
    sensuum defectui.

Genitori Genitoque
    laus et iubilatio,
salus, honor, virtus quoque
    sit et benedictio;
procedenti ab utroque
    compar sit laudatio.

> Thomas Aquinas, ca. 1263

B.

Of the glorious body telling,
    O my tongue, the mysteries sing;
and the blood, all price excelling,
    which for this world's ransoming,
in a noble womb once dwelling,
    he shed forth, the Gentiles' King.

Given for us, for us descending
    of a Virgin to proceed,
Man with man in converse blending
    scattered he his gospel seed;
till his sojourn drew to ending,
    which he closed in wondrous deed.

At the last great supper seated,
    circled by his brethren's band,
all the law required, completed
    in the feast its statutes planned;
to the twelve himself he meted
    for their food with his own hand.

Word made flesh, by word he maketh
    very bread his flesh to be;
man in wine Christ's blood partaketh,
    and if senses fail to see,
faith alone the true heart waketh
    to behold the mystery.

Therefore we, before it bending,
    this great sacrament adore;
types and shadows have their ending
    in the new rite evermore;
faith, our outward sense amending,
    maketh good defects before.

Honor, laud, and praise addressing
    to the Father and the Son,
might ascribe we, virtue, blessing,
    and eternal benison;
Holy Ghost, from both progressing,
    equal laud to thee be done!

translated, John Mason Neale
Medieval Hymns and Sequences, 1851

"*Pange lingua*" is probably the densest and most difficult hymn ever written, a characteristic product of the most massive intellect of the Middle Ages. St. Thomas was invited to write this and two other hymns for the Feast of Corpus Christi by Pope Urban IV. In "*Pange lingua*," poetry embraces not only history, but also theology and liturgical belief. While St. Thomas, in faultless Latin, conveys with precision every overtone of his thought, we can forgive poor Neale for being defeated. He makes St. Thomas just about singable in English, but he has to bend his vocabulary and submit to obscurity to an extent which he usually avoids.

Stanza 1: The Incarnation and the Atonement are at once brought together in lines 5–6.

Stanza 2: Similarly, the earthly ministry (lines 3–4) is joined on to the Last Supper (lines 5–6) which is seen as its climax.

Stanza 3: Here the Last Supper is the center of attention; the reference to "the law" recalls the fact that (as St. Thomas believed and as most agree) the Last Supper was a Passover meal, prescribed by Jewish custom, here transformed. St. Thomas is, of course, not quite faithful to Scripture in implying that all twelve disciples were present.

Stanza 4: In line 1, Christ is The Word, and the second "word" in the line is that "word of institution" (as liturgists call it) which gave the new significance to the bread and the wine. Transubstantiation, which St. Thomas himself clarified as a doctrine, is here affirmed to be a process which faith alone can comprehend.

Stanza 5: It is the sacrament, in Catholic liturgy, which is revered; hence Neale's "it" where the hymnals often write "him." Hebrews 8 lies behind the "types and shadows" passage.

165
Adoro Te Devote

A.

Adoro te devote, latens deitas,
te qui sub his figuris vere latitas:
tibi se cor meum totum subjicit,
quia te contemplans totum deficit.

Visus, tactus, gustus in te fallitur,
sed auditu solo tuto creditur;   (Rom. 10:10, 17)
credo quidquid dixit Dei Filius,
nil hoc verbo veritatis verius.

In cruce latebat sola deitas,   (Matt. 27:40)
at hic latet simul et humanitas;
ambo tamen credens atque confitens,
peto quod petivit latro poenitens.   (Luke 23:42)

Plagas, sicut Thomas, non intueor,   (John 20:29)
Deum tamen meum te confiteor;   (John 20:28)
fac me tibi semper magis credere,
in te spem habere, te diligere.

O memoriale mortis Domini,
panis veram, vitam praestans homini,
praesta meae menti de te vivere
et te illi semper dulce sapere.   (Ps. 33:9)

Pie pelicane, Jesu Domine,
me immundum munda tuo sanguine,
cuius una stilla salvum facere
totum mundum posset omni scelere.

Jesu, quem velatum nunc aspicio,
oro fiat illud quod tam sitio;
ut te revelata cernens facie,
visu sim beatus tuae gloriae.

anonymous, first in a manuscript of 1323

The (incomplete) translation of this most used in church, "Thee we adore," is by J. R. Woodford, 1852, and it forms a satisfactory vehicle of public devotion, even if—possibly because—it steers carefully round the more inaccessible subtleties of the original. Since it has inspired two of England's greatest poets who would otherwise not appear in this collection, we give below the translation first of Crashaw, and then, in the original meter, of Gerard Manley Hopkins.

B.

With all the powers my poor soul hath
of humble love and loyal faith,
thus low, my God, I bow to thee,
whom too much love bowed lower for me.

Down, down, proud sense, discourses die,
and all adore faith's mystery!
Faith is my skill, faith can believe
as fast as love new laws can give.

Faith is my force, faith strength affords
to keep pace with those powerful words;
and words more sure, more sweet than they
love could not think, truth could not say.

O dear memorial of that death,
which still survives, and gives us breath,
live ever, bread of life, and be
my food, my joy, my all to me.

O soft-self-wounding Pelican!
whose breast weeps balm for wounded man,
that blood, whose least drops sovereign be
to wash my worlds of sin from me.

Come, glorious Lord, my hopes increase,
and fill my portion in thy peace;
come, hidden life, and that long day
for which I languish, come away;

when this dry soul those eyes shall see,
and drink the unsealed source of thee;
when glory's sun faith's shade shall chase,
then for thy veil give me thy face.

translated, Richard Crashaw
Steps to the Temple, 1646
altered by John Austin
Devotions in the Antient Way of Offices, 1668
The final two stanzas translate stanza 7 of the original.

C.

Godhead here in hiding, whom I do adore
masked by these bare shadows, shape and nothing
                      more,
see, Lord, at thy service low lies here a heart
lost, all lost in wonder at the God thou art.

Seeing, touching, tasting are in thee deceived;
how says trusty hearing? That shall be believed;
what God's Son hath told me, take for truth I do;
truth himself speaks truly, or there's nothing true.

On the cross thy Godhead made no sign to men;
here thy very manhood steals from human ken;
both are my confession, both are my belief,
and I pray the prayer of the dying thief.

I am not like Thomas, wounds I cannot see,
but can plainly call thee Lord and God as he;
this faith each day deeper be my holding of,
daily make me harder hope and dearer love.

O thou our reminder of Christ crucified,
living Bread, the life of us for whom he died,
lend this life to me then; feed and feast my mind,
there be thou, the sweetness man was meant to find.

Bring the tender tale true of the Pelican;
bathe me, Jesus Lord, in what thy bosom ran—
blood that but one drop of has the power to win
all the world forgiveness of its world of sin.

Jesus whom I look at shrouded here below,
I beseech thee send me what I thirst for so,
some day to gaze on thee face to face in light
and be blest for ever with thy glory's light.

> translated, Gerard Manley Hopkins
> *Collected Poems*, 1918

166
Stabat Mater

The Latin hymn is a prayer to the Virgin; in Anglican use it was so
translated as to keep clear of that worship of the Virgin which some
felt unable to accept. The following translation is that used in *The
English Hymnal*, which contains elements from the earlier work of one
Anglican and one Roman Catholic translator.

A.

Stabat Mater dolorosa
iuxta crucem lacrimosa,
    dum pendebat Filius;
cuius animam gementem,
contristantem et dolentem,
    pertransivit gladius.   (Luke 2:35)

O quam tristis et afflicta
fuit illa benedicta
    Mater unigeniti!
Quae maerebat et dolebat,
pia Mater, dum videbat
    nati poenas inclyti!

Quis est homo qui non fleret,
Matrem Christi si videret
    in tanto supplicio?
Quis non posset contristari,
Christi Matrem contemplari
    dolentem cum Filio?

Pro peccatis suae gentis
vidit Jesum in tormentis,
    et flagellis subditum.
Vidit suum dulcem natum
morientem desolatum
    dum emisit spiritum.

Eia Mater, fons amoris,
me sentire vim doloris
    fac, ut tecum lugeam.
Fac ut ardeat cor meum
in amando Christum Deum
    ut sibi complaceam.

Sancta Mater, istud agas,
crucifixi fige plagas
    cordi meo valide.
Tui nati vulnerati,
tam dignati pro me pati,
    poenas mecum divide.

Fac me tecum pie flere,
crucifixo condolere,
    donec ego vixero;
juxta crucem tecum stare,
et me tibi sociare
    in planctu desidero.

Virgo virginum praeclara
mihi iam non sis amara,
    fac me tecum plangere.
Fac ut portem Christi mortem,
passionis fac consortem
    et plagas recolere.

Fac me plagis vulnerari,
fac me cruce inebriari
    et cruore Filii.
Flammis ne urar succensus,
per te, Virgo, sim defensus
    in die iudicii.

Christe, cum sit hinc exire,
da per Matrem me venire
    ad palmam victoriae.
Quando corpus morietur,
fac ut animae donetur
    paradisi gloria.

attributed to Jacopone of Todi

B.

At the cross her station keeping
stood the mournful Mother weeping,
    close to Jesus at the last,
through her soul, of joy bereaved,
bowed with anguish, deeply grieved,
    now at length the sword hath passed.   (Luke 2:35)

O that blessed one, grief-laden,
blessed Mother, blessed Maiden,
    Mother of th' all-holy One;
O that silent, ceaseless mourning,
O those dim eyes, never turning
    from that wondrous, suffering Son.

Who on Christ's dear Mother gazing,
in her trouble so amazing,
    born of woman, would not weep?
Who on Christ's dear Mother thinking,
such a cup of sorrow drinking,
    would not share her sorrow deep?

For his people's sins, in anguish,
there she saw the Victim languish,
    bleed in torments, bleed and die;
saw the Lord's anointed taken;
saw her Child in death forsaken;
    heard his last expiring cry.

In the passion of my Maker
be my sinful soul partaker,
    may I bear with her my part;
of his passion bear the token,
in a spirit bowed and broken
    bear his death within my heart.

May his wounds both wound and heal me,
he enkindle, cleanse, anneal me,
    be his cross my hope and stay.
May he, when the mountains quiver,
from that flame which burns for ever
    shield me on the judgment day.

Jesu, may thy cross defend me,
and thy saving death befriend me,
    cherished by thy deathless grace;
when to dust my soul returneth
grant a soul that to thee yearneth
    in thy paradise a place.

composite translation: Richard Mant, 1837; Aubrey de Vere, 1884;
and the compilers of *The English Hymnal*, 1906.
A translation was made by Edward Caswall in 1849,
in the meter 77.7.77.7.

167

The Length, the Breadth, the Height

A.

O amor quam ecstaticus!
quam effluens, quam nimius!
qui Deum Dei Filium
unum fecit mortalium!

Non invisit nos angelo,
seu supremo seu infimo,
carnis assumens pallium
venit ad nos per se ipsum.

Nobis baptisma suscipit,
nobis jejunans esurit,
nobis et Satan hunc tentat,
nobis tentantem superat.

Nobis orat et praedicat,
pro nobis cuncta factitat,
verbis, signis et actibus
nos quaerens, non se, penitus.

Pro nobis comprehenditur,
flagellatur, conspuitur,
crucis perfert patibulum,
pro nobis tradit spiritum.

Nobis surgit a mortuis,
nobis se transfert superis,
nobis suum dat Spiritum,
in robur, in solatium.

Deo Patri sit gloria
per infinita saecula,
cuius amore nimio
salvu sumus in Filio.

Thomas of Kempen (Thomas à Kempis)

B.

O Love, how deep, how broad, how high,
it fills the heart with ecstasy,
that God, the Son of God, should take
our mortal form for mortals' sake.

He sent no angel to our race
of higher or of lower place,
but wore the robe of human frame
himself, and to this lost world came.

For us he was baptized, and bore
his holy fast, and hungered sore;
for us temptation sharp he knew,
for us the tempter overthrew.

For us he prayed, for us he taught,
for us his daily works he wrought,
by words and signs and actions thus
still seeking not himself, but us.

For us to wicked men betrayed,
scourged, mocked, in purple robe arrayed,
he bore the shameful cross and death,
for us at length gave up his breath.

For us he rose from death again;
for us he went on high to reign;
for us he sent his Spirit here
to guide, to comfort, and to cheer.

To him whose boundless love has won
salvation for us through his Son,
to God the Father, glory be
both now and through eternity.

translated, Benjamin Webb
The Hymnal Noted, 1854

Later Latin Lyrics

168
Ye Sons and Daughters

A.

Alleluia! Alleuia! Alleluia!

O filii et filiae,
rex caelestis, rex gloriae,
morte revixit hodie.

Et Maria Magdalene   (Mark 16:1)
et Jacobi et Salome
venerunt corpus ungere.

In albis sedens angelus   (Mark 16:7)
praedixit mulieribus,
"In Galilaea est Dominus."

Discipulis adstantibus   (John 20:19)
in medio stetit Christus,
dicens, "Pax vobis omnibus."

Postquam audivit Didymus   (John 20: 24)
quia surrexerat Jesus,
remansit fide dubius.

"Vide, Thoma, vide latus,   (John 20:27)
vide pedes, vide manus;
noli esse incredulus."

Quando Thomas vidit Christum,
pedes, latus suum, manus,
dixit, "Tu es Deus meus."

Beati, qui non viderunt   (John 20:29)
et firmiter crediderunt;
vitam aeternam habebunt.

In hoc festo sanctissimo
sit laus et iubilatio;
benedicamus Domino.

Jean Tisserand

B.

Alleluia! Alleuia! Alleluia!

O sons and daughters, let us sing!
the King of heaven, the glorious King
o'er death today rose triumphing.

That Easter morn, at break of day
the faithful women went their way
to seek the tomb where Jesus lay.

An angel clad in white they see,
who sat, and spake unto the three,
"Your Lord doth go to Galilee."

That night th' apostles met in fear;
amidst them came their Lord most dear,
and said, "My peace be on all here."

When Thomas first the tidings heard,
how they had seen the risen Lord,
he doubted the disciples' word.

"My pierced side, O Thomas, see;
my hands, my feet, I show to thee;
not faithless, but believing be."

No longer Thomas then denied;
he saw the feet, the hands, the side;
"Thou art my Lord and God," he cried.

How blest are they who have not seen,
and yet whose faith hath constant been,
for they eternal life shall win.

On this most holy day of days,
to God your hearts and voices raise
in laud and jubilee and praise.

translated, John Mason Neale
Medieval Hymns and Sequences, 1851
as altered for *Hymns Ancient and Modern*, 1861

169
Food for Travelers

A.

O esca viatorum,
o panis angelorum,
        o manna caelitum,
esurientes ciba,
dulcedine non priva
        cor te quaerentium.

O lympha, fons amoris,
qui puro salvatoris
        e corde profluis,
te sitientes pota;
haec sola nostra vota;
        his una sufficis.

O Jesu, tuum vultum
quem colimus occultum
        sub panis specie,
fac ut remoto velo
aperta nos in caelo
        cernamus acie.

anonymous, ca. 1661

B.

O food of men wayfaring,
the bread of angels sharing,
        O manna from on high!
We hunger; Lord, supply us,
nor thy delights deny us,
        whose hearts to thee draw nigh.

O stream of love past telling,
O purest fountain, welling
        from out the Savior's side!
We faint with thirst, revive us,
of thine abundance give us,
        and all we need provide.

O Jesu, by thee bidden,
we here adore thee, hidden
        'neath forms of bread and wine.
Grant, when the veil is riven,
we may behold, in heaven,
thy countenance divine.

translated, Athelstan Riley
The English Hymnal, 1906

C.

O bread to pilgrims given,
        O food that angels eat,
O manna sent from heaven
        for heaven-born natures meet;
give us, for thee long pining,
        to eat till richly filled;
till, earth's delights resigning,
        our every wish is stilled.

O fountain, purely flowing
        forth from that sacred heart,
our Savior's grace bestowing,
        true wine of life thou art.
O let us, freely tasting
        our spirit's thirst assuage;
thy goodness, never wasting,
        avails from age to age.

Jesus, this feast receiving,
        we thee unseen adore;
thy faithful word believing,
        we take, and doubt no more;
give us, thou true and loving,
        on earth to live in thee;
then, death the veil removing,
        thy glorious face to see.

translated, Ray Palmer
The Sabbath Hymn Book, 1858
stanza 2 altered as in *Hymns for Celebration*, 1974
stanza 2 © 1974, Royal School of Church Music
(admin. GIA Publications, Inc.)

170
The Power of the Word

A.

Supreme quales, arbiter
tibi ministros eligis,
tuas opes qui vilibus
vasis amas committere!   (2 Cor. 4:7)

Haec nempe plena lumine
tu vase frangi praecipis;
lux inde magna rumpitur,
ceu nube scissa fulgura.

Totum per orbem nuntii
nubes velut citi colant;
verbo graves, Verbo Deo,
tonant, coruscant, perpluunt.

Christum sonant: versae ruunt
arces superbae daemonum;
circum tubis clangentibus   (Josh. 6:20)
sic versa quondam moenis.

Fac, Christe, caelestes tubae
somno graves nos excitent;
accensa de te lumina
pellant tenebras mentium.

Uni sit et trino Deo
supreme laus, summum decus,
de nocte qui nos ad suae
lumen vocavit gloriae.   (1 Pet. 2:9)

Jean Baptiste de Santeüil
Cluniac *Breviary*, 1686

B.

Disposer supreme, and Judge of the earth
    who choosest for thine the meek and the poor;
to frail earthen vessels, and things of no worth,
    entrusting thy riches which aye shall endure;

those vessels soon fail, though full of thy light,
    and at thy decree are broken and gone;
thence brightly appeareth thy truth in its might
    as through the clouds riven the lightnings have
                                           shone.

Like clouds are they borne to do thy great will,
    and swift as the winds about the world go;
the Word with his wisdom their spirits doth fill;
    they thunder, they lighten, their waters o'erfiow.

Their sound goeth forth, "Christ Jesus the Lord!"
    then Satan doth fear, his citadels fall;
as when the dread trumpets went forth at thy word,
    and one long blast shattered the Canaanite's
                                           wall.

O loud be their trump, and stirring their sound,
    to rouse us, O Lord, from slumber of sin!
The lights thou hast kindled in darkness around,
    O may they awaken our spirits within!

All honor and praise, dominion and might,
    to God, Three in One, eternally be,
who round us hath shed his own marvelous light
    and called us from darkness his glory to see.

translated, Isaac Williams
The British Magazine, 1836

171
Veiled in Flesh

A.

Divine crescebas puer;
crescendo discebas mori;
haec destinata tune erant
mortis tuae praeludia.

Satus Deo, volens tegi,
elegit obscurum patrem;
qui fecit aeternas domos
domo latet sub paupere.

Caelum menus quae sustinent
fabrile contrectant opus;
supremus astrorum parens
fit ipse vilis artifex.

Tremenda cuius praepetes
mandata portant spiritus,
cui pronus orbis subditur,
se sponte fabro subicut.

Qui natus es de virgine,
Jesu, tibi sit gloria
cum Patre cumque Spiritu
in sempiterna saecula.

Jean Baptiste de Santeüil
Hymni sacri et novi, 1689

B.

In stature grows the heavenly child,
    with death before his eyes;
a Lamb unblemished, meek and mild,
    prepared for sacrifice.

The Son of God his glory hides
    with parents mean and poor;
and he who made the heaven abides
    in dwelling-place obscure.

Those mighty hands that stay the sky
    no earthly toil refuse;
and he who set the stars on high
    an humble trade pursues.

He before whom the angels stand,
    at whose behest they fly,
now yields himself to man's command,
    and lays his glory by.

Jesu, the Virgin's holy Son,
    we praise thee and adore,
who art with God the Father One
    and Spirit evermore.

translated, John Chandler
Hymns of the Primitive Church, 1837

172
Veni Emmanuel

A.

Veni, veni Emmanuel;
captivum solve Israel,
qui gemit in exilio,
privatus Dei Filio.

    Gaude, gaude, Emmanuel
    nascetur pro te, Israel.

Veni, o Jesse Virgula;
ex hostis tuos ungula,
de specu tuos tartari
educ et antro barathri.

Veni, veni, o Oriens;
solare nos adveniens;
noctis depelle nebulas
dirasque noctis tenebras.

Veni, Clavis Davidica,
regna reclude caelica;
fac iter tutum superum,
at claude vias inferum.

Veni, veni, Adonai,
quo populo in Sinai
legem dedisti vertice
in maiestate gloriae.

anonymous
Psalteriolum Cantionum Catholicarum, 1710

B.

O come, O come, Emmanuel (Isa. 7:14)
and ransom captive Israel
that mourns in lonely exile here
until the Son of God appear.

        Rejoice Rejoice! Emmanuel
        shall come to thee, O Israel.

O come, thou Rod of Jesse, free (Isa. 11:1)
thine own from Satan's tyranny;
from depths of hell thy people save
and give them victory o'er the grave.

O come, thou Dayspring, come and cheer (Luke 1:78)
our spirits by thine advent here;
disperse the gloomy clouds of night
and death's dark shadows put to flight.

O come, thou Key of David, come, (Isa. 22:22)
and open wide our heavenly home; (Rev. 3:7)
make safe the way that leads on high,
and close the path to misery.

O come, O come, thou Lord of might, (Exod. 20)
who to thy tribes on Sinai's height
in ancient times didst give the law
in cloud and majesty and awe.

        translated, John Mason Neale
        The Hymnal Noted, 1851
        as altered for *Hymns Ancient and Modern*, 1861

173
God from on High Hath Heard

A.

Iam desinant suspiria;
audivit ex alto Deus:
caeli patescunt; en adest
promissa pax mortalibus.

Profunda noctis otia
caelestis abrumpit chorus,
natumque festo carmine
annuntiat ferris Deum.

Specum sacratum pervigil
dum turba pastorum subit,
eamus et castis pia
cunis feramus oscula.

At qualis nobis panditur
instantibus spectaculum
praesepe, faenum, fasciae,
parens inops, infans puer.

Tunc ille, Christe, Filius
et splendor aeterni Patris?
Illumne cerno, qui levi
orbem pugillo sustinet?

Sic est; verenda, quies lates,
fides penetrat nubila;
agnosco quem proni vident
tremunt, adorant angeli.

Agis magistrum vel tacens;
ex hac cathedra nos doces
vitare quod carni placet,
caro quod horret perpeti.

Castos amores nutriens,
sanans tumentes spiritus,
divine nostris O puer
praecordiis innascere.

Charles Coffin
Paris Breviary, 1736

B.

God from on high hath heard!
    let sighs and sorrows cease;
the skies unfold, and lo!
    descends the gift of peace!

Hark on the midnight air
    celestial voices swell;
the hosts of heaven proclaim
    "God comes on earth to dwell."

Haste with the shepherds; see
    the mystery of grace;
a manger-bed, a child
    is all the eye can trace.

Is this the eternal Son
    who on the starry throne
before the world began
    was with the Father one?

Yes, faith can pierce the cloud
    which shrouds his glory now;
and hail him Lord and God
    to whom all creatures bow.

Faith sees the sapphire throne
    where angels evermore
adoring, tremble still,
    and trembling still, adore.

O Child! thy silence speaks
    and bids us not refuse
to bear what flesh would shun,
    to spurn what flesh would choose.

Fill us with holy love,
    heal thou our earthly pride;
be born within our hearts,
    and ever there abide.

translated, James Russell Woodford
Hymns Arranged for Sundays, 1852

174
A Christian Community

A.

O quam iuvat fratres, Deus,
unum quibus Christus caput
vitale robur sufficit,
uno moveri spiritu.

Quam dulce laudes dicere
una tibi cunctos domo,
precumque ceu facta manu,
inferre vim gratam tibi.

Hanc quisque diligat domum,
hanc pace concors recreet;
vae dire qui spargit malus
dissensionum semina.

Sed damna cedunt in lucrum
te, Christe, diligentibus;
augent coronas praelia;
prosuntque, dum nocent, mali.

Vox blanda saevit tristius,
dum pectus incautum subit,
lapusque caeco dulcibus
laudum venenis inficit.

Praesta, beata Trinitas,
ut caritate mutua
prosimus alter alteri,
regnemus at polo simul.

Charles Coffin
Paris Breviary, 1736

B.

Christ is our head, our strength, our life,
    our only and sufficient good;
then, Lord, let unity inspire
    and aid our common brotherhood.

Melodious let our mingled praise
    from this fair house to thee ascend;
and our petitions, strong as deeds,
    in thine approving presence blend.

Let here tranquility abound,
    as all in loving concord strive;
no bitter seed of enmity
    unto a baleful harvest thrive.

Yet unto those who love thee, Lord,
    all things together work for good;
from injuries we gain a spur,
    a crown by agony and blood.

More grievous is the cruel tongue
    that flatters with envenomed art—
with honeyed insincerity
    corrupts the blind and heedless heart.

Here then, O Trinity most blest,
    the humble grace to each be given
to love his neighbor as himself,
    till thou enthrone us all in heaven.

translated, Leslie H. Bunn
French Diocesan Hymns, 1954

175
O Come, All Ye Faithful

A.

Adeste fideles,
laeti triumphantes,
venite, venite in Bethlehem;
natum videte
regem angelorum.

Venite, adoremus Dominum.

Deum de Deo,
lumen de lumine,
gestant puellae viscera;
Deum verum,
genitum, non factum.

En grege relicto
humiles ad cunas
vocati pastores approperant;
et nos ovanti
gradu festinemus.

Stella duce Magi
Christum adorantes
aurum thus et myrrham dant munera.
Jesu infanti
corda praebeamus.

Aeterni parentis
splendorem aeternum
velatum sub carne videbimus;
Deum infantem
pannis involutum.

Pro nobis egenum
et foeno cubantem,
piis foveamus amplexibus;
sic nos amantem
quis non redamaret?

Cantet nunc "Io"
chorus angelorum;
cantet nunc aula coelestium.
Gloria
in excelsis Deo!

Ergo qui natus
die hodierna,
Jesu, tibi sit gloria;
Patris aeterni
verbum caro factum!

stanzas 1, 2, 7, and 8, John Francis Wade, 1743
stanzas 3, 5, and 6, Etienne Jean-François Borderies, 1793
Office de St. Omer, 1822
stanza 4, anonymous
Paroissien Romain, 1868

B.

O come, all ye faithful,
joyful and triumphant,
O come ye, O come ye to Bethlehem;
come and behold him
born the King of angels:

      O come, let us adore him, Christ the Lord.

God of God,
Light of light,
Lo! he abhors not the Virgin's womb;
Very God
begotten, not created.

See how the shepherds,
summoned to his cradle,
leaving their flocks, draw nigh with lowly fear;
we too will thither
bend our joyful footsteps.

Lo, star-led chieftains,
magi, Christ adoring,
offer him incense, gold, and myrrh;
we to the Christ-Child
bring our hearts' oblations:

The splendor eternal
of eternal Godhead
veiled with infirmities of flesh we see;
hiding his glory,
swaddling clothes he weareth:

Child, for us sinners,
poor and in the manger,
fain we embrace thee with awe and love;
who would not love thee,
loving us so dearly?

Sing, choirs of angels,
sing in exultation,
sing, all ye citizens of heaven above:
"Glory to God
in the highest!"

Yea, Lord, we greet thee,
born this happy morning,
Jesu, to thee be glory given;
Word of the Father
now in flesh appearing.

stanzas 1, 2, 7, and 8 translated, Frederick Oakeley, 1841
The Hymnal for Use in the English Church, 1852
altered for *Hymns Ancient and Modern,* 1861
stanzas 3, 4, and 6 translated, Percy Dearmer
The English Hymnal, 1906
stanza 5 translated, Ronald A. Knox
The Westminster Hymnal, 1940
stanza 5 © Continuum International Publishing Group, Ltd.

176
The Heart of Jesus

A.

Summi parentis Filio,
patri futuri saeculi,
pacis beatae principi,
promamus ore canticum.

Qui vulneratus pectore
amoris ictum pertulit,
amoris urens ignibus
ipsum qui amantem diligunt.

Jesu, doloris victima,
quis te innocentem compulit
dura ut apertum lancea
latus pateret vulneri?

O fons amoris inclyte,
o vena aquarum limpida,
a flamma adurens crimina,
o cordis ardens caritas!

In corde, Jesu, iugiter
reconde nos, et uberi
dono fruamur gratiae
caelique tandem praemiis.

anonymous
Roman Breviary (Lisbon), 1736

B.

To Christ, the Prince of Peace,
and Son of God most high,
the Father of the world to come,
we lift our joyful cry.

Deep in his heart for us
the wound of love he bore,
that love which he enkindles still
in hearts that him adore.

O Jesu, Victim blest,
what else but love divine
could thee constrain to open thus
that sacred heart of thine?

O wondrous fount of love,
O well of waters free,
O heavenly flame, refining fire,
O burning charity!

Hide us in thy dear heart,
Jesu, our Savior blest,
so shall we find thy plenteous grace
and heaven's eternal rest!

translated, Edward Caswall
Lyra Catholica, 1849
altered for *Hymns Ancient and Modern,* 1861

Chapter 12:
Hymns from Greek Sources (177–187)

The hymnody of the Greek-speaking church has contributed less to Western hymnody than that of the Latin church for reasons which, after reading chapter 11, will be obvious. Greek hymnody took forms quite different from the Latin and was used for quite different purposes. The short selection we here give shows how diverse those forms and purposes were.

The "Lamplighting Hymn" (177) was already well known in about A.D. 365, when St. Basil mentions it as a familiar hymn. It certainly goes back into the days when Christians worshiped "underground" (literally so when they were in the catacombs), and when "light" had a special significance for people whose only safe place of worship was in the dark. It is also just about the first Greek hymn to find an English translation. John Keble (see chapter 9) made a version of it in what approximates to the original meter. His translation is slightly obscure here and there, and we add a second which is more literal and was made for a modern recension of the original Greek melody. Robert Bridges also translated it metrically, to go with the Genevan tune for the "Nunc dimittis" in his Yattendon Hymnal; this, "O gladsome Light," appears in many current hymnals.

We may suppose that there were plenty of hymns before this one. The New English Bible translation of Ephesians 5:13–14 makes it quite clear that the quotation "Awake thou that sleepest" is presumed by those translators to be from a hymn. Many other passages in the Epistles and Revelation are thought similarly to be fragments of hymns.

But nothing that one can call organized hymnody appeared until the seventh century at earliest. The period 700–900 saw the writing and singing of massive festal songs known as Canons and Contakions consisting of long odes with florid music, mostly referring to the Resurrection, and especially associated with Easter. Our 178 and 179 come from two of these. The originals are in wayward meters which cannot be reproduced for English singing, so John Mason Neale took his own line about meter, and, as always when he allowed himself to do that, produced translations which run beautifully and catch the festive spirit of the originals.

Other English hymns have been made out of Greek prayers: liturgical, like 180–182, or private, like 183–185. We owe most of these to Oxford Movement translators who valued the originals for their liturgical and devotional messages, and certainly in 180–182 we have a trio of magnificent liturgical hymns. The translations by the Scottish minister John Brownlie are also very valuable, 184 and 185 being particularly good, and also "O King, enthroned on high" (The English Hymnal, 454). The original of 184 is a poem by one of the outstanding Christian Greek poets; that of 185 is now unascertainable.

Neale's delicious carol "A great and mighty wonder" (186) was written in this meter because he tended to use it when he was free to choose; the arrangement with a refrain made out of stanza 3, for the SPOTLESS ROSE tune, was a happy inspiration of the editors of The English Hymnal.

Of 187, and one or two others, including "Art thou weary," Neale wrote that since they bore no closer relation to a Greek original than having been suggested by a single phrase, they ought to be regarded as hymns mostly of his own invention. This, in his favorite meter again, is a particularly pleasant one.

We provide a literal translation of the Greek originals, where it is appropriate, to compare with the versification that follows.

177

At the Lighting of the Lamps: Phos Hilaron

A.

Hail, gladdening light, of his pure glory poured
who is the immortal Father, heavenly, blest;
Holiest of holies, Jesus Christ our Lord!

Now we are come to the sun's hour of rest,
the lights of evening round us shine,
we hymn the Father, Son, and Holy Spirit divine.

Worthiest art thou at all times to be sung with
                              undefiled tongue,
Son of our God, giver of life, alone:
therefore in all the world thy glories, Lord, they own.

> translated, John Keble
> *The British Magazine*, 1834
> This, the earliest English translation,
> follows the line-scheme of the Greek.

B.

Christ, gladdening light of holy glory,
glory of God, heavenly Father immortal,
the holy blessed one, our Lord Jesus Christ:

we come now to the peaceful hour of sunset;
we see the star of evening shine;
we sing to the Father, the Son, and the Holy Spirit,
                                    one God.

You are worthy at all times to be praised
and honored with pure and pious songs,
God's only Son, our only life-giver:
wherefore all the world gives glory to you, its Master.

> translated, Erik Routley, ca. 1972
> *Christian Hymns Observed*, 1982
> © 1990, Hope Publishing Company
> The translation follows the meter of the Greek
> as set to the original tune.

C.

O gladsome light, O grace
of God the Father's face,
the eternal splendor wearing:
celestial, holy, blest,
our Savior, Jesus Christ,
joyful in thine appearing;

now ere day fadeth quite
we see the evening light,
our wonted hymn outpouring;
Father of might unknown,
thee, his incarnate Son
and Holy Spirit adoring.

To thee of right belongs
all praise of holy songs,
O Son of God, Lifegiver;
thee therefore, O most high,
the world doth glorify
and shall exalt for ever.

> translated, Robert Bridges
> *The Yattendon Hymnal*, 1899
> This translation was designed to match the
> Genevan tune for the *"Nunc dimittis."*

178
Easter Hymn

A.

All peoples: let us sing praise to him who has delivered Israel from Pharaoh's bitter bondage, and who has led him through the depths of the sea dry-shod, by a way of victory, to his glory.

Today is the spring of souls, for Christ, like the sun shining after a dark winter, has shone out again after three days, driving away the winter of our sin; we sing praise to him, to his glory.

On this royal light-bringing day of days, the gift-bearing Queen of seasons brings joy to the chosen people of the church, ceaselessly praising the risen Christ.

Neither the gates of death, nor the seals on the tomb, nor the keys of its doors, held you back, O Christ; but risen, Master, you gave your peace to your friends, a gift which exceeds all understanding.

> John of Damascus
> translated, Erik Routley

B.

Come, ye faithful, raise the strain
    of triumphant gladness!
God has brought us, Israel,
    into joy from sadness:
loosed from Pharaoh's bitter yoke
    Jacob's sons and daughters,
led them with unmoistened foot
    through the Red Sea waters.

'Tis the spring of souls today:
    Christ hath burst his prison;
and from three days' sleep in death
    as a sun hath risen.
All the winter of our sins,
    long and dark, is flying
from his light, to whom we give
    laud and praise undying.

Now the queen of seasons bright
    with the day of splendor,
with the royal feast of feasts,
    comes its joy to render:
comes to glad Jerusalem,
    who with true affection
welcomes, in unwearied strains
    Jesus' resurrection.

Neither might the gates of death,
    nor the tomb's dark portal
nor the watchers, nor the seal
    hold these as a mortal;
but today amidst thy friends
    thou didst stand, bestowing
that thy peace, which evermore
    passeth human knowing.

> translated, John Mason Neale
> *Hymns of the Eastern Church*, 1862
> Neale's original of line 4:5 read "but today amidst the twelve."

179
The Day of Resurrection

A.

    A day of resurrection! People, proudly tell of it. A Passover, a Passover of the Lord! For Christ, who is God, has brought us over from death to life, from earth to heaven, and we are singing songs of victory.

    Let us purify our affections, as we prepare to see the risen Christ flashing in the unapproachable light of his resurrection, and as we prepare to hear him clearly saying, "Greeting to you!" so we sing songs of victory.

    Let the heavens be duly joyful; let the earth exult; let the universe, visible and invisible, keep festival; for Christ our eternal joy is risen.

> John of Damascus
> translated, Erik Routley

B.

The day of Resurrection!
    Earth! tell it out abroad!
The Passover of gladness!
    the Passover of God!
From death to life eternal,
    from this world to the sky,
our Christ hath brought us over
    with hymns of victory.

Our hearts be pure from evil,
    that we may see aright
the Lord in rays eternal
    of resurrection-light:
and, listening to his accents,
    may hear so calm and plain
his own "All hail!" and hearing
    may raise the victor strain!

Now let the heavens be joyful!
    let earth her song begin!
Let the round earth keep triumph,
    and all that is therein:
Invisible and visible,
    their notes let all things blend—
for Christ the Lord hath risen—
    our joy that hath no end.

translated, John Mason Neale
Hymns of the Eastern Church, 1862
altered as in *Parish Hymn Book,* 1863
Neale's opening line was "'Tis the day of Resurrection."

180
Let All the Earth Keep Silence before Him

Let all mortal flesh keep silence,
    and with fear and trembling stand;
ponder nothing earthly-minded,
    for with blessing in his hand
Christ our God to earth descendeth,
    our full homage to demand.

King of kings, yet born of Mary,
    as of old on earth he stood,
Lord of lords, in human vesture—
    in the body and the blood—
he will give to all the faithful
    his own self for heavenly food.

Rank on rank the host of heaven
    spreads its vanguard on the way,
as the Light of Light descendeth
    from the realms of endless day,
that the powers of hell may vanish
    as the darkness clears away.

At his feet the six-winged seraph:
    Cherubim with sleepless eye,
veil their faces to the Presence,
    as with ceaseless voice they cry,
"Alleluia! Alleluia! Alleluia!
    Lord most high."

from the prayer at the opening of the Eucharist in the Liturgy of St.
James, found in both Greek and Syriac in the mid–fourth century
translated, Gerard Moultrie
Lyra Eucharistica, 1864

181
After Communion

Strengthen for service, Lord, the hands
    that holy things have taken;
let ears that now have heard thy songs
    to clamor never waken.

Lord, may the tongues which "Holy" sang
    keep free from all deceiving;
the eyes which saw thy love be bright,
    thy blessed hope perceiving.

The feet that tread thy holy courts
    from light do thou not banish;
the bodies by thy body fed
    with thy new life replenish.

Pearcy Dearmer
The English Hymnal, 1906
based on Charles Williams Humphrey's versification
of a prose translation by John Mason Neale
original in Syriac, from a closing prayer at the Eucharist in the
liturgy of Malabar, observed in the fifth century in the
Nestorian Church of South India.

182
From Glory to Glory

A.

Making the journey from glory to glory, we sing praise to you, the Savior of our souls. Glory to the Father, and to the Son, and to the Holy Spirit, now and always to ages of ages. We praise you, Savior of our souls.

Making the journey from strength to strength, completing all our service in your temple, we now pray you, Lord our God, to count us worthy of your utter love for mankind; make straight our journey; plant us firmly in the fear of you, and deem us worthy of the heavenly Kingdom, in Christ Jesus our Lord, with whom you are to be praised, and with the all-holy, righteous, and life-giving Spirit, now and always, to ages of ages.

> from the closing prayer at the Eucharist in the Liturgy of St. James,
> fourth century
> translated, Erik Routley

B.

From glory to glory advancing, we praise thee, O
       Lord;
thy name with the Father and Spirit be ever adored.

From strength unto strength we go forward on Sion's
       highway,
to appear before God in the city of infinite day.

Thanksgiving and glory and worship, and blessing
       and love
one heart and one song have the saints upon earth
       and above.

Evermore, O Lord, to thy servants thy presence be
       nigh;
ever fit us by service on earth for thy service on high.

> translated, Charles William Humphreys
> *The English Hymnal*, 1906

183
The Prayer of Bishop Synesius

A.

Christ, Son of the most high God, remember your servant, a man of sinful heart, who writes this; send deliverance from sorrows and griefs to my soul, born in sin; Jesus, Savior, grant me to see your divine radiance, so that having seen, I may sing a song, praises in my soul, praises in my body, to the Father with the great Holy Spirit.

> Synesius of Cyrene
> translated, Erik Routley

B.

Lord Jesus, think on me,
 and purge away my sin;
from earthborn passions set me free,
 and make me pure within.

Lord Jesus, think on me,
 with care and woe oppressed;
let me thy loving servant be,
 and taste thy promised rest.

Lord Jesus, think on me,
 amid the battle's strife;
in all my pain and misery
 be thou my health and life.

Lord Jesus, think on me,
 nor let me go astray;
through darkness and perplexity
 point thou my heavenly way.

Lord Jesus, think on me,
 when flows the tempest high;
when on doth rush the enemy,
 O Savior, be thou nigh.

Lord Jesus, think on me,
that, when the flood is past,
I may th' eternal brightness see,
and share thy joy at last.

translated, Allen William Chatfield
Songs and Hymns of Earliest Greek Christian Poets, 1876

184
Prayer for Purity

O Light that knew no dawn,
that shines to endless day,
all things in earth and heaven
are lustered by thy ray;
no eye can to thy throne ascend,
nor mind thy brightness comprehend.

Thy grace, O Father, give,
that I may serve with fear.
above all boon, I pray,
grant me thy voice to hear;
from sin thy child in mercy free
and let me dwell in light with thee;

that, cleansed from stain of sin,
I may meet homage give,
and, pure in heart, behold   (Matt. 5:3)
thy beauty while I live;
clean hands in holy worship raise   (Ps. 26:6)
and thee, O Christ my Savior, praise.

In supplication meek
to thee I bend the knee;
O Christ, when thou shalt come   (Luke 23:42)
in love remember me,
and in thy kingdom, by thy grace
grant me a humble servant's place.

Thy grace, O Father, give,
I humbly thee implore,
and let thy mercy bless
thy servant more and more.
All grace and glory be to thee
from age to age eternally.

Gregory of Nazianzus
translated, John Brownlie
Hymns of the Early Church, 1900

185
The King in His Beauty

The King shall come when morning dawns
and light triumphant breaks,
when beauty gilds the eastern hills
and life to joy awakes.

Not as of old a little child
to bear and fight and die,
but crowned with glory, like the sun
that lights the morning sky.

O brighter than the rising morn
when he, victorious, rose,
and left the lonesome place of death
despite the rage of foes.

O brighter than that glorious morn
shall this fair morning be
when Christ our King in beauty comes,
and we his face shall see!   (Isa. 33:20)

The King shall come when morning dawns,
and light and beauty brings;
Hail, Christ the Lord! thy people say,
come quickly, King of kings.

anonymous
translated, John Brownlie
Hymns from the East, 1907

186
The Divine Paradox

A.

Today is achieved a great and unimaginable wonder: a Virgin gives birth, her maidenhood intact; the Word is made flesh, and yet is not separated from the Father. Angels sing praises with the shepherds, and we shout with them: "Glory to God in the highest, and peace upon earth."

All the angels are dancing in heaven, and keep festival today; the whole creation rejoices, since our Savior, the Lord, is born in Bethlehem; the age of the idols comes to an end, and Christ reigns for ever.

Germanus of Constantinople
translated, Erik Routley

B.

A great and mighty wonder!
    a full and holy cure!
the Virgin bears the Infant
    with Virgin-honor pure!

The Word becomes incarnate,
    and yet remains on high:
and cherubim sing anthems
    to shepherds from the sky.

And we with them triumphant
    repeat the hymn again:
"To God on high be glory,
    and peace on earth to men!"

While thus they sing your Monarch,
    those bright angelic bands,
rejoice, ye vales and mountains!
    ye oceans, clap your hands!

Since all he comes to ransom,
    by all be he adored,
the Infant born in Bethlehem,
    the Savior and the Lord!

And idol forms shall perish,
    and error shall decay
and Christ shall wield his scepter,
    our Lord and God for aye.

translated, John Mason Neale
Hymns from the Eastern Church, 1862

187
The Weight of Glory

O happy band of pilgrims,
    if onward ye will tread,
with Jesus as your Fellow,
    to Jesus as your Head!

O happy if ye labor
    as Jesus did for men;
O happy if ye hunger
    as Jesus hungered then.   (Matt. 4:1)

The cross that Jesus carried
    he carried as your due;
the crown that Jesus weareth,
    he weareth it for you.

The faith by which ye see him,
    the hope in which ye yearn,
the love that through all troubles
    to him alone will turn,

what are they but vaunt-couriers   (Heb. 11:1)
    to lead you to his sight?
what are they save the effluence
    of uncreated light?

The trials that beset you,
    the sorrows ye endure,
the manifold temptations
    that death alone can cure,

what are they but his jewels
    of right celestial worth?
what are they but the ladder   (Gen. 28:20)
    set up to heaven on earth?

O happy band of pilgrims,
    look upward to the skies,
where such a light affliction   (2 Cor. 4:17)
    shall win you such a prize!

John Mason Neale
Hymns of the Eastern Church, 1862
suggested by the Canon of Saints Chrysanthus and Daria

Chapter 13:
Hymns from German and Italian Sources (188–205)

Perhaps it is harder for most hymn singers to imagine a world without "Now thank we all our God" than a world without "All glory, laud, and honor"; but the historical fact is that before the mid–nineteenth century virtually no hymns from the German language were known in England. The exceptions were John Wesley's translations (55–56, 195C, 202C) and possibly a stray translation from Paul Gerhardt by Augustus Montague Toplady, "Holy Ghost, dispel our sadness," which is now better known in America than in England.

The reason for the midcentury interest in German hymnody is quite different from that which produced the Latin and Greek hymns in the preceding section. John Mason Neale and company made versions of the Latin and Greek hymns because they deplored the historical and religious isolationism of the English church and sought to recover the liturgical disciplines—and with them, the hymnody—of the Middle Ages. The German originals are not medieval but post-Lutheran, not Catholic but Protestant, and the protest of the translators of these, who were contemporaries of the liturgical translators, was against England's geographical isolationism. Or you can say that a general interest in foreign travel and the beginning of the process which has so recently produced political and economic efforts towards European unity aroused in the English a new desire to share the praises of that country which was the real birthplace of congregational hymnody. German scholarship, especially in theology, was becoming known in England, and very disturbing the English often found it. German literature was beginning to find a response. German music, of course, was insisting on being heard.

Catherine Winkworth (1827–1878) is the translator from German who corresponds to J. M. Neale in the Latin field. Her *Lyra Germanica*, in two parts (1855, 1858), contains her first attempts to communicate German lyric to English readers. But that is exactly how to put it: the *Lyra Germanica* was not intended as a book to sing from, and it contained no music. Therefore it did not matter too much that fairly often she did not reproduce the German meters. She was usually fairly close to them but did not feel it necessary to be precise. (See her translation at 197B for an example of this.) In adjusting meters to make it easier to write in familiar English styles, she followed John Wesley, who made less attempt than she did to preserve original meters.

Personal contact with Christian Karl Josias, Baron von Bunsen, the Prussian ambassador to Britain, inspired this work, but contact with musicians immediately after it was published persuaded her that a hymnal consisting of her translations with music would fill a need. So she produced the *Chorale-Book for England* in 1863, containing two hundred pieces. Some were new (such as 196B and 199B, the two most famous of all her translations), but some were revised versions of pieces in the earlier books, adjusted to carry their proper German tunes. (English readers can see an example of this happening by turning to 159 in the *Methodist Hymn Book*, which is the 1858 version, and comparing it with 381 in *Congregational Praise*, which is the 1863 revision, of her translation of Luther's 130th Psalm, for the original of which see 2A in this collection.) She was very fortunate in her musical collaborators: Sterndale Bennett, one of the best English composers of his time; and Otto Goldschmidt (husband of Jenny Lind), one of the best musicologists. The 1863 book therefore becomes one of the most fertile sources of familiar hymnody from the German.

Before this time, the only English translator of German hymns whose work has lasted was John Wesley, who, just before his "conversion" in 1738, translated many German pieces, especially from the work of Pietist authors who were almost his contemporaries. (In the Wesley corpus it is usually understood that Charles Wesley wrote original hymns while John was content to translate.) The style of these translations is always lofty and eloquent—see our 195C and 202C—but Wesley always felt free not only to use meters which would in those days carry tunes familiar to the English singers but also to paraphrase. In 1774, Toplady, author of "Rock of Ages," translated a Gerhardt hymn, "Holy Ghost, dispel our sadness," without in his own works acknowledging that it was a translation. Nowadays this is normally sung not in his (or Gerhardt's) original meter but as rearranged in 8.7.8.7.D. (See, for example, *Worshipbook*, 342, which carries two of the original seven stanzas.) These apart, it was Catherine Winkworth's contemporaries who supplemented her own great work: Emma Frances Bevan (201B); the Scottish sisters Sarah Findlater ("Jesus, still lead on") and Jane Borthwick (203); and Frances E. Cox (whose "Jesus lives!" is especially fine; and see also our 198B). Another Scot, Richard Massie, often achieves an eloquence which translators usually find it necessary to renounce (see our 1 and 2), and of course *Ein feste Burg* generated many excellent translations, of which yet another Scot, Thomas Carlyle, wrote that which is most famous in Britain. We have included this in our Scottish section at 330, but the American translation is at 4B, and both these come slightly before the main wave of English translations, "*Ein feste Burg*" being, as we said in chapter 1, something of a special case.

Apart from that, and one other (190C) which we are about to mention, English translation from German was really begun in the 1850s, and historically it was a function of the new interest in Britain in foreign literature and in scholarship. But it brought into English hymnody a new strain of devotion which only the Germans of the period 1650–1750 (plus a few earlier pioneers) could provide.

We said in chapter 1 that Luther's personal contribution to hymnody, mainly dogmatic and creedal though with some surprising and lively

excursions into other areas, discouraged other sixteenth-century writers from adding much. And really nothing of great importance happens in German hymnody until the great Pietist movement of the mid–seventeenth century. But although it was Gerhardt (193A, 194C, 195A) who, in *Praxis Pietatis Melica* (first edition, 1644 [lost]; subsequent editions, 1647, 1653, and later), set the tone of German hymnody for nearly two centuries, there were signs before him of the new style, and the secret of this is that it was generated by intense public suffering.

It is for this reason that we have waited so long before presenting the two immortal pieces which are all that, so far as we know, Philipp Nicolai, pastor of Unna in Westphalia, wrote. Brooding in 1597 over the tragedy which had caused so much death in his congregation, a pestilence of the kind so common in those days, he wrote the music and the words of "*Wachet auf*" and "*Wie schön leuchtet*" (188A, 189A), which we give in full here. The tunes are in Luther's style, and perhaps no single tune has generated so much inspiration in subsequent composers as that of "*Wie schön leuchtet.*" But the texts are something quite new: "*Wachet auf*" is a visionary and intensely scriptural song of the Second Coming and the comfort which suffering mortals can take in the thought of it; "*Wie schön*" is a passionate hymn of personal devotion to Christ (which is now almost always sung by English-speaking congregations in a totally altered version by the eighteenth-century hymn writer Johannes Schlegel). These two spacious and magnificent odes come out of deep suffering, and they stand by themselves. Yet they forecast what happened a generation later when the whole of Germany was engulfed by the Thirty Years' War (1618–1648).

Perhaps no war until World War I generated such a mountain of human suffering as did this one. Hymnody reflects this in its response. What one might well expect is what one gets: hymns of intense personal devotion; hymns of passionate defiance; and hymns of rich and persevering praise. One might also expect just what one gets at the conclusion of the war: a radical reassessment of religion. Christianity had, for Protestants, been subjected to fierce and distorting pressures during the period 1618–1648, not least because that war was mostly a religious war. So at the end of it people looked for a religion more personal and more practical than that which mainstream Lutheranism had bequeathed. What came of it was a culture which the English would call Evangelical, but which they called Pietist, from the *Collegium Pietatis*, founded by Jakob Spener in 1670. This was not a campus but an "order," something like Methodism (which it so richly inspired) in England, or, though not in its theology, the Iona Community movement in twentieth-century Scotland: a way of life which people, clerical and lay, could choose to follow. Its chief notes were deep personal devotion, hopeful and optimistic religious behavior, Christian good works, and a special devotion to the crucified (rather than the risen) Christ.

A glance at our 190–197 will illustrate this. You can see it foreshadowed in "Ah, holy Jesus" (191) and in the angry defiance of "Lord of our life" (190). In respect of that second one, we must say that in order to get the sense of the original one must read Catherine Winkworth's translation; the other, better literature to be sure, was made earlier by an English statesman and scholar, Philip Pusey, who applied the "war" image to the new crusade which the Tractarians of the Church of England were pursuing against unbelief and, as he surely thought, against misconceived nonconformist religion in their own country. But Pusey captures very well the truculence of the original. All that is about 1630; and then we come to 192, the most famous now of all German hymns (much more often sung than "*Ein feste Burg*"), which was originally written as a grace at table in the darkest days of the war.

With Gerhardt, 193–195, we begin to emerge. The truculent note fades, the personal and hopeful note is heard more strongly. The communion hymn, 196, expresses all the new personal radiance; and the Passiontide hymn, 194, itself a translation from the Latin (and which, therefore, in English uses a double translation), the devotion to the Crucified. Everyday religion under pressure is classically celebrated in 195. Numbers 193–196 all come from Gerhardt's great collection in which, in the end, 123 of his own hymns appeared, as well as many by other authors of like mind, and many magnificent settings by Johann Crüger.

This practical, personally oriented Christian culture was attractive not only to Protestants but also to many Catholics who had so lately been at war for their faith. The mid-seventeenth century was the period of Port Royal and the Jansenist controversies, and the same tendency was noticeable there: impatience with an institutional religion which had cracked under the pressures of war (so far, anyhow, as the personal faith of Christians went), and a tendency to look for small groups ("churches within the church") which would really foster true religion. This again is very close to the Methodist style of the Wesleys. The Polish-born aristocrat Johann Scheffler (Angelus Silesius) was received into the Jesuit order at age 29 (1652) and thereafter wrote a great deal of devotional poetry of which our 197, in the beautiful Winkworth version, is the best known in English. Its style is indistinguishable from that of the Protestant Pietists.

Joachim Neander was a young and religiously ardent schoolmaster who was dismissed from his post at the age of thirty for his religious extravagances, as the authorities saw them, and died a few months later of exposure after attempting to live in a cave. He leaves us, in 199 and 200, two jewels of "religious radiance," both with an intensely personal accent. Even 198, another fine extrovert hymn of praise by a distinguished layman (evangelicals often produce good lay hymnodists), is really a personal prayer.

The stream flows strongly from there on. Our 201 is an evangelical piece written by a Lutheran minister whose interesting connection with J. S. Bach is mentioned in the *Hymnal Guide*; then appear the two great aristocrats, Tersteegen and Zinzendorf, who so peculiarly impressed John Wesley. Gerhard Tersteegen (55, 202) was the primary poet and benefactor of eighteenth-century Pietism; Nicholas Ludwig, Count von Zinzendorf (56), the refounder of Moravianism, an evangelical culture which traced its ancestry back to John Hus (fifteenth century) and which now flourishes very strongly in Eastern Pennsylvania as well as less conspicuously in England. Between them they produced a volume of hymnody which, with small additions only, kept the German-speaking Protestants fully supplied until the mid-twentieth century found that country reacting to World War II much as it had reacted to the Thirty Years' War: undergoing a profound and creative reassessment of its national religion. (*Cantate Domino*, 1974/1980, which we encounter in chapter 28, carries many examples of the "new deal" German hymnody, and it is perhaps worth recording that in the construction of that book the German members of the editorial board refused to countenance "*Schmücke dich*" and permitted "*Jesu meine Freude*" and "*Ein feste Burg*" only under protest.) But we are able to include 203, which is a very unusual German piece indeed, being the only hymn from the period of "Enlightenment," the new scientific and philosophical humanism, which has found its way into English currency.

Nobody will be surprised to find that in the nineteenth century German was the only European language to furnish material for translation in any quantity. Only Protestant cultures were generating vernacular hymnody, and the Lutheran churches of Scandinavia and the Reformed churches of Holland leaned so heavily on their respective parent traditions that they produced little of their own. We have one Danish hymn in our repertory here (233A), and more recently American Lutherans have explored Scandinavian writers, especially Nicolai Grundtvig, for the purposes of translation,

not with widespread success. Nowadays, of course, the activities of the World Council of Churches and postwar revisions of theology and liturgy have caused a good deal more traffic between these cultures and those outside so that Scandinavia, especially Sweden, is producing much original and interesting hymnody; and the Dutch, for so long wedded to the Genevan Psalter, have been making important contributions.

But two pieces from medieval Italy have found their way into the English repertory, and this is as good a place as any to consider them. Of the famous "Canticle of the Sun," by St. Francis of Assisi, the celebrated version, "All creatures of our God and King," is so universally accessible that we have here given the first English translation made of it, by Matthew Arnold. (A musical setting for this is at *Songs of Praise*, 434.) "Come down, O love divine" is the only piece from the medieval *Laudi spirituali*—sacred songs associated chiefly with fringe movements in the thirteenth and fourteenth centuries who began even then to explore the idea of "alternative churches" which we have just been mentioning in the German connection—which is generally familiar. Vaughan Williams's famous tune was and has remained the reason for the availability of this exquisitely translated piece. As yet we have nothing from Italian Protestant traditions. The Waldensians have their hymnal, but a good deal of it is translated from non-Italian Protestant sources, and the rest has up to now been judged of historic interest only. We must finally add, in reference to the St. Francis hymn, that two other English translations ought certainly to be compared with the famous one that is generally sung: that of George Radcliffe Woodward at 406 in *Songs of Syon*; and that of Howard Chandler Robbins at 307 in the American Episcopal *Hymnal 1940*.

188

Of the Voice at Midnight and the Wise Virgins Who Meet Their Heavenly Bridegroom. Matthew 25

A.

"Wachet auf", ruft uns die Stimme,
der Wächter sehr hoch auf der Zinne,
    "wach auf, du Stadt Jerusalem!
Mitternacht heißt diese Stunde;"
sie rufen uns mit hellem Munde:
    "Wo seid ihr klugen Jungfrauen?
        Wohlauf, der Bräutgam kömmt,
        steht auf, die Lampen nehmt!
          Halleluja!
Macht euch bereit zu der Hochzeit,
ihr müsset ihm entgegengehn!"

Zion hört die Wächter singen,
das Herz tut ihr vor Freude springen,
    sie wachet und steht eilend auf.
Ihr Freund kommt vom Himmel prächtig,
von Gnaden stark, von Wahrheit mächtig,
    ihr Licht wird hell, ihr Stern geht auf.
        Nun komm, du werte Kron,
        Herr Jesu, Gottes Sohn!
          Hosianna!
Wir folgen all zum Freudensaal
und halten mit das Abendmahl.

Gloria sei dir gesungen
mit Menschen- und mit Engelzungen,
    mit Harfen und mit Zimbeln schön.
Von zwölf Perlen sind die Pforten
an deiner Stadt, sind wir Konsorten
    der Engel hoch um deinen Thron.
        Kein Aug, hat je gespürt,
        kein Ohr hat je gehört
          solche Freude.
Des sind wir froh, io, io!
ewig in dulci jubilo.

Philipp Nicolai
Frewden-Spiegel dess ewigen Lebens, 1599

The initial letters of the stanzas form an acrostic, in reverse, on Graf zu Waldeck, the title of Wilhem Ernst, who had been a pupil of Nicolai.

The original third stanza is often replaced by a later revision, the source of which is unknown:

Gloria sei dir gesungen
mit Menschen- und mit Engelzungen,
    mit Harfen und mit Zimbeln schön.
Von zwölf Perlen sind die Tore
an deiner Stadt; wir stehn in Chore
    der Engel hoch um deinen Thron.
        Kein Aug hat je gespürt,
        kein Ohr hat mehr gehört
          solche Freude.
Des jauchzen wir und singen dir
das Halleluja für und für.

B.

Wake, O wake! with tidings thrilling
the watchmen all the air are filling,
    arise, Jerusalem, arise!
Midnight strikes! no more delaying,
"The hour has come!" we hear them saying.
    Where are ye all, ye virgins wise?
      The Bridegroom comes in sight,
      raise high your torches bright!
        Alleluia!
The wedding song swells loud and strong:
Go forth and join the festal throng.

Sion hears the watchmen shouting,
her heart leaps up with joy undoubting,
    she stands and waits with eager eyes;
see her Friend from heaven descending,
adorned with truth and grace unending!
    Her light burns clear, her star doth rise.
      Now come, thou precious Crown,
      Lord Jesu, God's own Son!
        Hosanna!
Let us prepare to follow there
where in thy supper we may share.

Every soul in thee rejoices;
from men and from angelic voices
    be glory given to thee alone!
Now the gates of pearl receive us,
thy presence never more shall leave us,
    we stand with angels round thy throne.
      Earth cannot give below
      the bliss thou dost bestow.
        Alleluia!
Grant us to raise to length of days
the triumph-chorus of thy praise.

translated, Francis C. Burkitt
The English Hymnal, 1906

C.

"Sleepers, wake!" A voice astounds us,
the shout of rampart-guards surrounds us:
    "Awake, Jerusalem, arise!"
Midnight's peace their cry has broken,
their urgent summons clearly spoken:
    "The time has come, O maidens wise!
      Rise up, and give us light;
      the Bridegroom is in sight.
        Alleluia!
Your lamps prepare and hasten there,
that you the wedding feast may share."

Zion hears the watchmen singing;
her heart with joyful hope is springing,
    she wakes and hurries through the night.
Forth he comes, her Bridegroom glorious
in strength of grace, in truth victorious:
    Her star is risen, her light grows bright.
      Now come, most worthy Lord,
      God's Son, Incarnate Word,
        Alleluia!
We follow all and heed your call
to come into the banquet hall.

Lamb of God, the heavens adore you;
let saints and angels sing before you,
    as harps and cymbals swell the sound.
Twelve great pearls, the city's portals:
Through them we stream to join th' immortals
    as we with joy your throne surround.
      No eye has known the sight,
      no ear heard such delight:
        Alleluia!
Therefore we sing to greet our King;
for ever let our praises ring.

translated, Carl P. Daw, Jr., 1982
A Year of Grace, 1990
© 1982, Hope Publishing Company

189

A Spiritual Bridal Song of the Believing Soul Concerning Jesus Christ, Her Heavenly Bridegroom: Based on the 45th Psalm of the Prophet David

A.

Wie schön leuchtet der Morgenstern
voll Gnad und Wahrheit von dem Herrn,
    die süße Wurzel Jesse.
Du Sohn Davids aus Jakobs Stamm,
mein König und mein Bräutigam,
    hast mir mein Herz besessen;
        lieblich, freundlich,
        schön und herrlich,
        groß und ehrlich,
        reich an Gaben,
hoch und sehr prächtig erhaben.

Ei meine Perl, du werte Kron,
wahr' Gottes und Marien Sohn,
    ein hochgeborner König!
Mein Herz heißt dich ein Himmelsblum;
dein süßes Evangelium
    ist lauter Milch und Honig.
        Ei mein Blümlein,
        Hosianna!
        Himmlisch Manna,
        das wir essen,
deiner kann ich nicht vergessen.

Geuß sehr tief in das Herz hinein,
du leuchtend Kleinod, edler Stein,
    mir deiner Liebe Flamme,
daß ich, O Herr, ein Gliedmaß bleib
an deinem auserwählten Leib,
    ein Zweig an deinem Stamme.
        Nach dir wallt mir
        mein Gemüte,
        ewge Güte,
        bis es findet
dich, des Liebe mich entzündet.

Von Gott kommt mir ein Freudenschein,
wenn du mich mit den Augen dein
    gar freundlich tust anblicken.
O Herr Jesu, mein trautes Gut,
dein Wort, dein Geist, dein Leib und Blut
    mich innerlich erquicken.
        Nimm mich freundlich
        in dein Arme,
        Herr, erbarme
        dich in Gnaden;
auf dein Wort komm ich geladen.

Herr Gott Vater, mein starker Held,
du hast mich ewig vor der Welt
    in deinem Sohn geliebet.
Dein Sohn hat mich ihm selbst vertraut,
er ist mein Schatz, ich seine Braut,
    drum mich auch nichts betrübet.
        Eia, eia,
        himmlisch Leben
        wird er geben
        mir dort oben;
ewig soll mein Herz ihn loben.

Zwingt die Saiten in Cythara
und laßt die süße Musika
    ganz freudenreich erschallen,
daß ich möge mit Jesulein,
dem wünderschönen Bräut'gam mein,
    in steter Liebe wallen.
        Singet, springet,
        jubilieret,
        triumphieret,
        dankt dem Herren;
groß ist der König der Ehren.

Wie bin ich doch so herzlich froh,
daß mein Schatz ist das A und O,   (Rev. 1:8)
   der Anfang und das Ende.
Er wird mich doch zu seinem Preis
aufnehmen in das Paradeis;
   des klopf ich in die Hände.
     Amen, amen,
     komm, du schöne
     Freudenkrone,
     bleib nicht lange;
deiner wart ich mit Verlangen.

Philipp Nicolai
Frewden-Spiegel dess ewigen Lebens, 1599
The initial letters of the stanzas form an acrostic on Wilhelm Ernst,
Graf und Herr zu Waldeck, who had been a pupil of Nicolai.

B.

How lovely shines the morning star!
The nations see and hail afar
   the light in Judah shining.
Thou David's Son of Jacob's race,
my Bridegroom and my King of grace,
   for thee my heart is pining.
     Lowly, holy,
     great and glorious,
     thou victorious
     Prince of graces,
filling all the heavenly places.

O highest joy by mortals won,
thou Son of God and Mary's Son,
   thou highborn King of ages!
Thou art my heart's most beauteous flower,
and thy blest gospel's saving power
   my raptured soul engages.
     Thou mine, I thine:
     Sing hosanna!
     Heavenly manna
     tasting, eating,
whilst thy love in songs repeating.

Now richly to my waiting heart,
O thou my God, deign to impart
   the grace of love undying.
In thy blest body let me be,
e'en as the branch is in the tree,
   thy life my life supplying.
     Sighing, crying
     for the savor
     of thy favor;
     resting never,
till I rest in thee forever.

A pledge of peace from God I see
when thy pure eyes are turned to me
   to show me thy good pleasure.
Jesus, thy Spirit and thy Word,
thy body and thy blood, afford
   my soul its dearest treasure.
     Keep me kindly
     in thy favor,
     O my Savior!
     Thou wilt cheer me;
thy word calls me to draw near thee.

Thou, mighty Father, in thy Son
didst love me ere thou hadst begun
   this ancient world's foundation.
Thy Son hath made a friend of me,
and when in spirit him I see,
   I joy in tribulation.
     What bliss is this!
     He that liveth
     to me giveth
     life for ever;
nothing me from him can sever.

Lift up the voice and strike the string,
let all glad sounds of music ring
  in God's high praises blended.
Christ will be with me all the way,
today, tomorrow, every day,
  till traveling days be ended.
    Sing out, ring out
    triumph glorious,
    O victorious
    chosen nation;
praise the God of your salvation.

O joy to know that thou, my Friend,
art Lord, Beginning without end,
  the First and Last, eternal!
And thou at length—O glorious grace!—
wilt take me to that holy place,
  the home of joys supernal.
    Amen, amen!
    Come and meet me!
    Quickly greet me!
    With deep yearning,
Lord, I look for thy returning.

composite translation
The Lutheran Hymnal, 1941
© 1941, Concordia Publishing House

190

Sapphic Ode. For Spiritual and Temporal Peace

A.

Christe, du Beistand deiner Kreuzgemeine,
eile, mit Hilf und Rettung uns erscheine.
Steure den Feinden, ihre Blutgedichte
  mache zunichte.

Streite doch selber für uns arme Kinder,
wehre dem Teufel, seine Macht verhinder;
alles, was kämpfet wider deine Glieder,
  stürze darnieder.

Frieden bei Kirch und Schule uns beschere,
Frieden zugleich der Obrigkeit gewähre.
Frieden dem Herzen, Frieden dem Gewissen
  gib zu genießen.

Also wird zeitlich deine Güt erhoben,
also wird ewig und ohn Ende loben
dich, o du Wächter deiner armen Herde,
  Himmel und Erde.

Matthäus Apelles von Löwenstern, 1630
Kirchen- und Haus-Music, 1644

B.

Christ, thou the champion of that war-worn host
who bear thy cross, haste, help, or we are lost;
the scheme of those who long our blood have sought
  bring thou to nought.

Do thou thyself for us thy children fight,
withstand the Devil, quell his rage and might,
whate'er assails thy members left below
  do thou o'erthrow:

and give us peace: peace in the church and school,
peace to the powers who o'er our country rule,
peace to the conscience, peace within the heart,
  do thou impart.

So shall thy goodness here be still adored,
thou guardian of thy little flock, dear Lord,
and heaven and earth through all eternity
  shall worship thee.

translated, Catherine Winkworth
Lyra Germanica, 1855

C.

Lord of our life and God of our salvation,
Star of our night, and Hope of every nation,
hear and receive thy church's supplication,
  Lord God Almighty.

See round thine ark the hungry billows curling,
see how thy foes their banners are unfurling;
Lord, while their darts envenomed they are hurling,
  thou canst preserve us.

Lord, thou canst help when earthly armor faileth,
Lord, thou canst save when deadly sin assaileth;
Christ, o'er thy Rock nor death nor hell prevaileth;
  Grant us thy peace, Lord.

Peace in our hearts, our evil thoughts assuaging,
peace in thy church, where brothers are engaging,
peace when the world its busy war is waging:
  calm thy foes' raging.

Grant us thy help till backward they are driven,
grant them thy truth, that they may be forgiven;
grant peace on earth, and after we have striven,
  peace in thy heaven.

  translated and paraphrased, Philip Pusey, 1834
  Psalm and Hymn Tunes, 1840

191

The Cause of the Bitter Sufferings of Jesus Christ and Consolation from His Love and Grace. From Augustine

A.

Herzliebster Jesu, was hast du verbrochen,
daß man ein solch scharf Urteil hat gesprochen?
Was ist die Schuld? In was für Missetaten
  bist du geraten?

Du wirst gegeißelt und mit Dorn' gekrönet,
ins Angesicht geschlagen und verhöhnet,
du wirst mit Essig und mit Gall getränket,
  ans Kreuz gehenket.

Was ist doch wohl die Ursach solcher Plagen?
Ach meine Sünden haben dich geschlagen;
ach mein Herr Jesu, ich hab dies verschuldet,
  was du erduldet.

Wie wunderbarlich ist doch diese Strafe!
Der gute Hirte leidet für die Schafe,
die Schuld bezahlt der Herre, der Gerechte,
  für seine Knechte.

Der Fromme stirbt, der recht und richtig wandelt,
der Böse lebt, der wider Gott mißhandelt;
der Mensch verwirkt den Tod und ist entgangen,
  Gott wird gefangen.

Ich war von Fuß auf voller Schand und Sünden,
bis zu dem Scheitel war nichts Gut's zu finden;
dafür hätt ich dort in der Hölle müssen
  ewiglich büßen.

O große Lieb, o Lieb ohn alle Maße,
die dich gebracht auf diese Marterstraße!
Ich lebte mit der Welt in Lust und Freuden,
  und du mußt leiden.

Ach großer König, groß zu allen Zeiten,
wie kann ich gnugsam solche Treu ausbreiten?
Keins Menschen Herz vermag es auszudenken,
  was dir zu schenken.

Ich kanns mit meinen Sinnen nicht erreichen,
womit doch dein Erbarmung zu vergleichen;
wie kann ich dir denn deine Liebestaten
  in Werk erstatten?

Doch ist noch etwas, das dir angenehme:
wenn ich des Fleisches Lüste dämpf und zähme,
dass sie aufs neu mein Herze nicht entzünden
  mit alten Sünden.

Weils aber nicht besteht in eignen Kräften,
fest die Begierden an das Kreuz zu heften,
so gib mir deinen Geist, der mich regiere,
    zum Guten führe.

Alsdann so werd ich deine Huld betrachten,
aus Lieb zu dir die Welt für nichts erachten.
bemühen werd ich mich, Herr, deinen Willen
    stets zu erfüllen.

Ich werde dir zu Ehren alles wagen,
kein Kreuz nicht achten, keine Schmach und Plagen,
nichts von Verfolgung, nichts von Todesschmerzen
    nehmen zu Herzen.

Dies alles, obs gering zwar ist zu schätzen,
wirst du es doch nicht gar beiseitesetzen;
in Gnaden wirst du dies von mir annehmen,
    mich nicht beschämen.

Wann, o Herr Jesu, dort von deinem Throne
wird stehn auf meinem Haupt die Ehrenkrone,
da will ich dir, wenn alles wird wohl klingen,
    Lob und Dank singen.

Johann Heermann, 1630
Devoti Musica Cordis, Hauss- und Hertz-Musica, 1630
Based on a text, probably by Jean de Fécamp (d. 1078), from
Meditationes, a fifteenth-century anthology falsely attributed to
Augustine of Hippo.
See also 410.

B.

Alas, dear Lord, what law then hast thou broken,
that such sharp sentence should on thee be spoken?
Of what great crime hast thou to make confession—
    what dark transgression?

They crown his head with thorns, they smite, they
    scourge him,
with cruel mockings to the cross they urge him,
they give him gall to drink, they still decry him,—
    they crucify him.

Whence come these sorrows, whence this mortal
    anguish?
It is my sins for which my Lord must languish;
yes, all the wrath, the woe he doth inherit
    'Tis I do merit!

What strangest punishment is suffered yonder!
The Shepherd dies for sheep that loved to wander!
The Master pays the debts his servants owe him,
    who would not know him.

There was no spot in me by sin unstained,
sick with its venom all my heart had fainted;
my heavy guilt to hell had well-nigh brought me,
    such woe it wrought me.

O wondrous love! whose depths no heart hath
    sounded,
that brought thee here by foes and thieves
    surrounded;
all worldly pleasures, heedless, I was trying
    while thou wast dying!

O mighty King! no time can dim thy glory!
How shall I spread abroad thy wondrous story?
How shall I find some worthy gift to proffer?
    What dare we offer?

For vainly doth our human wisdom ponder—
thy woes, thy mercy, still transcend our wonder.
Oh, how should I do aught that could delight thee?
    Can I requite thee?

Yet unrequited, Lord, I would not leave thee,
I can renounce whate'er doth vex or grieve thee,
and quench with thoughts of thee and prayers most
    lowly
    all fires unholy.

But since my strength alone will ne'er suffice me
to crucify desires that still entice me,
to all good deeds, O let thy Spirit win me,
    and reign within me!

I'll think upon thy mercy hour by hour,
I'll love thee so that earth must lose her power;
to do thy will shall be my sole endeavor
      henceforth for ever.

Whate'er of earthly good this life may grant me
I'll risk for thee—no shame, no cross shall daunt me;
I shall not fear what man can do to harm me,
      nor death alarm me.

But worthless is my sacrifice, I own it,
yet, Lord, for love's sake thou wilt not disown it;
thou wilt accept my gift in thy great meekness,
      nor shame my weakness.

And when, dear Lord, before thy throne in heaven
to me the crown of joy at last is given,
where sweetest hymns thy saints for ever raise thee,
      I too shall praise thee!

      translated, Catherine Winkworth
      The Chorale Book for England, 1863

C.

Ah, holy Jesus, how hast thou offended
that man to judge thee hath in hate pretended?
By foes derided, by thine own rejected,
      O most afflicted.

Who was the guilty? Who brought this upon thee?
Alas, my treason, Jesus, hath undone thee;
'twas I, Lord Jesus, I it was denied thee:
      I crucified thee.

Lo, the good Shepherd for the sheep is offered,
the slave hath sinned, and the Son hath suffered.
For man's atonement, while he nothing heedeth,
      God intercedeth.

For me, kind Jesus, was thine incarnation,
thy mortal sorrow and thy life's oblation;
thy death of anguish and thy bitter passion
      for my salvation.

Therefore, kind Jesus, since I cannot pay thee
I do adore thee, and will ever pray thee,
think on thy pity and thy love unswerving,
      not my deserving.

      paraphrased, Robert Bridges
      The Yattendon Hymnal, 1899
Bridges' first stanza follows the first of Winkworth; his second, her
third; his third, her fourth. His fourth is more freely constructed. His
fifth stanza follows Winkworth's thirteenth.

192
A Little Table Prayer

A.

Nun danket alle Gott
mit Herzen, Mund und Händen,
    der große Dinge tut
an uns und allen Enden,
    der uns von Mutterleib
    und Kindesbeinen an
    unzählig viel zugut
    und noch jetzund getan.

Der ewigreiche Gott
woll uns bei unserm Leben
    ein immer fröhlich Herz
und edlen Frieden geben
    und uns in seiner Gnad
    erhalten fort und fort
    und uns aus aller Not
    erlösen hier und dort.

Lob, Ehr und Preis sei Gott,
dem Vater und dem Sohne
    und dem, der beiden gleich
im höchsten Himmelsthrone,
    dem dreimal einen Gott,
    wie es ursprünglich war
und ist und bleiben wird
jetzund und immerdar.

Martin Rinckart, 1636
Praxis Pietatis Melica (Crüger), 1647

B.

Now thank we all our God
with heart and hands and voices,
    who wondrous things hath done,
in whom his world rejoices;
    who from our mother's arms
    hath blessed us on our way
with countless gifts of love
and still is ours today.

O may this bounteous God
through all our life be near us
    with ever joyful hearts
and blessed peace to cheer us;
    and keep us in his grace,
    and guide us when perplexed,
    and free us from all ills
    in this world and the next.

All praise and thanks to God
the Father now be given,
    the Son, and him who reigns
with them in highest heaven,
    the one eternal God,
    whom heaven and earth adore,
    for thus it was, is now,
    and shall be evermore.

translated, Catherine Winkworth
Lyra Germanica, 1858

193
Now All the Woods Are Sleeping

A.

Nun ruhen alle Wälder,
Vieh, Menschen, Städt und Felder,
    es schläft die ganze Welt;
ihr aber, meine Sinnen,
    auf, auf, ihr sollt beginnen,
was eurem Schöpfer wohlgefällt.

Wo bist du, Sonne, blieben?
Die Nacht hat dich vertrieben,
    die Nacht, des Tages Feind.
Fahr hin; ein andre Sonne,
    mein Jesus, meine Wonne,
gar hell in meinem Herzen scheint.

Der Tag ist nun vergangen
die güldnen Sternlein prangen
    am blauen Himmelssaal;
also werd ich auch stehen,
    wann mich wird heißen gehen
mein Gott aus diesem Jammertal.

Der Leib eilt nun zur Ruhe,
legt ab das Kleid und Schuhe,
    das Bild der Sterblichkeit;
die zieh ich aus, dagegen
    wird Christus mir anlegen
den Rock der Ehr und Herrlichkeit.

Das Haupt, die Füß und Hände
sind froh, daß nun zum Ende
    die Arbeit kommen sei.
Herz, freu dich, du sollst werden
    vom Elend dieser Erden
und von der Sünden Arbeit frei.

Nun geht, ihr matten Glieder,
geht hin und legt euch nieder,
    der Betten ihr begehrt.
Es kommen Stund und Zeiten,
da man euch wird bereiten
zur Ruh ein Bettlein in der Erd.

Mein Augen stehn verdrossen,
im Nu sind sie geschlossen,
    Wo bleibt dann Leib und Seel?
Nimm sie zu deinen Gnaden,
sei gut für allen Schaden,
du Aug und Wäcther Israel'.

Breit aus die Flügel beide,
o Jesu, meine Freude,
    und nimm dein Küchlein ein.
Will Satan mich verschlingen,
so laß die Englein singen:
"Dies Kind soll unverletzet sein."

Auch euch, ihr meine Lieben,
soll heute nicht betrüben
    kein Unfall noch Gefahr.
Gott laß euch selig schlafen,
stell euch die güldnen Waffen
ums Bett und seiner Engel Schar.

Paul Gerhardt, 1647
Praxis Pietatis Melica (Crüger), 1648
There is strong similarity to Virgil, *Aeneid*, IV, 522–528.

O sun, where art thou vanished?
The night thy reign hath banished,
    thy ancient foe, the night.
Farewell, a brighter glory
my Jesus sheddeth o'er me,
all clear within me shines his light.

Now thought and labor ceases,
for night the tired releases
    and bids sweet rest begin:
my heart, there comes a morrow
shall set thee free from sorrow
and all the dreary toil of sin.

My Jesus, stay thou by me,
and let no foe come nigh me,
    safe sheltered by thy wing,
but would the foe alarm me,
O let him never harm me,
but still thine angels round me sing.

My loved ones, rest securely,
from every peril surely
    our God will guard your heads;
and happy slumbers send you,
and bid his hosts attend you,
and golden-armed, watch o'er your heads.

translated, Catherine Winkworth
based on stanzas 1, 2, 5, 8, and 9 of Gerhardt's text
Lyra Germanica, 1856
as revised in this reprint of the 1855 edition

B.

Now all the woods are sleeping,
and night and stillness creeping
    o'er city, man, and beast;
but thou, my soul, awake thee,
to prayer awhile betake thee,
and praise thy Maker ere thou rest.

C.

The duteous day now closeth,
each flower and tree reposeth,
    shade creeps o'er wild and wood:
Let us as night is falling,
on God our Maker calling,
give thanks to him, the Giver good.

Now all the heavenly splendor
breaks forth in starlight tender
 from myriad worlds unknown;
and man, the marvel seeing,
forgets his selfish being
for joy of beauty not his own.

His care he drowneth yonder,
lost in th' abyss of wonder;
 to heaven his soul doth steal:
this life he disesteemeth,
the day it is that dreameth,
that doth from truth his vision seal.

Awhile his mortal blindness
may miss God's lovingkindness,
 and grope in faithless strife:
but when life's day is over
shall death's fair night discover
the fields of everlasting life.

Robert Bridges
The Yattendon Hymnal, 1899
Stanzas 1 and 2 are based loosely on Gerhardt.

194
Rhythmic Prayer. To the Face

A.

Salve caput cruentatum,
totum spinis coronatum,
conquassatum, vulneratum,
harundine verberatum,
facie sputis ilitia.
Salve, cuius dulcis vultus
immutatus et incultus
immutavit suum florem
totus versus in pallorem,
quem caeli tremit curia.

Omnis vigor atque viror
hinc recessit, non admiror,
mors apparet in aspectu,
totus pendens in defectu
attritus aegra macie.
sic affectus, sic despectus,
propter me sic interfectus,
peccatori tam indigno
cum amoris in te signo
appare clara facie.

In hac tua passione
me agnosce, pastor bone;
cujus sumpsi mel ex ore,
haustum lactis ex dulcore
prae omnibus deliciis.
Non me reum asperneris,
nec indignum dedigneris,
morte tibi jam vicina
tuum caput hic inclina,
in meis pausa bracchiis.

Tuae sanctae passioni
me gauderem interponi,
in hac cruce tecum mori
praesta crucis amatori,
sub cruce tua moriar:
morti tuae jam amarae
grates ago, Jesu care;
qui es clemens, pie Deus
fac quod petit tuus reus,
ut absque te non finiar.

Dum me mori est necesse,
noli mihi tunc deesse;
in tremenda mortis hora
veni Jesu! absque mora
tuere me et libera.
Cum me iubes emigrare
Jesu! care! tunc appare,
o amator amplectende
temet ipsum tunc ostende
in cruce salutifera.

anonymous Latin
sometimes attributed to Bernard of Clairvaux

B.

O sacred Head, sore wounded,
    defiled and put to scorn;
O kingly Head surrounded
    with mocking crown of thorn.
What sorrow mars thy grandeur?
    Can death thy bloom deflower?
O countenance, whose splendor
    the hosts of heaven adore!

Thy beauty, long-desired
    hath vanished from our sight;
thy power is all expired,
    and quenched the Light of light.
Ah me! for whom thou diest,
    hide not so far thy grace:
show me, O Love most highest,
    the brightness of thy face.

I pray thee, Jesus, own me,
    me, Shepherd good, for thine;
who to thy fold hast won me,
    and fed with truth divine.
Me, guilty me, refuse not,
    incline thy face to me,
this comfort that I lose not,
    on earth to comfort thee.

In thy most bitter passion
    my heart to share doth cry,
with thee for my salvation
    upon the cross to die.
Ah, keep my heart thus moved
    to stand thy cross beneath,
to mourn thee, well-beloved,
    yet thank thee for thy death.

My days are few, O fail not,
    with thine immortal power,
to hold me that I quail not
    in death's most fearful hour:
that I may fight befriended,
    and see in my last strife
to me thine arms extended
    upon the cross of life.

translated, Robert Bridges
The Yattendon Hymnal, 1899

C.

O Haupt voll Blut und Wunden,
    voll Schmerz und voller Hohn;
o Haupt, zum Spott gebunden
    mit einer Dornenkron;
o Haupt, sonst schön gezieret
    mit höchster Ehr und Zier,
jetzt aber hoch schimpfieret:
    gegrüßet seist du mir!

Du edles Angesichte,
    davor sonst schrickt und scheut
das große Weltgewichte:
    wie bist du so bespeit,
wie bist du so erbleichet!
    Wer hat dein Augenlicht,
dem sonst kein Licht nicht gleichet,
    so schändlich zugericht'?

Die Farbe deiner Wangen,
    der roten Lippen Pracht
ist hin und ganz vergangen;
    des blassen Todes Macht
hat alles hingenommen,
    hat alles hingerafft,
und daher bist du kommen
    von deines Liebes Kraft.

Nun, was du, Herr, erduldet,
    ist alles meine Last;
ich hab es selbst verschuldet,
    was du getragen hast.
Schau her, hier steh ich Armer,
    der Zorn verdienet hat.
Gib mir, o mein Erbarmer,
    den Anblick deiner Gnad.

Erkenne mich, mein Hüter,
    mein Hirte, nimm mich an.
Von dir, Quell aller Güter,
    ist mir viel Guts getan;
dein Mund hat mich gelabet
    mit Milch und süßer Kost,
dein Geist hat mich begabet
    mit mancher Himmelslust.

Ich will hier bei dir stehen,
    verachte mich doch nicht;
von dir will ich nicht gehen,
    wenn dir dein Herze bricht;
wenn dein Haupt wird erblassen
    im letzten Todesstoß,
alsdann will ich dich fassen
    in meinen Arm und Schoß.

Es dient zu meinen Freuden
    und tut mir herzlich wohl,
wenn ich in deinem Leiden,
    mein Heil, mich finden soll.
Ach möcht ich, o mein Leben,
    an deinem Kreuze hier
mein Leben von mir geben,
    wie wohl geschähe mir!

Ich danke dir von Herzen,
    o Jesu, liebster Freund,
für deines Todes Schmerzen,
    da du's so gut gemeint.
Ach gib, daß ich mich halte
    zu dir und deiner Treu
und, wenn ich nun erkalte,
    im dir mein Ende sei.

Wenn ich einmal soll scheiden,
    so scheide nicht von mir,
wenn ich den Tod soll leiden,
    so tritt du dann herfür;
wenn mir am allerbängsten
    wird um das Herze sein,
so reiß mich aus den Ängsten
    kraft deiner Angst und Pein.

Erscheine mir zum Schilde,
    zum Trost in meinem Tod
und laß mich sehn dein Bilde
    in deiner Kreuzesnot.
Da will ich nach dir blicken,
    da will ich glaubensvoll
dich fest an mein Herz drücken.
    Wer so stirbt, der stirbt wohl.

Paul Gerhardt, 1653
Praxis Pietatis Melica (Crüger), 1656
based on *"Salve caput cruentatum"*

D.

O sacred Head! now wounded,
 with grief and shame weighed down;
now scornfully surrounded
 with thorns, thy only crown;
O sacred Head! what glory,
 what bliss till now was thine!
I read the wondrous story!
 I joy to call thee mine!

O noblest brow and dearest!
 in other days the world
all feared when thou appearedst;
 what shame on thee is hurled!
How art thou pale with anguish,
 with sore abuse and scorn;
how does that visage languish
 which once was bright as morn!

What thou, my Lord, hast suffered
 was all for sinners' gain;
mine, mine was the transgression,
 but thine the deadly pain.
Lo! here I fall, my Savior!
 'Tis I deserve thy place;
look on me with thy favor,
 vouchsafe to me thy grace.

What language shall I borrow
 to thank thee, dearest Friend,
for this, thy dying sorrow,
 thy pity without end?
O make me thine for ever!
 and should I fainting be,
Lord, let me never, never
 outlive my love to thee!

Be near when I am dying,
 O show thy cross to me!
and for my succor flying,
 come, Lord, to set me free.
These eyes, new faith receiving,
 from Jesus shall not move,
for he who dies believing
 dies safely through thy love.

translated, James Waddell Alexander, 1830
The Christian Lyre, 1831
based on stanzas 1, 3, 4, 8, and 10 of Gerhardt's text
Lines 2:1–3 are from lines 9–10 of the Latin.

195
A Hymn of Trust

A.

Befiehl du deine Wege
 und was dein Herze kränkt
der allertreusten Pflege
 des, der den Himmel lenkt.
Der Wolken, Luft und Winden
 gibt Wege, Lauf und Bahn,
der wird auch Wege finden,
 da dein Fuß gehen kann.

Dem Herren mußt du trauen,
 wenn dirs soll wohlergehn;
auf sein Werk mußt du schauen,
 wenn dein Werk soll bestehn.
Mit Sorgen und mit Grämen
 und mit selbsteigner Pein
läßt Gott sich gar nichts nehmen,
 es muß erbeten sein.

"Dein ewge Treu und Gnade,
 o Vater, weiß und sieht,
was gut sei oder schade
 dem sterblichen Geblüt;
und was du dann erlesen,
 das treibst du, starker Held,
und bringst zum Stand und Wesen,
 was deinem Rat gefällt.

Weg hast du allerwegen,
    an Mitteln fehlt dirs nicht;
dein Tun ist lauter Segen,
    dein Gang ist lauter Licht,
dein Werk kann niemand hindern,
    dein Arbeit darf nicht ruhn,
wenn du, was deinen Kindern
    ersprießlich ist, willst tun."

Und ob gleich alle Teufel
    ier wollten widerstehn,
so wird doch ohne Zweifel
    Gott nicht zurücke gehn;
was er sich vorgenommen
    und was er haben will,
das muß doch endlich kommen
    zu seinem Zweck und Ziel.

Hoff, o du arme Seele,
    hoff und sei unverzagt!
Gott wird dich aus der Höhle,
    da dich der Kummer plagt,
mit großen Gnaden rücken;
    erwarte nur die Zeit,
so wirst du schon erblicken
    die Sonn der schönsten Freud.

Auf, auf, gib deinem Schmerze
    und Sorgen gute Nacht,
laß fahren, was das Herze
    betrübt und traurig macht;
bist du doch nicht Regente,
    der alles führen soll,
Gott sitzt im Regimente
    und führet alles wohl.

Ihn, ihn laß tun und walten,
    er ist ein weiser Fürst
und wird sich so verhalten,
    daß du dich wundern wirst,
wenn er, wie ihm gebühret,
    mit wunderbarem Rat
das Werk hinausgeführet,
    das dich bekümmert hat.

Er wird zwar eine Weile
    mit seinem Trost verziehn
und tun an seinem Teile,
    als hätt in seinem Sinn
er deiner sich begeben
    und, sollst du für und für
in Angst und Nöten schweben,
    als frag er nichts nach dir.

Wirds aber sich befinden,
    daß du ihm treu verbleibst,
so wird er dich entbinden,
    da du's am mindsten gläubst;
er wird dein Herze lösen
    von der so schweren Last,
die du zu keinem Bösen
    bisher getragen hast.

Wohl dir, du Kind der Treue,
    du hast und trägst davon
mit Ruhm und Dankgeschreie
    den Sieg und Ehrenkron;
Gott gibt dir selbst die Palmen
    in deine rechte Hand,
und du singst Freudenspsalmen
    dem, der dein Leid gewandt.

"Mach End, o Herr, mach Ende
    mit aller unsrer Not;
stärk unsre Füß und Hände
    und laß bis in den Tod
uns allzeit deiner Pflege
    und Treu empfohlen sein,
so gehen unsre Wege,
    gewiß zum Himmel ein."

Paul Gerhardt, 1653
Praxis Pietatis Melica (Crüger), 1656
The first words of the stanzas form an acrostic on Luther's version of
Psalm 37:5, "Befiehl dem Herren deine Wege und hoffe auf ihn, er
wirds wohl machen," with "dem Herren" at the beginning of stanza 2.

B.

Commit thou all that grieves thee
    and fills thy heart with care
to him whose faithful mercy
    the skies above declare,
who gives the winds their courses,
    who points the clouds their way;
'tis he will guide thy footsteps
    and be thy staff and stay.

O trust the Lord then wholly,
    if thou wouldst be secure;
his work must thou consider
    for thy work to endure.
What profit doth it bring thee
    to pine in grief and care?
God only sends his blessing
    in answer to thy prayer.

Thy lasting truth and mercy,
    O Father, see aright
the needs of all thy children,
    their anguish or delight:
What loving wisdom chooseth,
    redeeming might will do,
and bring to sure fulfillment
    thy counsel good and true.

Hope on, then, broken spirit;
    hope on, be not afraid:
Fear not the griefs that plague thee
    and keep thy heart dismayed:
Thy God, in his great mercy,
    will save thee, hold thee fast,
and in his own time grant thee
    the sun of joy at last.

translated, Arthur W. Farlander and Winfred Douglas, 1939
based on stanzas 1, 2, 3, and 6 of Gerhardt's text
The Hymnal 1940, 1943
© 1940, The Church Pension Fund

C. Trust in Providence. From the German

Commit thou all thy griefs
    and ways into his hands;
to his sure truth and tender care,
    who earth and heaven commands.

Who points the clouds their course,
    whom winds and seas obey,
he shall direct thy wandering feet,
    he shall prepare thy way.

Thou on the Lord rely,
    so safe shalt thou go on;
fix on his work thy steadfast eye,
    so shall thy work be done.

No profit canst thou gain
    by self-consuming care;
to him commend thy cause; his ear
    attends the softest prayer.

Thy everlasting truth,
    Father, thy ceaseless love,
sees all thy children's wants, and knows
    what best for each will prove.

And whatsoe'er thou will'st,
    thou dost, O King of kings;
what thy unerring wisdom chose
    thy power to being brings.

Thou everywhere hast sway,
    and all things serve thy might;
thy every act pure blessing is,
    thy path unsullied light.

When thou arisest, Lord,
    what shall thy work withstand?
When all thy children want thou giv'st,
    who, who shall stay thy hand?

Give to the winds thy fears;
    hope, and be undismayed;
God hears thy sighs, and counts thy tears,
    God shall lift up thy head.

Through waves and clouds and storms
    he gently clears thy way;
wait thou his time, so shall this night
    soon end in joyous day.

Still heavy is thy heart?
    Still sink thy spirits down?
Cast off the weight, let fear depart,
    and every care be gone.

What though thou rulest not?
    Yet heaven, and earth, and hell
proclaim, God sitteth on the throne,
    and ruleth all things well!

Leave to his sovereign sway
    to choose and to command;
so shalt thou wondering own his way
    how wise, how strong his hand.

Far, far above thy thought
    his counsel shall appear,
when fully he the work hath wrought
    that caused thy needless fear.

Thou seest our weakness, Lord,
    our hearts are known to thee;
O lift thou up the sinking hand,
    confirm the feeble knee!

Let us in life, in death,
    thy steadfast truth declare,
and publish with our latest breath
    thy love and guardian care!

translated, John Wesley, ca. 1737
Hymns and Sacred Poems, 1739

196
A Preparation for the Lord's Supper

A.

Schmücke dich, o liebe Seele,
laß die dunkle Sündenhöhle,
komm ans helle Licht gegangen,
fange herrlich an zu prangen!
Denn der Herr voll Heil und Gnaden
will dich jetzt zu Gaste laden;
der den Himmel kann verwalten,
will jetzt Herberg in dir halten.

Eile, wie Verlobte pflegen,
deinem Bräutigam entgegen,
der da mit dem Gnadenhammer
klopft an deine Herzenskammer!
Öffn' ihm bald des Geistes Pforten,
red ihn an mit schönen Worten:
Komm, mein Liebster, laß dich küssen,
laß mich deiner nicht mehr mißen!

Zwar in Kaufnung teurer Waren
pflegt man sonst kein Geld zu sparen;
aber du willst für die Gaben
diener Huld kein Geld night haben,
weil in allen Bergwerksgründen
kein solch Kleinod ist zu finden,
das die blutgefüllten Schalen
und dies Manna kann bezahlen.

Ach wie hungert mein Gemüte,
Menschenfreund, nach deincr Güte;
ach wie pfleg ich oft mit Tränen
mich nach dieser Kost zu sehnen;
ach wie pfleget mich zu dürsten
nach dcm Trank des Lebensfürsten,
Wunsche stets, daß meine Gebeine
Sic durch Gott mit Gott vereine.

Beides Lachen und auch Zittern
läßet sich in mir jetzt wittern;
Das Geheimnis dieser Speise
und die unerforschte Weise
machet, daß ich früh vermerke,
Herr, die Größe deiner Stärke.
Ist auch wohl ein Mensch zu finden,
der dein Allmacht sollt ergründen?

Nein, Vernunft die muß hier weichen,
kann dies Wunder nicht erreichen,
daß dies Brot nie wird verzehret,
ob es gleich viel Tausend nähret,
und daß mit dem Saft der Reben
uns wird Christi Blut gegeben.
O der großen Heimlichkeiten,
dir nur Gottes Geist kann deuten!

Jesu, meine Lebenssonne,
Jesu, meine Freud und Wonne,
Jesu, du mein ganz Beginnen,
Lebensquell und Licht der Sinnen:
hier fall ich zu deinen Füßen;
laß mich würdiglich genießen
dieser deiner Himmelsspeise
mir zum Heil und dir zum Preise.

Herr, es hat dein treues Lieben
dich vom Himmel hergetrieben,
daß du willig hast dein Leben
in den Tod für uns gegeben
und dazu ganz unverdrossen,
Herr, dein Blut für uns vergossen,
das uns jetzt kann kräftig tränken,
deiner Liebe zu gedenken.

Jesu, wahres Brot des Lebens,
hilf, daß ich doch nich vergebens
oder mir viellicht zum Schaden
sei zu deinem Tisch geladen.
Laß mich durch dies Seelenessen
deine Liebe recht ermessen,
daß ich auch, wie jetzt auf Erden,
mög dein Gast im Himmel werden.

Johann Franck, 1649
Praxis Pietatis Melica (Crüger), 1653

B.

Deck thyself, my soul, with gladness,
leave the gloomy haunts of sadness,
come into the daylight's splendor,
there with joy thy praises render
unto him whose grace unbounded
hath this wondrous banquet founded;
high o'er all the heavens he reigneth,
yet to dwell with thee he deigneth.

Hasten as a bride to meet him,
and with loving reverence greet him,
for with words of life immortal
now he knocketh at thy portal;
haste to ope the gates before him,
saying, whilst thou dost adore him,
"Suffer, Lord, that I receive thee,
and I never more will leave thee."

Ah, how hungers all my spirit
for the love I do not merit!
Oft have I, with sighs fast thronging
thought upon this food with longing,
in the battle well nigh worsted,
for this cup of life have thirsted,
for the Friend, who here invites us
and to God himself unites us.

Now I sink before thee lowly,
filled with joy most deep and holy,
as with trembling awe and wonder
on thy mighty works I ponder,
how, by mystery surrounded,
depths no man hath ever sounded,
none may dare to pierce unbidden
secrets that with thee are hidden.

Sun, who all my life dost brighten,
Light, who dost my soul enlighten,
Joy, the sweetest man e'er knoweth,
Fount, whence all my being floweth,
at thy feet I cry, "My Maker,
let me be a fit partaker
of this blessed food from heaven,
for our good, thy glory given."

Jesus, Bread of Life, I pray thee,
let me gladly here obey thee,
never to my hurt invited,
be thy love with love requited;
from this banquet let me measure,
Lord, how vast and deep the treasure;
through the gifts thou here dost give me
as thy guest in heaven receive me.

> translated, Catherine Winkworth, 1858, revised, 1863
> based on stanzas 1, 2, 4, 5, 7, and 9 of Franck's text
> *Chorale Book for England*, 1863

197

The Soul Gives Itself to Eternal Love

A.

Liebe, die du mich zum Bilde
    deiner Gottheit hast gemacht,
Liebe, die du mich so milde
    nach dem Fall hast wiederbracht:

    Liebe, dir ergeb ich mich,
    dein zu bleiben ewiglich.

Liebe, die du mich erkoren,
    eh ich noch geschaffen war,
Liebe, die du Mensch geboren
    und mir gleich wardst ganz und gar:

Liebe, die für mich gelitten
    und gestorben in der Zeit,
Liebe, die mir hat erstritten
    ewge Lust und Seligkeit:

Liebe, die du Kraft und Leben,
    Licht und Wahrheit, Geist und Wort,
Liebe, die sich ganz ergeben
    mir zum Heil und Seelenhort:

Liebe, die mich hat gebunden
    an ihr Joch mit Leib und Sinn,
Liebe, die mich überwunden
    und mein Herz hat ganz dahin:

Liebe, die mich ewig liebet
    und für meine Seele bitt',
Liebe, die das Lösgeld gibet
    und mich kräftiglich vertritt:

Liebe, die mich wird erwecken
    aus dem Grab der Sterblichkeit,
Liebe, die mich wird umstecken
    mit dem Laub der Herrlichkeit:

> Johann Scheffler (Angelus Silesius), 1657
> stanzas 1–3 and 5–7, *Heilige Seelenlust*, 1657
> stanza 4, probably not by Scheffler, *Geistriches Gesangbuch*, 1695

B.

O Love, who formedst me to wear
    the image of thy Godhead here;
who soughtest me with tender care
    through all my wanderings wild and drear:

    O Love, I give myself to thee,
    thine ever, only thine to be.

O Love, who ere life's earliest dawn
  on me thy choice hast gently laid,
O Love, who here as man wast born
  and like to us in all things made;

O Love, who once in time wast slain,
  pierced through and through with bitter woe;
O Love, who wrestling thus didst gain
  that we eternal joy might know;

O Love, of whom is truth and light,
  the Word and Spirit, life and power,
whose heart was bared to them that smite,
  to shield us in our trial hour,

O Love, who thus hast bound me fast,
  beneath that gentle yoke of thine;
Love, who hast conquered me at last
  and rapt away this heart of mine.

O Love, who lovest me for aye,
  who for my soul dost ever plead;
O Love, who didst my ransom pay,
  whose power sufficeth in my stead;

O Love, who once shalt bid me rise
  from out this dying life of ours;
O Love, who once above the skies
  shalt set me in the fadeless bowers:

translated, Catherine Winkworth
Lyra Germanica, 1858

198
Hymn of Praise

A.

Sei Lob und Ehr dem höchsten Gut,
  dem Vater aller Güte,
dem Gott, der alle Wunder tut,
  dem Gott, der mein Gemüte
mit seinem reichen Trost erfüllt,
dem Gott, der allen Jammer stillt.
  Gebt unserm Gott die Ehre!

Es danken dir die Himmelsheer,
  o Herrscher aller Thronen;
und die auf Erden, Luft und Meer
  in deinem Schatten wohnen,
die preisen deine Schöpfermacht,
die alles also wohl bedacht.
  Gebt unserm Gott die Ehre!

Was unser Gott geschaffen hat,
  das will er auch erhalten,
darüber will er früh und spat
  mit seiner Gnade walten.
In seinem ganzen Königreich
ist alles recht, ist alles gleich.
  Gebt unserm Gott die Ehre!

Ich reif zum Herrn in meiner Not:
  "Ach Gott, vernimm mein Schreien!"
Da half mein Helfer mir vom Tod
  und ließ mir Trost gedeihen.
Drum dank, ach Gott, drum dank ich dir;
ach danket, danket Gott mit mir!
  Gebt unserm Gott die Ehre!

Der Herr ist noch und nimmer nicht
    von seinem Volk geschieden;
er bleibet ihre Zuversicht,
    ihr Segen, Heil und Frieden.
Mit Mutterhänden leitet er
die Seinen stetig hin und her.
    Gebt unserm Gott die Ehre!

Wenn Trost und Hülf ermangeln muß,
    die alle Welt erzeiget,
so kommt, so hilft der Überfluß,
    der Schopfer selbst, und neiget
die Vateraugen denem zu,
die sonsten nirgends finden Ruh.
    Gebt unserm Gott die Ehre!

Ich will dich all mein Leben lang,
    o Gott, von nun an ehren,
man soll, o Gott, dein Lobgesang
    an allen Orten hören.
Mein ganzes Herz ermuntre sich,
mein Seel und Leib erfreue dich!
    Gebt unserm Gott die Ehre!

Ihr, die ihr Christi Namen nennt,
    gebt unserm Gott die Ehre;
ihr, die ihr Gottes Macht bekennt,
    gebt unserm Gott die Ehre!
Die falschen Götzen macht zu Spott;
der Herr ist Gott, der Herr ist Gott !
    Gebt unserm Gott die Ehre!

So kommet vor sein Angesicht
    mir jauchzenvollen Springen;
bezahlet die gelobte Pflicht
    and laßt uns fröhlich singen:
Gott hat es alles wohl bedacht
und alles, alles recht gemacht.
    Gebt unserm Gott die Ehre!

Johann Jakob Schütz, 1673
Christliches Gedenkbüchlein, 1675

B.

Sing praise to God who reigns above,
    the God of all creation,
the God of power, the God of love,
    the God of our salvation;
with healing balm my soul he fills,
and every faithless murmur stills.
    To God all praise and glory!

The angel host, O King of kings,
    thy praise for ever telling,
in earth and sky all living things
    beneath thy shadow dwelling,
adore the wisdom which could span,
and power which formed creation's plan.
    To God all praise and glory!

What God's almighty power hath made
    his gracious mercy keepeth;
by morning glow or evening shade
    his watchful eye ne'er sleepeth;
within the kingdom of his might,
lo! all is just, and all is right.
    To God all praise and glory!

I cried to God in my distress—
    in mercy hear my calling—
my Savior saw my helplessness,
    and kept my feet from falling.
For this, Lord, thanks and praise to thee!
Praise God, I say, praise God with me!
    To God all praise and glory!

The Lord is never far away,
    throughout all grief distressing,
an ever-present help and stay,
    our peace and joy and blessing;
as with a mother's tender hand
he leads his own, his chosen band.
    To God all praise and glory!

When every earthly hope has flown
    from sorrow's sons and daughters,
our Father from his heavenly throne
    beholds the troubled waters;
and, at his word, the storm is stayed
which made his children's hearts afraid.
    To God all praise and glory!

Then all my gladsome way along
    I sing aloud thy praises,
that men may hear the grateful song
    my voice unwearied raises:
Be joyful in the Lord, my heart,
both soul and body, bear your part!
    To God all praise and glory!

O ye who name Christ's holy name,
    give God all praise and glory;
all ye who own his power, proclaim
    aloud the wondrous story.
Cast each false idol from his throne:
The Lord is God and he alone:
    To God all praise and glory!

translated, Frances Elizabeth Cox
based on stanzas 1 through 8 of Schütz's text
Hymns from the German, 1864

199

And All That Is within Me, Bless His Holy Name. Psalm 103

A.

Lobe den Herren, den mächtigen König der Ehren,
meine geliebete Seele, das ist mein Begehren.
    Kommet zuhauf,
    Psalter und Harfe, wacht auf,
    lasset den Musicam hören.

Lobe den Herren, der alles so herrlich regieret,
der dich auf Adelers Fittichen sicher geführet,
    der dich erhält,
    wie es dir selber gefällt;
    hast du nicht dieses verspüret?

Lobe den Herren, der künstlich und fein dich
    bereitet,
der dir Gesundheit verliehen, dich freundlich
    geleitet.
    In wieviel Not
    hat nicht der gnädige Gott
    über dir Flügel gebreitet!

Lobe den Herren, der deinen Stand sichtbar
    gesegnet,
der aus dem Himmel mit Strömen der Liebe
    geregnet.
    Denke daran,
    was der Allmächtige kann,
    der dir mit Liebe begegnet.

Lobe den Herren, was in mir ist, lobe den Namen.
Alles, was Odem hat, lobe mit Abrahams Samen.
    Er ist dein Licht,
    Seele, vergiß es ja nicht.
    Lobende, schließe mit Amen.

Joachim Neander
Glaub- und Liebesübung, 1680

B.

Praise to the Lord! the Almighty, the King of
    Creation!
O my soul, praise him, for he is thy health and
    salvation!
    All ye who hear,
    now to his temple draw near,
    join me in glad adoration.

Praise to the Lord! who o'er all things so
        wondrously reigneth,
shelters thee under his wings, yea, so gently
        sustaineth;
    Hast thou not seen
    how thy desires e'er have been
    granted in what he ordaineth?

Praise to the Lord! who doth prosper thy work
        and defend thee,
surely his goodness and mercy here daily attend thee;
    Ponder anew
    what the Almighty can do
    if with his love he befriend thee!

Praise to the Lord! O let all that is in me adore him!
All that hath life and breath, come now with praises
        before him!
    Let the "Amen"
    sound from his people again,
    gladly for aye we adore him!

> translated, Catherine Winkworth
> *Chorale Book for England*, 1863
> Winkworth's 4-stanza translation combines in its second stanza ideas
> from the original stanzas 2 and 3.

C.

Sing praise to God, who has shaped and sustains
        all creation!
Sing praise, my soul, in profound and complete
        adoration!
    Gladsome rejoice—
    organ and trumpet and voice—
    joining God's great congregation.

Praise God, our guardian, who lovingly offers
        correction,
who, as on eagle's wings, saves us from sinful
        dejection.
    Have you observed,
    how we are always preserved
    by God's parental affection?

Sing praise to God, with sincere thanks for all your
        successes.
Merciful God ever loves to encourage and bless us.
    Only conceive,
    what godly strength can achieve:
    strength that would touch and caress us.

Sing praise, my soul, the great name of your high
        God commending.
All that have life and breath join you, their notes
        sweetly blending.
    God is your light!
    Soul, ever keep this in sight:
    amen, amen never ending.

> translated, Madeleine Forell Marshall, 1993
> *The New Century Hymnal*, 1995
> © 1993, Madeleine Forell Marshall

200
Thanks following the Meal. I Timothy 6:17

A.

Meine Hoffnung stehet feste
    auf dem lebendigen Gott;
er ist mir der allerbeste
    der mir beisteht in der Not;
      er allein
      soll es sein
    den ich nur von Hertzen mein.

Sag't mir wer kan doch vertrauen
    auf ein schwaches Menschen-Kind?
Wer kan feste Schlößer bauen
    in der Luft und in dem Wind?
      Es vergeht
      nichts besteht
    was ihr auf der Erden seh't.

Aber Gottes Güte währet
    immer und in Ewigkeit;
Vieh und Menschen er ernehret
    durch erwünschte Jarhes-Zeit
        alles hat
        seine Gnad
    dargereichet früh und spat.

Giebet er nicht alles reichlich
    und mit großem Uberfluß?
Seine Lieb' is unvergleichlich
    wie ein starcker Wasserguß:
        Luft und Erd
        uns ernehr't
    wann es Gottes Gunst begehr't.

Danket nun dem großem Schöpfer
    durch den wahren Menschen Sohn
der us wie ein freier Töpfer
    hat gemacht aus Erd und Ton;
        groß von Rat
        stark von Tat
    ist der uns gespeiset hat.

Joachim Neander
Glaub- und Liebesübung, 1680

B.

All my hope on God is founded;
    he doth still my trust renew.
Me through change and chance he guideth,
    only good and only true.
        God unknown,
        he alone
calls my heart to be his own.

Pride of man and earthly glory,
    sword and crown betray his trust;
what with care and toil he buildeth,
    tower and temple fall to dust.
        But God's power,
        hour by hour,
is my temple and my tower.

God's great goodness aye endureth,
    deep his wisdom passing thought;
splendor, light, and life attend him,
    beauty springeth out of nought.
        Evermore
        from his store
newborn worlds rise and adore.

Daily doth the almighty Giver
    bounteous gifts on us bestow;
his desire our soul delighteth,
    pleasure leads us where we go.
        Love doth stand
        at his hand;
joy doth wait at his command.

Still from man to God eternal
    sacrifice of praise be done,
high above all praises praising
    for the gift of Christ his Son.
        Christ doth call
        one and all:
ye who follow shall not fall.

Robert Bridges
based on Neander
The Yattendon Hymnal, 1899

201
This man receiveth sinners. Luke 15:1–10

A.

Jesus nimmt die Sünder an.
Saget doch dies Trostwort allen,
   welche von der rechten Bahn
auf verkehrten Weg verfallen.
   Hier ist, was sie retten kann:
   Jesus nimmt die Sünder an.

Keiner Gnade sind wir wert;
doch hat er in seinem Worte
   eidlich sich dazu erklärt.
Sehet nur, die Gnadenpforte
   ist hier völlig aufgetan:
   Jesus nimmt die Sünder an.

Wenn ein Schaf verloren ist,
suchet es ein treuer Hirte;
   Jesus, der uns nie vergißt,
suchet treulich das Verirrte,
   daß es nicht verderben kann:
   Jesus nimmt die Sünder an.

Kommet alle, kommet her,
kommet irh betrübten Sünder!
   Jesus rufet euch, und er
macht aus Sündern Gottes Kinder.
   Glaubets doch und denket dran:
   Jesus nimmt die Sünder an.

Ich Betrübter komme hier
und bekenne meine Sünden;
   laß, mein Heiland, mich bei dir
Gnade zur Vergebung finden,
   daß dies Wort mich trösten kann:
   Jesus nimmt die Sünder an.

Ich bin ganz getrosten Muts:
ob die Sünden blutrot wären,
   müssen sie kraft deines Bluts
dennoch sich in schneeweiß kehren,
   da ich gläubig sprechen kann:
   Jesus nimmt die Sünder an.

Mein Gewissen beisst mich nicht,
Moses darf mich nicht verklagen;
   der mich frei und ledig spricht,
hast die Schulden abgetragen,
   daß mich nichts verdammen kann:
   Jesus nimmt die Sünder an.

Jesus nimmt die Sünder an;
mich hat er auch angenommen
   und den Himmel aufgetan,
daß ich selig zu ihm kommen
   und auf den Trost sterben kann:
   Jesus nimmt die Sünder an.

Erdmann Neumeister
Evangelische Nachklang, 1718

B. Song of Welcome

Sinners Jesus will receive—
say this word of grace to all,
who the heavenly pathway leave,
all who linger, all who fall!
   This can bring them back again,
   Christ receiveth sinful men.

We deserve no help, no love,
yet his changeless word is given,
that his grace shall not remove:
No man at the gate of Heaven
   in his name shall knock in vain—
   Christ receiveth sinful men.

Shepherds seek their wandering sheep
o'er the mountains bleak and cold—
Jesus such a watch doth keep
o'er the lost ones of his fold;
    seeking them o'er moor and fen:
    Christ receiveth sinful men.

Come, and he will give you rest,
sorrow-stricken, sin-defiled—
he can make the sinfulest
God the Father's blessed child:
    Trust him, for his word is plain,
    Christ receiveth sinful men.

Sick and sorrowful and blind,
I with all my sins draw nigh—
O my Savior, thou canst find
help for sinners such as I.
    Speak that word of love again:
    Christ receiveth sinful men.

Yea, my soul is comforted,
for thy blood hath washed away
all my sins, though crimson red,
and I stand in white array,
    purged from every spot and stain:
    Christ receiveth sinful men.

Now my heart condemns me not,
pure before the law I stand;
he who cleansed me from all spot
satisfied its last demand.
    Who shall dare accuse me then?
    Christ receiveth sinful men.

Christ receiveth sinful men—
even me with all my sin;
openeth to me heaven again,
with him I may enter in.
    Death hath no more sting nor pain;
    Christ receiveth sinful men.

translated, Emma Frances Shuttleworth Bevan
Songs of Eternal Life, 1858

208

202

Remembrance of the Glorious and Delightful Presence of God

A.

Gott ist gegenwärtig. Lasset uns anbeten
und in Ehrfurcht vor ihn treten.
Gott ist in der Mitten. Alles in uns schweige
und sich innigst vor ihm beuge.
Wer ihn kennt,
wer ihn nennt,
schlag die Augen nieder;
kommt, ergebt euch wieder.

Gott ist gegenwärtig, dem die Cherubinen
Tag und Nacht gebücket dienen.
Heilig, heilig, heilig! singen ihm zur Ehre
aller Engel hohe Chöre.
Herr, vernimm
nsre Stimm,
da auch wir Geringen
unsre Opfer bringen.

Wir entsagen willig allen Eitelkeiten,
aller Erdenlust und Freuden;
da liegt unser Wille, Seele, Leib und Leben
dir zum Eigentum ergeben.
Du allein
sollst es sein,
unser Gott und Herre,
dir gebührt die Ehre.

Majestätisch Wesen, möcht ich recht dich preisen
und im Geist dir Dienst erweisen.
Möcht ich wie die Engel immer vor dir stehen
und dich gegenwärtig sehen.
Laß mich dir
für und für
trachten zu gefallen,
liebster Gott, in allem.

Luft, die alles füllet, drin wir immer schweben,
aller Dinge Grund und Leben,
Meer ohn Grund und Ende, Wunder aller Wunder:
ich senk mich in dich hinunter.
Ich in dir,
du in mir,
laß mich ganz verschwinden,
dich nur sehn und finden.

Du durchdringest alles; laß dein schönstes Lichte,
Herr, berühren mein Gesichte.
Wie die zarten Blumen willig sich entfalten
und der Sonne stille halten,
laß mich so
still und froh
deine Strahlen fassen
und dich wirken lassen.

Mache mich einfältig, innig, abgeschieden,
sanft und still in deinem Frieden;
mach mich reines Herzens, daß ich deine Klarheit
schauen mag in Geist un Wahrheit;
laß mein Herz
überwärts
wie ein Adler schweben
und in dir nur leben.

Herr, komm in mir wohnen, laß mein' Geist auf Erden
dir ein Heiligtum noch werden;
komm, du nahes Wesen, dich in mir verkläre,
daß ich dich stets lieb und ehre.
Wo ich geh,
sitz und steh,
laß mich dich erblicken
und vor dir mich bücken.

Gerhardt Tersteegen
Geistliches Blumengärtlien, 1729

B.

God reveals his presence, let us now adore him,
and with awe appear before him:
God is in his temple, all in us keep silence
and before him bow with reverence.
Him alone
God we own;
he's our Lord and Savior:
praise his name for ever.

God reveals his presence, whom the angelic legions
serve with awe in heavenly regions.
"Holy, holy, holy!" sing the hosts of heaven,
"Praise to God be ever given."
Condescend
to attend
Graciously, O Jesus,
to our songs and praises.

O majestic Being, were but soul and body
thee to serve at all times ready;
might we like the angels who behold thy glory,
with abasement sink before thee,
and through grace
be always
in our whole demeanor
to thy praise and honor.

translated, Frederick William Foster and John Miller, 1789
A Collection of Hymns, 1789
as altered by William Mercer in *The Church Psalter
and Hymn Book*, 1854
The original translation consisted of five stanzas
based on stanzas 1, 2, 4, 7, and 8 of Tersteegen's text.

C.

Lo, God is here! let us adore,
and own how dreadful is this place!   (Gen. 28:22)
Let all within us feel his power
and silent bow before his face;
Who know his power, his grace who prove,
serve him with awe, with reverence love.

Lo, God is here! him day and night
    the united choirs of angels sing;
to him, enthroned above all height
    heaven's hosts their noblest praises bring.
Disdain not, Lord, our meaner song,
who praise thee with a stammering tongue.

Gladly the toys of earth we leave,
    wealth, pleasure, fame, for thee alone;
to thee our will, soul, flesh we give;
    O take! O seal them for thine own!
Thou art the God; thou art the Lord;
be thou by all thy works adored.

Being of beings, may our praise
    thy courts with grateful fragrance fill;
still may we stand before thy face,
    still hear and do thy sovereign will.
To thee may all our thoughts arise,
ceaseless, accepted sacrifice.

In thee we move. All things of thee
    are full, thou source and life of all!
Thou vast, unfathomable sea!
    all prostrate, lost in wonder fall,
ye sons of men; for God is man!
All may we lose, so thee we gain!

As flowers their opening leaves display,
    and glad drink in the solar fire,
so may we catch thy every ray,
    so may thy influence us inspire,
thou beam of the eternal beam,
thou purging fire, thou quick'ning flame!

translated, John Wesley
Hymns and Sacred Poems, 1739

203
Praise and Prayer. 2 Corinthians 5:17

A.

O treuer Heiland Jesu Christ,
    wir danken deiner Treu
für Alles, was vergangen ist
    und was geworden neu.

Vergangen ist die Sicherheit,
    darin wir lang gesteckt;
du hast zu ihrer Seligkeit
    die Schläfer ausgeweckt.

Neu ist das Sehnen, das sich hin
    zu ewgen Gütern lenkt,
du hast dazu in Herz und Sinn
    der Gnade Trieb gesenkt.

Doch wie viel Altes muss vergehn,
    wie viel noch werden neu,
eh wir in dich verkläret stehn,
    zum Breife deiner Treu'!

Der du das Sehnen weckst und stillst,
    nimm auch des unsern wahr,
und wie du gern uns haben willst,
    so stelle selbst uns dar.

Erweck uns täglich, halt uns wach
    und heil'ge Seel und Leib;
ach, hör nicht auf und laß nicht nach,
    durch Güt und Ernst uns treib.

Mach du dem Geiste lieblich doch,
    was unserm Fleisch verhasst;
mach du uns sanft der Wahrheit Joch
    und liecht der Liebe Last.

Verleid uns, was uns trennt von dir,
    es sei auch, was es sei;
Zieh uns dir nach, so laufen wir
    den Berg des Lebens frei.

Ach, mach aus uns, was dir gefällt,
    uns in dein Bild verklär;
Gieb Kräfte der zukünftgen Welt,
    hilf uns von oben her.

Karl Johann Philipp Spitta, 1843
Psalter und Harfe, 1865

B.

We praise and bless thee, gracious Lord,
    our Savior kind and true,
for all the old things passed away,
    for all thou hast made new.

The old security is gone
    in which so long we lay;
the sleep of death thou hast dispelled,
    the darkness rolled away.

New hopes, new purposes, desires
    and joys, thy grace has given;
old ties are broken from the earth,
    new ties attach to heaven.

But yet how much must be destroyed,
    how much renewed must be,
ere we can fully stand complete
    in likeness, Lord, to thee.

Ere to Jerusalem above,
    the holy place, we come,
where nothing sinful or defiled
    shall ever find a home!

Thou, only thou, must carry on
    the work thou hast begun;
of thine own strength thou must impart
    in thine own ways to run.

Ah! leave us not—from day to day
    revive, restore again;
our feeble steps do thou direct,
    our enemies restrain.

Whate'er would tempt the soul to stray,
    or separate from thee,
that, Lord, remove, however dear
    to the poor heart it be!

When the flesh sinks, then strengthen thou
    the spirit from above;
make us to feel thy service sweet,
    and light thy yoke of love.

So shall we faultless stand at last
    before thy Father's throne,
the blessedness for ever ours,
    the glory all thine own.

translated, Jane Laurie Borthwick
Hymns from the Land of Luther, 1855

204
Canticle of Brother Sun and of All Creatures

A.

Altissimu, omnipotente, bonsignore,
tue sono le laude,
la gloria elhonore
et omne benedictione.

Ad te solo, Altissimo, se Konfano
et nullu homo enne dignu
te mentovare.

Laudato se, misignore, com tucte le tue creature,
spetialmente messer lo frate sole,
loquale iorno et allumini noi par loi.

Et ellu ebellu eradiante cum grande splendore:
de te, Altissimo, porta significatione.

Laudato si, misignore, per sora luna ele stelle:
in celu lai formate clarite
et pretiose et belle.

Laudato si, misignore, per frate vento,
et per aere et nubilo
et sereno et omne tempo
per loquale a le tue creature
dai sustentatamento.

Laudato si, misignore, per sor aqua,
laquale e multo utile et humile
et pretiosa et casta.

Laudato si, misignore, per frate focu,
per loquale ennalumini la nocte:
edello ebello et iocundo
et robustoso et forte.

Laudato si, misignore, per sora nostra matre terra,
laquale ne sustenta et governa,
et produce diversi fructi
con coloriti flori et herba.

Laudato si, misignore, per quelli ke perdonano
per lo tuo amore
et sostengo infirmitate
et tribulatione.

Beate quelli kel sosterrano in pace,
ke da te, Altissimo,
sirano incoronati.

Laudato si, misignore, per sora nostra
morte corporale,
da laquale nullu homo
vivente poskappare.

Gai acqueli ke morrano
ne le peccato mortali!

Beati quelli ke trovarane
le tue sanctissime voluntati
ke la morte secunda
nol farra male.

Laudate et benedictite, misignore,
et rengratiate et servaite li
cum grande humilitate.

Francis of Assisi, 1225

B.

O most high, almighty, good Lord God, to thee belong praise, glory, honor and all blessing!

Praised be my Lord God, with all his creatures; and specially our brother the sun, who brings us the day, and who brings us the light; fair is he, and shining with a very great splendor: O Lord, he signifies to us thee!

Praised be my Lord for our sister the moon, and for the stars, the which he has set clear and lovely in heaven.

Praised be my Lord for our brother the wind, and for air and cloud, calms and all weather, by the which thou upholdest in life all creatures.

Praised be my Lord for our sister water, who is very serviceable unto us, and humble, and precious and clean.

Praised be my Lord for our brother fire, through whom thou givest us light in the darkness; and he is bright, and pleasant, and very mighty, and strong.

Praised be my Lord for our mother the earth, the which doth sustain us and keep us, and bringeth forth divers fruits, and flowers of many colors, and grass.

Praised be my Lord for all those who pardon one another for his love's sake, and who endure weakness and tribulation; blessed are they who peaceably shall endure, for thou, O most Highest, shalt give them a crown!

Praised be my Lord for our sister, the death of the body, from whom no man escapeth. Woe to him who dieth in mortal sin! Blessed are they who are found walking by thy most holy will, for the second death shall have no power to do them harm.

Praise ye, and bless ye the Lord, and give thanks unto him, and serve him with great humility.

translated, Matthew Arnold, 1865
This translation, from the first volume of Arnold's *Essays in Criticism*,
reflects the rhythm and spirit of the original.

C.

All creatures of our God and King,
lift up your voice and with us sing
    Alleluia, alleluia!
Thou burning sun with golden beam,
thou silver moon with softer gleam,

    O praise him, O praise him,
    alleluia, alleluia, alleluia!

Thou rushing wind that art so strong,
ye clouds that sail in heaven along,
    O praise him, alleluia!
Thou rising morn, in praise rejoice,
ye lights of evening, find a voice.

Thou flowing water, pure and clear,
make music for thy Lord to hear,
    alleluia, alleluia!
Thou fire so masterful and bright,
thou givest man both warmth and light!

Dear mother earth, who day by day
unfoldest blessings on our way,
    O praise him, alleluia!
The flowers and fruits that in thee grow,
let them his glory also show.

And all ye men of tender heart,
forgiving others, take your part,
    O sing ye, alleluia!
Ye who long pain and sorrow bear,
praise God and on him cast your care.

And thou most kind and gentle death,
waiting to hush our latest breath,
    O praise him, alleluia!
Thou leadest home the child of God,
and Christ our Lord the way hath trod.

Let all things their Creator bless,
and worship him in humbleness,
    O praise him, alleluia!
Praise, praise the Father, praise the Son,
and praise the Spirit, Three in One.

translated, William H. Draper
The Public School Hymn Book, 1919

205
Come Down, O Love Divine

A.

Discendi, amor santo
visita la mie mente
del tuo amore ardente,
si che di te m'infiammi tutto quanto.

Vienne, consolatore,
nel mio cuor veramente:
del tuo ardente amore
ardel veracemente:
del tuo amor cocente
si forte sie ferito;
vada come smarrito
dentro e di fuore ardendo tutto quanto.

Arda si fortemente
che tutto mi consumi:
si che veracemente
lassi mondan costumi;
li splendienti lumi
lucenti, illuminanti
mi stien sempre davanti,
per il quali mi vesta il vero manto.

E'l manto ch'i'mi vesta
sie la carità santa:
sott'una bigia vesta
umilità si canta,
la qual mai non si vanta
per se nullo ben fare,
non si sa inalzare,
ma nel profondo scende con gran pianto.

Nel fondo più profondo
discende nel suo cuore:
di ciascun uom del mondo
sè ved'esser minore:
non si cura d'onore,
ma le vergogne brama:
di se vendetta chiama,
odio se stesso sempre in ogni canto.

Se dagli altri è inalzato
nel cuor sempre discende,
del ben che'gli ha, ingrato
sè esser sempre intende.
Chi tale stato prende
già ma'non può perire:
vita si gli è'l morire,
morendo vive e vivend'è poi santo.

In queste duo colonne
si ferman gil amadori,
perchè son le madonne
sopra l'altre migliori:
chi ben c'è ferm', ardori
si grandi sente al cuore,
che grida per amore,
che sostener nol può, si è tamanto.

Si grande è quel disio
ch'allor l'anima sente,
che dir nol sapre' io,
a ciò non son potente:
nulla umana mente
entender noi potria,
se noi gustasse pria
per la vertù dello Spirito Santo.
    Deo gracias.

Bianco of Siena, ca. 1367
Laudi spirituali del Bianco da Siena, 1851

Let holy charity
  mine outward vesture be
and lowliness become mine inner clothing:
  true lowliness of heart,
  which takes the humbler part
and o'er its own shortcomings weeps with loathing.

And so the yearning strong
  with which the soul will long
shall far outpass the power of human telling;
  nor none can guess its grace
  till he become the place
wherein the Holy Spirit makes his dwelling.

translated, Richard Frederick Littledale
The People's Hymnal, 1867

B.

Come down, O love divine,
  seek thou this soul of mine
and visit it with thine own ardor glowing;
  O Comforter, draw near,
  within my heart appear
and kindle it, thy holy flame bestowing.

O let it freely burn
  till earthly passions turn
to dust and ashes in thy heat consuming;
  and let thy glorious light
  shine ever on my sight
and clothe me round, the while my path illuming.

Chapter 14:
The Victorian Age, 1837–1906
(206–269)

In every respect the English Victorian age was an age of energy and confidence. Until its very last years, England was involved in no major war, and during the sixty-four years 1837–1901, which are those strictly to be called "Victorian," the country experienced an immense growth in population, economics, and invention. Virtually everything which was "success" to the Victorians has come to be questioned in the twentieth century. But the fashionable use of the word "Victorian" to describe what is stolid, philistine, and unimaginative is a dangerous half-truth which, whatever the intellectuals may say, is now being protested against by the addiction of large numbers of people, in Britain and America, to documentary entertainments (chiefly on television) which expose with remarkable fidelity, and not without affection, the true texture of Victorian life.

In hymnody the period conveniently ends at 1906, the year of *The English Hymnal*; but in this and the next two sections only a handful of hymns actually fall outside the reign of the most famous of English queens. And in hymnody the energy and enterprise of that age is very fully reflected.

In that age of energy there was much controversy. The hymns in this section respond to three great disputes: (1) that centered in the Oxford Movement which, after 1833, looked for and achieved nothing less than a revival of religion in the Church of England; (2) the passion of the Christian Socialists against social abuses; and (3), late in the age, what Robert Schumann would have called the "march of the armies of David against the Philistines" (the gestures of the literate against the cheapening of style that was overtaking hymnody itself).

"Cheapening" was the great blessing and the great peril. It became easy, in the early nineteenth century, to print and distribute books and especially to print music. Coincident with this came a new and clamorous demand for hymnody in the Church of England. Halfway through the age came several waves of evangelical revival, mostly aimed from America. A study of the enormous number of hymnals and songsheets produced from about 1860 onwards speedily convinces the reader that in hymnody, as in much else, you could get away with almost anything. A parallel situation developed in the later twentieth century where again a new kind of demand produced a massive output, and again standards fell to alarming depths. It was with music as it was with texts; and our third point of controversy was the inevitable response to a feeling, by 1900, that the too liberally sown and too casually tended garden of hymnody needed weeding.

It is a curious and rather mournful fact that literary and theological critics in church circles are still saying what secular criticism and popular taste have now rejected, that the nineteenth century has virtually nothing to offer in the way of good hymnody. Perhaps, in the field of correcting misconceptions, we have no more important chapter in this book than this present one, for it is designed to show what the Victorians were trying to do and what, when they were at their best, they achieved.

This is predominantly the age of Anglican hymnody. The famous case in the church courts which finally legitimized hymnody opened a gate, and the Romantics (chapter 9) rode through it, liberating hymnody through their special talents (see 116–124 for particular examples). (The law against hymnody had long been a dead letter, but members of Thomas Cotterill's congregation in Sheffield chose to make a test case out of the hymnal that their vicar was inviting them to use, and the archbishop in the end, after a nice piece of ecclesiastical diplomacy, ruled that hymnody was no longer illegal.)

The first wave of energy was directed at translation work, which we dealt with in chapters 11–13. To this Richard Mant made an early, and now mostly forgotten, contribution: his excellent "Bright the vision" (206) comes from his *Ancient Hymns* of 1837, its place there no doubt being justified by its being based on the *tersanctus* in Isaiah 6. But it is a generation before much original work comes from the Anglicans.

Therefore, after 206 we do not meet an Oxford Movement hymn again until 220. Nonconformity produced many hymnals during the early Victorian time, not least among them being private hymnals for wealthy and populous chapels, the most famous of which was the *Leeds Hymn Book* of 1853, one of whose editors produced the very spirited text of 218. But the creativity of nonconformity was somewhat muted by their eighteenth-century heritage: the Wesleys for the Methodists, and Watts for the Congregationalists and Baptists. Unitarians, however, produced some choice pieces, like 207, from one of their best minds, which well illustrates the special interest of nineteenth-century Unitarians in high culture.

But the most productive non-Anglican area turned out to be that of the Roman Catholic Church. This communion, released by emancipation from positive illegality in 1833 and reestablishing its hierarchy in 1850, produced one hymn writer in Frederick W. Faber (208–212) who had exactly the gift that was needed in that company. Roman Catholics were mostly poor, often immigrants, and in their newfound religious freedom concerned with two great issues: eucharistic devotion, and their mission to convert others to the Catholic faith. Both these notes are sounded by Faber, who had in his makeup a strong influence from evangelicalism. Hymns were, of course, not needed for the Mass, but vernacular hymnody at popular services has never been forbidden to English Catholics, and Faber's purpose, as he said, was to do for his people what the *Olney Hymns*, which he knew and admired, had done for Olney. His talent was equal to neither that of Newton nor that of Cowper, and he was fatally garrulous, so that his hymns usually need pruning

for public use; that is just as well, because he is capable of writing fairly expert doggerel. But on the other hand, there are stanzas in "My God, how wonderful thou art" and "O come and mourn with me awhile" which are profoundly beautiful and which sound an ecstatic note that the anti-enthusiastic Anglicans tended to avoid. The argumentative and conversational character of some of the others has an endearing quality, even if it does not always make very polished hymnody. Matthew Bridges's "Crown him with many crowns" (214) is at a loftier level; it is not too often found now in its original form, many editors preferring the diluted though still serviceable version with stanzas by Godfrey Thring.

With Thomas Toke Lynch (215–217) we stumble on a curious piece of church history. Lynch, a gentle Congregational minister, produced his collection of hymns, *The Rivulet*, in 1855 and enlarged it in 1856. A glance at the texts will indicate a certain nervous originality, a preoccupation with natural imagery, a readiness to deal with religious doubt and hesitation. (216 might have been a text for the 1963 *Honest to God* controversy.) As one of the few nonconformist writers of that time with anything new to say, he commands respect, and one forgives him some bad lines for an equal number of really inspired epigrams, like that at the end of stanza 3 of 215, or of stanza 3 of 217. One would not put it higher than that, were it not that the book chanced to fall into the hands of one John Campbell, the Scottish Calvinist editor of a denominational paper, whose native heresy-hunting instincts it aroused to such purpose that he reviewed it for seven consecutive weeks, tearing every page to theological shreds. The members of the Congregational Assembly were soon brought to such a tension of dispute between those who thought Campbell a monster and those who thought Lynch an enemy of right-thinking Christians that, in the words of the denomination's best historian of the incident, Albert Peel, the Assembly was "almost wrecked." Only Thomas Binney (130) prevailed to secure a peaceful settlement on the second occasion when the matter was debated. Such was the flammable atmosphere in which a nonconformist hymn writer worked; it is hardly surprising that we do not hear much from any but Lynch and Rawson (218) who, in the north country, seem to have kept safely clear of theological storm centers. The pale examples of Lynch's work that modern hymnals are content with hardly lead anyone to suspect what trouble he got into; we leave those for readers to discover for themselves.

Two "angry" hymns, 213 and 219, represent, in this early period, the mind of those who sought to issue calls to social action. Ebenezer Elliott's once famous piece, "When wilt thou save the people," is passionate and is also superbly written. Not less so is the only hymn by the author of *Tom Brown's Schooldays* (219), a text which squeamish editors often modify in order to get rid of the rhetorical questions and other acerbities; but they should leave it as it is and sing it to the tune MARTYRS.

And now, with *Hymns Ancient and Modern* (trial edition, 1860; first full edition, 1861), the Anglicans come into their own. Many hymnals had appeared during the fifties taking the quite new line which *Hymns A & M* made famous and standard, that of printing each hymn with a tune appropriate to it, instead of printing a words-edition for the congregation and a tune-book for the precentor, organist, or choir. But, as we have already often seen, it was not the earliest which made the headlines. *Hymns A & M*, with 273 hymns in the 1861 edition, very largely translations from Latin, with a sparing selection from the eighteenth-century Evangelicals, proved so abundantly successful that an enlarged edition (with a supplement bringing the total to 386) had to be brought out in 1868, a complete revision (473) in 1875, a supplement to the second edition (score 638) in 1889. The 1875 edition was perhaps the normative one; it was this edition which all editors—Anglican or not—felt they must measure up to, improve on, or react against. It was this edition that made "Abide with me" (27) and "O God, our help in ages past" [*sic*] (165) the kind of detail that caused people to protest with almost savage violence when the second revision of 1904 rationalized and updated the book and—to their horror—changed all the numbers. To that extent it was a British institution. (It still is; plenty of churches still use the edition which leaves 27 and 165 where you expect them, and the 1950 revision, while changing much, didn't dare to change those.)

The hymnody there required was a decorous adornment to the Prayer Book. Reacting against the "enthusiasm" of the evangelicals, these editors said that if we must have hymnody we must avoid the excesses into which it had led those Methodists whom, as agents for the reconversion of England, they most feared. So the book is arranged just as the Prayer Book is arranged, with hymns for matins coming first, then those for evensong, then those for the little hours (should anyone wish to observe them), then—corresponding to the "Collect, Epistle and Gospel" section of the Prayer Book—hymns for the church's year. Then, for Sundays after Trinity, "General Hymns," roughly arranged according to subject; then hymns for the sacraments, for special rites and occasions (corresponding to the "Occasional Prayers"), a long section of hymns for saints' days, and a handful of litanies.

Although the next series of hymns in this section comes from all manner of sources, the great majority of them appeared at some time in *Hymns A & M* and nearly all the authors have a place there up to 1904. Every one of the authors is in one or the other of the editions up to 1950. *Hymns A & M* was directed by a small committee whose leader was the Reverend Sir Henry Baker, a country parson in one of England's remotest counties—Herefordshire. And the ethos of the book is strictly that of the cozy, conservative, country parish church, the gathering place of those communities which were led by people who had a stake in the land rather than in industry. Not that they sang about the countryside any more than they sang about the city. They sang about what was in the Prayer Book, and therefore about what was in the Bible so interpreted.

Perhaps 220 is a good place to begin: a tolerable hymn, for a society that depended so much on the sea but that didn't go to sea much itself, to a rousing pictorial tune that sent shivers down decorous church-going spines. Numbers 221 and 222, by one of the very few laymen (an insurance manager) whom we meet in this section, show the "domestic" style at its best: neatly written, doctrinal, singable. Numbers 223 and 224 bring in one of the many high dignitaries who contributed to Victorian hymnody; Bishop Christopher Wordsworth could be dry and could indeed be trivial (there can hardly be a more lamentable travesty of 1 Corinthians 13 than "Gracious Spirit, Holy Ghost"); but he could also be magnificent, as in the massive and scriptural Ascension hymn, or that perfect miniature written for a confirmation, 224. John S. B. Monsell, Vicar of Guildford, wrote pleasant lyrics without attempting profundity (226–227). Dean Edward Plumptre again produced good serviceable material; the hymn about knowledge handles a subject unusual for the time and style (and it did not get into *Hymns A & M*); 229 is like a very well-dressed and well-starched version of 215. But schools and hospitals were multiplying at that time, and most Victorian attempts to meet their needs were far more pedestrian than these. Not so 245, however, which is by an author who knew how to write well and economically. (This was written for the opening of a hospital, though which one it is now difficult to determine—see the *Hymnal Guide*.)

Bishop William Walsham How is another typical gap-filler, always competent and honest, probably never inspired. Perhaps there is something impressive about the full version of 230 which is to some extent lost when the procession of apostles, evangelists, and martyrs is, as always now, dropped out (those stanzas do sit ill on Vaughan Williams's popular tune). Number 231 is a good example of the pictorial hymn so much loved by Victorians (indeed,

it is, like 262, based on an actual picture, and a very dubious one at that); one can hardly feel that it adequately transmits the message of Revelation 3:20, but at one time it was immensely popular.

Then comes the good Sabine Baring-Gould, a man of so many aesthetic interests, leading the children and congregation of his church round the village of Horbury Bridge on Sunday School Procession Day, with the great Tractarian Cross at the head, to the rousing, if mostly superficial, words of "Onward, Christian soldiers" (232). Processions, indoors or out, were a great matter for the Oxford Movement. Hardly less strenuous—beginning tolerably, touching real solid scriptural ground, then wilting at the end—is his translation from the Danish (233), still the only hymn we know from that language and so clearly the work of somebody whose culture was wider ranging than that of the usual parson. "For the beauty of the earth" (234), now a popular nature hymn, becomes, if you have its full and original text, an earnest eucharistic hymn of considerable dignity.

More pictorial imagery and sonorous language in 235, perhaps the best piece of literature Dean Henry Alford provided for hymnals. (His universally known harvest hymn is disqualified for inclusion here by its calamitous third stanza.) "Amen! Come, Lord Jesus" deserves to have had a longer life than in fact it got. "The Church's one foundation" (236) is one of the most theologically substantial of all Victorian hymns and thoroughly deserves its continued popularity. Written by a still young priest in reaction to the Colenso controversy (a heresy hunt in the Church of England focused on a popular, tough-minded, and unfortunate South African bishop who was removed from his see for saying that Moses did not write Deuteronomy because it contains an account of his own funeral) and on the side of that controversy with which few people would now be in sympathy, it has become a universal hymn of celebration for great church occasions. Within the author's lifetime such occasions became greater and the processions longer, and to meet organizers' requests he inflated the text to ten verses (see Julian, *Dictionary of Hymnology*); but they are hack work, new pieces on an old garment, and they have very properly fallen away.

Bishop Edward Henry Bickersteth (238), best known for "Peace, perfect peace," was a hymnal editor and an evangelical, and his style was usually trivial and overemotional. This is probably his best work, forgotten in Britain now, though still to be found in America.

It is late in the day to mention Sir Henry Baker as a writer (239, 240); he did indeed contribute one or two pieces to the 1861 *Hymns A & M* which had a certain vogue. But it seems right, here, to quote his best-known hymn followed by his best hymn, and these came later. What could be more typical of countryside Anglicanism than the domesticizing of the 23rd Psalm in 239? King David is no longer "in presence of his enemies" but at the communion rail. Number 240 is surely Baker's soundest piece of teaching, with a very well-turned lyric imagination.

Canon John Ellerton (246–247) was editor and hymnologist—one of the first—as well as a prolific author. Here again, as with How and Monsell, we have decent middle-of-the-road hymnody for parishes. "The day thou gavest" is still one of the authentic "Anglican sounds" and so is "Savior, again to thy dear name we raise." We offer here two saints' day hymns to show how sensibly Ellerton tackled a subject which too often produced platitude in hymnals. The opening of the third stanza of 247 has a touch of modest genius. Much of his work is still in hymn books and easily come by.

Dean Arthur Stanley (248) always seems to have written weightily; he used this ponderous verse-form more than once. This is cathedral-style writing, needing room to speak and space to ponder: urbane and dignified and decent. William Bright has in 249 and 250 a touch more warmth; 249 is unequal in a fashion that almost makes one welcome the absence of parsonic gloss; 250 is brilliant in its way, a really distinguished saints' day

hymn with a splendid climax to the whole argument in the last stanza.

Archbishop William Maclagan is now fast disappearing from hymnals, but 251 is worth attention for its very unusual subject: a really brave attempt to write a lyric on the mysteries of Holy Saturday. (Read also, should you have the chance, his workmanlike and unusual piece on St. Luke, at 420 in the standard edition of *Hymns A & M*.) William Romanis's hymn for St. James is another beautiful piece for a saint's day. The gifted scholar and historian Edwin Hatch is now universally famous for "Breathe on me" (253), whose unfortunate marriage to a detestable tune has hampered its message in America and in parts of England.

So much for the hymns along the main stream of Oxford Movement thinking. But now we must go back and pick up those we omitted.

Francis Turner Palgrave, of the *Golden Treasury*, knew his poetry and could write it. His book of that name is the *Golden Treasury of Shorter Poems*, but he compiled also a similar *Treasury* of longer poems, and a *Treasury of Sacred Song*, and from a standpoint near the Unitarian culture he looked pretty objectively at the fashionable hymnody of his time. Almost nothing of his is now sung, except 237 which surely is beautiful literature and beautiful thinking.

Another swimmer-against-the-stream is Henry Twells, an Anglican priest who did not quite fit into the Tractarian picture. I have not seen a picture of him so I do not know positively whether he had two vertical furrows between his eyebrows, but in his famous hymn, 241, we certainly see a very searching and prayerful imagination, and in 242 it is more prominent still. What other hymns for evensong deal with this aspect of Christ's ministry, or what other penitential hymns ask forgiveness for our religion? As for 243: meat too strong for any hymnal except the 1904 and 1916 editions of *Hymns A & M*, written a few days before he died. Why, this is one of the very few Victorian hymns which a frowning contemporary would surely have been proud to have written. Twells is a Victorian who should be looked at again by editors.

The stream of nonconformist hymnody between 1860 and 1890 becomes a mere trickle, but Congregationalism did produce one hymn writer who really seems to have taken it on himself to become that communion's Bishop How. Thomas Hornblower Gill wrote middle-of-the-road material; I cannot recall any inspired lines in his fairly generous output, but judiciously pruned (he was a bit garrulous), 244 still makes a sturdy hymn for occasions when history is being celebrated.

At 254 we begin to turn new pages. Before the great protest of Robert Bridges, to which we are just coming, there were signs that Anglicans wanted hymnody in new styles and on new subjects. One of these is in Ernest Edward Dugmore's two hymns here given. Number 254 waited a long time before becoming as popular as it now is, and it was the Scots, who put it into their 1927 Church Hymnary with a singable tune, who mostly contributed to that. A patristic theologian has pointed out to me that its first two stanzas reflect very vividly the theology of Gregory of Nyssa, one of the abler and more imaginative of the fourth-century Greek speaking teachers; and as it goes on it does reach out towards the Monday-to-Saturday world, a thing which, excluding the few "protesters," had rarely been done since Charles Wesley (67), and which is hardly attempted by the 1950 Hymns A & M. So it had been a long wait. In the far less familiar 255, Dugmore is experimenting with that meter which most nearly reflects the ethos of the heroic couplet (on which we commented in chapter 4), and there are lines there, in this immensely sonorous piece, which really do suggest the idiom of Alexander Pope.

Rudyard Kipling may or may not have intended 256 to be sung; it found a tune in the year of its first publication, and has been uneasily wedded to different partners for two generations since. Though its historic relevance has been forgotten and the presuppositions of stanza 4 are quite impossible for modern singers, it can still be read as great literature and as a remarkable penitential utterance for a writer so closely associated with celebrations of empire. Coming on this after reading some other Victorians is like touching real bone after being accustomed to plastic; look at those alliterations, those concrete and clanging monosyllables! Whatever else it may not be, this is real writing, and for about forty years hymnal editors found it irresistible.

And this brings us to the poet laureate Robert Bridges, whose single-handed contribution to the history of hymnody in *The Yattendon Hymnal* we must not here take too much space to celebrate. Here was the man who wrote in a letter, later published, the famous words: "All I can urge is that they should have at least *one* service a week where people like myself can attend without being offended or moved to laughter." He wrote that in 1911, when he was already famous—or notorious—for what he had said and done about Victorian hymnody. He was a trained physician, a leader in the world of letters, fifty-five years old, living on a hill outside Oxford and one of the two or three educated people attending the small parish church at Yattendon when, in 1899, he produced *The Yattendon Hymnal*. The full music edition of this hymnal is set out on a page thirteen inches by eleven, in open score, in an antique typeface which he invented, with full scholarly notes—sometimes perverse, always trenchant—on each hymn, and contains only two or three tunes later than 1750 (written by his friend H. Ellis Wooldridge, the Slade Professor of Fine Art at Oxford). The texts are nearly all by himself, designed to carry the original versions of tunes which were either unknown or known only in deformed versions.

His message was: Recover the treasures, not of the theological middle ages, but of the literary and musical past when these two arts were showing a true combination of maturity and innocence. All his material is slightly "old fashioned," written by the rules of eighteenth-century rather than nineteenth-century versifying, written to carry old tunes, written to translate or, more often, paraphrase old hymns in other languages. Two hymns of his are rewritings of Isaac Watts. There is a certain kind of profundity you look for in vain in Bridges. He had no ear for the deep notes of devotion in Watts and Wesley; it was not this that he wished to recover. At his best he is gently imaginative and ruthlessly craftsmanlike. His metricization is beautiful; he can write in strange meters, or in familiar ones with the unusual accents demanded by an old tune, as in 257, with effortless ease. But it is hymnody for "people like him," for the urbane and cultivated. Uneducated people can grasp Watts and Wesley; the cultivated enjoy Bridges. And why not? It is quite undeniable that up to the time of Karl Barth the settled habit of the church's teaching and preaching was to tell cultivated people to leave their culture and maturity in the church porch. You needed to be a man of the power, the audacity, the opinionated brusqueness, and, one must add, the worldly substance of Bridges to lift up a voice against that.

What Bridges did for texts, Vaughan Williams did for music, and the whole movement to make liturgy humane as well as correct and to bring good taste to the congregations, fused into a success under the guidance of Percy Dearmer, who began his crusade for culture by producing *The English Hymnal* in 1906. Under this spur of new zeal, perhaps the greatest activity was in retranslating some of the old Latin hymns that had been rather woodenly handled by the earlier translators. Our 137 and 145B are examples of the new style. *The English Hymnal* contained relatively few new texts and tunes—surprisingly few, considering its place as the second most influential hymnal in our history. But it did match Bridges's impertinent plea with Vaughan Williams's equally famous and equally alarming dictum, that good taste is a moral matter. And it did include a good deal of Bridges;

it produced Athelstan Riley's festive doxology (266) that made the tune LASST UNS ERFREUEN so famous; it printed some of Dearmer's own early work, and Scott Holland's sturdy "Judge eternal" (265); and above all, it discovered G. K. Chesterton (269) and printed the only hymn he ever wrote for congregational singing, one of the literary masterpieces of the whole field of hymnody.

Another editor was working quietly away, independent at first of this aristocratic movement, though when he finished his work he won their respect; he also was recovering the ancient melodies and (as Dearmer was later to do) reviving the old carols. G. R. Woodward (263–264), who first came out with *Carols for Eastertide* in 1894 containing the now well-known "This joyful Eastertide," went on to produce the *Cowley Carol Book* (1902) and *Songs of Syon* (1904, 1910). The expanded edition of this is a collection of over 400 pieces, all set to tunes of exquisite remoteness from the experience of ordinary congregations, many of the texts being his own. He had a style more eloquently antiquated than that of Bridges, and really the book is a collection of sacred madrigals for domestic devotion rather than a parish hymnal. But his contribution to the opening up of the field which Victorian decorum had so rigidly enclosed was substantial enough to earn him a place in the history of the subject, and if the reader is able to hear the incomparable sound of the FIRST GENEVAN PSALM behind the affectionate text of 264 he will see what Woodward was about.

These dedicated eccentrics, so different from the Ellertons and Hows and Wordsworths in their view of life and their demands of hymnody, rescued English hymnody from the becalmed condition into which some of its text writers (most of whom are not featured in this book at all) and nearly all its musicians had brought it.

206
Hymn Commemorative of the "Thrice Holy"

Bright the vision that delighted
 once the sight of Judah's seer;
sweet the countless tongues united
 to entrance the prophet's ear.

Round the Lord in glory seated
 cherubim and seraphim
filled his temple, and repeated
 each to each the alternate hymn:

"Lord, thy glory fills the heaven,
 earth is with its fullness stored;
unto thee be glory given,
 holy, holy, holy, Lord!"

Heaven is still with glory ringing,
 earth takes up the angels' cry,
"Holy, holy, holy" singing,
 "Lord of hosts, the Lord most high."

With his seraph train before him,
 with his holy church below
thus conspire we to adore him,
 bid we thus our anthem flow:

"Lord, thy glory fills the heaven;
 earth is with its fullness stored;
unto thee be glory given:
 Holy, holy, holy, Lord!'

Richard Mant
Ancient Hymns, 1837

207
Gethsemane

A voice upon the midnight air,
 where Kedron's moonlit waters stray (John 18:1)
weeps forth in agony of prayer,
 "O Father, take this cup away."

Ah, thou who sorrowest unto death,
 we conquer in thy mortal fray;
and earth for all her children saith,
 "O God, take not this cup away."

O Lord of sorrow! meekly die:
 thou'lt heal or hallow all our woe;
thy name refresh the mourner's sigh,
 thy peace revive the faint and low.

Great Chief of faithful souls, arise;
 none else can lead the martyr-band,
who teach the brave, how peril flies
 when faith unarmed uplifts the hand.

O King of earth! the cross ascend;
 o'er climes and ages 'tis thy throne;
where'er thy fading eye may bend
 the desert blooms, and is thine own. (Isa. 35:1)

Thy parting blessing, Lord, we pray;
 make but one fold below, above: (John 10:16)
and when we go the last lone way
 O give the welcome of thy love!

James Martineau
Hymns for the Christian Church and Home, 1840

208
Our Heavenly Father

My God! how wonderful thou art,
 thy majesty how bright,
how beautiful thy mercy seat
 in depths of burning light!

How dread are thine eternal years,
 O everlasting Lord!
by prostrate spirits day and night
 incessantly adored!

How beautiful, how beautiful
    the sight of thee must be,
thine endless wisdom, boundless power,
    and aweful purity!

Oh, how I fear thee, living God!
    with deepest, tenderest fears,
and worship thee with trembling hope
    and penitential tears.

Yet I may love thee, Living God!
    almighty as thou art,
for thou hast stooped to ask of me
    the love of my poor heart.

Oh, then this worse than worthless heart
    in pity deign to take
and make it love thee, for thyself
    and for thy glory's sake.

No earthly father loves like thee,
    no mother half so mild
bears and forbears, as thou hast done,
    with me, thy sinful child.

Only to sit and think of God,
    oh, what a joy it is!
To think the thought, to breathe the Name,
    earth has no higher bliss!

Father of Jesus, love's reward,
    what rapture will it be,
prostrate before thy throne to lie,
    and gaze, and gaze on thee!

Frederick William Faber
Jesus and Mary, 1849

209
Faith of Our Fathers

A. For England

Faith of our fathers! living still
    in spite of dungeon, fire, and sword:
Oh, how our hearts beat high with joy
    whene'er we hear that glorious word.

    Faith of our fathers! Holy Faith!
    We will be true to thee till death.

Our fathers, chained in prisons dark,
    were still in heart and conscience free:
how sweet would be their children's fate.
    if they, like them, could die for thee!

Faith of our fathers! Mary's prayers
    shall win our country back to thee;
and through the truth that comes from God
    England shall then indeed be free.

Faith of our fathers! We will love
    both friend and foe in all our strife:
and preach thee too, as love knows how,
    by kindly words and virtuous life:

B. For Ireland

The first four stanzas are much the same, with these differences:

1:3 Oh! Ireland's hearts beat high with joy
3:2 shall keep our country fast to thee;
3:4 Oh, we shall prosper and be free.
4:1 Faith of our fathers! We must love

to which are added these three stanzas:

Faith of our fathers! Guile and force
    to do thee bitter wrong unite;
but Erin's saints shall fight for us,
    and keep undimmed thy blessed light.

Faith of our fathers! Distant shores
    their happy faith to Ireland owe;
then in our home, O shall we not
    break the dark plots against thee now?

Faith of our fathers! Days of old
    within our hearts speak gallantly;
for ages thou hast stood by us,
    dear faith! and we will stand by thee.

Frederick William Faber
Jesus and Mary, 1849

210

The Right Must Win

Oh, it is hard to work for God,
    to rise and take his part
upon this battlefield of earth
    and not sometimes lose heart!

He hides himself so wondrously,
    as though there were no God;
he is least seen when all the powers
    of ill are most abroad.

Or he deserts us at the hour
    the fight is all but lost
and seems to leave us to ourselves
    just when we need him most.

Yes, there is less to try our faith,
    in our mysterious creed,
than in the godless look of earth
    in these our hours of need.

Ill masters good; good seems to change
    to ill with greatest ease;
and worst of all, the good with good
    is at cross purposes.

The church, the sacraments, the faith,
    their uphill journey take,
lose here what there they gain, and, if
    we lean upon them, break.

It is not so, but so it looks,
    and we lose courage then;
and doubts will come if God hath kept
    his promises to men.

Ah! God is other than we think;
    his ways are far above,
far beyond reason's height, and reached
    only by childlike love.

The look, the fashion of God's ways
    love's lifelong study are;
she can be bold, and guess, and act,
    when reason would not dare.

She has a prudence of her own;
    her step is firm and free;
yet there is cautious science too
    in her simplicity.

Workmen of God! O lose not heart,
    but learn what God is like;
and in the darkest battlefield
    thou shalt know when to strike.

Thrice blest is he to whom is given
    the instinct that can tell
that God is on the field when he
    is most invisible.

Blest too is he who can divine
    where real right doth lie,
and dares to take the side that seems
    wrong to man's blindfold eye.

Then learn to scorn the praise of men,
    and learn to lose with God;
for Jesus won the world through shame
    and beckons thee his road.

God's glory is a wondrous thing,
    most strange in all its ways,
and, of all things on earth, least like
    what men agree to praise.

As he can endless glory weave
    from what men reckon shame,
in his own world he is content
    to play a losing game.

Muse on his justice, downcast soul;
    muse and take better heart;
back with thine angel to the field
    and bravely do thy part.

God's justice is a bed, where we
    our anxious hearts may lay
and, weary with ourselves, may sleep
    our discontent away.

For right is right, since God is God,
    and right the day must win;
to doubt would be disloyalty,
    to falter would be sin.

Frederick William Faber
Jesus and Mary, 1849

211
Come to Jesus

Souls of men! why will ye scatter
    like a crowd of frightened sheep?
Foolish hearts! why will ye wander
    from a love so true and deep?

Was there ever kindest shepherd
    half so gentle, half so sweet,
as the Savior who would have us
    come and gather round his feet?

It is God: His love looks mighty
    but is mightier than it seems:
'Tis our Father: And his fondness
    goes far out beyond our dreams.

There's a wideness in God's mercy
    like the wideness of the sea:
There's a kindness in his justice
    which is more than liberty.

There is no place where earth's sorrows
    are more felt than up in heaven;
there is no place where earth's failings
    have such kindly judgment given.

There is welcome to the sinner,
    and more graces for the good;
there is mercy with the Savior;
    there is healing in his blood.

There is grace enough for thousands
    of new worlds as great as this;
there is room for fresh creations
    in that upper home of bliss.

For the love of God is broader
    than the measures of man's mind;
and the heart of the Eternal
    is most wonderfully kind.

But we make his love too narrow
    by false limits of our own;
and we magnify his strictness
    with a zeal he will not own.

There is plentiful redemption
    in the blood that has been shed;
there is joy for all the members
    in the sorrows of the Head.

'Tis not all we owe to Jesus;
    it is something more than all;
greater good because of evil,
    larger mercy through the fall.

225

Pining souls! come nearer Jesus,
    and O come not doubting thus,
but with faith that trusts more bravely
    his huge tenderness for us.

If our love were but more simple
    we should take him at his word;
and our lives would be all sunshine
    in the sweetness of our Lord.

Frederick William Faber
Hymns, 1862

212

Jesus Crucified

O come and mourn with me awhile!
    See, Mary calls us to her side;
O come and let us mourn with her;
    Jesus, our Love, is crucified!

Have we no tears to shed for him?
    while soldiers scoff and Jews deride?
Ah! look how patiently he hangs;
    Jesus, our Love, is crucified!

How fast his hands and feet are nailed;
    his blessed tongue with thirst is tied;
his failing eyes are blind with blood;
    Jesus, our Love, is crucified!

His mother cannot reach his face;
    she stands in helplessness beside;
her heart is martyred with her Son's;
    Jesus, our Love, is crucified!

Seven times he spoke, seven words of love,
    and all three hours his silence cried
for mercy on the souls of men;
    Jesus, our Love, is crucified!

What was thy crime, my dearest Lord?
    By earth, by heaven, thou hast been tried,
and guilty found of too much love;
    Jesus, our Love, is crucified!

Found guilty of excess of love,
    it was thine own sweet will that tied
thee tighter far than helpless nails;
    Jesus, our Love, is crucified!

Death came, and Jesus meekly bowed;
    his falling eyes he strove to guide
with mindful love to Mary's face;
    Jesus, our Love, is crucified!

O break, O break, hard heart of mine!
    Thy weak self-love and guilty pride
his Pilate and his Judas were;
    Jesus, our Love, is crucified!

Come, take thy stand beneath the cross,
    and let the blood from out that side
fall gently on thee drop by drop;
    Jesus, our Love, is crucified!

A broken heart, a fount of tears,
    ask, and they will not be denied;
a broken heart Love's cradle is;
    Jesus, our Love, is crucified!

O Love of God! O sin of man!
    in this dread act your strength is tried;
and victory remains with Love;
    for he, our Love, is crucified!

Frederick William Faber
Jesus and Mary, 1849

213
When Wilt Thou Save the People

When wilt thou save the people?
    O God of mercy, when?
not kings and lords, but nations,
    not thrones and crowns, but men!
Flowers of thy heart, O God, are they,
let them not pass, like weeds, away,
their heritage a sunless day.
    God save the people!

Shall crime bring crime for ever,
    strength aiding still the strong?
Is it thy will, O Father,
    that men should toil for wrong?
"No!" say thy mountains, "No!" thy skies,
man's clouded sun shall brightly rise
and songs be heard instead of sighs.
    God save the people!

When wilt thou save the people?
    O God of mercy, when?
The people, Lord! the people!—
    not thrones and crowns, but men!
God save the people; thine they are,
thy children, as thy angels fair;
from vice, oppression, and despair,
    God save the people!

Ebenezer Elliott
More Verse and Prose, 1850
first as a hymn in *The Congregational Church Hymnal*, 1887

214
Third Sorrowful Mystery, Song of the Seraphs. Revelation 19:12

Crown him with many crowns,
    the Lamb upon his throne;
hark, how the heavenly anthem drowns
    all music but its own:
    Awake, my soul, and sing
    of him who died for thee,
and hail him as thy matchless King
    through all eternity.

Crown him the Virgin's Son,
    the God incarnate born,
whose arm those crimson trophies won
    which now his brow adorn:
    fruit of the mystic Rose   (Song 2:1)
    as of that Rose the Stem;   (Isa. 11:1)
the Root whence mercy ever flows,
    the Babe of Bethlehem.

Crown him the Lord of love!
    Behold his hands and side,
rich wounds yet visible above
    in beauty glorified:
    No angel in the sky
    can fully bear that sight,
but downward bends his burning eye
    at mysteries so bright.

Crown him the Lord of peace,
    whose power a scepter sways
from pole to pole, that wars may cease   (Ps. 46:9)
    absorbed in prayer and praise:
    His reign shall know no end,
    and round his pierced feet
fair flowers of paradise extend
    their fragrance ever sweet.

Crown him the Lord of years,
    the Potentate of time,
Creator of the rolling spheres,
    ineffably sublime.
Glassed in a sea of light,   (Rev. 4:6)
    where everlasting waves
reflect his throne—the Infinite,
    who lives—and loves—and saves.

Crown him the Lord of heaven,
    one with the Father known,
and the blest Spirit through him given
    from yonder triune throne:
All hail, Redeemer, hail!
    for thou hast died for me!
Thy praise shall never, never fail
    throughout eternity.

Matthew Bridges
Hymns of the Heart, 1851
This hymn often appears with some quatrains inserted from a similar
hymn written in 1874 by Godfrey Thring; these can be identified by
comparison with the above, which is the original text.

215
Christ Walking on the Sea

Oh, where is he that trod the sea,
    Oh, where is he that spake?—
and demons from their victims flee,
    the dead their slumbers break;
the palsied rise in freedom strong,
    the dumb men talk and sing,
and from blind eyes, benighted long,
    bright beams of morning spring.

Oh, where is he that trod the sea,
    Oh, where is he that spake?—
and piercing words of liberty
    the deaf ears open shake;
and mildest words arrest the haste
    of fever's deadly fire,
and strong ones heal the weak, who waste
    their lives in sad desire.

Oh, where is he that trod the sea,
    Oh, where is he that spake?—
and dark waves, rolling heavily,
    a glassy smoothness take;
and lepers, whose own flesh has been
    a living loathsome grave,
see with amaze that they are clean,
    and cry, "'Tis he can save."

Oh, where is he that trod the sea?—
    'tis only he can save;
to thousands hungering wearily
    a wondrous meal he gave;
full soon, celestially fed,
    their rustic fare they take;
'twas springtide when he blessed the bread,
    and harvest when he brake.

Oh, where is he that trod the sea?—
    my soul, the Lord is here:
Let all thy fears be hushed in thee,
    to leap, to look, to hear
be thine: Thy needs he'll satisfy:
    Art thou diseased or dumb?
or dost thou in thy hunger cry?
    "I come," saith Christ, "I come."

Thomas Toke Lynch
The Rivulet, 1856

216
Resignation and Hope

Where is thy God, my soul?
    is he within thy heart?
or ruler of a distant realm
    in which thou hast no part?

Where is thy God, my soul?
    only in stars and sun?
or have the holy words of truth
    his light in every one?

Where is thy God, my soul?
    confined to Scripture's page?
or does his Spirit check and guide
    the spirit of each age?

O Ruler of the sky,
    rule thou within my heart;
O great Adorner of the world,
    thy light of life impart.

Giver of holy words,
    bestow thy holy power;
and aid me, whether work or thought
    engage the varying hour.

In thee I have my help,
    as all my fathers had;
I'll trust thee when I'm sorrowful,
    and serve thee when I'm glad.

Thomas Toke Lynch
The Rivulet, 1855

217
Advent

Lift up your heads, rejoice,
    redemption draweth nigh;
now breathes a softer air,
    now shines a milder sky;
the early trees put forth
    their new and tender leaf;
hushed is the moaning wind
    that told of winter's grief.

Lift up your heads, rejoice,
    redemption draweth nigh;
now mount the laden clouds,
    now flames the darkening sky;
the early scattered drops
    descend with heavy fall,
and to the waiting earth
    the hidden thunders call.

Lift up your heads, rejoice,
    redemption draweth nigh;
O note the varying signs
    of earth, and air, and sky: (Luke 12:54)
The God of glory comes
    in gentleness and might,
to comfort and alarm,
    to succor and to smite.

He comes, the wide world's King;
    he comes, the true heart's Friend;
new gladness to begin
    and ancient wrong to end;
he comes, to fill with light
    the weary, waiting eye:
Lift up your heads, rejoice,
    redemption draweth nigh.

Thomas Toke Lynch
The Rivulet, 1856

218
We Limit Not the Truth of God

We limit not the truth of God
    to our poor reach of mind,
by notions of our day and sect,
    crude, partial, and confined;
no, let a new and better hope
    within our hearts be stirred:

    The Lord hath yet more light and truth
        to break forth from his word.

Who dares to bind to his dull sense
    the oracles of heaven,
for all the nations, tongues, and climes
    and all the ages given?
That universe—how much unknown!
    that ocean unexplored!

Darkling our great forefathers went
    the first steps of the way;
'twas but the dawning, yet to grow
    into the perfect day.
And grow it shall; our glorious Sun
    more fervid rays afford:

The valleys past, ascending still,
    our souls would higher climb,
and look down from supernal heights
    on all the bygone time.
Upward we press; the air is clear,
    and the sphere-music heard:

O Father, Son, and Spirit, send
    us increase from above;
enlarge, expand all Christian souls
    to comprehend thy love;
and make us all go on to know
    with nobler powers conferred—

George Rawson
Leeds Hymn Book, 1853
Above the text, the author placed this quotation: "He charged us
before God, and his blessed angels, if God should reveal anything to us
by any other instrument of his, to be as ready to receive it as any truth
by his ministry; for he was very confident that Lord had more light and
truth yet to break forth our his holy word." —narrative of Pastor
Robinson's address to the Pilgrim Fathers, 1620.

219
The Word of God Conquering by Sacrifice

O God of truth, whose living word
    upholds whate'er hath breath,
look down on thy creation, Lord,
    enslaved by sin and death.

Set up thy standard, Lord, that we
    who claim a heavenly birth,
may march with thee to smite the lies
    that vex thy groaning earth.

Ah! would we join that blest array
    and follow in the might
of him, the Faithful and the True   (Rev. 19:11)
    in raiment clean and white?

We fight for truth? We fight for God?
    poor slaves of lies and sin!
He who would fight for thee on earth
    must first be true within.   (Ps. 51:6)

Then, God of truth, for whom we long,
    thou who wilt hear our prayer,
do thine own battle in our hearts
    and slay the falsehood there.

Still smite, still burn, till naught is left
    but God's own truth and love;
then, Lord, as morning dew come down,   (Hos. 6:3)
    rest on us from above.

Yea, come! then tried as in the fire   (1 Cor. 3:13)
    from every lie set free,
thy perfect truth shall dwell in us,
    and we shall live in thee.

Thomas Hughes
Lays of the Sanctuary, 1859

220
For Those at Sea

Eternal Father, strong to save,
whose arm doth bind the restless wave,
who bidd'st the mighty ocean deep
its own appointed limits keep: (Ps. 104:9)
O hear us when we cry to thee
for those in peril on the sea.

O Savior, whose almighty word
the winds and waves submissive heard,
who walkedst on the foaming deep   (Matt. 14:25)
and calm amidst its rage didst sleep;   (Mark 4:38)
O hear us when we cry to thee
for those in peril on the sea.

O sacred Spirit, who didst brood
upon the chaos dark and rude,   (Gen. 1:3)
who bad'st its angry tumult cease
and gavest light and life and peace:
O hear us when we cry to thee
for those in peril on the sea.

O Trinity of love and power,
our brethren shield in danger's hour,
from rock and tempest, fire and foe,
protect them wheresoe'er they go:
and ever let there rise to thee
glad hymns of praise from land and sea.

William Whiting, 1860
altered in *Hymns Ancient and Modern*, 1861

As they offered gifts most rare
at that manger rude and bare;
so may we with holy joy,
pure and free from sin's alloy,
all our costliest treasures bring,
Christ! to thee our heavenly King.

Holy Jesus, every day
keep us in the narrow way;
and, when earthly things are past,
bring our ransomed souls at last
where they need no star to guide,
where no clouds thy glory hide.

In the heavenly country bright
need they no created light;
thou, its light, its joy, its crown,
thou its sun which goes not down;
there for ever may we sing
alleluias to our King.

William Chatterton Dix, 1860
Hymns Ancient and Modern, 1861

221
Epiphany

As with gladness men of old
did the guiding star behold,
as with joy they hailed its light,
leading onward, beaming bright,
so, most gracious Lord, may we
evermore be led to thee.

As with joyful steps they sped
to that lowly manger-bed,
there to bend the knee before
him whom heaven and earth adore;
so may we with willing feet
ever seek the mercy seat.

222
Redemption by the Precious Blood

Alleluia, sing to Jesus,
    his the scepter, his the throne;
alleluia, his the triumph,
    his the victory alone:
Hark the songs of peaceful Zion
    thunder like a mighty flood;
Jesus, out of every nation,
    hath redeemed us by his blood.   (Rev. 7:9)

Alleluia, not as orphans
 are we left in sorrow now;
alleluia, he is near us:
 faith believes, nor questions how;
though the cloud from sight received him
 when the forty days were o'er, (Acts 1:9)
shall our hearts forget his promise,
 "I am with you evermore"? (Matt. 28:20)

Alleluia, Bread of angels, (Ps. 78:25)
 thou on earth our food, our stay;
alleluia, here the sinful
 flee to thee from day to day;
Intercessor, Friend of sinners,
 earth's Redeemer, plead for me
where the songs of all the sinless
 sweep across the crystal sea. (Rev. 4:6)

Alleluia, King eternal,
 thee the Lord of lords we own;
alleluia, born of Mary,
 earth thy footstool, heaven thy throne:
Thou within the veil hast entered,
 robed in flesh, our great High Priest. (Heb. 10:20)
Thou on earth both priest and victim
 in the eucharistic feast.

William Chatterton Dix, 1866
Altar Songs, 1867

223
Ascension

See the Conqueror mounts in triumph,
 see the King in royal state
riding on the clouds his chariot
 to his heavenly palace gate;
hark! the choirs of angel voices
 joyful alleluias sing
and the portals high are lifted
 to receive their heavenly King. (Ps. 24:7)

Who is he that comes in glory
 with the trump of jubilee?
Lord of battles, God of armies,
 he has gained the victory. (Ps. 98:2)
He who on the cross did suffer,
 he who from the grave arose,
he has vanquished sin and Satan,
 he by death has spoiled his foes.

While he lifts his hands in blessing
 he is parted from his friends; (Luke 24:50–1)
while their eager eyes behold him,
 he upon the clouds ascends;
he, who walked with God and pleased him,
 preaching truth and doom to come,
he, our Enoch, is translated
 to his everlasting home. (Gen. 5:24)

Now our heavenly Aaron enters
 with his blood within the veil (Heb. 5:4; 10:20)
Joshua now is come to Canaan,
 and the kings before him quail. (Josh. 5:1)
Now he plants the tribes of Israel
 in their promised resting place;
now our great Elijah offers
 double portion of his grace. (2 Kings 2:9–11)

He has raised our human nature
 on the clouds to God's right hand;
there we sit in heavenly places;
 there with him in glory stand:
Jesus reigns, adored by angels:
 Man with God is on the throne; (Heb. 1:5–8)
mighty Lord, in thine ascension
 we by faith behold our own.

Holy Ghost, Illuminator,
 shed thy beams upon our eyes,
help us to look up with Stephen,
 and to see, beyond the skies, (Acts 7:55–56)
where the Son of Man in glory
 standing is at God's right hand,
beckoning on his martyr army,
 succoring his faithful band.

See him, who is gone before us,
    heavenly mansions to prepare.   (John 14:2)
See him, who is ever pleading
    for us with prevailing prayer.   (Heb. 7:23)
See him, who with sound of trumpet
    and with his angelic train
summoning the world to judgment,
    on the clouds will come again.   (Mark 13:26)

Lift us up from earth to heaven,
    give us wings of faith and love,
gales of holy aspirations
    wafting us to heaven above;
that with hearts and minds uplifted,
    we with Christ our Lord may dwell
where he sits enthroned in glory
    in his heavenly citadel.

So at last, when he appeareth,
    we from out our graves may spring,   (Isa. 40:29)
with our youth renewed like eagles,
    flocking round our heavenly King
caught up on the clouds of heaven,
    and may meet him in the air,   (1 Thess. 4:17)
rise to realms where he is reigning,
    and may reign for ever there.

Glory be to God the Father;
    glory be to God the Son,
dying, risen, ascending for us,
    who the heavenly realm has won;
glory to the Holy Spirit;
    to One God in persons Three;
glory both in earth and heaven,
    glory, endless glory be.

Christopher Wordsworth
The Holy Year, 1862
Line 8:4 paraphrases the collect for Ascension Day.

224
At Confirmation

Lord, be thy word my rule,
    in it may I rejoice;
thy glory be my aim,
    thy holy will my choice;

thy promises my hope;
    thy providence my guard;
thine arm my strong support;
    thyself, my great reward.

Christopher Wordsworth
The Holy Year (6th ed.), 1872

225
Mark 4:37–40

Fierce raged the tempest o'er the deep,
watch did thine anxious servants keep;
but thou wast wrapped in guileless sleep,
    calm and still.

"Save, Lord, we perish!" was their cry,
"O save us in our agony!"
Thy word above the storm rose high,
    "Peace, be still."

The wild winds hushed, the angry deep
sank like a little child to sleep.
The sullen billows ceased to leap
    at thy will.

So, when our life is clouded o'er,
and storm winds drift us from the shore,
say, lest we sink to rise no more,
    "Peace, be still."

Godfrey Thring
The Congregational Hymn and Tune Book, 1862

226
Fight the Good Fight

Fight the good fight with all thy might,   (1 Tim. 6:12)
Christ is thy strength, and Christ thy right;
lay hold on life, and it shall be
thy joy and crown eternally.

Run the straight race through God's good grace,
lift up thine eyes, and see his face;
life with its way before us lies,
Christ is the path, and Christ the prize.

Cast care aside, and on thy Guide
lean, and his mercy will provide;
lean, and the trusting soul shall prove
Christ is its life, and Christ its love.

Faint not nor fear, his arms are near,
he changeth not, and thou art dear;
only believe, and thou shalt see
that Christ is all in all to thee.   (Col. 3:11)

John Samuel Bewley Monsell
Hymns of Love and Praise, 1863

227
Gifts

O worship the Lord in the beauty of holiness!
bow down before him, his glory proclaim;
with gold of obedience, and incense of lowliness,
kneel and adore him: The Lord is his name!

Low at his feet lay thy burden of carefulness,
high on his heart he will bear it for thee,
comfort thy sorrows and answer thy prayerfulness,
guiding thy steps as may best for thee be.

Fear not to enter his courts in the slenderness
of the poor wealth thou wouldst reckon as thine:
truth in its beauty, and love in its tenderness,
these are the offerings to lay on his shrine.

These, though we bring them in trembling and
fearfulness,
he will accept for the name that is dear;
mornings of joy give for evenings of fearfulness,
(Ps. 30:6)
trust for our trembling, and hope for our fear.

O worship the Lord in the beauty of holiness!
bow down before him, his glory proclaim;
with gold of obedience, and incense of lowliness
kneel and adore him, the Lord is his name!

John Samuel Bewley Monsell
Hymns of Love and Praise, 1863

228
The Teacher's Prayer

O Lord of hosts, all heaven possessing,
behold us from thy sapphire throne,
in doubt and darkness dimly guessing,
we might thy glory half have known;
but thou in Christ hast made us thine,
and on us all thy beauties shine.

Illumine all, disciples, teachers,
thy law's deep wonders to unfold;
with reverent hand let wisdom's preachers
bring forth their treasures, new and old;
(Matt. 13:52)
let oldest, youngest, find in thee
of truth and love the boundless sea.

Let faith still light the lamp of science,
and knowledge pass from truth to truth,
and wisdom, in its full reliance
renew the primal awe of youth;
so holier, wiser may we grow,
as time's swift currents onward flow.

Bind thou our life in fullest union
 with all thy saints from sin set free;
uphold us in that blest communion
 of all thy saints on earth with thee;
keep thou our souls, or there, or here,
in mightiest love, that casts out fear.   (1 John 4:18)

Edward Hayes Plumptre
Lazarus and Other Poems, 1864

229

A Hymn Used in the Chapel of King's College Hospital

Thine arm, O Lord, in days of old
 was strong to heal and save;
it triumphed o'er disease and death,
 o'er darkness and the grave;
to thee they went, the blind, the dumb,
 the palsied and the lame,
the leper with his tainted life,
 the sick with fevered frame.

And lo! thy touch brought life and health,
 gave speech, and strength, and sight;
and youth renewed and frenzy calmed
 owned thee the Lord of light;
and now, O Lord, be near to bless,
 Almighty as of yore,
in crowded streets, by restless couch,
 as by Gennesaret's shore.

Be thou our great deliverer still,
 thou Lord of life and death;
restore and quicken, soothe and bless
 with thine almighty breath;
to hands that work, and eyes that see,
 give wisdom's heavenly lore,
that whole and sick, the weak and strong
 may praise thee evermore.

Edward Hayes Plumptre
Lazarus and Other Poems (2nd ed.), 1865

230

For All the Saints

For all thy saints, who from their labors rest,
who thee by faith before the world confessed,
thy name, O Jesus, be for ever blessed.
 Alleluia!

Thou wast their rock, their fortress, and their might;
thou, Lord, their captain in the well-fought fight;
thou in the darkness drear their one true Light.
 Alleluia!

For the apostles' glorious company,
who bearing forth the cross o'er land and sea,
shook all the mighty world, we sing to thee: (Acts 17:6)
 Alleluia!

For the evangelists, by whose pure word,
like fourfold stream, the garden of the Lord (Gen. 2:10)
is fair and fruitful, be thy name adored.
 Alleluia!

For martyrs, who with rapture-kindled eye
saw the bright crown descending from the sky
and, seeing, grasped it, thee we glorify. (Acts 7:55)
 Alleluia!

O may thy soldiers, faithful, true, and bold,
fight as the saints who nobly fought of old,
and win with them the victors' crown of gold. (Rev. 2:10)
 Alleluia!

O blest communion! fellowship divine!
We feebly struggle, they in glory shine!
Yet all are one in thee, for all are thine! (John 17:22)
 Alleluia!

And when the strife is fierce, the warfare long,
steals on the ear the distant triumph-song,
and hearts are brave again, and arms are strong!
 Alleluia!

The golden evening brightens in the west;
soon, soon to faithful warriors cometh rest:
Sweet is the calm of paradise the blest.
      Alleluia!

But lo! there breaks a yet more glorious day;
the saints triumphant rise in bright array;
the King of glory passes on his way!
      Alleluia!

From earth's wide bounds, from ocean's farthest coast,
through gates of pearl streams in the countless host,
singing to Father, Son, and Holy Ghost:
      Alleluia!

William Walsham How
Hymn for Saints' Days, and other Hymns, 1864
The more familiar "the" for "thy" in 1:1 is How's revision.

231
Behold, I Stand at the Door, and Knock. Revelation 3:20

O Jesus, thou art standing
    outside the fast-closed door,
in lowly patience waiting
    to pass the threshold o'er.
Shame on us, Christian brothers,
    his name and sign who bear,
O shame, thrice shame upon us
    to keep him standing there!

O Jesus, thou art knocking:
    and lo! thy hand is scarred,
and thorns thy brow encircle,
    and tears thy face have marred:
O love that passeth knowledge,
    so patiently to wait!
O sin that hath no equal
    so fast to bar the gate!

O Jesus, thou art pleading
    in accents meek and low,
"I died for you, my children,
    and will ye treat me so?"
O Lord, with shame and sorrow
    we open now the door:
dear Savior, enter, enter,
    and leave us never more.

William Walsham How
suggested by "Brothers, and a Sermon," a poem by Jean Ingelow
Psalms and Hymns, Supplement, 1867

232
Onward, Christian Soldiers

Onward, Christian soldiers!
    marching as to war,
with the cross of Jesus
    going on before.
Christ the royal Master
    leads against the foe;
onward into battle
    see, his banners go!

    Onward, Christian soldiers!
      marching as to war,
    with the cross of Jesus
      going on before.

Like a mighty army
    moves the church of God;
brothers, we are treading
    where the saints have trod;
we are not divided,
    all one body we,
one in hope and doctrine   (Eph. 4:4)
    one in charity.

At the sign of triumph
 Satan's legions flee;
on, then, Christian soldiers,
 on to victory.
Hell's foundations quiver
 at the shout of praise;
brothers, lift your voices,
 loud your anthems raise.

What the saints established
 that I hold for true,
what the saints believed
 that believe I too.
Long as earth endureth
 men that faith will hold—
kingdoms, nations, empires,
 in destruction rolled.

Crowns and thrones may perish,
 kingdoms rise and wane,
but the church of Jesus
 constant will remain;
gates of hell can never
 'gainst that church prevail;
we have Christ's own promise
 and that cannot fail.

Onward then, ye people,
 join our happy throng,
blend with ours your voices
 in the triumph song;
Glory, laud, and honor
 unto Christ the King;
this through countless ages
 men and angels sing:

Sabine Baring-Gould
The Church Times, October 15, 1864

233
Unity and Progress
Ephesians 4:4

A.

Igjennem Nat og Trängsel
 gaar Själens Valfartsgang
med stille Haab og Längsel,
 med dyb Forventningssang
Det gjennem Natten luer,
 det lysner gjennem Sky,
til Broder Broder skuer
 og kjender ham paany.

Vor Nat det Lys oplive,
 som aldrig slukkes ud!
Eet sind os alle give
 i Trängsel Trøstens Gud!
Eet Hjerte khärligt lue
 i hver Korsdragers Bryst!
Een Gud, til hvem vi skue!
 een Tro, eet Haab, een Trøst!

Een Røst fra tusind Munde!
 een Aand i Tusinds Røst!
Een Fred, hvortil vi stunde!
 Een Frelsens, Naadens Kyst!
Een Sorg, eet Savn, een Längsel!
 Een Fader her og hist!
Een Udgang af al Trängsel!
 Eet Liv i Jesu Christ!

Saa gaa vi med hverandre
 den store Pilgrimsang!
Til Golgatha vi vandre
 i Aand, med Bøn og Sang!
Fra Kors fra Grav vi stige
 med salig Lov og Pris
til den Opstandnes Rige,
 til Frelsens Paradis!

Bernhardt Severin Ingemann, 1825
Høimesse-Psalmer, Anden Udgave med et Tallaeg, 1843

237

B.

Through the night of doubt and sorrow
    onward goes the pilgrim band
singing songs of expectation,
    marching to the Promised Land.
Clear before us through the darkness
    gleams and burns the guiding Light;
brother clasps the hand of brother,
    stepping fearless through the night.

One the light of God's own presence
    o'er his ransomed people shed,
chasing far the gloom and terror,
    brightening all the path we tread:
One the object of our journey,
    one the faith which never tires,
one the earnest looking forward,
    one the hope our God inspires.

One the strain that lips of thousands
    lift as from the heart of one:
One the conflict, one the peril,
    one the march in God begun:
one the gladness of rejoicing
    on the far eternal shore,
where the one almighty Father
    reigns in love for evermore.

Onward therefore, pilgrim brothers,
    onward with the cross our aid,
bear its shame and fight its battle
    till we rest beneath its shade.
Soon shall come the great awaking,
    soon the rending of the tomb,
then the scattering of all shadows
    and the end of toil and gloom.

translated, Sabine Baring-Gould
The People's Hymnal, 1867

234
The Sacrifice of Praise

For the beauty of the earth,
    for the beauty of the skies,
for the love which from our birth
    over and around us lies:

        Christ our God, to thee we raise
        this, our sacrifice of praise.

For the beauty of each hour
    of the day and of the night,
hill and vale, and tree and flower,
    sun and moon and stars of light:

For the joy of ear and eye,
    for the heart and brain's delight,
for the mystic harmony
    linking sense to sound and sight:

For the joy of human love,
    brother, sister, parent, child,
friends on earth, and friends above,
    for all gentle thoughts and mild:

For each perfect gift of thine,
    to our race so freely given,
graces human and divine,
    flowers of earth and buds of heaven:

For thy bride that evermore
    lifteth holy hands above,
offering up on every shore
    this pure sacrifice of love:

For the martyrs' crown of light,
    for thy prophets' eagle eye,
for thy bold confessors' might,
    for the lips of infancy: (Ps. 8:4)

For thy virgins' robes of snow,
      for thy Maiden-Mother mild,
for thyself, with hearts aglow,
      Jesus, Victim undefiled:

Folliott Sandford Pierpoint
Lyra Eucharistica, 1864
The second phrase in the refrain is taken from the eucharistic prayer
in the *Book of Common Prayer*, which echoes Hebrews 13:15.

235

Amen! Come, Lord Jesus

Ten thousand times ten thousand,   (Rev. 5:11)
      in sparkling raiment bright,
the armies of the ransomed saints
      throng up the steeps of light;
'tis finished, all is finished,
      their fight with death and sin;
fling open wide the golden gates
      and let the victors in.

What rush of alleluias
      fills all the earth and sky!
what ringing of a thousand harps
      bespeaks the triumph nigh!
O day for which creation
      and all its tribes were made!
O joy, for all its former woes
      a thousandfold repaid!

Oh, then, what raptured greetings
      on Canaan's happy shore,
what knitting severed friendships up,
      where partings are no more!
Then eyes with joy shall sparkle
      that brimmed with tears of late;
orphans no longer fatherless
      nor widows desolate.

Bring near thy great salvation,
      thou Lamb for sinners slain,
fill up the roll of thine elect,
      then take thy power and reign!
Appear, Desire of nations,
      thine exiles long for home;
show in the heavens thy promised sign:
      thou Prince and Savior, come!

Henry Alford
stanzas 1–3, 1866
The Year of Praise, 1867
stanza 4, 1870
Life, Journal, and Letters, 1872

236

The Holy Catholic Church: The Communion of Saints. "He is the Head of the Body, the Church."

The Church's one foundation
      is Jesus Christ her Lord;   (1 Cor. 3:11)
she is his new creation
      by water and the Word;   (Eph. 5:26)
from heaven he came and sought her
      to be his holy bride,
with his own blood he bought her
      and for her life he died.

Elect from every nation,
      yet one o'er all the earth,
her charter of salvation,
      one Lord, one faith, one birth;   (Eph. 4:4)
one holy name she blesses,
      partakes one holy food,
and to one hope she presses
      with every grace endued.

Though with a scornful wonder
    men see her sore oppressed,
by schisms rent asunder,
    by heresies distressed,
yet saints their watch are keeping,
    their cry goes up, "How long?"   (Rev. 6:9–10)
and soon the night of weeping
    shall be the morn of song.   (Ps. 30:5)

Mid toil and tribulation
    and tumult of her war
she waits the consummation
    of peace for evermore;
till with the vision glorious
    her longing eyes are blest,
and the great church victorious
    shall be the church at rest.

Yet she on earth hath union
    with God the Three in One   (Eph. 5:26)
and mystic sweet communion
    with those whose rest is won:
O happy ones and holy!
    Lord, give us grace, that we,
with them, the meek and lowly,
    on high may dwell with thee.

Samuel John Stone, 1866
Lyra Fidelium: *Twelve Hymns on the Twelve Articles
of the Apostles' Creed*, 1866
as revised for *Appendix to Hymns Ancient and Modern*,
1868, omitting stanzas 3 and 6 of the original seven

Where'er the gentle heart
    finds courage from above,
where'er the heart forsook
    warms with the breath of love;
where faith bids fear depart,
City of God, thou art.

Thou art where'er the proud
    in humbleness melts down;
where self itself yields up,
    where martyrs win their crown;
where faithful souls possess
themselves in perfect peace;   (Luke 21:19)

where in life's common ways
    with cheerful feet we go;
where in his steps we tread
    who trod the way of woe;
where he is in the heart,
City of God, thou art.

Not throned above the skies,
    nor golden walled afar,
but where Christ's two or three   (Matt. 18:20)
    in his name gathered are,
be in the midst of them,
God's own Jerusalem.

Francis Turner Palgrave
Hymns, 1867

237

The Kingdom of God Within

O thou not made with hands,
    not throned above the skies,
nor walled with shining walls,
    nor framed with stones of price,
more bright than gold or gem,
God's own Jerusalem!—

238

For the Last Sunday of the Year

O God, the rock of ages,   (Ps. 90:1)
    who evermore hast been,
what time the tempest rages,
    our dwelling-place serene:
before thy first creations,
    O Lord, the same as now,
to endless generations
    the everlasting thou!

Our years are like the shadows (Ps. 90:5–9)
    on sunny hills that lie,
or grasses in the meadows
    that blossom but to die;
a sleep, a dream, a story
    by strangers quickly told,
an unremaining glory
    of things that soon are old.

O thou who canst not slumber (Ps. 121:4)
    whose light grows never pale,
teach us aright to number (Ps. 90:12)
    our years before they fail.
On us thy mercy lighten,
    on us thy goodness rest,
and let thy Spirit brighten
    the hearts thyself hast blest.

Lord, crown our faith's endeavor
    with beauty and with grace (Ps. 90:17)
till, clothed in light for ever,
    we see thee face to face:
A joy no language measures,
    a fountain brimming o'er;
an endless flow of pleasures,
    an ocean without shore.

Edward Henry Bickersteth, 1860/1862
Psalms and Hymns, 1867

239
Psalm 23

The King of love my Shepherd is,
    whose goodness faileth never;
I nothing lack if I am his
    and he is mine for ever.

Where streams of living water flow
    my ransomed soul he feedeth,
and where the verdant pastures grow
    with food celestial feedeth.

Perverse and foolish oft I strayed,
    but yet in love he sought me,
and on his shoulder gently laid,
    and home, rejoicing, brought me. (Matt. 18:12)

In death's dark vale I fear no ill
    with thee, dear Lord, beside me;
thy rod and staff my comfort still,
    thy cross before to guide me.

Thou spread'st a table in my sight;
    thy unction grace bestoweth:
and, oh, what transport of delight
    from thy pure chalice floweth!

And so through all the length of days
    thy goodness faileth never;
Good Shepherd, may I sing thy praise
    within thy house for ever!

Henry Williams Baker
Appendix to Hymns Ancient and Modern, 1868

240
The Holy Spirit

O Holy Ghost, thy people bless
    who long to feel thy might,
and fain would grow in holiness
    as children of the light. (Eph. 5:8)

To thee we bring, who art the Lord,
    our selves to be thy throne;
let every deed and thought and word
    thy pure dominion own.

Life-giving Spirit, o'er us move
    as on the formless deep;
give life and order, light and love (Gen. 1:3)
    where now is death or sleep.

Great gift of our ascended King   (John 16:7–8)
    his saving truth reveal;
our tongues inspire his praise to sing,
    our hearts his love to feel.

True wind of heaven, from south or north
    for joy or chastening, blow;   (Song 4:16)
the garden spices shall spring forth
    if thou wilt bid them flow.

O Holy Ghost, of sevenfold might,   (Isa. 11:2)
    all graces come from thee;
grant us to know and serve aright
    our God in Persons Three.

Henry Williams Baker
Monkland Parish Magazine, June 3, 1873

241
At Even, Ere the Sun Was Set

At even, when the sun was set,   (Mark 1:32)
    the sick, O Lord, around thee lay,
Oh, in what divers pains they met!
    Oh, with what joy they went away!

Once more 'tis eventide, and we
    oppressed with various ills draw near;
what if thy form we cannot see?
    We know and feel that thou art here.

O Savior Christ! our woes dispel:
    for some are sick, and some are sad,
and some have never loved thee well,
    and some have lost the love they had;

and some are pressed with worldly care,
    and some are tried with sinful doubt;
and some such grievous passions bear
    that only thou canst cast them out;

and some have found the world is vain,
    yet from the world they break not free;
and some have friends who give them pain,
    yet have not sought a friend in thee;

and none, O Lord, have perfect rest,
    for none are wholly free from sin;
and they who fain would serve thee best
    are conscious most of wrong within.

O Savior Christ, thou too art man;
    thou hast been troubled, tested, tried;
thy kind but searching glance can scan
    the very wounds that shame would hide.

Thy touch has still its ancient power;
    no word from thee can fruitless fall:
Hear in this solemn evening hour,
    and in thy mercy save us all.

Henry Twells, 1868
Appendix to Hymns Ancient and Modern, 1868
The original first line was "At even, ere the sun was set."
Stanza 4, part of Twells's original text, was not in the 1868 publication,
but was restored in *Church Hymns*, 1871.

242
Forgive Us Our Righteousness

Not for our sins alone
    thy mercy, Lord, we sue;
let fall thy pitying glance
    on our devotions too,
what we have done for thee,
    and what we think to do.

The holiest hours we spend
    in prayer upon our knees,
the times when most we deem
    our songs of praise will please,
thou searcher of all hearts,
    forgiveness pour on these.

And all the gifts we bring,
    and all the vows we make,
and all the acts of love
    we plan for thy dear sake,
into thy pardoning thought,
    O God of mercy, take.

And most, when we, thy flock,
    before thine altar bend,
and strange, bewildering thoughts
    with those sweet moments blend,
by him whose death we plead,
    Good Lord, thy help extend.

Bow down thine ear and hear!
    Open thine eyes and see!
Our very love is shame,
    and we must come to thee
to make it of thy grace
    what thou wouldst have it be.

Henry Twells
Hymns Ancient and Modern, 1889

243

The Voice Says, "Cry!" Isaiah 40:6

The voice says, "Cry!" What shall we cry?
    "All flesh is grass, and like the flower
its glories droop, its pleasures die,
    its joys but last one fleeting hour."

The voice says, "Cry!" O piteous cry!
    and are there none to help and save?
Have all that live below the sky
    no other prospect but a grave?

The voice says, "Cry!" Yet glorious cry!
    the Word of God can never fall,
and tells how Jesus, throned on high,
    holds out eternal life to all.

The voice says, "Cry!" Who heeds the cry?
    O brother man! Who heeds it not?
By countless millions, far and nigh,
    'tis still unheard, despised, forgot.

The voice says, "Cry!" What stops the cry?
    Our greed of wealth, our love of ease,
our lack of earnest will to try
    mankind to save, and God to please.

The voice says, "Cry!" O let us cry!
    though standing on death's awful brink,
men feast, they jest, they sell, they buy,   (Luke 17:28)
    and cannot see, and will not think.

The voice says, "Cry!" Lord, we would cry,
    but of thy goodness teach us how;
for fast the hours of mercy fly,
    and, if we cry, it must be now!

Henry Twells, 1900
*Hymn, Sonnets, and Other Poems for the Bicentenary of the Society
for the Propagation of the Gospel*, 1900

244

The People of God

We come unto our fathers' God,
    their Rock is our salvation;
th' eternal arms their dear abode,
    we make our habitation.
We bring thee, Lord, the praise they brought;
we seek thee as thy saints have sought
    in every generation.

Unto thy people we belong,
    elect, redeemed, renewed;
we join the blessed pilgrim throng
    with thine own hand endued.
Our hands their tasks divine essay;
our feet pursue the heavenly way
    their steadfast feet pursued.

The fire divine, their steps that led   (Exod. 40:38)
    still goeth bright before us;
the heavenly shield, around them spread
    is still high holden o'er us.
The grace those sinners that subdued,
the strength those weaklings that renewed,
    doth vanquish, doth restore us.

The cleaving sins that brought them low
    are still our souls oppressing;
the tears that from their eyes did flow
    fall fast, our shame confessing.
As with thee, Lord, prevailed their cry,
so our strong prayer ascends on high
    and bringeth down thy blessing.

The precious things on us bestowed
    the same dear Lord discover;
the joy wherewith their souls o'erflowed
    makes our glad hearts run over.
Their fire of love in us doth burn;
as yearned their hearts, our hearts do yearn
    after the heavenly Love.

Their joy unto our Lord we bring;
    their song to us descendeth:
the Spirit who in them did sing
    to us his music lendeth.
His song in them, in us, is one;
we raise it high, we send it on—
    the song that never endeth!

Ye saints to come, take up the strain—
    the same sweet theme endeavor!
Unbroken be the golden chain!
    Keep on the song for ever!
Save in the same dear dwelling place   (Ps. 90:1)
rich with the same eternal grace,
    bless the same boundless Giver!

Thomas Hornblower Gill, 1868
The Golden Chain of Praise, 1868

245
Skill and Science

Accept this building, gracious Lord,
    no temple though it be;
we raise it for our suffering kin,
    and so, good Lord, for thee.

Accept our little gift, and give
    to all who here may dwell,
the will and power to do their work,
    or bear their sorrows well.

From thee all skill and science flow,
    all pity, care, and love,
all calm and courage, faith and hope—
    O pour them from above!

And part them, Lord, to each and all,
    as each and all shall need
to rise, like incense, each to thee,
    in noble thought and deed.

And hasten, Lord, that perfect day,
    when pain and death shall cease,
and thy just rule shall fill the earth
    with health, and light, and peace;

when ever blue the sky shall gleam,
    and ever green the sod,
and man's rude work deface no more
    the paradise of God.

Charles Kingsley, 1870/1871
Collected Poems, 1889
The common version of the hymn omits the first two stanzas.

246
Saint Barnabas

O Son of God, our Captain of Salvation, (Heb. 2:10)
    thyself by suffering schooled to human grief,
we bless thee for thy sons of consolation, (Acts 4:36)
    who follow in the steps of thee, their Chief.

Those whom thy Spirit's dread vocation severs
    to lead the vanguard of thy conquering host;
whose toilsome years are spent in brave endeavors
    to bear thy saving name from coast to coast.

Those whose bright faith makes feeble hearts grow
                        stronger,
    and sends fresh warriors to the great campaign,
bids the lone convert feel estranged no longer,
    and wins the sundered to be one again;

and all true helpers, patient, kind, and skillful,
    who shed thy light across our darkened earth,
counsel the doubting, and restrain the willful,
    soothe the sickbed, and share the children's
                        mirth.

Such was thy Levite, strong in self-oblation,
    to cast his all at thine apostles' feet;
he whose new name through every Christian nation
    from age to age our thankful strains repeat.

Thus, Lord, thy Barnabas in memory keeping,
    still be thy church's watchword, "Comfort ye";
              (Isa. 40:1)
till in our Father's house shall end our weeping,
    and all our wants be satisfied in thee.

John Ellerton, 1871
Church Hymns, 1871

247
Conversion of Saint Paul

We sing the glorious conquest
    before Damascus gate,
when Saul, the church's spoiler
    came breathing threats and hate; (Acts 9:1)
the ravening wolf rushed forward
    full early to the prey; (John 10:11–12)
but lo! the Shepherd met him
    and bound him fast today!

O Glory most excelling
    that smote across his path!
O Light that pierced and blinded
    the zealot in his wrath!
O Voice that spoke within him
    the calm reproving word!
O Love that sought and held him
    the bondman of the Lord!

O Wisdom, ordering all things
    in order strong and sweet,
what nobler spoil was ever
    cast at the Victor's feet?
What wiser master-builder (1 Cor. 3:10)
    e'er wrought at thine employ,
than he, till now so furious
    thy building to destroy?

Lord, teach thy church the lesson,
    still in her darkest hour
of weakness and of danger
    to trust thy hidden power.
Thy grace by ways mysterious
    the wrath of man can bind, (Ps. 76:10)
and in thy boldest foeman
    thy chosen saint can find!

John Ellerton, 1871
Church Hymns, 1871

The Victorian Age, 1837–1906

248
Hymn for Advent

The Lord is come! on Syrian soil,
the child of poverty and toil;
the Man of sorrows, born to know
each varying shade of human woe:
His joy, his glory to fulfill,
in earth and heaven, his Father's will;
on lonely mount, by festive board,
on bitter cross, despised, adored.

The Lord is come! In him we trace
the fullness of God's truth and grace;
throughout those words and acts divine
gleams of the eternal splendor shine;
and from his inmost spirit flow,
as from a height of sunlit snow,
the rivers of perennial life,
to heal and sweeten nature's strife.

The Lord is come! in every heart
where truth and mercy claim a part;
in every land where right is might,
and deeds of darkness shun the light;
in every church where faith and love
lift heavenward thoughts to things above;
in every holy, happy home
we bless thee, Lord, that thou hast come.

Arthur Penryhn Stanley
Macmillan's Magazine, December 1872
as in *The English Hymnal*, 1906

249
The Eucharistic Presentation

'Tis said, 'tis done: and like as we believe
    that he, true God, became for us true Man;
as, clinging to the cross, our souls receive
    the mysteries of his redemptive plan;
as we confess, "He rose, and burst the tomb—
went up on high—will come to speak the doom";

so may we see the bright harmonious line
    of all those marvels stretching on to this,
a kindred master-work of power divine,
    that yields a foretaste of our country's bliss,
when pilgrim hearts discern from earthly food
the quickening essence of his flesh and blood.

Wherefore, we sinners, mindful of the love
    that bought us, once for all, on Calvary's tree,
and having with us him that pleads above (Heb. 7:23)
    we here present, we here set forth to thee
that only Offering perfect in thine eyes,
the one true pure immortal Sacrifice.

Look, Father, look on his anointed face,
    and only look on us as found in him;
look not on our misusings of thy grace,
    our prayer so languid, and our faith so dim;
for lo! between our sins and their reward
we set the passion of thy Son our Lord.

And then, for those, our dearest and our best,
    by this prevailing presence we appeal;
O fold them closer to thy mercy's breast,
    O do thine utmost for their souls' true weal:
from tainting mischief keep them white and clear,
and crown thy gifts with strength to persevere.

And so we come: O draw us to thy feet,
    most patient Savior, who canst love us still;
and by this food, so awful and so sweet,
    deliver us from every touch of ill:
In thine own service make us glad and free,
and grant us never more to part with thee.

William Bright
The Monthly Packet, October 1873
The common version, from *Hymns Ancient and Modern*,
1875, omits the first two stanzas and begins,
"And now, O Father, mindful of the love."

250
Saint Matthew

He sat to watch o'er customs paid,
a man of scorned and hardening trade;
alike the symbol and the tool
of foreign masters' hated rule.

But grace within his breast had stirred;
there needed but the timely word;
it came, true Lord of souls, from thee,
that royal summons, "Follow me."

Enough, when thou wast passing by,
to hear thy voice, to meet thine eye:
He rose, responsive to the call,
and left his task, his gains, his all.

O wise exchange! with these to part,
and lay up treasure in thy heart; (Matt. 6:21)
with twofold crown of light to thine
amid thy servants' foremost line.

Come, Savior, as in days of old:
Pass where the world has strongest hold,
and faithless fear and selfish greed
are thorns that choke the holy seed. (Matt. 13:22)

Who keep thy gifts, O bid them claim
the steward's, not the owner's name;
who yield all up for thy dear sake,
let them of Matthew's wealth partake.

William Bright
Hymns Ancient and Modern, 1889

251
Holy Saturday

It is finished! blessed Jesus,
    thou hast breathed thy latest sigh,
teach us, the sons of Adam,
    how the Son of God can die.

Lifeless lies the pierced body,
    resting in its rocky bed;
thou hast left the cross of anguish
    for the mansions of the dead.

In the hidden realms of darkness
    shines a light unseen before,
when the Lord of dead and living
    enters at the lowly door.

Lo! in spirit, rich in mercy
    comes he from the world above,
preaching to the souls in prison (1 Pet. 3:19)
    tidings of his dying love.

Lo! the heavenly light around him,
    as he draws his people near;
all amazed they come rejoicing
    at the gracious words they hear.

Patriarch and priest and prophet
    gather round him as he stands,
in adoring faith and gladness
    hearing of the pierced hands.

There in lowliest joy and wonder
    stands the robber by his side,
reaping now the blessed promise
    spoken by the Crucified. (Luke 23:43)

Jesus, Lord of our salvation,
    let thy mercy rest on me;
grant me too, when life is finished,
    rest in paradise with thee.

William Dalrymple Maclagan
Hymns Ancient and Modern, 1875
revised by Maclagan for *Hymns Ancient and Modern, 1904*

252
Saint James

Lord, who shall sit beside thee,   (Mark 10:37–38)
     enthroned on either hand,
when clouds no longer hide thee,
     'mid all thy faithful band?

Who drinks the cup of sorrow
     thy Father gave to thee
'neath shadows of the morrow,
     in dark Gethsemane;

who on thy passion thinking
     can find in loss a gain,   (Phil. 3:7)
and dare to meet unshrinking
     thy baptism of pain.

O Jesu, form within us
     thy likeness clear and true,
by thine example win us
     to suffer or to do.

This law itself fulfilleth—
     Christlike to Christ is nigh,
and where the Father willeth
     shall sit with Christ on high.

William Romanis
Wigston Magna School Hymns, 1878

253
The Breath of the Spirit

Breathe on me, Breath of God,
     fill me with life anew,
that I may love what thou dost love
     and do what thou wouldst do.

Breathe on me, Breath of God,
     until my heart is pure,   (Matt. 5:3)
until with thee I will one will
     to do or to endure.

Breathe on me, Breath of God,
     till I am wholly thine,
till all this earthly part of me
     glows with thy fire divine.

Breathe on me, Breath of God,
     so shall I never die,
but live with thee the perfect life
     of thine eternity.

Edwin Hatch
Between Doubt and Prayer, 1878
The original line 3:2, "blend all my soul with thine," was altered in
The Congregational Psalmist Hymnal, 1886.

254
For the Opening of an Exhibition

Almighty Father of all things that be,
our life, our work, we consecrate to thee,
whose heavens declare thy glory from above,
whose earth below is witness to thy love.

For well we know this weary, soiled earth
is yet thine own by right of its new birth   (Isa 65:1)
since that great cross upreared on Calvary   (Rev. 21:2)
redeemed it from its sin and shame to thee.

Thine still the changeful beauty of the hills,
the purple valleys flecked with silver rills,
the ocean glistening 'neath the golden rays,
they all are thine, and, voiceless, speak thy praise.
                 (Ps. 19:4)

Thou dost the strength to workman's arm impart;
from thee the skilled musician's mystic art,
the grace of poet's pen or painter's hand
to teach the loveliness of sea or land.

Then grant us, Lord, in all things thee to own,
to dwell within the shadow of thy throne,
to speak and work, to think, and live, and move,
reflecting thine own nature, which is love;   (1 John 4:7)

that so, by Christ redeemed from sin and shame,
and hallowed by thy Spirit's cleansing flame,
ourselves, our work, and all our powers may be
a sacrifice acceptable to thee.   (Rom. 12:1)

Ernest Edward Dugmore, 1884
Hymns and Litanies, 1885
altered in *Hymns Ancient and Modern*, 1904

255
To the Eternal Father

Almighty Father, unoriginate,
 whom no man hath seen, ever, nor can see;
who reignest blessed and only Potentate,
 light unapproachable encircling thee;
almighty Father, hallowed be thy name,
who ever art, unchangeably the same.   (James 1:17)

Thou lovest us, else had we never been:
 before we were, in ages long ago,
thy love had us and all our wants foreseen,
 creating us that we thy love might know.
Yea, Father, thou, in whom we live and move,
hast loved us with an everlasting love.   (Acts 17:28)

Thou madest man immortal at the first,
 an image of thine own eternity,   (Gen. 1:26)
and when he fell from life, through sin accurst,
 and lost his right to the life-giving tree,   (Gen. 3:8)
thy love, unconquered, would to him restore
his life ennobled and for evermore.

Such was thy love, thou didst not even spare
 thy Best-Beloved, but gav'st him for us all;
to live that human life beyond compare,   (Rom. 8:32)
 and dying, by his death retrieve our fall.
In him thy love unbounded we behold,
for, giving him, thou canst not aught withhold.

Thou knowest what we are, how frail and blind,
 thou still rememberest that we are but dust:
        (Ps. 103:14)
Like as a father pitieth, thou art kind,
 thy justice kindness, and thy kindness just,
Then hear thy children's prayer from heaven thy
         throne;
"Father, thy kingdom come; thy will be done!"
        (Luke 11:2)

Ernest Edward Dugmore
Hymns of Adoration, 1900
altered in *Hymns Ancient and Modern*, 1904

256
Recessional

God of our fathers, known of old,
 Lord of our far-flung battleline,
beneath whose awful hand we hold
 dominion over palm and pine—
Lord God of hosts, be with us yet,
lest we forget—lest we forget!

The tumult and the shouting dies;
 the captains and the kings depart:
Still stands thine ancient sacrifice,
 an humble and a contrite heart.   (Ps. 51:17)
Lord God of hosts, be with us yet—
lest we forget—lest we forget!

Far-called, our navies melt away:
 on dune and headland sinks the fire:
Lo, all our pomp of yesterday
 is one with Nineveh and Tyre!
Judge of the nations, spare us yet,
lest we forget—lest we forget!

If, drunk with sight of power, we loose
 wild tongues that have not thee in awe,
such boastings as the Gentiles use,
 or lesser breeds without the law—
Lord God of hosts, be with us yet,
lest we forget—lest we forget!

For heathen heart that puts her trust
    in reeking tube and iron shard,
all valiant dust that builds on dust,
    and guarding, calls not thee to guard,
for frantic boast and foolish word,
thy mercy on thy people, Lord!

Rudyard Kipling
The Times, July 17, 1897

257
Amor Patris et Filii, Veri Splendor

Love of the Father, love of God the Son,
from whom all came, in whom was all begun;
who formest heavenly beauty out of strife,
creation's whole desire and breath of life;

thou the all-holy, thou supreme in might,
thou dost give peace, thy presence maketh right;
thou with thy favor all things dost enfold,
with thine all-kindness free from harm wilt hold.

Hope of all comfort, splendor of all aid,
that dost not fail nor leave the heart afraid;
to all that cry thou dost all help afford,
the angels' armor, and the saints' reward.

Purest and highest, wisest and most just,
there is no truth save only in thy trust;
thou dost the mind from earthly dreams recall,
and bring through Christ to him, for whom are all.

Eternal glory, all men thee adore,
who art and shalt be worshiped evermore;
us whom thou madest, comfort with thy might,
and lead us to enjoy thy heavenly light.

Robert Bridges
suggested by the anonymous twelfth-century
Latin text named in his heading
The Yattendon Hymnal, 1899

258
Love, unto Thine Own Who Camest

Love, unto thine own who camest
    condescending,
    whom thine own received not: (John 1:11)
light, that shinedst in the darkness,
    but the darkness
    thy splendor perceived not: (John 1:5)

O blessed were they who saw thee,
    who were chosen
    first saints of thy saving word:
blessed they who have not seen thee,
    yet believing   (John 20:29)
    are called by thee, O Lord.

Like stars in the night appearing,
    some are shining,
    leaders high of man's desire:
saints are some, in silent temples
    ever burning,
    bright lamps of love's living fire.

Thou hidest them, Love almighty,
    in thy presence,
    from this world's provoking wrongs:
sheltered in thy quiet haven
    thou dost keep them
    from strife of ungodly tongues.

Love, unto thine own who camest,
    may thy servants
    thy great love receive aright:
grant, O grant that out of darkness
    all creation
    may come to thy marvelous light.   (1 Pet. 1:12)

Robert Bridges
The Yattendon Hymnal, 1899

259

In Time of War

Rejoice, O land, in God thy might;
his will obey, him serve aright;
for thee the saints lift up their voice.
Fear not, O land, in God rejoice.

Glad shalt thou be, with blessing crowned,
with joy and peace thou shalt abound.
Yea, love with thee shall make his home
until thou see God's kingdom come.

He shall forgive thy sins untold.
Remember thou his love of old.
Walk in his way, his word adore,
and keep his truth for evermore.

Robert Bridges, 1897
The Yattendon Hymnal, 1899

260

Thee Will I Love

Thee will I love, my God and King,
thee will I sing,
my strength and tower;
for evermore thee will I trust,
O God most just
of truth and power;
who all things hast
in order placed
who for thy pleasure hast created;
and on thy throne,
unseen, unknown,
reignest alone
in glory seated.

Set in my heart thy love I find,
my wandering mind
to thee thou leadest:
my trembling hope, my strong desire
with heavenly fire
thou kindly feedest.
Lo, all things fair
thy path prepare,
thy beauty to my spirit calleth
thine to remain
in joy or pain
and count it gain
whate'er befalleth.

O more and more thy love extend,
my life befriend
with heavenly pleasure;
that I may win thy paradise,
thy pearl of price,
thy countless treasure;
since but in thee
I can go free
from earthly care and vain oppression,
this prayer I make
for Jesus' sake,
that thou me take
for thy possession.

Robert Bridges
The Yattendon Hymnal, 1899

261

Our Father, Who Art in Heaven

Eternal Father, who didst all create,
in whom we live, and to whose bosom move,
to all men be thy name known, which is Love,
till its loud praises sound at heaven's gate.

Perfect thy kingdom in our passing state,
that here on earth thou may'st as well approve
our service, as thou ownest theirs above,
whose joy we echo and in pain await.

Grant body and soul each day their daily bread:
    and should in spite of grace fresh woe begin,
even as our anger soon is past and dead,
    be thy remembrance mortal of our sin:

By thee in paths of peace thy sheep be led,
and in the vale of terror comforted.

Robert Bridges, 1876
The Growth of Love, 1876
First as a hymn in *Songs of Praise*, 1931, it having been previously
discovered by the editors of *The English Hymnal* (see 411)
that a sonnet could be sung as a hymn.

262
The Adoration of the Lamb

The church of God a kingdom is,
    where Christ in power doth reign,
where spirits yearn till seen in bliss
    their Lord shall come again.

Glad companies of saints possess
    this church below, above;
and God's perpetual calm doth bless
    their paradise of love.

An altar stands within the shrine,
    whereon, once sacrificed,
is set, immaculate, divine,
    the Lamb of God, the Christ.

There rich and poor, from countless lands,
    praise Christ on mystic rood;
there nations reach forth holy hands
    to take God's holy food.

There pure life-giving streams o'erflow
    the sower's garden-ground;
and faith and hope fair blossoms show,
    and fruits of love abound.

O King, O Christ, this endless grace
    to us and all men bring,
to see the vision of thy face
    in joy, O Christ our King.

Lionel Brulton Campbell Lockhart Muirhead
The Yattendon Hymnal, 1899
The title of the hymn is that of the painting by Huybrecht and
Jan van Eyck, which was the inspiration of this hymn.

263
Gloria in Excelsis

Praise ye the Lord, ye servants of the Lord:
    praise ye his name; his lordly honor sing:
    thee we adore, to thee glad homage bring;
thee we acknowledge: God to be adored
for thy great glory, Sovereign, Lord, and King.

Father of Christ—that Lamb with blemish none,
    that took the sins of all mankind away—
    to thee belongeth worship, day by day;
yea, Holy Father, everlasting Son,
and Holy Ghost, all praise be thine for aye!

George Ratcliffe Woodward
Songs of Syon, 1904
based on the *Apostolic Constitutions*, fourth century

264
How Dazzling Fair Art Thou

    How dazzling fair art thou, my Life, my Light!
    How comely is thy countenance, how bright!
Sun uncreate, how keen is the enjoyment
that saints and angels find in thine employment!
    In view whereof sing I, by day and night,
    "How dazzling fair art thou, my Life, my Light!"

My soul, O Lord, is still athirst for thee: (Ps. 42)
  my heart doth yearn thy seemly face to see:
dim is my sight; but one ray of thy kindness
should quickly skill to cure me of thy blindness:
  meanwhile my song and my complaint shall be,
  "My soul, O Lord, is sore athirst for thee."

How lordly are thy mansions, King of love!
  How worshipful thy courts in realms above! (Ps. 84:1)
Say, Lord, when shall I come to stand before thee,
and in thy gallant gates and walls adore thee?
  Meantime I mourn, as doth the plaintive dove,
  "How lordly are thy mansions, King of love!"

When shall I come to hear the angel-song?
  Nay, swell the chorus of the heavenly throng?
When join the noble company of sages
who chant thy lauds through everlasting ages?
  Now every day methinks, and all day long,
  "When shall I come to hear that angel-song?"

For songs of Syon, Lord, my soul prepare,
  part in that never-ending round to bear;
to cry, with men of humble heart and lowly, (Ps. 148:13)
to thy great glory, "Holy, holy, holy"; (Isa. 6:3)
  meanwhile shall be the tenor of mine air,
  "For songs of Syon, Lord, my soul prepare."

George Ratcliffe Woodward
Songs of Syon, 1910
based on Johann Scheffler's
"Wie schön bist du, mein Leben und mein Licht"

265
Judge Eternal, Throned in Splendor

Judge eternal, throned in splendor,
  Lord of lords and King of kings,
with thy living fire of judgment
  purge this realm of bitter things,
solace all its wide dominion
  with the healing of thy wings.

Still the weary folk are pining
  for the hour that brings release.
and the city's crowded clangor
  cries aloud for sin to cease;
and the homesteads and the woodlands
  plead in silence for thy peace.

Crown, O God, thine own endeavor:
  cleave our darkness with thy sword;
feed the faint and hungry heathen
  with the richness of thy Word:
Cleanse the body of this empire
  through the glory of the Lord.

Henry Scott Holland
The Commonwealth, July 1902

266
The Choir of Heaven

Ye watchers and ye holy ones, (Dan. 4:23)
bright seraphs, cherubim, and thrones,
  raise the glad strain, alleluia!
Cry out, dominions, princedoms, powers,
virtues, archangels, angels' choirs,

    Alleluia, alleluia, alleluia, alleluia, alleluia!

O higher than the cherubim,
more glorious than the seraphim,
  lead their praises, alleluia!
Thou bearer of the eternal Word,
most gracious, magnify the Lord, (Luke 1:46)

Respond, ye souls in endless rest,
ye patriarchs and prophets blest,
  Alleluia! alleluia!
Ye holy twelve, ye martyrs strong,
all saints triumphant, raise the song,

O friends, in gladness let us sing
supernal anthems echoing,
   Alleluia! alleluia!
To God the Father, God the Son,
and God the Spirit, Three in One,

Athelstan Riley
The English Hymnal, 1906

267
At Catechism

Jesus, good above all other,
gentle Child of gentle Mother,
in a stable born our Brother,
   give us grace to persevere.

Jesus, cradled in a manger,
for us facing every danger,
living as a homeless stranger,
   make we thee our King most dear.

Jesus, for thy people dying,
risen Master, death defying,
Lord in heaven, thy grace supplying,
   keep us by thine altar near.

Jesus, who our sorrows bearest,
all our thoughts and hopes thou sharest,
thou to man the truth declarest;
   help us all thy truth to hear.

Lord, in all our doings guide us,
pride and hate shall ne'er divide us;
we'll go on with thee beside us,
   and with joy we'll persevere!

Percy Dearmer
borrowing lines from "Jesus, kind above all others," a cento from
"Gabriel from heaven descending," John Mason Neale's translation of
the sequence of Adam of St. Victor
The English Hymnal, 1906
Line 3:4 was subsequently altered by the author to
"keep us to thy presence near."

268
It Is Finished

"It is finished!" Christ hath known
all the life of men wayfaring,
human joys and sorrows sharing,
   making human needs his own.
Lord, in us thy life renewing,
   lead us where thy feet have trod,
till, the way of truth pursuing,
   human souls find rest in God.

"It is finished!" Christ is slain
on the altar of creation,
offering for a world's salvation
   sacrifice of love and pain.
Lord, thy love through pain revealing,
   purge our passions, scourge our vice,
till, upon the tree of healing
   self is slain in sacrifice.

"It is finished!" Christ our King
wins the victor's crown of glory;
sun and stars recite his story;
   floods and fields his triumph sing.
Lord, whose praise the world is telling,
   Lord, to whom all power is given   (Matt. 28:19)
by thy death, hell's armies quelling,
   bring thy saints to reign in heaven.

George Gabriel Scott Gillett
The English Hymnal, 1906

269

O God of Earth and Altar

O God of earth and altar,   (Exod. 20:24)
    bow down and hear our cry,
our earthly rulers falter,
    our people drift and die;
the walls of gold entomb us,
    the swords of scorn divide,
take not thy thunder from us,
    but take away our pride.

From all that terror teaches,
    from lies of tongue and pen,
from all the easy speeches
    that comfort cruel men,
from sale and profanation
    of honor and the sword,
from sleep and from damnation
    deliver us, good Lord!

Tie in a living tether
    the prince and priest and thrall,
bind all our lives together,
    smite us and save us all;
in ire and exultation,
    aflame with faith, and free,
lift up a living nation,
    a single sword to thee.

Gilbert Keith Chesterton
The Commonwealth, 1906

Chapter 15:
Women Writers before 1906
(270–295)

Half of my readers will bristle at this title, but there is no help for it. The Victorian age talked dogmatically about men, women, and children as three distinct species of the genus human, and history insists that until the opening of the twentieth century, at least in hymnology, the women and (in the succeeding chapter) the children be so treated.

By way of prologue, we present 270–272, which come from an earlier period. Hardly any hymnody by women comes from the eighteenth century or earlier, and only two or three such compositions have survived at all in modern use. We are obliged to begin with Madame Jeanne Marie Bouvier de La Motte Guyon, about whom Ronald Knox wrote in *Enthusiasm* (1950) so entertainingly and naughtily. She was the leader of the French "Quietist" movement and personally something of an eccentric. If she had lived in the English nineteenth century she would probably have got a good deal out of her system by writing novels; in the twentieth, she would have gone to America and started a movement. As it was, she paraded a somewhat paranoid religiosity, and of her many literary works, Knox says,

> they give an impression of extraordinary glibness . . . of eccentricity rather than originality, of very mediocre taste. Her poems seem to me frankly dull; nor did Cowper, who admired them, manage to make a great deal of them in translation.

Well, 270 comes out as a harmless devotional piece, perhaps not much more than that.

Anne Steele, our first English woman hymnodist, writing surprisingly early, places us on firmer ground in 271, which is still popular; and Anna Barbauld, 272, gives us a hymn which,

though rather long, is more impressive in its original than in the truncated version still to be found in hymnals. It is a hymn for springtime or for the late winter, very realistic, and strikingly unsentimental.

Harriet Auber (273–274) still falls technically outside the Victorian era. The less-known of the two hymns we here cite is probably the stronger; there are good thoughts and bad lines in 274, which will probably never be divorced now from a disastrous tune.

The tendency for women writers to use meters ending with a short line is something of a curiosity in the nineteenth century. Charlotte Elliott constantly did it. "Just as I am" (275), if one uses the whole text, has a very good shape and a telling climax (it again has suffered from abominable tunes). Number 276 is even stronger; in stanza 4— oh, if only she had written "all with one great voice" instead of "sweet voice"! That word "sweet" was run to death by Victorian writers of both sexes. But here is a still sturdy hymn full of good teaching (and there is a good tune for this, though few know it).

Now one must understand that the separation of women in our context reflects the simple fact that women and men in English bourgeois society—hymns don't come from any other section— lived totally different lives. So you find here no echo at all of the controversies that gave the age its energy. On the contrary, you are reminded of the separateness of women by the very titles of some of the sources: Look at the source of 275, and of 289. Or look at the novelists, and consider the predicament of any middle-aged woman in Trollope or Dickens or Thackeray. Except when they deal with the "lower orders" or with country folk who are really rustics, one doesn't know whether to be more terrified of their triviality, if they are trivial, or their officiousness, if they are of the managing kind. At their best they are pictured as dedicated to home and family, or, if unmarried, to good works, which in the best hands really meant disciplined and sacrificial compassion.

It is hardly surprising that with such a complexity of spiritual and mental hazards to negotiate, the one faculty which a Victorian bourgeois woman should have had time to nourish is in fact so lacking in the hymnody she mostly produced: imagination. However, there is imagination in the best Victorian women's hymns; it is there in Charlotte Elliott, and it is there in the Unitarian Sarah Adams, whose "Nearer, my God, to thee," if separated from sentimental music (the musicians really did treat these women badly) and from historical association, turns out to be strong literature.

Sunday schools, of course, gave the ladies plenty to do. Number 278 is a famous hymn from that field written by Miss Mary Fawler Maude when she was ill and separated from her class for three months, in each week of which she wrote them a letter. The letters were later collected and published, and this little piece was among them. Miss Anna Laetitia Waring (279) produced a number of poems, some of which are hymns of a pastoral, meditative, and hopeful kind.

But this brings us to Mrs. Cecil Frances Alexander, and the more one sees of her work, the more one is convinced that for sheer honesty and straightforwardness she is the leading Victorian woman hymn writer. She is, indeed, worth closer study than we can here give her. People are often too easily labeled by the part of their work which captures a fickle public imagination; Mrs. Alexander is, to most people, a writer of children's hymns. Well, when she was Miss Humphreys, that was what she was. See 306–308 for some famous examples from her early collection of 1848. But the great thing about her children's hymns is their directness and candor. It does not always suit us now; perhaps it is because several of her children's hymns, like all three of those we cite in the next section, have been appropriated by adults that we look patronizingly upon them. Certainly "Once in royal David's city," which begins and ends so well, has one dreadful line: "mild, obedient, good";

certainly "There is a green hill" doesn't say all that can be said about the mystery of the Atonement. Equally certainly she perpetrated "We are but little children weak," which has an alarming first line, though much sound stuff further on, and "Within the churchyard side by side are many long, low graves"; but no, even there one has to appreciate the straightforwardness and the candor. In one respect Mrs. Alexander was fortunate: she was rarely let down by the musicians. That could be said of one hideous tune to 280, "Jesus calls us," which has to be divorced from its *Hymns A & M* tune before it can be seen for the sound piece it is; but for sheer simplicity, 281 is hard to beat, and so is the soundly scriptural 282. When we come to 320 we shall have more to say—that is her greatest piece, written forty-one years later than her children's series (see chapters 16 and 17).

Frances Ridley Havergal (283–284) was an extraordinary person. A maiden lady all her fairly short life, she devoted herself from her early adult years to private evangelism. Not all of us are sure that she might not have proved a somewhat overwhelming guest (read what is said in the *Hymnal Guide* about "Take my life"), but one can only admire—even if one keeps a safe distance— her zeal and sincerity. She was a facile writer and fairly frequently wrote doggerel. Our 283, her first hymn, is a modest and moving piece, and 284, one of her best known, shows that, if she did equate Christian service with religious proselytizing, she did at least mean what she said. Among Evangelicals her hymnody is always welcome, and certainly it strikes sounder notes than much that Evangelicals are now fed with.

Number 285 has greater artistry than Miss Havergal could compass; it is a series of compact and balanced statements so adroitly arranged as to make an eloquent hymn. The comma between stanzas 5 and 6, after the buttoned-up neatness of the first four stanzas, is most dramatic; conviction at last breaks through decorum. Sung to the tune HEINLEIN this is magnificent.

Number 286 became a hymn after its author's death, and perhaps it would have been equally appropriate in chapter 21; but it is, in its manner, strictly in line with the feminine hymnody of the period. It has to be delivered from the efforts of musicians to overdo the sentiment, but it is a beautiful meditation.

Miss Elizabeth Cecilia Clephane, the short-lived evangelical hymnist who wrote 287 and 313, became after her death one of the most sought-after authors of the evangelical missions of the seventies. Text 287 is a highly personalized, atonement-centered piece characteristic of the piety generated by those revivals. This is Evangelicalism, the almost direct opposite of resurrection-centered Calvinism, and at the same time the opposite (if such multidimensional geometry be permitted) of demure Anglicanism. This has much in common with those "Gospel Songs" which are dealt with later in chapter 19.

Could anything be more different from that than the contemplative and charming manner of 288? This poetess, Dora Greenwell, who began her life in Northumbria, a part of England not rich in hymnic associations, embraces the liberal rather than the Evangelical culture and presents a human and living Christ rather than a dying Christ. Hymnals have usually rearranged the stanzas, but in those few places where it is still known it brings a message quite unusual in the female hymnody of the time.

Equally unusual is the monumental 289—the only completely objective theological hymn to come from the hand of a nineteenth-century woman writer. No hymnal includes all the stanzas, and yet, which can really be spared without damaging the shape of the whole?

Christina Rossetti probably did not think of herself as a hymn writer, but from *The English Hymnal* onwards, fragments of her poetic output have been sought after by singers. The subtle variety in 290–294 (see also 309), her special facility for writing short, epigrammatic poems of

true lyric quality, and her profound evangelical diction combine to make her the most literate and poetically gifted of all these women. She, like Mrs. Alexander, has usually been happy in her partnerships with musicians, but she can especially be read for devotional purposes without thought of music, for there is plenty of depth in her words.

Our section ends (295) with Mrs. Ada Rundall Greenaway's hymn on the first word from the cross, a successful handling of a meter which often leads writers into exuberant platitude, and one of the very few new texts introduced in the 1904 *Hymns A & M* which has survived into later collections.

270

O Thou by Long Experience Tried

O thou by long experience tried,
near whom no grief can long abide,
my Lord! how full of sweet content
my years of pilgrimage are spent.

All scenes alike engaging prove
to souls impressed with sacred love;
where'er they dwell, they dwell with thee,
in heaven, in earth, or in the sea.

To me remains nor place nor time;
my country is in every clime;
I can be calm and free from care
on any shore, since God is there.

While place we seek or place we shun,
the soul finds happiness in none;
but with my God to guide my way
'tis equal joy to go or stay.

Could I be cast where thou art not,
that were indeed a dreadful lot:
But regions none remote I call,
secure of finding God in all.

Then let me to his throne repair,
and never be a stranger there:
Then love divine shall be my guard,
and peace and safety my reward.

Jeanne Marie Bouvier de La Motte Guyon
translated, William Cowper
*Poems: Translated from the French of
Madame de La Mothe Guyon*, 1801

271

The Excellency of the Holy Scriptures

Father of mercies, in thy word
    what endless glory shines!
For ever be thy name adored
    for these celestial lines.

Here mines of heavenly wealth disclose
    their bright, unbounded store:
The glittering gem no longer glows,
    and India boasts no more.

Here may the wretched sons of want
    exhaustless riches find:
riches, above what earth can grant,
    and lasting as the mind.

Here, the fair tree of knowledge grows,
    and yields a free repast,
sublimer sweets than nature knows
    invite the longing taste.

Here may the blind and hungry come,
    and light and food receive;
here shall the meanest guest have room,
    and taste, and see, and live.

Amidst these gloomy wilds below,
    when dark and sad we stray;
here beams of heaven relieve our woe,
    and guide to endless day.

Here springs of consolation rise
    to cheer the fainting mind;
and thirsty souls receive supplies,
    and sweet refreshment find.

When guilt and terror, pain and grief,
    united rend the heart,
here sinners meet divine relief,
    and cool the raging smart.

Here the Redeemer's welcome voice
    spreads heavenly peace around;
and life, and everlasting joys,
    attend the blissful sound.

But when his painful sufferings rise
    (delightful, dreadful scene!),
angels may read with wondering eyes
    that Jesus died for men.

O may these heavenly pages be
    my ever dear delight;
and still new beauties may I see,
    and still increasing light.

Divine instructor, gracious Lord,
    be thou for ever near;
teach me to love thy sacred word,
    and view my Savior there.

Anne Steele
Poems on Subjects Chiefly Devotional, 1760

272

Praise to God in Prosperity and Adversity

Praise to God, immortal praise
for the love that crowns our days!
Bounteous source of every joy,
let thy praise our tongues employ.

For the blessings of the field,
for the stores and gardens yield;
for the vine's exalted juice,
for the generous olive's use;

flocks that whiten o'er the plain;
yellow sheaves of ripened grain;
clouds that drop their fattening dews;
suns that temperate warmth diffuse;

all that spring with bounteous hand
scatters o'er the smiling land;
all that liberal autumn pours
from her rich o'erflowing stores:

These to thee, my God, we owe,
source whence all our blessings flow;
and for these my soul shall raise
grateful vow and solemn praise.

Yet, should rising whirlwinds tear   (Hab. 3:17)
from its stem the ripening ear;
should the fig tree's blasted shoot
drop her green untimely fruit,

should the vine put forth no more,
nor the olive yield her store;
though the sickening flocks should fall
and the herds desert the stall;

should thine altered hand restrain   (James 5:7)
th' early and the latter rain;
blast each opening bud of joy,
and the rising year destroy,

yet to thee my soul should raise
grateful vows and solemn praise;
and, when every blessing's flown,
love thee for thyself alone!

Anna Laetitia Aikin Barbauld
Hymns for Public Worship, 1772

273
Psalm 78

O praise our great and gracious Lord,
    and call upon his name;
to strains of joy tune every chord,
    his mighty acts proclaim;
tell how he led his chosen race
    to Canaan's pleasant land;
tell how his covenant of grace
    unchanged shall ever stand.

He gave the shadowing cloud by day,
    the moving fire by night;
to guide his Israel in their way,
    he made their darkness light;
and have we not a sure retreat,
    a Savior ever nigh,
the same clear light to guide our feet,
    the Dayspring from on high?   (Luke 1:78)

We too have manna from above,
    the Bread that came from heaven;
to us the same kind hand of love
    hath living waters given.
A Rock we have, from whence the spring
    in rich abundance flows;
that Rock is Christ, our Priest, our King,   (1 Cor. 10:4)
    who life and health bestows.

O let us prize this blessed food,
    and trust our heavenly Guide;
so shall we find death's fearful flood
    serene as Jordan's tide,
and safely reach that happy shore,
    the land of peace and rest,
where angels worship and adore
    in God's own presence blest.

Harriet Auber
The Spirit of the Psalms, 1829

274
Whitsunday

Our blest Redeemer, ere he breathed
    his tender, last farewell,
a Guide, a Comforter bequeathed   (John 16:7)
    with us to dwell.

He came in semblance of a dove,   (Mark 1:10)
    with sheltering wings outspread,
the holy balm of peace and love
    on earth to shed.

He came in tongues of living flame   (Acts 2:3)
    to teach, convince, subdue:
all-powerful as the wind he came,   (Acts 2:2)
    as viewless too.   (John 3:8)

He came sweet influence to impart,
    a gracious, willing guest,
while he can find one humble heart
    wherein to rest.

And his that gentle voice we hear,
    soft as the breath of even,
that checks each fault, that calms each fear,
    and speaks of heaven.

And every virtue we possess,
    and every victory won,
and every thought of holiness
    are his alone.

Spirit of purity and grace,
    our weakness, pitying, see;
O make our hearts thy dwelling-place
    and worthier thee.

Harriet Auber
The Spirit of the Psalms, 1829

275
Him That Cometh unto Me I Will in No Wise Cast Out

Just as I am, without one plea,
but that thy blood was shed for me,
and that thou bid'st me come to thee,
    O Lamb of God, I come.

Just as I am, and waiting not
to rid my soul of one dark blot,
to thee, whose blood can cleanse each spot,
    O Lamb of God, I come.

Just as I am, though tossed about
with many a conflict, many a doubt,
fightings and fears within, without,
    O Lamb of God, I come.

Just as I am, poor, wretched, blind;
sight, riches, healing of the mind,
yea, all I need, in thee to find,
    O Lamb of God, I come.

Just as I am, thou wilt receive,
wilt welcome, pardon, cleanse, relieve,
because thy promise I believe,
    O Lamb of God, I come.

Just as I am, thy love unknown
has broken every barrier down;   (Eph. 2:13)
now to be thine, yea, thine alone,
    O Lamb of God, I come.

Just as I am, of that free love
the breadth, length, depth, and height to prove
here for a season, then above,   (Eph. 3:18)
    O Lamb of God, I come.

Charlotte Elliott, 1836
stanzas 1–6, *The Invalid's Hymn Book*, 1836
stanza 7, *Hours of Sorrow Cheered and Comforted*, 1836

276

Watch and Pray That Ye Enter Not into Temptation

"Christian! seek not yet repose,"
    hear thy guardian angel say,
"thou art in the midst of foes:
      Watch and pray!"

Principalities and powers,   (Eph. 6:12)
    mustering their unseen array,
wait for thine unguarded hours:
      Watch and pray!

Gird thy heavenly armor on,
    wear it ever night and day;
ambushed lies the evil one:
      Watch and pray!

Hear the victors who o'ercame;
    still they mark each warrior's way: (Heb. 12:1)
All with one sweet voice exclaim,
      "Watch and pray!"

Hear, above all, hear thy Lord,
    him thou lovest to obey;
hide within thy heart his word,
      "Watch and pray!"

Watch, as if on that alone
    hung the issue of the day:
pray that help may be sent down:
      Watch and pray!

Charlotte Elliott
Morning and Evening Hymns for a Week, 1839

277

Nearer, My God, to Thee

Nearer, my God, to thee,
    nearer to thee!
E'en though it be a cross
    that raiseth me:
Still all my song would be,
nearer, my God, to thee—
    nearer to thee!

Though, like the wanderer,   (Gen. 28:20)
    the sun gone down,
darkness be over me,
    my rest a stone;
yet in my dreams I'd be
nearer, my God, to thee—
    nearer to thee!

There let the way appear
    steps unto heaven;
all that thou send'st to me
    in mercy given:
Angels to beckon me
nearer, my God, to thee—
    nearer to thee!

Then with my waking thoughts
    bright with thy praise,
out of my stony griefs,
    Bethel I'll raise;
so by my woes to be
nearer, my God, to thee—
    nearer to thee.

Or if on joyful wing
    cleaving the sky,
sun, moon, and stars forgot,
    upwards I fly:
Still all my song shall be,
nearer, my God, to thee—
    nearer to thee.

Sarah Fuller Flower Adams, 1840
Hymns and Anthems, 1841

278
Thine for Ever, God of Love

Thine for ever, God of love,
hear us from thy throne above;
thine for ever may we be
here and in eternity.

Thine for ever! Lord of life,
shield us through our earthly strife;
thou the Life, the Truth, the Way   (John 14:6)
guide us to the realms of day.

Thine for ever! Oh, how blest
they who find in thee their rest!
Savior, Guardian, heavenly Friend,
O defend us to the end.

Thine for ever! Savior, keep
us thy frail and trembling sheep;
safe alone beneath thy care
let us all thy goodness share.

Thine for ever; thou our Guide,
all our wants by thee supplied,
all our sins by thee forgiven,
lead us, Lord, from earth to heaven.

Mary Fawler Hooper Maude, 1847
Twelve Letters on Confirmation, 1848

Church Hymns, 1871, transposed stanzas 2 and 3, and omitted these
two final stanzas:

Thine forever in that day
when the world shall pass away,
when the trumpet note shall sound
and the nations underground

shall that awful summons hear
which proclaims the judgment near.
Thine forever! 'Neath thy wing
hide and save us, King of kings.

279
I Will Fear No Evil, for Thou Art with Me.
Psalm 23:4

In heavenly love abiding
    no change my heart shall fear;
and safe is such confiding,
    for nothing changes here:
The storm may roar without me,
    my heart may low be laid;
but God is round about me,
    and can I be dismayed?

Wherever he may guide me,
    no want shall turn me back;
my Shepherd is beside me,
    and nothing can I lack;
his wisdom ever waketh,
    his sight is never dim;
he knows the way he taketh,
    and I will walk with him.

Green pastures are before me,
    which yet I have not seen;
bright skies will soon be o'er me,
    where the dark clouds have been:
My hope I cannot measure,
    my path to life is free;
my Savior hath my treasure,
    and he will walk with me.

Anna Laetitia Waring
Hymns and Meditations, 1850

280
Follow Me. For Saint Andrew's Day

Jesus calls us; o'er the tumult
    of our life's wild restless sea;
day by day his sweet voice soundeth,
    saying "Christian, follow me";

as of old Saint Andrew heard it   (Mark 1:16)
    by the Galilean lake,
turned from home, and toil, and kindred,
    leaving all for his dear sake.

Jesus calls us from the worship
    of this vain world's golden store,
from each idol that would keep us,
    saying "Christian, love me more."   (John 21:15)

In our joys and in our sorrows,
    days of toil and hours of ease,
still he calls, in cares and pleasures,
    that we love him more than these.

Jesus calls us: By thy mercies,
    Savior, make us hear thy call,
give our hearts to thine obedience,
    serve and love thee best of all.

Cecil Frances Humphreys Alexander
Hymns for Public Worship, 1852

281
The Ascension

The golden gates are lifted up,
    the doors are opened wide,
the King of glory is gone in
    unto his Father's side.

Thou art gone up before us, Lord,
    to make for us a place,
that we may be where now thou art,
    and look upon God's face.

And ever on our earthly path
    a gleam of glory lies;
a light still breaks behind the cloud
    that veils thee from our eyes.

Lift up our hearts, lift up our minds,
    let thy dear grace be given,
that, while we wander here below,
    our treasure be in heaven;   (Matt. 6:21)

that where thou art at God's right hand,
    our hope, our love may be,
dwell thou in us, that we may dwell
    for evermore in thee.

Cecil Frances Humphreys Alexander
Hymns Descriptive and Devotional, 1858
An earlier version, published in *Hymns* (Society for Promoting
Christian Knowledge), 1852, began "The eternal gates
lift up their heads."

282
For Saints Philip and James

There is one Way, and only one,   (John 14:6)
    out of our gloom, and sin, and care,
to that far land where shines no sun   (Rev. 21:23)
    because the face of God is there.

There is one Truth, the truth of God,
    that Christ came down from heaven to show,
one Life, that his redeeming blood
    has won for all his saints below.

The lore from Philip once concealed,   (John 14:8–9)
    we know its fullness now in Christ;
in him the Father is revealed,
    and all our longing is sufficed.

And still unwavering faith holds sure
    the words that James wrote sternly down:
        (James 5:7)
except we labor and endure
    we cannot win the heavenly crown.

O Way divine, through gloom and strife
    bring us thy Father's face to see;
O heavenly Truth, O precious Life,
    at last, at last we rest in thee.

Cecil Frances Humphreys Alexander
Hymns Ancient and Modern, 1875

283

This I Have Done for Thee. What Hast Thou Done for Me?

Thy life was given for me,
    thy blood, O Lord, was shed,
that I might ransomed be,
    and quickened from the dead;
thy life was given for me:
what have I given for thee?

Long years were spent for me
    in weariness and woe,
that through eternity
    thy glory I might know;
long years were spent for me;
have I spent one for thee?

Thy Father's home of light,
    thy rainbow-circled throne
were left for earthly night,
    for wanderings sad and lone;
yea, all was left for me;
have I left aught for thee?

Thou, Lord, hast borne for me
    more than my tongue can tell
of bitterest agony,
    to rescue me from hell;
thou sufferedst all for me;
what have I borne for thee?

And thou hast brought to me
    down from thy throne above
salvation full and free,
    thy pardon and thy love;
great gifts thou broughtest me:
what have I brought to thee?

O let my life be given,
    my years for thee be spent;
world-fetters will be riven,
    and joy with suffering blent;
thou gav'st thyself for me;
I give myself to thee.

Frances Ridley Havergal, 1858
Good Words, February 1860

The title, though not applied directly to the text by Havergal, is that of a painting of the crucifixion that inspired it. The common form of the hymn, altered with the author's permission for *Hymns Ancient and Modern*, 1875, begins, "I gave my life for thee."

284

A Worker's Prayer: None of Us Liveth unto Himself. Romans 14:7

Lord, speak to me, that I may speak
    in living echoes of thy tone;
as thou hast sought, so let me seek
    thy erring children, lost and lone.

O lead me, Lord, that I may lead
    the wandering and the wavering feet;
O feed me, Lord, that I may feed
    thy hungering ones with manna sweet.

O strengthen me, that while I stand
    firm on the rock and strong in thee,
I may stretch out a loving hand
    to wrestlers with the troubled sea.

O teach me, Lord, that I may teach
    the precious things thou dost impart;
and wing my words, that they may reach
    the hidden depths of many a heart.

O give thine own sweet rest to me,
  that I may speak with soothing power
a word in season, as from thee,   (Isa. 50:5)
  to weary ones, in needful hour.

O fill me with thy fullness, Lord,
  until my very heart o'erflow
in kindling thought and glowing word,
  thy love to tell, thy praise to show.

O use me, Lord, use even me
  just as thou wilt, and when, and where,
until thy blessed face I see,
  thy rest, thy joy, thy glory share.

Frances Ridley Havergal, 1872
Under the Surface, 1874

285
Never Further than Thy Cross

Never further than thy cross,
  never higher than thy feet;
here earth's precious things seem dross,   (Gal. 6:14)
  here earth's bitter things grow sweet.

Gazing thus, our sin we see,
  learn thy love while gazing thus—
sin, which laid the cross on thee,
  love, which bore the cross for us.

Here we learn to serve and give,
  and, rejoicing, self deny;
here we gather love to live,
  here we gather faith to die.

Symbols of our liberty
  and our service here unite:
captives, by thy cross set free,
  soldiers of thy cross, we fight.

Pressing onwards as we can,
  still to this our hearts must tend,
where our earliest hopes began,
  there our last aspirings end,

till amid the hosts of light
  we in thee redeemed, complete,
through thy cross made pure and white,
  cast our crowns before thy feet.

Elisabeth Rundle Charles
The Family Treasury, February 1860

286
On the Love of Christ

And didst thou love the race that loved not thee?
  And didst thou take to heaven a human brow?
Dost plead with man's voice by the marvelous sea?
  Art thou his kinsman now?

O God, O Kinsman loved, but not enough!
  O Man, with eyes majestic after death,
whose feet have toiled along our pathways rough,
  whose lips drawn human breath,

by that one likeness which is ours and thine,
  by that one nature which doth hold us kin,
by that high heaven where, sinless, thou dost shine
  to draw us sinners in;

by thy last silence in the judgment hall,
  by long foreknowledge of the deadly tree,
by darkness, by the wormwood and the gall,
  I pray thee visit me.

Come, lest this heart should, cold and cast away,
  die ere the guest adored she entertain;
lest eyes which never saw thine earthly day
  should miss thy heavenly reign.

Jean Ingelow
Poems, 1863
from a longer poem, beginning, "On the love of Christ"
first as a hymn in *The Congregational Church Hymnal*, 1887
this cento, *The Congregational Hymnary*, 1916

287
Beneath the Cross of Jesus

Beneath the cross of Jesus
    I fain would take my stand—
the shadow of a mighty Rock   (Isa. 32:2)
    within a weary land;
a home within a wilderness,
    a rest upon the way,
from the burning of the noontide heat
    and the burden of the day.

O safe and happy shelter!
    O refuge tired and sweet!
O trysting-place where heaven's love
    and heaven's justice meet!
As to the exiled patriarch   (Gen. 28:20)
    that wondrous dream was given,
so seems my Savior's cross to me
    a ladder up to heaven.

There lies within its shadow,
    but on the further side,
the darkness of an open grave
    that gapes both deep and wide;
and there, between us and the cross
    two arms outstretched to save,
like a watchman set to guard the way
    from that eternal grave.

Upon the cross of Jesus
    mine eyes at times can see
the very dying form of One
    who suffered there for me.
And from my stricken heart, with tears,
    two wonders I confess—
the wonders of redeeming love
    and my own worthlessness.

I take, O cross, thy shadow,
    for my abiding place;
I ask no other sunshine than
    the sunshine of his face:
Content to let the world go by,
    to know no gain or loss—
my sinful self my only shame,
    my glory all the cross!

Elizabeth Cecilia Douglas Clephane, 1868
The Family Treasury, 1872

288
Immanuel

And art thou come with us to dwell,
    our prince, our guide, our love, our Lord?
And is thy name Immanuel,
    God present with his world restored?

The world is glad for thee; the heart
    is glad for thee, and all is well
and fixed, and sure, because thou art
    whose name is called Immanuel.

The heart is glad for thee: It knows
    none now shall bid it err or mourn,
and o'er its desert breaks the rose   (Isa. 35:1)
    in triumph o'er the grieving thorn.

The world is glad for thee! The rude
    wild moor, the city's crowded pen;
each waste, each peopled solitude
    becomes a home for happy men.

Thou bringest all again; with thee
    is light, is space, is breadth and room
for each thing fair, beloved, and free
    to have its hour of life and bloom.

Each heart's deep instinct unconfessed;
    each lowly wish, each daring claim;
all, all that life hath long repressed
    unfolds, undreading blight or blame.

Thy reign eternal will not cease;
    thy years are sure and glad and slow;
within thy mighty world of peace
    the humblest flower hath leave to blow.

Then come to heal thy people's smart,
    and with thee bring thy captive train;
come, Savior of the world and heart,
    come, mighty Victor over pain.

Dora Greenwell
Carmina Crucis, 1869

289

Processional Hymn for Ascension Day

At the name of Jesus   (Phil. 2:1)
    every knee shall bow,
every tongue confess him
    King of glory now.
'Tis the Father's pleasure
    we should call him Lord
who from the beginning
    was the mighty Word.   (John 1:1)

Mighty and mysterious
    in the highest height,
God from everlasting,
    very Light of light:
in the Father's bosom
    with the Spirit blest.
love, in love eternal,
    rest, in perfect rest.

At his voice creation   (John 1:3)
    sprang at once to light,
all the angel faces,
    all the hosts of light,
thrones and dominations,
    stars upon their way,
all the heavenly orders
    in their great array.

Humbled for a season
    to receive a name
from the lips of sinners
    unto whom he came,
faithfully he bore it
    spotless to the last,
brought it back victorious
    when from death he passed.

Bore it up triumphant
    with its human light,
through all ranks of creatures
    to the central height,
to the throne of Godhead,
    to the Father's breast:
filled it with the glory
    of that perfect rest.

Name him, brothers, name him
    with love as strong as death,
but with awe and wonder,
    and with bated breath;
he is God the Savior,
    he is Christ the Lord,
ever to be worshiped,
    trusted, and adored.

In your hearts enthrone him;
    there let him subdue
all that is not holy,
    all that is not true:
Crown him as your captain
    in temptation's hour;
let his will enfold you
    in its light and power.

Brothers, this Lord Jesus
   shall return again,
with his Father's glory,
   with his angel-train;
for all wreaths of empire
   meet upon his brow
and our hearts confess him
   King of glory now.

Caroline Maria Noel
The Name of Jesus, and Other Verses for the Sick and Lonely, 1870
The original first word, "in," was altered in
Hymns Ancient and Modern, 1875.

290
A Christmas Carol

In the bleak midwinter
   frosty wind made moan;
earth stood hard as iron,
   water like a stone;
snow had fallen, snow on snow,
   snow on snow,
in the bleak midwinter,
   long ago.

Our God, heaven cannot hold him,
   nor earth sustain;
heaven and earth shall flee away
   when he comes to reign:
In the bleak midwinter
   a stable-place sufficed
the Lord God Almighty—
   Jesus Christ.

Enough for him whom cherubim
   worship night and day,
a breastful of milk
   and a mangerful of hay;
enough for him whom angels
   fall down before,
the ox and ass and camel
   which adore.

Angels and archangels
   may have gathered there,
cherubim and seraphim
   thronged the air;
but only his mother
   in her maiden bliss
worshiped the Beloved
   with a kiss.

What can I give him,
   poor as I am?
If I were a shepherd
   I would bring a lamb;
if I were a wise man
   I would do my part,
yet what I can, I give him—
   give my heart.

Christina Georgina Rossetti
Scribner's Monthly, January 1872

291
Saint Michael and All Angels

Service and strength, God's angels and archangels;
   his seraphs fires, and lamps his cherubim:
Glory to God from highest and from lowest,
   glory to God in everlasting hymn
      from all his creatures.

Princes that serve, and powers that work his
         pleasure,
   heights that soar toward him, depths that sink
         toward him;
flames fire out-flaming, chill beside his essence;
   insight all-probing, save where scant and dim
      toward its Creator.

Sacred and free exultant in God's pleasure,
   his will their solace, thus they wait on him,
and shout their shout of ecstasy eternal,
   and trim their splendors that they burn not dim
      toward their Creator.

Wherefore with angels, wherefore with archangels,
with lofty cherubs, loftier seraphim,
we laud and magnify our God almighty,
and veil our faces rendering love to him
with all his creatures.

Christina Georgina Rossetti
Called to Be Saints, 1881

292
Christmastide

Love came down at Christmas,
Love all lovely, Love divine;
Love was born at Christmas,
star and angels gave the sign.

Worship we the Godhead,
Love incarnate, Love divine;
worship we our Jesus:
But wherewith for sacred sign?

Love shall be our token,
love be yours and love be mine,
love to God and all men,
love for plea and gift and sign.

Christina Georgina Rossetti
Time Flies, 1885
revised in 1893 edition

293
None Other Lamb

None other Lamb, none other Name,
none other Hope in heaven or earth or sea,
none other Hiding-place from guilt and shame,
none beside thee.

My faith burns low, my hope burns low,
only my heart's desire cries out in me
by the deep thunder of its want and woe,
cries out to thee.

Lord, thou art Life, though I be dead,
love's Fire thou art however cold I be:
nor heaven have I, nor place to lay my head,
nor home, but thee.

Christina Georgina Rossetti
The Face of the Deep, 1892

294
A Song for the Feast of All Saints

Love is the key of life and death,
of hidden heavenly mystery:
of all Christ is, of all he saith,
love is the key.

As three times to his saint he saith,   (John 21:15)
he saith to me, he saith to thee,
breathing his grace-conferring breath:
"Lovest thou me?"

Ah, Lord, I have such feeble faith,
such feeble hope to comfort me,
but love it is, is strong as death,
and I love thee.

Christina Georgina Rossetti
The Face of the Deep, 1892

295
Father, Forgive Them, for They Know Not What They Do. Luke 23:34

O word of pity, for our pardon pleading,
breathed in the hour of loneliness and pain;
O voice, which through the ages interceding,
calls us to fellowship with God again;

O word of comfort, through the silence stealing,
as the dread act of sacrifice began;
O infinite compassion, still revealing
the infinite forgiveness won for man;

O word of hope, to raise us nearer heaven,
    when courage fails us, and when faith is dim;
the souls for whom Christ prays to Christ are given,
                     (John 17:12)
    to find their pardon and their joy in him.

O Intercessor, who art ever living
    to plead for dying souls that they may live,
teach us to know our sin which needs forgiving,
    teach us to know the love which can forgive.

Ada Rundall Greenaway
Hymns Ancient and Modern, 1904

Chapter 16:
Hymns for Children,
1715–1900 (296–319)

While hymns specially written for children came into their own only after the invention of Sunday schools by late-eighteenth-century Evangelicals, the young were not overlooked either by Watts or by Wesley. In the 1790 edition of Charles Wesley's children's hymns, published by his brother John after Charles had died, John wrote—and it must have been among the last things he did write—in the preface:

> There are two ways of writing or speaking to children; the one is, to let ourselves down to them; the other, to lift them up to us. Dr. Watts has wrote in the former way, and has succeeded admirably well, speaking to children as children, and leaving them as he found them. The following hymns are written on the other plan: they contain strong and manly sense, yet expressed in such plain and easy language as even children can understand. But when they do understand them, they will be children no longer, only in years and stature.

Wise old John! As usual, he sees further than most people of his age. Now, in thus writing of Watts I suspect that he did not have in mind our 296 which, as 2 in his *Divine Songs for Children*, is the only piece from either that or the second part of the same little volume, *Moral Songs*, which survives (with two stanzas omitted) in modern books; and when there, it is always treated as an adult hymn. Rather he will have been thinking of the more popular moralistic pieces which very specifically address the condition of children, like

> Let dogs delight to bark and bite,
>   for God hath made them so;
> let bears and lions growl and fight,
>   for 'tis their nature too.

But, children, you should never let
    such angry passions rise;
your little hands were never made
    to tear each other's eyes.

Looking at most of Watts's children's pieces one sees what John Wesley meant. And one sees the contrast in that part of Charles's famous "Gentle Jesus," which we quote as 297. Even more, of course, one sees it in 72, which it is difficult to think of as having been written for children, but which was, apparently, so devised.

But the axis discerned by John Wesley has continued to be a pattern of children's hymn writing, and during the nineteenth century, with so many books being published for Sunday school use, one sees a fairly heavy emphasis on the "Watts" principle. Nowadays the question is put a little differently, though it is the same question; we now ask whether or not children are part of the whole worshiping congregation, and whether it is wise to invite them to sing what their elders—especially those only just older than children—will be embarrassed to sing with them. It is one thing, and a quite legitimate thing, to talk to children as children when only they are present; it is another to do that when one is also addressing adults. And plenty of educationists will now admit that it is the great adult hymns—it hardly matters how profound provided their language is sufficiently evocative of the imagination—that, if they are presented to children, really build up their faith. This is a variation on the "Wesley" principle.

In the work of the two sisters, Ann and Jane Taylor (Ann having later become Mrs. Gilbert), one sees a real attempt to help the children express large thoughts about central things, stilted though the language sometimes is (298–299). In Mary Duncan's tiny piece we have simply a small child being put to bed at home and being given the simplest words for its prayer. Mrs. Jemima Luke's very well-known piece on the ministry of Christ (301) has the great merit of making the human

Jesus real to children, though its language has a cooing archness that sounds odder now than it would have done then. The diction of Jane Leeson's equally well-known hymn (304) is by contrast chaste and restrained and seems to treat a child with just that much more respect.

John Mason Neale, some may be surprised to learn, wrote his first hymns for children long before he began his translations, and at the age of twenty-four. These contain straight teaching; no searching here for ideas and pictures that will appeal especially to children, just a presentation in simple language of the church's teaching. Such of these as now survive are normally used as adult hymns (302–303).

Number 305 is an odd case which we include for textual reasons. This again is, in either form, a very small child's hymn making a simple moral point which could easily appeal to the very young.

Mrs. Cecil Frances Alexander (306–308) is the most famous of all children's hymn writers, and she is undoubtedly a "Wesley-principle" author. These were her earliest hymns, and they are designed to illustrate the catechism. Once again, this is "Wesley-style" material, upon which we have already commented in chapter 15. This, too, is usually classed in modern hymnals as suitable for adults.

It will be easy for the reader to assign the rest to their separate categories. We take no account of the terrible rubbish which was so often written for and fed to Victorian children; about each of our examples there is at least a touch of honest work-manship. Baring-Gould's "Now the day is over" (312) should be especially studied as a model of unaffected simplicity; and Elizabeth Clephane's evangelical song "There were ninety and nine" (313) raises the point that there is often something strictly juvenile about the hymnody associated with evangelical missions. This, now thought of as very much a "mission" hymn, was originally a children's hymn. We shall have to take up this point again when we come to Gospel Songs (chapter 19). Note

the grave and simple language of the two children's hymns by writers best known for their adult work, How (315) and Ellerton (317); the open-air touch of 316, by R. S. Hawker, reputedly, in his Cornwall parish, the inventor of the English "Harvest Festival"; and, above all, the quite remarkable felicity of 319, one of the very few hymns available on that aspect of our Lord's life which Scripture hides from us but which appeals especially to youthful imaginations: "What was he like when he was eleven years old?"

The writing of children's hymns, like any other aspect of education, needs gifts which not all writers possess. The fatal habit of Victorians was to do what Wesley says Watts did, and do it much worse. Their hymns are littered with the adjective "little"—and what child wants to think of itself as little? What child of healthy mind wants to stay little? Hymnals in use still contain a good deal of this unhealthy stuff, and the worst incongruities appear when they are used at school assemblies. I cannot easily forgive the authorities who were content to invite my own boys in the 1960s, teenagers then, to rush into school with their breakfast in their throats and bawl

> Our hands are so small,
>   and our words are so weak:
>   we cannot teach others;
>   how then shall we seek
>   to work for our Lord in his harvest?

There is something truly solemn about the complex infelicities of that in a school housing about 1,600 young Scotsmen. No wonder creatures so trained grow up to despise hymns!

296

Praise for Creation and Providence

I sing the almighty power of God,
    that made the mountains rise;
that spread the flowing seas abroad
    and built the lofty skies.

I sing the wisdom that ordained
    the sun to rule by day;
the moon shines full at his command,
    and all the seas obey.

I sing the goodness of the Lord,
    that filled the earth with food;
he formed the creatures with his word,
    and then pronounced them good.

Lord, how thy wonders are displayed
    where'er I turn mine eye;
if I survey the ground I tread,
    or gaze upon the sky!

There's not a plant or flower below,
    but makes thy glories known;
and clouds arise, and tempests blow
    by order from thy throne.

Creatures (as numerous as they be)
    are subject to thy care;
there's not a place where we can flee
    but God is present there.

In heaven he shines with beams of love,
    with wrath in hell beneath;
'tis on his earth I stand or move,
    and 'tis his air I breathe.

His hand is my perpetual guard,
    he keeps me with his eye;
why should I then forget the Lord
    who is for ever nigh?

Isaac Watts
Divine Songs for Children, 1715

297

Gentle Jesus

Lamb of God, I look to thee
thou shalt my example be;
thou art gentle, meek, and mild,
thou wast once a little child.

Fain I would be, as thou art,
give me thine obedient heart;
thou art pitiful and kind,
let me have thy loving mind.

Meek and lowly may I be,
thou art all humility;
let me to my betters bow,
subject to thy parents thou.

Let me above all fulfill
God my heavenly Father's will,
never his good spirit grieve,
only to his glory live.

Thou didst live to God alone,
thou didst never seek thine own;
thou thyself didst never please,
God was all thy happiness.

Loving Jesu, gentle Lamb,
in thy gracious hands I am,
make me, Savior, what thou art,
live thyself within my heart.

I shall then show forth thy praise,
serve thee all my happy days;
then the world shall ever see,
Christ, the holy Child, in me.

Charles Wesley
Hymns and Sacred Poems, Abridged, 1742
This is the second part of a text that begins "Gentle Jesus,
meek and mild." The original was divided in *Hymns for Children*, 1763.

298
Providence

Lord, I would own thy tender care,
    and all thy love to me;
the food I eat, the clothes I wear,
    are all bestowed by thee.

'Tis thou preservest me from death
    and dangers every hour;
I cannot draw another breath
    unless thou give me power.

Kind angels guard me every night,
    as round my bed they stay;
nor am I absent from thy sight
    in darkness or by day.

My health and friends and parents dear
    to me by God are given;
I have not any blessing here
    but what is sent from heaven.

Such goodness, Lord, and constant care,
    a child can ne'er repay;
but may it be my daily prayer
    to love thee and obey.

Jane Taylor
Hymns for Infant Minds, 1809

299
Our Father, Which Art in Heaven

Great God, and wilt thou condescend
to be my Father and my Friend?
I a poor child, and thou so high,
the Lord of earth, and air, and sky.

Art thou my Father? Canst thou bear
to hear my poor, imperfect prayer?
Or wilt thou listen to the praise
that such a little one can raise?

Art thou my Father? Let me be
a meek, obedient child to thee;
and try, in word and deed and thought,
to serve and please thee as I ought.

Art thou my Father? I'll depend
upon the care of such a Friend;
and only wish to do and be
whatever seemeth good to thee.

Art thou my Father? Then at last
when all my days on earth are past,
send down and take me in thy love
to be thy better child above.

Ann Taylor Gilbert
Hymns for Infant Minds (2nd ed.), 1810

300
An Evening Prayer

Jesus, tender Shepherd, hear me,
    bless thy little lamb tonight;
through the darkness be thou near me,
    watch my sleep till morning light.

All this day thy hand has led me,
    and I thank thee for thy care;
thou hast clothed me, warmed and fed me,
    listen to my evening prayer.

Let my sins be all forgiven,
    bless the friends I love so well;
take me, when I die, to heaven,
    happy there with thee to dwell.

Mary Lundie Duncan, 1839
Memoir, 1841

301
Child's Desire

I think, when I read that sweet story of old,
    when Jesus was here among men,
how he called little children as lambs to his fold,
    I should like to have been with him then.
I wish that his hands had been placed on my head,
    that his arm had been thrown around me,
and that I might have seen his kind look when he
                      said,
    "Let the little ones come unto me."

Yet still to his footstool in prayer I may go,
    and ask for a share in his love;
and if I now earnestly seek him below,
    I shall see him and hear him above,
in that beautiful place he has gone to prepare
    for all that are washed and forgiven.
And many dear children are gathering there,
    "For of such is the kingdom of heaven."

But thousands and thousands who wander and fall
    never heard of that heavenly home
I should like them to know there is room for them all,
    and that Jesus had bid them to come.
I long for the joy of that glorious time,
    the sweetest, and brightest, and best,
when the dear little children of every clime
    shall crowd to his arms and be blest.

Jemima Thompson Luke
Sunday School Teacher's Magazine, March 1841

302
In Passion Week

O thou, who through this Holy Week
    didst suffer for us all;
the sick to cure, the lost to seek,
    to raise up them that fall:

We cannot understand the woe
    thy love was pleased to bear:
O Lamb of God! we only know
    that all our hopes are there!

Thy feet the path of suffering trod,
    thy hand the victory won;
what shall we render to our God
    for all that he hath done?

To God the Father, God the Son,
    and God the Holy Ghost,
by men on earth be honor done
    and by the heavenly host.

John Mason Neale
Hymns for Children, 1842

303
Good Friday

A time to watch, a time to pray,
a day of wonders is today;
the saddest, yet the sweetest too,
that ever man or angel knew:

The saddest; for our Savior bore
his death, that man might die no more:
the agony, the scourge, the fear,
the crown of thorns, the cross, the spear;

and yet the sweetest; for today
our load of sin was borne away;
and hopes of joy that never dies
hang on our Savior's sacrifice.

Like straying sheep we wandered wide;   (Isa. 53:6)
thy laws we broke, thy name defied;
on thee the guilt of all was laid;
by thee the debt of all was paid.

O Savior, blessed be thy name!
Thine is the glory, ours the shame;
by all the pains thy love endured,
let all our many sins be cured.

> John Mason Neale
> *Hymns for Children*, 1842
> The hymn ended with Thomas Ken's doxology, 29D.

304

My Sheep Hear My Voice, and I Know Them, and They Follow Me

Loving Shepherd of thy sheep,
keep thy lamb, in safety keep;
nothing can thy power withstand,
none can pluck me from thy hand.

Loving Savior, thou didst give
thine own life that we might live;
and the hands outstretched to bless
bear the cruel nails' impress.

I would bless thee every day,
gladly all thy will obey,
like thy blessed ones above,
happy in thy precious love.

Loving Shepherd, ever near,
teach thy lamb thy voice to hear;
suffer not my steps to stray
from the straight and narrow way.

Where thou leadest I will go,
walking in thy steps below,
till before my Father's throne
I shall know as I am known.

> Jane Eliza Leeson
> *Hymns & Scenes of Childhood*, 1842
> altered in *Hymns Ancient and Modern*, 1875

305

Little Drops of Water

This is a curiosity. The form which was very much used in England a generation or two ago is by an American writer, Mrs. Julia A. Carney; it was published in Boston in 1845. A quite different version, but using the same first stanza, was written by Dr. Ebenezer Cobham Brewer in a magazine, *Reading and Spelling*, published in England in 1848. The whole story has to be chased through four separate entries in Julian's *Dictionary*, which more than once insists on the superiority of the American version, even when in the earlier edition (1892) Julian believed the American version to be later than the English, and an adaptation of it. Mrs. Carney gets the credit only in the last edition of 1907.

A.

Little drops of water
    little grains of sand,
make the mighty ocean,
    make the beauteous land.

And the little moments,
    humble though they be,
make the mighty ages
    of eternity.

Little deeds of kindness,
    little words of love,
make our earth an Eden
    like the heaven above.

So our little errors
    lead the soul away
from the paths of virtue
    into sin to stray.

Little seeds of mercy,
    sown by youthful hands
grow to bless the nations
    far in heathen lands.

> Julia Abigail Fletcher Carney
> *Reader*, 1845

B.

Little drops of water,
    little grains of sand
make the mighty ocean
    and the beauteous land.

Straw by straw the sparrow
    builds its cozy nest;
leaf by leaf the forest
    stands in verdure dressed.

Letter after letter
    words and books are made;
little and by little
    mountains level laid.

Drop by drop is iron
    worn in time away;
perseverance, patience
    ever win their way.

Every finished labor
    once did but begin;
try and go on trying:
    that's the way to win.

Ebenezer Cobham Brewer
Reading and Spelling, 1848

306

Suffered under Pontius Pilate; Was Crucified, Dead, and Buried

There is a green hill far away,
    without a city wall,
where the dear Lord was crucified,
    who died to save us all.

We may not know, we cannot tell
    what pains he had to bear,
but we believe it was for us
    he hung and suffered there.

He died that we might be forgiven,
    he died to make us good,
that we might go at last to heaven
    saved by his precious blood.

There was no other good enough
    to pay the price of sin;
he only could unlock the gate
    of heaven, and let us in.

Oh, dearly, dearly has he loved,
    and we must love him too;
and trust in his redeeming blood
    and try his works to do.

Cecil Frances Humphreys Alexander
Hymns for Little Children, 1848

307

Who Was Conceived of the Holy Ghost, Born of the Virgin Mary

Once in royal David's city
    stood a lowly cattle shed,
where a Mother laid her Baby
    in a manger for his bed;
Mary was that Mother mild,
Jesus Christ her little Child.

He came down to earth from heaven,
    who is God and Lord of all,
and his shelter was a stable,
    and his cradle was a stall;
with the poor, and mean, and lowly
lived on earth our Savior holy.

And through all his wondrous childhood
    he would honor and obey,
love and watch the lowly Maiden
    in whose gentle arms he lay;
Christian children all must be
mild, obedient, good as he.

For he is our childhood's pattern,
    day by day like us he grew,
he was little, weak, and helpless,
    tears and smiles like us he knew;
and he feeleth for our sadness;
and he shareth in our gladness.

And our eyes at last shall see him,
    through his own redeeming love,
for that Child, so dear and gentle,
    is our Lord in heaven above;
and he leads his children on
to the place where he is gone.

Not in that poor lowly stable,
    with the oxen standing by,
we shall see him; but in heaven
    set at God's right hand on high;
when like stars his children crowned,
robed in white shall wait around.

Cecil Frances Humphreys Alexander
Hymns for Little Children, 1848

308

God the Father, Maker of Heaven and Earth

All things bright and beautiful,
    all creatures great and small,
all things wise and wonderful,
    the Lord God made them all.

Each little flower that opens,
    each little bird that sings,
he made their glowing colors,
    he made their tiny wings.

The rich man in his castle,
    the poor man at his gate,
God made them, high or lowly,
    and ordered their estate.

The purple-headed mountain,
    the river running by,
the sunset and the morning
    that brightens up the sky;

the cold wind in the winter,
    the pleasant summer sun,
the ripe fruits in the garden—
    he made them every one;

the tall trees in the greenwood,
    the meadows where we play,
the rushes by the water
    we gather every day;

he gave us eyes to see them,
    and lips that we might tell
how great is God Almighty
    who has made all things well.

Cecil Frances Humphreys Alexander
Hymns for Little Children, 1848

309

A Christmas Carol. For My Godchildren

The shepherds had an angel,
    the wise man had a star;
but what have I, a little child,
    to guide me home from far,
where glad stars sing together
    and singing angels are?

Lord Jesus is my guardian,
     so I can nothing lack;   (Ps. 23:1)
the lambs lie in his bosom,   (Isa. 40:11)
     along life's dangerous track;
the willful lambs that go astray
     he, bleeding, fetches back.   (Matt. 18:12)

Lord Jesus is my guiding star,
     by beacon light in heaven;
he leads me step by step along
     the path of life uneven;
he, true light, leads me to that land
     whose day shall be as seven.

Those shepherds, through the lonely night
     sat watching by their sheep,   (Luke 2:15)
until they saw the heavenly host
     who neither tire nor sleep;
all singing, "Glory, glory,"
     in festival they keep.

Christ watches me, his little lamb,
     cares for me day and night,
that I may be his own in heaven:
     So angels clad in white
shall sing their "Glory, glory"
     for my sake in the height.

Lord, bring me nearer day by day,
     till I my voice unite,
and sing my "Glory, glory,"
     with angels clad in white.
All "Glory, glory," given to thee,
     through all the heavenly height.

Christina Georgina Rossetti, 1856
Poetical Works, 1894

310

There's a Friend for Little Children

There's a Friend for little children
     above the bright blue sky,
a Friend who never changes,
     whose love will never die;
our earthly friends may fail us,
     and change with changing years,
this Friend is always worthy
     of that dear name he bears.

There's a rest for little children
     above the bright blue sky,
who love the blessed Savior
     and to the Father cry;
a rest from every trouble,
     from sin and danger free,
where every little pilgrim
     shall rest eternally.

There's a home for little children
     above the bright blue sky,
where Jesus reigns in glory,
     a home of peace and joy;
no home on earth is like it,
     nor can with it compare;
and every one is happy
     nor could be happier there.

There's a crown for little children
     above the bright blue sky,
and all who look to Jesus
     shall wear it by and by;
a crown of brightest glory,
     which he will then bestow
on those who found his favor
     and loved his name below.

There's a song for little children
    above the bright blue sky,
a song that will not weary,
    though sung continually;
a song which even angels
    can never, never sing;
they know not Christ as Savior,
    but worship him as King.

There's a robe for little children
    above the bright blue sky,
and a harp of sweetest music,
    and palms of victory.
All, all above is treasured
    and found in Christ alone;
O come, dear little children,
    that all may be your own.

Albert Midlane, 1859
Good News for the Little Ones, December 1859
The original order of stanzas, which is never preserved
in hymnals, was 2, 3, 1, 4, 5, 6. Observe the way in which a
thought expressed more profoundly by Isaac Watts in 40 above
is reflected in the second half of stanza 5.

311
I Love to Hear the Story

I love to hear the story
    which angel voices tell,
how once the King of glory
    came down on earth to dwell.
I am both weak and sinful,
    but this I surely know,
the Lord came down to save me
    because he loved me so.

I'm glad my blessed Savior
    was once a child like me,
to show how pure and holy
    his little ones might be;
and if I try to follow
    his footsteps here below,
he never will forsake me,
    because he loves me so.

To tell his love and mercy
    my sweetest songs I'll raise;
and though I cannot see him,
    I know he hears my praise;
for he himself has promised
    that even I may go
to sing among his angels,
    because he loves me so.

Emily Huntington Miller
The Little Corporal, 1867

312
Now the Day Is Over

Now the day is over,
    night is drawing nigh,
shadows of the evening
    steal across the sky.

Now the darkness gathers,
    stars begin to peep,
birds and beasts and flowers
    soon will be asleep.

Jesu, give the weary
    calm and sweet repose;
with thy tenderest blessing
    may our eyelids close.

Grant to little children
    visions bright of thee;
guard the sailors tossing
    on the deep blue sea.

Comfort every sufferer
    watching late in pain;
those who plan some evil
    from their sin restrain.

Through the long night watches
    may thine angels spread
their white wings above me
    watching round my bed.

When the morning wakens,
    then may I arise
pure, and fresh, and sinless
    in thy holy eyes.

Glory to the Father,
    glory to the Son,
and to thee, blest Spirit
    whilst all ages run.

Sabine Baring-Gould, 1865
The Church Times, February 16, 1867

313
The Lost Sheep

There were ninety and nine that safely lay
    in the shelter of the fold,
and one was out on the hills away,
    far off from the gates of gold;
away on the mountains wild and bare,
away from the tender Shepherd's care.

"Lord, thou hast here thy ninety and nine;
    are they not enough for thee?"
But the Shepherd made answer: "This of mine
    has wandered away from me;
and although the road be rough and steep
I go to the desert to find my sheep."

But none of the ransomed ever knew
    how deep were the waters crossed;
nor how dark the night that the Lord passed through
    ere he found his sheep that was lost.
Out in the desert he heard its cry—
sick and hopeless, and ready to die.

"Lord, whence are those blood-drops all the way,
    that mark out the mountain's track?"
"They were shed for one that had gone astray
    ere the Shepherd could bring him back."
"Lord, whence are thy hands so rent and torn?"
"They are pierced tonight by many a thorn."

And all through the mountains, thunder-riven,
    and up from the rocky steep,
there arose a cry to the gates of heaven,
    "Rejoice! I have found my sheep!"
And the angels echoed around the throne,
"Rejoice, for the Lord brings back his own."

(Luke 15:10)

Elizabeth Cecilia Douglas Clephane, 1868
The Children's Hour, 1868

314
God, Who Made the Earth

God, who made the earth,
    the air, the sky, the sea,
who gave the light its birth,
    careth for me.

God, who made the grass,
    the flower, the fruit, the tree,
the day and night to pass,
    careth for me.

God, who made the sun,
    the moon, the stars, is he
who, when life's clouds come on,
    careth for me.

God, who made all things,
    on earth, in air, in sea,
who changing seasons brings,
    careth for me.

God, who sent his Son
    to die on Calvary,
he if I lean on him
    will care for me.

When in heaven's bright land
    I all his loved ones see,
I'll sing with that blest band,
    "God cared for me."

Sarah Betts Bradshaw Rhodes, 1870
Methodist Sunday School Hymn Book, 1879

315
Herein Is Love. 1 John 4:10

It is a thing most wonderful,
    almost too wonderful to be,
that God's own Son should come from heaven
    to die to save a child like me.

And yet I know that it is true;
    he chose a poor and humble lot,
and wept, and toiled, and mourned, and died
    for love of those who loved him not.

I cannot tell how he could love
    a child so weak and full of sin;
his love must be most wonderful
    if he could die my love to win.

I sometimes think about the cross,
    and shut my eyes, and try to see
the cruel nails and crown of thorns,
    and Jesus crucified for me.

But even could I see him die,
    I could but see a little part
of that great love, which, like a fire
    is always burning in his heart.

It is most wonderful to know
    his love for me so free and pure;
but 'tis more wonderful to see
    my love for him so faint and poor.

And yet I want to love thee, Lord;
    O light the flame within my heart,
and I will love thee more and more
    until I see thee as thou art.

William Walsham How
Children's Hymns, 1872

316
The Song of the School:
Saint Mark's, Morwenstow

Sing to the Lord the children's hymn,
    his gentle love declare,
who bends amid the seraphim
    to hear the children's prayer.

He at a mother's breast was fed,
    though God's own Son was he;
he learnt the first small words he said
    at a meek mother's knee.

He held us to his mighty breast,
    the children of the earth;
he lifted up his hands and blessed
    the babes of human birth.

Lo! from the stars his face will turn
    on us with glances mild;
the angels of his presence yearn
    to bless the little child.

Keep us, O Jesus, Lord, for thee,
    that so, by thy dear grace,
we, children of the font, may see
    our heavenly Father's face.

Robert Stephen Hawker
Poetical Works, 1879

317
Hail to the Lord Who Comes

Hail to the Lord who comes,
    comes to his temple gate!
Not with his angel host
    not in his kingly state;
no shouts proclaim him nigh,
    no crowds his coming wait;

but borne upon the throne
 of Mary's gentle breast,
watched by her duteous love,
 in her fond arms at rest;
thus to his Father's house,
 he comes, the heavenly Guest.

There Joseph at her side
 in reverent wonder stands;
and, filled with holy joy,
 old Simeon in his hands   (Luke 2:28)
takes up the promised child,
 the glory of all lands.

Hail to the great First-born
 whose ransom price they pay!
The Son before all worlds   (John 8:58)
 the Child of man today,
that he might ransom us
 who still in bondage lay!

O Light of all the earth,
 thy children wait for thee!
Come to thy temples here   (Mal. 3:1)
 that we, from sin set free,
before thy Father's face
 may all presented be!

John Ellerton, 1880
The Children's Hymn Book, 1881

318
The Children's Friend

Jesus, Friend of little children,
 be a friend to me;
take my soul, and ever keep me
 close to thee.

Show me what my love should cherish,
 what, too, it should shun;
lest my feet for poison flowers
 swift should run.

Teach me how to grow in goodness,
 daily as I grow;
thou hast been a Child, and surely
 thou shouldst know.

Fill me with thy gentle meekness,
 make my heart like thine;
like an altar lamp, then let me
 burn and shine.

Step by step, O lead me onward,
 upward into youth;
wiser, stronger, still becoming
 in thy truth.

Never leave me, nor forsake me,
 ever be my Friend;
for I need thee from life's dawning
 to its end.

Walter John Mathams
Psalms and Hymns for School and Home, 1882

319
The Childhood of Christ

Ye fair green hills of Galilee,
 that girdle quiet Nazareth,
what glorious vision did ye see
 when he who conquered sin and death
your flowery slopes and summits trod,
and grew in grace with man and God?

We saw no glory crown his head,
 as childhood ripened into youth;
no angels on his errands sped;
 he wrought no sign. But meekness, truth
and duty marked each step he trod,
and love to man, and love to God.

Jesus! my Savior, Master, King,
    who didst for me the burden bear,
while saints in heaven thy glory sing,
    let me on earth thy likeness wear.
Mine be the path thy feet have trod—
duty and love to man and God.

Eustace Rogers Conder
The Congregational Church Hymnal, 1887

Chapter 17:
Irish and Scottish Hymnody
(320–348)

Scotland and Ireland share a basic Celtic tradition which in Ireland is kept culturally separate from the Protestant tradition of Ulster while in Scotland it is mixed much more freely with the Nordic. Tradition has it that St. Patrick (320) took Christianity to Ireland from Gaul (France) in the late fourth century and founded the Catholic-Celtic pattern of Christianity which is still so peculiarly and natively Irish. Tradition also says (history cannot be asked to document it) that St. Patrick wrote the old Irish original of the "Breastplate" under circumstances recounted in the *Hymnal Guide*.

Whatever historians may eventually find to confirm or refute this, the two versions of the "Breastplate" now in currency make two fine and spacious hymns. Mrs. Cecil Frances Alexander's translation, easily her finest piece of hymnic literature and written forty years after she began writing hymns, makes of it a credal recitation, entirely appropriate to the ancient rites of baptism (and supremely appropriate to the celebrations of Holy Saturday, or Easter Eve, which are so closely associated in the early church with baptism and confirmation). The Scottish translation of Robert A. S. Macalister is closer to the original and has a slightly greater emphasis on the form of incantation, a primitive song by which the singer warded off the evil spirits and demons whose design was to frustrate his faith. But in both there is a very primitive blending of supernatural faith and natural experience; whether it is a matter of "binding to myself" or "arising in the strength of" the subjects of the verses, the sea and rocks and sun and moon are treated on equal terms with the articles of the faith. Since Christian faith is not least a matter of coming to proper terms with the created world, there is nothing theologically improper in this; on the contrary, both hymns in a way not found elsewhere bring heaven and earth together.

St. Columba marked the next step in the evangelization of the Celts in taking the faith from Ireland to the west of Scotland and from his center at Iona dispersing the faith to the mainland. If he is responsible for the Latin original of 321 and the Irish of 322, he has left us two vividly contrasted poems; the Latin one being dogmatic; the Irish one, a song of experience.

Numbers 323 and 324, the former probably medieval, the latter undated, follow the manner of 322 in their highly personal diction, and it will be seen that the Latin poem of Columba is an exception to the normal manner of Celtic song.

Of course, none of this is, in the modern sense, hymnody until it has been translated into hymn form by English-speaking scholars. The Celtic church was not a hymn-singing church, but the Celts are an essentially poetic people, full of rhyme and music, and this handful of poems, which in translation now enrich the repertory of hymns, brings to that repertory a touch of homespun earthiness that is very welcome when it is contrasted with the rigid liturgical hymnody of the Latin-speaking church, or indeed with the over-spiritualized songs which tend to be contemporary with the translations.

Number 325 is from a Gaelic original written by a relatively modern Gaelic bard; this and the now well-known carol, 326, are about all we have from Gaelic singers of the nineteenth century. Number 325 is a most attractive piece, based so clearly in the Psalter; and 326 has made its way through being wedded to a haunting tune, as has 324.

If a first appearance in a manuscript from an Irish monastery is evidence of Irish origin, then the original of the communion hymn, "Draw nigh and take the body of the Lord" (*The English Hymnal*, 307), and the carol, "*Angelus ad virginem*" (*Oxford Book of Carols*, 52), should be added to this list.

But in Scotland the Celtic culture has long had its competitors. There has always been a Catholic stream outside the Gaelic-speaking tradition. There is no direct evidence that William Drummond of

Hawthornden was himself a Catholic; but his translation of 327 (which could have been in chapter 11 but is included here for its Scottish origin) appeared in an English *Primer of the Blessed Virgin* with eighteen other hymns and translations ascribed to him, and the making of English versions of medieval Office Hymns was not an activity characteristic of Scottish Protestants of the time. This tiny but exquisite piece contains more poetry than most such translations. Apart from this we have no poetry from English-speaking Catholic Scotland.

Far more characteristic, of course, is metrical psalmody (see chapter 2), and we offer one example of King James VI's complete psalter to show how this exalted writer went to work. The reader will find no difficulty in deducing why the Assembly, hard pressed by one party to adopt this as the authorized psalter, could not see its way to doing so. Musicians would have been hard pressed finding workable tunes for meters like this. The Protestant, Edinburgh-based Scotland of John Knox had no need for hymns; private versions of the psalter were the only variations on psalmody we find until the "Paraphrases" were authorized in 1781 (see chapter 8). Our 329, which jerks us abruptly into the conventional hymn-singing culture, is the work of an early Scottish Congregationalist and appeared in one of the first hymnals used by that denomination, which, quite unlike the English form of this church order, was an evangelical reaction *against* Calvinism that began shortly before 1800.

Number 330 was a private venture by a leading Scottish man of letters who was learned in the lore of Europe at a time when few people were, and it remains for Britishers the accepted translation of "*Ein feste Burg*," more rugged and eloquent than the American version but at one or two points less easy to sing as hymnody—lines 5–8 of the last stanza are a very awkward corner. The zealous and short-lived Robert M. M'Cheyne, one of Scotland's most strenuous and celebrated preachers and evangelists, wrote 331 as a devotional poem; its intense spiritual power has attracted the notice of a few hymnal editors, who occasionally adjust the meter of stanza 1 to accommodate the singers. This has a touch of the Wesleys in it and, though hardly intended as a hymn, remains one of the greatest devotional pieces Scotland produced in that age.

Nor was 332 aimed at a hymn book—hymns were still not wanted in Scotland—but it was not long after the authorization of hymnody in Scotland that editors grabbed it. Its author was a professor of classics at Edinburgh, and he allows himself a grand freedom of language in his versification of the "*Benedicite.*" George Macdonald, more a novelist and philosopher than a poet, wrote a few hymns at an early stage (he was for a year or two a Congregational minister in England) of which perhaps it is 333 that is the most useful. And Scotland certainly did produce some good translators: Jane Borthwick (334) and her sister Sarah Findlater in *Hymns from the Land of Luther* (4 vols., 1854–1862) very ably supported the work of Catherine Winkworth (see chapter 13).

But it is really Horatius Bonar (335–338) who must be called Protestant Scotland's first hymn writer. He was a minister of the Free Church, this communion being the product of the "Disruption" of 1843 when the Scottish Church split almost down the middle on theological grounds, leaving on one side the Church of Scotland, espousing the conservative cause, and on the other the Free Kirk, which gathered in people of more liberal view. It is natural that the first substantial contribution to hymnody from Scotland should come from that side. Bonar was facile and suffered much from too little self-criticism; too often the contents of *Hymns of Faith and Hope*, three plump little volumes, are garrulous and unevenly written. And not seldom they drink over-deeply of sentimentality. But as an Evangelical Romantic, Bonar produced work which, with careful pruning, appealed very widely. Number 335 is a good romantic ballad; 336 I should judge his finest piece, and 337, with half its stanzas taken out, remains deservedly popular. Number 338 comes from a much later date and competes with 336 for the first place; perhaps its unusual modesty and contemplative gentleness gives it the right to be thought of as his best. It is not easy to forgive a writer who could describe the Eucharist, as he did in one of his very well-known hymns, as "this brief, bright hour of fellowship with thee," but one can imagine that if hymnody for Scotland was in any sense liberated by him, the very pressure generated by three centuries of prohibition might produce occasional lightheadedness in the writing.

If Bonar is the Free Kirk's first hymnist, James Burns (339–340) is usually regarded as the Church of Scotland's first. Compared with Bonar he was less prolific, though hardly more inspired. He shows the same tendency to slip into overamiable language; 339 was at one time very popular, and history explains why. Number 340 is more vivid and pictorial, a very good children's hymn still, once the lines in stanza 2 have been altered from their original form, which caused too many sniggers amongst the young to be allowed to survive:

> The old man meek and mild,
>   the priest of Israel slept,
> his watch the temple child,
>   the little Levite kept.

(Less casual study of the Scripture forbids us to insist that Samuel at the time was anything younger than a teenager—but never mind.)

With 341 we meet something very different. It can always be shown that when Scotland imitates England it corrupts itself, and that is certainly the case with hymn writers. But in these stanzas from a much longer poem made by Mrs. Anna Cousin out of sayings of the venerable seventeenth-century sage, Samuel Rutherford, we have a warmth and vision that are from beginning to end strictly Scottish. Anyone who can read stanzas 2 and 4 unmoved has no soul for prayer.

Number 342 should give the reader a moment's pause. Most readers will think they know this hymn,

the work of another Free Kirk minister. But it never now appears as its author wrote it, and a closer look at it in its fuller form shows that it was by no means designed to be one of those general hymns of praise that the parson slams into the praise list when he is in too much of a hurry to think of anything else but a hymn about the reading of Scripture. Just occasionally editorial tinkering changes the whole personality of a hymn; it has certainly done so here.

We are back to personal devotion with 343–344. Principal Shairp, Scottish man of letters, one of the very few Scottish laymen who ever wrote a hymn, takes in 343 much the same line as Burns did in 339, but he does it with greater poise. The end of stanza 2 has quite unusual distinction. With the more famous George Matheson, we are back in the Kirk of Scotland, and indeed in the parish manse. Number 344 is the one everybody knows. It won a famous tune immediately after being written, and perhaps so delicate a piece should not have ever been exposed to the draughts of congregational singing; but it is real writing, without a word out of place, the work of a natural lyricist. Perhaps one needs to know the delectable folk song "The Queen's Maries" (all about Mary Queen of Scots and three other friends called Mary) to appreciate the artistry of 345, a poem which only one editor, English, but possibly the greatest of them all, spotted for a hymnal (it is in *Worship Song*). The better-known 346 expresses a theology which, at the turn of this century, was very popular, went later into complete eclipse, and has now almost entirely returned to favor. But this hymn got lost in the Barthian period.

Number 347 is known only in America as a hymn; it owes something to the great "Breastplate," and has a lyric, almost runic rhythm which is rather captivating. Number 348 is the best known of Nicol Macnicol's translations from the works of Nārāyan Vāman Tilak, an Indian Christian whom we shall meet again in chapter 28.

Scottish hymnody, then, is never a very broad stream, though the evangelical revivals generated a good deal of it, and the offerings of Scottish liberals were gratefully received by English editors who wanted relief from episcopal and decanal pedagogy. It might have continued in the same placid way had it not been for the development which we shall celebrate in chapter 23.

320
Saint Patrick's Breastplate
Irish: Atromriug indiu niurt tren

A.

I bind unto myself today
    the strong name of the Trinity,
by invocation of the same
    the Three in One and One in Three.

I bind this day to me for ever
    by power of faith, Christ's incarnation;
his baptism in Jordan river,
    his death on cross for my salvation;
his bursting from the spiced tomb,
    his riding up the heavenly way,
his coming at the day of doom.
    I bind unto myself today.

I bind unto myself the power
    of the great love of cherubim;
the sweet "Well done" in judgment hour,
    the service of the seraphim,
confessors' faith, apostles' word,
    the patriarchs' prayers, the prophets' scrolls,
all good deeds done unto the Lord
    and purity of virgin souls.

I bind unto myself today
    the virtues of the star-lit heaven,
the glorious sun's life-giving ray,
    the whiteness of the moon at even,
the flashing of the lightning free,
    the whirling wind's tempestuous shocks,
the stable earth, the deep salt sea
    around the old eternal rocks.

I bind unto myself today
    the power of God to hold and lead,
his eye to watch, his might to stay,
    his ear to hearken to my need.
The wisdom of my God to teach,
    his hand to guide, his shield to ward;
the word of God to give me speech,
    his heavenly host to be my guard.

Against the demon snares of sin,
    the vice that gives temptation force,
the natural lusts that war within,
    the hostile men that mar my course;
or few or many, far or nigh,
    in every place and in all hours,
against their fierce hostility
    I bind to me those holy powers.

Against all Satan's spells and wiles,
    against false words of heresy,
against the knowledge that defiles,
    against the heart's idolatry,
against the wizard's evil craft,
    against the death-wound and the burning,
the choking wave, the poisoned shaft,
    protect me, Christ, till thy returning.

Christ be with me, Christ within me,
    Christ behind me, Christ before me,
Christ beside me, Christ to win me,
    Christ to comfort and restore me.
Christ beneath me, Christ above me,
    Christ in quiet, Christ in danger,
Christ in hearts of all that love me,
    Christ in mouth of friend and stranger.

I bind unto myself the name,
    the strong name of the Trinity,
by invocation of the same,
    the Three in One and One in Three,
of whom all nature hath creation,
    eternal Father, Spirit, Word:
Praise to the Lord of my salvation,
    salvation is of Christ the Lord.

> Patrick of Ireland, 432
> translated, Cecil Frances Alexander, 1899
> *Writings of St. Patrick*, Appendix, 1889

B.

Today I arise
invoking the blessed Trinity,
confessing the blessed Unity,
Creator of all the things that be.

Today I arise
by strength of Christ and his mystic birth,
by his passion and triumph's saving worth,
by his coming again to judge the earth.

Today I arise
by seraphs serving the Lord above,
by truths his ancient heralds prove,
by saints in purity, labor, love.

Today I arise
by splendor of sun and flaming brand,
by rushing wind, by lightning grand,
by depth of sea, by strength of land.

Today I arise
with God my steersman, stay, and guide,
to guard, to counsel, to hear, to bide,
his way before, his hosts beside.

Protecting me now
from crafty wiles of demon crew,
from foemen, be they many or few,
from lusts that I can scarce subdue.

Lord Jesus the Christ,
today surround me with thy might;
before, behind, on left and right,
be thou in breadth, in length, in height.

Direct and control
the minds of all who think on me,
the lips of all who speak to me,
the eyes of all who look on me.

Today I arise,
invoking the blessed Trinity,
confessing the blessed Unity,
Savior, on us salvation be!

> translated, Robert Alexander Stewart Macalister, 1927
> *The Church Hymnary*, 1927

321
The Hymns of Saint Columba
Latin: In te, Christe, credentium

A.

Have mercy, Christ, have mercy
    on all that trust in thee,
for thou art God in glory,
    to all eternity.

O God, make speed to save us
    in life's abounding throes;
O God, make haste to help us
    in all our weary woes.

O God, thou art the Father
    of all that have believed;
from whom all hosts of angels
    have life and power received.

O God, thou art the Former
    of all created things:
the righteous Judge of judges,
    the Almighty King of kings.

The God whose power and glory
 thy countless creatures show—
the love of all above us,
 the dread of all below.

High in the heavenly Sion
 thou reignest God adored;
and in the coming glory
 thou shalt be sovereign Lord.

Beyond our ken thou shinest,
 the everlasting light;
ineffable in loving,
 unthinkable in might.

Thou to the meek and lowly
 thy secrets dost unfold;
O God, thou knowest all things,
 all things both new and old.

I walk secure and blessed,
 in every clime and coast,
in Name of God the Father
 and Son and Holy Ghost.

B.

Christ is the world's Redeemer,
 the lover of the pure,
the font of heavenly wisdom,
 our trust and hope secure;

the armor of his soldiers,
 the Lord of earth and sky;
our health while we are living,
 our life when we shall die.

Christ hath our host surrounded
 with clouds of martyrs bright,
who wave their palms in triumph
 and fire us for the fight.

Christ the red cross ascended
 to save a world undone,
and suffering for the sinful
 our full redemption won.

Down in the realm of darkness
 he lay, a captive bound,
but at the hour appointed
 he rose a victor crowned.

And now to heaven ascended,
 he sits upon the throne,
whence he had ne'er departed,
 his Father's and his own.

All glory to the Father,
 the unbegotten One;
all honor be to Jesus,
 his sole-begotten Son;

and to the Holy Spirit—
 the perfect Trinity,
let all the worlds give answer—
 "Amen. So let it be!"

attributed to Columba of Iona, sixth century
translated, Duncan MacGregor, 1897
Saint Columba: A Record and a Tribute, 1897

322

A Hymn of Trust
Irish: Im aonarán dom ins an slied

Alone with none but thee, my God,
 I journey on my way;
what need I fear, when thou art near,
 O King of night and day?
More safe am I within thy hand
than if a host did round me stand.

My destined time is fixed by thee,
    and death doth know his hour.
Did warriors strong around me throng,
    they could not stay his power;
no walls of stone can man defend
when thou thy messenger dost send.

My life I yield to thy decree,
    and bow to thy control
in peaceful calm, for from thine arm
    no power can wrest my soul.
Could earthly omens e'er appall
a man that heeds the heavenly call!

The child of God can fear no ill,
    his chosen dread no foe;
we leave our fate with thee, and wait
    thy bidding when to go.
'Tis not from chance our comfort springs:
thou art our Trust, O King of kings

attributed to Columba of Iona, sixth century
translated, William T. Cairns
Church Hymnal, 1919

323

Consecration
Irish: Daot an crorohe, a mhic dé

How great the tale, that there should be
in God's Son's heart a place for me!
That on a sinner's lips like mine
the cross of Jesus Christ should shine!

Christ Jesus, bend me to thy will,
my feet to urge, my griefs to still;
that e'en my flesh and blood may be
a temple sanctified to thee.

No rest, no calm, my soul may win,
because my body craves to sin;
till thou, dear Lord, thyself impart
peace to my head, light to my heart.

May consecration come from far,
soft shining like the evening star!
My toilsome path make plain to me,
until I come to rest in thee.

Murdoch (Muiredhach) O'Daly of Connaucht, thirteenth century
translated, Eleanor Henrietta Hull, 1912
Poem-Book of the Gael, 1912
This text has also been attributed to Muiredhach's brother,
Donnchadh O'Daly.

324

Be Thou My Vision
Irish: Rob tu mo bhoile, a Comdi cride

Be thou my Vision, O Lord of my heart,
naught be all else to me, save that thou art;
thou my best thought in the day and the night,
waking or sleeping, thy presence my light.

Be thou my Wisdom, be thou my true Word,
I ever with thee, and thou with me, Lord;
thou my great Father, and I thy dear son,
thou in me dwelling, and I with thee one.

Be thou my breastplate, my sword for the fight,
be thou my armor, and be thou my might;
thou my soul's shelter, and thou my high tower,
raise thou me heavenward, O Power of my power.

Riches I heed not, nor man's empty praise,
thou mine inheritance through all my days;
thou, and thou only, the first in my heart,
high King of heaven, my treasure thou art!

High King of heaven, when the battle is done,
grant heaven's joys to me, O bright heaven's sun!
Heart of my own heart, whatever befall,
still be my Vision, O Ruler of all.

anonymous, eighth century
translated, Mary Elizabeth Byrne, 1905
versified, Eleanor Henrietta Hull, 1912
Poem-Book of the Gael, 1912
as adapted in *Church Hymnal*, 1919

325
O Lord, I Sing Thy Praises
Gaelic: A Schlànuighear ro ghlòrmhor

O Lord, I sing thy praises,
    who art my strength and stay,
my leader through life's mazes,
    to bring me to thy way;
thou didst not leave me straying
    when I afar would go   (Matt. 18:12)
with heedless footsteps playing
    upon the brink of woe.

For thou, thy glory showing,
    mad'st me thy beauty see;
thy love has been bestowing
    new life and joy on me.
Thou grace and glory givest,   (Ps. 84:11)
    thou art a Sun and Shield,
thou only ever livest,
    thy words salvation yield.

O Lord, do not forsake me,
    but guide me as a friend;
and strong in heart still make me
    for what thy love may send.
When seized by sore diseases,
    which no kind hand allays,
make thou my bed, Lord Jesus,
    and hear me sing thy praise.

When friends, with grief high swelling,
    have laid me 'neath the sod,
the grave shall be my dwelling
    until the day of God.
Through death's dark vale victorious,
    O let me lean on thee,
and let me see thee glorious
    through all eternity.

Peter Grant of Strathspey
translated, Lachlan Macbean, 1900
Songs and Hymns of the Gael, 1900

326
Child in the Manger
Gaelic: Leanbh an àigh

Child in the manger,
infant of Mary;
outcast and stranger,
    Lord of all!
Child who inherits
all our transgressions,
all our demerits
    on him fall.

Monarchs have tender
delicate children,
nourished in splendor,
    proud and gay;
death soon shall banish
honor and beauty,
pleasure shall vanish,
    forms decay.

But the most holy
Child of salvation
gently and lowly
    lived below;
now as our glorious
mighty Redeemer,
see him victorious
    o'er each foe.

Prophets foretold him
infant of wonder;
angels behold him
    on his throne;
worthy our Savior
of all their praises;
happy for ever
    are his own.

Mary McDougall Macdonald
translated, Lachlan Macbean, 1888
Songs and Hymns of the Gael, 1888

327
O Trinity, O Blessed Light

A.

O lux beata Trinitas,
et principalis unitas,
iam sol recedit igneus,
infunde lumen cordibus.

Te mane laudum carmine,
te deprecamur vespere,
te nostra supplex gloria
per cuncta laudet saecula.

Deo patri sit gloria,
eiusque soli Filio,
cum Spiritu Paraclito,
et nunc et in perpetuum.

anonymous Latin, middle period

B.

O Trinity, O blessed Light,
    O Unity, most principal,
the fiery sun now leaves our sight:
    cause in our hearts thy beams to fall.

Let us with songs of praise divine
    at morn and evening thee implore;
and let our glory, bowed to thine,
    thee glorify for evermore.

To God the Father glory great,
    and glory to his only Son,
and to the Holy Paraclete
    both now and still while ages run.

translated, William Drummond of Hawthornden
Primer, or Office of the Blessed Virgin Mary, 1619

328
Psalm 1

This is displayed with the original spelling.

That mortal man most happy is and blest
    who in the wickeds counsals doth not walk,
nor zit in sinners wayis doth stay and rest   (that)
    Nor sittis in seatis of skornful men in talk
        but contrair fixis his delicht
            into Jehouas law
        and on his law, both day and nicht,
            to think is neuer slaw.   (slow)

He salbe lyk a plesant plantit tree   (shall be)
    vpon a reuer syde incressing tal,   (river)
that yieldis his fruit in saison dew, we see;
    whose plesant leif doth neuer fade nor fal.
        Now this is surely for to say
            that quhat he takis in hand,
        it sal withoutin doute alway
            most prosperously stand.

Bot wicked men ar nowayis of that band;
    but as the caffe quhich be the wind is tost
                                        (chaff . . . by)
thairfor they sall not in that iugement stand
    nor yett among the iust be sinneris lost.
        For gret Jehoua cleirly knowis
            the iust mens way vpricht,
        but sure the wickeds way that throwis
            sall perish be his micht.

James VI of Scotland
Psalms, 1631

329
Let God Arise

O Lord our God, arise!
    the cause of truth maintain,
and wide o'er all the peopled world
    extend her blessed reign.

Thou Prince of life, arise!
    nor let thy glory cease;
far spread the conquests of thy grace,
    and bless the earth with peace.

Thou Holy Ghost, arise!
    Expand thy quickening wing,
and o'er a dark and ruined world
    let light and order spring.

All on the earth, arise!
    To God the Savior sing:
From shore to shore, from earth to heaven,
    let echoing anthems ring.

Ralph Wardlaw
A Collection of Hymns for the Use of the Tabernacles in Scotland, 1800

330
Ein feste Burg

A safe stronghold our God is still,
    a trusty shield and weapon;
he'll help us clear from all the ill
    that hath us now o'ertaken.
        The ancient prince of hell
        hath risen with purpose fell;
    strong mail of craft and power
    he weareth in this hour;
on earth is not his fellow.

With force of arms we nothing can,
    full soon were we downridden;
but for us fights the proper Man,
    whom God himself hath bidden.
        Ask ye, who is this same?
        Christ Jesus is his name,
    the Lord Sabaoth's Son,
    he and no other one
shall conquer in the battle.

And were this world all devils o'er,
    and watching to devour us;
we lay it not to heart so sore;
    not they can overpower us
        and let the prince of ill
        look grim as e'er he will,
    he harms us not a whit;
    for why—his doom is writ;
a word shall quickly slay him.

God's word, for all their craft and force
    one moment shall not linger,
but, spite of hell, shall have its course:
    'Tis written by his finger.
        And though they take our life,
        goods, honor, children, wife,
    yet is their profit small;
    these things shall vanish all:
The city of God remaineth.

Martin Luther, 1528
translated, Thomas Carlyle
Fraser's Magazine, 1831
See Luther's original at 4A and Hedge's translation at 4B.

331
I Am Debtor

When this passing world is done,
when has sunk yon glaring sun,
when we stand with Christ in glory,
looking o'er life's finished story,
then, Lord, shall I fully know—
not till then—how much I owe.   (Luke 7:43)

When I hear the wicked call
on the rocks and hills to fall,
when I see them start and shrink
on the fiery deluge brink,
then, Lord, shall I fully know—
not till then—how much I owe.

When I stand before the throne,
dressed in beauty not my own,
when I see thee as thou art,
love thee with unsinning heart,
then, Lord, shall I fully know—
not till then—how much I owe.

When the praise of heaven I hear,
loud as thunders to the ear,
loud as many waters' noise,
sweet as harp's melodious voice,
then, Lord, shall I fully know—
not till then—how much I owe.

Even on earth, as through a glass (1 Cor. 13:8)
darkly, let thy glory pass, (Exod. 33:18)
make forgiveness feel so sweet,
make thy Spirit's help so meet,
even on earth, Lord make me know
something of how much I owe.

Chosen not for good in me,
wakened up from wrath to flee,
hidden in the Savior's side,
by the Spirit sanctified,
teach me, Lord, on earth to show,
by my love, how much I owe.

Oft I walk beneath the cloud,
dark as midnight's gloomy shroud;
but, when fear is at the height,
Jesus comes, and all is light:
Blessed Jesus! bid me show
doubting saints how much I owe.

When in flowery paths I tread,
oft by sin I'm captive led;
oft I fall, but still arise;
the Spirit comes—the tempter flies;
blessed Spirit! bid me show
weary sinners all I owe.

Oft the nights of sorrow reign—
weeping, sickness, sighing, pain,
but a night thine anger burns—
morning comes, and joy returns:
God of comforts! bid me show
to thy poor, how much I owe.

Robert Murray M'Cheyne, 1837
The Scottish Christian Herald, May 20, 1837
Stanzas 1, 3, 4, and 5 (and sometimes 6) constitute the selection in
most current hymnals.

332
Benedicite Omnia Opera

Angels holy,
high and lowly,
sing the praises of the Lord!
earth and sky, all living nature,
man, the stamp of thy Creator,
praise ye, praise ye God the Lord!

Sun and moon bright,
night and noonlight,
starry temples, azure-floored,
cloud and rain, and wild wind's madness,
breeze that floats with genial gladness,
praise ye, praise ye God the Lord!

Ocean hoary,
tell his glory;
cliffs, where tumbling seas have roared,
pulse of waters, blithely beating,
wave advancing, wave retreating,
praise ye, praise ye God the Lord!

Rock and high land,
wood and island,
crag, where eagle's pride hath soared,
mighty mountains, purple-breasted,
peaks cloud-cleaving, snowy-crested,
praise ye, praise ye God the Lord!

Rolling river,
 praise him ever,
  from the mountain's deep vein poured;
silver fountain, clearly gushing,
troubled torrent madly rushing,
 praise ye, praise ye God the Lord!

 Bond and free man,
  land and sea man,
   earth with peoples widely stored,
wanderer lone o'er prairies ample,
full-voiced choir in costly temple,
  praise ye, praise ye God the Lord!

  Praise him ever,
   bounteous giver:
    praise him, Father, Friend, and Lord;
each glad soul its free course winging,
each blithe voice its free song singing,
  praise the great and mighty Lord!

John Stuart Blackie
The Inquirer, 1840

333

Blessed Are the Poor in Spirit

Our Father, hear our longing prayer,
 and help this prayer to flow,
that humble thoughts, which are thy care
 may live in us and grow.

For lowly hearts shall understand
 the peace, the calm delight
of dwelling in thy heavenly land,
 a pleasure in thy sight.

Give us humility, that so
 thy reign may come within,
and when thy children homeward go
 we too may enter in.

Hear us, our Savior; ours thou art,
 though we are not like thee;
give us thy Spirit in our heart,
 large, lowly, trusting, free.

George Macdonald
Hymns and Sacred Songs for Sunday Schools and School Worship, 1855

334

Submission. Luke 21:19

Be still, my soul: The Lord is on thy side;
 bear patiently the cross of grief or pain;
leave to thy God to order and provide;
 in every change he faithful will remain.
Be still, my soul: Thy best, thy heavenly Friend
through thorny ways leads to a joyful end.

Be still, my soul: Thy God doth undertake
 to guide the future as he has the past.
Thy hope, thy confidence let nothing shake;
 all now mysterious shall be bright at last.
Be still, my soul: The waves and winds still know
his voice who ruled them while he dwelt below.
(Mark 4:41)

Be still, my soul: When dearest friends depart,
 and all is darkened in the vale of tears,
then shalt thou better know his love, his heart,
 who comes to soothe thy sorrow and thy fears.
Be still, my soul: Thy Jesus can repay,
from his own fullness, all he takes away.

Be still, my soul: The hour is hastening on
 when we shall be for ever with the Lord,
when disappointment, grief, and fear are gone,
 sorrow forgot, love's purest joys restored.
Be still, my soul: When change and tears are past,
all safe and blessed we shall meet at last.

Be still, my soul: Begin the song of praise
    on earth, be leaving, to thy Lord on high;
acknowledge him in all thy words and ways,
    so shall he view thee with a well-pleased eye.
Be still, my soul: The Sun of life divine
through passing clouds shall but more brightly shine.

translated, Jane Laurie Borthwick
Hymns from the Land of Luther, 2nd series, 1855
from *"Stille, mein Wille, dein Jesus hilft siegen,"* by Katharina Amalia
Dorothea von Schlegel, which appeared in *Neue Sammlung geistliche
Lieder*, 1752

335
The Voice from Galilee

I heard the voice of Jesus say,
    "Come unto me and rest,   (Matt. 11:28)
lay down, thou weary one, lay down
    thy head upon my breast."
I came to Jesus, as I was,
    weary, and worn, and sad;
I found in him a resting place,
    and he has made me glad.

I heard the voice of Jesus say,
    "Behold, I freely give   (Rev. 22:17)
the living water: Thirsty one
    stoop down, and drink, and live."
I came to Jesus, and I drank
    of that life-giving stream;
my thirst was quenched, my soul revived,
    and now I live in him.   (Gal. 2:20)

I heard the voice of Jesus say,
    "I am this dark world's light;   (John 8:12)
look unto me, thy morn shall rise,
    and all the day be bright."
I looked to Jesus, and I found
    in him my Star, my Sun;
and in that Light of life I'll walk
    till traveling days are done.

Horatius Bonar
Hymns, Original and Selected, 1846

336
The Love of God

O Love of God, how strong and true!
eternal and yet ever new,
uncomprehended and unbought,
beyond all knowledge and all thought!

O love of God, how deep and great!
far deeper than man's deepest hate;
self-fed, self-kindled like the light
changeless, eternal, infinite!

O heavenly love, how precious still
in days of weariness and ill,
in nights of pain and helplessness,
to heal, to comfort, and to bless!

O wide-embracing, wondrous love,
we read thee in the sky above,
we read thee in the earth below,
in seas that swell and streams that flow.

We read thee in the flowers, the trees,
the freshness of the fragrant breeze,
the songs of birds upon the wing,
the joy of summer and of spring.

We read thee best in him who came
to bear for us the cross of shame,
sent by the Father from on high,
our life to live, our death to die.

We read thee in the manger-bed
on which his infancy was laid;
and Nazareth that love reveals,
nestling amid its lonely hills.

We read thee in the tears once shed   (Luke 19:41)
over doomed Salem's guilty head,
in the cold tomb of Bethany,
and blood-drops of Gethsemane.

We read thy power to bless and save
ev'n in the darkness of the grave;
still more in resurrection light
we read the fullness of thy might.

O love of God, our shield and stay,
through all the perils of our way;
eternal love, in thee we rest,
for ever safe, for ever blest!

Horatius Bonar
Hymns of Faith and Hope, 2nd series, 1861

337

Life's Praise

Fill thou my life, O Lord my God,
    in every part with praise,
that my whole being may proclaim
    thy being and thy ways.

Not for the lip of praise alone,
    nor even the praising heart
I ask, but for a life made up
    of praise in every part:

Praise in the common things of life,
    its goings out and in,
praise in each duty and each deed,
    however small and mean;

praise in the common words I speak,
    life's common looks and tones,
in intercourse at hearth or board
    with my beloved ones;

not in the temple-crowd alone,
    where holy voices chime,
but in the silent paths of earth,
    the quiet rooms of time;

upon the bed of weariness,
    with fevered eye and brain;
or standing by another's couch
    watching the pulse of pain;

enduring wrong, reproach, or loss,
    with sweet and steadfast will;
loving and blessing those who hate,
    returning good for ill;

surrendering my fondest will
    in things or great or small,
seeking the good of others still,
    nor pleasing self at all.

Fill every part of me with praise;
    let all my being speak
of thee and of thy love, O Lord,
    poor though I be and weak.

So shalt thou, Lord, from me, ev'n me,
    receive the glory due,
and so shall I begin on earth
    the song for ever new.

So shall each fear, each fret, each care,
    be turned into song;
and every winding of the way
    the echo shall prolong.

So shall no part of day or night
    from sacredness be free,
but all my life, in every step,
    be fellowship with thee.

Horatius Bonar
Hymns of Faith and Hope, 3rd series, 1866

338
Beloved, Let Us Love

Beloved, let us love: Love is of God; (1 John 4:7)
in God alone hath love its true abode.

Beloved, let us love: For they who love,
they only, are his sons, born from above. (John 3:7)

Beloved, let us love: For love is rest,
and he who loveth not abides unblest. (1 John 4:8)

Beloved, let us love: In love is light,
and he who loveth not dwelleth in night. (1 John 2:11)

Beloved, let us love: For only thus
shall we be with that God who loveth us.

Horatius Bonar
Supplement to Psalms and Hymns, 1880

339
Childlike Trust

As helpless as a child who clings
     fast to his father's arm,
and casts his weakness on the strength
     that keeps him safe from harm,
so I, my Father, cling to thee,
     and thus I every hour
would link my earthly feebleness
     to thine almighty power.

As trustful as a child who looks
     up to his mother's face,
and all his little griefs and fears
     forgets in her embrace,
so I to thee, my Savior, look,
     and in thy face divine
can read the love that will sustain
     as weak a faith as mine.

As loving as a child who sits
     close by his parent's knee,
and knows no want while he can have
     that sweet society,
so, sitting at thy feet, my heart
     would all its love outpour,
and pray that thou wouldst teach me, Lord,
     to love thee more and more.

James Drummond Burns
The Evening Hymn, 1857

340
The Child Samuel. I Samuel 3

Hushed was the evening hymn,
     the temple courts were dark,
the lamp was burning dim
     before the sacred ark;
when suddenly a voice divine
rang through the silence of the shrine.

The priest of Israel slept,
     the old man meek and mild,
watch in the temple kept
     the little Levite child;
and what from Eli's sense was sealed
to Hannah's son the Lord revealed.

O give me Samuel's ear,
     the open ear, O Lord,
alive and quick to hear
     each whisper of thy word;
Like him to answer to the call,
and to obey thee first of all.

O give me Samuel's heart,
     a lowly heart that waits
when in thy house thou art,
     or watches at thy gates;
by day and night a heart that still
moves at the breathing of thy will.

O give me Samuel's mind,
    a sweet unmurmuring faith
obedient and resigned
    to thee in life and death;
that I may read with childlike eyes
truths that are hidden from the wise.   (Luke 10:21)

James Drummond Burns
The Evening Hymn, 1857
altered in *The Congregational Hymnary*, 1916
See the narrative above, p. 289, for the original version of lines 2:1–4.

341

Immanuel's Land

The sands of time are sinking;
    the dawn of heaven breaks;
the summer morn I've sighed for,
    the fair, sweet morn, awakes.
Dark, dark hath been the midnight;
    but dayspring is at hand,
and glory, glory dwelleth
    in Immanuel's land.

The King there in his beauty   (Isa. 33:17)
    without a veil is seen;
it were a well-spent journey
    though seven deaths lay between:
the Lamb, with his fair army,
    doth on Mount Zion stand,
and glory, glory dwelleth
    in Immanuel's land.

O Christ! he is the fountain,
    the deep, sweet well of love;
the streams on earth I've tasted,
    more deep I'll drink above:
There to an ocean fullness
    his mercy doth expand,
and glory, glory dwelleth
    in Immanuel's land.

With mercy and with judgment
    my web of time he wove,
and aye the dews of sorrow
    were lustered with his love;
I'll bless the hand that guided,
    I'll bless the heart that planned,
when throned where glory dwelleth
    in Immanuel's land.

The bride eyes not her garment,
    but her dear bridegroom's face;
I will not gaze at glory
    but on my King of grace.
Not at the crown he giveth,
    but on his pierced hand:
The Lamb is all the glory
    of Immanuel's land.

I've wrestled on towards heaven,
    'gainst storm and wind and tide;
now, like a weary traveler
    that leaneth on his guide,
amid the shades of evening
    while sinks life's lingering sand,
I hail the glory dwelling
    in Immanuel's land.

Anne Ross Cundell Cousin
The Christian Treasury, December 1857
revised by the author for *The Baptist Church Hymnal*, 1900
fashioned out of thoughts and phrases in *Letters and Dying Sayings of
Samuel Rutherford*, 1600–1661

342

Now unto the King Eternal, Immortal, Invisible, the Only Wise God. I Timothy 1:17

A. Original

Immortal, invisible, God only wise,
in light inaccessible hid from our eyes,
most blessed, most glorious, the Ancient of Days,
                                          (Dan. 7:9)
Almighty, victorious, thy great name we praise.

Unresting, unhasting, silent as light,
nor striving, nor wasting, thou rulest in might;
thy justice like mountains soaring above   (Ps. 36:6)
thy clouds which are fountains of goodness and love.

To all life thou givest, both great and small;
in all life thou livest, true life of all;
thy blossom and flourish only are we,
to wither and perish—but nought changeth thee.

Today and tomorrow with thee still are now;
nor trouble, nor sorrow, nor care, Lord, hast thou;
nor passion doth fever, nor age can decay,
the same God for ever as on yesterday.

Great Father of glory, Father of light,
thine angels adore thee, veiling their sight;
but of all thy good graces this grace, Lord, impart—
take the veil from our faces, the veil from our heart.

(2 Cor. 3:15)

All laud we would render; O help us to see,
'tis only the splendor of light hideth thee;
and so let thy glory to our gaze unroll
through Christ in the story, and Christ in the soul.

Walter Chalmers Smith
Hymns of Christ and the Christian Life, 1867

B. As altered by the author

Immortal, invisible, God only wise,
in light inaccessible hid from our eyes,
most blessed, most glorious, the Ancient of Days,
Almighty, victorious, thy great name we praise.

Unresting, unhasting, and silent as light,
nor wanting, nor wasting, thou rulest in might;
thy justice like mountains high soaring above
thy clouds which are fountains of goodness and love.

To all life thou givest—to both great and small;
in all life thou livest, the true life of all;
we blossom and flourish as leaves in the tree,
and wither and perish—but nought changeth thee.

Today and tomorrow with thee still are now;
nor trouble, nor sorrow, nor care, Lord, hast thou;
nor passion doth fever, nor age can decay,
the same God for ever that was yesterday.

Great Father of glory, pure Father of light,
thine angels adore thee, all veiling their sight;
but of all thy good graces this grace, Lord, impart—
take the veil from our faces, the veil from our heart.

All laud we would render; O help us to see,
'tis only the splendor of light hideth thee;
and so let thy glory almighty impart
through Christ in the story, thy Christ to the heart.

altered by Smith at the request of Garrett Horder for
Congregational Hymns, 1884

343
Changeless Love

'Twixt gleams of joy and clouds of doubt
    our feelings come and go;
our best estate is tossed about
    in ceaseless ebb and flow.
No mood of feeling, form of thought,
    is constant for a day:
But thou, O Lord, thou changest not:
    The same thou art alway.

I grasp thy strength, make it mine own,
    my heart with peace is blest;
I lose my hold, and then comes down
    darkness, and cold unrest.
Let me no more my comfort draw
    from my frail hold of thee;
in this alone rejoice with awe,
    thy mighty grasp of me.

Out of that weak, unquiet drift
    that comes but to depart,
to that pure heaven my spirit lift
    where thou unchanging art.
Lay hold of me with thy strong grasp,
    let thy almighty arm
in its embrace my weakness clasp,
    and I shall fear no harm.

Thy purpose of eternal good
    let me but surely know;
on this I'll lean—let changing mood
    and feeling come and go—
glad when thy sunshine fills my soul,
    not lorn when clouds o'ercast,
since thou within thy sure control
    of love dost hold me fast.

John Campbell Shairp, 1871
Glen Dessaray and Other Poems, 1888

344

O Love, That Wilt Not Let Me Go

O Love, that wilt not let me go,
    I rest my weary soul in thee;
I give thee back the life I owe,
that in thine ocean depths its flow
    may richer, fuller be.

O Light that followest all my way,
    I yield my flickering torch to thee;
my heart restores its borrowed ray,
that in thy sunshine's blaze its day
    may brighter, fairer be.

O Joy that seekest me through pain,
    I cannot close my heart to thee;
I trace the rainbow through the rain,
and feel the promise is not vain,
    that morn shall tearless be.   (Ps. 30:11)

O Cross that liftest up my head,
    I dare not ask to fly from thee;
I lay in dust life's glory dead,
and from the ground there blossoms red
    life that shall endless be.

George Matheson, 1881
Life and Work, January 1882
Matheson revised his original line 3:3, "I climb," to "I trace" for
The Scottish Hymnal, 1884.

345

Three Doors

Three doors there are in the temple,
    where men go up to pray,
and they that wait at the outer gate
    may enter by either way.

O Father, give each his answer,
    each in his kindred way;
adapt thy light to his form of night,
    and grant him his needed day.

O give to the yearning spirits
    that only thy rest desire,
the power to bask in the peace they ask,
    and feel the warmth of thy fire.

Give to the soul that seeketh   (Luke 11:9)
    'mid cloud, and doubt, and storm,
the glad surprise of the straining eyes,
    to see on the waves thy form.   (John 21:7)

Give to the heart that knocketh
    at the doors of earthly care
the strength to tread in the pathway spread
    by the flowers thou hast planted there.

For the middle wall shall be broken,   (Eph. 2:13)
   and the light expand its ray,
when the burdened of brain and the soother of pain
   shall be ranked with them that pray.

George Matheson
Sacred Songs, 1890

346

Gather Us In, Thou Love That Fillest All

Gather us in, thou Love that fillest all,
   gather our rival faiths within thy fold,
rend each man's temple's veil and bid it fall,
   that we may know that thou hast been of old:
      Gather us in.

Gather us in: We worship only thee;
   in varied names we stretch a common hand;
in diverse forms a common soul we see;
   in many ships we seek our spirit-land:
      Gather us in.

Each sees one color of thy rainbow-light,
   each looks upon one tint and calls it heaven;
thou art the fullness of our partial sight;
   we are not perfect till we find the seven:
      Gather us in.

Thine is the mystic life great India craves,
   thine is the Parsee's sin-destroying beam,
thine is the Buddhist's rest from tossing waves,
   thine is the empire of vast China's dream:
      Gather us in.

Thine is the Roman's strength without his pride,
   thine is the Greek's glad world without its
                    graves,
thine is Judea's law with love beside,
   the truth that censures and the grace that saves:
      Gather us in.

Some seek a Father in the heavens above,
   some ask a human image to adore,
some crave a spirit vast as life and love;
   within thy mansions we have all and more:
      Gather us in.

George Matheson
Sacred Songs, 1890

347

Thraldom

I bind myself this tide
to the Galilean's side,
to the wounds of Calvary,
to the Christ who died for me.

I bind my soul this day
to the brother far away,
to the brother near at hand,
in this town and in this land.

I bind my heart in thrall
to the God, the Lord of all,
to the God, the poor man's friend,
and the Christ whom he did send.

I bind myself to peace,
to make strife and envy cease;
God, knit thou sure the cord
of my thraldom to the Lord!

Lauchlan MacLean Watt
The Tryst, 1907

348

Hymn of Penitence
Marathi: Sisyahi ganaya nahi yogya jo tayala

One who is all unfit to count
   as scholar in thy school,
thou of thy love hast named a friend—
   O kindness wonderful!

So weak am I, O gracious Lord,
    so all unworthy thee,
that e'en the dust upon thy feet
    outweighs me utterly.

Thou dwellest in unshadowed light,
    all sin and shame above—
that thou shouldst bear our sin and shame,
    how can I tell such love?

Ah, did not he the heavenly throne   (Phil. 2:5ff)
    a little thing esteem,
and not unworthy for my sake
    a mortal body deem?

When in his flesh they drove the nails
    did he not all endure?
What name is there to fit a life
    so patient and so pure?

So Love itself in human form,
    for love of me he came;
I cannot look upon his face
    for shame, for bitter shame.

If there is aught of worth in me
    it comes from thee alone;
then keep me safe, for so, O Lord,
    thou keepest but thine own.

Nārāyan Vāman Tilak
translated, Nicol Macnicol
The Life of Tilak, 1920

Chapter 18:
American Hymnody to 1900 (349–389)

No adjective is so difficult to define as "American." At different periods in history it means several different things. America (we are bound here to mean by that the United States) is now a complex society in which no civilized race on earth is unrepresented; and if it be said that it was never a racially homogeneous society, the truth is that that complexity has been admitted and has been reflected in an "American culture" only in the twentieth century.

Nobody thinks that the Pilgrim Fathers discovered America. But they did introduce Protestantism to America, and therefore the first nearly three centuries of American hymnody are entirely a story of what came from, and what reacted against, their influence. Huge tracts of America were unaffected by any such influence at the time of the foundation of the United States in 1776; but those who lived in these tracts were either Catholics or unevangelized Indians or subject blacks serving white masters who were solidly Protestant.

It is only in the years after about 1950 that American hymnody provides anything but a very one-sided view of American culture. The whole of this present section is concerned with a society which has now virtually passed away: the all-dominating culture of New England and the eastern seaboard down to Baltimore.

New England was colonized by Calvinistic Protestants, and therefore the public praise of the majority of Christians was psalmody. The first book to be printed in this part of America was the "Bay Psalm Book" (1640), a psalter based on the "Old Version" of Sternhold and Hopkins and designed as a simpler and more tractable replacement for Ainsworth's Psalter of 1612, which the Pilgrim Fathers had brought with them. In the eighteenth century the Episcopalians were almost confined to Tate and Brady's "New Version," which, on the whole, got a more hospitable reception in America than in its own country. And if there was any hymnody here or there it was Watts or Wesley. John Wesley, as we saw earlier (chapter 5), edited his own hymnal for his Georgia mission and had it printed at Charlestown [Charleston], South Carolina, in 1737. This predated all Charles Wesley's work and was mostly Watts and members of the Wesley family with incursions into George Herbert. Indeed, we look in vain for native American hymnody in the colonial days, except for the quite remarkable and finely wrought hymn of Samuel Davies (349), which stands out as a landmark. It has some of the authentic power of Watts himself. Whether it was ever sung in its author's brief lifetime we cannot tell; it was not printed until some years after his death. But there it stands, monumental and severe, quite unique among American hymns for its theological weight and grandeur.

While psalmody was suffocating hymnody in the cultivated Northeast, hymnody began to flourish in the "southern states" (this is the term applied in America to what is geographically the Southeast); but since hardly anybody apart from scholars knew anything about the folk hymnody of North Carolina, Tennessee, and Kentucky before the second half of our own century, we are leaving that, and the parallel development of the Black Spiritual, to chapter 19.

Our 350, some fifty years younger than 349, was born of psalmody in that when the American Congregationalists wanted a revision of the Watts psalter they entrusted the work to President Timothy Dwight, part of whose task was to make versions of those psalms which Watts had never versified. "I love thy kingdom," still one of America's favorites, is, surprisingly enough, his version of Psalm 137. Clearly he was almost as hopelessly defeated by that psalm as Watts had been, for his product is strictly a hymn, further away from the psalm than Watts would ever have allowed himself to go. But it alone of his work has survived, and so it is there as another lonely milestone.

One of the earliest hymn writers of the newly formed United States must have been John Quincy Adams, son of the second president and himself president from 1825 to 1829. He wrote a complete metrical psalter and a small number of original hymns which were published after his death; none of this is interesting enough literature to merit a place here.

We may say that the main stream begins to flow with the two Unitarian ministers whose work is exemplified in 351 and 352. If 351 looks a rather eccentric production (what tune the author can have ever heard it sung to remains a mystery), 352 gives a very clear indication of how things are going to go. For we are going to find, and our quoted texts will prove it, that the style of hymnody affected by the Unitarian, Congregational, and Presbyterian divines of the American nineteenth century was, until the century was well advanced, far better literature than the English Anglicans were providing in the same period. Theologically it had its dubious moments, but these New England Calvinists knew how to handle words. It is indeed interesting that so many of these hymns have now been forgotten in America, 351 perhaps understandably, good writing though it is, but 352 incomprehensibly. We shall come to the reasons for this later on.

American hymnody did not make a real impact on English congregations until the century was well advanced, but 353 and 360 have the distinction of being the two American hymns admitted to the first edition (1861) of *Hymns Ancient and Modern*. That hymnal was always slow in admitting American influence, and it was not until its 1950 edition that American work was taken seriously by its editors. One curious point is that these two hymns, the first of which certainly has great distinction, were written by authors who were twenty-five and nineteen years old, respectively, at the time of their publication; the careful reader will note that eleven of the hymns in this section were written by authors who were less than thirty years old.

Number 354 is another very youthful piece, very mature and poised writing, typical again of the New England style.

Ray Palmer, Congregationalist, is certainly one of America's leading hymn writers. He made a very good beginning with his youthful "My faith looks up to thee" (355), and his work in the other examples (356 and 357, with which should be taken 163D and 169C) shows very well his unusually contemplative manner. If American hymnody was subject to any special temptation, it was to the production of surface gloss concealing intellectual commonplaceness. One never finds this in Palmer.

More Unitarian work will be found at 358, 372, 373 (one of the first Christmas hymns with a social message), 374 (unusual and charming), 378, 379, and 380, in all of which there is some very good literature. "City of God" (379) is perhaps the most typical example of a fine lyric whose theological judgments are entirely questionable; the humanistic optimism in this material has found less acceptance in the late twentieth century than it naturally found in the mid-nineteenth. Perhaps 381 qualifies to be called one of the six best American hymns ever written, for here undoubtedly we have a firm base in Scripture and dogma on which a sonorous and beautiful lyric is built; despite the long lines there is not a word wasted here.

The American men of letters contributed plenty to the hymn treasury. Compare that with our Victorian age in which, even if we do steal the occasional piece from Tennyson, no major poet ever wrote a hymn. Emerson, the famous essayist, did not perhaps distinguish himself in hymnody, but 359, an early work written for a local church celebration, has honest candor.

The unwillingness of American editors, both in the nineteenth century and in this, to fashion hymnody out of the work of recognized poets in the manner we shall investigate in chapter 20 was no doubt partly the consequence of Puritan prejudice; but the high lyric talent of the American nineteenth-century writers must have had something to do with it. But there are two large exceptions among the well-known hymns from America: "Once to every man and nation" (which we shall examine shortly) and "Dear Lord and Father of mankind."

John Greenleaf Whittier was a Quaker poet who was, in the earlier years of a long life, very active in the Abolitionist movement and who spent his later years as a full-time man of letters. His work in current hymnals is the great American exception to the generalization we have just made. In later life he did write one or two hymns, of which "All things are thine" is the best known; but he wrote those at the wish of people who had already discovered what good hymns could be made out of poetry he did not design for singing. His Quaker background was, of course, not a hymn-singing culture, and it was for quite other purposes that he wrote the poems from which his best "hymns" actually come. For if nowadays "Dear Lord and Father" and "O brother man" are probably his best-known hymns in his own country, it is in the selections given at 362–366 that we see the best of his contribution to hymnody. These five pieces are, as the notes show, stanzas selected from three long poems which run in total to 77 Common Meter stanzas and which declare his mature faith. Only "Immortal love," the best and most widely used of these selections (363), uses the first stanza of any of these poems.

Two things will at once occur to a thoughtful reader. The first is that if one can make serviceable hymns out of seven-stanza selections so wild and apparently arbitrary as these are, the style of the originals must be fairly loose. The second is that by making such centos the editors have probably altered the thought of the originals to some extent. The first of these notions is only partly true, and the truth about it gives the answer to the second. The original poems are all to some extent argumentative, consisting of the juxtaposition of two opposed ideas of faith. The editors have boiled off the argument, leaving only the positive faith, which, of course, is better for singing than the

argument. The controversial elements have not wholly disappeared from the selections we have offered (which will be found at some points different from those in many hymnals); stanza 3 of 365, for example, lifts the curtain for a moment. But it does remain true that Whittier is the only reputable author whose work has been so extensively and at the same time so successfully rearranged in this fashion by hymnal editors.

The "argument" is, in Whittier, always that of the liberal and cultivated man against doctrinaire rigorism. In true Quaker fashion, what Whittier has to say he says very gently. But "The Eternal Goodness," from which we take our 366, opens, in our selection, with stanza 4. Here are the first three:

> O friends! with whom my feet have trod
> the quiet aisles of prayer,
> glad witness to your zeal for God
> and love of man I bear.

> I trace your lines of argument;
> your logic linked and strong
> I weigh as one who dreads dissent,
> and fears a doubt as wrong.

> But still my human hands are weak
> to hold your iron creeds;
> against the words ye bid me speak
> my heart within me pleads.

> Who fathoms the eternal thought? . . .

Our selection ends at stanza 20. There follow these:

> O brothers! if my faith is vain,
> if hopes like these betray,
> pray for me that my feet may gain
> the sure and safer way.

> And thou, O Lord, by whom are seen
> thy creatures as they be,
> forgive me if too close I lean
> my human heart on thee!

Whittier cannot be called "orthodox" in his approach to creeds and liturgies, and this is not the place to argue whether it is legitimate to extract stanzas from longer works and, by omitting one strain of thought, modify their author's message. Your present writer's personal opinion is that when this is done with Whittier it is less unsuccessful than we shall find it when we come to Russell Lowell, because the manner of Whittier is gentle, where Lowell's, in the poem from which "Once to every man and nation" came, is polemical. If one wants a complete Whittier poem, one has one in the very late devotional lyric, 367, which certainly now is a piece for private reading rather than devotional song. If one wants him in a more muscular mood, then the early poem 361 gives us that—almost unknown now, recovered only by Garrett Horder in England [and reworked by him as 361B], never now sung in the USA. And if there is a case against "Dear Lord and Father," which in all conscience is an excellent piece of word-spinning, perhaps it is that there Whittier was writing a polemical piece, a poetic tract contrasting the serenity and sanity of the Christian faith with the vaporings of a kind of drug-addictive transcendental meditation associated with the drinking of "soma," a potation designed to induce visions. The quietism of the hymn as we know it (it is in fact the last six stanzas, or selections from them, of the poem) takes on a very different tone when its context is made explicit.

American Episcopalians did not make a large contribution to nineteenth-century hymnody; their great days were about 1940. We have already touched on 353 and 360 which no doubt made the grade in *Hymns A & M* because of their Episcopal origin; for its first century that book was always inhospitable to non-Episcopal writing. Bishop Arthur Cleveland Coxe has a style much less even, much more rugged, than that of the liberals. "Savior, sprinkle many nations" is well known to many singers; it is a tolerable hymn somewhat disfigured by an opening line which means nothing

much, being based on a venerable mistranslation in the Bible. Number 369 is much more fierce, written by him when he was 26, and passionately interpreting the dark prophecies in Isaiah 63. Nobody knew this in Britain until Vaughan Williams married it to the Welsh tune EBENEZER in *The English Hymnal*, and it proved to be too strong meat for any other hymnal to take it up.

Oliver Wendell Holmes, one of the country's greatest men of letters, is justly famous for "Lord of all being," 375; here and in several other hymns he shows the characteristic "Unitarian" polish and also the length of vision which in less sure hands became sentimental and antidogmatic. It is not so here. The "Battle Hymn of the Republic" (376) is almost too well-known to stand comment, and yet, even here, in a piece that has become so popular, what admirable writing in the expansive nineteenth-century style! Just occasionally, perhaps, it is overexuberant (the "jubilant feet" and the "glorious bosom" are not quite up to standard), but few national songs come near this in literary quality. The final stanza, whose authenticity has sometimes been doubted, is perfectly genuine, though the author was unsure whether in the end to include it or not.

Yet another noncleric, the essayist and journalist William Cullen Bryant, produced several good pieces. We choose 368 for its social emphasis, which redresses some of the balance against the tendency to overspiritual writing we have been conscious of up to now. (Great poets do not often make good hymn writers, but the Americans show, and the English showed in James Montgomery and G. K. Chesterton, how very well the best journalist can rise to the occasion.) Miss Eliza Scudder was chiefly a hymn writer. Her vogue has now disappeared, but 380 has plenty of solid merit in the now-familiar style.

This brings us to "Once to every man and nation," which must be, apart from the two Christmas hymns, the most popular nineteenth-century hymn in late twentieth-century America;

and possibly American readers will be surprised to learn that the hymn they know so well was really fashioned in England. Russell Lowell's eloquent poem on the Mexican War which we reprint in full at 370A is full of that colorful language and moral hyperbole in which the Boston school of writers excelled; but as it stands it is hardly a hymn.

It was the English editor William Garrett Horder (1845–1919) who, except for the two hymns so mysteriously annexed earlier by English Episcopalians, really introduced American hymnody to England. In *The Hymn Lover*, his book on hymnody, he gave many pages to American hymn writers, and in *Worship Song* (1905) and the collections which preceded it he transcribed scores of these hymns. *Worship Song*, the only hymnal with music that he edited, was a fairly obscure book, but Percy Dearmer, who edited *The English Hymnal*, knew it and admired it, and in 1906 the book that was destined to become England's most enduring hymnal carried many of these hymns which he had learned from Horder's pages. It was Horder who recast Lowell's poem in the form now well known, and it was Dearmer (in a later hymnal, *Songs of Praise*, 1925) who set it to the Welsh tune EBENEZER from which in the USA it is now never separated. Further bibliographical information about this extraordinary piece, which combines at a high pressure theological perverseness and trenchant language, will be found in the *Hymnal Guide*. In 371 we are able to provide a Lowell hymn rather less well-known but at least designed to be sung and of considerable lyric warmth.

The same rich feeling for words is to be found in William Henry Burleigh's poem at 382 and in Edmund H. Sears's and Phillips Brooks's famous Christmas hymns (373 and 383), both of which, when sung in full, have a social emphasis uncommon up to that time in Christmas songs.

With the Congregationalist Samuel Wolcott's "Christ for the world" (384) perhaps we detect a slight falling off into platitudinousness; and the evangelical note appears in Miss Mary Artemisia Lathbury's 386, which, with "Day is dying in the west," she wrote for the Chautauqua Convention, the pioneer of that endless network of conference centers for revival and study which now covers the USA. Possibly it was evangelical influences after 1870 that caused hymn writers to turn away from the high-toned style of Boston. Frederick L. Hosmer (387, 388) is the last of the Unitarians to rise to it. His writing is impeccable, his cast of mind optimistic and, like that of most of the others, wholly unfashionable nowadays. But apart from him we begin now to descend rather steeply into a more conventional hymn style. The euphoria of the Centennial in 1876 may perhaps be blamed for the rather inflated language of 385, and a similar, more local celebration for that of 389; but this, compared with the speculative and imaginative style of the earlier New England work, is poor stuff, associated, unfortunately, with lamentably bombastic music. Both are the work of Episcopalians.

I have drawn attention here to the special virtues of the New England style partly because so much of this hymnody has actually passed out of the American repertory now, and much of it got a pretty poor showing in English books. The reason for this extinction of the style in twentieth-century hymnals is the changing of a theological fashion. It is entirely understandable that the successive traumas of the twentieth century, coming so rudely upon the euphoria of the nineteenth, should cause people to turn their backs on this sort of material. Whittier's hymn, with its opening verse,

O sometimes gleams upon our sight,
　　through present wrong, the eternal right,
and step by step, since time began,
　　we see the steady gain of man . . .

expresses a sentiment which the twentieth century caused a whole generation to consider almost blasphemous. Where the English writers were disciplined by their prayer books and Bibles and so largely guided by the ideals of the Oxford

Movement, the Americans knew no such "movement" and mostly no such liturgies. So their thoughts turned naturally to speculation, and they were always vulnerable to the taunt "It's all very well for you New Englanders; you can afford to talk that way."

Reflecting the theological stance of the new orthodoxy of 1925–1945, critics like Bernard Manning depreciated this kind of material and exalted Watts, Wesley, and the other English Calvinists and early Evangelicals. Nobody (for me) can speak or write too affectionately about those people, but as the twentieth century enters its last quarter it is easier than it was forty years before to see certain qualities in the American hymnody which have lately been undervalued. Present-day casualness of language, theological unimaginativeness, seminarial pedagogy, and hatred of poetry and history, not to mention our total aesthetic anarchy, throw a shadow in which the professional literary standards and the religious assurance of the old American writers begin, after being painted gray by our early twentieth-century theologians, to glow again with a light we were formerly too complacent to notice.

In a moment we shall see what else happened to American hymnody in the nineteenth century which will redress to some extent any disbalance a fastidious reader may complain of so far.

And as a postscript: In case anyone accuses the present editor of undue admiration for American work, he will state (following the lead of that great hymnologist, the late Millar Patrick) that that wretched travesty of the 23rd Psalm, "Father, hear the prayer we offer," being among the American pieces introduced to England by Garrett Horder and Percy Dearmer, appeals to him as being by far the worst hymn of the century written in either country. For this, the reader will set the dogs on him from a quite different quarter, but at least he will enjoy the change of ground.

349
The Glories of God in Pardoning Sinners

Great God of wonders! all thy ways
    are matchless, godlike, and divine,
but the fair glories of thy grace
    more godlike and unrivaled shine:

      Who is a pardoning God like thee?
      or who has grace so rich and free?

Crimes of such horror to forgive,
    such guilty, daring worms to spare,
this is thy grand prerogative,
    and none shall in the honor share.

Angels and men, resign your claim
    to pity, mercy, love, and grace,
these glories crown Jehovah's name
    with an incomparable blaze.

In wonder lost, with trembling joy,
    we take the pardon of our God,
pardon for crimes of deepest dye,
    a pardon bought with Jesus' blood.

O may this strange, this matchless grace,
    this godlike miracle of love,
fill the wide world with grateful praise,
    and all the angelic hosts above!

Samuel Davies
Hymns Adapted to Divine Worship, 1769
Line 2:2 is usually altered to read "daring souls."

350
Love to the Church. Psalm 137. Part 3.

I love thy kingdom, Lord,
    the house of thine abode,
the church our blest Redeemer saved
    with his own precious blood.

I love thy church, O God;
her walls before thee stand,
dear as the apple of thine eye, (Deut. 32:10)
and graven on thy hand. (Isa. 49:16)

If e'er to bless thy sons
my voice, or hands, deny,
these hands let useful skill forsake,
this voice in silence die.

If e'er my heart forget
her welfare, or her woe,
let every joy this heart forsake,
and every grief o'erflow.

For her my tears shall fall,
for her my prayers ascend,
to her my cares and toils be given,
till toils and cares shall end.

Beyond my highest joy
I prize her heavenly ways;
her sweet communion, solemn vows,
her hymns of love and praise.

Jesus, thou Friend divine,
our Savior and our King,
thy hand from every snare and foe
shall great deliverance bring.

Sure as thy truth shall last
to Zion shall be given
the highest glories earth can yield,
and brighter bliss of heaven.

Timothy Dwight
The Psalms of David Imitated (Dwight's edition of Watts), 1801

351
Easter

Lift your glad voices in triumph on high,
for Jesus has risen, and man cannot die;
Vain were the terrors that gathered around him,
and short the dominion of death and the
grave;
he burst from the fetters of darkness that bound
him,
resplendent in glory to live and to save;
Loud was the chorus of angels on high,
"The Savior hath risen, and man shall not die!"

Glory to God, in full anthems of joy;
the being he gave us death cannot destroy;
sad were the life we must part with tomorrow,
if tears were our birthright and death were
our end. (1 Cor. 15:10)
But Jesus hath cheered the dark valley of sorrow
(Ps. 23:4)
and made us, immortal, to heaven ascend.
Lift then your voices in triumph on high,
for Jesus hath risen, and man shall not die!

Henry Ware, Jr.
The Christian Disciple, 1817

352
Universal Worship

O thou, to whom in ancient time
the lyre of Hebrew bards was strung,
whom kings adored in songs sublime
and prophets praised with glowing tongue;

not now on Zion's height alone
thy favored worshipers may dwell, (John 4:21)
nor where at sultry noon thy Son (John 4:5)
sat weary by the patriarch's well;

from every place below the skies
 the grateful song, the fervent prayer,
the incense of the heart may rise
 to heaven, and find acceptance there.

To thee shall age with snowy hair
 and strength and beauty bow the knee,
and childhood lisp with reverent air
 its praises and its prayers to thee.

O thou, to whom in ancient time
 the lyre of prophet bards was strung,
to thee at last, in every clime
 shall temples rise, and praise be sung.

John Pierpont, 1824
Psalms and Hymns, 1840

353
Christ the Way

Thou art the Way; to thee alone
 from sin and death we flee;
and he who would the Father seek
 must seek him, Lord, by thee.

Thou art the Truth; thy word alone
 true wisdom can impart;
thou only canst inform the mind
 and purify the heart.

Thou art the Life; the rending tomb
 proclaims thy conquering arm,
and those who put their trust in thee
 nor death nor hell can harm.

Thou art the Way, the Truth, the Life;
 grant us that way to know,
that truth to keep, that life to win
 whose joys eternal flow.

George Washington Doane
Songs by the Way, 1824

354
The Divine Compassion

Thou who didst stoop below
 to drain the cup of woe,
wearing the form of frail mortality;
 thy blessed labors done,
 thy crown of victory won,
hast passed from earth, passed to thy throne on high.

Our eyes behold thee not,
 yet hast thou not forgot
those who have placed their hope, their trust in thee.
 Before thy Father's face
 thou hast prepared a place
that where thou art, there they may also be.

(John 14:1–2)

It was no path of flowers
 which, through this world of ours.
beloved of the Father, thou didst tread;
 and shall we, in dismay,
 shrink from the narrow way
when clouds and darkness are around it spread?

O thou who art our life,
 be with us through the strife;
the holy head by earth's fierce storms was bowed:
 raise thou our eyes above,
 to see a Father's love,
beam, like a bow of promise, through the cloud.

(Gen. 8:22)

And O, if thoughts of gloom
 should hover o'er the tomb,
he light of love our guiding star shall be;
 our spirit shall not dread
 the shadowy path to tread,
Friend, Guardian, Savior, which doth lead to thee.

Sarah Elizabeth Appleton Miles
The Christian Examiner, 1827

355
My Faith Looks Up to Thee

My faith looks up to thee,
thou Lamb of Calvary,
    Savior divine!
Now hear me when I pray,
take all my guilt away,
O let me from this day
    be wholly thine.

May thy rich grace impart
strength to my fainting heart,
    my zeal inspire;
as thou hast died for me,
O may thy love to me
pure, warm, and changeless be,
    a living fire.

While life's dark maze I tread,
and griefs around me spread,
    be thou my guide;
bid darkness turn to day,
wipe sorrow's tears away,
nor let me ever stray
    from thee aside.

When ends life's transient dream,
when death's cold sullen stream
    shall o'er me roll,
blest Savior, then in love
fear and distrust remove;
O bear me safe above,
    a ransomed soul.

Ray Palmer, 1830
Spiritual Songs for Social Worship, 1831

356
Whom Having Not Seen, Ye Love. I Peter 1:8

Jesus, these eyes have never seen
    that radiant form of thine;
the veil of sense hangs dark between
    thy blessed face and mine.

I see thee not, I hear thee not,
    yet art thou oft with me;
and earth hath ne'er so dear a spot
    as where I met with thee.

Like some bright dream that comes unsought,
    when slumbers o'er me roll,
thine image ever fills my thought,
    and charms my ravished soul.

Yet, thou I have not seen, and still
    must rest in faith alone,
I love thee, dearest Lord, and will,
    unseen, but not unknown.

When death these mortal eyes shall seal,
    and still this throbbing heart,
the rending veil shall thee reveal
    all glorious as thou art.

Ray Palmer
The Sabbath Hymn Book, 1858

357
How Unsearchable Are His Judgments!
Romans 11:31

Lord, my weak thought in vain would climb
    to search the starry vault profound;
in vain would wing her flight sublime
    to find creation's utmost bound.

But weaker yet that thought must prove
    to search thy grand eternal plan,
thy sovereign counsels, born of love,
    long ages ere the world began.

When my dim reason would demand
    why that, or this, thou dost ordain,
by some vast deep I seem to stand,
    whose secrets I must ask in vain.

When doubts disturb my troubled breast,
    and all is dark as night to me,
here, as on solid rock, I rest—
    that thus it seemeth good to thee.

Be this my joy, that evermore
    thou rulest all things at thy will;
thy sovereign wisdom I adore,
    and calmly, sweetly, trust thee still.

Ray Palmer
The Sabbath Hymn Book, 1858

358
Christ on the Road to Emmaus

Hath not thy heart within thee burned   (Luke 24:32)
    at evening's calm and holy hour,
as if its inmost depths discerned
    the presence of a loftier Power?

Hast thou not heard 'mid forest glades,
    while ancient rivers murmured by,
a voice from the eternal shades
    that spake a present Deity?

And as upon the sacred page
    thine eye in rapt attention turned
o'er records of a holier age,
    hath not thy heart within thee burned?

It was the voice of God, that spake
    in silence to thy silent heart;
and bade each holier thought awake,
    and every dream of earth depart.

Voice of our God, O yet be near!
    In low sweet accents whisper peace;
direct us on our pathway here;
    then bid in heaven our wanderings cease.

Stephen G. Bulfinch
Contemplations of the Savior, 1832

359
The House of God

We love the venerable house
    our fathers built to God:
in heaven are kept their grateful vows,
    their dust endears the sod.

Here holy thoughts a light have shed
    from many a radiant face,
and prayers of tender hope have spread
    a perfume through the place.

And anxious hearts have pondered here
    the mystery of life,
and prayed the eternal Light to clear
    their doubts and aid their strife.

From humble tenements around
    came up the pensive train,
and in the church a blessing found
    that filled their homes again;

for faith, and peace, and mighty love,
    that from the Godhead flow,
showed them the life of heaven above
    springs from the life below.

They live with God, their homes are dust;
　　yet here their children pray,
and in this fleeting lifetime trust
　　to find the narrow way.

On him who by the altar stands,
　　on him thy blessing fall!
Speak through his lips thy pure commands,
　　thou Heart, that lovest all.

Ralph Waldo Emerson, 1833
Hymns of the Spirit, 1864

360
Take Up Thy Cross

"Take up thy cross," the Savior said,
　　"if thou wouldst my disciple be;
take up thy cross with willing heart
　　and humbly follow after me."　　　(Mark 8:34)

Take up thy cross; let not its weight
　　fill thy weak spirit with alarm;
his strength shall bear thy spirit up,
　　and brace thy heart, and nerve thine arm.

Take up thy cross, nor heed the shame,　　(Heb. 12:2)
　　nor let thy foolish pride be still;
the Lord refused not e'en to die
　　upon the cross, on Calvary's hill.

Take up thy cross, then, in his strength
　　and calmly sin's wild deluge brave;
'twill guide thee to a better home,
　　and point to glory o'er the grave.

Take up thy cross, and follow on,
　　nor think till death to lay it down;
for only he who bears the cross
　　may hope to wear the glorious crown.

Charles William Everest
Visions of Death, and Other Poems, 1833

361
My Triumph

A. Original poem

The autumn-time has come;
on woods that dream of bloom,
and over purpling vines,
the low sun fainter shines.

The aster-flower is failing,
the hazel's gold is paling;
yet overhead more near
the eternal stars appear!

And present gratitude
insures the future's good,
and for the things I see
I trust the things to be;

that in the paths untrod,
and the long days of God,
my feet shall still be led,
my heart be comforted.

O living friends who love me!
O dear ones gone above me!
careless of other fame,
I leave to you my name.

Hide it from idle praises,
save it from evil phrases:
Why, when dear lips that spake it
are dumb, should strangers wake it?

Let the thick curtain fall;
I better know than all
how little I have gained,
how vast the unattained.

Not by the page word-painted
let life be banned or sainted:
deeper that written scroll
the colors of the soul.

Sweeter than any sung
my songs that found no tongue;
nobler than any fact
my wish that failed of act.

Others shall sing the song,
others shall right the wrong—
finish what I begin,
and all I fail of win.

What matter, I or they?
mine or another's day,
so the right word be said
and life the sweeter made?

Hail to the coming singers!
Hail to the brave light-bringers!
Forward I reach and share
all that they sing and dare.

The airs of heaven blow o'er me;
a glory shines before me
of what mankind shall be—
pure, generous, brave, and free.

A dream of man and woman
diviner but still human,
solving the riddle old,
shaping the age of gold!

The love of God and neighbor;
and equal-handed labor;
the richer life, where beauty
walks hand in hand with duty.

Ring, bells in unreared steeples,
the joy of unborn peoples!
Sound, trumpets far off blown,
your triumph is my own!

Parcel and part of all,
I keep the festival,
Forereach the good to be,
and share the victory.

I feel the earth move sunward,
I join the great march onward,
and take, by faith, while living,
my freehold of thanksgiving.

John Greenleaf Whittier
Ballads of New England, 1870

B. Reworked as a hymn

Lord, for the things we see
we trust the things to be;
and present gratitude
insures the future's good.
So in the paths untrod
and the long days of God
our feet shall still be led,
our hearts be comforted.

Others shall sing the song,
others shall right the wrong—
finish what we begin,
and all we fail of, win.
What matter, we or they?
ours or another's day,
so the right word be said
and life the sweeter made?

Hail to the coming singers!
Hail to the brave light-bringers!
forward we reach and share
all that they sing or dare.
The airs of heaven blow o'er us,
a glory shines before us
of what mankind shall be—
pure, generous, brave, and free.

The love of God and neighbor,
an equal band at labor,
the richer life where beauty
walks hand in hand with duty.
We feel the earth move sunward,
we join the great march onward,
and take by faith, while living
our freehold of thanksgiving!

W. Garrett Horder
Worship Song, 1905
Horder used lines 11–12, 9–10, 13–16, 37–52, 57–60, and 69–72 of
Whittier's original, changed first-person singular to first-person plural,
and made other smaller alterations.

362

from My Psalm

All as God wills, who wisely heeds
    to give or to withhold,
and knoweth more of all my needs
    than all my prayers have told!

Enough that blessings undeserved
    have marked my erring track;
that wheresoe'er my feet have swerved,
    his chastening turned me back;

that more and more a Providence
    of love is understood,
making the springs of time and sense
    sweet with eternal good;

that death seems but a covered way
    which opens into light,
wherein no blinded child can stray
    beyond the Father's sight;

that care and trial seem at last
    through memory's sunset air,
like mountain ranges overpast,
    in purple distance fair;

that all the jarring notes of life
    seem blending in a psalm,
and all the angles of its strife
    slow rounding into calm;

and so the shadows fall apart,
    and so the west winds play;
and all the windows of my heart
    I open to the day.

John Greenleaf Whittier, 1859
The Works of John Greenleaf Whittier, 1892–1894
These are stanzas 11–17 of the 17-stanza text that begins, "I mourn no
more my vanished years."

363

from Our Master

Immortal love, forever full,
    forever flowing free,
forever shared, forever whole,
    a never-ebbing sea!

Our outward lips confess the name
    all other names above;
love only knoweth whence it came
    and comprehendeth love.

We may not climb the heavenly steeps   (Rom. 10:6–7)
    to bring the Lord Christ down;
In vain we search the lowest deeps,
    for him no depths can drown.

But warm, sweet, tender, even yet
    a present help is he;
and faith has still its Olivet,
    and love its Galilee.

The healing of his seamless dress   (Mark 5:27)
    is by our beds of pain;
we touch him in life's throng and press,
    and we are whole again.

Through him the first fond prayers are said
    our lips of childhood frame,
the last low whispers of our dead
    are burdened with his name.

Alone, O love ineffable!
    thy saving name is given;   (Acts 4:12)
to turn aside from thee is hell,
    to walk with thee is heaven.

> John Greenleaf Whittier, 1866
> *The Independent*, November 1, 1866
> *The Works of John Greenleaf Whittier*, 1892–1894
> These are stanzas 1–2, 5, 13–15, and 31 of the 38-stanza text.

Yet weak and blinded though we be,
    thou dost our service own;
we bring our varying gifts to thee
    and thou rejectest none.

To thee our full humanity,
    its joys and pains, belong;
the wrong of man to man on thee
    inflicts a deeper wrong.

Who hates, hates thee: who loves, becomes
    therein to thee allied: (1 John 4:20)
all sweet accords of hearts and homes
    in thee are multiplied.

Apart from thee all gain is loss,
    all labor vainly done;
the solemn shadow of the cross
    is better than the sun.

> John Greenleaf Whittier, 1866
> *The Independent*, November 1, 1866
> *The Works of John Greenleaf Whittier*, 1892–1894
> These are stanzas 16–18, 20–22, and 30 of the 38-stanza text.

364
from Our Master

Our Lord and Master of us all,
    whate'er our name or sign,
we own thy sway, we hear thy call,
    we test our lives by thine.

Thou judgest us; thy purity
    doth all our lusts condemn;
the love that draws us nearer thee
    is hot with wrath to them;

our thoughts lie open to thy sight;
    and, naked to thy glance,
our secret sins are in the light
    of thy pure countenance.

365
from Our Master

O Love! O Life! our faith and sight
    thy presence maketh one,
as through transfigured clouds of white
    we trace the noonday sun.

So to our mortal eyes subdued,
    flesh-veiled, but not concealed,
we know in thee the fatherhood
    and heart of God revealed.

Our Friend, our Brother, and our Lord,
    what may thy service be?
Not name, nor form, nor ritual word,
    but simply following thee.

Thy litanies, sweet offices
 of love and gratitude;
thy sacramental liturgies,
 the joy of doing good.

The heart must ring thy Christmas bells,
 thy inward altars raise;
its faith and hope thy canticles,
 and its obedience, praise.

Blow, winds of God, awake, and blow
 the mists of earth away;
shine out, O Light divine, and show
 how wide and far we stray.

We faintly hear, we dimly see,
 in differing phrase we pray;
but, dim or clear, we own in thee
 the Light, the Truth, the Way!   (John 14:6)

John Greenleaf Whittier, 1866
The Independent, November 1, 1866
The Works of John Greenleaf Whittier, 1892–1894
These are stanzas 24–25, 34, 36, 38, 3, and 26 of the 38-stanza text.

366
from The Eternal Goodness

Who fathoms the eternal thought?
 who talks of scheme and plan?
The Lord is God! He needeth not
 the poor device of man.

Yet in the maddening maze of things,
 and tossed by storm and flood,
to one fixed ground my spirit clings;
 I know that God is good.

I long for household voices gone,
 for vanished smiles I long;
but God hath led my dear ones on,
 and he can do no wrong.

I know not what the future hath
 of marvel or surprise,
assured alone that life and death
 his mercy underlies.

And if my heart and flesh are weak
 to bear an untried pain,
the bruised reed he will not break,   (Isa. 42:3)
 but strengthen and sustain.

And so beside the silent sea
 I wait the muffled oar;
no harm from him can come to me
 on ocean or on shore.

I know not where his islands lift
 their fronded palms in air;
I only know I cannot drift
 beyond his love and care.

John Greenleaf Whittier, 1865
The Works of John Greenleaf Whittier, 1892–1894
These are stanzas 4, 11, 15–17, and 19–20 of the 22-stanza text
beginning, "O friends! with whom my feet have trod."

367
At Last

When on my day of life the night is falling,
 and, in the winds from unsunned spaces blown,
I hear far voices out of darkness calling
 my feet to paths unknown,

thou who hast made my home of life so pleasant,
 leave not its tenant when its walls decay;
O Love Divine, O Helper ever present,
 be thou my strength and stay!

Be near me when all else is from me drifting:
 earth, sky, home's pictures, days of shade and
 shine,
and kindly faces to my own uplifting
 the love which answers mine.

I have but thee, my Father; let thy spirit
    be with me then to comfort and uphold;
no gate of pearl, no branch of palm I merit,
        nor street of shining gold.

Suffice it if—my good and ill unreckoned,
    and both forgiven through thy abounding
                grace—
I find myself by hands familiar beckoned
      unto my fitting place.

Some humble door among thy many mansions,
           (John 14:2)
    some sheltering shade where sin and striving
                cease,
and flows for ever, through heaven's green
             expansions,   (Rev. 22:1)
      the river of thy peace.

There, from the music round about me stealing,
    I fain would learn the new and holy song,
and find at last, beneath thy trees of healing,
      the life for which I long.

John Greenleaf Whittier, 1882
The Works of John Greenleaf Whittier, 1892–1894

368
Home Mission

Look from thy sphere of endless day,
    O God of pity and of might;
in pity look on those who stray
    benighted, in this land of light.

In peopled vale, in lonely glen,
    in crowded mart, by stream or sea,
how many of the sons of men
    hear not the message sent from thee.

Send forth thy heralds, Lord, to call
    the thoughtless young, the hardened old,
a scattered homeless flock, till all
    be gathered to thy peaceful fold.

Send them thy mighty word to speak,
    till faith shall dawn, and doubt depart,
to awe the bold, to stay the weak,
    and bind and heal the broken heart.

Then all these wastes, a dreary scene,
    that make us sadden as we gaze,
shall grow, with living waters green
    and lift to heaven the voice of praise.

William Cullen Bryant, 1840
Songs for the Sanctuary, 1865

369
Who Is This, with Garments Gory

Who is this, with garments gory,   (Isa. 63:1–6)
    triumphing from Bozrah's way;
this that weareth robes of glory
    bright with more than victory's ray?
Who is this unwearied corner
    from his journey's sultry length,
traveling through Idumè's summer
    in the greatness of his strength?

Wherefore red in thine apparel
    like the conquerors of earth,
and arrayed like those who carol
    o'er the reeking vineyard's mirth?
Who art thou, the valleys seeking   (Isa. 63:14)
    where our peaceful harvests wave?
"I, in righteous anger speaking,
    I the mighty One to save;

"I, that of the raging heathen
    trod the winepress all alone   (Isa. 63:3)
now in victor-garlands wreathen
    coming to redeem my own:
I am he with sprinkled raiment,
    glorious for the vengeance-hour,
ransoming, with priceless payment,
    and delivering with power."

Hail, all hail! thou Lord of Glory!
    thee our Father, thee we own;   (Isa. 63:16)
Abram heard not of our story,
    Israel ne'er our name hath known,
but, Redeemer, thou hast sought us,
    thou hast heard thy children's wail,
thou with thy dear blood hast bought us:
    Hail, thou mighty Victor, hail!

Arthur Cleveland Coxe
Hallowe'en, a Romaunt, with Lays Meditative and Devotional, 1844

370
Once to Every Man and Nation

A. The Present Crisis

When a deed is done for freedom, through the
    broad earth's aching breast
runs a thrill of joy prophetic, trembling on from
    east to west,
and the slave, where'er he cowers, feels the soul
    within him climb
to the awful verge of manhood, as the energy
    sublime
of a century bursts full-blossomed on the thorny
    stem of time.

Through the walls of hut and palace shoots the
    instantaneous throe,
when the travail of the ages wrings earth's systems
    to and fro;
at the birth of each new era, with a recognizing
    start,
nation wildly looks at nation, standing with mute
    lips apart,
and glad truth's yet mightier man-child leaps
    beneath the future's heart.

So the evil's triumph sendeth, with a terror and a
    chill,
under continent to continent the sense of coming
    ill,
and the slave, where'er he cowers, feels his
    sympathies with God
in hot teardrops ebbing earthward, to be drunk up
    by the sod,
till a corpse crawls round unburied, delving in the
    nobler clod.

For mankind are one in spirit, and an instinct
    bears along,
round the earth's electric circle, the swift flash of
    right or wrong;
whether conscious or unconscious, yet humanity's
    vast frame
through its ocean-sundered fibers feels the gush of
    joy or shame;—
in the gain or loss of one race all the rest have
    equal claim.

*Once to every man and nation comes the
    moment to decide,
*in the strife of truth with falsehood, for the good
    or evil side;
*some great cause, God's new Messiah, offering
    each the bloom or blight,
parts the goats upon the left hand, and the sheep
    upon the right,
*and the choice goes by for ever 'twixt that darkness
    and that light.

Hast thou chosen, O my people, on whose party
    thou shalt stand,
ere the doom from its worn sandals shakes the
    dust against our land:
*Though the cause of evil prosper, yet 'tis truth
    alone is strong,
and, albeit she wander outcast now, I see around
    her throng
troops of beautiful, tall angels, to enshield her
    from all wrong.

Backward look across the ages and the beacon-
    moments see,
that, like peaks of some sunk continent, jut
    through oblivion's sea;
not an ear in court or market for the low fore-
    boding cry
of those crises, God's stern winnowers, from
    whose feet earth's chaff must fly;
never shows the choice momentous till the
    judgment hath passed by.

Careless seems the great Avenger; history's pages
    but record
one death-grapple in the darkness 'twixt old
    systems and the Word;
* truth forever on the scaffold, wrong for ever on
    the throne,—
* yet that scaffold sways the future, and, behind the
    dim unknown,
* standeth God within the shadow, keeping watch
    above his own.

We see dimly in the present what is small and
    what is great,
slow of faith how weak an arm may turn the iron
    helm of fate,
but the soul is still oracular; amid the market's
    din,
list the ominous stern whisper from the Delphic
    cave within,—
"They enslave their children's children who make
    compromise with sin."

Slavery, the earthborn cyclops, fellest of the giant
    brood,
sons of brutish force and darkness, who have
    drenched the earth with blood,
famished in his self-made desert, blinded by our
    purer day,
gropes in yet unblasted regions for his miserable
    prey;—
shall we guide his gory fingers where our helpless
    children play?

* Then to side with truth is noble when we share
    her wretched crust,
* ere her cause bring fame and profit, and 'tis
    prosperous to be just;
* then it is the brave man chooses, while the
    coward stands aside,
doubting in his abject spirit, till his Lord is
    crucified,
* and the multitude make virtue of the faith they
    had denied.

Count me o'er earth's chosen heroes,—they were
    souls that stood alone,
while the men they agonized for hurled the
    contumelious stone,
stood serene, and down the future saw the golden
    beam incline
to the side of perfect justice, mastered by their
    faith divine,
by one man's plain truth to manhood and to
    God's supreme design.

* By the light of burning heretics Christ's bleeding
    feet I track,
* toiling up new Calvaries ever with the cross that
    turns not back,
and these mounts of anguish number how each
    generation learned
one new word of that grand credo which in
    prophet-hearts hath burned
since the first man stood God-conquered with his
    face to heaven upturned.

For humanity sweeps onward: where today the
    martyr stands,
on the morrow crouches Judas with the silver in
    his hands;
far in front the cross stands ready and the crackling
    fagots burn,
while the hooting mob of yesterday in silent awe
    return
to glean up the scattered ashes into history's
    golden urn.

'Tis as easy to be heroes as to sit the idle slaves of
    a legendary virtue carved upon our
    fathers' graves,
worshipers of light ancestral make the present
    light a crime;——
was the Mayflower launched by cowards, steered
    by men behind their time?
Turn those tracks toward past or future, that make
    Plymouth Rock sublime?

They were men of present valor, stalwart old
    iconoclasts,
unconvinced by axe or gibbet that all virtue was
    the past's;
but we make their truth our falsehood, thinking
    that hath made us free,
hoarding it in moldy parchments, while our
    tender spirits flee
the rude grasp of that great impulse which drove
    them across the sea.

They have rights who dare maintain them; we are
    traitors to our sires,
smothering in their holy ashes freedom's new-lit
    altar-fires;
shall we make their creed our jailer? Shall we, in
    our haste to slay,
from the tombs of the old prophets steal the
    funeral lamps away
to light up the martyr-fagots round the prophets
    of today?

*New occasions teach new duties; time makes
    ancient good uncouth;
*they must upward still, and onward, who would
    keep abreast of truth;
lo, before us gleam her campfires! We ourselves
    must Pilgrims be,
launch our Mayflower, and steer boldly through
    the desperate winter sea,
nor attempt the future's portal with the past's
    blood-rusted key.

James Russell Lowell
Boston Courier, December 11, 1845

B. The hymn devised by Horder

Once to every man and nation
    comes the moment to decide,
in the strife of truth with falsehood,
    for the good or evil side;
some great cause, God's new Messiah,
    off'ring each the bloom or blight,—
and the choice goes by for ever
    'twixt that darkness and that light.

Then to side with truth is noble,
    when we share her wretched crust,
ere her cause bring fame and profit
    and 'tis prosperous to be just;
then it is the brave man chooses,
    while the coward stands aside,
till the multitude make virtue
    of the faith they had denied.

By the light of burning martyrs,
    Jesus' bleeding feet I track,
toiling up new Calvaries ever
    with the cross that turns not back;
new occasions teach new duties;
    time makes ancient good uncouth;
they must upward still and onward
    who would keep abreast of truth.

Though the cause of evil prosper
    yet 'tis truth alone is strong;
though her portion be the scaffold
    and upon the throne be wrong,
yet that scaffold sways the future,
    and behind the dim unknown,
standeth God within the shadow,
    keeping watch above his own.

W. Garrett Horder
Hymns Supplemental to Existing Collections, 1894
using the lines marked by asterisks in Lowell's poem

371
Epiphany

"What means this glory round our feet,"
    the magi mused, "more bright than morn?"
And voices chanted clear and sweet,
    "Today the Prince of Peace is born."

"What means that star," the shepherds said,
    "that brightens through the rocky glen?"
And angels answering overhead
    sang, "Peace on earth, good will to men."

'Tis eighteen hundred years and more
    since those sweet oracles were dumb;
we wait for him, like them of yore;
    alas! he seems so slow to come.

But it was said in words of gold,
    no time or sorrow e'er shall dim,
that little children might be bold,
    in perfect trust to come to him.   (Mark 10:14)

All round about our feet shall shine
    a light like that the wise man saw,
if we our willing hearts incline
    to that sweet life which is the law.

So shall we learn to understand
    the simple faith of shepherds then,
and, kindly clasping hand in hand,
    sing, "Peace on earth, good will to men."

For they who to their childhood cling,
    and keep their natures fresh as morn
once more shall hear the angels sing,
    "Today the Prince of Peace is born."

James Russell Lowell
Songs of the Sanctuary, 1865

372
Who Hearest Prayer

No human eyes thy face may see;   (Exod. 33:20)
    no human thought thy form may know;
but all creation dwells in thee,
    and thy great life through all doth flow!

And yet, O strange and wondrous thought!—
    thou art a God who hearest prayer   (Ps. 65:2)
and every heart with sorrow fraught
    to seek thy present aid may dare.

And though most weak our efforts seem
    into one creed these thoughts to bind,
and vain the intellectual dream
    to see and know th' Eternal Mind;

yet thou wilt not turn them aside
    who cannot solve thy life divine,
but would give up all reason's pride
    to know their hearts approved by thine.

So though we faint on life's dark hill,
    and thought grow weak and knowledge flee,
yet faith shall teach us courage still,
    and love shall guide us on to thee.

Thomas Wentworth Higginson
A Book of Hymns for Public and Private Devotion, 1846

373
It Came upon the Midnight Clear

It came upon the midnight clear,
    that glorious song of old,
from angels bending near the earth
    to touch their harps of gold—
"Peace on the earth, good will to men   (Luke 2:15)
    from heaven's all gracious King."
The world in solemn stillness lay
    to hear the angels sing.

Still through the cloven skies they come,
    with heavenly wing unfurled,
and still their heavenly music floats
    o'er all the weary world;
above its sad and lonely plains
    they bend on hovering wing,
and ever o'er its Babel-sounds   (Gen. 11:1ff)
    the blessed angels sing.

Yet, with the woes of sin and strife
    the world has suffered long;
beneath the angel-strain have rolled
    two thousand years of wrong;
and man, at war with man, hears not
    the love song which they bring:
O hush the noise, ye men of strife,
    and hear the angels sing!

And ye, beneath life's crushing load,
    whose forms are bending low,
who toil along the climbing way
    with painful steps and slow,—
look now, for glad and golden hours
    come swiftly on the wing:
O rest beside the weary road,
    and hear the angels sing!

For lo! the days are hastening on
    by prophet bards foretold   (Virgil, *Eclogue IV*)
when with the ever-circling years
    comes round the age of gold:
when peace shall over all the earth
    her ancient splendors fling,
and the whole world give back the song
    which now the angels sing.

Edmund Hamilton Sears
The Christian Register, December 29, 1849

374
Cana

Dear Friend, whose presence in the house,
    whose gracious word benign,
could once, at Cana's wedding feast
    turn water into wine,   (John 2:1–11)

come, visit us, and when dull work
    grows weary, line on line,   (Isa. 28:10)
revive our souls, and make us see
    life's water turn to wine.

Gay mirth shall deepen into joy,
    earth's hope shall grow divine
when Jesus visits us, to turn
    life's water into wine.

The social talk, the evening fire,
    the homely household shrine,
shall glow with angel visits when
    the Lord pours out the wine.

For when self-seeking turns to love,
    which knows not mine and thine,
the miracle again is wrought,
    and water changed to wine.

James Freeman Clarke
Lyra Sacra Americana, 1855

375
A Sunday Hymn

Lord of all being, throned afar,
thy glory flames from sun and star
center and soul of every sphere,
yet to each loving heart how near;

sun of our life, thy quickening ray
sheds on our path the glow of day;
star of our hope, thy softened light
cheers the long watches of the night.

Our midnight is thy smile withdrawn,
our noontide is thy gracious dawn,
our rainbow arch, thy mercy's sign;   (Gen. 8:22)
all, save the clouds of sin, are thine.

Lord of all life, below, above,
whose light is truth, whose warmth is love,
before thy ever-blazing throne
we ask no luster of our own.

Grant us thy truth to make us free   (John 8:32)
and kindling hearts that burn for thee,
till all thy living altars claim
one holy light, one heavenly flame.

Oliver Wendell Holmes, 1848
The Atlantic Monthly, December 1859

The first publication of this text came at the end of one of his "Professor at the Breakfast Table" essays, preceded by these words:

Peace be to all such as may have been vexed in spirit by any utterance the pages may have repeated! They will doubtless forget for the moment the difference in the hues of truth we look at through our human prisms, and join in singing (inwardly) this hymn to the Source of light we all need to lead us, and the warmth which alone can make us brothers.

376
The Battle Hymn of the Republic

Mine eyes have seen the glory of the coming of the
                                                    Lord;
he is trampling out the vintage where the grapes of
                                        wrath are stored (Isa. 63:3)
he hath loosed the fateful lightning of his terrible
                                                    swift sword:
            His truth is marching on.

I have seen him in the watch fires of a hundred
                                            circling camps;
they have builded him an altar in the evening dews
                                                and damps;
I have read his righteous sentence in the dim and
                                                flaring lamps;
            his day is marching on.

I have read a fiery gospel, writ in burnished rows of
                                                    steel;
As ye deal with my contemners, so with you my
                                            grace shall deal:
Let the hero born of woman crush the serpent with
                                    his heel; (Gen. 3:15)
            our God is marching on.

He has sounded forth the trumpet that shall never
                                            call retreat;
he is sifting out the hearts of men before his
                                            judgment seat;
O be swift, my soul, to answer him, be jubilant, my
                                                    feet:
            Our God is marching on.

In the beauty of the lilies Christ was born across
                                                the sea
with a glory in his bosom that transfigures you and
                                                    me;
as he died to make men holy, let us die to make
                                                men free:
            Our God is marching on.

He is coming like the glory of the morning on the
                                        wave, (Hos. 6:3)
he is wisdom to the mighty, he is succor to the
                                                    brave;
so the world shall be his footstool, and the soul of
                                                time his slave:
            Our God is marching on.

Julia Ward Howe, 1861
The Atlantic Monthly, February 1862
The authenticity of the final stanza is disputed.

377
Looking to God

I look to thee in every need,
    and never look in vain;
I feel thy strong and tender love
    and all is well again:
The thought of thee is mightier far
than sin and pain and sorrow are.

Discouraged in the work of life,
    disheartened by its load,
shamed by its failures and its fears,
    I sink beside the road;
but let me only think of thee,
and then new heart springs up in me.

Thy calmness bends serene above,
    my restlessness to still;
around me flows thy quickening life,
    to nerve my faltering will;
thy presence fills my solitude;
thy providence turns all to good.

Embosomed deep in thy dear love,
    held in thy law, I stand;
thy hand in all things I behold,
    and all things in thy hand;
thou leadest me by unsought ways,
and turnst my mourning into praise.   (Ps. 30:11)

Samuel Longfellow
Hymns of the Spirit, 1864

378
Inspiration

Life of ages, richly poured,
    love of God, unspent and free,
flowing in the prophet's word
    and the people's liberty!

Never was to chosen race
    that unstinted tide confined;
thine is every time and place,
    fountain sweet of heart and mind!

Secret of the morning stars,
    motion of the oldest hours,
pledge through elemental wars
    of the coming spirit's powers!

Rolling planet, flaming sun,
    stand in nobler man complete;
prescient laws thine errands run,
    frame the shrine for Godhead meet.

Homeward led, the wondering eye
    upward yearned in joy or awe,
found the love that waited nigh,
    guidance of thy guardian law.

In the touch of earth it thrilled;
    down from mystic skies it burned;
right obeyed and passion stilled
    its eternal gladness earned.

Breathing in the thinker's creed,
    pulsing in the hero's blood,
nerving simplest thought and deed,
    freshening time with truth and good,

consecrating art and song,
    holy book and pilgrim track,
hurling floods of tyrant wrong
    from the sacred limits back—

Life of ages, richly poured,
    love of God, unspent and free,
flow still in the prophet's word,
    and the people's liberty!

Samuel Johnson
Hymns of the Spirit, 1864

379
The Church, the City of God

City of God, how broad and far
    outspread thy walls sublime!
The true thy chartered freemen are
    of every age and clime.

One holy church, one army strong,
    one steadfast high intent,
one working band, one harvest song.
    One King omnipotent!

How purely hath thy speech come down
    from man's primeval youth!
How grandly hath thine empire grown
    of freedom, love, and truth!

How gleam thy watch fires through the night
    with never-fainting ray!
How rise thy towers, serene and bright
    to greet the dawning day!

In vain the surges' angry shock,
    in vain the drifting sands;
unharmed upon the eternal Rock,
    the eternal City stands.

Samuel Johnson
Hymns of the Spirit, 1864

380
The Spirit of Truth

Thou, long disowned, reviled, oppressed,
    strange friend of humankind,
seeking through weary years a rest
    within our hearts to find;

how late thy bright and awful brow
    breaks through these clouds of sin!
Hail, Truth Divine! we know thee now;
    Angel of God, come in!

Come, though with purifying fire
    and desolating sword,
thou of all nations the desire!   (Hag. 2:4)
    Earth waits thy cleansing word.

Struck by the lightning of thy glance,
    let old oppressions die;
before thy cloudless countenance
    let fear and falsehood fly.

Anoint our eyes with healing grace   (Rev. 3:18)
    to see, as ne'er before,
our Father in our brother's face,
    our Maker in his poor.

Flood our dark life with golden day;
    convince, subdue, enthrall;
then to a mightier yield thy sway,
    and Love be all in all.

Eliza Scudder
Hymns of the Spirit, 1864

381
We Would Be One

Eternal Ruler of the ceaseless round
    of circling planets singing on their way,
Guide of the nations from the night profound
    into the glory of the perfect day;
rule in our hearts, that we may ever be
guided, and strengthened, and upheld by thee.

We are of thee, the children of thy love,
    the brothers of thy well-beloved Son;
descend, O Holy Spirit, like a dove.
    into our hearts, that we may be as one,—
as one with thee, to whom we ever tend;
as one with him, our Brother and our Friend.

We would be one in hatred of all wrong,
    one in the love of all things sweet and fair,
one with the joy that breaketh into song,
    one with the grief that trembles into prayer,
one in the power that makes thy children free
to follow truth, and thus to follow thee.

O clothe us with thy heavenly armor, Lord— (Eph. 6:10)
    thy trusty shield, thy sword of love divine;
our inspirations be thy constant word,
    we ask no victories that are not thine.
Give or withhold, let pain or pleasure be:
enough to know that we are serving thee.

> John White Chadwick, 1864
> *Singers and Songs of the Liberal Church*, 1875
> first as a hymn in *Congregational Hymns*, 1884

382
A Prayer for Guidance

Lead us, O Father, in the paths of peace; (Luke 1:79)
    without thy guiding hand we go astray,
and doubts appall, and sorrows still increase;
    lead us through Christ, the true and living Way.

Lead us, O Father, in the paths of truth;
    unhelped by thee, in error's maze we grope,
while passion stains and folly dims our youth,
    and age comes on uncheered by faith and hope.

Lead us, O Father, in the paths of right;
    blindly we stumble when we walk alone,
involved in shadows of a darksome night,
    only with thee we journey safely on.

Lead us, O Father, to thy heavenly rest,
    however rough and steep the path may be.
through joy or sorrow, as thou deemest best,
    until our lives are perfected in thee.

> William Henry Burleigh
> *The New Congregational Hymn Book*, 1859

383
O Little Town of Bethlehem

O little town of Bethlehem,
    how still we see thee lie!
above thy deep and dreamless sleep
    the silent stars go by.
Yet in thy dark streets shineth
    the everlasting light;
the hopes and fears of all the years
    are met in thee tonight.

For Christ is born of Mary;
    and gathered all above,
while mortals sleep the angels keep
    their watch of wondering love.
O morning stars together
    proclaim the holy birth!
and praises sing to Christ the King,
    and peace to men on earth.

How silently, how silently
    the wondrous gift is given;
so God imparts to human hearts
    the blessings of his heaven.
No ear may hear his coming;
    but in this world of sin,
where meek hearts will receive him still,
    the dear Christ enters in.

Where children pure and happy
     pray to the blessed Child,
where misery cries out to thee,
     son of the undefiled;
where charity stands watching
     and faith holds wide the door,
the dark night wakes, the glory breaks,
     and Christmas comes once more.

O holy Child of Bethlehem,
     descend on us, we pray;
cast out our sin, and enter in,
     be born in us today.
We hear the Christmas angels
     the great glad tidings tell;
O come to us, abide with us,
     our Lord, Immanuel.

Phillips Brooks, 1868

The Church Porch, 1874

Line 4:4 was subsequently changed by Brooks to
"son of the mother mild."

384
Christ for the World, and the World for Christ

Christ for the world, we sing!
the world to Christ we bring
     with loving zeal;
the poor and them that mourn,
the faint and overborne,
sin-sick and sorrow-worn,
     whom Christ doth heal.

Christ for the world, we sing!
The world to Christ we bring
     with fervent prayer;
the wayward and the lost,
by restless passions tossed,
redeemed at countless cost
     from dark despair.

Christ for the world we sing!
the world to Christ we bring
     with one accord;
with us the work to share,
with us reproach to dare,
with us the cross to bear
     for Christ our Lord.

Christ for the world we sing!
the world to Christ we bring
     with joyful song;
the newborn souls, whose days
reclaimed from error's ways,
inspired with hope and praise,
     to Christ belong.

Samuel Wolcott, 1869

Song Garland, or Singing for Jesus, 1869

385
Centennial Hymn

God of our fathers, whose almighty hand
leads forth in beauty all the starry band
of shining worlds in splendor through the skies,
our grateful songs before thy throne arise.

Thy love divine hath led us in the past:
In this free land by thee our lot is cast;
be thou our Ruler, Guardian, Guide, and Stay;
thy word our law, thy paths our chosen way.

From war's alarms, from deadly pestilence,
be thy strong arm our ever sure defense;
thy true religion in our hearts increase,
thy bounteous goodness nourish us in peace.

Refresh thy people on their toilsome way,
lead us from night to never-ending day;
fill all our lives with love and grace divine,
and glory, laud, and praise be ever thine.

Daniel Crane Roberts, 1876

The Hymnal, 1892

386
Break Thou the Bread of Life

Break thou the bread of life,
    dear Lord, to me,
as thou didst break the loaves
    beside the sea;
beyond the sacred page
    I seek thee, Lord;
my spirit longs for thee,
    O living Word.

Bless thou the truth, dear Lord,
    to me, to me,
as thou didst bless the bread
    by Galilee;
then shall all bondage cease,
    all fetters fall;
and I shall find my peace,
    my All in All.

Mary Artemisia Lathbury, 1877
The Chautauqua Carols, 1877

387
The Larger Faith

We pray no more, made lowly wise,
    for miracle and sign;
anoint our eyes to see within
    the common, the divine.

"Lo, here, lo there," no more we cry   (Matt. 24:23)
    dividing with our call
the mantle of thy presence, Lord,
    that seamless covers all.

We turn from seeking thee afar
    and in unwonted ways,
to build from out our daily lives
    the temples of thy praise.

And if thy casual comings, Lord,
    to hearts of old were dear,
what joy shall dwell within the faith
    that feels thee ever near!

And nobler yet shall duty grow,
    and more shall worship be,
when thou art found in all our life,
    and all our life in thee.

Frederick Lucian Hosmer, 1879
The Christian Register, March 22, 1879

388
The Day of God

"Thy kingdom come," on bended knee
    the passing ages pray;
and faithful souls have yearned to see
    on earth that kingdom's day.

But the slow watches of the night
    not less to God belong,
and for the everlasting right
    the silent stars are strong.

And lo! already on the hills
    the flags of dawn appear;
gird up your loins, ye prophet souls,
    proclaim the day is near;

the day in whose clear-shining light
    all wrong shall stand revealed,
when justice shall be clothed with might,
    and every hurt be healed;

when knowledge, hand in hand with peace   (Ps. 85:12)
    shall walk the earth abroad—
the day of perfect righteousness,
    the promised day of God.

Frederick Lucian Hosmer, 1891
The Thought of God in Hymns and Poems, 2nd series, 1894

389
Ancient of Days

Ancient of Days, who sittest throned in glory,
    to thee all knees are bent, all voices pray; (Dan. 7:9)
thy love has blest the wide world's wondrous story
    with light and life since Eden's dawning day.

O holy Father, who hast led thy children
    in all the ages, with the fire and cloud, (Exod. 40:38)
through seas dry-shod and weary wastes bewild'ring;
    to thee, in reverent love our hearts are bowed.

O holy Jesus, Prince of Peace and Savior,
    to thee we owe the peace that still prevails,
stilling the rude wills of men's wild behavior,
    and calming passion's fierce and stormy gales.

O Holy Ghost, the Lord and the Life-giver,
    thine is the quickening power that still prevails,
from thee have flowed, as from a pleasant river,
    our plenty, wealth, prosperity, and peace.

O Triune God, with heart and voice adoring,
    praise we the goodness that doth crown our days;
pray we that thou wilt hear us, still imploring
    thy love and favor, kept to us always.

        William Croswell Doane, 1886; revised, 1892
        Hymnal, 1892

Chapter 19:
Black and White Spirituals and Gospel Songs (390–408)

Very little commentary is needed on these three groups of regional or sectional hymnody peculiar to America. They all have this in common: They depend far more on their music than on their texts for their effect. Less than any other of the material in this collection can they be read without musical association.

For the elements of the history of Black Spirituals, see the *Hymnal Guide* entry on "Go, tell it on the mountain," and for ampler and more authoritative information, *120 Negro Spirituals*, by Alexander Sandilands. Essentially they are the songs of the black people who were brought to America originally from Africa as slaves; the Kentucky revivals at the end of the eighteenth century did much to begin to form them into a religious community and to appeal to the instincts which their condition had sought to suppress. We here give only a few texts which seem to be representative of the character of these haunting songs. They are, broadly speaking, (a) scriptural, with a strong emphasis on the liberation of the Exodus (390–391); (b) strongly heaven-centered, as the songs of people in such dismal earthly circumstances well might be (392); (c) full of appeal to the Savior as comforter of sufferings (393); (d) evangelically crucifixion-centered (394); (e) very simply didactic (395–396); or (f) hopeful and nursery-rhyme-like (397–398). Almost always they had refrains, as was appropriate to songs for people who were largely illiterate, and they were always vivid, often conversational and even humorous, in their language. Usually they were songs of desperate courage, and often they had an educational slant to give a hopeful pattern to life and to make simple the stories of the Scriptures for the comfort of the slaves.

The use of such songs as these as hymns in the worship of congregations not racially or socially subject to the conditions that generated them is a fairly recent development and is, as much as anything, a gesture of solidarity. Sometimes—though not in the examples here given—the texts are written in a dialect which is really a "white" transcription of the pronunciation customary among blacks from the southern states. And of course more modern songs, like "O, Freedom," have been written in the style of the "black classics." But they remain a regional and subcultural form of hymnody whose simple words and music make it perhaps the most powerful section of pure folk song—material sung before being written down—in the whole literature.

Tunes and texts remain together, and there are hardly any instances at all of a "black" tune being set to a "white" text. The most famous exception is the "black" tune MCKEE, now often sung to "In Christ there is no East nor West."

The White Spiritual is so called by analogy with the more primitive Black Spiritual, but it is something quite different. This is a generic name sometimes given to the hymnody of the white settlers in the so-called southern states (that expression really means the old slave states), lying either side of the southern Appalachians. This hymnody mostly used texts from evangelical English sources: Isaac Watts most frequently, Charles Wesley sometimes, Toplady and Newton occasionally. Through social and historical accidents, it was known, until recently, only to those communities that lay in that part of the United States, and its special quality is not in its texts but in its music. Certain tunes have now escaped from that closed environment and found their way all over America, one or two, like the tune of "Amazing grace" (whose words are from the *Olney Hymns*, 1779), all over the world. These tunes are actually in the idiom of the Scottish, Welsh, and Irish folk music of the eighteenth century, when they are not modeled on the evangelical fuguing tunes used by the Methodists—and disapproved by Wesley—from about 1770 onwards.

The communities that use this music are still exceedingly remote, inbred, mentally conservative, rather antieducational, and primitive in their religious customs. They devote themselves to agriculture, being the descendants of those British settlers who entered North Carolina and slowly thrust their way through the forests and over the highest range of the Appalachians, which reaches 6,000 feet in several places and is thickly forested to the summit, into Tennessee and Kentucky. They were not slave owners—they had not the affluence nor stability for that. They were rude pioneers whose behavior to the Indians in the early stages has been matched in later years, their successors claim without much accuracy, by the brutality of the strip-mining industrialists to them. In Tennessee they still gather for immense hymn-singing marathons, using hymnals that are reprinted without alteration from original editions a hundred and more years old. They sing in a strange nasal style from music books set out in "shape note" characters, a device that in the United States corresponds to the British sol-fa system as an assistance to easy music reading—and in fact is a great deal better. Their solid conservatism and resistance to change very naturally extinguishes any need for new hymnody, and one rarely finds a native text. When one does, it is distinguished from the Black Spiritual and the Gospel Song by hardly ever having a chorus, for these people could read, and could read music. But when the tune is of the "English," rather than of the other British kinds, you often find endless repetitions of words in a Common Meter stanza to accommodate it, and everything in these fascinating old books, which remain monolithically unchangeable in type and temperament, suggests that these songs, for these people, are the whole of their aesthetic culture; they are their drama, their poetry, their symphonies, their pop music. The music itself, having come into their culture from the main stream of British hymnody and folk song, ran back naturally into the wider culture as soon as it was rediscovered, to the enrichment of everybody concerned. But when sung by people elsewhere in

the world it sounds entirely different from what one hears in one of these tiny, primitive, southern churches or at one of their marathon united hymn-singing festivals on a summer night in the countryside.

The Gospel Song (402–408) is the third native contribution of Americans to the treasury of hymnody, and it has something in common with both the Black Spiritual and the White Spiritual. It has the simplicity, the repetitiveness, and the addiction to refrains of the black song, since it is largely aimed at those who cannot read, or do not propose to. It has the obsessive, ingrown, and entirely petrified character of the White Spiritual in that it never changes its style, as we can easily demonstrate by presenting songs of this kind ranging over a period of almost a century.

Like the black songs, it is atonement-centered and often didactic, but the only human suffering it knows about is the supposed suffering of the sinner. It is the music of an uncomplicated activist religion that has little time for subtleties, doubts, or speculations and is the reverse of contemplative. A hint was thrown out when we passed 313 of an affinity between this style and that of children's hymns—and indeed there is a ministry to immaturity for which these songs were originally designed. They became known on both sides of the Atlantic through the missions of Moody and Sankey from 1870 onwards and also through the famous traveling choir, the Jubilee Singers from the (black) Fisk University in Nashville, Tennessee. Their repetitiveness and their very limited vocabulary, nicely combining a very narrow range of words and expressions with just enough theological technicality ("blood," "the Lamb") to attract the uninitiated, made them an ideal vehicle for mass-mission in the industrial parts of both our countries. The music matched, in its unchanging, repetitive, and uncomplicated style, the set of the words.

It was, one need hardly say, very easy to write such lyrics as these. Fanny Crosby (Mrs. Frances Jane van Alstyne) is said to have composed more lyrics than Charles Wesley, but it is hardly unfair to say that when you have seen one you have seen them all (403). Ira D. Sankey, the evangelistic singer, composed relatively few, and his style had a certain homespun innocence that often avoided sheer platitude; his associate, P. P. Bliss (404), was more prolific and less inventive. The early international success of these songs distinguishes them totally from the spirituals. In all the decades that followed their first appearance, they have appealed to many and have had such success that nobody has seriously considered any adaptation of their message to changing situations. They therefore have their special place among those religious groups which see the Gospel as a static, unchanging body of truth to which everybody is, in their special language, invited to come. The one variation on the strictly "Gospel" aspect of these songs turns out to be a naturalistic sentimentality which can plumb alarming depths (406), and it is depressingly true that the integrity of both the Black Spiritual and the Gospel Song has been dangerously compromised by a textual—and far more a musical—concession to the worst of commercialized bad taste. It is no bad exercise to look over the handful of such songs that was admitted to *The English Hymnal* and consider on what grounds the highly sensitive editors of that book thought these the best examples; the ground will be found to be, on the whole, sound. *Hymns Ancient and Modern*, England's monument of hymnic propriety, only ever admitted one such song, our 402, and it disappeared in 1950.

390
Go Down, Moses

When Israel was in Egypt's land,
   Let my people go!
oppressed so hard they could not stand.
   Let my people go!

Go down, Moses,
   way down in Egypt land,
   tell old Pharaoh:
   "Let my people go!"

No more shall they in bondage toil;
let them come out with Egypt's spoil.

Oh, 'twas a dark and dismal night,
when Moses led the Israelites.

The Lord told Moses what to do,
to lead the children of Israel through

"O come along, Moses, you'll not get lost."
"Stretch out your rod and come across."

And when they reached the other shore,
they sang a song of triumph o'er.

Pharaoh said he would go across,
but Pharaoh and his host were lost.

O let us all from bondage flee,
and let us all in Christ be free.

oral tradition, based on Exodus 7:1–15, 19

391
Deep River

Deep river,
   my home is over Jordan,
Deep river,
   Lord, I want to cross over into campground.

Oh, don't you want to go to that Gospel feast,
that promised land where all is peace?
Oh, deep river, Lord,
   I want to cross over into campground.

oral tradition, based on Deuteronomy 11:31

392
Swing Low, Sweet Chariot

Swing low, sweet chariot,
    coming for to carry me home!
Swing low, sweet chariot,
    coming for to carry me home!

I looked over Jordan, and what did I see,
    coming for to carry me home?
A band of angels coming after me,
    coming for to carry me home.

If you get there before I do,
tell all my friends I'm coming too.

The brightest day that ever I saw,
when Jesus washed my sins away.

I'm sometimes up and sometimes down,
but still my soul feels heavenly bound.

oral traditional, based on 2 Kings 2:11

393
Nobody Knows the Trouble I See

Nobody knows the trouble I see, Lord,
    nobody knows the trouble I see,
nobody knows the trouble I see, Lord,
    nobody knows like Jesus.

Brothers, will you pray for me,
brothers, will you pray for me,
brothers, will you pray for me
    and help me to drive old Satan away?

Sisters, will you pray for me?

Mothers, will you pray for me?

Preachers, will you pray for me?

oral tradition, based on Revelation 2:2, 9 and 1 Thessalonians 5:25
Some versions give "I've seen" for "I see."

394
Were You There

Were you there when they crucified my Lord?
Were you there when they crucified my Lord?
Oh, sometimes it causes me to tremble, tremble,
                             tremble,
Were you there when they crucified my Lord?

Were you there when they nailed him to the tree?

Were you there when they pierced him in the side?

Were you there when the sun refused to shine?

Were you there when they laid him in the tomb?

Were you there when he rose up from the dead?

oral tradition, based on Matthew 27:32–61

395
Going to Write to Master Jesus

Going to write to Master Jesus,
    to send some valiant soldiers,
to turn back Pharaoh's army, hallelu!
to turn back Pharaoh's army, hallelujah!
to turn back Pharaoh's army, hallelu!

If you want your souls converted,
you'd better be a-praying.

When the children were in bondage,
they cried unto the Lord.

You say you are a soldier,
fighting for your Savior.

oral tradition, based on Exodus 14:10 and Deuteronomy 26:7

396
Walk You in the Light

Walk you in the light,
walk you in the light,
walk you in the light,
walking in the light of God.

O children, do you think it's true?
walking in the light of God,
that Jesus Christ did die for you?
walking in the light of God?

I think I heard some children say,
that they never heard their parents pray:

O parents, that is not the way,
but teach your children to watch and pray.

I love to shout and I love to sing,
I love to praise my heavenly King.

O sisters, can't you help me sing,
for Moses' sister did help him.

oral tradition, based on John 12:35 and Exodus 15:20ff
Some versions give the repeating phrase as
"We are walking in the light."

397
We Are Climbing Jacob's Ladder

We are climbing Jacob's ladder,
we are climbing Jacob's ladder,
we are climbing Jacob's ladder,
soldiers of the cross.

Every round goes higher, higher.

Sinner, do you love my Jesus?

If you love him, why not serve him?

Do you think I'd make a soldier?

We are climbing higher, higher.

oral tradition, based on Genesis 28:12

398
Let Us Break Bread Together on Our Knees

Let us break bread together on our knees,
let us break bread together on our knees.
When I fall on my knees
with my face to the rising sun,
O Lord, have mercy on me.

Let us drink wine together on our knees,

Let us praise God together on our knees,

oral tradition, based on Acts 20:7 and 1 Corinthians 11:23ff

399
What Wondrous Love Is This

What wondrous love is this,
O my soul!
What wondrous love is this
that caused the Lord of bliss
to send this precious peace
to my soul!

When I was sinking down,
sinking down;
when I was sinking down
beneath God's righteous frown,
Christ laid aside his crown
for my soul!

Ye winged seraphs, fly,
  bear the news.
Ye winged seraphs, fly
like comets through the sky,
Fill vast eternity
  with the news!

Ye friends of Zion's King,
  join his praise;
ye friends of Zion's King,
with hearts and voices sing,
and strike each tuneful string
  in his praise!

To God and to the Lamb
  I will sing;
to God and to the Lamb,
who is the great I AM,
while millions join the theme,
  I will sing!

And while from death I'm free,
  I'll sing on;
and while from death I'm free,
I'll sing and joyful be,
and through eternity
  I'll sing on.

anonymous
A General Selection of the Newest and Most Admired Hymns and Spiritual Songs Now in Use (Stith Mead), 2nd edition, 1811

The text appeared the same year in *A Selection of Hymns and Spiritual Songs from the Best Authors* (Starke Dupuy). Dupuy's version differs in these lines: 1:5, "to bear the dreadful curse"; 4:1–2, "Ye sons of Zion's King, join the praise"; and 5:4. "and to the great I AM"; 6:1, "And when from death I'm free." Dupuy also reverses the order of stanzas 4 and 5, and adds this final stanza:

And when to that bright world
  we arrive,
when to that world we go,
free from all pain and woe,
we'll join the happy throng,
  and sing on.

400
The Wicked Kingdom

See how the wicked kingdom
  is falling every day!
and still our blessed Jesus
  is winning souls away:
But, oh, how I am tempted,
  no mortal tongue can tell!
So often I'm surrounded
  with enemies from hell.

With weeping and with praying,
  my Jesus I have found
to crucify old nature,
  and make his grace abound.
Dear children, don't be weary,
  but march on in the way;
for Jesus will stand by you,
  and be your guard and stay.

If sinners will serve Satan,
  and join with one accord,
dear brethren, as for my part,
  I'm bound to serve the Lord;
and if you will go with me,
  pray give to me your hand,
and we'll march on together,
  unto the promised land.

Through troubles and distresses,
  we'll make our way to God;
though earth and hell oppose us,
  we'll keep the heavenly road.
Our Jesus went before us,
  and many sorrows bore,
and we who follow after,
  can never meet with more.

Thou dear to me, my brethren,
    each one of you I find.
My duty now compels me
    to leave you all behind:
But while the parting grieves us,
    I humbly ask your prayers,
to bear me up in trouble,
    and conquer all my fears.

And now, my loving brothers,
    I bid you all farewell!
With you my loving sisters,
    I can no longer dwell.
Farewell to every mourner!
    I hope the Lord you'll find,
to ease you of your burden,
    and give you peace of mind.

Farewell, poor careless sinners!
    I love you dearly well;
I've labored much to bring you
    with Jesus Christ to dwell;
I now am bound to leave you—
    O tell me, will you go?
But if you won't decide it,
    I'll bid you all adieu!

We'll bid farewell to sorrow,
    to sickness, care, and pain,
and mount aloft with Jesus
    forevermore to reign;
we'll join to sing his praises
    above the ethereal blue,
and then, poor careless sinners,
    what will become of you?

anonymous, attributed to *Baptist Harmony*
The Southern Harmony and Musical Companion, 1835

401
Safe in the Promised Land

Where are the Hebrew children?   (Dan. 3)
    Safe in the promised land.
Though the furnace flamed around them,
God, while in their troubles, found them,
he with love and mercy bound them.
    Safe in the promised land.

Where are the twelve apostles?
    Safe in the promised land.
They went up through pain and sighing,
scoffing, scourging, crucifying,
nobly for their Master dying.
    Safe in the promised land.

Where are the holy martyrs?
    Safe in the promised land.
They went up through flaming fire,
trusting in their great Messiah,
who by grace will raise them higher.
    Safe in the promised land.

Where are the holy Christians?
    Safe in the promised land.
Those who've washed their robes and made them
white, and spotless pure, and laid them   (Rev. 7)
where no earthly stain can fade them.
    Safe in the promised land.

attributed to Peter Cartwright
The Sacred Harp, 1844

402
Rescue the Perishing

Rescue the perishing, care for the dying,
    snatch them in pity from sin and the grave;
weep o'er the erring one, lift up the fallen,
    tell them of Jesus the mighty to save.

Rescue the perishing, care for the dying;
Jesus is merciful, Jesus will save.

Though they are slighting him, still he is waiting,
    waiting the penitent child to receive;
plead with them earnestly, plead with them gently,
    he will forgive if they only believe.

Down in the human heart, crushed by the tempter,
    feelings lie buried that grace can restore;
touched by a loving heart, wakened by kindness,
    chords that are broken will vibrate once more.

Rescue the perishing, duty demands it;
    strength for thy labor the Lord will provide;
back to the narrow way, patiently win them;
    tell the poor wand'rer a Savior has died.

Fanny Crosby, 1869
Songs of Devotion, 1870

403
Blessed Assurance

Blessed assurance, Jesus is mine!
Oh, what a foretaste of glory divine!
Heir of salvation, purchase of God,
born of the Spirit, washed in his blood.

    This is my story, this is my song,
    praising my Savior, all the day long;
    this is my story, this is my song,
    praising my Savior all the day long.

Perfect submission, perfect delight,
visions of rapture now burst on my sight:
angels descending bring from above   (John 1:51)
echoes of mercy, whispers of love.

Perfect submission, all is at rest,
I in my Savior am happy and blest;
watching and waiting, looking above,
filled with his goodness, lost in his love.

Fanny Crosby, 1873
Gems of Praise, 1873

404
Whosoever Will

"Whosoever heareth," shout, shout the sound!
spread the blessed tidings all the world around;
tell the joyful news wherever man is found,
    "Whosoever will may come."   (Rev. 22:17)

    "Whosoever will, whosoever will,"
    send the proclamation over vale and hill;
    'Tis a loving Father calls the wand'rer home:
    "Whosoever will may come."

Whosoever cometh need not delay,
now the door is open, enter while you may;
Jesus is the true, the only living Way;
    "Whosoever will may come."

"Whosoever will," the promise is secure;
"whosoever will," for ever must endure;
"Whosoever will!" 'tis life for evermore:
    "Whosoever will may come."

Philip Paul Bliss, 1870
The Prize, 1870

405
There Is Power in the Blood

Would you be free from the burden of sin?
    There's power in the blood, power in the blood;
would you o'er evil a victory win?
    There's wonderful power in the blood.

There is power, power, wonder-working power
    in the blood of the Lamb;
There is power, power, wonder-working power
    in the precious blood of the Lamb.

Would you be free from your passion and pride?
Come for a cleansing to Calvary's side.

Would you be whiter, much whiter than snow? (Isa. 1:18)
Sin stains are lost in its life-giving flow.

Would you do service for Jesus your King?
Would you live daily his praises to sing?

Lewis Edgar Jones
Songs of Praise and Victory, 1899

406
In the Garden

I come to the garden alone,
    while the dew is still on the roses;
and the voice I hear, falling on my ear,
    the Son of God discloses.

    And he walks with me, and he talks with me,
        and he tells me I am his own,
    and the joy we share as we tarry there
        none other has ever known.

He speaks and the sound of his voice
    is so sweet the birds hush their singing;
and the melody that he gave to me
    within my heart is ringing.

I'd stay in the garden with him,
    though the night around me be falling;
but he bids me go; through the voice of woe
    his voice to me is calling.

C. Austin Miles, 1912
The Gospel Message, No. 2, 1912

407
Lord, Lay Some Soul upon My Heart

Lord, lay some soul upon my heart,
    and love that soul through me;
and may I bravely do my part
    to win that soul for thee.

    Some soul for thee, some soul for thee,
        this is my earnest plea;
    help me each day on life's highway
        to win some soul for thee.

Lord, lead me to some soul in sin,
    and grant that I may be
endued with power and love to win
    that soul, dear Lord, for thee.

To win that soul for thee alone
    will be my constant prayer;
that when I've reached the great white throne
    I'll meet that dear one there.

stanza 1, anonymous
stanzas 2 and 3, Mack Weaver and B. B. McKinney, 1939
Broadman Hymnal, 1940
© 1940, 1968, Broadman Press

408
Jesus Is Lord of All

Jesus is Savior and Lord of my life,
    my hope, my glory, my all;
wonderful Master in joy and in strife,
    on him you too may call.

    Jesus is Lord of all,
    Jesus is Lord of all,
    Lord of my thoughts and my service each day.
    Jesus is Lord of all.

Blessed Redeemer, all glorious King,
　　worthy of reverence I pay;
tribute and praises I joyfully bring
　　to him, the Life, the Way.

Will you surrender your all to him now?
　　Follow his will and obey,
crown him as Sovereign, before his throne bow;
　　give him your heart today.

LeRoy McClard, 1966
Songs of Salvation, No. 3, 1966
© 1966, Broadman Press

Chapter 20: Hymns from the Poets (409–448)

If any reader has been reading this book continuously, at this point he will encounter a complete change of pace, something almost like a new start. We are shifted back to England and back to 1600. No poetry anthology would need to put up with any such anomaly; in the history of hymnody it is absolutely inevitable.

More than once we have remarked that great poets, even great lyric poets, are not normally successful hymn writers. That proposition has a positive and a negative sense. Hymn writing, and abundant examples have surely proved it, is a branch of versifying which requires special gifts, special experience, special knowledge. It requires a subordination of many of the poet's natural instincts to the demands of sacred ballad. He cannot do just what he would normally have a right to do with meter, rhyme, and stanza-shape. When one adds to these restrictions the undoubted fact that so much hymn writing has come from people who have a religious experience which their friends would call intense and their enemies narrow or even bigoted, you have adequate explanation of the reason why what we can now call good hymnody is only the tip of an iceberg whose nether parts are nothing but a congealed mass of bad poetry and worse thinking. If one were attempting to compile an anthology of bad and risible hymnody, the temptation to make it ten times the size of this one would be almost overwhelming. There is indeed terrible Watts and terrible Wesley, and ten times more terrible material from people whose names we do not even refer to here. And yet in its upper reaches, as we have tried to show, the restricted art of the hymn writer produces as excellent material for its purpose as the restricted art of the sonnet writer. It was strictly the hymn-writing tradition, and nothing else, that led to "Ride on, ride on in majesty," a hymn by a writer almost all the rest of whose work is not worth mentioning.

If the reader turns back for a moment to chapter 14, right at the end of that article we mentioned Robert Bridges, and the last few hymns in chapter 14 were mentioned as examples of the reaction against mediocre hymnody on the part of men of letters. The contents of this present section are as much the contribution to hymnody of those counter-revolutionaries as of their own writers; for we have collected here a group of forty hymns not one of which was intended by its author to be sung, or—with, I think, less than half a dozen exceptions—ever so sung in its author's lifetime.

Once again our historical principle applies: The use of the work of older lyric poets as hymnody was not invented by Bridges, Percy Dearmer, and Garrett Horder, although they were the most successful promoters of this particular kind of hymnology; the practice in fact goes right back to John Wesley, who included a good deal of George Herbert in his Charlestown hymn book of 1737. But he hardly ever did so without alteration, sometimes so drastic as to make the text unrecognizable. (If anybody ever asked John Wesley how he reconciled this treatment with his very famous passage in the 1780 preface where he remonstrates with people who alter his own and his brother's hymns, did he ever say, "Ah, but that was before my conversion"?) None the less, the way he went beyond the hymnody of his own family and of Watts to enrich his hymnal shows how different his approach to the business was from that of most Evangelicals who followed him.

And here and there one will find poems made into hymns well before 1900. Indeed, to make the picture as clear as possible, we provide the date of the book in which, so far as can be ascertained, the poem did first appear as a hymn (excluding, in the case of George Herbert, the Wesley book because of its drastic alterations). These dates form a code which can be unraveled as follows:

1855: *The New Congregational Hymn Book*
1861: *Hymns Ancient and Modern*, 1st edition

It will at once be seen that *The English Hymnal* and *Songs of Praise* are by far the richest quarries. Indeed, there is far more material from the poets in *Songs of Praise* (1931 edition) than we have given here, since that book, like its remarkable successor, the *Cambridge Hymnal*, 1967 (from a quite different editorial stable), was designed for educational purposes. In both of these one finds a wealth of exquisite material which any hymn lover should study even if there are not many chances of actually hearing it sung. What we have here is a selection of those hymns taken from the poets that seem to have found most congregational favor, or to deserve it. They will be more familiar to the English than to the Americans. This is probably understandable. If it was true to say, in the last chapter but one, that Americans became accustomed to a very polished style of writing and perhaps were less exposed to doggerel than the English in the nineteenth century, they may have felt less of an urge to nourish hymnody by exploring the poets. But in later years, when this is what they might have done, interest in the texts of hymns was almost extinguished by the custom of making them unreadable by always including them within the music staves of a hymnal. Yet 447 and 448 indicate grounds for hope.

It is unnecessary to comment on each item in the present section; it will be better to let the reader read them and allow them to speak for themselves. But one point of guidance may well be useful. It is always necessary to notice that a true poet uses words as precision instruments and often condenses complex ideas into short and memorable phrases. It is always unwise to read—or to sing—the poets too quickly. To take the most obvious example: George Herbert's "Come, my way" (415) is a tiny poem in which only one word is not a monosyllable. It needs to be read or sung very slowly in order that the words may expand and give off their aroma. Give the whole poem a chance to breathe! And where there is an obscurity, the reader may trust the poet to be delivering good sense instead of—as he might do with a more conventional hymn writer—dismissing him in haste.

It is proper, however, to give some account of the way in which some of these pieces came into the treasury of hymnody. We begin with "God be in my head," which is, in musical use, less a hymn than an anthem, for it is always sung to a through-composed setting. This was first used in a hymnal in *The Oxford Hymn Book*, 1908, and since then has had several settings.

"Jerusalem, my happy home" (410) has constantly attracted the attention of editors. See the *Hymnal Guide* for a brief account of the way in which it has been used, altered, adapted, and built on. But the first hymnal to include the whole text unaltered was *The English Hymnal*, and while its homely quaintness is sometimes too much for congregations to adjust to, it is something beautiful to read; the imagery of heaven in terms of an English garden, peopled by cheerful saints, has a touch of pathos if it can be believed—it is certainly plausible—that it was composed by a priest in prison under sentence of death.

The Edmund Spenser sonnet (411) has found its way into many books since *The English Hymnal* editors hit on the happy solution of the problem of setting fourteen lines to a four-line tune, namely, by repeating the tune's second half for the final couplet (which in a sonnet always sums up the thought of the whole). It was this that prompted the same editors, in *Songs of Praise*, to use a Bridges sonnet (our 261), and indeed, more daringly, a Shakespeare one (*Songs of Praise*, 622).

The Thomas Campion songs, part of a delicious little group, were domestic songs to be sung with a lute; *Songs of Praise* took them over as hymns. Of the George Herbert poems, 414, "Antiphon" is here printed as the author wrote it. *Hymns Ancient and Modern* seems to have been the first collection (1889) to use it as a hymn, and they did this by repeating the "antiphon" at the beginning of verse 2. All hymnals have done this since except *Hymns for Church and School* (1964), which sets the hymn twice, once in the corrupt way and once in the original way, offering a new tune which so sets it. (An earlier one did appear privately about 1920 but has not survived.) "King of glory" (416) drops one stanza to make a 24-line hymn which since 1906 has been very popular in England, and appears in every British hymnal now, but hardly ever in the U.S.A.

For 417 and 418 we have to thank the Congregationalists who, in the second edition of their hymn book in 1855, plundered John Milton, their own great poet, to excellent purpose. The youthful "Let us with a gladsome mind," written when the poet was 15, needed to have some metrical irregularities ironed out in order to become singable; the 1855 editors perhaps went further than they needed, and the most faithful hymn text available is that of *The English Hymnal*. But a comparison of the hymn with its original shows how irresistible the old editors must have found Milton's juvenile venture.

Number 418, almost equally well known now, comes from the same source. Some nameless genius extracted these six stanzas from Milton's version of Psalms 80–88, made in 1648 in strict conformity with the requirements of metrical psalters. Hardly any words are here altered except in the first stanza. The hymn begins with the last lines of Psalm 85, which originally ran:

Before him righteousness shall go,
   his royal harbinger,
then will he come, and not be slow,
   his footsteps cannot err.

Thereafter the editors took verses 10–11 of Psalm 85, verse 8 of Psalm 82, and verses 9–10 of Psalm 86, and, except for the omission sometimes of their stanza 2, it has stayed like that ever since.

The next one needing comment is 424, "Pray that Jerusalem . . . ," which of course could have appeared among the Scottish psalms in chapter 2. But although the Scottish Psalter was virtually unknown in England in the nineteenth century, this three-stanza fragment was given as a hymn in C. H. Spurgeon's *Our Own Hymn-Book* (1866); it was picked up by *The English Hymnal* and is the only fragment of a Scottish psalm in that book. It has a curiously haunting quality, as if for this one moment in spite of themselves the metricizers broke into poetry. Here and there in later hymnals it is expanded by the use of verses from other psalms, rather in the manner of 418.

Number 425B is one of our few examples of a poem successfully rewritten; we did not care for John Wesley's way of doing it, but the author of this (Earl Horatio Nelson, whose version was later amended in details) has produced a magnificent hymn out of the irregular but beautiful original. This first appeared in ten-syllable lines in 1868 as "Descend to thy Jerusalem, O Lord"; the first appearance of the version which has now found most favor (the one we give) seems to have been in *The Congregational Hymnary*, 1916. It has been picked up by one or two American hymnals, but is never there found in its full 5-stanza form.

Henry Vaughan's "My soul, there is a country" caught the eye of Garrett Horder, who put it into *Worship Song* in 1896; he thought it wise to alter stanza 3, to keep the meter and to write "afar" in stanza 1. *Songs of Praise* in 1925 restored the true text but kept Horder's tune.

The Richard Baxter poems at 428 and 429 are parts of much longer pieces. Baxter was splendid but incredibly prolix in prose and verse. In an age before typewriters, he must have been one of the most industrious authors who ever lived, but he is hardly ever damaged by abridgment. It is interesting to note that "Lord, it belongs not . . ." was picked up as early as the 1868 *Hymns A & M*. Probably both these hymns have missed some measure of popularity through beginning with somewhat austere opening lines. One has to pause to recall that "it belongs not to my care" means not "I don't care," but "it is not my business," and that "He wants not friends" doesn't mean that "he is too high minded to bother with friends," but "he is never without friends." Once over those initial hurdles, what priceless beauties one enjoys in the rest! As for the superb 430—hardly any of it is actually Baxter. John Hampden Gurney based his hymn on some Baxter verses of which he kept hardly a line intact, and yet he breathes the Puritan spirit of indomitable cheerfulness as if he had been Baxter's close friend. By the way, "sight" in stanza 2, line 6 is certainly the true reading, despite the faithfulness of many hymnals to the oldest existing text (surely misprinted) in writing the foolish rhyme, "light."

It is not quite certain that "My song is love unknown" (431) was never sung in its author's lifetime. It just might have been sung privately, to Lawes's tune for Psalm 47, as some believe. But it did not become a regular hymn until 1868 and perhaps began to be really popular after the Congregationalists took it in 1887. It is always sad when any stanza of this is left out by modern editors.

The two John Bunyan hymns (433, 434) speak for themselves. Undoubtedly it was the Dearmer version which made the thing popular, with Vaughan Williams's tune. Americans now always use Dearmer; English editors almost always Bunyan, hobgoblins and all.

The reader may be glad to be reminded that Kit Smart (435, 436), who ended his days insane, was the poet who wrote the poems that form the libretto for Benjamin Britten's *Rejoice in the Lamb*. Number 435 is the selection made in *Songs of Praise* except that we restore (for reading) "He sang" for their "We sing," a decent emendation for congregational use.

William Blake (437) would have been surprised to find himself in a hymnal; he would have been staggered—probably into apoplexy—to find himself the author of the text for a second English national anthem, first so used at a rally in support of Women's Guilds in 1916; this is what the song known as "Jerusalem" amounts to. Whether this is a great poem and a great piece of music which should never have met is an arguable point and one which will not interest American readers. We are here content with the mystical song from *Songs of Innocence* which *The English Hymnal* so felicitously made into a hymn.

Number 439 is a late addition to this company, having first appeared as a hymn in *The BBC Hymn Book* of 1951. This is another poet who went out of his mind; but this beautiful pastoral, with its dying fall, has proved very popular lately, beginning "A Stranger once did bless . . ." and with some of the preceding verses written in, it recovers its original pathos.

John Henry Newman is one of the few poets who, writing verse he did not design as hymnody, heard it sung as hymnody within his own lifetime. "Lead, kindly light" was a personal poem written under circumstances that are well enough known (see the *Hymnal Guide*); he was often in later years heard to say that it was because of Dykes's tune that everybody loved it, and, when asked what the angel faces in the last verse were, he admitted that by that time he had forgotten. *Hymns Ancient and Modern* picked this up in its first edition, and in its second effort of 1868 netted a much more substantial treasure in "Praise to the Holiest" (442). This is the last part of the 35-stanza "Hymn of the Angelicals" in *The Dream of Gerontius* (1865), and is made into a hymn by repeating its first stanza—which is the first stanza of each of the five parts of the hymn in the original drama—at the end. Those early *Hymns A & M* editors were not concerned to quarry among the older poets, but these two, from the intellectual leader of that Oxford Movement which the book served, were something which, despite their author's allegiance to the Church of Rome, the editors could not miss. It is truly astonishing that 442 is not known at all in America outside the Episcopal Church. The third poem of Newman, also from *Gerontius* (441), had to wait till 1906 for its release as a hymn. It is worth observing that both 441 and 442 come from a dramatic poem about an old man who is facing his own death; there are important references to death in both. (The stanza that refers to it in 441 is never used in the hymn version.)

Tennyson could have heard his *In Memoriam* "Prologue" (443) sung as a hymn if (as was most unlikely) at the end of his life he went into a Congregational church that had laid in its new hymnal, for the 1887 *Congregational Church Hymnal* seems to have been the first such book to set it to music. It made an instant appeal to the people who were enjoying the speculative, liberal hymnody in which the Americans excelled. And, of course, it is beautiful writing. Theologians are worried by "seemest" in stanza 3, but the rest of it has perhaps not wholly deserved the relegation which it has suffered in Britain. There is less to argue about in 444 and more in which to take the purest pleasure. But Tennyson would not have heard this sung; it waited for 1909 to get into a hymnal.

Number 445, which has some fine lofty lines, was first used as a hymn in *The Congregational Hymnary* of 1916, and 446, whose author's untimely death in the First World War alone prevented his living to hear sung, was taken by *Songs of Praise* in 1925. It is, as far as we can find, the earliest-dated hymn to address the Deity in the "you" form, though not quite the only one in the 1925 book to do so.

A few pages back we said that the use of poetry as hymns has appealed less to Americans, but we end our section with two pieces which owe their place in this anthology mostly to American enterprise. W. H. Auden's fragment (447) was actually first included as a hymn in the 1967 *Cambridge Hymnal*, but Auden became an American citizen in 1938; Elizabeth Poston, joint editor of *The Cambridge Hymnal*, was probably the English musician who knew most about American literature at that time. Moreover, it was its inclusion, with a wholly manageable tune, in the American *Worshipbook* (1972), rather than the Cambridge association, or its appearance in the Episcopal supplement of 1971, that really launched it on its hymnic career. A younger author, and a less recondite text, appears at 448; Richard Wilbur is a wholly American poet, and since the poem was first set to music for use as a hymn in the Lutheran *Contemporary Worship I* in 1969, it has been much sought after. It uses the meter of the German carol *"Es ist ein Ros entsprungen,"* and, if the Auden is regarded as not wholly American, it may be the first instance (apart from the Whittier poems which were made into hymns by English editors) of American nonhymnic poetry entering the field of hymnody. There is much more to find in English books, and the plundering of the poets was rarely ill-judged. (It is something quite different from decontexting attractive tunes from symphonic classics.) Its purpose was to cleanse the stream of hymnic literature through a new appreciation of poetic precision. You cannot be a poet and write clichés, or write carelessly, or write—at least before 1900—in-group language. Poets make the faith public. They minister to the educated and the educable. This enrichment was greatly needed in the early twentieth century.

409
God Be in My Head

A.

Jésus soit en ma teste et mon entendement.
Jésus soit en mes yeux et mon regardement.
Jésus soit en ma bouche et en mon parlement.
Jésus soit en mon coeur et en mon pensement.
Jésus soit en ma vie et mon trespassement.

> anonymous
> *Horae beate ad virginis*, printed for Antoine Verard, ca. 1497
> This, one of several such collections from this period,
> is in the British Library.

B.

God be in my heed
    and in myn understandynge
God be in myn eyen
    and in my lokynge
God be in my mouthe
    and in my spekynge
God be in my herte
    and in my thynkynge
God be at myn ende
    and my departynge.

> translated, anonymous
> *Horae beate virginis marie ad usum in signis ac*
> *preclare ecclesie Sarum*, 1514

C.

God be in my head
    and in my understanding;
God be in my eyes
    and in my looking;
God be in my mouth
    and in my speaking.
God be in my heart
    and in my thinking.
God be at my end
    and at my departing.

> *Sarum Primer*, 1558
> first as a hymn in *The Oxford Hymn Book*, 1908

410
Jerusalem, My Happy Home

Jerusalem, my happy home,
    when shall I come to thee?
when shall my sorrows have an end?
    thy joys when shall I see?

O happy harbor of the saints!
    O sweet and blessed soil!
in thee no sorrow may be found,
    no grief, no care, no toil.

In thee no sickness may be seen,
    no hurt, no ache, no sore;
in thee there is no dread of death,
    but life for evermore.

No dampish mist is seen in thee,
    no cold nor darksome night
there every soul shines as the sun;
    there God himself gives light.

There lust and lucre cannot dwell;
    there envy bears no sway,
there is no hunger, heat, nor cold,
    but pleasure every way.

Jerusalem, Jerusalem,
    God grant I once may see
thy endless joys, and of the same
    partaker aye may be.

Thy walls are made of precious stones,
    thy bulwarks diamonds square;
thy gates are of right Orient pearl,
    exceeding rich and rare;

thy turrets and thy pinnacles
    with carbuncles do shine;
thy very streets are paved with gold
    surpassing clear and fine;

thy houses are of ivory,
    thy windows crystal clear;
thy tiles are made of beaten gold—
    O God, that I were there!

Within thy gates no thing doth come
    that is not passing clean,
no spider's web, no dirt, no dust,
    no filth may there be seen.

Ah, my sweet home, Jerusalem,
    would God I were in thee!
would God my woes were at an end,
    thy joys that I might see!

Thy saints are crowned with glory great:
    They see God face to face;
they triumph still, they still rejoice;
    most happy is their case.

We that are here in banishment
    continually do mourn;
we sigh and sob, we weep and wail,
    perpetually we groan.

Our sweet is mixed with bitter gall,
    our pleasure is but pain,
our joys scarce worth the looking on,
    our sorrows still remain.

But there they live in such delight,
    such pleasure and such play,
as that to them a thousand years
    doth seem as yesterday.   (Ps. 90:4)

Thy vineyards and thy orchards are
    most beautiful and fair,
full furnished with trees and fruits,
    most wonderful and rare;

thy gardens and thy gallant walks
    continually are green;
there grow such sweet and pleasant flowers
    as nowhere else are seen.

There's nectar and ambrosia made,
    there's musk and civet sweet;
there many a fair and dainty drug
    is trodden under feet.

There cinnamon, there sugar grows,
    there nard and balm abound;
what tongue can tell, or heart conceive
    the joys that there are found!

Quite through the streets with silver sound
    the flood of life doth flow,   (Rev. 22:1)
upon whose banks on every side
    the wood of life doth grow.

There trees for evermore bear fruit,
    and evermore do spring;
there evermore the angels sit,
    and evermore do sing;

there David stands with harp in hand
    as master of the choir:
Ten thousand times that man were blest
    that might this music hear.

Our Lady sings Magnificat   (Luke 1:46)
    with tune surpassing sweet;
and all the virgins bear their parts
    sitting about her feet.

Te Deum doth Saint Ambrose sing,
    Saint Austin doth the like;
old Simeon and Zachary   (Luke 1:68, 2:29)
    have not their songs to seek.

There Magdalene hath left her moan
    and cheerfully doth sing
with blessed saints, whose harmony
    in every street doth ring.

Jerusalem, my happy home,
    would God I were in thee!
Would God my woes were at an end,
    thy joys that I might see!

"F. B. P.," who may have been a Catholic priest under sentence of
death in London, ca. 1593
based on a passage in the *Liber Meditationum*,
often ascribed, erroneously, to Augustine of Hippo
manuscript in the British Library, ca. 1616
Lines 24:1–2 refer to a tradition that the *Te Deum* was composed by
Saints Ambrose and Augustine singing antiphonally. This is no more
than a pious and affectionate legend.
See also 191A.

411
Sonnet 68

Most glorious Lord of life, that on this day
    didst make thy triumph over death and sin,
and, having harrowed hell, didst bring away
    captivity thence captive, us to win:

This joyous day, dear Lord, with joy begin,
    and grant that we, for whom thou diddest die
being with thy dear blood clean washed from sin,
    may live for ever in felicity:

And that thy love we weighing worthily,
    may likewise love thee for the same again;
and for thy sake that all like dear didst buy
    with love may one another entertain.

So let us love, dear love, like as we ought:
Love is the lesson which our Lord us taught.

Edmund Spenser
Amoretti and Epithalamion, 1595
first as a hymn in *The English Hymnal*, 1906

412
O Come Quickly

Never weather-beaten sail more willing bent to
    shore,
never tired pilgrim's limbs affected slumber more,
than my wearied sprite now longs to fly out of my
    troubled breast.
O come quickly, sweetest Lord, and take my soul to
    rest.

Ever blooming are the joys of heaven's high
    paradise,
cold age deafs not there our ears, nor vapor dims
    our eyes;
glory there the sun outshines; whose beams the
    blessed only see;
O come quickly, glorious Lord, and raise my sprite
    to thee.

Thomas Campion
First Booke of Ayres; Containing Divine and Morall Songs, ca. 1613
first as a hymn in *Songs of Praise*, 1931

413
Sing a Song of Joy

Sing a song of joy,
praise our God with mirth.
His flock who can destroy?
Is he not Lord of heaven and earth?

Sing we then secure,
tuning well our strings,
with voice as echo pure,
let us renown the King of kings.

First who taught the day
from the east to rise?
whom doth the sun obey
when in the seas his glory dies?

He the stars directs
that in order stand:
Who heaven and earth protects
but he that formed them with his hand?

All that dread his name,
and his hests observe,
his arm will shield from shame,
their steps from truth shall never swerve.

Let us then rejoice,
sounding loud his praise,
so will he hear our voice,
and bless on earth our peaceful days.

Thomas Campion
First Booke of Ayres; Containing Divine and Morall Songs, ca. 1613
first as a hymn in *Songs of Praise,* 1931

414
Antiphon

Let all the world in every corner sing,
my God and King!

The heavens are not too high,
his praise may thither fly;
the earth is not too low,
his praises there may grow.

Let all the world in every corner sing,
my God and King!

The church with psalms must shout,
no door can keep them out;
but, above all, the heart
must bear the longest part.

Let all the world in every corner sing
my God and King!

George Herbert
The Temple, 1633
first as a hymn in *Hymns Ancient and Modern,* 1889

415
The Call

Come, my Way, my Truth, my Life: (John 14:6)
such a way as gives us breath,
such a truth as ends all strife,
such a life as killeth death.

Come, my light, my feast, my strength:
such a light as shows a feast,
such a feast as mends in length,
such a strength as makes his guest.

Come, my joy, my love, my heart:
such a joy as none can move,
such a love as none can part,
such a heart as joys in love.

George Herbert
The Temple, 1633
first as a hymn in *Songs of Praise,* 1925

416
Praise

King of glory, King of peace,
    I will love thee;
and that love may never cease,
    I will move thee.
Thou hast granted my request,
    thou hast heard me;
thou didst note my working breast,
    thou hast spared me.

Wherefore with my utmost art
    I will sing thee,
and the cream of all my heart
    I will bring thee.
Though my sins against me cried,
    thou didst clear me;
and alone, when they replied,
    thou didst hear me.

Seven whole days, not one in seven,
    I will praise thee;
in my heart, though not in heaven
    I can raise thee.
Small it is, in this poor sort
    to enroll thee:
E'en eternity's too short
    to extol thee.

George Herbert
The Temple, 1633
first as a hymn in *The Yattendon Hymnal*, 1899

This form, which pairs Herbert's common-meter stanzas, omits the
original sixth stanza:

Thou grew'st soft and moist with tears,
    thou relentedst:
and when justice called for fears,
    thou dissentedst.

417
Psalm 136

A. Complete

Let us with a gladsome mind
praise the Lord, for he is kind;

        for his mercies aye endure,
        ever faithful, ever sure.

Let us blaze his name abroad,
for of gods he is the God;

O let us his praises tell,
that doth the wrathful tyrants quell;

That with his miracles doth make
amazed heaven and earth to shake;

That by his wisdom did create
the painted heavens so full of state;

That did the solid earth ordain
to rise above the wat'ry plain;

That by his all-commanding might
did fill the new-made world with light;

The floods stood still like walls of glass,
while the Hebrew bands did pass;

But full soon they did devour
the tawny king with all his power;

His chosen people he did bless
in the wasteful wilderness;

In bloody battle he brought down
kings of prowess and renown;

He foiled bold Seon and his host
that ruled the Amorrean coast;

And large-limbed Og he did subdue
with all his over-hardy crew;

And to his servant, Israel,
he gave their land therein to dwell;

And caused the golden-tressed sun
all the day long his course to run;

The horned moon to shine by night
amongst her spangled sisters bright;

He with his thunder-clasping hand
smote the first born of Egypt land;

And in despite of Pharaoh fell,
he brought from thence his Israel;

The ruddy waves he cleft in twain
of the Erythracean main;

He hath with a piteous eye
beheld us in our misery;

And freed us from the slavery
of the invading enemy;

All living creatures he doth feed,
and with full hand supplies their need;

Let us therefore warble forth
his mighty majesty and worth;

That his mansion hath on high
above the reach of mortal eye.

John Milton, 1623
Poems of Mr. John Milton, 1645

B. Edited as a hymn

Let us with a gladsome mind
praise the Lord, for he is kind:

> for his mercies shall endure,
> ever faithful, ever sure.

Let us sound his name abroad,
for of gods he is the God.

He with all-commanding might
filled the new-made world with light.

He the golden-tressed sun
caused all day his course to run.

He his chosen race did bless
in the wasteful wilderness.

He hath, with a piteous eye
looked upon our misery.

All things living he doth feed;
his full hand supplies their need.

Let us then with gladsome mind
praise the Lord, for he is kind.

first as a hymn in The New Congregational Hymnal, 1855

418
Nine of the Psalms Done into Metre

The Lord will come, and not be slow,
  his footsteps cannot err;
before him righteousness shall go,
  his royal harbinger.

Mercy and truth, that long were missed,
    now joyfully are met;
sweet peace and righteousness have kissed,
    and hand in hand are set.

Truth from the earth like to a flower
    shall bud and blossom then,
and justice from her heavenly bower
    look down on mortal men.

Rise, God, judge thou the earth in night,
    this wicked earth redress,
for thou art he who shalt by right
    the nations all possess.

The nations all whom thou hast made
    shall come, and all shall frame
to bow them low before thee, Lord,
    and glorify thy name.

For great thou art, and wonders great
    by thy strong hand are done;
thou in thy everlasting seat
    remainest God alone.

> John Milton, 1648
> *Poems, Etc. upon Several Occasions*, 1673
> first as a hymn in *The Congregational Hymn Book*, 1855,
> being a cento of selections from Psalms 80 through 88

419

A Hymne to God the Father

Wilt thou forgive that sin, where I begun,
    which was my sin, though it were done before?
Wilt thou forgive those sins, through which I run,
    and do run still; though still I do deplore?
      When thou hast done, thou hast not done,
        for I have more.

Wilt thou forgive that sin by which I've won
    others to sin? and made my sin their door?
Wilt thou forgive that sin which I did shun
    a year or two: but wallowed in, a score?
      When thou hast done, thou hast not done,
        for I have more.

I have a sin of fear, that when I've spun
    my last thread, I shall perish on that shore;
swear by thyself, that at my death thy Son
    shall shine as he shines now, and heretofore;
      and having done that, thou hast done:
        I fear no more.

> John Donne, 1623
> *Poems*, 1633
> first as a hymn in *The English Hymnal*, 1906

420

Hymn

Drop, drop, slow tears,
    and bathe those beauteous feet
which brought from heaven
    the news and Prince of Peace:
cease not, wet eyes,
    his mercy to entreat;
to cry for vengeance
    sin doth never cease.
In your deep floods
    drown all my faults and fears;
nor let his eye
    see sin, but through my tears.

> Phineas Fletcher
> *Piscatorial Eclogs and other Poetical Miscellanies*, 1633
> first as a hymn in *The English Hymnal*, 1906

421
Why Dost Thou Shade Thy Lovely Face

Why dost thou shade thy lovely face? Oh, why
does that eclipsing hand so long deny
the sunshine of thy soul-enlivening eye?

Without that light, what light remains in me?
Thou art my life, my way, my light: In thee
I live, I move, and by thy beams I see.

Thou art my life; if thou but turn away
my life's a thousand deaths: Thou art my way;
without thee, Lord, I travel not, but stray.

My light thou art; without thy glorious sight,
my eyes are darkened with perpetual night.
My God, thou art my way, my life, my light.

Thou art my way; I wander, if thou fly:
Thou art my light; if hid, how blind am I!
Thou art my life; if thou withdraw, I die.

Mine eyes are blind and dark, I cannot see;
to whom, or whither should my darkness flee,
but to the light? and who's that light but thee?

My oath is lost, my wandering steps do stray;
I cannot safely go, nor safely stay;
whom should I seek but thee, my path, my way?

[stanzas 8–14 omitted]

Thou art the pilgrim's path, the blind man's eye;
the dead man's life: On thee my hopes rely;
if thou remove, I err, I grope, I die.

Disclose thy sunbeams, close thy wings and stay:
See, see how I am blind and dead, and stray,
O thou that art my light, my life, my way.

Francis Quarles
Emblemes Divine and Moral, 1635.
first as a hymn in *Songs of Praise*, 1931, using stanzas 3–5 and 16

422
Hymn

A. Original

Lord, when the wise men came from far,
led to thy cradle by a star,
then did the shepherds too rejoice,
instructed by thy angel's voice.
Blest were the wise men in their skill,
and shepherds in their harmless will.

Wise men in tracing nature's laws
ascend unto the highest cause,
shepherds with humble fearfulness
walk safely, though their light be less:
Though wise men better know the way,
it seems no honest heart can stray.

There is no merit in the wise
but love, the shepherds' sacrifice.
Wise men, all ways of knowledge past,
to the shepherds' wonder come at last;
to know can only wonder breed,
and not to know is wonder's seed.

A wise man at the altar bows
and offers up his studied vows
and is received. May not the tears
which spring too from a shepherd's fears,
and sighs upon his frailty spent,
though not distinct, be eloquent?

'Tis true, the object sanctifies
all passions which within us rise,
but since no creature comprehends
the Cause of causes, End of ends,
he who himself vouchsafes to know
best pleases his Creator so.

357

When then our sorrows we apply
to our own wants and poverty,
when we look up in all distress
and our own misery confess,
sending both thanks and prayers above,
then, though we do not know, we love.

Sidney Godolphin
Caroline Poets (G. Saintsbury), 1906

B. 1925 cento

Lord, when the wise men came from far,
led to thy cradle by a star,
shepherds with humble fearfulness
walked safely, though their light was less.

Wise men in tracing nature's laws
ascend unto the highest cause,
though wise men better know the way,
it seems no honest heart can stray.

And since no creature comprehends
the Cause of causes, End of ends,
he who himself vouchsafes to know
best pleases his Creator so.

There is no merit in the wise
but love, the shepherds' sacrifice;
wise men, all ways of knowledge past
to the shepherds' wonder came at last.

altered by Percy Dearmer
first as a hymn in *Songs of Praise*, 1925
The whole poem appears in *School Worship*, 1926.

423
The White Island: or Place of the Blest

In this world (the Isle of Dreams)
while we sit by sorrow's streams,
tears and terrors are our themes
            reciting:

But when once from hence we fly,
more and more approaching nigh
unto young eternity
            uniting:

In that whiter island, where
things are evermore sincere;
candor here, and luster there
            delighting:

There no monstrous fancies shall
out of hell a horror call,
to create (or cause at all)
            affrighting.

There in calm and cooling sleep
we our eyes shall never steep;
but eternal watch shall keep
            attending

pleasures, such as shall pursue
me immortalized, and you:
and fresh joys, as never to
            have ending.

Robert Herrick
Noble Numbers, 1647
first as a hymn in *Songs of Praise*, 1925

424
Psalm 122

Pray that Jerusalem may have
      peace and felicity:
let them that love thee and thy peace
      have still prosperity.

Therefore I wish that peace may still
      within thy walls remain,
and ever may thy palaces
      prosperity retain.

Now for my friends' and brethren's sake,
    "Peace be in thee," I'll say;
and for the house of God our Lord
    I'll seek thy good alway.

The Psalms of David in Meeter (Scottish Psalter), 1650
This fragment (stanzas 6–9) appears in *Our Own Hymn-Book*
(Spurgeon), 1866.

425
The Second Advent; or, Christ's Coming to Jerusalem in Triumph

A. Original poem

Lord! come away!
    Why dost thou stay?
Thy road is ready; and thy paths made straight
    with longing expectation wait
the consecration of thy beauteous feet!
Ride on triumphantly! Behold, we lay
    our lusts and proud wills in thy way!

Hosanna! Welcome to our hearts! Lord, here
thou hast a temple too; and full as dear
as that of Sion, and as full of sin;
nothing but thieves and robbers dwell therein:
enter, and chase them forth, and cleanse the floor!
Crucify them, that they may never more
        profane that holy place
    where thou hast chose to set thy face!
And then, if our stiff tongues shall be
mute in the praises of thy Deity,
    the stones out of the temple wall
        shall cry aloud, and call
"Hosanna!" and thy glorious footsteps greet! Amen!

Jeremy Taylor
The Golden Grove, 1655

B. Revised as a hymn

"Draw nigh to thy Jerusalem, O Lord,"
thy faithful people cry with one accord:
"Ride on in triumph; Lord, behold, we lay
our passions, lusts, and proud wills in thy way."

Thy road is ready; and thy paths, made straight,
with longing expectation seem to wait
the consecration of thy beauteous feet,
and silently thy promised advent greet.

Hosanna! Welcome to our hearts; for here
thou hast a temple too, as Sion dear;
yes, dear as Sion, and as full of sin:
how long shall thieves and robbers dwell therein?

Enter and chase them forth, and cleanse the floor;
o'erthrow them all, that they may never more
profane with traffic vile that holy place
where thou hast chosen, Lord, to set thy face.

And then, if our stiff tongues shall faithlessly
be mute in praises of thy Deity,
the very temple stones shall loud repeat
"Hosanna!" and thy glorious footsteps greet.

Horatio Nelson
first as a hymn in *The Sarum Hymnal*, 1868
altered in *The Congregational Hymnary*, 1916

426
Peace

My soul, there is a country
    afar beyond the stars,
where stands a winged sentry
    all skillful in the wars.

There, above noise and danger,
    sweet Peace sits crowned with smiles,
and One born in a manger
    commands the beauteous files.

He is thy gracious Friend,
    and—O my soul, awake—
did in pure love descend
    to die here for thy sake.

If thou canst get but thither,
    there grows the flower of peace,
the Rose that cannot wither,
    thy fortress and thy ease.

Leave then thy foolish ranges,
    or none can thee secure,
but One, who never changes,
    thy God, thy Life, thy Cure.

Henry Vaughan
Silex Scintillans, 1655
first as a hymn in *Worship Song*, 1896

427
Psalm for Christmas Day

Fairest of morning lights, appear,
    thou blest and gaudy day,
on which was born our Savior dear;
    arise and come away!

This day prevents his day of doom;
    his mercy now is nigh;
the mighty God of Love is come,
    the Dayspring from on high!

Behold, the great Creator makes
    himself a house of clay;
a robe of Virgin-flesh he takes
    which he will wear for aye.

Hark, hark, the wise Eternal Word
    like a weak infant cries:
In form of servant is the Lord,
    and God in cradle lies.

This wonder struck the world amazed,
    it shook the starry frame;
squadrons of spirits stood and gazed,
    then down in troops they came.

Glad shepherds ran to view this sight;
    a choir of angels sings;
and eastern sages with delight
    adore this King of kings.

Join then, all hearts that are not stone,
    and all our voices prove
to celebrate this Holy One,
    the God of peace and love.

Thomas Pestel
Sermons and Devotions Old and New, 1659
first as a hymn in *The English Hymnal*, 1906, beginning with stanza 3

428
from The Resolution

He wants not friends that hath thy love,
    and may converse and walk with thee
and with thy saints, here and above,
    with whom for ever I must be.

In the communion of saints
    is wisdom, safety, and delight;
and when my heart declines and faints,
    it's raised by their heat and light.

As for my friends, they are not lost;
    the several vessels of thy fleet,
though parted now, by tempests tossed,
    shall safely in the haven meet.

Still we are centered all in thee,
    members, though distant, of one Head;
in the same family we be,
    by the same faith and Spirit led.

Before thy throne we daily meet
    as joint petitioners to thee;
in spirit we each other greet,
    and shall again each other see.

The heavenly hosts, world without end,
    shall be my company above;
and thou, my best and surest friend,
    who shall divide me from thy love?   (Rev. 8:37)

Richard Baxter, 1663
Poetical Fragments, 1681
first as a hymn in *The English Hymnal*, 1906
This is a cento from the text beginning,
"Lord, I have cast up my account."

429

from London, at the Door of Eternity, August, 7, 1681: Heart-Employment with God and Itself: The Concordant Discord of a Broken-Hearted Heart

Lord, it belongs not to my care,
    whether I die or live;
to love and serve thee is my share:
    And this thy grace must give.

If life be long, I will be glad
    that I may long obey:
If short, yet why should I be sad,
    to soar to endless day?

Christ leads me through no darker rooms
    than he went through before;
he that into God's kingdom comes
    must enter by that door.

Come, Lord, when grace hath made me meet
    thy blessed face to see:
For if thy work on earth be sweet,
    what will thy glory be?

Then shall I end my sad complaints,
    and weary, sinful days:
And join with the triumphant saints,
    that sing Jehovah's praise.

My knowledge of that life is small;
    the eye of faith is dim;
but 'tis enough that Christ knows all,
    and I shall be with him.

Richard Baxter, 1681
Poetical Fragments, 1681
this version first as a hymn in *The New Congregational Hymn Book*, 1855
Line 2:4 was altered from "that shall have the same pay" in
Hymns Ancient and Modern, 1868.
This is a cento from the text beginning, "My whole though broken
heart, O Lord," with the first line of the selection altered from
"Now it belongs not to my care." The complete text may be seen
in *The Hymnal 1940 Companion*.

430

Ye Holy Angels Bright

Ye holy angels bright,
    who wait at God's right hand,
or through the realms of light
    fly at your Lord's command,
        assist our song,
            for else the theme
              too high doth seem
        for mortal tongue.

Ye blessed souls at rest,
    who ran this earthly race,
and now, from sin released
    behold your Father's face,
        his praises sound,
            as in his sight
              with sweet delight
    ye do abound.

Ye saints, who toil below,
 adore your heavenly King,
and onward as ye go
 some joyful anthem sing;
  take what he gives,
   and praise him still
   through good or ill,
  whoever lives.

My soul, bear thou thy part,
 triumph in God above,
and with a well-tuned heart
 sing thou the songs of love.
  Let all thy days
   till life shall end,
   whate'er he send,
  be filled with praise.

John Hampden Gurney
based on Richard Baxter's 16-stanza poem, "A Psalm of Praise, to the
Tune of Psalm 148"
The Poor Man's Family Book, 1672
first as a hymn in *Collection of Hymns for Public Worship*, 1838
altered in *Hymns Ancient and Modern*, 1889

431
My Song Is Love Unknown

My song is love unknown,
 my Savior's love to me,
love to the loveless shown
 that they might lovely be.
  Oh, who am I,
   that for my sake
   my Lord should take
  frail flesh, and die?

He came from his blest throne
 salvation to bestow;
but men made strange, and none
 the longed-for Christ would know.
  But, O my Friend,
   my Friend indeed,
   who at my need
  his life did spend!

Sometimes they strew his way
 and his sweet praises sing;
resounding all the day
 hosannas to their King.
  Then "Crucify!"
   is all their breath,
   and for his death
  they thirst and cry.

Why, what hath my Lord done?
 what makes this rage and spite?
He made the lame to run,
 he gave the blind their sight.
  Sweet injuries!
   Yet they at these
   themselves displease
  and 'gainst him rise.

They rise, and needs will have
 my dear Lord made away;
a murderer they save,
 the Prince of life they slay.
  Yet cheerful he
   to suffering goes   (Heb. 12:2)
   that he his foes
  from thence might free.

In life no house, no home
　　my Lord on earth might have;
in death, no friendly tomb
　　but what a stranger gave.
　　　　What may I say?
　　　　　　heaven was his home;
　　　　　　but mine the tomb
　　　　wherein he lay.

Here might I stay and sing
　　no story so divine;
never was love, dear King,
　　never was grief like thine.
　　　　This is my Friend,
　　　　　　in whose sweet praise
　　　　　　I all my days
　　　　could gladly spend.

Samuel Crossman
The Young Man's Meditation, 1664
first as a hymn in *The Anglican Hymn Book*, 1868

432
Incarnation

The holy Son of God most high,
　　for love of Adam's lapsed race
quit the sweet pleasures of the sky
　　to bring us to that happy place.

His robes of light he laid aside,
　　which did his majesty adorn,
and the frail state of mortals tried
　　in human flesh and figure born.　　(Phil. 2:5–11)

Whole choirs of angels loudly sing
　　the mystery of his sacred birth,
and the blest news to shepherds bring,
　　filling their watchful souls with mirth.

The Son of God thus man became,
　　that men the sons of God might be,
and by their second birth regain
　　a likeness to his deity.

Henry More
cento from *Divine Hymns*, 1668
first as a hymn in *Songs of Praise*, 1925

433
The Shepherd Boy's Song
in the Valley of Humiliation

He that is down needs fear no fall,
　　he that is low, no pride;
he that is humble ever shall
　　have God to be his guide.

I am content with what I have,
　　little be it or much;
and, Lord, contentment still I crave,
　　because thou savest such.

Fullness to such a burden is
　　that go on pilgrimage;
here little, and hereafter bliss
　　is best from age to age.

John Bunyan
The Pilgrim's Progress, Part II, 1684

434
Valiant for Truth

A.

Who would true valor see,
　　let him come hither;
one here will constant be,
　　come wind, come weather;
there's no discouragement
shall make him once relent
his first avowed intent
　　to be a pilgrim.

Whoso beset him round
　　with dismal stories,
do but themselves confound;
　　his strength the more is.
No lion can him fright,
he'll with a giant fight,
but he will have a right
　　to be a pilgrim.

Hobgoblin nor foul fiend
　　can daunt his spirit;
he knows he at the end
　　shall life inherit.
Then fancies fly away!
He'll fear not what men say;
he'll labor night and day
　　to be a pilgrim.

John Bunyan
The Pilgrim's Progress, Part II, 1684
first as a hymn in *The Congregational Hymnary*, 1916

B.

He who would valiant be
　　'gainst all disaster,
let him in constancy
　　follow the Master.
There's no discouragement
shall make him once relent
his first avowed intent
　　to be a pilgrim.

Who so beset him round
　　with dismal stories,
do but themselves confound—
　　his strength the more is.
No foes shall stay his might,
though he with giants fight:
He will make good his right
　　to be a pilgrim.

Since, Lord, thou dost defend
　　us with thy Spirit,
we know we at the end
　　shall life inherit.
Then fancies flee away!
I'll fear not what men say,
I'll labor night and day
　　to be a pilgrim.

altered, Percy Dearmer, 1904
The English Hymnal, 1906

435
Song of David

He sang of God, the mighty Source
of all things, the stupendous force
　　on which all strength depends,
from whose right arm, beneath whose eyes,
all period, power, and enterprise
　　commences, reigns, and ends.

Glorious the sun in mid career,
glorious th' assembled stars appear,
　　glorious the comet's train,
glorious the trumpet and alarm,
glorious th' almighty outstretched arm,
　　glorious th' enraptured main.

The world, the clustering spheres he made,
the glorious light, the soothing shade,
　　dale, champaign, grove, and hill,
the multitudinous abyss,
where secrecy remains in bliss,
　　and wisdom hides her skill.

Strong is the lion, like a coal
his eyeball, like a bastion's mole
　　his chest against the foes:
Strong the gier-eagle on his sail;
strong against tide the enormous whale
　　emerges as he goes;

but stronger still—in earth and air
and in the sea—the man of prayer;
    and far beneath the tide,
and in the seat to faith assigned,
where ask is have, where seek is find,
    where knock is open wide.

Christopher Smart
Song to David, 1763
These are stanzas 18, 84, 21, 76, and 78 of the original 86, and were
first published as a hymn in *Songs of Praise*, 1925,
where the hymn version begins, "We sing . . . ."

436
Easter Day

Awake, arise! lift up thy voice,
    which as a trumpet swell!
Rejoice in Christ! again rejoice,
    and on his praises dwell!

Let us not doubt, as doubted some,
    when first the Lord appeared;
but full of faith and reverence come,
    what time his voice is heard.

And ev'n as John, who ran so well,
    confess upon our knees
the Prince who locks up death and hell,
    and has himself the keys.

And thus through gladness and surprise
    the saints their Savior treat;
nor will they trust their ears and eyes
    but by his hands and feet:

Those hands of liberal love indeed
    in infinite degree,
those feet still frank to move and bleed
    for millions and for me.

O Dead, arise! O Friendless, stand
    by seraphim adored!
O Solitude, again command
    thy host from heaven restored!

Christopher Smart
A *Translation of the Psalms of David*, 1765
first as a hymn in *Songs of Praise*, 1925

437
The Divine Image

To Mercy, Pity, Peace, and Love,
    all pray in their distress,
and to these virtues of delight
    return their thankfulness.

For Mercy, Pity, Peace, and Love
    is God our Father dear;
and Mercy, Pity, Peace, and Love
    is Man, his child and care.

For Mercy has a human heart,
    Pity, a human face;
and Love, the human form divine;
    and Peace, the human dress.

Then every man, of every clime,
    that prays in his distress,
prays to the human form divine:
    Love, Mercy, Pity, Peace.

And all must love the human form,
    in heathen, Turk, or Jew;
where Mercy, Love, and Pity dwell,
    there God is dwelling too.

William Blake
Songs of Innocence, 1789
first as a hymn in *The English Hymnal*, 1906

438
Thy Heaven, on Which 'Tis Bliss to Look

Thy heaven, on which 'tis bliss to look
shall be my pure and shining book,
where I shall read, in words of flame
the glories of thy wondrous name.

There's nothing brought, above, below,
from flowers that bloom to stars that glow,
but in its light my soul can see
some feature of thy deity:

There's nothing dark, below, above,
but in its gloom I trace thy love,
and meekly wait that moment, when
thy touch shall turn all bright again.

Thomas Moore
Sacred Songs, 1810
first as a hymn in *Songs of Praise*, 1925
These are stanzas 4, 6, and 7 of Moore's 7-stanza poem, which begins
"The turf shall be my fragrant shrine."
Thomas Hastings, in his *Spiritual Songs*, 1832, altered the first two of
the stanzas above and added a third of his own, creating a version
often found in collections in the United States.

439
The Stranger

When trouble haunts me, need I sigh?
    no, rather smile away despair;
for those have been more sad than I,
    with burdens more than I could bear;
aye, gone rejoicing under care
where I had sunk in black despair.

When pain disturbs my peace and rest,
    am I a hopeless grief to keep,
when some have slept on torture's breast
    and smiled as in the sweetest sleep,
aye, peace on thorns, in faith forgiven,
and pillowed on the hope of heaven?

Though low and poor and broken down
    am I to think myself distressed?
No, rather laugh where others frown
    and think my being truly blest;
for others I can daily see
more worthy riches worse than me.

Aye, once a Stranger blest the earth
    who never caused a heart to mourn,
whose very voice gave sorrow mirth—
    and how did earth his worth return?
It spurned him from its lowliest lot,
the meanest station owned him not;

an outcast thrown in sorrow's way,
    a fugitive that knew no sin,
yet in lonely places forced to stay—
    men would not take the Stranger in.
Yet peace, though much himself he mourned,
was all to others he returned.

His presence was a peace to all,
    he bade the sorrowful rejoice.
Pain turned to pleasure at his call,
    health lived and issued from his voice.
He healed the sick and sent abroad
the dumb rejoicing in the Lord.

The blind met daylight in his eye,
    the joys of everlasting day;
the sick found health in his reply;
    the cripple threw his crutch away.
Yet he with troubles did remain
and suffered poverty and pain.

Yet none could say of wrong he did,
    and scorn was ever standing by;
accusers by their conscience chid,
    when proof was sought, made no reply.
Yet without sin, he suffered more
than ever sinners did before.

John Clare
The Village Minstrel, 1821

first as a hymn in *The BBC Hymn Book*, 1951, beginning with stanza 4, its first line rephrased as "A Stranger once did bless the earth," and with the following stanza replacing the final one above:

It was for sin he suffered all
    to set the world-imprisoned free,
to cheer the weary when they call—
    and who could such a stranger be?
The God, who hears each human cry,
and came, a Savior, from on high.

440
Faith—Heavenly Leadings

Lead, kindly Light, amid the encircling gloom,
    lead thou me on;
the night is dark, and I am far from home,
    lead thou me on.
Keep thou my feet; I do not ask to see
the distant scene; one step enough for me.

I was not ever thus, nor prayed that thou
    shouldst lead me on;
I loved to choose and see my path; but now
    lead thou me on.
I loved the garish day, and, spite of fears,
pride ruled my will: Remember not past years.

So long thy power hath blest me, sure it still
    will lead me on
o'er moor and fen, o'er crag and torrent, till
    the night is gone,
and with the morn those angel faces smile
which I have loved long since, and lost awhile.

John Henry Newman
The British Magazine, March 1834
first as a hymn in *Hymns Ancient and Modern*, 1861

441
Sanctus Fortis

    Sanctus fortis, sanctus Deus,
        de profundis oro te,
    miserere, Judex meus,
        parce mihi, Domine.

Firmly I believe and truly,
    God is Three and God is One;
and I next acknowledge duly
    manhood taken by the Son.

And I trust and hope most fully
    in that manhood crucified;
and each thought and deed unruly
    do to death, as he has died.

Simply to his grace and wholly
    light and life and strength belong,
and I love, supremely, solely,
    him the holy, him the strong.

    Sanctus fortis, sanctus Deus,
        de profundis oro te,
    miserere, Judex meus,
        parce mihi, Domine.

And I hold in veneration
    for the love of him alone,
holy church, as his creation,
    and her teachings, as his own.

And I take with joy whatever
    now besets me, pain or fear,
and with a strong will I sever
    all the ties which bind me here.

Adoration aye be given
    with and through the angelic host
to the God of earth and heaven,
    Father, Son, and Holy Ghost.

Sanctus fortis, sanctus Deus,
de profundis oro te,
miserere, Judex meus,
mortis in discrimine.

John Henry Newman
The Dream of Gerontius, 1865, lines 72–107, sung by Gerontius
first as a hymn in *The English Hymnal*, 1906, using the stanzas in
English, except that beginning "And I take with joy whatever"

442

Praise to the Holiest in the Height

Praise to the Holiest in the height
and in the depth be praise,
in all his words most wonderful,
most sure in all his ways.

O loving wisdom of our God!
when all was sin and shame
a second Adam to the fight
and to the rescue came.

O wisest love! that flesh and blood
which did in Adam fail,
should strive afresh against the foe,
should strive and should prevail;

and that a higher gift than grace
should flesh and blood refine,
God's presence and his very self,
and essence all-divine.

O generous love! that he who smote
in man for man the foe,
the double agony in man
for man should undergo;

and in the garden secretly,
and on the cross on high,
should teach his brethren and inspire
to suffer and to die.

John Henry Newman
The Dream of Gerontius, 1865, lines 790–813,
sung by the Choir of Angelicals
first as a hymn in *Hymns Ancient and Modern*, 1868,
repeating the first stanza at the end

443

Strong Son of God

Strong Son of God, immortal love,
whom we, that have not seen thy face,
by faith, and faith alone, embrace,
believing where we cannot prove;

thou wilt not leave us in the dust:
Thou madest man, he knows not why;
he thinks he was not made to die;
and thou hast made him: Thou art just.

Thou seemest human and divine,
the highest, holiest manhood, thou;
our wills are ours, we know not how;
our wills are ours, to make them thine.

Our little systems have their day;
they have their day and cease to be:
They are but broken lights of thee,
and thou, O Lord, art more than they.

We have but faith: We cannot know;
for knowledge is of things we see;
and yet we trust it comes from thee,
a beam in darkness: Let it grow.

Let knowledge grow from more to more,
but more of reverence in us dwell;
that mind and soul, according well,
may make one music as before,

but vaster. We are fools and slight;
    we mock thee when we do not fear;
    but help thy foolish ones to bear—
help thy vain worlds to bear thy light.

Alfred, Lord Tennyson, 1849
In Memoriam, 1850
first as a hymn in *The Congregational Church Hymnal*, 1887, in this
form, which omits stanzas 2 and 9–11 of the 11 in Tennyson's prologue

444
Ring Out, Wild Bells

Ring out, wild bells, to the wild sky,
    the flying cloud, the frosty light:
    The year is dying in the night;
ring out, wild bells, and let him die.

Ring out the grief that saps the mind,
    for those that here we see no more;
    ring out the feud of rich and poor,
ring in redress to all mankind.

Ring out a slowly dying cause,
    and ancient forms of party strife;
    ring in the nobler modes of life,
with sweeter manners, purer laws.

Ring out false pride in place and blood,
    the civic slander and the spite;
    ring in the love of truth and right,
ring in the common love of good.

Ring out old shapes of foul disease;
    ring out the narrowing lust of gold;
    ring out the thousand wars of old,
ring in the thousand years of peace.

Ring in the valiant man and free,
    the larger heart, the kindlier hand;
    ring out the darkness of the land,
ring in the Christ that is to be.

Alfred, Lord Tennyson
In Memoriam, 1850
first as a hymn in *The Fellowship Hymn Book*, 1909, in this form, which
omits stanzas 2 and 5 of the 8 in Tennyson's section 106

445
Hark, What a Sound

Hark, what a sound, and too divine for hearing,
    stirs on the earth and trembles in the air!
Is it the thunder of the Lord's appearing?
    Is it the music of his people's prayer?

Surely he cometh, and a thousand voices
    shout to the saints, and to the deaf are dumb;
surely he cometh, and the earth rejoices,
    glad in his coming who hath sworn, "I come."

This hath he done, and shall we not adore him?
    This shall he do, and can we still despair?
Come, let us quickly fling ourselves before him,
    cast at his feet the burden of our care.

Yea, through life, death, through sorrow and
through sinning
    he shall suffice me, for he hath sufficed:
Christ is the end, for Christ was the beginning,
    Christ the beginning, for the end is Christ.

Frederick William Henry Myers
St. Paul, 1867
first as a hymn in *Hymns for Use in St. Olave's Grammar School*, 1903
These are stanzas 142–144 and 146 of the 146 in Myers's first edition
of this text, which he revised several times.

446
Lord of the Strong

Lord of the strong, when earth you trod
    you calmly faced the angry sea,
    the fierce unmasked hypocrisy,
        the traitor's kiss, the rabble hiss,
    the awful death upon the tree:
        All glory be to God.

Lord of the weak, when earth you trod,
    oppressors writhed beneath your scorn;
    the weak, despised, depraved, forlorn
        you taught to hope and know the scope
of love divine for all who mourn:
        All glory be to God.

Lord of the rich, when earth you trod,
    to mammon's power you never bowed,
    but taught how men with wealth endowed
        in meekness' school might learn to rule
the demon that enslaves the proud:
        All glory be to God.

Lord of the poor, when earth you trod,
    the lot you chose was hard and poor;
    you taught us hardness to endure,
        and so to gain through hurt and pain
the wealth that lasts for evermore:
        All glory be to God.

Lord of us all, when earth you trod,
    the life you led was perfect, free,
    defiant of all tyranny;
        now give us grace that we may face
our foes with like temerity,
        and glory give to God.

Donald Hankey
The Spectator, ca. 1915
first as a hymn in *Songs of Praise*, 1925

447
He Is the Way

He is the Way.
Follow him through the Land of Unlikeness;
you will see rare beasts and have unique adventures.

He is the Truth.
Seek him in the Kingdom of Anxiety;
you will come to a great city that has expected your
             return for years.

He is the Life.
Love him in the World of the Flesh;
and at your marriage all its occasions shall dance
             for joy.

Wystan Hugh Auden, 1942
For the Time Being, 1945
first as a hymn in *The Cambridge Hymnal*, 1967

448
A Christmas Hymn

A stable-lamp is lighted
whose glow shall wake the sky;
the stars shall bend their voices,
and every stone shall cry.
And every stone shall cry,
and straw like gold shall shine;
a barn shall harbor heaven,
a stall become a shrine.

This child through David's city
shall ride in triumph by;
the palm shall strew its branches,
and every stone shall cry.
And every stone shall cry,
though heavy, dull, and dumb,
and lie within the roadway
to pave his kingdom come.

Yet he shall be forsaken,
and yielded up to die;
the sky shall groan and darken,
and every stone shall cry.
And every stone shall cry
for stony hearts of men:
God's blood upon the spearhead,
God's blood refused again.

But now, as at the ending,
the low is lifted high;
the stars shall bend their voices
and every stone shall cry.
And every stone shall cry
in praises of the child
by whose descent among us
the worlds are reconciled.

Richard Wilbur, 1958
Advice to a Prophet and Other Poems, 1961
first as a hymn in *Contemporary Worship*, 1969
© 1961, 1989, Richard Wilbur

Chapter 21:
English Hymnody, 1906–1951
(449–479)

This period defines itself very naturally. It begins with *The English Hymnal*, where chapter 14 left off, and ends with the first wave of new hymnals after the Second World War. It is dominated by *Songs of Praise*, which appeared first in 1925 and in its enlarged and extremely successful edition in 1931; if one compares that book with *The English Hymnal*, to which it owed so much and with which it shares its general editor and musical editor (Percy Dearmer and Ralph Vaughan Williams), one sees at once the direction of the main thrust of hymnody during the first quarter of the century: from liturgical richness towards aesthetic and intellectual liberalism.

That indeed is the shape of Dearmer's own development. It is as if, having written *The Parson's Handbook* and got *The English Hymnal* rolling, he felt free to develop that crusade against the enthronement of religious cant which was his other passion. His is one of the most interesting spiritual stories of that time. Some have judged that he abandoned his earlier liturgical interests for the social gospel, but that is putting it far too naively. Throughout his very busy and creative life, a life during which admittedly he became more and more of a misfit so far as orthodox Anglicanism was concerned, he was saying, "If you are going to do it at all, do it, for heaven's sake, *right*." His liturgical work had a social gospel at its very heart; he used to storm at all those who wanted the Catholic liturgies for sentimental reasons and who put up cheap buildings and devised cheap vestments, whose cheapness, he was never tired of saying, was achieved by sweated labor. Similarly, he detested cheap music and cheap piety, and the musicians he gathered round him, Vaughan Williams and, even more, Martin Shaw, abetted the crusade by campaigning vigorously in favor of the proposition that what was popular need not be trivial, which

meant in practice a reevaluation of the folk song heritage of a much earlier Britain.

The hymnody of these very important years is divided simply into that which was and that which was not directly influenced by Dearmer and his group. Broadly speaking this means a division between the Anglican and the non-Anglican, though when one realizes how much Dearmer did to bring the work of American Unitarians into English currency, one has to judge him an ecumenical Christian. His eyes were turned towards literature and away from the in-group language of the Evangelicals. He had little use for Watts, not very much more for Wesley; Doddridge was mostly a closed book to him. The one way in which he noticeably changed in his theology is that in his later books he would never have dreamed of including Cowper's "There is a fountain," and would no longer countenance in "O for a thousand tongues" the stanza "his blood availed for me."

Take first the group composed of 452, 454, and 456–458, the first three of which were in the earlier edition of *Songs of Praise*. Numbers 452 and 454 come from the First World War and are petitions for peace, Clifford Bax's poem being very largely humanistic, Laurence Housman's being decisively Christian, both exquisitely written, both lyrical—and, one has to add, both now more sung in America than in England. The First World War lent impetus to the movement for the revival of English art which was focused, just after its end, in the League of Arts. Both these pieces were much promoted in their literature (which itself had much influence on the contents of the early *Songs of Praise*). In Dearmer's own work, of which in the later *Songs of Praise* there is, perhaps, too much, we see a strenuous forward thrust and a tendency to pull congregations away from that which is bigoted and philistine. Number 456 really does bring John the Baptist into the twentieth century (he is ill served elsewhere by hymn writers); 457, based on a famous passage in the second-century *Didache* (cf. 552), removes mystery from the Eucharist and substitutes the atmosphere of the primitive love-feast in a manner one would have expected more of a neosacramental Nonconformist. And as for 458, which thanks God for prophets and philosophers but not for Jesus Christ, this takes the Dearmer style as far in the direction of "mission to pagans" as it ever went. Incidentally it also illustrates a habit which he formed of writing new hymns based on the opening words, and singable to the tunes, of hymns already well known (cf. 198), a practice which brought down on him much puristic wrath at the time.

Puristic wrath and pedantic contempt are quite the wrong response to Dearmer, exasperating though his orthodox colleagues must have found him in some ways. The real essence of Dearmer's contribution to religious culture is to be found in *The Oxford Book of Carols* (1928), whose preface is one of the classics of carol literature. We must add to that what we demonstrated in chapter 20: the way he threw great lyric poetry at his singers, especially at the schools for which *Songs of Praise* was partly devised. Thirdly, we must celebrate the work of other authors whom he urged to write for him. Having discovered G. K. Chesterton's "O God of earth and altar" in 1906, he commissioned or promoted such excellent things as Charter Piggott's memorial hymn (459), by far the best and healthiest of such hymns available; Bishop G. K. Allen Bell's magnificent ecumenical celebration, 465 (now becoming very popular through the rearrangement of its lines to carry a simpler tune than any to be found in its original meter); and the often delicious pieces of Jan Struther, of which I take 466 to be the best and sanest of all marriage hymns. Piggott was a well-known Congregationalist preacher (see also 481), Bell the most dedicated and outspoken of all his Episcopal contemporaries, and Jan Struther a virtually humanist novelist. Dearmer spread his net wide, and in respect of Jan Struther, whom we shall meet once more, we may perhaps offer a word in defense of a writer who was especially singled out for vilification by the many

enemies which Dearmer's work made. If there is any place for hymns (like 458) which can be sung communally by gatherings including a proportion of uncertain and not yet fully-committed Christians, hymns which perhaps at a more mature stage such people may, if they ever reach it, leave behind, the delicacy and metrical skill of Jan Struther was a talent which such songs could especially use.

George Wallace Briggs became at a later stage a colleague of the *Songs of Praise* team. A much more evangelical Anglican than Dearmer, he was even more of an educationist. A navy chaplain during the war, Briggs developed his hymn writing in the twenties, and was the kind of Christian minister who is often heard using the word "manly." He had a much higher respect for Wesley than Dearmer had (this increased as he got older), and his work is much less experimental and trendy than most of Dearmer's. At its best it has a very successful combination of virility and tenderness. Number 460, one of his earlier and one of his best, has a Wesleyan touch in its use of massive words in the last stanza (and in its meter) and the teacher's touch in the narrative style of its earlier stanzas. Number 461, very popular now, is in the old-fashioned biblical style, very simple and direct. Number 462 is a good example of his later work, a meditation on the new terrors of the nuclear bomb; 463, which may be his last hymn, first printed when he was 82, may also be his very finest. One can see how with advancing years he went back towards the style of Cowper, Wesley, and the other great Evangelicals. Yet it is not imitative stuff. It is strictly twentieth-century hymnody, succeeding through the simplicity of its expression. He is now easily the most sought-after of the writers of his time, and with full justice.

Geoffrey Anketell Studdert-Kennedy, the author of 455, was one of the major lyricists of the First World War and one of the two best-known military chaplains. (The other was Philip B. Clayton, founder of "Toc H.") He had a vivid, slashing style in which he often expressed his—and everybody's—indignation at the folly of war. This piece, which Dearmer collected from an Industrial Christian Fellowship leaflet, is one of three he included in *Songs of Praise*; theologians may hesitate at stanza 5, but this is one of the first English hymns to use the modern urban imagery which the Americans had already begun to attempt, and of which we shall shortly hear more.

Bishop Timothy Rees (453), of whose work Dearmer does not seem to have known, was a monk of the Community of the Resurrection at Mirfield, Yorkshire, an Anglo-Catholic body dedicated to missions at home and abroad. The preaching of these talented men often took them to places where Gospel Songs and highly seasoned evangelical or eucharistic hymnody were the normal fare, and their first hymn book (1922), which included this piece, is generously endowed with material of that kind. Rees's "God of love" could be called the greatest of all "Gospel Songs"; it has their rhythmic and repetitive simplicity, but it adds a severity and concreteness which they never attempt, and now (1951) that it has received a worthy musical setting it has begun to travel far.

Number 467 is something quite unique, in being a collaboration between two able hymn writers. Ronald Knox was in his day equal to G. K. Chesterton in his fame as a Catholic apologist; witty, urbane, with a crossword-puzzle mind, he wrote satire, detective stories, theological works, and many hymn translations. Cyril Argentine Alington, Head Master of Eton, later Dean of Durham, was also an able hymn writer, several of whose pieces have appeared in many books. Knox, when he collaborated in this, was probably still an Anglican. (He joined the Catholic Church in 1918, being himself the son of the Bishop of Manchester.) The remarkable thing about this composition is its use of Scripture, which is more strictly exegetical and interpretative than anything since Charles Wesley (223 would be its only competitor). It was first included in a hymnal for

schools and is less well known than it deserves to be. Alington's "solo" at 468 is again closely and devoutly scriptural, though elsewhere his work is more lyrical and less didactic.

The BBC Hymn Book of 1951, a very brave attempt to provide an ecumenical book with some of the characteristics of *Songs of Praise* and designed primarily for use at the daily broadcast service, was again musically adventurous but at its best in selecting from older hymns rather than in devising new texts. It suddenly comes to life in its harvest section, however, producing Andrew Young's exquisite poem (474) for the first time as a hymn, and three tiny gems by the journalist and sports commentator John Arlott, of which we have two at 475 and 476. All our three examples show a special sense of the beauty of words and have nourished with sanity the harvest observances in church which were until so recently disfigured by the use of hymns of an oppressively moralistic kind.

Something of the same gift—less impressive, perhaps, and a little more ecclesiastical in tone, but often producing some excellent hymns——is found in the underused author Thomas C. Hunter Clare who, in a series of privately printed booklets for his parish, included several pieces which are only now coming into their own. "God of the pastures" (472) is an excellent hymn about the blessing of labor, and 473 is a welcome respite from the trivial piece by Wordsworth on the same passage.

Apart from the prodigious and sometimes eccentric labors of Dearmer and the substantial contribution of Briggs, the Anglicans were not writing a great deal in these years. The one other tradition that produced anything like a steady stream was that of the Congregationalists. With a single exception, all the rest of the hymns in this section come from them.

The Congregational Hymnary of 1916 showed no sign of being influenced by the Dearmer group. It appeared in the depths of World War I, its musical taste was already rather dated, and it produced very little in the way of enduring new texts. But it did have its moments. The now-accepted version of 425 was one of them. Its most distinguished contribution, however, was in making known some of the hymns of Howell Elvet (Hywel Elfed) Lewis, the leading Welsh poet and preacher of his time. Elfed, to give him his bardic name, wrote in Welsh and in English, but normally he did not translate his own work from one language to the other; his English hymns do not have any special Welsh accent. He has his place in this section because it is strictly the twentieth century that has appreciated him, but actually 450 was written in 1883. It was a memorable experience to hear him broadcasting a sermon seventy years later, only a month or two before he died at 93, in which he quoted this hymn and told how he wrote it for the first church in which he ministered. It is still an admirable piece and too little known. Number 451 is much more widely used, and the *Hymnary* was the first to print it.

Number 449 was also first printed in the *Hymnary* and is the work of a minister whose most famous charge was in Bristol; the only known hymn of this author, it has real distinction. In some books it begins "Lord Christ, who . . . ," but the alteration is entirely unnecessary, and this is still one of the most satisfying hymns of Christian service. Doddridge showed the right path (51), but ever since his day Christian writers on this subject, following Wesley, tended to equate the life of service with the specific purpose of making conversions. This one shows the liberal mind at its graceful best.

Number 459, also by a Congregationalist, we have already mentioned. The three authors represented in 469–471 and 477–479, virtually representing three generations, are an interesting trio. Henry Carter (477), minister for thirty-seven years of his denomination's most eminent campus church (Cambridge), wrote only two published hymns; but this, a new interpretation of a passage in Scripture which Charles Wesley had handled in a famous hymn "Soldiers of Christ, arise," is great

writing; "The whole armor of God" is here expounded by a lifelong pacifist, and, to tell the truth, it communicates the sense of that passage to the twentieth century better than the older and better-known text.

Albert Bayly (469–471) has proved to be the most sought-after writer of his generation. He is a Congregational minister who has spent a long working life in a succession of small charges, mostly in the country. In *Rejoice, O People*, a privately published collection he put out in 1950, he showed himself to be a writer who could successfully handle what were then modern ideas and modern language. Number 469, with its astronomical context, makes a good Christian layman's prayer in a scientific milieu; 470 is one of a whole series he wrote on the minor prophets and expounds Scripture with admirable directness and candor; 471 is a lyric in an unusual meter written much later.

The third one of the trio, George Caird, revives for the twentieth century the tradition of the scholar-poet, and in this, in this century, he is unique. He is, at the time of writing, Dean Ireland Professor of New Testament in the University of Oxford, having spent all but three years of his working life in matters academic and having established himself as one of the international leaders in biblical studies. The merest glance at the texts of 478 and 479 shows him to be capable of handling Scripture as subtly and tellingly as Charles Wesley himself; he may indeed be the last of the great line of hymn writers whose language and thought are wholly inspired by the King James Version. Both these weighty, condensed, shapely pieces were written before his thirtieth year—478 when he was a student, 479 during his first years as a minister—and both were answers to challenges, the earlier having been written for a college hymn-writing competition (in a meter suggested by a friend [Routley] who wanted to get a great tune into currency), the latter on a friend's suggestion that the great epigram of Pastor Robinson famously expounded in 218 could bear a new interpretation in the twentieth century. (Numbers 479 and 218 should be compared.)

This leaves only that strange and lonely figure, Thomas Tiplady, whom we certainly must not overlook (464). Tiplady was unusual in most ways. He was just about the only early twentieth-century Methodist to dare to write hymns at all; the shadow of the great Charles Wesley still shut out most of the sun. And, very unusually for a Methodist, he spent twenty-three years in one place, a mission on the south bank of the Thames within sight of the Archbishop's palace. Here he held evening services directly aimed at the unchurched heathen and the poor; he used to say that it was not unusual for men to come in smoking cigarettes and keeping their caps on. He found nothing in the traditional services of his church that would serve, so he held services featuring films (he was one of the very first to do this, though later many did), and he found no hymns to speak to their condition, so he wrote his own for them. These he published in small booklets, and they are found to be hymns dealing quite directly with the kind of life and world known to the underprivileged of Lambeth. Normally their style is less interesting than their subject matter, and they suffer from a certain casualness and, often, shallowness. During his lifetime his own countrymen never took to his work, though he was able to say that eleven American hymnals used it. (None of the more recent American books does.) In 1944 his mission was completely destroyed in an air raid, but he battled on for several years after this, picking up the pieces. And in 464 we surely have a charming miniature which would grace anybody's hymnal. It is our tribute, anyhow, to one of the most courageous and offbeat ministers in that very orthodox age and among that then very orthodox Protestant communion.

The emphasis, then, in these early twentieth-century hymns is either towards culture (in the Anglicans) or towards the restatement of theology in orthodox but up-to-date language (in the Nonconformists). On all sides there is a quietening down after the explosion of the nineteenth century, not least due to the quite new standards which seemed now to be applicable to hymn writing after Dearmer had made his gestures. Fewer people perhaps wanted to do it, but fewer people thought they had the capacity to do it, and this application of the brake was probably a healthy sign.

449
Service

Brother, who on thy heart didst bear
    the burden of our shame and sin,
and stoopest ever still to share
    the fight without, the fear within;

whose patience cannot know defeat,
    whose pity will not be denied,
whose loving kindness is so sweet,
    whose tender mercies are so wide:

O Brother man, for this we pray,
    thou brother Man and sovereign Lord,
that we thy brethren, day by day
    may follow thee and keep thy word;

that we may care, as thou hast cared,
    for sick and lame and maimed and blind,
and freely share, as thou hast shared
    in all the woe of all mankind;

that ours may be the holy task
    to help and bless, to heal and save;
this is the privilege we ask,
    and this the happiness we crave.

So in thy mercy make us wise,
    and lead us in the ways of love,
until, at last, our wondering eyes
    look on thy glorious face above.

Henry Arnold Thomas
The Congregational Hymnary, 1916

450
A Psalm of Cheerful Trust

The days that were, the days that are,
  they all are days of God;
with psalms of cheerful trust we tread
  where Christ's own freemen trod.

We bless the love of larger noon
  that moved the loyal heart
in evil times to trust the true
  and choose the better part.

God of the fathers! God of Christ!
  keep us in simple ways;
and in the calm of silent hours
  train us for clamorous days.

For those who find the tempest strong,
  make us a hiding place,
a shadow in a weary land
  for healing and for grace.

When love for man is growing cold,
  and many faithless prove,
then may the Man of Sorrows come
  and teach us how to love.

We tarry, Lord, thy leisure still,
  the best is yet to be;
naught ever comes too late for man
  that is in time for thee.

God of our fathers, God of Christ!
  keep us in simple ways;
and may the sharpness of the strife
  be to thy greater praise.

Howell Elvet (Hywel Elfed) Lewis, 1883
Cheltenham Ladies' College Hymnal, 1892
Lewis changed line 3:3 from "silent hills" to the form above.

451
Thy Will Be Done

Lord of light, whose name outshineth
  all the suns and stars of space,
deign to make us thy coworkers
  in the kingdom of thy grace;
use us to fulfill thy purpose
  in the gift of Christ thy Son;

  Father, as in highest heaven
  so on earth thy will be done.

By the toil of lowly workers
  in some far outlying field;
by the courage where the radiance
  of the cross is still revealed;
by the victories of meekness,
  through reproach and suffering won:

Grant that knowledge, still increasing,
  at thy feet may lowly kneel;
with thy grace our triumphs hallow,
  with thy charity our zeal;
lift the nations from the shadows
  to the glory of the sun:

By the prayers of faithful watchmen,
  never silent day or night;
by the cross of Jesus bringing
  peace to men, and healing light;
by the love that passeth knowledge,
  making all thy children one:

Howell Elvet (Hywel Elfed) Lewis
The Congregational Hymnary, 1916

452
Turn Back, O Man

Turn back, O man, forswear thy foolish ways.
Old now is earth, and none may count her days,
    yet thou, her child, whose head is crowned
                    with flame,
    still wilt not hear thine inner God proclaim—
"Turn back, O man, forswear thy foolish ways."

Earth might be fair, and all men glad and wise.
Age after age her tragic empires rise,
    built while they dream, and in that dreaming
                    weep:
    Would man but wake from out his haunted
                    sleep,
earth might be fair, and all men glad and wise.

Earth shall be fair, and all her people one:
Nor till that hour shall God's whole will be done.
    Now, even now, once more from earth to sky
    peals forth in joy man's old undaunted cry—
"Earth shall be fair, and all her people one!"

Clifford Bax, 1916
Motherland Song Book, 1919
first as a hymn in *Songs of Praise*, 1925

453
Hallowed Be Thy Name

God of love and truth and beauty,
    hallowed be thy name,
fount of order, law, and duty,
    hallowed be thy name.
As in heaven thy hosts adore thee,
and their faces veil before thee,
so on earth, Lord, we implore thee,
    hallowed be thy name.

Lord, remove our guilty blindness,
    hallowed be thy name.
Show thy heart of lovingkindness,
    hallowed be thy name.
By our heart's deep-felt contrition,
by our mind's enlightened vision,
by our will's complete submission,
    hallowed be thy name.

In our worship, Lord most holy,
    hallowed be thy name.
In our work, however lowly,
    hallowed be thy name.
In each heart's imagination,
in the church's adoration,
in the conscience of the nation,
    hallowed be thy name.

Timothy Rees, 1916
Mirfield Mission Hymn Book, 1922

454
Peace

Father eternal, Ruler of creation,
    Spirit of life, which moved ere form was made,
through the thick darkness covering every nation,
    light to man's blindness, O be thou our aid:

        Thy kingdom come,
        O Lord, thy will be done.

Races and peoples, lo, we stand divided,
    and, sharing not our griefs, no joy can share;
by wars and tumults love is mocked, derided;
    his conquering cross no kingdom wills to bear.

Envious of heart, blind-eyed, with tongues
                    confounded,
    nation by nation still goes unforgiven,
in wrath and fear, by jealousies surrounded,
    building proud towers which shall not reach to
                    heaven.

Lust of possession worketh desolations;
 there is no meekness in the sons of earth;
led by no star, the rulers of the nations
 still fail to bring us to the peaceful birth:

How shall we love thee, holy, hidden Being,
 if we love not the world which thou hast made?
O give us brother-love for better seeing
 thy Word made flesh, and in a manger laid:

Laurence Housman, 1919
Songs of Praise, 1925

455
His Coming

When through the whirl of wheels, and engines
      humming,
 patiently powerful for the sons of men,
peals like a trumpet promise of his coming
 who in the clouds is pledged to come again;

when through the night the furnace fires a-flaring,
 shooting out tongues of flame like leaping blood,
speak to the heart of Love, alive and daring,
 sing of the boundless energy of God;

when in the depths the patient miner striving
 feels in his arms the vigor of the Lord,
strikes for a kingdom and his King's arriving,
 holding his pick more splendid than the sword;

when in the sweat of labor and its sorrow,
 toiling in twilight flickering and dim,
flames out the sunshine of the great tomorrow
 when all the world looks up because of him—

then will he come with meekness for his glory,
 God in a workman's jacket as before,
living again the eternal gospel-story,
 sweeping the shavings from his workshop floor.

Geoffrey Anketell Studdert-Kennedy
Industrial Christian Fellowship hymn leaflet, 1921

456
Make Straight the Way

Lo, in the wilderness a voice
 "Make straight the way," is crying:
when men are turning from the light
 and hope and love seem dying,
the prophet comes to make us clean,
"There standeth one you have not seen,
 whose voice you are denying."

God give us grace to hearken now
 to those who come to warn us,
give sight and strength, that we may kill
 the vices that have torn us,
lest love professed should disappear
in creeds of hate, contempt, and fear
 that crash and overturn us.

When from the vineyard cruel men
 cast out the heavenly powers
and Christendom denies its Lord,
 the world in ruin cowers.
Now come, O God, in thy great might!
Unchanged, unchanging is thy right,
 unswayed thy justice towers.

Percy Dearmer
Songs of Praise, 1925
revised in *Songs of Praise*, 1931
© 1931, Oxford University Press

457
The Love Feast

As the disciples, when thy Son had left them,
 met in a love feast, joyfully conversing,
all the stored memory of the Lord's last supper
    fondly rehearsing;
so may we here, who gather now in friendship,
 seek for the spirit of those earlier churches,
welcoming him who stands and for an entrance
   patiently searches.   (Rev. 3:20)

As, when their converse closed and supper ended,
    taking the bread and wine they made
        thanksgiving,
breaking and blessing, thus to have communion
        with Christ the living;
so may we here, a company of brothers,
    make this our love feast and commemoration,
that in his Spirit we may have more worthy
        participation.

And as they prayed and sang to thee rejoicing,
    ere in the nightfall they embraced and parted,
in their hearts singing as they journeyed homeward,
        brave and true-hearted;
so may we here, like corn that once was scattered
    over the hillside, now one bread united,
led by the Spirit, do thy work rejoicing, lamps filled
    and lighted.

Percy Dearmer
Songs of Praise, 1931
© 1931, Oxford University Press

458
Sing Praise to God

Sing praise to God, who spoke through man
    in differing times and manners   (Heb. 1:1)
for those great seers who've led the van,
    truth writ upon their banners;
for those who once blazed out the way,
for those who still lead on today,
    to God be thanks and glory.

For Amos, of the prophets first
    the vast confusion rending
of many gods that blessed or cursed,
    to find one, good, transcending;
for all who taught mankind to rise
out of the old familiar lies,
    to God be thanks and glory.

For Socrates who, phrase by phrase,
    talked men to truth, unshrinking,
and left for Plato's mighty grace
    to mold our ways of thinking;
for all who wrestled, sane and free,
to win the unseen reality,
    to God be thanks and glory.

For all the poets, who have wrought
    through music, words, and vision
to tell the beauty of God's thought
    by art's sublime precision,
who bring our highest dreams to shape
and help the soul in her escape,
    to God be thanks and glory.

Percy Dearmer
Songs of Praise, 1931
© 1931, Oxford University Press

459
For Those We Love within the Veil

For those we love within the veil,
    who once were comrades of our way,
we thank thee, Lord; for they have won
        to cloudless day;

and life for them is life indeed,
    the splendid goal of earth's strait race;
and where no shadows intervene,
        they see thy face.

Not as we knew them any more,
    toilworn, and sad with burdened care:
erect, clear-eyed, upon their brows
        thy name they bear.

Free from the fret of mortal years,
    and knowing now thy perfect will,
with quickened sense and heightened joy
        they serve thee still.

381

Oh, fuller, sweeter is that life,
    and larger, ampler is the air;
eye cannot see nor heart conceive
      the glory there,

nor know to what high purpose thou
    dost yet employ their ripened powers,
nor how at thy behest they touch
      this life of ours.

There are no tears within their eyes;
    with love they keep perpetual tryst;
and praise and work and rest are one
      with thee, O Christ.

William Charter Piggott, 1915
Songs of Praise, 1925
© Oxford University Press

460
His Ministry

Son of the Lord most high,
    who gave the worlds their birth,
he came to live and die,
    the Son of man on earth.
In Bethlehem's stable born was he
and humbly bred in Galilee.

Born in so low estate,
    schooled in a workman's trade,
not with the high and great
    his home the Highest made:
But laboring by his brethren's side
life's common lot he glorified.

Then, when his hour was come
    he heard his Father's call;
and leaving friends and home,
    he gave himself for all;
good news to bring, the lost to find,
to heal the sick, the lame, the blind.

Toiling by night and day,
    himself oft burdened sore,
where hearts in bondage lay,
    himself their burden bore:
Till, scorned by them he died to save;
himself in death, as life, he gave.

O lowly majesty,
    lofty in lowliness!
Blest Savior, who am I
    to share thy blessedness?
Yet thou hast called me, even me,
Servant divine, to follow thee.

George Wallace Briggs
Prayers and Hymns for Use in Schools, 1927

461
The Light of the World

Christ is the world's true light,
    its Captain of salvation,
the Daystar clear and bright
    of every man and nation;
new life, new hope awakes
    where'er men own his sway;
freedom her bondage breaks
    and night is turned to day.

In Christ all races meet,
    their ancient feuds forgetting,
the whole round world complete
    from sunrise to its setting:
When Christ is throned as Lord,
    men shall forsake their fear,
to plowshare beat the sword,
    to pruning hook the spear.

One Lord, in one great name
    unite us all who own thee;
cast out our pride and shame
    that hinder to enthrone thee;
the world has waited long,
    has travailed long in pain;
to heal its ancient wrong
    come, Prince of Peace, and reign.

George Wallace Briggs
Songs of Praise, 1931
© 1931, Oxford University Press

462
Science

God, who hast given us power to sound
    depths hitherto unknown:
to probe earth's hidden mysteries,
    and make their might our own:

Great are thy gifts: Yet greater far
    this gift, O God, bestow,
that as to knowledge we attain
    we may in wisdom grow.

Let wisdom's godly fear dispel
    all fears that hate impart;
give understanding to the mind,
    and with new mind, new heart.

So for thy glory and man's good
    may we thy gifts employ, lest,
maddened by the lust of power
    man shall himself destroy.

George Wallace Briggs
The Times, January 10, 1954
revised in *Hymns of Faith*, 1957
© Oxford University Press

463
The Friend of Sinners

Jesus, whose all-redeeming love
    no penitent did scorn,
who didst the stain of guilt remove
    till hope anew was born:

To thee, Physician of the soul,
    the lost, the outcast came:
Thou didst restore and make them whole,
    disburdened of their shame.

'Twas love, thy love, their bondage brake,
    whose fetters sin had bound:
For faith to love did answer make,
    and free forgiveness found.

Thou didst rebuke the scornful pride
    that called thee "sinners' friend,"
thy mercy as the Father's wide,
    God's mercy without end.

Along life's desecrated way
    where man despairing trod,
thy love all-pitying did display
    the pitying love of God.

Jesus, that pardoning grace to find,
    I too would come to thee:
O merciful to all mankind,
    be merciful to me.

George Wallace Briggs
Hymns of Faith, 1957
© Oxford University Press

464
Christ Walks in Beauty

From Nazareth the Lord has come,
    and walks in Galilee
along the narrow, crowded streets,
    and by the tideless sea.
The people throng to hear his words
    of sweet celestial grace;
and, by the way he leaves behind,
    his pathway all may trace.

            Christ walks in beauty, grace, and power
                along life's common ways,
            and, like the dawn in summertime
                awakes the voice of praise.

From Galilee, the Risen Lord
    now comes to every land,
to share his love with every race
    and lead it by the hand;
no more in darkness shall men grope,
    for he their light shall be;
and, from the bonds of sin and fear
    the truth shall make them free.   (John 8:36)

Thomas Tiplady
The Lambeth Book of Hymns and Solos, 1936

465
The Communion of Saints

Christ is the King! O friends, rejoice;
brothers and sisters, with one voice,
let all men know he is your choice.
Ring out, ye bells, give tongue, give tongue!
Let your most merry peal be rung,
while our exultant song is sung.

O magnify the Lord, and raise
anthems of joy and holy praise
for Christ's brave saints of ancient days,
who with a faith for ever new
followed the King, and round him drew
thousands of faithful men and true.

O Christian women, Christian men,
all the world over, seek again
the way disciples followed then.
Christ through all ages is the same;
place the same hope in his great name,
with the same faith his word proclaim.

Let Love's unconquerable might
your scattered companies unite
in service to the Lord of light;
so shall God's will on earth be done,
new lamps be lit, new tasks begun,
and the whole church at last be one.

George Kennedy Allen Bell
Songs of Praise, 1931
© 1931, Oxford University Press

466
Marriage

God, whose eternal mind
        rules the round world over,
    whose wisdom underlies
        all that men discover:
Grant that we, by thought and speech,
may grow nearer each to each;
    Lord, let sweet converse bind
        lover unto lover.
            Bless us, God of loving.

Godhead in human guise
    once to earth returning,
daily through human eyes
    joys of earth discerning:
Grant that we may treasure less
passion than true tenderness,
    yet never, Lord, despise
      heart to sweetheart turning.
        Bless us, God of loving.

God, whose unbounded grace
    heaven and earth pervadeth,
whose mercy doth embrace
    all thy wisdom madeth:
Grant that we may, hand in hand,
all forgive, all understand;
    keeping, through time and space,
      trust that never fadeth.
        Bless us, God of loving.

God, who art Three in One,
    all things comprehending,
wise Father, valiant Son
    in the Spirit blending:
Grant us love's eternal three—
friendship, rapture, constancy;
    Lord, till our lives be done,
      grant us love unending.
        Bless us, God of loving.

Jan Struther (Joyce Anstruther Maxtone Graham Placzek)
Songs of Praise, 1931
© 1931, Oxford University Press

467
Prophecy

Awake, awake, put on thy strength, O Zion. (Isa. 52:1)
    God's purpose tarries, but his will stands fast;
                (Hab. 2:3)
of Judah's tribe is born the mighty Lion,
             (Gen. 49:9; Rev. 5:5)
    and Man shall bruise the serpent's head at last.
            (Gen. 3:15)

    Promise and covenant God surely keeps;
              (Ps. 111:9)
    he watching o'er us slumbers not nor sleeps.
             (Ps. 121:4)

Ho, ye that thirst, the pleasant fountains wait you;
              (Isa. 55:1)
    ye that are poor, ye shall be freely fed;
why give ye gold for wine that cannot sate you?
            (Isa. 55:2)
    Why strive your hands for that which is not
          bread? (John 6:27)

For now the low estate of his handmaiden
    God hath regarded and she shall be blest;
            (Luke 1:48)
hear him that saith, "Come, all ye heavy laden,
    come unto me and I will give you rest."
           (Matt. 11:28)

Scornful we looked, and lo! his face was stained,
            (Isa. 53:4)
    his visage marred beyond the sons of men;
           (Isa. 53:23)
yet those his stripes our life and peace regained,
           (Isa. 53:6)
    those hands shall heal us that were pierced then.

Arise and shine, thy battlements are shining, (Isa. 60:1)
    upon thee breaks the glory of the Lord;
and from the east, thy royalty divining,   (Isa. 60:2–7)
    the Gentiles come to see thy peace restored.

Ronald A. Knox and Cyril Argentine Alington, 1918
The Public School Hymn Book, 1919

468
Kings and Priests

Ye that know the Lord is gracious,   (1 Pet. 2:4–10)
   ye for whom a cornerstone
stands, of God elect and precious,
   laid that ye may build thereon,
see that on that sure foundation
   ye a living temple raise,
towers that may tell forth salvation,   (Isa. 60:18)
   walls that may re-echo praise.

Living stones, by God appointed
   each to his appointed place,
kings and priests, by God anointed,
   shall ye not declare his grace?
Ye, a royal generation,
   tell the tidings of your birth,
tidings of a new creation   (2 Cor. 5:17)
   to an old and weary earth.

Tell the praise of him who called you
   out of darkness into light,
broke the fetters that enthralled you,
   gave you freedom, peace, and sight:
Tell the tale of sins forgiven,
   strength renewed and hope restored,   (Isa. 40:28)
till the earth, in tune with heaven,
   praise and magnify the Lord!

Cyril Argentine Alington, 1950
Hymns Ancient and Modern, 1950
© Hymns Ancient and Modern Ltd.

469
Lord of the Universe

O Lord of every shining constellation
   that wheels in splendor through the midnight
           sky;
grant us thy Spirit's true illumination
   to read the secrets of thy work on high.

And thou who mad'st the atom's hidden forces,
   whose laws its mighty energies fulfill;
teach us, to whom thou giv'st such rich resources,
   in all we use, to serve thy holy will.

O Life, awaking life in cell and tissue,
   from flower to bird, from beast to brain of man;
O help us trace, from birth to final issue,
   the sure unfolding of thine ageless plan.

Thou, who hast stamped thine image on thy
           creatures,   (Gen. 1:26)
   and though they marred that image, lov'st them
           still;
uplift our eyes to Christ, that in his features
   we may discern the beauty of thy will.

Great Lord of nature, shaping and renewing,
   who mad'st us more than nature's sons to be;
help us to tread, with grace our souls enduing,
   the road to life and immortality.

Albert Frederick Bayly, 1949
Rejoice, O People, 1950
© Oxford University Press

470
Do Justly, Love Mercy. Micah 6:6–8

A. Original

What doth the Lord require
   for praise and offering?
What sacrifice, desire,
   or tribute bid thee bring?

   Do justly;
   love mercy;
walk humbly with thy God.

Rulers of men, give ear!
    Should you not justice know?
Will God your pleading hear,
    while crime and cruelty grow?

Masters of wealth and trade;
    all you for whom men toil:
think not to win God's aid
    if lies your commerce soil.

Still down the ages ring
    the prophet's stern commands.
To merchant, worker, king
    he brings God's high demands.

How shall my soul fulfill
    God's law so hard and high?
Let Christ endue thy will
    with grace to fortify.

      Then justly;
      in mercy;
      thou'lt humbly walk with God.

Albert Frederick Bayly, 1949
Rejoice, O People, 1950
© Oxford University Press

B. As revised by the author

What does the Lord require
    for praise or offering?
What sacrifice, desire,
    or tribute bid you bring?

      Do justly;
      love mercy;
      walk humbly with your God.

Rulers of earth give ear!
    Should you not justice know?
Will God your pleading hear,
    while crime and cruelty grow?

All who gain wealth by trade,
    for whom the worker toils,
think not to win God's aid,
    if greed your commerce soils.

Still down the ages ring
    the prophet's stern commands:
To merchant, worker, king,
    he brings God's high demands:

How shall our life fulfill
    God's law so hard and high?
Let Christ endue our will
    with grace to fortify.

      Then justly,
      in mercy,
      we'll humbly walk with God.

100 Hymns for Today, 1969
© Oxford University Press

471
Springs of Joy

Joy wings to God our song,
    for all life holds
      to stir the heart,
      to light the mind
and make our spirit strong.

Joy wings our grateful hymn,
    for home and friends,
      and all the love
      that fills our cup
of gladness to the brim.

Joy wings to God our praise,
    for wisdom's wealth,
      our heritage
      from every age,
to guide us in his ways.

Joy wings to God our prayer.
 All gifts we need
  of courage, faith,
   forgiveness, peace,
are offered by his care.

Joy wings our heart and voice
 to give ourselves
  to Christ who died
   and, risen, lives
that we may all rejoice.

Albert Frederick Bayly, 1972
Rejoice in God, 1977
© Oxford University Press

472
God of All

God of the pastures, hear our prayer,
 Lord of the growing seed,
bless thou the fields, for to thy care
 we look in all our need.

God of the rivers in their course,
 Lord of the swelling sea,
where man must strive with nature's force,
 do thou his guardian be.

God of the dark and somber mine,
 Lord of its hard-won store,
in toil and peril all be thine;
 thy help and strength are sure.

God of the city's throbbing heart,
 Lord of its industry,
bid greed and base deceit depart,
 give true prosperity.

God of authority and right,
 Lord of all earthly power,
to those who rule us grant thy light,
 thy wisdom be their dower.

God of the nations, King of men,
 Lord of each humble soul,
we seek thy gracious aid again:
 Come down and make us whole.

Thomas C. Hunter Clare
The Voice of Melody, 1949
© 1976 Stainer & Bell Ltd. (admin. Hope Publishing Company)

473
The Gift of Love

Lord, thy word hath taught
 that our deeds are naught
if no flame of love doth fire us,
nor with godly grace inspire us:
 From thy holy hill
 love in us instill.

Send thy Spirit down,
 and thy children crown
with this jewel best and rarest,
in thy diadem the fairest,
 rich all gold above,
 gracious, holy love.

Faith and hope beyond,
 of true peace the bond,
all man's virtues love uniteth
and thine image in him writeth,
 who hath not its light
 lives not in thy sight.

Hear us for his sake,
 who our flesh did take,
send us love that never faileth,
love that o'er all foes prevaileth;
 through thy Son our Lord
 this great gift afford.

Thomas C. Hunter Clare
The Voice of Praise, 1950
© Thomas C. Hunter Clare

474
Lord, by Whose Breath

Lord, by whose breath all souls and seeds are living
    with life that is and life that is to be,
firstfruits of earth we offer with thanksgiving
    for fields in flood with summer's golden sea.

Lord of the earth, accept these gifts in token
    thou in thy works art to be all-adored,
from whom the light as daily bread is broken,
    sunset and dawn as wine and milk are poured.

Poor is our praise, but these shall be our psalter;
    lo, like thyself they rose up from the dead;
Lord, give them back when at thy holy altar
    we feed on thee, who art our living Bread.

Andrew Young
The BBC Hymn Book, 1951
© 1951, Oxford University Press

475
A Country Hymn

We watched the winter turn its back,
    its grip is loosened now,
and shoot and leaf have signed their green
    on brown of field and bough.

From ambushed frost that kills by night,
    and storm with bludgeoned hand,
from soft and secret-moving blight,
    dear God, protect our land,

and send soft rain to feed the crops,
    sun-warm them gold and red;
so grant the prayer we learned from Christ,
    give us our daily bread.

John Arlott, 1950
The BBC Hymn Book, 1951
© Estate of John Arlott

476
A Country Hymn

God, whose farm is all creation,
    take the gratitude we give;
take the finest of our harvest,
    crops we grow that men may live.

Take our plowing, seeding, reaping,
    hopes and fears of sun and rain,
all our thinking, planning, waiting,
    ripened in this fruit and grain.

All our labor, all our watching,
    all our calendar of care,
in these crops of your creation,
    take, O God; they are our prayer.

John Arlott, 1950
The BBC Hymn Book, 1951
© Estate of John Arlott

477
The Whole Armor of God

Give me, O Christ, the strength that is in thee,
    that I may stand in every evil hour;
faints my poor heart except to thee I flee,
    resting my weakness in thy perfect power.

Give me to see the foes that I must fight,
    powers of the darkness, throned where thou
                      shouldst reign,
read the directings of thy wrath aright,
    lest, striking flesh and blood, I strike in vain.

Give me to wear the armor that can guard,
    over my breast thy blood-bought righteousness,
faith for my shield, when fiery darts rain hard,
    girded with truth, and shod with zeal to bless.

(Eph. 6:10–15)

Give me to wield the weapon that is sure,
    taking, through prayer, thy sword into my hand,
word of thy wisdom, peaceable and pure,
    so, Christ my Conqueror, I shall conqueror stand.

Henry Child Carter
Congregational Praise, 1951
© 1951, The United Reformed Church

478
Stewardship

Almighty Father, who for us thy Son didst give
that men and nations in his precious death might
                                                live,
in mercy guard us, lest by sloth and selfish pride
we cause to stumble him for whom the Savior died.
(1 Cor. 8:9)

We are thy stewards; thine our talents, wisdom, skill;
(Matt. 18:24)
our only glory that we may thy trust fulfill;
that we thy pleasure in our neighbors' good pursue,
(Matt. 19:19)
if thou but workest in us both to will and do.
(Phil. 2:13)

On just and unjust thou thy care dost freely shower;
(Matt. 5:45)
make us thy children, free from greed and lust for
                                                power,
lest human justice, yoked with man's unequal laws,
oppress the needy, and neglect the humble cause.

Let not thy worship blind us to the claims of love;
but let thy manna lead us to the feast above,
(Heb 9:4,11)
to seek the country which by faith we now possess,
(Heb. 11:14)
where Christ our treasure reigns in peace and
                                                righteousness.

George Bradford Caird, 1942
Congregational Praise, 1951
© George Bradford Caird

479
More Light and Truth

Not far beyond the sea, nor high
above the heavens, but very nigh   (Deut. 30:11–14)
    thy voice, O God, is heard.
For each new step of faith we take
thou hast more light and truth to break
    forth from thy holy Word.

The babe in Christ thy Scriptures feed   (Heb. 5:13–14)
with milk sufficient for his need,
    the nurture of the Lord.   (Eph. 6:4)
Beneath life's burden and its heat   (Matt. 20:12)
the full-grown man finds stronger meat
    in thy unfailing Word.

Rooted and grounded in thy love,   (Eph. 3:17–18)
with saints on earth and saints above
    we join in full accord
to grasp the breadth, length, depth, and height,
the crucified and risen might
    of Christ, the Incarnate Word.

Help us to press toward that mark,   (Phil. 3:14)
and, though our vision now is dark,   (1 Cor. 13:12)
    to live by what we see.
So, when we see thee face to face,
thy truth and light our dwelling-place
    for ever more shall be.

George Bradford Caird, 1945
New Songs, 1962
© George Bradford Caird

Chapter 22:
Hymns for Children,
1906–1951 (480–486)

This very brief selection does scanty justice to the development of thinking about children's hymns during this period, which in hymnody was one of its most important aspects.

The English Hymnal had a strictly Victorian selection of children's hymns. It is a poor selection, but it is good compared with what was offered by the book universally popular in nonconformist Sunday schools, *The Sunday School Hymnary*, 1905, which packed its section for older children with "junior Gospel Songs" and moralistic doggerel. The temptation to include in chapter 20 Henry Wadsworth Longfellow's "Tell me not in mournful numbers," which this book picked up, was easy to resist.

It may well have been because parents after 1914 had a good deal more contact with their own children than, in the hymn writing section of society, they had earlier, that children's hymnody took on so decisive a new look. Dearmer, in his educational phase, had a good deal to do with it too. In *Songs of Praise*, his children's section, especially in the 1931 edition, is strictly for young children and shows the results of good searching for good children's poetry.

We had had enough, anyhow, of "writing down" to children. The offensive aspect of it was not so much when adults spoke their language in front of children (which children don't mind) but when they seemed, in the stilted and pompous language they affected, not to be taking children seriously. Many new books of children's hymns appeared between about 1920 and 1950, all of which were doing their best to find the right balance in this delicate form of communication. Undoubtedly the two most interesting were *The Church and School Hymnal* and *School Worship*, the one Anglican, the other Congregationalist, both of which came out in 1926.

Number 480 is a good example of the kind of material that appeared in *The Church and School Hymnal* and 481 of that which appeared in *School Worship*. Number 480 is very good, sturdy and swinging, with a very pictorial and at the same time faithful handling of Scripture. Perhaps 481 is, here and there, a little overdone; the "chivalry" motif was, in this and many other hymns of the period, a concession to Romanticism by people who had been brought up on Tennyson. But at least it takes trouble and takes the youngsters seriously.

Number 482, from *School Worship* again, is really remarkable; its author was the Public Orator in the University of Cambridge, a classical scholar, and a Baptist. He builds up, for small children, a vivid picture of the youth of Jesus in a manner which shows the influence of the Schweitzerian *Quest for the Historical Jesus* and of the preaching which was influenced by that line of thought. This book, though getting old now, is still worth careful study by people looking for children's hymns.

With 483 and 484 we return to the Anglican book and introduce that remarkable children's poet, Canon J. M. C. Crum. We shall probably never be able to decide whether 483 goes well over the edge of risibility, or whether it just gets by. Its genial, frankly humorous approach to the sort of thing that Isaac Watts wrote about in his *Divine Songs* certainly sounds a new note and a refreshing one. Its author would have been the last person to expect us to take it very seriously. He always had a very delicate and serene style, and a feeling for the right word, and in 484, which surely is entirely beautiful, he shows us what heights he could reach. Fairly often elsewhere he is a bit arch and sometimes sentimental, but hardly in the ponderous way which the older books insisted was the right way.

Lesbia Scott's hymn of the saints, 485, was written in England but first published in America and much later taken back to England. She here has a slightly Crum-like twinkle. (One supposes an American would now have to read "planes" for "trains" in stanza 3, line 6; and what he does about "tea" is his own problem.) Perhaps "just like me" in the last line but one is a shade questionable; but at the time it was certainly a very good effort at clearing cant out of children's hymnody.

Number 486 is our one example from *Songs of Praise*, but we would gladly suggest that the reader look carefully at the 1931 edition of that book. Here is chivalry again, which nowadays will hardly do as a Christian image; but here also is rhythmical, friendly writing which children have in fact always fallen for. We should add that G. W. Briggs (460–463) wrote some of the best children's hymns that are available, and that they are in *Songs of Praise*.

But this should be enough to alert the reader to the fact, which he will find confirmed in the hymnals of this period, that if the Victorians were in danger always of being stuffy and repressive, the later writers were in equal danger of being sweet and overmellifluous. One healthy sign in the hymnals of this period is the way in which they tend to shorten their children's sections and to close the gap between what is appropriate to children above the age of about ten and what is appropriate for everybody. The adults have for a long time been appropriating the best children's hymns ("Once in royal David's city" is still a children's hymn in *Hymns Ancient & Modern*, but not so elsewhere), and increasingly those who look after children know that children will always welcome the most direct and commanding of the adult hymns. Now that a family is a family and not so much a household, this is as it should be.

480
David and His Son

O David was a shepherd lad,
    and guarded well the sheep;
by night and day, good times or bad,
    his watch he used to keep.
But David's less than David's Son,
    though a shepherd too is he;
through all the world his pastures run,
    and of his flock are we.

O David was a shepherd lad,
    and more he dared to do;
Goliath all in armor clad
    with sling and stone he slew.
But David's Son, more daring yet,
    put weapons all away;
all evil things with goodness met,
    and stronger was than they.

O David was a shepherd lad,
    and a kingdom he attained;
and gold and glory great he had,
    and forty years he reigned.
But David's Son is rich in love,
    and reigns eternally;
for King he is in heaven above,
    and on the earth shall be

Charles Erskine Clarke
The Church and School Hymnal, 1926

481
The Holy War

Christ rides to the holy war again,
leading his own to a new campaign;
for love of God and for love of man,
who will be with him and lead the van?

The Master leads as of old he led
the hero band of our hallowed dead;
to help the poor and the overborne,
who rides with him in the breaking dawn?

To free the body as once the soul,
making like happy and sweet and whole,
to give to labor its heritage,
who will with him in the work engage?

To give to the children smiles for tears,
glad rest for care to the hoary years,
to woman peace, and to manhood power,
who follows him in the present hour?

For Christ is out, and he turns not back,
though fierce the war and though long the track,
till he makes an end of want and woe—
who, then, is ready with him to go?

Yes, Christ is out, and when he comes in
he comes victorious over sin,
as Lord and Brother of love-bound men,
who will go with him and stay till then?

William Charter Piggott
School Worship, 1926

482
Jesus and Joseph

Jesus and Joseph day after day
chiseled and planed and hammered away
in the shop at Nazareth.   (Matt. 13:55)

Mary the Mother ground at the mill;
eight little hungry mouths she must fill
in the home at Nazareth.

Four little boys for kindling were sent;
pulling the grasses and flowers they went
o'er the hills at Nazareth.

Grasses and flowers so pretty and gay,
packed in the oven they smolder away   (Matt. 6:30)
in the yard at Nazareth.

Soon it grows hot, her loaves she can bake;
bread, and not stones, for dinner they take   (Matt. 7:9)
in the home at Nazareth.

"Where is the coin that fell?" with her broom
Mary goes sweeping over the room   (Luke 15:8)
in the home at Nazareth.

"Look! There it is!" She ran in her joy
telling the news to the man and the boy
in the shop at Nazareth.

Patching their clothes by the candle's light (Matt. 9:16)
Mary would sew far into the night
in the home at Nazareth.

Games in the market—what did they play? (Matt. 11:16)
Weddings and funerals, that was their way,
boys and girls at Nazareth.

So he grew up, our Savior dear   (Luke 2:52)
sharing the life of all of us here
in his home at Nazareth.

All that he did, he did for our sake,
seeking a home for us all to make
in heaven like that at Nazareth.

Terrot Reaveley Glover
School Worship, 1926

483
Nature's Good Humor

Oh, once in a while
  we obey with a smile
and are ever so modest and prudent,
but it's not very long
  before something is wrong,
  and somebody's done what he shouldn't.

In meadow and wood
  the cattle are good
and the rabbits are thinking no evil;
the anemones white
  are refined and polite,
  and all the primroses are civil.

O Savior, look down
  when we sulk or we frown
and smooth into kindness our quarrels;
till our heart is as light
  as a little bird's flight
  and our life is as free as a squirrel's!

John McLeod Campbell Crum
The Church and School Hymnal, 1926

484
Love Is Our Shepherd

Love is our shepherd. All is well.
  By meadow green and quiet pool
on summer noons he'll make us lie
  among the elm tree shadows cool.

And when the surly winter comes
  and all the shade is bleak with snows,
Love is our Shepherd, we'll not fear
  to go where Love our Shepherd goes.

For he'll not suffer one lost lamb
  to wander bleating on the fell;
he'll lift it up and bear it home.
  Love is our Shepherd. All is well.

John McLeod Campbell Crum
The Church and School Hymnal, 1926

485
Saints Now

I sing a song of the saints of God,
  patient and brave and true,
who toiled and fought and lived and died
  for the Lord they loved and knew.
And one was a doctor and one was a queen,
and one was a shepherdess on the green:
They were all of them saints of God; and I mean,
  God helping, to be one too.

They loved their Lord so good and dear,
  and his love made them strong;
and they followed the right, for Jesus' sake,
  the whole of their good lives long.
And one was a soldier, and one was a priest,
and one was slain by a fierce wild beast:
And there's not any reason, not the least
  why I shouldn't be one too.

They lived not only in ages past,
  there are hundreds of thousands still;
the world is bright with the joyous saints
  who love to do Jesus' will.
You can meet them in school, or in lanes, or at sea,
in church, or in trains, or in shops, or at tea,
for the saints of God are just like me,
  and I mean to be one too.

Lesbia Lesley Locket Scott
Everyday Hymns for Children, 1929

486
Chivalry

When a knight won his spurs, in the stories of old,
he was gentle and brave, he was gallant and bold;
with a shield on his arm and a lance in his hand
for God and for valor he rode through the land.

No charger have I, and no sword by my side,
yet still to adventure and battle I ride,
though back into storyland giants have fled,
and the knights are no more and the dragons are
dead.

Let faith be my shield and let joy be my steed
'gainst the dragons of anger, the ogres of greed;
and let me set free, with the sword of my youth,
from the castle of darkness the power of the truth.

Jan Struther (Joyce Anstruther Maxtone Graham Placzek)
Songs of Praise, 1931
© 1931, Oxford University Press

Chapter 23:
British Hymnody, 1952–1975
(487–520)

Following the year 1951, in which the first wave of postwar hymnals spent its force, the period of consolidation continued for a while. Then came the beginnings of a revolution. This was, in the first place, musical, and the first shots were fired with the publication in 1957 of the *Folk Mass* by Geoffrey Beaumont (1906–1971), which at once raised the question whether styles up to then regarded as quite alien to English church music could be used in worship and which also gave at once a new connotation to the word "folk."

Since the first phases of this were all musical—devising new tunes for hymns already well known—they do not here concern us. And when the quest for new texts began, its early phases produced texts that went with new kinds of (in the new sense) folk music. These we shall consider in the next chapter.

What concerns us here is that in the years 1956–1965 English hymnody took what one can only describe as a pasting. Many people were saying that the new styles must irretrievably replace the old. Many hasty judgments were made, both by those who espoused them and those who rejected them. It looked as if the main stream of hymnody might dry up.

As it turned out this was certainly not the case, and we must here, in introducing a set of hymns from the period 1964–1975, recount one or two of the events which released again the stream of "straight" hymnody. As will be seen, it began to flow perhaps more clearly and unpollutedly than it had done for many years.

The first thing to say about the years 1964–1975 is that they are the beginning of the age of "supplements." The earlier years had seen a considerable production and marketing of informal books of religious songs; but the red light of inflation had already begun to glow. The consequence

was that, what with the considerable store of new material that was coming, the difficulty of judging its durability in a hurry, the danger that too much hospitality to it might empty the hymnals of too much that was classic and still valuable, and the cost of making full hymnals, the major denominations all decided that the right thing to do was to produce an updating supplement to be used alongside the existing book. This had immense advantages: The editors of a new supplement could concentrate on what was new, without feeling that one new piece meant the extinction of one old one; and the relatively inexpensive supplement might be renewable in a shorter time than economics would dictate in the case of a full-sized book.

But, while the fashion of supplements was introduced by two major collections which appeared almost simultaneously in 1969, *Hymns and Songs* (Methodist) and *100 Hymns for Today* (Anglican, primarily for *Hymns A & M*), the story really begins in 1962 in a remote and pleasant Scottish village called Dunblane. So important is this story in the recent history of hymnody that it must here be recounted by one who was privileged to be a participant in the enterprise.

Around 1960, a row of cottages in Dunblane, about forty miles from both Edinburgh and Glasgow, was bought by the Scottish Churches' Council, a new ecumenical body representing the seven major denominations in Scotland, as a small retreat house and conference center. Pleasantly furnished and equipped with a small chapel in a cave which was reputedly the cell of the medieval Saint Blane, this house was placed in the charge of Dr. Ian Fraser (see 488–489), a minister of the Church of Scotland who had served in a dockside parish at Rosyth. His brief was to organize a program of conferences—what in America are called workshops—to discuss and report on any issue of importance that might be appropriate, either from study of ancient matters or from examination of new political, economic, or ecclesiastical problems that came from time to time. In his wisdom Dr. Fraser, himself not a musician, decided that one of these workshops should be devoted to church music. As will have already been seen, no time in history since the sixteenth century was a better one for the close and zealous examination of the place of music in the church.

It should be understood that the background of this was a feeling that the church must change its shape, its manner, and its attitudes. They were saying the same thing at the time at the Second Vatican Council in Rome, and everybody was saying it. So what was the musician's response? Dr. Fraser himself was and remains—though he is not now in charge at Dunblane—an able disciple of the Iona Community, which from its foundation by Dr. George (later Lord) McLeod was the most active and successful instrument of renewal in the Church of Scotland and collected members from all denominations and from all over the world.

So the spirit in which some twenty-four people, half musicians and half clergy (not excluding several clerical musicians), met was a spirit of excitement and expectation. Now what must here be said, and must be said by a partisan with all possible objectivity, is that the "report" which this workshop was to produce was from the first designed to be a collection of experimental hymns, or whatever other church music occurred to it, for the consideration of the authorities of the Church of Scotland, who were known to be already working on a revision of their official hymn book, *The Church Hymnary*. The question remained open whether whatever Dunblane produced should be issued as a supplemental book by that church or incorporated into its thinking for the new book. The issue, which was known publicly only in 1973 when *The Church Hymnary, Third Edition*, was published, was that, with the single exception of the Rimaud-Langlais hymn (570 in our collection), this is the only major hymnal in recent years which totally ignored the products of the Dunblane group.

However, that is jumping ahead in the story. The conference set up a small working party, after some close thinking about principles, who were to search for or, if necessary, write new material. The products of the first working party appeared in a very informal booklet—hastily written out in the secretary's abominable manuscript and on an electric typewriter—called *Dunblane Praises*. Issued in an edition of 200 copies in 1964, it was retailed at (what used to be) two shillings, about twenty cents. It was distributed to churches and individuals who wanted it, and the edition had to be reprinted until a halt was called at 1,400 copies. There were 16 pieces, of which eight were new tunes to old hymns; but our 497 was in it, and this, with 498, has traveled a long distance since then.

The whole enterprise was repeated in 1966, and the product of that was *Dunblane Praises, 2* (1967); and a third meeting produced some more material, mostly in the form of canticles and responsive music, which was taken by Galliard Ltd. (now Stainer & Bell/Galaxy) and published as *New Songs for the Church I* and *II*, together with gleanings from the two *Dunblane Praises* books.

Now, considering that this material was produced by a fairly small bunch of writers and musicians from several denominations under pressure—they were in any case busy people who could only spare about 48 hours at a time for meetings—the modest success of their materials is, I think, fit to celebrate. As it happens, the only texts we have by members of that working party are 488, 489, and 504; but the ascriptions of several others will indicate that they were collected and first published by this group.

At this point it is worth looking at the two pieces by Dr. Fraser, 488 and 489; if Scotland had been tardy in producing literature in hymnody, in the person of Ian Fraser it certainly woke up. He has written much more than this (see also 530, 708, and 709). He has a zestful style, a poetic imagination, and an impatience of cliché which produces sometimes a most endearing roughness of texture. As for 504, all that needs to be said is that we include it here because it qualifies for inclusion in the *Hymnal Guide*, which see for a note on the odd circumstances of its composition.

But, going on from there, the Congregationalist minister John Geyer, a very able theologian, was laid under contribution in 491; and his other hymn, 492, first in *Hymns and Songs* (1969), has traveled some distance since. These are both weighty theological utterances saying quite new things about their subjects.

Brian Wren (497) was in the 1964 booklet, and we hardly knew then that we were coming in on the early work of a writer who was to achieve major importance. But since then he has done so. Wren, Kaan, and Pratt Green (to whom we shall come almost at once) are the leading triumvirate of English hymn writers at the moment (1975), and each has his special gifts. Wren's is for the felicitous expression of profound theological ideas. His communion hymn (498) brings together as no other does the equally important individual and communal factors in the grace that the sacrament confers: "I" becomes, before the end, "we," a beautiful piece of timing and reconciliation. We present 499 for the same kind of reason; who else has written a hymn on the subject, "How dare you presume to serve?" Place this alongside, say, 284, and see what has happened. And in 500 we have one of many hymns, and the best so far, on the now fashionable subject of ecology; note again the disciplined choice of words, and the lyric passion that compensates entirely for the absence of rhyme.

Number 503, one of many hymns written by Ian Ferguson, an ex–classics professor who is now Dean of Arts in the Open University in England, is probably the best known of all the Dunblane products. Informality masks a ferocious seriousness in this characteristically social-oriented poem.

That disposes of Dunblane. Before turning to the supplements of the more official sort, we must mention 487, which comes from a book prepared for public (residential) schools in 1964, a book which remains the model for all future editors in matters of style, presentation, and precision of textual reading. The new texts in this book are not many, or specially distinguished, but their finest discovery was Donald Hughes, who just before his untimely death had begun to develop a very promising gift for hymnody. Hughes was a Methodist Head Master, a devoted admirer of Charles Wesley and of Bernard Manning, and in 487 (which he wrote in "thou," but his executor has authorized the perfectly natural changes to "you") he produced a perfect lyric, serious but hopeful, not a word out of place, with a Wesley-like balance between the massive words and the small ones.

One other important hymnal of the same period is the *Anglican Hymn Book* (1965), a book for Anglican Evangelical congregations containing a good deal more of the classic Calvinist and Methodist hymnody than one finds in the other two hymnals used in that church. Among the new texts to be found there is 501, by an author, Timothy Dudley-Smith, who here and later elsewhere proves himself to have a polished and direct style. "Tell out, my soul" is no doubt the first hymn to be directly inspired by the text of the New English Bible (compare 517) and has become very popular. Less well known, but often equally admirable, is his work in *Psalm Praise* (1973), a book of hymns, often in popular style, based on the Psalter. Number 502 is an example of this, and his work is easily the most valuable in that collection.

The first of the official supplements to appear, *Hymns and Songs*, virtually introduced the work of Fred Pratt Green. It is true that one of his pieces was in the *Methodist School Hymn Book* of 1950, but it is only since 1969 that, having been before a poet and dramatist as well as a minister, he emerged as one of the leaders among hymn writers. That he undoubtedly now is. It is safe to say that no hymnal that ignores him can claim to be fully literate. He has one very unusual gift: he especially enjoys writing "to order" and does his best work when so stimulated. In such circumstances he always writes at once and sends a revision a few days later. Number 505 was written to carry a certain tune, CHRISTE SANCTORUM, and how majestically simple and trenchant it is. It has a timeless quality and yet could only have been written in the mid-twentieth century because of the especially modern juxtaposition of ancient ideas that it achieves. Number 506 is one of his finest pieces, and again note now, by the use of none but simple words, he tells the singer so much about the doctrine of the Trinity—even, in stanza 2, its history—that nobody else tells him. From the now considerable bulk of his work I chose 507, published previously only on a leaflet printed for the occasion it celebrates, for its beautiful combination of sheer ingenuity and hymnic eloquence. It is unlikely that the original version will be much sung, for you have to know a little of the Lady Julian to catch its allusions, especially in stanza 4. But even if one doesn't know Julian, one can appreciate the climax of that stanza. The more general version once again says quite new things about saints. (What an unsmiling and fraught company they are in the more pedestrian of the Victorian hymns!)

Both the Methodist supplement and *100 Hymns for Today* carry 508 and 509, featuring two of our most gifted women writers. Rosamond Herklots mostly writes hymns for children, but this admirable piece (508) has gone far enough to get into the *Hymnal Guide*. Miss Chisholm's very dramatic piece on Peter (509), written originally with a special dramatic ceremony in mind, is full of telling and alarming messages and is also proving a good traveler.

Numbers 510–514 are our first encounters with the new Catholic hymnody. It will later be necessary to say that Vatican II, with its liberation of vernacular hymnody, has yet to liberate any good texts in the USA, but England and Scotland have been more fortunate. James Quinn, of the Lauriston Jesuit Fathers in Edinburgh, produced single-handedly a book in 1969 which contained a hundred pieces, some translations, some original, in a very finished and professional style, thus giving his coreligionists a good start. In England, although an understandable eagerness to cash in on the new hymnic permissiveness produced a certain amount

of hastily written material and hastily edited literature, the *New Catholic Hymnal* of 1971, a learned and demanding collection mostly showing fairly lofty taste, discovered a brilliant new writer in Brian Foley; and *Praise the Lord*, a more parish-oriented collection put together by three youthful scholars, gives us some fine material in a different key. The two Foley pieces (512 and 513) are very polished, modest, and moving; the energy and rhythm of the two from *Praise the Lord* (514 and 515) have already evoked some fascinating music, and deservedly so. Ever since 1964, Protestants have hoped that Catholics would avoid the errors into which Protestants fell in their hymn-singing customs. That was, it turned out, too much to hope for, but the excellent example of these two books and of *Worship II* in America and the *Catholic Book of Worship* (1972) in Canada is one that we all hope will be widely followed.

The third edition of *The Church Hymnary* in Scotland admitted relatively few new texts and, as we said, missed many chances, but here and there it provides a new text worth anybody's respect. Dr. Archibald M. Hunter, very well known as a scholar in New Testament studies, paraphrases what all his pupils know to be his favorite biblical passage in 516, in a most unusual and entirely appropriate meter. Ian Pitt-Watson, perhaps Scotland's most accomplished minister-musician, has metricized three psalms (see 517) using the language of the New English Bible and surprising many by finding so much poetry there. His versions are beautifully done and are a good augury for any revision of the Scottish Psalter that may, within the next thousand years or so, be in view.

Some of the "supplement" material already mentioned appears in *New Church Praise* (1975), such as our 500. Of the many authors appearing there for the first time, it is, we hope, not invidious to select the two who seem to be the best metrists. John Gregory (518, written long before publication) takes a Genevan meter otherwise handled only by Bridges (260) for his spacious communion hymn, and Caryl Micklem, English scholar and musician (519), shows considerable versatility in his substantial contribution to that book, not least in writing for children (535). He is one of the very few authors outside the "folk" circle who successfully write their own music for their lyrics.

This leaves us only with the fascinating and unclassifiable Fred Kaan. Kaan, as many already know, is a Dutch-born minister of the United Reformed Church (formerly Congregationalist) who began in the 1960s writing hymns for his own congregation in Plymouth, England. He has never written hymns in his own language, but he has made English so much his own as to have developed a quite inimitable and distinctive style. His hymns up to 1971 were collected in the last edition of *Pilgrim Praise* (Galliard), but he issued some of them privately at an earlier stage in an informal typescript booklet and then in a printed booklet, neither of which needed music because he always wrote in the meter of a well-known hymn tune.

What Kaan has done primarily is to focus the contemporary desire for hymns about modern ideas and situations, especially hymns about the city, and respond to it. Two of his best-known hymns are "Sing we of the modern city" and "Sing we a song of high revolt"; I happen to think that both contain blemishes which make them less appropriate for inclusion here than the four I have ventured to choose from the collection of sixty-eight. These, surely, repay careful attention.

The one to look at first is 495, and the line to note is "and for the love we owe the modern city," which in its context is pure, vintage Kaan. Then look at 496, the very simple communion hymn, and notice how naturally and yet how dramatically the "machine" is accommodated in it; also the wonderful phrase, "Pass from hand to hand the living love of Christ." After this consider 493. Here one sees the other special gift of Kaan, which is a feeling for words so intense as to produce strange and often exhilarating word-associations. His title, "Come to Your Senses," is a good example of the

ambiguity he loves to play with. And the spirit of joyful surprise is nowhere better communicated than in the first and last stanzas of this. Even more elusive, perhaps, is 494, in which the word "tree" takes on a dreamlike, shifting quality, prepared for by the image of the "gardener." Among his many remarkable compositions I believe this to be the most searching and distinguished. In Kaan we have indeed the archetypal "new-European" hymn writer. He will appear again in chapter 28.

The reader is, of course, encouraged to look about in contemporary books for new material, and if he does so he will encounter plenty more not only from the authors mentioned but from others. The third quarter of the twentieth century, after a quiet start followed by an alarming episode, has brought out of English hymn-writers a form of song which is at the same time traditional in form and new and fresh in content. Especially it expresses contemporary doubts (and, at its best, their resolutions), contemporary hesitations (and, at its best, penitence), and contemporary observation (and, at its best, concreteness).

The signature hymn for some people for the whole of this modern movement is 490, perhaps the most famous of all "contemporary" hymns in traditional form. The reader must decide whether the author has succeeded in making poetry out of motorways and pylons and railways; every new hymnal has it and almost always to a different tune. The best comment on it is what one young scientist of semiagnostic cast of mind is known to have said when it first appeared: "This is the first time the church has said anything that indicates that it, or God, is interested in what I do with my life." "God of concrete" is the central and archetypal hymn of mission to technology, and as such it deserves honor. Its author is a Methodist; Charles Wesley might possibly knit his brows over it, but John, whose special genius was in being observant and in despising cant, would certainly have responded with a surprised and delighted chuckle.

487
Penitence

Creator of the earth and skies,
    to whom the words of life belong,   (John 6:67)
grant us your truth to make us wise;
    grant us your power to make us strong.

Like theirs of old, our life is death,
    our light is darkness, till we see   (John 9:41)
the eternal Word made flesh and breath,
    the God who walked by Galilee.

We have not known you; to the skies
    our monuments of folly soar,
and all our self-wrought miseries
    have made us trust ourselves the more.

We have not loved you; far and wide
    the wreckage of our hatred spreads,
and evils wrought by human pride
    recoil on unrepentant heads.

For this, our foolish confidence,
    our pride of knowledge, and our sin,
we come to you in penitence;
    in us the work of grace begin.   (Phil 1:6)

Teach us to know and love you, Lord,
    and humbly follow in your way.
Speak to our souls the quickening word,
    and turn our darkness into day.

Donald W. Hughes
Hymns for Church and School, 1964
altered, 1969
© Paul Hughes

488
Christ, Burning

Christ, burning
    past all suns,
stars beneath thy feet
    like leaves on forest floor:
Man, turning
    spaceward, shuns
knowledge incomplete,
    fevered, to explore.

Christ, holding
    atoms in one
loom of light and power
    to weave creation's life:
Man, molding
    rocket, gun,
turns creation sour,
    plots dissolving strife.

Christ, festive
    in gay bird,
rush of river flood,
    joy on lovers' part:
Youth, restive
    seeks new word,
beat of life in blood,
    chill of death in heart.

Christ, humble
    on our side,
snatching death's grim keys,
    ending Satan's scope:
We gamble
    on our Guide,
inch our gains of peace,
    work a work of hope.

Ian M. Fraser
Dunblane Praises 1, 1964
© 1972, Stainer & Bell Ltd. (admin. Hope Publishing Company)

489
Lord, Bring the Day to Pass

Lord, bring the day to pass
 when forest, rock, and hill,
the beasts, the birds, the grass
 will know your finished will:
When man attains his destiny
and nature its lost unity.

Forgive our careless use
 of water, ore, and soil—
the plenty we abuse
 supplied by others' toil:
Save us from making self our creed,
turn us towards our brother's need.

Give us, when we release
 creation's secret powers,
to harness them for peace,
 our children's peace, and ours:
Teach us the art of mastering
which makes life rich, and draws death's sting.

Creation groans, travails;   (Rom. 8:22)
 futile its present plight,
bound—till the hour it hails
 the newborn sons of light
who enter on their true estate.
Come, Lord: New heavens and earth create!

          (Rev. 21:1)

Ian M. Fraser
New Songs for the Church, 1969
© 1969, Stainer & Bell Ltd. (admin. Hope Publishing Company)

490
The Earth Is the Lord's

God of concrete, God of steel,
God of piston and of wheel,
God of pylon, God of steam,
God of girder and of beam,
God of atom, God of mine,
all the world of power is thine.

Lord of cable, Lord of rail,
Lord of motorway and mail,
Lord of rocket, Lord of flight,
Lord of soaring satellite,
Lord of lightning's livid line,
all the world of speed is thine.

Lord of science, Lord of art,
God of map and graph and chart,
Lord of physics and research,
word of Bible, faith of church,
Lord of sequence and design,
all the world of truth is thine.

God, whose glory fills the earth,
gave the universe its birth,
loosed the Christ with Easter's might,
saves the world from evil's blight,
claims mankind by grace divine,
all the world of love is thine.

Richard G. Jones, 1962
Methodist Recorder, 1964
© 1968, Stainer & Bell Ltd. (admin. Hope Publishing Company)

491
Our Risen Lord We Will Adore

Our risen Lord we will adore
 who broke the gates of hell;
the Tyrant's power shall hold no more,
 and earth with praise shall swell.

So great the Lord is, and our King
    in majesty doth reign;   (Ps. 99:1)
all men his greatness ever sing
    and shout aloud his name.

The elemental powers are dead,   (Gal. 4:9)
    the rule of sin and fear,
all by our God are captive led,   (Ps. 68:18)
    his kingdom now draws near.

The powers of war and peace are caught,
    all other fame is loss;   (Phil. 3:8)
the stonied soul, her freedom bought,   (Job 17:8)
    rejoices in his cross.

With all your being show his praise,
    who feeds us with his leaven;   (1 Cor. 5:8)
in song his mighty deeds upraise
    and rise with him to heaven.

John Brownlow Geyer
Dunblane Praises 1, 1964
© 1969, Stainer & Bell Ltd. (admin. Hope Publishing Company)

492
We Know That Christ Is Raised and Dies No More

We know that Christ is raised and dies no more.
Embraced by futile death he broke its hold;   (Rom. 6:9)
and man's despair he turned to blazing joy.
        Alleluia!

We share by water in his saving death.
This union brings to being one new cell,
a living and organic part of Christ.
        Alleluia!

The Father's splendor clothes the Son with life.
The Spirit's fission shakes the Church of God.
Baptized we live with God the Three-in-One.
        Alleluia!

A new Creation comes to life and grows
as Christ's new Body takes on flesh and blood.
The universe restored and whole will sing:
        Alleluia!

John Brownlow Geyer, 1967
Hymns and Songs, 1969
© John Brownlow Geyer

493
Come to Your Senses

If you have ears, then listen
    to what the Spirit says
and give an open hearing
    to wonder and surprise.

If you have eyes for seeing
    the word in human form,
then let your love be telling
    and your compassion warm.

If you have buds for tasting
    the apple of God's eye,
then go, enjoy creation
    and people on the way.

If you have hands for caring,
    then pray that you may know
the tender art of loving
    our world of touch and go.

If you can smell the perfume
    of life, the feast of earth,
then sow the seeds of laughter
    and tend the shoots of mirth.

Come, people, to your senses,
    and celebrate the day!
For God gives wine for water,   (John 2:1–12)
    the gift of light for gray.

Fred Kaan, 1970
Pilgrim Praise, 1968
© 1972, Hope Publishing Company

494

The Tree Springs to Life

We meet you, O Christ,
in many a guise;
your image we see
in simple and wise.
You live in a palace,
exist in a shack.
We see you, the gardener,   (John 20:15)
a tree on your back.

In millions alive,
away and abroad;
involved in our life
you live down the road.
Imprisoned in systems
you long to be free.
We see you, Lord Jesus,
still bearing your tree.   (Luke 23:26)

We hear you, O man,
in agony cry.
For freedom you march,
in riots you die.
Your face in the papers
we read and we see.
The tree must be planted
by human decree.

You choose to be made
at one with the earth;
the dark of the grave
prepares for your birth.
Your death is your rising,
creative your word;
the tree springs to life and
our hope is restored.

Fred Kaan, 1966
Pilgrim Praise, 1968
© 1968, Hope Publishing Company
In *The Only Earth We Know*, 1999, Kaan made these changes: line 2:7,
"We witness you, Jesus"; line 3:1, "Man" or "Christ" for "man."

495

From Worship to Service

Lord, as we rise to leave this shell of worship,
called to the risk of unprotected living,
willing to be at one with all your people,
we ask for courage.

For all the strain with living interwoven,
for the demands each day will make upon us,
and for the love we owe the modern city,
Lord, make us cheerful.

Give us an eye for openings to serve you;
make us alert when calm is interrupted,
ready and wise to use the unexpected:
Sharpen our insight.

Lift from our life the blanket of convention;
give us the nerve to lose our life to others.
Be with your church in death and resurrection,
Lord of all ages!

Fred Kaan, 1966
Pilgrim Praise, 1968
© 1968, Hope Publishing Company

496

A Communion Hymn

As we break the bread
and taste the life of wine,
we bring to mind our Lord,
man of all time.

Grain is sown to die;   (John 11:24)
it rises from the dead,
becomes through human toil
our common bread.

Pass from hand to hand
    the living love of Christ!
Machine and man provide
    bread for this feast.

Jesus binds in one
    our daily life and work;
he is of all mankind
    symbol and mark.

Having shared the bread
    that died to rise again,
we rise to serve the world,
    scattered as grain.

Fred Kaan, 1965
Pilgrim Praise, 1968
© 1968, Hope Publishing Company
In subsequent publications, the author made these revisions: line 1:4,
"man" to "Man"; line 2:4, "our daily bread"; line 3:3, "machines and
people raise"; and, line 4:3, "he is of humankind."

497
Prayer for Unity

Lord Christ, the Father's mighty Son,
whose work upon the cross was done
    all men to receive,
make all our scattered churches one,
    that the world may believe.

To make us one your prayers were said.
To make us one you broke the bread
    for all to receive.
Its pieces scatter us instead:
    How can others believe?

Lord Christ, forgive us, make us new!
What our designs could never do
    your love can achieve.
Our prayers, our work, we bring to you
    that the world may believe.

We will not question or refuse
the way you work, the means you choose,
    the pattern you weave,
but reconcile our warring views
    that the world may believe.   (John 17:21)

Brian Wren, 1962
Dunblane Praises 1, 1964
© 1968, Hope Publishing Company
In *Faith Looking Forward*, 1983, Wren revised line 1:3 to read
"to give and receive."
A subsequent revision, beginning "Dear Christ, the Father's loving
Son," is found among the "Hymns Not Included" in
Piece Together Praise, 1996.

498
Christ Making Friends

A. Original

I come with joy to meet my Lord,
    forgiven, loved, and free,
in awe and wonder to recall
    his life laid down for me.

I come with Christians far and near,
    to find, as all are fed,
man's true community of love
    in Christ's communion bread.

As Christ breaks bread for men to share
    each proud division ends,
the love that made us, makes us one,
    and strangers now are friends.

And thus with joy we meet our Lord,
    his presence, always near,
is in such friendship better known:
    We see and praise him here.

Together met, together bound,
  we'll go our different ways,
and as his people in the world
  we'll live and speak his praise.

Brian Wren, 1968
The Hymn Book, 1971
© 1971, 1995, Hope Publishing Company

B. Christ's Freedom Meal

I come with joy, a child of God,
  forgiven, loved, and free,
the life of Jesus to recall,
  in love laid down for me.

I come with Christians far and near
  to find, as all are fed,
the new community of love
  in Christ's communion bread.

As Christ breaks bread, and bids us share,
  each proud division ends.
The love that made us makes us one,
  and strangers now are friends.

The Spirit of the risen Christ,
  unseen, but ever near,
is in such friendship better known,
  alive among us here.

Together met, together bound
  by all that God has done,
we'll go with joy, to give the world
  the love that makes us one.

Brian Wren, 1968; revised, 1977, 1993
Piece Together Praise, 1996
© 1971, 1995, Hope Publishing Company

499
Pilgrimage of Confession

A. Original

Lord Jesus, if I love and serve my neighbor
  out of my knowledge, leisure, power, or wealth,
open my eyes to understand his anger
  if from his helplessness he hates my help.

When I have met my brother's need with kindness
  and prayed that he could waken from despair,
open my ears if, crying now for justice,
  he struggles for the changes that I fear.

Lord, though I cling to safety or possessions,
  yet from the cross love's poverty prevails:
Open my heart to life and liberation,
  open my hands to bear the mark of nails.

Brian Wren, 1973
New Church Praise, 1975
© 1983, Hope Publishing Company
In *Faith Looking Forward*, 1983, Wren noted that the pronouns might
be male in stanza one and female in stanza two or vice versa.

B. Living with God

Spirit of Jesus, if I love my neighbor
  out of my knowledge, leisure, power, or wealth,
help me to understand the shame and anger
  of helplessness that hates my power to help.

And if, when I have answered need with kindness,
  my neighbor rises, wakened from despair,
keep me from flinching when the cry for justice
  requires of me the changes that I fear.

If I am hugging safety of possessions,
    uncurl my spirit, as your love prevails,
to join my neighbors, work for liberation,
    and find my freedom at the mark of nails.

> Brian Wren, 1973; revised, 1995, 1996
> *Piece Together Praise*, 1996
> © 1975, 1994, Hope Publishing Company

500
Caring for Planet Earth

Thank you, Lord, for water, soil, and air—
large gifts supporting everything that lives.
    Forgive our spoiling and abuse of them.
    Help us renew the face of the earth.

Thank you, Lord, for minerals and ores—
the basis of all building, wealth, and speed.
    Forgive our reckless plundering and waste.
    Help us renew the face of the earth.

Thank you, Lord, for priceless energy—
stored in each atom, gathered from the sun.
    Forgive our greed and carelessness of power.
    Help us renew the face of the earth.

Thank you, Lord, for weaving nature's life
into a seamless robe, a fragile whole.
    Forgive our haste, that tampers unawares.
    Help us renew the face of the earth.

Thank you, Lord, for making planet earth
a home for us and ages yet unborn.
    Help us to share, consider, save, and store.
    Come and renew the face of the earth.

> Brian Wren, 1973
> *New Church Praise*, 1975
> © 1975, Hope Publishing Company
> In *Faith Looking Forward*, 1983, Wren changed the address
> from "Lord" to "God."

501
Magnificat

Tell out, my soul, the greatness of the Lord!
    Unnumbered blessings give my spirit voice;
tender to me the promise of his word;
    in God my Savior shall my heart rejoice.

Tell out, my soul, the greatness of his name!
    make known his might, the deeds his arm has
                                            done;
his mercy sure, from age to age the same;
    his holy name—the Lord, the Mighty One.

Tell out, my soul, the greatness of his might!
    Powers and dominions lay their glory by.
Proud hearts and stubborn wills are put to flight,
    the hungry fed, the humble lifted high.

Tell out, my soul, the glories of his word!
    Firm is his promise, and his mercy sure.
Tell out, my soul, the greatness of the Lord
    to children's children and for evermore!

> Timothy Dudley-Smith, 1961
> based on New English Bible version of Luke 1:46–55
> *Anglican Hymn Book*, 1965
> © 1962, 1990, Hope Publishing Company

502
Non Nobis, Domine. Psalm 115

Not to us be glory given
    but to him who reigns above,
Glory to the God of heaven
    for his thankfulness and love!
What though unbelieving voices
    hear no word and see no sign,
still in God my heart rejoices,
    working out his will divine.

Not what human fingers fashion,
    gold and silver, deaf and blind,
dead to knowledge and compassion,
    having neither heart nor mind—
lifeless gods, yet men adore them,
    nerveless hands and feet of clay;
all become, who bow before them,
    lost indeed, and dead as they.

Not in them is hope of blessing—
    hope is in the living Lord!
High and low, his name confessing,
    find in him their shield and sword.
Hope of all whose hearts revere him,
    God of Israel, still the same!
God of Aaron! Those who fear him
    he remembers them by name.

Not the dead, but we the living
    praise the Lord with all our powers;
of his goodness freely giving—
    his is heaven: earth is ours.
Not to us be glory given
    but to him who reigns above;
Glory to the God of heaven
    for his faithfulness and love!

Timothy Dudley-Smith, 1970
Psalm Praise, 1973
© 1973, Hope Publishing Company

503
Am I My Brother's Keeper

"Am I my brother's keeper?"   (Gen. 4:9)
    the muttered cry was drowned
by Abel's life-blood shouting
    in silence from the ground.
For no man is an island,
    divided from the main;
the bell which tolled for Abel
    tolled equally for Cain.

The ruler called for water,
    and thought his hands were clean,   (Matt. 27:24)
Christ counted less than order,
    the man than the machine.
The crowd cried, "Crucify him!"
    their malice wouldn't budge,
so Pilate called for water,
    and history's his judge.

As long as people hunger,
    as long as people thirst,
and ignorance and illness
    and warfare do their worst,
as long as there's injustice
    in any of God's lands,
I am my brother's keeper;
    I dare not wash my hands.

John (Ian) Ferguson, 1966
Dunblane Praises 2, 1967
© 1969, Stainer & Bell Ltd. (admin. Hope Publishing Company)

504
The Lord Is There

All who love and serve your city,
    all who bear its daily stress,
all who cry for peace and justice,
    all who curse, and all who bless,

in your day of loss and sorrow,
    in your day of helpless strife,
honor, peace, and love retreating,
    seek the Lord, who is your life.

In your day of wealth and plenty,
    wasted work and wasted play,
call to mind the word of Jesus,
    Work ye yet while it is day."   (John 9:4)

For all days are days of judgment,
    and the Lord is waiting still,
drawing near to men who spurn him,   (Luke 19:41)
    offering peace on Calvary's hill.

Risen Lord, shall yet the city
    be the city of despair?
Come today, our Judge, our Glory,
    be its name, "The Lord is there."   (Ezek. 48:35)

Erik Routley, 1966
Dunblane Praises 2, 1967
© 1969, Stainer & Bell Ltd. (admin. Hope Publishing Company)
The form of the text above is that appearing in the first edition of this
book and in *Ecumenical Praise*, 1976. *Our Lives Be Praise*, 1990,
reproduces Routley's typescript, which has the heading "For the City"
and these differences: 2:3, "honor, love, and peace retreating"; 3:4, "'I
must work while it is day'"; 4:4, "offering peace from Calvary's hill";
and, 5:1, "Risen Lord! shall still the city."

505
The Uniqueness of Christ

Christ is the world's Light, he and none other;
born in the darkness, he became our Brother.
If we have seen him, we have seen the Father: (John 14:9)
    Glory to God on high.

Christ is the world's Peace, he and none other;
no man can serve him and despise his brother.   (1 John 4:20)
Who else unites us, one in God the Father? (John 17:21)
    Glory to God on high.

Christ is the world's Life, he and none other;
sold once for silver, murdered here, our Brother—
he who redeems us, reigns with God the Father:
    Glory to God on high.

Give God the glory, God and none other;
give God the glory, Spirit, Son, and Father;
give God the glory, God in Man my brother:
    Glory to God on high.

Fred Pratt Green, 1968
Hymns and Songs, 1969
© 1969, Hope Publishing Company

506
Hymn in Honor of the Holy and Undivided Trinity

Rejoice with us in God the Trinity,
    the Three for ever One, forever Three,
Fountain of Love, Giver of Unity!

We would rejoice again, and yet again
that God reveals his truth to mortal men,
    unveils for all to see,
in what he is, what man himself may be.

How long and earnestly the Fathers strove
to frame in words a faith we cannot prove;
    but, oh, how dead our creeds
unless they live in Christ-like words and deeds!

So let us all, rejecting none, remove
whatever thwarts a reconciling love,
    all ills that still divide
the fold of Christ, and all the world beside.

Rejoice with us that man may yet achieve
what God himself has dared us to believe:
    That many live as one,
each loving each, as Father, Spirit, Son.

Fred Pratt Green, 1970
26 Hymns, 1971
© 1971, Hope Publishing Company
In *The Hymns and Ballads of Fred Pratt Green*, 1983, the author
changed "man" to "we" in lines 1:4 and 4:1.

507

In Commemoration of Julian of Norwich

A. Original

Rejoice in God's saints
    this day of all days!
A world without saints
    forgets how to praise!
Rejoice in their courage,
    their spiritual skill;
in Julian of Norwich
    rejoice, all who will!

The candle she lit
    six centuries gone,
by darkness beset
    shines quietly on.
Her cell is no prison,
    though narrow and dim,
for Jesus is risen
    and she lives in him.

How bright in her cell
    the showings of God!
No writings could tell
    what love understood.
She suffers his passion,
    she grieves over sin,
and shares that compassion
    which makes us all kin.

How courteous is God!
    All love and all light!
In God's Motherhood
    she finds her delight.
She pleads for the sinner,
    she wrestles with hell;
God answers: *"All manner
    of things shall be well!"*

Dear Lord, we would learn
    to walk in this way,
with patience discern
    how best to obey.
The disciplined spirit,
    the saintly, how rare!
Lord, help us to wear it—
    the habit of prayer!

Written for a celebration at Norwich, England, of the 600th anniversary of the *Revelations of Divine Love*, which Lady Julian of Norwich wrote in 1373, this text incorporates many expressions and one direct quotation from the *Revelations*.

In *The Hymns and Ballads of Fred Pratt Green*, 1983, the author presented the final four lines in this form:

That call to perfection
    you taught us to face:
Lord, fix our direction,
    and keep us in grace.

B. For any saint's day

Rejoice in God's saints,
    this day of all days!
A world without saints
    forgets how to praise!
Their joy in exploring
    far reaches of prayer,
their depth of adoring,
    Lord, help us to share.

Rejoice in God's saints,
    the grave and the gay!
Some march with events,
    some live but to pray.
The world in its folly
    they wake from its dream:
In love that is holy
    there's power to redeem.

Rejoice in God's saints!
　　what patience is theirs!
They shame our complaints.
　　our comforts, our cares.
The disciplined spirit,
　　the saintly, how rare!
Lord, help us to wear it,
　　this habit of prayer!

Rejoice in God's saints
　　this day of all days!
A world without saints
　　forgets how to praise.
In loving, in living,
　　they prove it is true:
the way of self-giving,
　　Lord, leads us to you.

C. In Celebration of Saints

Rejoice in God's saints, today and all days!
A world without saints forgets how to praise.
Their faith in acquiring the habit of prayer,
their depth of adoring, Lord, help us to share.

Some march with events to turn them God's way;
some need to withdraw, the better to pray;
some carry the gospel through fire and through flood:
our world is their parish: Their purpose is God.

Rejoice in those saints, unpraised and unknown,
who bear someone's cross, or shoulder their own:
They shame our complaining, our comforts, our cares:
What patience in caring, what courage is theirs!

Rejoice in God's saints, today and all days!
A world without saints forgets how to praise.
In loving, in living, they prove it is true:
Their way of self-giving, Lord, leads us to you.

Fred Pratt Green, 1973, 1977
The Hymns and Ballads of Fred Pratt Green, 1983
© 1973, Hope Publishing Co.
Rewritten to widen its scope and displayed in this form in
The Hymns and Ballads of Fred Pratt Green, 1983.

508
The Unforgiving Heart

"Forgive our sins as we forgive,"
　　you taught us, Lord, to pray,
but you alone can grant us grace
　　to live the words we say.

How can your pardon reach and bless
　　the unforgiving heart
that broods on wrongs, and will not let
　　old bitterness depart?

In blazing light your cross reveals
　　the truth we dimly knew,
how small the debts men owe to us,
　　how great our debt to you.　　　(Luke 7:41–2)

Lord, cleanse the depths within our souls
　　and bid resentment cease;
then, reconciled with God and man,
　　our lives will spread your peace.

Rosamond E. Herklots, 1966
Hymns and Songs, 1969
© 1969, Oxford University Press

509
Peter Feared the Cross

Peter feared the cross for himself and his Master;
Peter tempted Jesus to turn and go back.
    O Lord, have mercy,
    lighten our darkness.
    We've all been tempters,
    our light is black.

Judas loved his pride and rejected his Master;
Judas turned a traitor, and lost his way back.
    O Lord, have mercy,
    lighten our darkness.
    We've all been traitors,
    our light is black.

Peter, James, and John fell asleep when their Master
asked them to be praying a few paces back.
    O Lord, have mercy,
    lighten our darkness.
    We've all been sleeping,
    our light is black.

Peter, vexed and tired, thrice denied his own Master;
said he never knew him, to stop a girl's clack.
    O Lord, have mercy,
    lighten our darkness.
    We've all denied you,
    our light is black.

Twelve all ran away, and forsook their dear Master;
left him, lonely prisoner, a lamb in wolves' pack.
    O Lord, have mercy,
    lighten our darkness.
    We've all been failures,
    our light is black.

Pilate asked the crowd to set free their good Master.
"Crucify!" they shouted, "we don't want him back!"
    O Lord, have mercy,
    lighten our darkness.
    We crucified you,
    our light is black.

We have watched the cross and we've scoffed at our
                                      Master:
thought the safe way better, and tried our own tack.
    O Lord, have mercy,
    lighten our darkness.
    We've all reviled you,
    our light is black.

Emily Chisholm, 1964
Hymns and Songs, 1969
© Hymns Ancient and Modern Ltd.

510
Ubi Caritas

God is love, and where true love is, God himself is
                                        there.
Here in Christ we gather, love of Christ our calling.
Christ, our love, is with us, gladness be his greeting.
Let us fear him, yes, and love him, God eternal.
Loving him, let each love Christ in all his brethren.

    God is love, and where true love is,
    God himself is there.

When we Christians gather, members of one body,
let there be in us no discord, but one Spirit.
Banished now be anger, strife, and every quarrel.
Christ, our God, be always present here among us.

Grant us love's fulfillment, joy with all the blessed,
when we see your face, O Savior, in its glory.
Shine on us, O purest Light of all creation,
be our bliss while endless ages sing your praises.

James Quinn
translated from the liturgy for Maundy Thursday
Hymns for All Seasons, 1969
© 1969, Continuum International Publishing Group, Ltd.

511
Forth in the Peace of Christ

Forth in the peace of Christ we go:
    Christ to the world with joy we bring;
Christ in our minds, Christ on our lips,
    Christ in our hearts, the world's true King.

King of our hearts, Christ makes us kings; (1 Pet. 2:9)
    kingship with him his servants gain;
with Christ the Servant-Lord of all,
    Christ's world we serve to share Christ's reign.

Priests of the world, Christ sends us forth
    the world of time to consecrate,
the world of sin by grace to heal,
    Christ's world in Christ to re-create. (2 Cor. 5:17)

Christ's are our lips, his word we speak;
    prophets are we whose deeds proclaim
Christ's truth in love that we may be
    Christ in the world, to spread Christ's name.

We are the church; Christ bids us show
    that in his church all nations find
their hearth and home where Christ restores
    true peace, true love, to all mankind.

James Quinn
Hymns for All Seasons, 1969
© 1969, Continuum International Publishing Group, Ltd.

512
See Christ Was Wounded for Our Sake

See, Christ was wounded for our sake,
    and bruised and beaten for our sin,
so by his sufferings we are healed,
    for God has laid our guilt on him.

Look on his face, come close to him—
    see, you will find no beauty there:
Despised, rejected, who can tell
    the grief and sorrow he must bear?

Like sheep that stray, we leave God's path
    to choose our own and not his will;
like sheep to slaughter he has gone,
    obedient to his Father's will.

Cast out to die by those he loved,
    reviled by those he died to save,
see how sin's pride has sought his death,
    see how sin's hate has made his grave.

For on his shoulders God has laid
    the weight of sin that we should bear;
so by his passion we have peace,
    through his obedience and his prayer.

Brian Foley
New Catholic Hymnal, 1971
© 1971, Faber Music, Ltd.

513
Lord, As I Wake I Turn to You

Lord, as I wake I turn to you,
    yourself the first thought of my day:
My King, my God, whose help is sure,
    yourself the help for which I pray.

There is no blessing, Lord, from you
    for those who make their will their way,
no praise for those who will not praise,
    no peace for those who will not pray.

Your loving gifts of grace to me,
    those favors I could never earn,
call for my thanks in praise and prayer,
    call me to love you in return.

Lord, make my life a life of love,
    keep me from sin in all I do;
Lord, make your law my only law,
    your will my will, for love of you.

Brian Foley
paraphrase of Psalm 5
New Catholic Hymnal, 1971
© 1971, Faber Music, Ltd.

514
Offertory

Reap me the earth as a harvest to God,
    gather and bring it again,
all that is his, to the Maker of all,
    lift it and offer it high.

        Bring bread, bring wine,
        give glory to the Lord.
        Whose is the earth but God's?
        Whose is the praise but his?

Go with your song and your music, with joy,
    go to the altar of God.
Carry your offerings, fruits of the earth,
    work of your laboring hands.

Gladness and pity and passion and pain,
    all that is mortal in man,
lay all before him, return him his gift,
    God, to whom all shall go home.

Peter Icarus (Luke Connaughton)
Sing a New Song to the Lord, 1970
© McCrimmon Publishing Co. Ltd.

515
Bread and Wine

Bread from the earth, wine from the soil, Adam
    made of clay:
Bring to the Lord—sing to the Lord!—gifts of red
    and gold.
Red is the wine, royal and rich, golden gleams the
    wheat.

Fashioned from dust, what can you give, man, so
    weak, so poor?
Bring to the Lord—sing to the Lord!—what he
    gave to you:
Spirit of flame, mastering mind, body fine and
    proud.

Cry on his name, worship your God, all who dwell
    on earth.
Bring to the Lord—sing to the Lord!—heart and
    voice and will.
Father and Son, Spirit most high, worship three in
    One.

Luke Connaughton
Praise the Lord, 1972
© Continuum International Publishing Group, Ltd.

516
Kenosis. Philippians 2:5–11

Though in God's form he was,
Christ Jesus would not snatch
at parity with God.

Himself he sacrificed,
taking a servant's form,
being born like every man;

revealed in human shape,
obediently he stooped
to die upon a cross.

Him therefore God raised high,
gave him the name of Lord,
all other names above;

that at the Savior's name
no knee might be unbowed
in heaven or earth or hell;

and every tongue confess,
to God the Father's praise,
that "Jesus Christ is Lord."

Archibald MacBride Hunter
The Church Hymnary, 1973
© Archibald MacBride Hunter

517
Psalm 139

Thou art before me, Lord, thou art behind,
    and thou above me hast spread out thy hand;
such knowledge is too wonderful for me,
    too high to grasp, too great to understand.

Then whither from thy Spirit shall I go,
    and whither from thy presence shall I flee?
If I ascend to heaven thou art there,
    and in the lowest depths I meet with thee.

If I should take my flight into the dawn,
    if I should dwell on ocean's farthest shore,
thy mighty hand would rest upon me still,
    and thy right hand would guard me evermore.

If I should say, "Darkness will cover me,
    and I shall hide within the veil of night,"
surely the darkness is not dark to thee,
    the night is as the day, the darkness light.

Search me, O God, search me and know my heart,
    try me, O God, my mind and spirit try;
keep me from any path that gives thee pain,
    and lead me in the everlasting way.

Ian Pitt-Watson
based on the New English Bible
The Church Hymnary, 1973
© David Pitt-Watson

518
Offertory

Good is our God who made this place
            whereon our race
        in plenty liveth.
Great is the praise to him we owe,
            that we may show
        'tis he that giveth.
            Then let who would
            for daily food
give thanks to God who life preserveth;
            offer this board
            to our good Lord,
            and him applaud
        who praise deserveth.

Praise him again whose sovereign will
            grants us the skill
        of daily labor;
whose blessed Son to our great good
            fashioned his wood
        to serve his neighbor.
            Shall we who sing
            not also bring
of this world's wages to the table?—
            giving again
            of what we gain,
            to make it plain
        God doth enable.

So let us our Creator praise
         who all our days
         our life sustaineth;
offer our work, renew our vow,
         adore him now
         who rightly reigneth;
         that we who break
         this bread, and take
this cup of Christ to our enjoyment,
         may so believe,
         so well receive,
         never to leave
         our Lord's employment.

John K. Gregory
New Church Praise, 1975
© Hymns Ancient and Modern Ltd.
The meter and rhyme scheme in this hymn follow exactly those of 260.

519

Think on These Things. Philippians 4:6–8

We praise you, Lord, for all that's true and pure—
clean lines, clear water, and an honest mind.
Grant us your truth, keep guard over our hearts,
    fill all our thoughts with these things.

We praise you, Lord, for all that's excellent—
high mountain peaks, achievement dearly won.
Lift up our eyes, keep guard over our hearts,
    fill all our thoughts with these things.

We praise you, Lord, for all of good report—
the spur to us of others' noble lives.
Show us your will, keep guard over our hearts,
    fill all our thoughts with these things.

We praise you, Lord, the man of Nazareth—
you lived for others, now you live for all.
Jesus, draw near, keep guard over our hearts,
    fill all our thoughts with these things.

Caryl Micklem
New Church Praise, 1975
© Ruth Micklem

520

Give to Me, Lord, a Thankful Heart

Give to me, Lord, a thankful heart
    and a discerning mind:
give, as I play the Christian's part,
the strength to finish what I start
    and act on what I find.

When, in the rush of days, my will
    is habit-bound and slow
help me to keep in vision still
what love and power and peace can fill
    a life that trusts in you.

By your divine and urgent claim
    and by your human face
kindle our seeking hearts to flame
and as you teach the world your name
    let it become your place.

Jesus, with all your church I long
    to see your kingdom come:
Show me your way of righting wrong
and turning sorrow into song
    until you bring me home.

Caryl Micklem
New Church Praise, 1975
© Ruth Micklem

Chapter 24:
English "Folk" Hymnody
(521–528)

There are special reasons why the representation of the English "folk" style in this collection is altogether disproportionate to the output of its promoters. One of the chief reasons is that almost always it means very little without its music. In all but one of the eight pieces we present here the music is composed by the author of the words, and this is the normal fashion, which at once distinguishes the style from that of "mainline" hymnody.

It is too early yet to judge how much of this material will prove to be enduring; our selection turns out to include three pieces from the founding father of the cult in England and five from three other authors who are far less celebrated than some of those we might have chosen. The point we hope to make will become clear after a little discussion of that extraordinary figure who during the 1960s leapt to fame and prominence in England, Sydney Carter.

Carter is a journalist and folksinger of whom in the year 1960 probably only his close friends had ever heard. By 1970 two or three of his pieces had been translated into many languages and were sought after by the editors of many hymnals. By then he had had several long-run programs on English television, and his songs had become well known through records mostly made either by himself or by his intimate friend, Donald Swann. His work, after first appearing in 1964 in a very modest booklet called 9 *Carols or Ballads*, was taken up by an enterprising English publisher and by 1970 was available in many books featuring songs of this kind written by what had by then become a fairly wide-ranging group of his disciples and imitators. The best collection of his songs, which includes a comment by himself on each piece, is *Green Print for Song* (Stainer & Bell, 1974); the sources of his songs apart from this are so numerous and followed each other so quickly that it is best now to give that as the definitive source.

The ingredients in what we call, for want of a better way of putting it, the "folk" style are informality and protest. Upon those two, one might say, hang all its subsidiary properties. Consider first some of Sydney Carter's very well-known songs—too well known to need including here—such as "Lord of the Dance," "When I needed a neighbor," and "No use knocking on the window." In these, as certainly also in 521, the informality breaks down into a sense of the physical, a sense of movement, and a free-ranging imaginative and—in Carter's case—poetic perception. The protest breaks down into a series of gestures against the overabstraction (antiphysical) and the conventionality (antimovement) of institutional religion. Consider that bird in 521: the image of the bird is free and outdoor; it is cruel to cage it. Consider two of Carter's favorite words, the noun "dance" and the verb "travel": negatively, English religion doesn't—in some cases mustn't—*dance*; positively, and here he is certainly on sound theological ground, it must always *travel*. One does, of course, notice in Carter a habit of impressionism in theology allied with a ruthless and severe concreteness in image and precept. The (assumed, not always fairly) callousness of Christians to the poor, the contrast between institutional opulence and practical meagerness, the shut-in quality of the kind of religion he seems to know most about are always under attack in his songs.

Now, these songs are an incursion into Christianity of a demotic art-form which has always had a vigorous underground existence. It derives from traditional folk song in being the product of a culture which depends on oral tradition rather than on writing. Carter always says it doesn't matter if you alter his words or how you harmonize his tunes; it is incongruous and inept ever to say "This, and this only, is the definitive text." It is not that world. It is the world of the young—specifically the young of the 1950s—who were learning to reject the conventional world, finding ways of lampooning its absurdities and demonstrating against its injustices, and, when met together in cellars in London and Newcastle, the two metropolitan centers of this culture, making up songs that expressed their aspirations. The essence of folk song is always that it is unprinted; it is hardly too much to say that at its most genuine it is unprintable! This is the world in which Carter had already found a sort of senior membership before he became famous as a Christian gadfly. The musical instrument of these singers was always the extremely portable and informal guitar—you can't carry a church organ down to the cellar. The language is conversational, and there is no reason why it should not be crude. It is as "in-group" as that of the lower grade of eighteenth-century Evangelical hymn, or as that of some of the Gospel Songs. It has no public manner because a public manner is just what the folk-people dislike and distrust.

Carter has professionalized all this to some extent. He has a public manner: a deadpan stance, a rasping voice, and a fairly settled frown. He is as near as we have ever seen in our time to the sort of Old Testament prophet who could produce the ironic and penetrating song in the beginning of Isaiah 5. He never tries to make a beautiful sound; he prints his songs in keys comfortable for him but hideous for any trained voice except a full bass; and although there is humor and a twinkle in many of his secular songs, in his religious pieces he never sings in any mood but that of exasperated censoriousness. (I am about to say that 522 is as near an exception to this as he ever gets.) Even "Lord of the Dance" is a protest; he sings as if dancing is the last thing his hearers will ever do.

Now this is no affectation. Every word of it is meant, and every word of it is, in a wry sense, inspired. In "The Bird of Heaven" you have the contrast he is always painting: a Blake-like picture of the imprisoned formal culture over against the blessed and joyful freedom he wants to communicate. A touch of this sanctified dissent is part of the equipment of any religious songwriter. There is something in the background he wants to change. Isaac Watts had it, gentle spirit that he

was, when he wrote of ineffable visions and impossible demands. Charles Wesley had it when he wrote of the inconceivable grace of Christ. Perhaps the almost-absence of it is what gives the great American Unitarians their vulnerability, for there indeed Carter would recognize "style and nothing more," at least in some cases, such as "Dear Lord and Father of mankind."

But it is this quality that produces the imagination that conceived "Every star" (522). "Why *shouldn't* there be an incarnation on Saturn?" asks Carter in his usual tone. He produces as a result of this question what some believe—I among them—to be his most innocent and lovable piece.

But not his greatest. Without question, that is 523, one of his earlier and most startling compositions. Here is a drama, here is irony, here is a theological exploration which opens up a terrifying vision of the real source of human grievance. "It's God they ought to crucify." Well, I know of two short theological books that are written with that song as their text. I know also of many people whom the song has offended because they mistook it for a piece in the same universe of discourse as "Praise, my soul." But this is Carter; he is a folk poet in that he expresses the unexpressed thoughts of ordinary human beings about Jesus, about grief, about the church, and even about the cross. He exposes them as alarmingly as this. In this he is in line with the greatest of hymn writers. But he has to be publicly sung with circumspection.

Carter is a layman. The next two authors might be described as laicized clergy in that both were ordained, and both are now serving the community in secular employment—Goodall in education, Stewart in the media—without in any sense having deserted the faith into which they were ordained. David Goodall, of whom more ought to have been heard, exercises still the professional ministry of the United Reformed Church in recognizable ways. Whether Goodall can be called a disciple of Carter is doubtful, for he was writing songs like 524 and 525 before Carter had become famous. But here again is civilized protest and baptized poetry. Goodall is a far more cultivated musician than Carter (as a matter of history he succeeded the British political leader Edward Heath as organ scholar at Balliol College, Oxford, in 1938), and a far subtler writer; in addition, he refuses to abandon his theological insights. The result in 524 is a very tight-knit piece expressing the deep Christian unease at the conventionalities of outward religion; and in 525 it is a beautifully witty and well-turned song of the Carter kind expressing the contradictions within the mind and intentions of what he calls "a not-quite Christian."

Malcolm Stewart, at one time a Roman Catholic priest and always a cultivated musician, in his *Gospel Songs for Today* (in America, called *Now Songs*), spends little time protesting and most of the time either gently musing or positively teaching. His best-known song is "When he comes back," which is a strictly scriptural homily in verse; one could say the same of 527. His 526 is more contemplative and narrative, but it has the same slightly wistful manner which makes him one of the most engaging of these singers.

There are, as we have said, dozens, scores, maybe by now hundreds of people writing in this style. One of the most reliable sources of modern carol and folk-song material is the three volumes called *Faith, Folk, and Clarity; . . . Nativity; . . . Festivity*, published in 1967–1969 by Stainer and Bell/Galaxy. From one of these we take 528, the only one of these pieces whose tune is not by its author. The tune here, which one has to have in mind when reading it, is "The Keel Row," the rollicking Northumbrian song whose accents and cadences Michael Hewlett, the one full-time clergyman in our group, has very carefully followed in his entertaining lyric.

In chapters 27 and 28 we shall glance at some products of this style outside England. Here it will be enough to say that without any doubt Sydney Carter and his circle made the style fit to mention as a genuine part of Christian hymnody, as sectional,

perhaps, as the Spirituals or the Gospel Songs, but no less authentic. Indeed, you might say that these are today's real Gospel Songs with their choruses, their informality, and their closeness to simple human emotions. It need not be stressed here, only gently admitted, that the style simply invites writers less disciplined than those we have quoted to indulge in every possible form of public sloth, bad manners, and unfair-mindedness. Most writers of this kind of material have failed to see that any artistic discipline is implied in the productions of the real creative artists. That, one must suppose, indicates the extent to which Carter and his circle are masters of the "art that conceals art."

521
Bird of Heaven

Catch the bird of heaven,
    lock him in a cage of gold;
look again tomorrow,
       and he will be gone.

      Ah! the bird of heaven!
        Follow where the bird has gone;
      Ah! the bird of heaven!
        keep on traveling on.

Lock him in religion,
    gold and frankincense and myrrh,
carry to his prison,
     but he will be gone.

Temple made of marble,
    beak and feather made of gold,
all the bells are ringing,
     but the bird has gone.

Bell and book and candle
   cannot hold him any more,
for the bird is flying
   as he did before.

Sydney Carter, ca. 1960
9 Carols or Ballads, 1964
© 1969, Stainer & Bell Ltd. (admin. Hope Publishing Company)

522
Every Star Shall Sing a Carol

Every star shall sing a carol.
   Every creature, high or low
come and praise the King of heaven
   by whatever name you know.

      God above, man below.
      Holy is the name I know.

When the King of all creation
   had a cradle on the earth,
holy was the human body,
   holy was the human birth.

Who can tell what other cradle
   high above the Milky Way
still may rock the King of heaven
   on another Christmas Day?

Who can count how many crosses,
   still to come or long ago
crucify the King of heaven?
   Holy is the name I know.

Who can tell what other body
   he will hallow for his own?
I will praise the Son of Mary,
   Brother of my blood and bone.

Every star and every planet,
   every creature high or low
come and praise the King of heaven
   by whatever name you know.

Sydney Carter, 1961
9 Carols or Ballads, 1964
© 1961, Stainer & Bell Ltd. (admin. Hope Publishing Company)

523
Friday Morning

It was on a Friday morning
   that they took me from the cell,
and I saw they had a carpenter
   to crucify as well.
You can blame it on to Pilate,
   you can blame it on the Jews,
you can blame it on the Devil,
   it's God I accuse.

      "It's God they ought to crucify
         instead of you and me,"
      I said to the carpenter
         a-hanging on the tree.

You can blame it on to Adam,
   you can blame it on to Eve,
you can blame it on the apple
   but that I can't believe.
It was God who made the devil,
   and the woman and the man,
and there wouldn't be an apple
   if it wasn't in the plan.

Now Barabbas was a killer,
   and they let Barabbas go.
But you are being crucified
   for nothing, here below.
Your God is up in heaven,
   and he doesn't do a thing:
With a million angels watching,
   and they never move a wing.

To hell with Jehovah,
  to the carpenter I said,
I wish that a carpenter
  had made the world instead.
Goodbye, and good luck to you,
  our ways will soon divide;
remember me in heaven,
  the man you hung beside.   (Luke 23:43)

Sydney Carter, 1959
9 Carols or Ballads, 1974
© 1960, Stainer & Bell Ltd. (admin. Hope Publishing Company)

524
Pious Prayers

When the pious prayers we make
  are a wall of pride,
lest the faithful few awake
  to the world outside;
when a man won't mix with a race
  which he disapproves,
only God descends to make clean the face
  of the world he loves.

Through the bright persuading voice
  of the lies we read,
in the self-deceiving choice
  of our lust and greed,
though the word of man is a mesh
  that our blindness proves,
we have seen the Word of the Lord made flesh
  in the world he loves.

Beat the dust and noisy pain
  of our town and street;
watch him flinching at the stain
  of our hands and feet;
hang the heart of God upon high
  though he reigns above—
and then see him conquering come to die
  for the world he loves.

David Stanton Goodall, 1962
Dunblane Praises 1, 1964
© 1969, Stainer & Bell Ltd. (admin. Hope Publishing Company)

525
Song for a Not-Quite-Convert

I want to go out,
I want to go home.
I want to be single,
I want to belong.
I want to grow up.
I want to stay young.
I want to do both and all at once and anything else
            that takes my fancy,
  whether it hurts or helps to pass the time of day:
    Show me the way!

Now tell me a tale,
or say me a prayer,
bring on the preacher
and let him declare,
"We're going to heaven,
  for heaven's up there."
But what of the folks who stay below and live and
            die and never
  recollect the tales they heard in their forgotten
                youth?
Tell them the truth!

One Saturday night
I sat all alone,
and when it was Sunday
went out on my own.
I came to the church,
they opened the door.
But when I got in the congregation looked the same
                                              as me and
    everyone as lonely as a man without a wife,
        looking for life.

    I want to get out,
    I want to stay here,
    I want to be welcomed,
    I want to keep clear:
    I want to believe,
    I want to be sure.
Show me the man who knows the way, the truth,
            the life, and who is   (John 14:6)
yesterday today and everlastingly the same.
    Tell me his name.   (Heb. 13:8)

W. Wynne Chester (David Stanton Goodall), 1966
British Weekly Book Supplement, April 21, 1966
© 1967, David Stanton Goodall

526
The Sun and the Hill

In a garden one night on a bed of bracken and grief
two men slept while another man cried in grief.
    Let them sleep and take their rest
    let him face his lonely test—
    for how could they understand
    that the hour of dark was close at hand
till they saw their friend carried off in the chains of
                                              a thief?

In an upstairs room where once was light and bread
two men sat and thought of one now dead.
    Two days and two nights till on the third,
    they heard tell of the woman's word
    but what else could it seem
    but that she's sown a wish to reap a dream?
For never in the world had such a thing been said.

Before that dawn, when the night hung over the hill,
those two men came running while the rest of the
                                              world lay still.
    They ran till they came to an open cave;
    all they found was an empty grave,
    then Peter and John both knew,
    Peter and John knew the word was true,
and Peter and John saw the sun come over the hill—
yes—Peter and John saw the sun come over the hill.

Malcolm Stewart
Gospel Songs for Today, 1969
© Continuum International Publishing Group, Ltd.

527
The Beatitudes

You are blessed who are poor in desires
never seeking the riches of earth, which the fires
    can consume, turn to dust,
    or the water of fortune can rust,
    the kingdom is yours, you are just.

You are blessed who are sad but whose crying
is not for yourself, for your self must be dying.
    Your tears shall have worth
    when they share in the cares of the earth,
    for a cross brings the kingdom to birth.

You are blessed who are gentle and meek,
for the war-cries of rage are the tunes of the weak.
    Your silence is long
    and the trumpets of anger blow strong;
    but the kingdom will dance to your song.

You are blessed, you who hunger and thirst
for the waters of love to abound. They are cursed
   who still foster and keep
   only deserts, and selfishness reap—
   in the kingdom love's waters run deep.

You are blessed who have mercy. So frail
is mankind, he must die if all pity should fail;
   For is there a name
   that can last down its years without shame?
   To a kingdom of mercy—your claim.

You are blessed who are pure, who control
and who make pastures rich of your body and soul.
   For those lands are laid waste
   where the beasts prowl to quench every taste.
   In a rich land the kingdom is placed.

You are blessed who make peace, who believe
not in weapons to conquer, to ravish, to grieve.
   You find your employ
   in creating what guns just destroy.
   The name of God's sons you'll enjoy.

You are blessed when they seek you to kill
and to wound like the Master himself on a hill.
   amid laughter and scorn;
   so his wounds as a mark must be worn
   to recall where the kingdom was born.

Malcolm Stewart
Gospel Songs for Today, 1969
© Continuum International Publishing Group, Ltd.

528
Song and Dance

When God almighty came to be one of us,
   masking the glory of his golden train,
dozens of plain things kindled by accident,
   and they will never be the same again.
     Sing, all you midwives, dance, all the
                    carpenters,
      sing, all the publicans and shepherds too,
     God in his mercy uses the commonplace,
      God on his birthday had a need of you.

Splendor of Rome and local authority,
   working on policy with furrowed head,
joined to locate Messiah's nativity,
   just where the prophets had already said.
     Sing, all you tax-men, dance, the
                   commissioners,
      sing, civil servants and policemen too,
     God for his purpose uses the governments,
      God on his birthday had a need of you.

Wise men they called them, earnest astrologers,
   watching for meaning in the moving stars'
science or fancy, learned or laughable,
   theirs was a vision that was brought to pass.
     Sing, all you wise men, dance, all the
                   scientists,
      whether your theories are false or true.
     God uses knowledge, God uses ignorance,
      God on his birthday had a need of you.

Sing, all creation, made for his purposes,
    called by his providence to live and move:
none is unwanted, none insignificant,
    Love needs a universe of folk to love.
        Old men and maidens, young men and
                    children   (Ps. 148:12)
        black ones and colored ones and white
                    ones too,
    God on his birthday, and to eternity,
        God took upon himself the need of you.

Michael Hewlett
Faith, Folk, and Festivity, 1969
© 1969, Stainer & Bell Ltd. (admin. Hope Publishing Company)
to be sung to the tune of "The Keel Row"

Chapter 25:
Hymns for Children,
1952–1975 (529–535)

Continuing from where we left off in chapter 22, we find that hymnody for children, after a period of considerable activity, did not make any noticeable progress until the later sixties. The period 1906–1951 was, we said, a pedagogic period, and while there was a great deal of progress then in writing hymns for children that at least achieved a tolerable style and got rid of the peculiar awkwardness of Victorian stiffness, a pedagogic period was not likely to be the period of real breakthrough in children's hymn writing.

What our small selection here seems to indicate is that during the later sixties a few writers, at least, managed to do the one thing that was required: lose their adult self-consciousness and really celebrate in a Christian way the thoughts that children might be thinking themselves. This is, for the first time, a third choice alongside the two that John Wesley offered: You can stoop down to the children, or you can lift them up to you, said he. In other words, you, an adult, can talk to children as children, or you can help them to talk as adults. But either way you are still talking to them. Is it possible to get them to say, as the ordinary hymn writer wants to get his singers to say, "*That's* what I meant; thank you for helping me to articulate it"?

Paul Townsend (529) produces a song which is partly carol, partly (but very little) hymn, to which one reacts by saying, "Yes, that's what a child might well say when learning for the first time about time zones." It is in a ballad style, varied by the extrametrical stanza 4, and it has been very delightfully set to music by Donald Swann. Ian Fraser of Dunblane succeeded in several children's hymns in getting inside the minds of children in the same way. One part of the Dunblane project (see chapter 23) was to try to invent new kinds of children's hymns; and all submissions were put before a Christian child psychologist before being published.

Number 531 also first appeared in the Dunblane book, but it originated in a class of children at Emmanual Church, Cambridge, where their leader, who is a professional musician, invited them as a group to invent a hymn by saying, "How should we thank God? How about thinking what the world would be, without—now what?" The full text was designed to be sung at intervals during a young people's service. The children also to some extent invented the music.

The short-lived Eric Reid left a little church music which indicated that had he been spared he would have been a major contributor in the field. Himself an educationist and teacher, he wrote a few of the Dunblane children's hymns, of which 532 and 533 are examples. Both of these are in *New Songs for the Church, Book I.* "Trotting," in itself a delightful conception, depends for its success partly on a remarkably graceful tune. The other one is a quite remarkable essay in interpreting the mystery of the Trinity to young minds.

A very creative and useful book for children ages eight to eleven is *New Orbit*, published in 1972 by Stainer & Bell; our 534, a kind of very simple junior *"Benedicite,"* is one sample from it; but several of the pieces in this and the preceding chapter are in it as well.

And from a more recent publication we offer Caryl Micklem's meditation on light from *New Church Praise.* There is no room for more, but in the best contemporary books this is the kind of material one may look for. It is partly the consequence of the liberation of vocabulary which the "folk" writers achieved (and "folk" at its best, of whatever period, is always a good nourishment for children!) and partly it comes from the new attitude to children in education and in church which has become normal since intelligent people who have families now have uninterrupted and direct contact with their children, a situation which, so evidently, did not apply in the nineteenth century.

529
The Clock Carol

When the bells chime noon in London,
New York begins its day,
good morning in Toronto spells
good night for Mandalay.

When the sun shines on the pyramids,
Alaska's in the dark;
at one tick of the clock God hears
both nightingale and lark.

For he is there through nights and days,
through rain and cold and heat;
behind the chatter of the clocks
we sense his timeless beat.

Midday, midnight, the bells are always ringing,
the world keeps turning into day and night:
Sunshine, moonshine, the light and shadow bringing,
patterns they make from God's one light.

While some work at their benches,
their brothers work in fields,
yet one Creator is the source
of what their labor yields.

Men of all kinds and colors,
in factory or field,
have on their faces, black or white,
God's image there revealed.

For East and West in him are one,
and color, race, and clime;
his love will reach beyond the bounds
of night and day and time.

Paul Townsend, 1965
Faith, Folk, and Clarity, 1967
© 1965, Donald Swann; 1968, Galliard Ltd.

530
Lord, I Love to Stamp and Shout

Lord, I love to stamp and shout
testing lungs and muscles out;
other times I curl up still
dreaming till I've had my fill
—still as mouse, or ranting free:
What strange mixture makes me me?

Lord, I love to watch things fly,
whizzing, zooming, flashing by;
engines, aircraft, speedboats, cars,
spacecraft shooting to the stars
—as I learn and think and grow
let my life say, "Go, man, go!"

Lord, I love to probe and pry,
seeking out the reason why;
looking inside things and out,
finding what they're all about
—make me curious to find
what will really bless mankind.

Lord, I'm many things and one,
though my life's not long begun;
you alone my secret see
what I am cut out to be:
take this life—it's almost new—
make your dreams for it come true.

Ian M. Fraser
Dunblane Praises 2, 1967
© 1969, Stainer & Bell Ltd. (admin. Hope Publishing Company)

531
Think of a World

Think of a world without any flowers,
    think of a world without any trees,
think of a sky without any sunshine,
    think of the air without any breeze.
We thank you, Lord, for flowers and trees and
                                sunshine,
we thank you, Lord, and praise your holy name.

Think of a world without any animals,
    think of a field without any herd,
think of a stream without any fishes,
    think of a dawn without any bird:
We thank you, Lord, for all your living creatures,
we thank you, Lord, and praise your holy name.

Think of a world without any paintings,
    think of a room where all the walls are bare,
think of a rainbow without any colors,
    think of the earth with darkness everywhere.
We thank you, Lord, for paintings and for colors,
we thank you, Lord, and praise your holy name.

Think of a world without any poetry,
    think of a book without any words,
think of a song without any music,
    think of a hymn without any verse.
We thank you, Lord, for poetry and music,
we thank you, Lord, and praise your holy name.

Think of a world without any science,
    think of a journey with nothing to explore,
think of a quest without any mystery,
    nothing to seek, and nothing left in store.
We thank you, Lord, for miracles of science,
we thank you, Lord, and praise your holy name.

Think of a world without any people
    think of a street with no one living there,
think of a town without any houses,
    no one to love, and nobody to care.
We thank you, Lord, for families and friendships,
we thank you, Lord, and praise your holy name.

Think of a world without any worship,
    think of a God without his only Son,
think of a cross without a resurrection,
    only a grave, and not a victory won.
We thank you, Lord, for showing us our Savior,
we thank you, Lord, and praise your holy name.

Thanks to our Lord for being here among us,
    thanks be to you for sharing all we do;
thanks for our Church and all the love we find
                                here,
    thanks for this place, and all its promise true.
We thank you, Lord, for life in all its richness,
we thank you, Lord, and praise your holy name.

Doreen Newport
Dunblane Praises 2, 1967
© 1969, Stainer & Bell Ltd. (admin. Hope Publishing Company)

532
Trotting, Trotting

Trotting, trotting through Jerusalem,
Jesus, sitting on a donkey's back,
children waving branches singing,
"Happy is he that comes in the name of the Lord!"

Many people in Jerusalem
thought he should have come on a mighty horse
leading all the Jews to battle—
"Happy is he that comes in the name of the Lord!"

Many people in Jerusalem
were amazed to see such a quiet man
trotting, trotting on a donkey,
"Happy is he that comes in the name of the Lord!"

Trotting, trotting through Jerusalem,
Jesus, sitting on a donkey's back,
let us join the children singing,
"Happy is he that comes in the name of the Lord!"

Eric Reid
Dunblane Praises 2, 1967
© 1969, Stainer & Bell Ltd. (admin. Hope Publishing Company)

533
Trinity

God is our Friend,
    Jesus is our Friend,
and the Holy Spirit is our Friend,
    all made into one.

God keeps us safe,
    God makes us strong;
he's very sad when he sees us go wrong,
    God will help us all.

Jesus like us
    played in the street,
grew up to heal, and made life complete
    helping everyone.

Nobody hears,
    nobody knows;
quiet as sunshine the Holy Spirit grows
    into everyone.

God is our Friend,
    Jesus is our Friend,
and the Holy Spirit is our Friend,
    all made into one.

Eric Reid
Dunblane Praises 2, 1967
© H. A. Reid

534
Bless the Lord

When I see the salmon leap the fall,
or the airplane's silver trail—
or a drop of water magnified,
    then my eyes and soul bless the Lord.

When I hear the frosty crunch of snow,
or the sun-drenched hum of the bee,
or a well-tuned engine whine with power,
    then my ears and soul bless the Lord.

After rain a smell of clean fresh air
blows soft and cool and free;
when the strawberries are turned to jam,
    then my nose and soul bless the Lord.

At the taste of berries gathered free,
or the tang of seafood, mint, or treacle,
touch of velvet, feel of cold smooth stones,
    hands and tongue and soul bless the Lord.

Gracie King
New Orbit, 1972
© 1972, Stainer & Bell Ltd. (admin. Hope Publishing Company)

535
All Kinds of Light

Father, we thank you—
for the light that shines all the day;
    for the bright sky you have given,
    most like your heaven;
        Father, we thank you.

Father, we thank you—
for the lamps that lighten the way;
    for human skill's exploration
    of your creation;
        Father, we thank you.

Father, we thank you—
for the friends who brighten our play;
for your command to call others
sisters and brothers;
Father, we thank you.

Father, we thank you—
for your love in Jesus today,
giving us hope for tomorrow
through joy or sorrow;
Father, we thank you.

Caryl Micklem
New Church Praise, 1975
© Ruth Micklem

Chapter 26: American Hymnody, 1901–1975 (536–559)

A subtle change comes over the story of American hymnody after the turn of the century, the center of gravity moving from the Unitarians towards the Episcopalians. Until about 1940 the best American writers were doing as well as, sometimes better than, their English cousins, though the stream begins to run rather less broadly.

True, the first six in our selection come from non-Anglicans, and indeed form a direct continuation of the tradition we celebrated in chapter 18. Louis Benson, a Presbyterian minister, is known as the founding father of serious American hymnology, and the library he bequeathed to Princeton Theological Seminary is one of the finest hymnological collections in the world. As 536 shows, he was also an excellent hymn writer; this one on the life of Christ is his best known, and is one of the best of its kind.

Frank Mason North (537) was a Methodist, and in his famous "city" hymn antedated the English city pioneers (Scott Holland and G. K. Chesterton) by a year or two. Perhaps it is now somewhat dated, especially in its assignation of work to men and tears to women in stanza 3, but it set the fashion which others followed more successfully. Shepherd Knapp (538) is another Presbyterian, and, using a meter which American writers were always partial to, he writes a typically fervent and forthright hymn for ministers. (This meter invites garrulousness, but he avoids it well.)

William P. Merrill, Presbyterian, is best known for his muscular, almost Pelagian, "Rise up, O men of God"; in his hymn for a national occasion, 539, he gives us what amounts to America's answer to Kipling's "Recessional" (256): less stirring literature, but better hymn writing. Yet another Presbyterian, Henry van Dyke, wrote a poem on the dignity of work from which different hymnals take different centos, of which 540 is one.

Americans, one sees, are developing in the first decade of the century a reaction to the overspiritualized manner of the great Unitarians. The same reaction is seen in the very warmly felt lines of the great Presbyterian missionary to Japan, William M. Vories (541), who wrote these lines while contemplating the power struggle in Europe which was, even in 1908, developing into a worldwide threat.

The Episcopal line begins with Walter Russell Bowie (542 and 543), a pastor of great distinction, who contributed in these two pieces not only two hymns of great power but two on strictly twentieth-century subjects. The "city" hymn is surely a long step forward from F. M. North: both more visionary and more concrete. And 543, written at the request of F. W. Dwelly, first Dean of Liverpool Cathedral in England, to try to say to this age what the *Dies irae* said to former generations, is a masterpiece which is as well known in England as in the USA.

Henry Hallam Tweedy (544), a Presbyterian professor, was the editor of a successful hymnal and the writer of a text which has also become as well known in England as in America; only one word mars it, "ban" in stanza 4, which one fervently wishes had been "shun" (banning ugliness just isn't possible); but the hymn was written when the Hymn Society of America advertised its search for modern missionary hymns, and as such it certainly says some quite new and very trenchant things. Even more famous, the best known of all twentieth-century American hymns, is Harry Fosdick's "God of grace" (545). This was written for the dedication of the enormous Riverside Church in New York, in 1930. It cannot be too often stated that the association of this text with the tune Cwm Rhondda was an association he deplored. During its fairly short life this admirably downright text has suffered more abuse by sentimental and careless choosers than it deserved.

Numbers 546–552 bring the Episcopalian contribution to its peak. Though a small Christian community in the USA and not generating a large number of hymn writers, it is probably fair to say that in the first half of this century it produced the half dozen finest hymns. For this, apart from Bowie already mentioned, we have chiefly to thank Howard Chandler Robbins and F. Bland Tucker. The contributions of Robbins to the 1940 Episcopal *Hymnal* all repay close study—especially his translation of St. Francis's "Canticle of the Sun," which is not better than Draper's, but certainly is a fascinating variation. We here include 546, his most daring and unusual composition; 547, a straightforward hymn of spiritual resolution; and 548, an unusually poetic miniature, to show what variety of styles he could handle.

Tucker is even finer. He often goes to ancient sources for his material. Number 549, from Abelard, is exquisite not only in its handling of the subject but in the unusually subtle way it disposes its important syllables; almost any good tune seems to give the "lift" required by the third line of each stanza. This admirable craftsmanship, this complete rejection of the cliché, is found all through his work. Number 550 paraphrases Philippians 2 most felicitously, though of course less closely than 516.

Number 551, from *Diognetus* (the most beautiful of all the sub-Apostolic writings) I find the most moving of all his texts, a tender and penetrating exposition of the idea in "They will reverence my Son" in the parable of the rebellious husbandmen. The famous 552, taken from another very early Christian source, is now, very properly, in all reputable hymnals. Again the author has seized upon the central idea in a fine passage of ancient literature. There is no better twentieth-century writing in either of our countries than is to be found in Tucker.

Georgia Harkness, the distinguished American scholar, wrote 553 for a promotion by the Hymn Society similar to that mentioned above under 544, and her hymn, perhaps not quite free from cliché but containing some fine lines, has found very wide acceptance in America. Women writers in the USA do not seem to flourish yet in great numbers.

The one later writer, however, who, in a very different way, can be thought of as standing alongside Tucker is the Lutheran Martin Franzmann (554 and 555). Lutherans, especially of the Germanic Missouri Synod, have not until very recently been energetic hymn writers; the Pietist chorales did for them what Wesley did for later Methodists. But Franzmann, whose style has a rough-cast ruggedness about it, certainly avoids cliché; indeed, it is so dense that it needs a good deal of careful thinking before it delivers its full message. His hymns seem always to frown before they smile, and this in itself is a refreshment after the fixed and euphoric beam that we get from some of the earlier American poets. (Incidentally, Franzmann has been served in both these pieces with special distinction by musicians whose settings exactly reflect the dark colors and bright endings of these fine poems.)

Of a very different kind, but from the same cultural background, is the impressionistic communion hymn, 556; one of the few hymns without a single finite verb and without any punctuation. It is something of a *tour de force* and another example of the new talent for poetry that Lutherans are fostering in America.

Finally, among orthodox American hymns, we offer two new pieces from the newest (at this date) American hymnal. This is the book that serves the church that contains the ex-Congregationalists of America as well as the Evangelical and Reformed Church; these two contrasted pieces, chosen with some difficulty from a very fair offering of good new material in this modest and fascinating hymnal, seem to pick up the best in those traditions. Number 558 is one of several by a distinguished academic who, following Tucker's lead, goes to ancient sources for his subjects and versifies them with considerable skill. In this case the difference between the use of analogies in the three stanzas is no fault of his; it faithfully reflects Cyprian, who wrote the tract *De unitate ecclesiae* in a mood of white-hot anger and probably did not give himself leisure to polish it. For sheer originality, expressed, we have to say, in poetry which aspires more often than it succeeds, the United Church of Christ *Hymnal* is a book to be respected.

In the matter of American folk hymnody we regret that technical difficulties prevent our offering any examples. This is material which in any case is difficult to present without music. Very often the text and the tune come from the same hand. Very often, too, they are skillful and trenchant. The best known of these pieces probably are James Thiem's "Sons of God," Ray Repp's "Clap Your Hands," and Peter Scholtes's "They'll Know We Are Christians by Our Love." It is, like its English counterpart, informal hymnody, and not infrequently the doctrinal and scriptural content of these modern Gospel Songs—for that is what they are—is impressive. In others there is a tendency to stray into romantic ecumenism and a somewhat unfocused zeal to serve those deemed to be under-privileged. At their worst they are crude, and it is probably fair to say that the Roman Catholic communities in America, with their sudden new need for hymns, have been the most vulnerable to the assaults of commercialized hymnody of this kind. That fact should not too much prejudice a reader against the whole genre, which at its best has brought much vitality to American worship. Our lack of representation of this kind of song must be taken in terms of the line we took about Spirituals and Gospel Songs: they are available everywhere; they need their music to make their effect; and sometimes they are hideously expensive to reprint.

The section ends with a tiny piece which is unique and unclassifiable and therefore anachronistically placed. Apart from the work of Whittier, American hymnbook editors have not plundered their poets as freely as have the English. But Sidney Lanier, short-lived and in his time obscure, left some haunting lines, including those here given (559), which were picked up by American Methodists in 1905 but otherwise have appeared more often in British than in American books. They fittingly conclude a section which illustrates the great variety of styles that has developed in America since 1900.

536
Earthly Life of Jesus

O sing a song of Bethlehem,
 of shepherds watching there,
and of the news that came to them
 from angels in the air;
the light that shone on Bethlehem
 fills all the world today;
of Jesus' birth and peace on earth
 the angels sing alway.

O sing a song of Nazareth,
 of sunny days of joy,
O sing of fragrant flowers beneath
 and of the sinless Boy:
For now the flowers of Nazareth
 in every heart may grow;
now spreads the fame of his dear name,
 on all the winds that blow.

O sing a song of Galilee,
 of lake and woods and hill,
of him who walked upon the sea
 and bade its waves be still:
For though, like waves on Galilee,
 dark seas of trouble roll,
when faith has heard the Master's word
 falls peace upon the soul.

O sing a song of Calvary,
 its glory and dismay,
of him who hung upon the tree
 and took our sins away;
for he who died on Calvary
 is risen from the grave,
and Christ our Lord, by heaven adored,
 is mighty now to save.

Louis F. Benson, 1899
The School Hymnal, 1899

435

537
A Prayer for the Multitudes

Where cross the crowded ways of life,
    where sound the cries of race and clan,
above the noise of selfish strife,
    we hear thy voice, O Son of Man.

In haunts of wretchedness and need,
    on shadowed thresholds dark with fears,
from paths where hide the lures of greed,
    we catch the vision of thy tears.   (Luke 19:41)

From tender childhood's helplessness,
    from woman's grief, man's burdened toil,
from famished souls, from sorrows stress,
    thy heart has never known recoil.

The cup of water given for thee   (Matt. 10:42)
    still holds the freshness of thy grace:
Yet long these multitudes to see
    the sweet compassion of thy face.

O Master, from the mountainside   (Mark 9:10ff)
    make haste to heal these hearts of pain;
among these restless throngs abide,
    O tread the city's streets again:

till sons of men shall learn thy love,
    and follow where thy feet have trod;
till glorious from thy heaven above,
    shall come the city of our God.   (Rev. 21:1ff)

Frank Mason North, 1903
The Christian City, June 1903

538
Christian Vocation

Lord God of hosts, whose purpose, never swerving,
    leads toward the day of Jesus Christ thy Son,
grant us to march among thy faithful legions,
    armed with thy courage, till the world is won.

Strong Son of God, whose work was his that sent
    thee,
    one with the Father, thought and deed and word,
one make us all, true comrades in thy service,
    and make us one in thee, with God the Lord.

O Prince of peace, thou bringer of good tidings,
    teach us to speak thy word of hope and cheer—
rest for the soul, and strength for all men's striving,
    light for the path of life, and God brought near.

Lord God, whose grace has called us to thy service,
    how good thy thoughts towards us, how great
    their sum!   (Ps. 139:17)
We work with thee, we go where thou wilt lead us,
    until in all the earth thy kingdom come.

Shepherd Knapp, 1907
The Hymnal, 1911

539
Thanksgiving

Not alone for mighty empire,
    stretching far o'er land and sea,
not alone for bounteous harvests,
    lift we up our hearts to thee.
Standing in the living present,
    memory and hope between,
Lord, we would with deep thanksgiving
    praise thee most for things unseen.

Not for battleship and fortress,
    not for conquests of the sword,
but for conquests of the spirit
    give we thanks to thee, O Lord,
For the heritage of freedom,
    for the home, the church, the school,
for the open door to manhood
    in a land the people rule.

For the armies of the faithful,
    souls that passed and left no name;
for the glory that illumines
    patriot lives of deathless fame;
for our prophets and apostles,
    loyal to the living word,
for all heroes of the spirit,
    give we thanks to thee, O Lord.

God of justice, save the people
    from the clash of race and creed,
from the strife of class and faction,
    make our nation free indeed;
keep her faith in simple manhood
    strong as when her life began,
till it find its full fruition
    in the brotherhood of man!

William Pierson Merrill, 1909
The Continent, 1911

540
The Dignity of Work

Jesus, thou divine companion,
    by thy lowly human birth
thou hast come to join the workers,
    burden-bearers of the earth.
Thou the carpenter of Nazareth,
    toiling for thy daily food,
by thy patience and thy courage
    thou hast taught us toil is good.

They who tread the path of labor
    follow where thy feet have trod;
they who work without complaining
    do the holy will of God.
Thou, the peace that passeth knowledge,
    dwellest in the daily strife;
thou, the Bread of heaven, art broken
    in the sacrament of life.

Every task, however simple,
    sets the soul that does it free;
every deed of love and kindness
    done to man is done to thee.   (Matt. 25:35)
Jesus, thou divine companion,
    help us all to work our best;
bless us in our daily labor,
    lead us to our sabbath rest.

Henry van Dyke
The Toiling of Felix, 1898
revised for *Hymns of the Kingdom of God*, 1909

541
Let There Be Light, Lord God of Hosts

Let there be light, Lord God of hosts,
    let there be wisdom on the earth;
    let broad humanity have birth,
let there be deeds, instead of boasts.

Within our passioned hearts instill
    the calm that endeth strain and strife;
    make us thy ministers of life;
purge us from lusts that curse and kill.

Give us the peace of vision clear
    to see our brothers' good our own,
    to joy and suffer not alone—
the love that casteth out all fear.

Let woe and waste of warfare cease,
    that useful labor yet may build
    its homes with love and laughter filled;
God, give thy wayward children peace.

William Merrill Vories, 1908
The Advocate of Peace, February 1909

542
O Holy City, Seen of John

O holy city, seen of John,
    where Christ the Lamb doth reign,   (Rev. 21)
within whose four-square walls shall come
    no night, nor need, nor pain,
and where the tears are wiped from eyes
    that shall not weep again!

Hark, how from men whose lives are held
    more cheap than merchandise;
from women struggling sore for bread,
    from little children's cries,
there swells the sobbing human plaint
    that bids thy walls arise!

O shame to us who rest content
    while lust and greed for gain
in street and shop and tenement
    wring gold from human pain,
and bitter lips in blind despair
    cry, "Christ hath died in vain!"

Give us, O God, the strength to build
    the city that hath stood
too long a dream, whose laws are love,
    whose ways are brotherhood,
and where the sun that shineth is
    God's brace for human good.

Already in the mind of God
    that city riseth fair:
Lo, how its splendor challenges
    the souls that greatly dare—
yea, bids us seize the whole of life
    and build its glory there.

Walter Russell Bowie, 1909
Hymns of the Kingdom of God, 1910

543
Dies Irae

Lord Christ, when first thou cam'st to men,
    upon a cross they bound thee,
and mocked thy saving kingship then
    by thorns with which they crowned thee;
and still our wrongs may weave thee now
new thorns to pierce that steady brow
    and robe of sorrow round thee.

O awful love, which found no room
    in life where sin denied thee,
and, doomed to death, must bring to doom
    the power which crucified thee,
till not a stone was left on stone,
and all a nation's pride, o'erthrown,
    went down to dust beside thee!

New advent of the love of Christ,
    shall we again refuse thee,
till in the night of hate and war
    we perish as we lose thee?
From old unfaith our souls release
to seek the kingdom of thy peace
    by which alone we choose thee.

O wounded hands of Jesus, build
    in us thy new creation;
our pride is dust, our vaunt is stilled,
    we wait thy revelation:
O Love that triumphs over loss,
we bring our hearts before thy cross
    to finish thy salvation.

Walter Russell Bowie, 1928
Songs of Praise, 1931
© Abingdon Press (admin. The Copyright Company)

544

Eternal God, Whose Power Upholds

Eternal God, whose power upholds
    both flower and flaming star,
to whom there is no here or there,
    no time, no near or far,
no alien race, no foreign shore,
    no child unsought, unknown,
O send us forth, thy prophets true,
    to make all lands thine own!

O God of love, whose spirit wakes
    in every human breast,
whom love, and love alone, can know,
    in whom all hearts find rest,
help us to spread thy gracious reign,
    till greed and hate shall cease,
and kindness dwell in human hearts,
    and all the earth be peace!

O God of truth, whom science seeks
    and reverent souls adore,
who lightest every earnest mind
    of every clime and shore,
dispel the gloom of error's night,
    of ignorance and fear,
until true wisdom from above
    shall make life's pathway clear!

O God of beauty, oft revealed
    in dreams of human art,
in speech that flows to melody,
    in holiness of heart;
teach us to ban all ugliness
    that blinds our eyes to thee,
till all shall know the loveliness
    of lives made fair and free.

O God of righteousness and grace,
    seen in the Christ, thy Son,   (John 14:9)
whose life and death reveal thy face,
    by whom thy will was done,   (John 4:34)
inspire thy heralds of good news
    to live thy life divine,
till Christ is formed in all mankind,
    and every land is thine!

Henry Hallam Tweedy, 1929
Hymn Society Bulletin, July 1929

545

God of Grace and God of Glory

God of grace and God of glory,
    on thy people pour thy power;
crown thine ancient church's story,
    bring her bud to glorious flower.
        Grant us wisdom,
        grant us courage,
    for the facing of this hour.

Lo! the hosts of evil round us
    scorn thy Christ, assail his ways!
Fears and doubts too long have bound us,
    free our hearts to work and praise.
        Grant us wisdom,
        grant us courage,
    for the living of these days.

Cure thy children's warring madness;
    bend our pride to thy control;
shame our wanton, selfish gladness,
    rich in things and poor in soul.
        Grant us wisdom,
        grant us courage,
    lest we miss thy kingdom's goal.

Set our feet on lofty places;
    gird our lives that we may be
armored with all Christ-like graces
    in the fight to set men free.
        Grant us wisdom,
        grant us courage,
    that we fail not man nor thee.

Save us from weak resignation
    to the evils we deplore;
let the search for thy salvation
    be our glory evermore.
        Grant us wisdom,
        grant us courage,
    serving thee whom we adore.

Harry Emerson Fosdick, 1930
Praise and Service, 1932
© 1930, Elinor Fosdick Downs

546
And Have the Bright Immensities

And have the bright immensities
    received our risen Lord,
where light-years frame the Pleiades
    and point Orion's sword?
Do flaming suns his footsteps trace
    through corridors sublime,
the Lord of interstellar space
    and Conqueror of time?

The heaven that hides him from our sight
    knows neither near nor far;
an altar candle sheds its light
    as surely as a star:
And where his loving people meet
    to share the gift divine,
there stands he with unhurrying feet;
    there heavenly splendors shine.

Howard Chandler Robbins
The Living Church, April 4, 1931
© Morehouse Group

547
Put Forth, O Lord, Thy Spirit's Might

Put forth, O Lord, thy Spirit's might
    and bid thy church increase,
in breadth and length, in depth and height,
    her unity and peace.

Let works of darkness disappear
    before thy conquering light;
let hatred and tormenting fear
    pass with the passing night.

Let what apostles learned of thee
    be ours from age to age;
their steadfast faith our unity,
    their peace our heritage.

O Judge divine of human strife!
    O Vanquisher of pain!
To know thee is eternal life,
    to serve thee is to reign.

Howard Chandler Robbins
New Church Hymnal, 1937

548
Sunset to Sunrise Changes Now

Sunset to sunrise changes now,
    for God doth make his world anew;
on the Redeemer's thorn-crowned brow
    the wonders of that dawn we view.

E'en though the sun withholds its light,
    lo! a more heavenly lamp shines here,
and from the cross, on Calvary's height
    gleams of eternity appear.

Here, in o'erwhelming final strife
    the Lord of life hath victory;
and sin is slain, and death brings life,
    and sons of earth hold heaven in fee.

translated, Howard Chandler Robbins, 1938
from original by Clement of Alexandria in *Protrepticus*, ca. 200
Preaching the Gospel, 1939
first as a hymn in *The Hymnal 1940*, 1943

549
Alone Thou Goest Forth, O Lord

Alone thou goest forth, O Lord,
    in sacrifice to die;
is this thy sorrow naught to us
    who pass unheeding by?

Our sins, not thine, thou bearest, Lord;
    make us thy sorrow feel,
till through our pity and our shame
    love answers love's appeal.

This is earth's darkest hour, but thou
    dost light and life restore;
then let all praise be given thee
    who livest evermore.

Give us compassion for thee, Lord,
    that, as we share this hour,
thy cross may bring us to thy joy
    and resurrection power.

translated, Francis Bland Tucker, 1938
from *"Solus ad victimam procedis"* by Peter Abelard in
Hymnaris Paraclitensis, ca. 1135
The Hymnal 1940, 1943
© 1940, The Church Pension Fund

550
All Praise to Thee, for Thou, O King Divine

All praise to thee, for thou, O King divine,
didst yield the glory that of right was thine,
that in our darkened hearts thy grace might shine.
    Alleluia!

Thou cam'st to us in lowliness of thought;
by thee the outcast and the poor were sought,
and by thy death was God's salvation wrought.
    Alleluia!

Let this mind be in us which was in thee,
who wast a servant that we might be free,
humbling thyself to death on Calvary.
    Alleluia!

Wherefore, by God's eternal purpose, thou
art high exalted o'er all creatures now,
and given the name to which all knees shall bow.
    Alleluia!

Let every tongue confess with one accord
in heaven and earth that Jesus Christ is Lord;
and God the Father be by all adored.
    Alleluia!

Francis Bland Tucker, 1938
based on Philippians 2:5–12
The Hymnal 1940, 1943
© 1940, The Church Pension Fund

551
The Great Creator of the Worlds

The great Creator of the worlds,
    the sovereign God of heaven,
his holy and immortal truth
    to men on earth hath given.

441

He sent no angel of his host
 to bear this mighty word,
but him through whom the worlds were made,
 the everlasting Lord.

He sent him not in wrath and power,
 but grace and peace to bring;
in kindness, as a king might send
 his son, himself a king.

He sent him down as sending God;
 as man he came to men;
as one with us he dwelt with us,
 and died and lives again.

He came as Savior to his own,
 the way of love he trod;
he came to win men by good will,
 for force is not of God.

Not to oppress, but summon men
 their truest life to find,
in love God sent his Son to save,
 not to condemn mankind.

translated and paraphrased, Francis Bland Tucker, 1939
from the *Epistle to Diognetus*, ca. 150
The Hymnal 1940, 1943
© 1940, The Church Pension Fund

For *The Hymnal 1982*, Tucker revised these lines:

1:4 to all on earth hath given.

4:2 in flesh to us he came;

4:4 and bore a human name.

5:3 he came to win us by good will,

6:1 not to oppress, but summon all

552
Father, We Thank Thee Who Hast Planted

Father, we thank thee who hast planted
 thy holy name within our hearts.
Knowledge and faith and life immortal
 Jesus thy Son to us imparts.
Thou, Lord, didst make all for thy pleasure,
 didst give man food for all his days,
giving in Christ the Bread eternal;
 thine is the power, be thine the praise.

Watch o'er thy church, O Lord, in mercy,
 save it from evil, guard it still,
perfect it in thy love, unite it,
 cleansed and conformed unto thy will.
As grain, once scattered on the hillsides,
 was in this broken bread made one,
so, from all lands thy church be gathered
 into thy kingdom by thy Son.

Francis Bland Tucker, 1939
based on prayers from the *Didache (The Teaching of the
Twelve Apostles)*, 2nd century
The Hymnal 1940, 1943
© 1940, The Church Pension Fund

553
Hope of the World

Hope of the world, thou Christ of great compassion,
 speak to our fearful hearts by conflict rent.
Save us, thy people, from consuming passion,
 who by our own false hopes and aims are spent.

Hope of the world, God's gift from highest heaven,
 bringing to hungry souls the bread of life,
still let thy Spirit unto us be given
 to heal earth's wounds and end her bitter strife.

Hope of the world, afoot on dusty highways,
 showing to wandering souls the path of light;
walk thou beside us lest the tempting byways
 lure us away from thee to endless night.

Hope of the world, who by thy cross didst save us
  from death and dark despair, from sin and guilt;
we render back the love thy mercy gave us;
  take thou our lives and use them as thou wilt.

Hope of the world, O Christ, o'er death victorious,
  who by this sign didst conquer grief and pain,
we would be faithful to thy gospel glorious:
  Thou art our Lord! Thou dost forever reign!

Georgia Harkness, 1953
The Hymn, July 1954
© 1954, 1982, The Hymn Society (admin. Hope Publishing Company)

554
O God, O Lord of Heaven and Earth

O God, O Lord of heaven and earth,
  thy living finger never wrote
  that life should be an aimless mote,
a deathward drift from futile birth.
Thy Word meant life triumphant hurled
through every cranny of thy world.
  Since light awoke and life began,
  thou hast desired thy life for man.

Our fatal will to equal thee,
  our rebel will wrought death and night.
  We seized and used in thy despite
thy wondrous gift of liberty.
We housed us in this house of doom,
where death had royal scope and room,
  until thy Servant, Prince of Peace,
  breached all its walls for our release.

Thou camest to our hall of death,
  O Christ, to breathe our poisoned air,
  to drink for us the dark despair
that strangled man's reluctant breath.
How beautiful the feet that trod
the road that leads us back to God.
  How beautiful the feet that ran
  to bring the great good news to man.

O Spirit, who didst once restore
  thy church that it might be again
  the bringer of good news to men,
breathe on thy cloven church once more,
that in these gray and latter days
there may be men whose life is praise,
  each life a high doxology
  to Father, Son, and unto thee.

Martin Franzmann, 1967
Worship Supplement, 1969
© 1967, Lutheran Council in the USA

555
Weary of All Trumpeting

Weary of all trumpeting,
  weary of all killing,
weary of all songs that sing
  promise, nonfulfilling,
we would raise, O Christ, one song;
  we would join in singing
that great music pure and strong,
  wherewith heaven is ringing.

Captain Christ, O lowly Lord,
  Servant King, your dying
bade us sheathe the foolish sword,
  bade us cease denying.
Trumpet with your Spirit's breath
  through each height and hollow;
into your self-giving death,
  call us all to follow.

To the triumph of your cross
  summon all men living;
summon us to live by loss,
  gaining all by giving,
suffering all, that men may see
  triumph in surrender;
leaving all, that we may be
  partners in your splendor.

Martin Franzmann, 1971
Worship II, 1975
© 1972, Inter-Lutheran Commission on Worship

556
Now

Now the silence
Now the peace
Now the empty hands uplifted

Now the kneeling
Now the plea
Now the Father's arms in welcome

Now the hearing
Now the power
Now the vessel brimmed for pouring

Now the body
Now the blood
Now the joyful celebration

Now the wedding
Now the songs
Now the heart forgiven leaping

Now the Spirit's visitation
Now the Son's epiphany
Now the Father's blessing

Now   Now   Now

Jaroslav J. Vajda, 1968
Worship Supplement, 1969
© 1969, Hope Publishing Company

557

The Mountains Rise in Ranges Far and High

The mountains rise in ranges far and high
above the walls men throw against the sky;
I cannot bid them stay on border lines,
embossing earth the way my will defines.

The mighty rivers cannot choose to flow
through this land, and through that refuse to go;
they take the water from one neighbor's rain,
and make another's desert green with grain.

I cannot cause a partial sun to shine
on those whose color is the same as mine,
and keep in darkness those who should be free
to build a better world along with me.

If neither mountain, flowing stream, nor sun
can choose one people and another shun,
then I, O Lord, must let no barrier stand
between me and my brother's outstretched hand.

William Nelson, 1967
The Hymnal of the United Church of Christ, 1974
© 1969, United Church Press/Pilgrim Press

558

The Church of Christ Is One

The church of Christ is one:
Many are the rays of the sun,
but only one parent light.
Take a ray from the sun,
uncleft the sun remains;
the church of Christ is bathed—
suffused in the Lord's undying light;
although on all the earth diffused,
ever its light is one.

The church of Christ is one:
Many are the branches of a tree,
but rooted in the earth one trunk.
Break a branch from the tree,
the branch will cease to grow;
the branches of the church
are spread through the earth, and still
the body of the church remains,
whole, unbroken, one.

The church of Christ is one:
Many are the streams of a spring:
The source undivided stands.
    Choke a stream at the source,
the stream will fail—go dry;
    the Wellspring of the church
outflows in many streams, and still
the Head thereof is always one,
    one alone the source.

translated, Ford L. Battles, 1971
from Cyprian of Carthage in *De unitate ecclesiae*, 252
The Hymnal of the United Church of Christ, 1974
© 1974, United Church Press/Pilgrim Press

559

A Ballad of Trees and the Master

Into the woods my Master went,
    clean forspent, forspent;
into the woods my Master came,
    forspent with love and shame;
but the olives they were not blind to him,
the little gray leaves were kind to him,
the thorn tree had a mind to him,
    when into the woods he came.

Out of the woods my Master went,
    and he was well content;
out of the woods my Master came,
    content with death and shame.
When death and shame would woo him last,
from under the trees they drew him last:
'twas on a tree they slew him last,
    when out of the woods he came.

Sidney Lanier, 1880
The Independent, December 23, 1880
Poems of Sidney Lanier, 1884
first as a hymn in *The Methodist Hymnal*, 1905

Chapter 27:
Canada and Australia to 1975
(560–569)

T. S. Eliot wrote rather austerely that a "classic" can emerge only from a society with a long historical tradition. This may explain why Canada, Australia, and other English-speaking communities in the British Commonwealth have not yet produced a Charles Wesley. Young cultures do produce hymnody, and the chapter after this one will indicate how picturesque and refreshing such hymnody can be. One must remember that in 1776, America south of the Canadian border was by no means a young culture; the vigor of USA hymnody in the nineteenth century can be ascribed largely to the high culture of that very unusual community which is New England and perhaps also to the simple fact that already a great many people were living there.

Canada has only recently emerged as a significant source of hymnody, and we have the very forward-looking enterprise of the 1971 *Hymn Book* jointly used by the United Church and the Anglican Church in Canada to thank for that. And it has to be said that the first two well-known Canadian hymns turn out to be by Britishers. One is Joseph M. Scriven's "What a friend we have in Jesus" (which combines very wide popularity with a fairly low level of literature and which therefore we did not feel it necessary to transcribe), and the other is the Duke of Argyll's version of Psalm 121 (560). The Duke was Governor General of Canada when he wrote it, and the hymn is among those most dearly loved by Canadians; he was, of course, a Scottish aristocrat, and the Scottish influence in Canada extended to a widespread Presbyterian suspicion of hymnody, which contributed to that country's slow start in hymnody but which this piece effectively challenged.

It is difficult to find anything distinguished from Canada until we come to authors who are, at the time of writing, still alive. Robert B. Y. Scott's

"O day of God" (561) has been on the road since 1938 and found its way to England for the first time in 1951 (*The BBC Hymn Book*). All the rest (562–565) are taken from the 1971 *Hymn Book* and represent only a small fraction of the new material to be found there. Not the least of the distinctions of that book is the set of translations of medieval hymns by John Willis Grant which it includes. And 565 features the youngest authors in our collection, a further indication of the versatility of the New Canadian hymnody. [Note: George Brandon, the author of 564, was not a Canadian but a citizen of the United States.]

Australia has been rather slower in getting off the ground, though there are indications that in a few years' time we may be able to say more than we can now. The one Australian hymn to achieve the status of a "classic" is that of Principal Ernest Merrington (566) in which there are four stanzas of universal value. *The Australian Hymn Book* (1977), however, has abundant signs of hope. Our 567–569 come from that book, 567 being by its general editor. This book, though in its contents very unlike the Canadian one of 1971, is like it in being an ecumenical publication designed for use in most of the major denominations in Australia, and in this it is a portent of hope.

560
Psalm 121

Unto the hills around do I lift up
      my longing eyes;
O whence for me shall my salvation come,
      from whence arise?
From God the Lord doth come my certain aid,
from God the Lord who heaven and earth hath made.

He will not suffer that thy foot be moved:
    Safe shalt thou be.
No careless slumber shall his eyelids close,
    who keepeth thee.
Behold our God, the Lord, he slumbereth ne'er,
who keepeth Israel in his holy care.

Jehovah is himself thy keeper true,
    thy changeless shade;
Jehovah thy defense on thy right hand
    himself hath made.
And thee no sun by day shall ever smite,
nor moon shall harm thee in the silent night.

From every evil shall he keep thy soul,
    from every sin;
Jehovah shall preserve thy going out,
    thy coming in.
Above thee watching, he whom we adore
shall keep thee henceforth, yea, for evermore.

John Douglas Sutherland Campbell, 1877
The Book of Psalms, 1877

561

The Day of the Lord

O Day of God, draw nigh
    in beauty and in power;
come with thy timeless judgment now
    to match our present hour.

Bring to our troubled minds,
    uncertain and afraid,
the quiet of a steadfast faith,
    calm of a call obeyed.

Bring justice to our land,
    that all may dwell secure,
and finely build for days to come
    foundations that endure.

Bring to our world of strife
    thy sovereign word of peace,
that war may haunt the world no more
    and desolation cease.

O Day of God, bring nigh
    thy bright and shining light,
to rise resplendent on the world
    and drive away the night.

Robert B. Y. Scott, 1937
Christian Social Order hymn sheet, 1937
© 1988, Emmanuel College, Toronto

Scott substituted a new final stanza for the first publication of this text in a hymnal, in *Hymns for Worship*, 1939:

O Day of God, draw nigh,
    as at creation's birth;
let there be light again, and set
    thy judgments in the earth.   (Ps. 105:7)

562

God, Who Hast Caused to Be Written

God, who hast caused to be written thy word for
                    our learning,
grant us that, hearing, our hearts may be inwardly
                    burning.   (Luke 24:32)
    Give to us grace,
    that in thy Son we embrace
life, all its glory discerning.

Now may our God give us joy, and his peace in
                    believing (Rom. 15:13)
all things were written in truth for our thankful
                    receiving.   (2 Tim. 3:16)
    As Christ did preach,
    from man to man love must reach:
Grant us each day love's achieving.

Lord, should the powers of the earth and the
               heavens be shaken,   (Heb. 12:26)
grant us to see thee in all things, our vision awaken.
          Help us to see,
        though all the earth cease to be,   (Matt. 5:18)
thy truth shall never be shaken.   (Ps. 117:2)

Herbert O'Driscoll, ca. 1967
from an ancient collect
The Hymn Book, 1971
© 1980, Herbert O'Driscoll
The author subsequently updated this text, by revising "who hast" to
"you have" in 1:1 and changing "thee" and "thy" to "you" and "your"
throughout. In stanza 2, "his peace" became "all peace"
and "from man to man" was rephrased as "through all the world."

563

In Thy Pentecostal Splendor

In thy Pentecostal splendor
    rise, O living God, arise;
smoke of battle blurs and blinds us,
    blow thy wind and clear our eyes:
        Alleluia!
    thou art God of victories.

Thou of old didst lead thy people
    through the desert as they went;
thou upon the mount to Moses
    didst thy tenfold rule present:
        Alleluia!
    Thou art law and covenant.

Him who stooped to die for sinners
    thou hast glorified again;
he, captivity led captive,
    now obtaineth gifts for men:
        Alleluia!
    Thou art giver, now as then!

Thou at Pentecost didst shower
    gracious rain from heaven above;
on all flesh didst pour thy Spirit,
    silver-winged, descending dove:
        Alleluia!
    Thou art liberty and love!

Let the fire of thy near presence
    melt our fears, like wax, away;
touch our lips with songs of courage,
    teach us with thy saints to say,
        Alleluia!
    Thou, God, lead'st us all the way!

John Edward Speers
based on Psalm 68
The Hymn Book, 1971
© John Edward Speers

564

O God, Whose Mighty Wisdom Moves

O God, whose mighty wisdom moves
    the minds of men to seek thy way,
by thee the fathers sought the law;
    Lord, keep us in that quest today,
that in thy light we yet may see
the path that leads through truth to thee.

O God, whose perfect holiness
    inspires our search to find thy will,
by thee the prophets spoke of old;
    Lord, let us hear them speaking still,
that in thy light we yet may see
the path that leads through right to thee.

O God, whose tender, yearning heart
    gave us a Son, the living word;
by thee men sent the good news forth;
    Lord, let this gospel now be heard,
that in thy light we yet may see
the path that leads through love to thee.

O God, whose surging Spirit stirs
    within the souls of all on earth,
by thee the Scriptures bring new life,
    and hopes forgotten find rebirth;
Lord, grant us in thy light to see
the path that leads through all to thee.

George Brandon, 1952
Ten New Hymns on the Bible, 1953
© 1953, 1981, The Hymn Society (admin. Hope Publishing Company)

565
On This Day of Sharing

On this day of sharing
    gladly do we come
to the Lord's own table,
    gathering as one.

See the table laden
    with the bread and wine,
sign of Christ's own presence,
    pledge of love divine!

Food and drink, symbolic
    of his life on earth:
Peace, goodwill to all men,
    promised from his birth.

In the bread that's broken,
    in the wine that's poured,
be the name of Jesus
    evermore adored!

Many urgent problems
    face the human race—
war and vice and hunger:
    God seems out of place.

Yet our Savior sends us
    to this world of sin,
calling men to Jesus:
    "Let Christ enter in!"

Then, depart to serve him;
    worship him as God;
follow as he leads us
    in the way he trod.

David Kenneth Bentley, Doreen Margaret Jeal,
Marsha Coburn Kahale, and Robert Kyba, 1966
The Hymn Book, 1971
© Rosedale United Church, Montreal

566
God of Eternity, Lord of the Ages

God of eternity, Lord of the ages,
    Father and Spirit and Savior of men!
Thine is the glory of time's numbered pages;
    thine is the power to revive us again.

Thankful we come to thee, Lord of the nations,
    praising thy faithfulness, mercy, and grace,
shown to our fathers in past generations,
    pledge of thy love to our people and race.

Far from our ancient home, sundered by oceans,
    Zion is builded and God is adored:
Lift we our hearts in united devotions!
    Ends of the earth, join in praise to the Lord! (Ps. 48:10)

Beauteous this land of ours, bountiful Giver!
    brightly the heavens thy glory declare;
streameth the sunlight on hill, plain, and river,
    shineth thy cross over fields rich and fair.

Pardon our sinfulness, God of all pity,
    call to remembrance thy mercies of old; (Ps. 25:6)
strengthen thy church to abide as a city
    set on a hill for a light to thy fold. (Matt. 5:14–15)

Head of the church on earth, risen, ascended!
　　thine is the honor that dwells in this place;
as thou hast blessed us through years that have
　　　　　　　　　　　　　　　　　　　ended,
　　still lift upon us the light of thy face.

Ernest Northcroft Merrington, 1912
The Church Hymnary, 1927

567
For Absent Friends

Our God, we know your providence
　　and love are everywhere,
the wheeling stars, a sparrow's fall
　　are equally your care.

Much more to us of little faith
　　your power and love extend:
The church is given your Spirit's power,
　　our loneliness, a friend.

No power on earth can separate
　　us from the love of God;
and in that love, though parted, we
　　in union tread his road.

Those absent from our family
　　we bring to you in prayer,
that where they are they'll seek and find
　　a present helper there.

Through Christ we pray for all we love—
　　his love is all our might;
increase our faith, confirm our trust,
　　surround us with your light.

Wesley Milgate, 1975
Australian Hymn Book, 1977
© Australian Hymn Book Company

568
A Song of Cosmic Praise

　　Sing a new song, sing a new song
　　　　and wait upon the promise of the Lord.

Creation sings a new song to the Lord,
the universal energies rejoice,
through all the magnitudes of space and time
　　creatures proclaim the grandeur of Christ.

The mountains and the valleys and the plains,
the cattle and the wild beasts and the birds,
the shadows and the clouds, the rain and snow,
　　praise and reflect the bounty of Christ.

The ocean deeps, the currents, and the tides,
the diatoms, the fishes, and the whale,
the storm, the reef, the waterspout, the calm
　　praise and reflect the wonder of Christ.

The fruit trees in their seasons and the vine,
the eucalypt, the cedar, and the palm,
the lotus and the orchid and the rose
　　praise and reflect the beauty of Christ.

The human eye, the shaping hand, the mind,
with number and with symbol and design,
in work and play and artistry and prayer
　　praise and reflect the wisdom of Christ.

The love of man and woman clear as dawn,
the will for truth and justice broad as day,
the wisdom of the heart profound as night
　　praise and reflect the glory of Christ.

James Phillip McAuley, ca. 1965
Australian Hymn Book, 1977
© Curtis Brown

569

A Lamp for Our Feet Has Been Given

A lamp for our feet has been given,
    a light has been set on a hill;
God's word in its truth may be trusted
    by all who surrender their will:
to order the chaos of darkness,
    give hope in the midst of despair,
to make of our lives new creations
    and lighten the burdens we bear.

Lord, worship and praise we would offer
    in thanks for the grace we've received;
your word is our rock and our tower,
    in trusting we are not deceived.
The prophets of old had their visions,
    your word often came in their dreams,
but we see the word now incarnate
    in Christ, and in those he redeems.

Lord, grant to us eyes ever watchful,
    and ears ever open to hear
the word that in love you are speaking,
    the word that defeats all our fear.
In suffering love you have claimed us,
    forgive us for flesh that is weak;
you know that our spirits are willing:
    Give strength with the word that you speak.

Granton Douglas Hay, 1975
Australian Hymn Book, 1977
© Australian Hymn Book Company

Chapter 28:
Cantate Domino: Hymns from Modern Foreign Sources (570–592)

This chapter is headed by the quotation from Psalm 96 which is also the title of the best-known international hymn book, and it contains a small handful of hymns all of which come from what are in some sense new hymn-cultures of non-English-speaking background.

Looking back over the whole story, we find that it is, naturally enough, centered in the English language. The only other language in which such a book as this could have been compiled is the German; there is a vast treasury of hymnody originating in that tongue. But even so it would have been a very different kind of book, for only in the English-speaking tradition has so much hymn writing been combined with so much translation. The German tradition is Lutheran or Reformed, and German hymnaries have never taken much notice of hymnody (other than medieval) from other languages. Until recently the same has been true of the Scandinavian language groups. As for the Catholic countries, until 1964 they had no tradition of hymnody apart from that which was founded and concluded in the Middle Ages.

The distinguishing quality of twentieth-century church life has been, as everyone knows, ecumenism. This means not only the meeting of Christians of hitherto hostile denominations, but also, in our field, the meeting of languages. The Ecumenical Movement found its focus in the conferences which led to the establishment in 1948 of the World Council of Churches, and it was its associated junior instrument (junior in standing but senior in foundation), the World Student Christian Federation, which produced the first editions (1924, 1930, 1951) of the multilingual and international hymnal, *Cantate Domino*. They appear to have invented the idea of collecting hymns that could be sung in several languages by groups representing many cultures, and their books in the successive editions have had a modest and significant success. This suggested to other groups the provision of similar books, like the hymnal *Laudamus* and the worship book *Venite Adoremus* of the World Lutheran Federation.

It was only, however, in 1974 that *Cantate Domino* could show the specially valuable fruits of Roman Catholic participation. This edition was published by the World Council of Churches, and a glance at it will show that it is ampler, and much further-ranging in styles and in places of origin, than its predecessors. Indeed, in the preparation of this book the Eastern Orthodox churches also participated for the first time, although, since they have no tradition of congregational hymnody, their contribution was confined to liturgical pieces.

Developments of this kind show that a new horizontal dimension has been introduced into hymnody in the twentieth century. It is no longer a single historical stream of the kind we have been following right up to this point. The Catholic churches have since 1964 been developing vernacular hymnody of a quite new kind. The churches in countries which were regarded not much more than a hundred years ago as mission-receiving countries are now developing indigenous qualities and indigenous hymnody. Even a generation ago it was difficult, with the best will in the world, to find true indigenous hymnody from Africa, India, and the Far East; it is not so now.

Profound difficulties remain and will become more intractable as communication increases. They are not only theological and ecclesiastical, although the more "indigenous" a church becomes, the stranger its ways of thinking may well appear to traditional "Western" minds. People from the southern hemisphere are now arguing forcibly with those who stand in the Latin tradition of Christianity on the most fundamental principles. But the aesthetic of these countries also creates difficulties of understanding, as when their traditional ideas of poetic expression, or of the musical scale, are wholly foreign to those of Europe. Naturally, all this has to be faced and will, one hopes, be creatively resolved in the many centuries that are left to our descendants. At the moment we are in a kind of "honeymoon" stage in which the excitement and newness of the hymnody that comes through from lands whose praise we never before shared overrides the difficulties.

Translation, of course, presents new hazards. Sometimes the originals are, so far as our present talents go, almost untranslatable into English. Or they look unusual and peculiar when so translated. Some of the best English pieces taken from foreign originals may be, like 586, paraphrases made by a poet, who does not know the original language, out of a prose translation furnished by a linguist.

The contents of this chapter are arranged roughly geographically, and they begin with two offerings from Catholic France. These show only a hint of the strenuous activity in psalmody and hymnody that has come from the *Centre nationale de pastorale liturgique* in Paris, whose chief poet is Didier Rimaud and whose leading musician, the celebrated Joseph Gelineau.

Number 570 is historic, in being a biblical canticle written before 1964. Its occasion was the conference on "Bible and Liturgy" held in Strasbourg in July 1957, when at the service of vigils before the high Mass the psalmody was entirely in the vernacular and included this specially composed hymn with music by Jean Langlais. The original French processional is in nine stanzas; the English translation, made for *Dunblane Praises 1*, 1964 (see chapter 23), uses that part of it which appears on a record made at the time.

Number 571 is another canticle, the most spacious and majestic of all the many such responsive songs written by the CNPL team. These canticles are always profoundly biblical, and therefore in the highest tradition of hymnody. Other work of the kind by Lucien Deiss has become very well known in Europe and America.

Numbers 572–574 are from Germany. In a quite understandable sense, the new German hymnody is a new culture. Right down to 1933, German hymnody was dominated by the chorale, where it was not corrupted by romantic perversions. It was isolated and remote; it used virtually no translations from contemporary sources. The first great break came with the Hitler persecutions, which forced the Confessing Church, the resisting part of the Lutheran communion, into reassessments of its customs and its role. Out of this came a small quantity of new hymnody, much of it by the heroic Bishop Otto Dibelius. It was almost all a throwback to the hymnody of the Thirty Years' War, and in their praise the new-style congregations revived the ancient chorales and rejected the romantic accretions. Number 572 is probably the only hymn from this period that has gone into English; it is translated by a writer who has written no other hymns, and it has appeared only in his translation of the original author's book, *The Iron Ration of a Christian*.

Number 573, by a martyr of the Resistance and the most influential theologian of his generation, Dietrich Bonhoeffer, was not designed as a hymn. It is part of a poem that was printed at the end of the book known in English as *Letters and Papers from Prison*. It has been used as a hymn in Germany, but the English translation was made for *Cantate Domino*. Another Bonhoeffer text, "Men go to God when they are sorely pressed," by the Canadian translator Walter Farquharson, is now deservedly finding acceptance.

But the most remarkable development in hymnody in Germany during the postwar years has been what we may for convenience call the *Kirchentag* style. The *Kirchentag* was originally a large convention of religious people from all over Europe, mostly young, who met for a quite unusual kind of religious revival. Immediately after World War II this enterprise, which organized several of these gatherings, was mostly organized by that great Christian, Reinold von Thadden. Outwardly, the sight of a hundred thousand people in a large German stadium met for religious purposes might suggest the kind of activity widely associated with the name of Billy Graham. But the tone was radical, not conservative; the politics were left, not right; the preaching was intellectual rather than emotional. And the hymnody was in a quite unusual way professional; it could not be less like the Lutheran or Pietist chorales. It was rhythmical and syncopated; it presupposed guitars rather than organs, sometimes indeed jazz groups; it was antiphonal, and, in abounding in refrains, it shared just one quality with Gospel Songs. Some of the most creative minds in German music contributed to these songs. The lyrics are almost always biblical and radical at the same time.

Long after the *Kirchentag* phase passed, this German version of "folk" or "pop" hymnody persisted, and indeed, it is still, in 1976, in full cry. There is much that we might have quoted, though like other folk material it loses much of its force when separated from its music and is usually, especially in translation, unsatisfactory for reading. But special honor should be done to Provost Dieter Trautwein of Frankfurt, who in earlier years was a distinguished leader in German religious youth work, who has composed a number of these new lyrics; we choose his communion hymn (574) because it seems to embody most of the characteristics of this style: new thinking, intimacy, informality, ruggedness, and sincerity.

The Netherlands, traditionally even more conservative than Germany in its public praise, since the Reformed church had the same addiction to metrical psalms that we found in the Church of Scotland, has been producing some excellent new material. Its best-known religious poet is Huub Oosterhuis (575), whose most famous hymn is here given; this one has traveled a long way.

Sweden, whose hymnody anybody in 1950 would have thought irretrievably petrified, has experienced a similar explosion of creativity. The recent *Psalmer och Visor* (1975) shows how violent the explosion has been. Olov Hartman, their best religious dramatist and poet, has written a number of hymns, and 576 exhibits their biblical background and imaginative quality. Anders Frostenson (577) is their most energetic hymn writer; a good deal of the lyric in *Psalmer och Visor* is his own, and here again we find a special celebration of the Bible, especially of the Old Testament, which makes his work unlike anything that the English-speaking writers are producing at the moment.

From here on we go farther from the English scene. Number 578 is, it has to be admitted, a paraphrase based on a prose translation, the text as you have it being the work of an author who does not know a word of Hungarian. It probably is as near the original as some of Robert Bridges's work was to his sources; that may well be the only context in which it would be decent to invoke the name of Bridges in this connection. But it is just about all that is yet available from Hungarian Protestantism.

Africa is producing a good deal of religious lyric. As yet in translation it is immature, though it is always zestful. Number 579 is from a French original by a minister who comes from and works in Cameroon, and it was written to be sung to the tune of a traditional funeral dance. (It will be readily recalled that funeral customs in those regions are a good deal less oppressive and decorous than ours.) It is a simple Easter narrative, with a double refrain; the absence of the refrain at the climactic point is especially dramatic.

We met the Indian poet Nārāyan Tilak at 348. In 580 he has another characteristic lyric, beautifully rendered by a different translator, and at 581 a third, in Nicol Macnicol's translation. Later Indian material is, as is fitting, dancelike and ecstatic and, more than most, needs its music to make its effect. We should mention the work of the Portuguese-Indian priest Christopher Coelho of Goa, who has written many antiphonal canticles with music that combine Western tonality with

Indian turns of phrase, and some of which may be found in *Cantate Domino*. We may hazard a guess that hymnody as understood by Western Protestants will not come easily to either of the two leading temperaments in the Indian subcontinent, the contemplative Hindu or the activist Muslim. But the Bible, especially the Book of Psalms, provides a good ground for some very vital new hymnody among the beleaguered Christians of that region.

Number 582 introduces that extraordinary ecumenical figure, Daniel Thambyrajah Niles, who, in editing the *East Asian Christian Conference Hymnal* (1963), circulated so many valuable translations of contemporary lyrics from India and the Far East. "Slaves of Christ" comes from that source and from the Tamil language. There is a touch of resemblance between some of this hymnody and the Negro Spiritual. In the next few years we are going to hear from these quarters a great deal about "liberation," a paratheological concept which is much exercising ecumenical Christians at present and which has the same origin as the liberation-yearning we hear from the first-generation black slaves.

China before 1948 was beginning to develop a hymnody of its own after being brought up, like all the farther regions, on translations of Watts, Wesley, and American Unitarians. Numbers 583–586 represent different strains in the very varied scene of Chinese Christianity. Probably it will be some time before Chinese Christians, who have now for so long been in exile or silence, develop what one could call an indigenous Christian style. They are, as here evidenced, very good pupils of Western preachers. Numbers 584 and 585 are translations by missionaries who knew the language; 583 and 586 are paraphrases, but both admirably done. (The *E. A. C. C. Hymnal*, the only source of 583, misses a point by providing a tune in the wrong meter.) The Korean hymn, 587, which many Western books have found useful, is even more obviously a Western Evangelical

product. It might be noted that it was written well before the 1950 Korean War.

Japan, perhaps religiously the most mysterious of all nations, not least because of the extraordinary Japanese capacity for assimilating the surface qualities of alien cultures, has produced a small quantity of Christian lyric, and it is certainly right for us to include the very forward-looking song about Christ's working life (588) and the haunting, though undogmatic, lines of that great Christian, Toyohiko Kagawa (589).

In this almost indecent scamper through the part of the world where the great majority of human beings actually live, we finally touch down in Latin America and in the Caribbean. Latin America—principally Brazil but including the central states—has a vigorous Protestant tradition, Presbyterian and Methodist, which until recently used Western Evangelical hymnody for its praise. But 590 is a quite remarkable departure from that style. The original is in Portuguese, and although it is pessimistic, it is certainly passionate.

Caribbean Christianity, where it is not of the black culture, is very largely the product of missions from Europe and the USA. Ethnically, those delicious islands are in the late twentieth century experiencing profound racial and political problems, and there is a certain tender pathos in the poem (591) by the exiled John Hoad, formerly a College Principal in Jamaica. Here, though it is the work of a white Christian, is something which really evokes the life of Jamaica in the way in which Kagawa evoked that of traditional Japan a page before.

Finally, in 592, we give the text of what seems to be one of the very best hymns written lately by an English missionary for a foreign country. Its author was the editor of that quite remarkable collection, *Africa Praise* (1968), and he contributed this to that book, most of which is strictly African and not material exported from Britain. He wrote it for an African tune; a rather beautiful British one appears with it in *The Church Hymnary*, third edition. The sharing of Western talent in this fashion is something quite different from the exporting of Western style hymnody, in the past, necessary, but now inappropriate.

This section is, in any case, only the prologue to a development in hymnody which is already energetic and will become decisive. Perhaps the very swiftness of the journey round the world, which has had a touch of Pan Am Flight One about it, will cause the reader to feel a due sense of the vastness of the field and the speed of progress. From the severe biblicism of Sweden to John Hoad's glowworms in the tropics—fifty years ago no English worshiper knew a word of this or conceived of its happening; even ten years ago we did not know much of it.

570

We Beheld His Glory
French: Dieu, nous avons vu ta gloire en ton Christ

God, your glory we have seen in your Son,
    full of truth, full of heavenly grace: (John 1:14)
      In Christ make us live, his love shine on
        our face,
    and the nations shall see in us the triumph you
      have won.

In the fields of this world his good news he has
      sown,
and sends us out to reap till the harvest is done.
                     (John 4:35–36)

In his love like a fire that consumes he passed by;
the flame has touched our lips; let us shout, "Here
      am I!"   (Isa. 6:8)

He was broken for us, God-forsaken his cry, Matt. 27:46)
and still the bread he breaks; to ourselves we must die.

He has trampled the grapes of new life on his cross;
                        (Isa. 63:3)
now drink the cup and live; he has filled it for us.

He has founded a kingdom that none shall destroy;
the cornerstone is laid; go to work, build with joy!

Didier Rimaud, 1957
translated, Brian Wren (stanzas) and Ronald Johnson (refrain), 1964
Cantate Domino, 1974
© 1974, Hope Publishing Company

571

Images of the Cross
French: Par le croix qui fit mourir le fis du Père

By the cross which did to death our only Savior,
this blessed vine from which grapes are gathered in:
    Jesus Christ, we thank and bless you!
By the cross which casts down fire upon our planet,
this burning bush in which love is plainly shown:
                    (Exod. 3:4)
    Jesus Christ, we glorify you!
By the cross on Calvary's hill securely planted,
this living branch which can heal our every sin:
    Conquering God, we your people proclaim you!

By the blood with which we marked the woode
                lintels,   (Exod. 12:21–22)
for our protection the night when God passed by:
    Jesus Christ, we thank and bless you!
By the blood, which in our Exodus once saved us,
when hell was sealed up by God's engulfing sea:
                    (Exod. 14:16)
    Jesus Christ, we glorify you!
By the blood which kills the poison in bad fruitage,
and gives new life to the dead sap in the tree:
    Conquering God, we your people proclaim you!

By the death on Calvary's hill of him the Firstborn,
who bears the wood and the flame for his own pyre:
    Jesus Christ, we thank and bless you!
By the death, amid the thorns, of God's own
                       Shepherd,
the Paschal Lamb who was pierced by our despair:
    Jesus Christ, we glorify you!
By the death of God's Beloved outside his vineyard,
                         (Mark 12:8)
that he might change us from murderer into heir:
    Conquering God, we your people proclaim you!

By the wood which sings a song of nuptial gladness,
of God who takes for bride our human race:
    Jesus Christ, we thank and bless you!
By the wood which raises up in his full vigor
the Son of Man who draws all men by his grace:
    Jesus Christ, we glorify you!   (John 12:32)
By the wood where he perfects his royal priesthood
in one High Priest who for sin is sacrifice: (Heb. 9:11–14)
    Conquering God, we your people proclaim you!

Holy tree which reaches up from earth to heaven
that all the world may exult in Jacob's God: (Gen. 28:10)
    Jesus Christ, we thank and bless you!
Mighty ship which snatches us from God's deep
                          anger,
saves us, with Noah, from drowning in the flood:
                       (1 Pet. 3:20)
    Jesus Christ, we glorify you!
Tender wood which gives to brackish water
                 sweetness,   (Exod. 15:25)
and from the Rock shall strike fountains for our good:
                        (1 Cor. 10:4)
    Conquering God, we your people proclaim you!

Didier Rimaud, ca. 1963
translated, Fred Pratt Green, 1972
Cantate Domino, 1974
© 1974, Hope Publishing Company

572
O Faithless, Fearful Army
German: Der Herr wird für dich streiten

A.

Der Herr wird für dich streiten,
    du angstverstörtes Heer,
und seinen Weg bereiten
    dir mitten durch das Meer;
das Eine und das Größte
    ließ er an dir gescheh'n,
der Gott, der dich erlöste,
    läßt dich nicht untergeh'n!

Warum willst du verzagen
    vor Feindes Übermacht,
als müßtest du nun schlagen
    mit deiner Kraft die Schlacht.
Und ob gleich Tod und Hölle
    die unausweichlich droh'n
er trat an deine Stelle,
    des Vaters einger Sohn.

Mit seinem Leib und Leben
    deckt er sein Eigentum,
du darfst dich ihm nur geben,
    er ist dein Heil und Ruhm!
Er ist der rechte Krieger
    in Gottes großer Schlacht—
Herr Christ, du bist der Sieger,
    dein Werk ist schon vollbracht!

Heinrich Vogel, 1936
Eiserne Ration eines Christen, 1936

B.

O faithless, fearful army,
    for you the Lord doth fight.
For you, through oceans stormy
    he cleaves his path of light.
Determined is the issue,
    the crucial victory past;
and God who has redeemed you
    upholds you to the last.

Why downcast, why despairing,
    in face of hostile power;
as though alone you're bearing
    the stresses of this hour?
To death and hell appointed—
    see, conquering in your place
the Son of God, the Anointed,
    elect by sovereign grace!

His death and resurrection
    he clothes upon his folk,
bound to him in subjection
    by faith and love and hope.
O Warrior true and glorious,
    thou hast God's battle won!
Lord Christ, for us victorious,
    thy perfect work is done.

translated, W. A. Whitehouse, 1941
The Iron Ration of a Christian, 1941

573
New Year 1945
German: Von guten Mächten wunderbar geboren

By gracious powers so wonderfully sheltered,
    and confidently waiting come what may,
we know that God is with us night and morning
    and never fails to greet us each new day.

Yet is this heart by its old foe tormented,
    still evil days bring burdens hard to bear.
O give our frightened souls the sure salvation
    for which, O Lord, you taught us to prepare.

And when this cup you give is filled to brimming
    with bitter suffering, hard to understand,
we take it thankfully, and without trembling
    out of so good, and so beloved, a hand.

Yet when again, in this same world, you give us
    the joy we had, the brightness of your sun,
we shall remember all the days we lived through,
    and our whole life shall then be yours alone.

Now, when your silence deeply spreads around us,
    O let us hear all your creation says—
that world of sound which soundlessly invades us,
    and all your children's highest hymns of praise.

Dietrich Bonhoeffer, 1944
translated, Geoffrey Winthrop Young
Prisoner for God, 1953 (subsequently published as
Letter and Prayers from Prison)
paraphrased, Fred Pratt Green, 1972
Cantate Domino, 1974
© 1974, Hope Publishing Co.

Green approved the following, written by Michael Ball for *Baptist Praise and Worship*, 1991, as a substitute for his own final stanza:

Now as your silence deeply spreads around us,
    open our ears to hear your children raise
from all the world, from every nation round us,
    to you their universal hymn of praise.

574

Honored Guest

German: Herr, du bist an vielen Tischen

Lord, you are at many tables
    an invited, honored Guest.
        Even of those, Lord,
    who are self-sufficient
    you let none bear you down.
Come, share the meal with us,
come, share the meal with us,
unite those who part without loving.

Lord, you are at many tables
    an invited, honored Guest.
        You also speak, Lord,
    to those who see nothing
    except tomorrow's cares.
Come, share the meal with us,
come, share the meal with us,
give light to the eyes of the weary.

Lord, you are at many tables
    an invited, honored Guest.
        You come to people
    who do without you.
    False piety, you hate.
Come, share the meal with us,
come, share the meal with us,
then, Lord, we shall trust what you offer.

Lord, you are at many tables
    an invited, honored Guest.
        But as our Host, Lord,
    you make sure we carry
    each other's load of care.   (Gal. 6:8)
Come, share the meal with us,
come, share the meal with us,
here, now, and at each of our tables.

Dieter Trautwein, 1967
translated, Dieter Trautwein
paraphrased, Fred Pratt Green, 1973
Cantate Domino, 1974
© 1974, Hope Publishing Company

575

A World Full of People

Dutch: Zo lang er mensen zijn op aarde

While still the earth is full of people,
    and earth to man her increase gives,
we give our thanks to you, the keeper
    and father God of all that lives.

As long as human words are spoken
    and for each other we exist,
you give your love as faithful token,
    we thank you in the name of Christ.

You feed the birds in tree and rafter,
    you clothe the flowers of the field.   (Matt. 6:25ff)
You shelter us now and hereafter,
    and to your care our days we yield.

You are our light and our salvation,
    you raise your people from the dead.
You gave your Son for every nation,
    his body is the living bread.

The world is bound to bow before you,
    you brought it by your love to birth;
you live among us, we adore you,
    we are your children down-to-earth.

Huub Oosterhuis, 1958
translated, Fred Kaan, 1968
Pilgrim Praise, 1968
© 1968, Hope Publishing Company

In *The Hymn Texts for Fred Kaan*, 1995, line 1:2 was revised to read:

    and mother-earth her increase gives,

and line 3:2 was changed to:

    you clothe the flower in the field.

The full music edition of *Cantate Domino*, 1980, has a different English translation by Redmond McGoldrick.

576

Babel

Swedish: Se här bygges Babels torn

See them building Babel's tower: (Gen. 11:3)
    Slaves the stones are carrying:
Here no man cares for brother man:
    Kyrieleison.

Far astray that upward road,
    man, become a stranger,
goes hungry at his brother's board:
    Kyrieleison.

"Brotherhood," forgotten word
    down the grassy hillside
rejected from that building lies.   (Mark 12:10)
    Kyrieleison.

Men one day will find it there
    and will recognize it
as keystone of God's hill and house.
    Hallelujah!

Then their cry will rise, and we,
    each in his own language   (Acts 2:11)
shall hear of brotherhood once more,
    Hallelujah!

Mighty wind of heaven's rule,
    storming every barrier
will blow for ever where it wills,   (John 3:8)
    Hallelujah!

So shall Babel come to naught.
    Where it stood shall flourish
the harvest of God's brotherhood.
    Hallelujah!

Olov Hartman, 1970
translated, Caryl Micklem and Ruth Micklem, 1972
Cantate Domino, 1974
© Ruth Micklem

577

Faith, While Trees Are Still in Blossom

Swedish: Tron sig sträcker efter frukten när i blomning trädet går

Faith, while trees are still in blossom,
    plans the picking of the fruit;
faith can feel the thrill of harvest
    when the buds begin to sprout.

Long before the dawn is breaking,
    faith anticipates the sun.
Faith is eager for the daylight,
    for the work that must be done.

Long before the rains were coming,
    Noah went and built an ark.   (Gen. 6:13)
Abraham, the lonely migrant,
    saw the light beyond the dark.   (Gen. 12:1)

Faith, uplifted, tamed the water
    of the undivided sea   (Exod. 14:15 16)
and the people of the Hebrews
    found the path that made them free.

Faith believes that God is faithful—   (Rom. 4:3)
    "He will be that he will be"—   (Exod. 3:14)
Faith accepts his call, responding,
    "I am willing: Lord, send me."   (Isa. 6:3)

Anders Frostenson, 1960
translated, Fred Kaan, 1972
Cantate Domino, 1974
© 1976, Hope Publishing Company

578

The Tree of Life
Hungarian: Paradicsomnak te szép élö fája

There in God's garden stands the tree of wisdom
(Gen. 2:16)
whose leaves hold forth the healing of the nations:
(Rev. 22:2)
tree of all knowledge, tree of all compassion,
tree of all beauty.

Its name is Jesus, name that says "Our Savior!"
(Matt. 1:21)
There on its branches see the scars of suffering;
see where the tendrils of our human selfhood
feed on its lifeblood.

Thorns not its own are tangled in its foliage;
our greed has starved it; our despite has choked it.
Yet, look, it lives! Its grief has not destroyed it,
nor fire consumed it.   (Exod. 3:2)

See how its branches reach to us in welcome;
hear what the voice says, "Come to me, ye weary!
(Matt. 11:28)
Give me your sickness, give me all your sorrow.
I will give blessing."

This is my ending; this my resurrection;
into your hands, Lord, I commit my spirit.   (Ps. 31:5)
This have I searched for; now I can possess it.
This ground is holy!   (Exod. 3:5)

All heaven is singing, "Thanks to Christ, whose
passion
offers in mercy healing, strength, and pardon.
All men and nations, take it, take it freely!" (Rev. 22:17)
Amen! My Master!

paraphrased, Erik Routley, 1971
based on a hymn by Imre Pécseli Király, ca. 1641
Cantate Domino, 1974
© 1976, Hinshaw Music, Inc.

579

Easter
French: Notre Dieu Sauveur est Jésus Seigneur

Our Jesus is Savior, Lord, and Friend;
he searched all our life from end to end.

And he came down to earth to shed his
blood on Calvary,
all to give life to men.

The city rejoices, the children sing:
"A day of joy: Behold, our King!"

The table is set in an upper room;
the bread and the wine foretell his doom.

In form of a servant he washes their feet,
and says, "Thus humbly each other greet."

They all go with him to Gethsemane,
but in Pilate's courts there is none but he.

"Not guilty!" says Pilate, and washes his hands.
"Away with him now!" the crowd demands.

Before evening falls, it all is done;
the tomb receives our Holy One.

Where are the disciples? Where now are his friends?
The Lord is dead, and here all hope ends.

[Pause; no refrain]

Two nights and a day, and the news is abroad:
Not end but beginning! Alive is the Lord!

Sing alleluia, for Christ the Lord is risen,
all to give life to men.

So praise we God's love for what Jesus has done.
Now death is defeated and victory won.

Abel Nkuinji, 1965
paraphrased, Erik Routley, 1972
Cantate Domino, 1974
© 1974, Hope Publishing Company

580

The Lowest Place

Grant me to give to men what they desire,
   and for my portion take what they do slight.
Grant me, my Lord, a mind that doth aspire
   to less than it may claim of proper right.

Rather, the lowest place, at all men's feet,
   that do thou graciously reserve for me.
This only bounty I would fain entreat,
   that thy will, O my God, my will may be.

Nārāyan Vāman Tilak
translated, John C. Winslow, 1920
The Life of Tilak, 1920
as adapted in *Cantate Domino*, 1951
© World Student Christian Federation

Winslow's translation consists of two unequal stanzas, the first encompassing the initial six lines, the second containing four lines, adding these after the final two above:

And yet one other boon must thou bestow;
I name it not, saith Dāsa—for thou dost know!

"Dāsa," meaning "servant," is Tilak's self-appellation.

581

As the Lyre to the Singer

As the lyre to the singer,
   as one's thought to spoken word,
as the rose to fragrant odor,
   so to me is Christ the Lord.

As the mother to the baby,
   as the traveler to his guide,
as the lake to streaming rainfall
   stands the Savior by my side.

As the sun to gladdening dayspring,
   as the oil is to the flame,
as the fish is to the water,
   so to me is his sweet name.

Bound to him and by him holden
   as the flute and breath accord,
his for now and his for ever
   is my soul to Christ the Lord.

Nārāyan Vāman Tilak
translated, Nicol Macnicol, 1922
E. A. C. C. *Hymnal*, 1963
© Christian Conference of Asia

582

Let Us Win the World for Jesus
Tamil: Dhaaseree yith therenniyei anbaai

Slaves of Christ, his mercy we remember,
and his will that our lands for him we win,
that he reign—our witness we shall bear,
        for all his brethren care,
        and his communion share
        in all our work and prayer.

    Slaves of Christ, his mercy we remember,
    and his will that our lands for him we win.

Calling men, the laboring and the laden,
to his feet that their burdens he may lift. (Matt. 11:28)
At his word—their sorrows fully past,
        their troubles on him cast,
        their sickness healed at last,
        will men to him hold fast.

Bringing him, our Master and our Savior,
where his sword must all false presences slay,
that his peace may shatter human pride,
   the right from wrong divide,
   the widow's cause decide,
   injustice set aside.

V. Santiago, 1920
translated and paraphrased, Daniel Thambyrajah Niles, 1962
E. A. C. C. Hymnal, 1963
© D. T. Niles

583

Saving Love
Mandarin: Ai zhi quan yuan jiu shi shen

God, the love that saved mankind,
 raised the cross upon life's road,
  guiding us through winding ways.
Praise we him who brought the blind
 grace, which to them sight restored
  by the truth he set ablaze.

Babel voices round us rise;
 grief and torment, blood and dust
  hide all meaning and all light.
Burdened hearts and aching eyes
 seek their Lord in love and trust,
  praying that he end their night.

Quiet from the earth is fled;
 vain is hope, and striving vain,
  like dead water and dead wood
severed from the fountainhead.
 Send thou down like healing rain
  grace that brings forth truth and good.

Where a crossroad comes we stand
 rent by inner questioning,
  aims that differ and delude.
Stretch thou forth thy guiding hand,
 and thy wandering people bring
  into peace and plenitude.

Free the vanquished and enslaved,
  and those sunk in pain and haste,
   by thy glorious sacrifice.
Lead thou them whom thou hast saved
  upward through the narrow gate
   to the joy of paradise.

anonymous, Chinese
paraphrased, Margaret Barclay, 1950
E. A. C. C. Hymnal, 1963
© World Student Christian Federation

584

My Heart Looks in Faith
Mandarin: Wo xin suo xiang xin

My heart looks in faith
 to the Lamb divine:
his precious blood he shed
 for this life of mine.

My heart waits in hope
 the great God to see;   (Ps. 42:2)
sure are his promises,
 they encompass me.

My heart dwells in love
 by the Spirit blest;
he heals my sicknesses,
 sets my soul at rest.

All faith, hope, and love
 are by Jesus given,
on earth to give us strength
 and his peace in heaven.

Tzu-ch'en Chao
Hymns for the People, 1931
translated, Frank W. Price, 1952
Chinese Christian Hymns, 1963
© Mrs. Frank W. Price

585

The Bread of Life

Mandarin: Jiu shi zhe shen, wei zhong shengij bokai

The bread of life, for all men broken!
　　He drank the cup on Golgotha.
His grace we trust, and spread with reverence
　　this holy feast, and thus remember.

With godly fear we seek thy presence;
　　our hearts are sad, people distressed.
Thy holy face is stained with bitter tears,
　　our human pain still bearest thou with us.

O Lord, we pray, come thou among us,
　　lighten our eyes, brightly appear!
Immanuel, heaven's joy unending,
　　our life with thine for ever blending.

Timothy Tingfang Lew, 1936
Hymns of Universal Praise, 1936
translated, Walter Reginald Oxenham Taylor, 1943
The BBC Hymn Book, 1951
© 1951, Oxford University Press

586

The Heavenly City

Salem, from heaven descending, (Rev. 21:1ff)
　　home, light, felicity,
beneath man's sore oppressions
　　our hearts cry out for thee.
The hope of thy pledged coming
　　assuages grief and pain,
kindles to high emprises,
　　the weak makes strong again.

Salem, from heaven descending,
　　here milk and honey flow,
here rules the Son of Mary
　　whose head was cradled low;
here sorrows shall be ended,
　　nor gold nor power divide,
nor brethren here be sundered
　　by huckster's guile or pride.

Salem, from heaven descending—
　　here reigns in joy and peace
the Lamb who bore our sorrows
　　that we might find release.
No more the lust of empire,
　　nor rift of race-disdain!
Sword shall be turned to plowshare (Isa. 2:4)
　　and slaughter shall be slain.

Salem, from heaven descending,
　　where heart and mind are free,
behold, the Word eternal
　　is Light and Lord to thee.
Here violence is vanquished,
　　nor bars nor bonds prevail;
and who now travel darkling
　　shall see without a veil.

Salem, from heaven descending,
　　home, light, beatitude,
the hopes of thy pledged coming
　　our grief and pain extrude.
On earth, as now in heaven,
　　God's holy will be done;
may we, from doubt delivered,
　　in toil and hope be one. (1 Cor. 15:58)

Timothy Tingfang Lew, 1936
Hymns of Universal Praise, 1936
paraphrased, Nathaniel Micklem, 1937
Edinburgh Conference of Churches leaflet, 1937
© Nathaniel Micklem

587
Redemption
Korean: Yil Yesu hul li pi

The Savior's precious blood
hath made all nations one,
united let us praise this deed
the Father's love hath done.

In this vast world of men,
a world so full of sin,
no other theme can be our prayer
than this: "Thy kingdom come!"

In this sad world of war
can peace be ever found?
Unless the love of Christ prevail,
true peace will not abound.

The Master's new command
was: "Love each other well." (John 13:34)
O brothers, let us all unite
to do his holy will.

Tai Jun Park, 1949
translated, William Scott and Yung Oon Kim, 1950
Cantate Domino, 1951
© World Student Christian Federation

588
Jesus in the Little Village of Nazareth
Japanese: Mukashi shu Iesu wa kusa fukaki

Long ago in little Nazareth lived the Son of Man,
planing wood, the carpenter, working to the plan
which his father gave him daily, whatever it was,
from his brow the sweat drops falling until evening's
pause.
God made a workman, occupied with human toil,
God here accepting as his own our blood and
soil.

God's salvation is no theory based on empty thought,
with his calloused working hands was salvation
wrought,
not in human wisdom, nor found in learned book,
but by Holy Spirit's fire within the flesh he took.
Man made a brother sharing life with God's
own son,
the laborer finding life anew in Christ begun.

Toiler, trader, peasant, farmer—each enriched by
grace
given freely, irrespective of man's name or place.
Let us then the hammer lift, or turn the heavy
wheels,
draw the water for the field, or hoe till evening
steals.
Work, for the Father worketh even until now.
(John 5:17)
He will the work complete. He only knoweth
how. (Phil. 1:6)

Gunpei Yamamuro, 1940
translated, Daniel Thambyrajah Niles, 1962
E. A. C. C. Hymnal, 1963
© Christian Conference of Asia

589
Black Soil
Japanese: Kurotsuchi

O black fruitful soil, presenting a gladsome scene,
dressed in garments green,
bedecking earth with beauty—tree and flower and
vine—
youth lead their cows to pasture in the bright
sunshine.

Revive the land where poverty lies,
for God, a Mother true, their every need
supplies,
and his grace is their perpetual surprise.

Come, brothers, unite to guard all our homes and
land,
joined in heart and hand,
that we may lift the burdens of the poor, the weak;
and, to the sick and lonely, words of comfort speak.

God's love, O, how deep! Unceasing the mercy
which
flows from Jesus rich;
when we through sin inflict on him most grievous
pain,
e'en then his love, unchanging, claims us once again.

Toyohiko Kagawa, 1938
translated, Vern Rossman, 1961
E. A. C. C. Hymnal, 1963
© Christian Conference of Asia

590
The Modern City
Portugese: Nesta grande ciadade vivemos

A. Original

Modern man has the city for his home
where his life is walled in by want and dread,
pained by nights without sleep and days of grinding
work,
in the struggle to earn his daily bread.

In our cities, immense and growing out,
there are millions from faith and love estranged,
who need to recapture hope of better things,
and whose hearts, by the grace of Christ, can
change.

In the dark of our noisy city life,
men and women are groping for the light,
human beings who hunger to see right prevail,
unaware of the liberating Christ.

In the great giant cities of our globe,
hollowed out by the ways of greed and crime,
we are set to reflect the likeness of our God
and to act out renewal's great design.

Grow then, cities, to house the world of man,
with your skyscrapers blotting out the sun.
Let Christ be the light to shine from human homes
in the high-rising blocks of steel and stone.

João Dias de Araújo, 1967
translated, Fred Kaan, 1972
Cantate Domino, 1974
© 1974, Hope Publishing Company

B. Revised by the translator

Modern people have cities for their home,
where their life is walled in by want and dread,
pained by nights without sleep and days of grinding
work,
in the struggle to earn their daily bread.

In our cities, immense and growing out,
there are millions from faith and love estranged,
who need to recapture thoughts of better things,
and whose hearts, by the grace of Christ, can
change.

In the dark of our noisy city life,
men and women are groping for the light,
human beings who hunger to see right prevail,
unaware of the liberating Christ.

In the great giant cities of our globe,
hollowed out by the ways of greed and crime,
we are set to reflect the likeness of our God
and to act out renewal's great design.

Grow then, cities, to house the human race,
    with your skyscrapers blotting out the sun.
Let Christ be the light to shine from all our homes
    in the high rising blocks of steel and stone.

translated, Fred Kaan, 1972, revised 1985
The Hymn Texts of Fred Kaan, 1985
© 1974, Hope Publishing Company

591

Take the Dark Strength of Our Nights

Take the dark strength of our nights,
soft with peeny-wallies' lights.
Take the star-signs wheeling round
while the steel drum melts to sound.
Take and weave a womb of night
        that we may live.

Take the protest of our need:
What the garden? What the weed?
Take the orb and break the chain,
break the shackles of the brain.
Take and weave a womb of right
        that we may live.

Take the islands' human skills,
dancing seas and wise old hills.
Take our Jesus and his power,
match his people to this hour.
Take and weave a womb of light
        that we may live.

John Hoad, 1971
© John Hoad

592

Yoruba Hymn to the Holy Spirit

[The publisher regrets the absence of this text. Permission to reprint, though granted for the original volume, was denied for this edition.]

Arthur Morris Jones
Africa Praise, 1968
© Lutterworth Press

Isaac Watts's "We give immortal praise," found at this point in the first edition as an epilogue and numbered 593, has been moved to the new epilogue and renumbered as 982.

Chapter 29:
Great Britain, 1976–2000
(593–716)

What has often been spoken of as the hymn "explosion" must now be reckoned a "renaissance," given its sustained productivity and continuing influence. Several writers who emerged in the 1960s and 1970s have continued to make substantial contributions over the subsequent decades. Among the more prolific and widely published are the "triumvirate" identified in chapter 23: Fred Pratt Green, Fred Kaan, and Brian Wren. Not only did these leading figures continue to write, but their work influenced and encouraged many others. There has also been much congregational song in styles influenced by popular culture, whose story was begun in chapter 24. Recent years have also seen significant attempts to blend these two types. In the wake of this activity, the age of supplements has continued, but there has also been a new generation of large collections incorporating the best from the provisional books.

The two historic Anglican hymn book traditions have continued. In the line of *Hymns Ancient and Modern* and *100 Hymns for Today* (1969) came a second supplement, *More Hymns for Today* (1980). These were consolidated with the inheritance of the larger book in the *New Standard Edition* of 1983. This was followed in 2000 by *Common Praise*, which, in something of a daring departure, left behind the family name in favor of a parallel to *Common Prayer*. Meanwhile, *The New English Hymnal* was released in 1986, following on a 1975 supplement, *English Praise*.

A different direction was taken by the Jubilate Hymns team, which consisted mostly of evangelical Anglicans under the leadership of Bishop Michael Baughen (b. 1930), but included participants from other traditions. This team has mixed popular and traditional styles, both in music and in texts, producing a stream of publications with different emphases. The defining collection of this group is *Hymns for Today's Church* (1982; revised, 1987). Inherited texts were vigorously modernized, to the delight of some and the distress of others. Many of the same persons were also involved in books that feature a less-formal style, beginning with *Youth Praise* (1966) and extending to the more comprehensive *Sing Glory* (1999).

In 1979, the same year in which the supplement *Partners in Praise* was released, the British Methodist Conference began work toward a new collection, with the intent that it include "the best in Methodist hymnody" while "making a contribution to the life and worship of the Church universal." Invitations to other groups brought into the editorial process representatives from United Reformed, Congregational Federation, Churches of Christ, Wesleyan Reform Union, Baptist, and Anglican traditions. Though the subsequent insistence by the Methodist conference of a stronger identity with its own heritage prompted the official withdrawal of the United Reformed Church, *Hymns and Psalms* was released in 1983 with the subtitle "A Methodist and Ecumenical Hymn Book." The book went through a remarkably open editing process, with draft versions made available for public comment. Three years after the 1972 union that created the United Reformed Church, the supplement *New Church Praise* was produced. The first comprehensive hymnal of this body is *Rejoice and Sing*, published in 1991, the same year in which the Baptist Union released *Baptist Praise and Worship*.

The texts of Fred Pratt Green have been widely published and sung, owing to his ability to infuse traditional form and style with fresh words and ideas. A good example is the harvest hymn at 593, which sets natural and spiritual dimensions as a frame around a theological call for justice and compassion. The last three lines of this text are as fine as anything else written in this period. The presence in the *Hymnal Guide* of a dozen texts in addition to those here and in chapters 23 and 28 is evidence of the broad acceptance of Green's work.

Several of his texts, such as 594 and "When the church of Jesus shuts its outer door," articulate the role of the church in ministry outside its walls. A similar theme is sounded in 595, prompted by a request from Erik Routley for a text to match Parry's REPTON. Green is in no way minimizing the significance of liturgy, however; 596 is a magisterial text about the place and purpose of the church gathered for worship.

Green has been likened to his Methodist forebear, Charles Wesley, in poetic skill and pastoral concern. Like Wesley, he is always conscious of the redemptive power of God's love. He is effective at biblical quotation and allusion, as in the marvelous turn of phrase in the last couplet of 597. His ability to paraphrase and interpret Scripture may be seen in 598, a commission for the 1989 hymnal of United Methodists in the United States, and in 599. He uses Scripture and structure in 600 to make an effective contrast of the biblical with the present, illuminating both in the process.

The range and pastoral sensitivity of Green's writing is seen in hymns as intimate as 597, which recognizes the disease of self-centeredness; as honest and mature as 601; and as expansive as 602, which has been used widely to articulate the role of music in the life of faith. In several of his texts, the author was willing to change language to accommodate the shift to inclusive language, though this sometimes came at the expense of diminished poetic impact. For example, the opening line of 602 originally juxtaposed "man's music" with "God is glorified."

Fred Kaan has continued to be a forceful voice for peace and justice—and one heard around the world. His passion is evident in 603, an early text that is perhaps his most widely used, and 604, with its brilliant last line, written for the 1983 Christian World Conference on Life and Peace. Kaan's hymns convey not only fervor, but also mood. This is exemplified in two texts related to communion. The overlapping mnemonic images of 605 communicate a tender touching, while 606, written for the 1975 meeting of the World Council of Churches in Nairobi, captures all the exuberant joy of its preexisting tune to proclaim the Good News. Kaan's involvement in and concern for the worldwide church and its life in community are demonstrated not only in original hymns, such as 607, but also in his work as a translator (see Index of Authors and Translators).

Kaan has written several texts that bring faith to bear on the poignant, even painful, parts of human experience. One such hymn is 608, which, acknowledging failure in relationship, prays for faith, hope, and love. Another powerful contemplative text, expressing the same theology while recognizing mortality, is 609. The mixed feelings that many encounter in the commercial—and even the churchly—buildup to Christmas are, in typical Kaan fashion, given shape and Scripture-grounded hope in 610.

Brian Wren has given sustained attention to the theology of worship and to its expression in both spoken and sung words. As his own ideas have evolved, he has not only written new texts, but has also revised his earlier work, resulting in the existence of multiple versions in print. For example, the texts at 497–500 have all been either significantly altered or withdrawn. In 1991 Wren moved permanently to the United States, first as an itinerant workshop leader and writer, later as a teacher of worship. A consistent theme in his writing is the relation of a realistic view of daily life to an optimistic theology. For example, the wedding text at 611 is both frank and hopeful in its tracing of the stages of marital love.

Wren's interest in redressing the balance of language for God is seen in 612, with its unexpected juxtapositions of human images, and in 613, with its revealing use of biblical scenes of darkness. He employs Gospel scenes involving women in 614 not only to bring into focus the ways in which Jesus related to females but also to reveal Jesus as the central figure. Wren's concern for immediacy of theological meaning produced 615, prompted by the assassination of Martin Luther

King, Jr. The same awareness of Christ's presence in human life, even despair, is seen in 616 and in the energetic language of 617, which vividly presents the transformation that this understanding of Jesus engenders in the believer's life.

The resonance of biblical theology in the contemporary world is presented in various ways. Hymn 618 articulates an understanding of the development of Scripture consonant with recent biblical study. The clarifying and confronting testimony of churches of the Third World resounds in 619. The text at 620 is, in the author's words, a "revisioning (not a replacement) of the central themes in Charles Wesley's hymn, 'And can it be that I should gain'" (58).

One other English hymnwriter of this period has had texts accepted as widely as Green, Kaan, and Wren: Anglican bishop Timothy Dudley-Smith, whose writing is more traditional in theology and style. He has great facility in the careful and consistent use of varied metric forms, many of which draw on historic patterns. In his text for the dedication of a children's hospital, 621, he strikes a profound balance between faith, science, and pastoral care, while skillfully negotiating the 6.6.6.6.4.4.4.4. meter. A more adventuresome use of form is seen in the additive Christmas text at 622, for which Routley composed a tune. The accelerating reiterations of 623 underscore the focus on Christ, who is the subject of the angels' song. A similar feeling for the pace of words brings energy to the singer's identification with the biblical characters in the Easter text at 624.

Dudley-Smith's hymns are richly biblical. The scriptural foundations of 501 and 502 are obvious. He often combines paraphrase and meditation, as in 625 and "I lift my eyes to the quiet hills." The writer's knowledge of devotional and theological literature underlies many texts, as in 626, which takes its first line from Albert Schweitzer's *Quest for the Historical Jesus*. One may find in 627 not only the words of Jesus, but also echoes of Bonar's "I heard the voice of Jesus say" (335).

Though the roles Erik Routley played in the "explosion" as scholar, critic, and encourager may be more obvious, his own hymn writing should not be overlooked. His paraphrase of Psalm 98 at 628, done for the 1974 edition of *Cantate Domino* (which Routley edited), has found wide use. It was for this same book that he prepared the English versions of 578 and 579. Another Psalm, 119, forms the background for 629. Three other texts by him are seen at 177B, 504, and 982. Routley's influence was complemented by that of composer, arranger, and editor John Wilson (1905–1992), who was also a great encourager and promoter. Together they edited *Hymns for Celebration* (1974). Wilson's scholarship and taste did much to shape the best aspects of new developments, as he was frequently called upon in the preparation of new collections, both in England and the United States.

Alan Luff, a participant at Dunblane, has been widely influential in liturgy and hymnology in such roles as Precentor of Westminster Abbey, Chairman of the Hymn Society of Great Britain and Ireland, and Chairman of the Pratt Green Trust. Luff has worked on projects as diverse as *Story Song* (with Donald Pickard, 1993), a collection of 100 songs designed to encourage participation in God's story; a monograph on *Welsh Hymns and Their Tunes*; and *HymnQuest*, an electronic compendium of hymns and information about them. His own texts demonstrate pastoral empathy for the complexities of personal and congregational life. From *Story Song* comes 630, the application of Jesus' healing of ten lepers to the need for openness and wholeness in the life of the church. "A Hymn for the Passage of Time" (631) is a thoughtful explication of faith for maturing years, with language that balances activity and security. The solid structure and argument of 632 present the place of worship as an opportunity for the people at worship to experience the Gospel story that is proclaimed.

The influence of the leaders of the renaissance on other writers has been strongest in the United Reformed Church. This is not surprising, given that

Routley, Kaan, and Wren are all of this tradition, which can trace its heritage to Watts. Alan Gaunt and Basil Bridge are the most visible of these, but there are several others.

Alan Gaunt was another participant at Dunblane. He has written on diverse topics and in a wide range of styles. There is a tender intimacy to his finest work, as seen in 633, with its revealing images of the open door, and 634, which, with its subtle transformations of "all shall be well," is based on Julian of Norwich. The word "helpless" receives similar effective treatment in 635, which had its origins at Dunblane and is one of many hymns by Gaunt that link the incarnation to our experience. Based on a Greek original, 636 finds that narrow space in which direct language about the crucifixion is vivid without becoming morbid.

This ability to narrow the gap between idea and worshiper is also employed to connect the singer with Scripture, as in 637, which reminds of the constant need to identify with Psalm 51:17, and 638, with its recurrent references emphasizing the "heart of God" lending perspective on Romans 8. In 639 Gaunt presents a distinctly nonsentimental definition of peace. His skillful work as a translator is seen in 640, one of several pieces from the eighteenth-century Welsh writer, Ann Griffiths.

Basil E. Bridge, also a minister, wrote 641 for a URC provincial project entitled "Faith Aflame." The three stanzas of this text address the members of the Trinity with scriptural images of fire (Exodus 3:2, Luke 12:49, Acts 2:3). The memorial acclamations form a refrain in 642, the third statement having been reshaped to echo 1 Corinthians 15:22. Both of these texts were revised for their publication in *Rejoice and Sing* in consultation with that book's editors. Another of Bridge's hymns, "The Son of God proclaim," is widely published.

Caryl Micklem, whose work as author and composer was noted in earlier chapters (see 519, 520, 535, and 576), more recently served as Chairman of the Hymn Society of Great Britain

and Ireland. His winning entry for a competition to celebrate the formation of the Council for World Mission, 643, traces ways in which the movements of history have shifted and broadened the church's understanding of mission.

Elizabeth Cosnett, a teacher of English and scholar of poets as hymn writers, succeeded Micklem as Executive President of the Hymn Society of Great Britain and Ireland. In her own writing, she is quite careful as to detail, while being adventuresome in topic and form. A striking example of this is 644, with its vivid acknowledgment that God is creator of all! This text ranges widely, likening depression to the despair of the psalmist (compare Psalm 69) and picking up the drumbeat of the heart—and of hope—in the last line. Cosnett echoes Job 11:7 in 645, with its probing of the limits of human knowledge. The opening line, the revision of which she has permitted but does not prefer, has provided a focus for a civil and thoughtful discussion of the matter of inclusive language, in which she has participated. A refrain structure, making a connection with the carol tradition, is employed in 646, with its recollection of biblical events for the Candlemas service.

It has been argued by some that the meaning of "kingdom" language has become either lost or distorted in our time. By using examples from the ministry of Jesus in 647, Bryn Austin Rees clarifies both present and eschatological meanings. Ian Alexander, a URC pastor, wrote 648 for his congregation. This eloquent prayer of forgiveness articulates those matters of attitude and will about which we often find it easy to deceive ourselves. University chaplain and teacher Colin Thompson is another writer from the United Reformed Church. He skillfully employs contrast in 649 to set spiritual and physical hunger in the context of the church's apparent affluence. The basis of 650 in *"Nada te turbe"* by Teresa of Ávila is seen in Thompson's choice to set in italics those lines that most strongly reflect her poem. David Fox, a translator of hymns from Welsh, as well as a minister, is the author of

651, with its presentation of the incarnation as the model for the church's work in reconciliation.

The hope following the Second Vatican Council for hymns from Roman Catholics that might be broadly shared has not been fulfilled to any great extent. The hymns of James Quinn, SJ, have, perhaps, achieved the widest use of any by a recent Roman Catholic author. In addition to those at 510 and 511, others from his 1969 collection have proven themselves useful. Among these is 652, an evening hymn that conveys comfort and trust. Quinn's keen ear for the weight of words has produced numerous skillful paraphrases, often unrhymed, of Scripture, liturgical texts, and Latin hymns. These connect historic devotional patterns of the church with worship in English. An example is his version of the canticle of Zechariah at 653. Names and titles of Jesus provide the form of 654, while it is the shifting images in 655 that guide meditation on the Word of God.

Luke Connaughton, a Roman Catholic journalist, was editor of *Sing a New Song to the Lord* (1970), which included nearly forty of his own texts. The size of his contribution was masked by the use of pseudonyms, such as J. Smith and Peter Icarus (see 514 and 515). In 656 the carefully wrought balance between a typical refrain structure and the repetitions of "Love" through a chain of word links is compelling.

Contemporary with the earlier of the more prolific hymnists discussed above were several writers who are known by fewer texts. Some of these were discussed in chapter 23, while others have become visible only through the most recent generation of hymnals. Rosamond E. Herklots, born in India, wrote more than a hundred texts, the best known of which is at 508. Though not as widely published, 657 enlarges our understanding of the incarnation by including the slaughter of the Innocents. J. R. Peacey, an Anglican college chaplain, wrote only eighteen hymns, all in the years following his retirement. Five of these were first published in *100 Hymns for Today*. In addition

to 658, which connects the contemporary church with Pentecost, "Awake, awake, fling off the night" has appeared in a number of collections. H. C. A. Gaunt, a schoolmaster before becoming Sacristan and, subsequently, Precentor of Winchester Cathedral, had several items in *100 Hymns for Today*. Among the better known of these is "Come, Lord, to our souls come down," not included here. The active devotion of 659, first published in *More Hymns for Today*, is cast in direct language, with short lines and simple images. As such, it is engaging and appropriate for children and adults alike.

William Hubert Vanstone's text at 660 is a powerful statement of God's unconditional love, hidden and revealed. A theologian, Vanstone wrote the text to fit a tune composed by his mother and subsequently used it to conclude his award-winning book, *Love's Endeavour, Love's Expense*, which takes its title from the hymn. Perhaps not since Watts's "Nature with open volume stands" (39) has this theme been addressed with such eloquence.

Allusions to several gospel passages and her own reflection are woven into 661, a hymn on the Beatitudes by Mollie Knight. Ann Phillips, an editor, librarian, teacher, and author of books for children, employs metaphor and vivid imagery to portray the order-bringing and life-giving roles of the Spirit in 662.

Several of the Jubilate team have been prolific in writing original texts. Dudley-Smith, though not a member of the group, has been associated with their work. Among the team members whose work has received broad acceptance are Christopher Idle, Michael Perry, Michael Saward, and David Mowbray, all Anglicans.

The strongest writing of Christopher Idle lies in his superb biblical paraphrases, such as 663, drawn from Isaiah 35, and 664, from Revelation 7. A skillful application, rather than a paraphrase, is 665, based on the wedding at Cana, with the telling phrase, "surprise our dullness." Idle's translations of historic texts are also effective. These include 666, based on a prayer by the eighth-century scholar, Alcuin, as well as versions of the "*Te Deum*" and "*Wachet auf.*" "Powerful in making us wise to salvation," a text about the nature, content, and application of Scripture, is found in many collections.

Like Idle, Michael Perry, editor of many of the Jubilate collections, wrote skillful paraphrases of psalms and other Scriptures. Many versions of his "*Benedictus*" (667) appear in recent books—the result of his frequent revision of the text. The direct and parallel petitions of 668 convey both intimacy and fervency. Given Perry's own untimely death from cancer, the opening strophe is particularly poignant, as is the middle stanza of 669, added a few years after the original outer ones. Well known, though not included here, are "How shall they hear the word of God" and "See him lying on a bed of straw." An interesting facet of Perry's work was his design of texts to fit music of Schubert, Brahms, Gounod—and Gershwin! Two hymns by Michael Saward have been found particularly useful by churches across a broad spectrum. The first, 670, is a straightforward confession of praise with a refrain, whose popularity has been encouraged by its match to John Barnard's GUITING POWER. The second, a baptism text, 671, recalls within a patterned structure symbols, actions, and New Testament interpretations of the rite.

Two texts by David Mowbray are notable for the ways in which they encompass a broad range of persons. Diverse talents are identified in 672, which invokes Spirit and Word in dedicating these gifts to God in worship and life. A refrain of praise is used in 673 as a response to stanzas that acknowledge God's grace through the stages of life. From *Story Song* come 674, with its concise, parallel statements about the uniqueness and compassion of Jesus, and 675, a moving reflection on the ministry of hospice care. The same collection contains texts by Mowbray inspired by Dietrich Bonhoeffer and Dag Hammerskjold.

While most of the attention drawn by *Hymns for Today's Church* was for its revisions or the new hymns by members of the Jubilate Group, this collection also presented some notable pieces by less well-known authors. Among these was 676, in which Edward Burns, an Anglican priest, places the human quest for knowledge within the context of faith. Burns is also the author of "We have a gospel to proclaim," a forthright declaration of the church's evangelistic mission. Paul Wigmore, a photographer and prolific writer, came to hymn writing rather late. His prayer for the gifts of the Spirit, 677, is gentle and elegant.

The Salvation Army, whose hymn writers are little known beyond their own circle, issued a new *Song Book* in 1986. Malcolm Bale, who held a series of editorial and administrative posts in the Army, wrote 678 to put in hymnic form the social conscience that characterizes its ministry.

Christopher Ellis is a Baptist pastor and educator whose writing was stimulated by ministry in an ecumenical congregation in which Fred Kaan was his colleague. Colorful vocabulary and rhythmic energy from words ending in "-ness" compensate for the lack of rhyme in 679, written to appropriate the liberation imagery of Exodus for a Maundy Thursday communion service. A quest for vitality in reading and heeding Scripture is the topic of 680. Its first two stanzas petition God to open the Scriptures to the singers, while the last one asks that the singers themselves be opened to become "doers and not hearers only." Joyce Woolford, a Baptist librarian and lay preacher, wrote 681 to heighten appreciation of the ways in which Jesus makes himself known in worship. Its short lines, each ending with a lift, communicate the excitement of the Emmaus experience.

Michael Forster was reared an Anglican and worked as a music teacher before preparing for the Baptist ministry. He has since become a mental health chaplain and a Methodist. His texts combine a nuanced understanding of the Scriptures with a sense of urgency about living their message.

The two hymns at 682 and 683, constructed on sayings from the cross, show different facets of his approach. The former explores community within the Trinity, a concept that has drawn attention from contemporary theologians. The latter traces the meaning of "completion" as "integrity" in the suffering of Jesus and in the life of faith. One of several pieces written for less-formal contexts, 684 first appeared in a musical. The ingenious turn of phrase that ends each stanza employs a biblical metaphor to make a significant theological statement in a text rich with biblical allusions.

Martin Leckebusch, a computer programmer, has been part of Anglican, Pentecostal, Methodist, and Baptist congregations. His writing shows the influence of Dudley-Smith in its conservative theology, biblical imagery, and structural ingenuity. He advocates a restoration of hymnody in traditional forms to the worship of those, who, like him, are in the charismatic wing of the church. To promote this, he provides texts such as 685, which joins biblical story, liturgical history, and contemporary application. Like Forster, he is keen to link scriptural warrant with daily experience. This is evident in 686, which moves from the tithe of the agricultural offering through New Testament references to giving to stewardship of the monthly pay cycle by which many reap their harvest.

Reflecting Praise, a volume of hymns by, for, and about women, was issued in 1993 by Women in Theology and Stainer and Bell. The editors, June Boyce-Tillman and Janet Wootton, both contributed texts embodying the collection's concern for feminist theology and inclusive language. The tone of the anthology is set by its first text, 687, by Wootton, a Congregational minister and theologian. In 688, she has produced a text rich with allusions to biblical covenants. Its recounting of convivial scenes that mingle joy and sorrow provides strong links to experiences of worship and daily life. Boyce-Tillman, a lecturer in music and authority on Hildegard of Bingen, wrote 689, with its dynamic images of the Spirit's transforming love.

Donald Pickard, a Methodist missionary and theological educator, and Luff's collaborator in editing *Story Song*, wrote 690 to encompass the lectionary themes for Advent. In language accessible to worshipers of all ages, it celebrates Immanuel, "love with a human face." In 691, Rosalind Brown traces acts and patterns of humility in the life of Jesus as models for Christian service by linking the *Kenosis* hymn of Philippians 2 to the account of Jesus' washing the disciples' feet. Brown, an Anglican priest, wrote this hymn while a member of the Episcopal Community of Celebration in Pennsylvania.

Informed by his background in the sciences, Methodist minister Andrew Pratt brings a distinctive voice to hymnody. His hymns give form to feelings of doubt and despair—even anger—in an age of technology. They frequently employ language that is deliberately secular. Many are reminiscent of the lamenting psalms, and some have an intensity better suited to private reading than to corporate worship. The experience of the adulterous woman to whom Jesus reached out is the substance of 692, an exceptional ballad. In 693 we gain insight—and perhaps the ability to deal in a healthier manner with our own feelings—into the role of anger in Jesus' ministry.

New directions in worship have brought new varieties of congregational song. One type is simple and brief, depending on repetition, sometimes with the substitution of words or phrases, for its effect. Another is more elaborate and soloistic, inviting responsorial participation through a chorus or refrain. Overlapping these forms and more traditional styles of hymns are a number of songs that are difficult to categorize. Some have characteristics of the ballad and are particularly effective in telling biblical stories. Others approach the casual style of popular song.

Peter Smith, a Methodist minister and folksinger, was editor of the *Faith, Folk and . . .* trilogy in the 1960s. His responsive ballad, 694, recounts several of Jesus' acts of healing. Written for a workshop at Iona in 1975, it has been published with many variants, demonstrating the vulnerability of this type of song to alteration by oral tradition. David Owen identifies the attractiveness of Jesus' parables in 695. Drawing from these stories, Patricia Hunt collects a series of metaphors for the kingdom in 696. The gardens of Eden, Gethsemane, and Golgotha form the outline of 697 by Hillary Greenwood. Her structure, though perhaps more direct, lacks the stronger narrative or logical coherence seen in other recent texts on the same scenes by Jaroslav Vajda (726) and Herman Stuempfle (770). Estelle White, a Roman Catholic who has written numerous songs for children, authored 698, a striking ballad, interesting in form and style. The scenes of God speaking, first as Creator, then as Companion, mark milestones on the journey in covenant with God. The facile rhymes and the refrain encourage participation.

A prominent figure in worship song is Graham Kendrick, the son of a Baptist minister. Certain of his texts provide greater depth than is typical of the genre, particularly as he responds to the human condition with empathy and theological perception. These are stated strongly in 699, with its repeated *kyries* in response to both a violent world and the judgment of God. God's compassion for persons and concern for creation are both declared and implored in 700. These two texts also show creativity in form: the first assigning portions of stanzas to men and women, the second calling for the refrain only after the second, fourth, and fifth stanzas. A more typical refrain form is used in 701, a confessional text that juxtaposes the humanity and divinity of Jesus.

The remarkable community at Iona has produced a vigorous body of congregational song that links creative worship to societal service, fired with passion for peace and justice. The music, often drawing on folk traditions, gives an air of informality, while the texts are infused with keen thought about the relationship of Scripture to life. Several collections of songs have been issued

through the community's Wild Goose Worship Group (which takes its name from a Celtic symbol of the Holy Spirit). These include the three volumes of *Wild Goose Songs: Heaven Shall Not Wait* (1987), *Enemy of Apathy* (1988), and *Love from Below* (1989), as well as other topical and seasonal collections. These books offer insight into the philosophy and process that lie behind the literature. With the aid of community members who serve around the world, they have also compiled congregational song from various cultures in *Many and Great* (1990) and *Sent by the Lord* (1991).

Though many persons in the Iona Community have contributed, directly and indirectly, to this effort, its leaders have been John Bell and Graham Maule. Their ability to combine in song elements that are both boldly engaging and deeply serious is evident in 702, with its genuine invitation to Christian transformation. The recollection of the sounds, sights, and symbols of the eucharist in 703 proclaims that all things cohere in Christ. The seriousness of self-examination and confession as preparation for the sacrament are poignantly portrayed in 704.

A delicate and realistic balance of faith and doubt is seen in these songs. Such is the case of 705, which finds its context in the community's healing services. This text, as many others from Iona, holds in dynamic tension the signs of compassion that are palpable alongside those that point to the unseen. Celtic language and imagery often enliven these texts, as seen in the aviary and female language for the Holy Spirit (compare the Hebrew, *ruach*) in 706. Another typical element is the vivid presentation of the biblical story, as in 707.

Ian Fraser was warden of the Scottish Churches' House at Dunblane, host to the seminal consultations, and the author of notable texts in those gatherings (488, 489, 530). Two of his more recent pieces for the Iona community are seen at 708 and 709. The former, using the building metaphor for the church, notes how individual differences may become strengths if valued in Christian community. The parable of the prodigal son lies behind 709.

Among the other members of the Iona Community who have written hymns are Douglas Galbraith, Kathy Galloway, Leith Fisher, and Anna Briggs. Galbraith, a musician and theologian trained in classics, was a participant at Dunblane. With John Bell, he edited *Common Ground* (1998), an ecumenical anthology for Scottish churches. The original text on which 710 is based was a call for justice, written upon hearing an account of the death in police custody of a South Korean student. The present version is a reworking for general use that alludes to several biblical texts which emphasize God's activity and compassion.

Another hymn that stresses the vitality of God's work in the present is 711 by Kathy Galloway, a liturgist and writer who was warden of Iona from 1983 to 1989. Her choice of a metric shape that matches LOBE DEN HERREN and her use of participles give energy to the expression in contemporary language of traditional divine attributes. In his exposition of Matthew 18:1–6 at 712, Leith Fisher suggests ways in which we may learn from Jesus and his teaching of children.

The theme of longing and the tone of tenderness are dominant in the texts of Anna Briggs. She recounts the many manifestations of brokenness in contemporary life and commits them to God in 713. The invocation of God's presence is intensified in the *Maranathas* of 714, a text written with the tune NUN KOMM DER HEIDEN HEILAND in mind. In 715 Briggs captures the thoughts of Mary, who not only ponders in her heart but senses in her body.

A final text related to Iona is 716, which addresses the differing situations of persons coming to worship on Remembrance Sunday and recognizes their common need for the peace of God. This hymn was developed by a worship group in Glasgow's Carnwadric Parish, under the leadership of John Bell and Mairi Munro, and is an example of the work done in particular situations by members of the community.

593
Harvest Hymn

For the fruits of his creation,
    thanks be to God;
for his gifts to every nation,
    thanks be to God;
for the plowing, sowing, reaping,
silent growth while we are sleeping,
future needs in earth's safe-keeping,
    thanks be to God.

In the just reward of labor,
    God's will is done;
in the help we give our neighbor,
    God's will is done;
in our worldwide task of caring
for the hungry and despairing,
in the harvests we are sharing,
    God's will is done.

For the harvests of the Spirit,
    thanks be to God;
for the good we all inherit,
    thanks be to God;
for the wonders that astound us,
for the truths that still confound us,
most of all that love has found us,
    thanks be to God.

Fred Pratt Green, 1970; revised, 1976, ca. 1982
Hymns and Psalms, 1983
© 1970, Hope Publishing Company

594
The Caring Church

The church of Christ in every age
    beset by change but Spirit led,
must claim and test its heritage
    and keep on rising from the dead.

477

Across the world, across the street,
    the victims of injustice cry
for shelter and for bread to eat,
    and never live until they die.

Then let the servant church arise,
    a caring church that longs to be
a partner in Christ's sacrifice,
    and clothed in Christ's humanity.

For he alone, whose blood was shed,
    can cure the fever in our blood,
and teach us how to share our bread
    and feed the starving multitude.

We have no mission but to serve
    in full obedience to our Lord:
To care for all, without reserve,
    and spread his liberating Word.

Fred Pratt Green, 1969; revised, ca. 1977
The Hymns and Ballads of Fred Pratt Green, 1982
© 1971, Hope Publishing Company

595
Our Christian Vocation

How clear is our vocation, Lord,
    when once we heed your call:
To live according to your word,
and daily learn, refreshed, restored,
    that you are Lord of all
    and will not let us fall.

But if, forgetful, we should find
    your yoke is hard to bear;
if worldly pressures fray the mind,
and love itself cannot unwind
    its tangled skein of care:
    Our inward life repair.

We marvel how your saints become
    in hindrances more sure;
whose joyful virtues put to shame
the casual way we wear your name,
    and by our faults obscure
    your power to cleanse and cure.

In what you give us, Lord, to do,
    together or alone,
in old routines and ventures new,
may we not cease to look to you,
    the cross you hung upon—
    all you endeavored done.

Fred Pratt Green, 1980
The Hymns and Ballads of Fred Pratt Green, 1982
© 1982, Hope Publishing Company

596
The Church of Christ

God is here! As we his people
    meet to offer praise and prayer,
may we find in fuller measure
    what it is in Christ we share.
Here, as in the world around us,
    all our varied skills and arts
wait the coming of his Spirit
    into open minds and hearts.

Here are symbols to remind us
    of our lifelong need of grace;
here are table, font, and pulpit;
    here the cross has central place.
Here in honesty of preaching,
    here in silence, as in speech,
here, in newness and renewal,
    God the Spirit comes to each.

Here our children find a welcome
    in the Shepherd's flock and fold,
here as bread and wine are taken,
    Christ sustains us as of old,
here the servants of the Servant
    seek in worship to explore
what it means in daily living
    to believe and to adore.

Lord of all, of church and kingdom,
    in an age of change and doubt,
keep us faithful to the gospel,
    help us work your purpose out.
Here, in this day's dedication,
    all we have to give, receive:
We, who cannot live without you,
    we adore you! we believe!

597
Here, Master, in This Quiet Place

Here, Master, in this quiet place,
    where anyone may kneel,
I also come to ask for grace,
    believing you can heal.

If pain of body, stress of mind,
    destroys my inward peace,
in prayer for others may I find
    the secret of release.

If self upon its sickness feeds
    and turns my life to gall,
let me not brood upon my needs,
    but simply tell you all.

You never said, "You ask too much"
    to any troubled soul.
I long to feel your healing touch—
    Will you not make me whole?

But if the thing I most desire
    is not your way for me,
may faith, when tested in the fire,
    prove its integrity.

Of all my prayers, may this be chief:
    Till faith is fully grown,
Lord, disbelieve my unbelief,
    and claim me as your own.

598
Judge Me Not by Human Standards

Seek the Lord who now is present,
    pray to One who is at hand;
let the wicked cease from sinning,
    evildoers change their mind.

On the sinful God has pity;
    those returning he forgives.
This is what the Lord is saying
    to a world that disbelieves:

"Judge me not by human standards!
    As the vault of heaven soars
high above the earth, so higher
    are my thoughts and ways than yours.

See how rain and snow from heaven
    make earth blossom and bear fruit,
giving you, before returning,
    seed for sowing, bread to eat:

So my word returns not fruitless;
    does not from its labors cease
till it has achieved my purpose
    in a world of joy and peace."

God is love! How close the prophet
    to that vital gospel word!
In Isaiah's inspiration
    it is Jesus we have heard!

Fred Pratt Green, 1987
based on Isaiah 55:6–13
Later Hymns and Ballads and Fifty Poems, 1989
© 1989, Hope Publishing Company
The author wished the last stanza to appear in italics to indicate that it
moves beyond the Isaiah passage.

599
The Baptism of Jesus

When Jesus came to Jordan
    to be baptized by John,
he did not come for pardon,
    but as his Father's Son.
He came to share repentance
    with all who mourn their sins,
to speak the vital sentence
    with which good news begins.

He came to share temptation,
    our utmost woe and loss,
for us and our salvation
    to die upon the cross.
So when the Dove descended
    on him, the Son of Man,
the hidden years had ended,
    the age of grace began.

Come, Holy Spirit, aid us
    to keep the vows we make,
this very day invade us,
    and every bondage break.
Come, give our lives direction,
    the gift we covet most:
To share the resurrection
    that leads to Pentecost.

Fred Pratt Green, 1973
The Hymns and Ballads of Fred Pratt Green, 1982
© 1980, Hope Publishing Company
The United Methodist Hymnal, 1989, altered line 1:4 to
"but as the sinless one."

600
The Mocking of Christ

To mock your reign, O dearest Lord,
    they made a crown of thorns;
set you with taunts along the road,
    from which no one returns.
They did not know, as we do now,
    how glorious is that crown:
That thorns would flower upon your brow,
    your sorrows heal our own.

In mock acclaim, O gracious Lord,
    they snatched a purple cloak,
your passion turned, for all they cared,
    into a soldier's joke.
They did not know, as we do now,
    that though we merit blame,
you will your robe of mercy throw
    around our naked shame.

A sceptered reed, O patient Lord,
    they thrust into your hand,
and acted out their grim charade
    to its appointed end.
They did not know, as we do now,
    though empires rise and fall
your kingdom shall not cease to grow
    till love embraces all.

Fred Pratt Green, 1972
based on Matthew 27:29
The Hymns and Ballads of Fred Pratt Green, 1982
© 1973, Hope Publishing Company

601
A Mature Faith

When our confidence is shaken
    in beliefs we thought secure;
when the spirit in its sickness
    seeks but cannot find a cure:
God is active in the tensions
    of a faith not yet mature.

Solar systems, void of meaning,
    freeze the spirit into stone;
always our researches lead us
    to the ultimate Unknown:
Faith must die, or come full circle
    to its source in God alone.

In the discipline of praying,
    when it's hardest to believe;
in the drudgery of caring,
    when it's not enough to grieve:
Faith maturing, learns acceptance
    of the insights we receive.

God is love; and he redeems us
    in the Christ we crucify:
This is God's eternal answer
    to the world's eternal why;
may we in this faith maturing
    be content to live and die.

Fred Pratt Green, 1971
The Hymns and Ballads of Fred Pratt Green, 1982
© 1971, Hope Publishing Company

602
Let the People Sing!

When, in our music, God is glorified,
and adoration leaves no room for pride,
it is as though the whole creation cried:
    Alleluia!

How often, making music, we have found
a new dimension in the world of sound,
as worship moved us to a more profound
    Alleluia!

So has the church, in liturgy and song,
in faith and love, through centuries of wrong,
borne witness to the truth in every tongue:
    Alleluia!

And did not Jesus sing a Psalm that night
when utmost evil strove against the light?
Then let us sing, for whom he won the fight:
    Alleluia!

Let every instrument be tuned for praise!
Let all rejoice who have a voice to raise!
And may God give us faith to sing always:
    Alleluia!

Fred Pratt Green, 1972; revised, ca. 1976
The Hymns and Ballads of Fred Pratt Green, 1982
© 1972, Hope Publishing Company

603

A Hymn on Human Rights

For the healing of the nations,
    Lord, we pray with one accord,
for a just and equal sharing
    of the things that earth affords.
To a life of love in action
    help us rise and pledge our word.

Lead us forward into freedom,
    from despair your world release,
that, redeemed from war and hatred,
    all may come and go in peace.
Show us how through care and goodness
    fear will die and hope increase.

All that kills abundant living,
    let it from the earth be banned:
Pride of status, race or schooling,
    dogmas that obscure your plan.
In our common quest for justice
    may we hallow life's brief span.

You, Creator-God, have written
    your great name on humankind;
for our growing in your likeness
    bring the life of Christ to mind;
that by our response and service
    earth its destiny may find.

Fred Kaan, 1965
The Only Earth We Know, 1999
© 1968, Hope Publishing Company

604

A Hymn on Life and Peace

We utter our cry: that peace may prevail,
    that earth will survive and faith must not fail.
We pray with our life for the world in our care,
for people diminished by doubt and despair.

We cry from the fright of our daily scene
    for strength to say "No!" to all that is mean:
Designs bearing chaos, extinction of life,
all energy wasted on weapons of death.

We lift up our hearts for children unborn:
    Give wisdom, O God, that we may hand on
—replenished and tended—this good planet earth,
preserving the future and wonder of birth.

Creator of life, come, share out, we pray
    your Spirit on earth, revealing the Way
to leaders conferring round tables for peace,
that they may from bias and guile be released.

Be there with your Love, in protest and march
    and help us to fire with passion your church,
to match all our statements and lofty resolve
with being—unresting—in action involved.

Whatever the ill or pressure we face,
    Lord, hearten and heal, give insight and grace
to think and make peace with each heartbeat and
                        breath,
choose Christ before Caesar and life before death!

Fred Kaan, 1983
The Only Earth We Know, 1999
© 1984, Hope Publishing Company

605

Hands Shaped like a Cradle

Put peace into each other's hands
    and like a treasure hold it,
protect it like a candle flame,
    with tenderness enfold it.

Put peace into each other's hands
    with loving expectation;
be gentle in your words and ways,
    in touch with God's creation.

Put peace into each other's hands
    like bread we break for sharing;
look people warmly in the eye:
    our life is meant for caring.

As at communion, shape your hands
    into a waiting cradle;
the gift of Christ receive, revere,
    united round the table.

Put Christ into each other's hands,
    he is love's deepest measure;
in love make peace, give peace a chance
    and share it like a treasure.

Fred Kaan, 1988
The Only Earth We Know, 1999
© 1989, Hope Publishing Company

606

Communion Calypso

Let us talents and tongues employ,
reaching out with a shout of joy:
Bread is broken, the wine is poured,
Christ is spoken and seen and heard.

    Jesus lives again, earth can breathe again,
    pass the Word around: Loaves abound!

Christ is able to make us one,
at the table he set the tone,
teaching people to live to bless,
love in word and in deed express.

Jesus calls us in—sends us out
bearing fruit in a world of doubt,
gives us love to tell, bread to share:
God (Immanuel!) everywhere.

Fred Kaan, 1975
The Only Earth We Know, 1999
© 1975, Hope Publishing Company

607

A Hymn for Harvest Thanksgiving

Now join we, to praise the Creator,
    our voices in worship and song;
we stand to recall with thanksgiving
    that to God all seasons belong:

We thank you, O Source of all goodness,
    for the joy and abundance of crops,
for food that is stored in our larders,
    for all we can buy in the shops.

But also of need and starvation
    we sing with concern and despair,
of skills that are used for destruction,
    of land that is burnt and laid bare.

We cry for the plight of the hungry
    while harvests are left on the field,
for orchards neglected and wasting,
    for produce from markets withheld.

The song grows in depth and in wideness;
    the earth and its people are one.
There can be no thanks without giving,
    no words without deeds that are done.

Then teach us, O God of the harvest,
    to be humble in all that we claim,
to share what we have with the nations,
    to care for the world in your name.

Fred Kaan, 1968; revised, 1998
The Only Earth We Know, 1999
© 1968, Hope Publishing Company

608

A Hymn for People Seeking Release from Broken Relationships, and Forgiveness for Having Failed Others

God! When human bonds are broken
    and we lack the love or skill
to restore the hope of healing,
    give us grace and make us still.

Through that stillness, with your Spirit
    come into our world of stress,
for the sake of Christ forgiving
    all the failures we confess.

You in us are bruised and broken:
    Hear us as we seek release
from the pain of earlier living;
    set us free and grant us peace.

Send us, God of new beginnings,
    humbly hopeful into life;
use us as a means of blessing:
    Make us stronger, give us faith.

Give us faith to be more faithful,
    give us hope to be more true,
give us love to go on learning:
    God! Encourage and renew!

Fred Kaan, 1988
The Only Earth We Know, 1999
© 1989, Hope Publishing Company

609

A Hymn in the First Person Singular

Today I live, but once shall come my death;
one day shall still my laughter and crying,
    bring to a halt my heartbeat and my breath:
O give me faith for living and for dying.

How I shall die, or when, I do not know,
nor where—for endless is the world's horizon;
    but save me, God, from thoughts that lay me low,
from morbid fears that freeze my powers of reason.

When earthly life shall close, as close it must,
let Jesus be my brother and my merit.
    Let me without regret recall the past
and then, into your hands commit my spirit.

Meanwhile I live and move and I am glad,
enjoy this life and all its interweaving;
    each given day, as I take up the thread,
let love suggest my mode, my mood of living.

Fred Kaan, 1975
The Only Earth We Know, 1999
© 1975, Hope Publishing Company

610

An Uneasy Carol

We come uneasy, God, this festive season,
    afraid that all may be just as before;
so hallow, help us use, each restive reason
    that makes us want to see through tale and lore.

We come uneasy, longing to be able
    to look beyond the symbols and the signs,
to find behind our carols and the bible
    the living Word, as read between the lines.

We come uneasy, asking for your leading
    to take our distance from the manger scene
and go into our mainstreets for our reading
    of all that can in people's eyes be seen.

We come, uneasy at the thought of knowing
    the child who suffers, all who die too soon:
You, earthy-Christ, in human likeness growing
    from cradle of the night to cross at noon.

We welcome you, uneasy at your coming,
    but reassured that you have come to stay
to bind together your and our becoming
    a sign of hope, a light to save the day.

Then free us from traditions that diminish
    the glory of your Christmas to a farce;
make good our will, from yearly start to finish
    to "see this thing that (daily!) comes to pass."

Fred Kaan, 1980
The Only Earth We Know, 1999
© 1981, Hope Publishing Company

611
When Love Is Found

When love is found
    and hope comes home,
sing and be glad
    that two are one.
When love explodes
    and fills the sky,
praise God, and share
    our Maker's joy.

When God has flowered
    in trust and care,
build both each day,
    that love may dare
to reach beyond
    home's warmth and light,
to serve and strive
    for truth and right.

Where love is tried
    as loved ones change,
hold still to hope,
    though all seems strange,
till ease returns
    and love grows wise
through listening ears
    and opened eyes.

When love is torn,
    and trust betrayed,
pray strength to love
    till torments fade,
till lovers keep
    no score of wrong,
but hear through pain
    love's Easter song.

Praise God for love,
    praise God for life,
in age or youth,
    in calm or strife.
Lift up your hearts!
    Let love be fed
through death and life
    in broken bread.

Brian Wren, 1978; revised, 1992
Piece Together Praise, 1996
© 1983, Hope Publishing Company

612
Bring Many Names

Bring many names,
    beautiful and good,
celebrate, in parable and story,
    holiness in glory,
    living, loving God.
Hail and hosanna!
Bring many names!

Strong mother God,
    working night and day,
planning all the wonders of creation,
    setting each equation,
    genius at play:
Hail and hosanna,
strong mother God!

Warm father God,
    hugging every child,
feeling all the strains of human living,
    caring and forgiving
    till we're reconciled:
Hail and hosanna,
warm father God!

Old, aching God,
    gray with endless care,
calmly piercing evil's new disguises,
    glad of good surprises,
    wiser than despair:
Hail and hosanna,
old, aching God!

Young, growing God,
    eager, on the move,
saying no to falsehood and unkindness,
    crying out for justice,
    giving all you have:
Hail and hosanna,
young, growing God!

Great, living God,
    never fully known,
joyful darkness far beyond our seeing,
    closer yet than breathing,
    everlasting home:
Hail and hosanna,
great, living God!

Brian Wren, 1986; revised, 1987, 1988, 1994
Piece Together Praise, 1996
© 1989, 1994, Hope Publishing Company

613
Joyful Is the Dark

Joyful is the dark,
    holy, hidden God,
rolling cloud of night beyond all naming:
    Majesty in darkness,
    Energy of love,
Word-in-Flesh, the mystery proclaiming.

Joyful is the dark
    Spirit of the deep,
winging wildly o'er the world's creation,
    silken sheen of midnight,
    plumage black and bright,
swooping with the beauty of a raven.

Joyful is the dark,
    shadowed stable floor;
angels flicker, God on earth confessing,
    as with exultation,
    Mary, giving birth,
hails the infant cry of need and blessing.

Joyful is the dark
    coolness of the tomb,
waiting for the wonder of the morning;
    never was that midnight
    touched by dread and gloom:
Darkness was the cradle of the dawning.

Joyful is the dark
    depth of love divine,
roaring, looming thundercloud of glory,
    holy, haunting beauty,
    living, loving God.
Hallelujah! Sing and tell the story!

Brian Wren, 1986
Piece Together Praise, 1996
© 1989, Hope Publishing Company

614

Woman in the Night

Woman in the night,
    spent from giving birth,
    guard our precious light;
peace is on the earth.

        Come and join the song,
            women, children, men.
        Jesus makes us free to live again!

Woman in the crowd,
    creeping up behind,
    touching is allowed:
Seek and you will find!

Woman at the well,
    question the Messiah;
    find your friends and tell:
Drink your heart's desire!

Woman at the feast,
    let the righteous stare;
    come and go in peace;
love him with your hair!

Woman in the house,
    nurtured to be meek,
    leave your second place,
listen, think, and speak!

Women on the road,
    from your sickness freed,
    witness and provide,
joining word and deed:

Women on the hill,
    stand when men have fled;
    Christ needs loving still,
though your hope is dead.

Women in the dawn,
    care and spices bring,
    earliest to mourn,
earliest to sing!

Brian Wren, 1983
Piece Together Praise, 1996
© 1983, Hope Publishing Company

615

Christ Is Alive!

Christ is alive! Let Christians sing.
    The cross stands empty to the sky.
Let streets and homes with praises ring.
    Love, drowned in death, shall never die.

Christ is alive! No longer bound
    to distant years in Palestine,
but saving, healing, here and now,
    and touching every place and time.

In every insult, rift, and war,
    where color, scorn, or wealth divide,
Christ suffers still, yet loves the more,
    and lives, where even hope has died.

Women and men, in age and youth,
    can feel the Spirit, hear the call,
and find the way, the life, the truth,
    revealed in Jesus, freed for all.

Christ is alive, and comes to bring
    good news to this and every age,
till earth and sky and ocean ring
    with joy, with justice, love, and praise.

Brian Wren, 1968; revised, 1978, 1989, 1993
Piece Together Praise, 1996
© 1975, 1995, Hope Publishing Company

616

Here Hangs a Man Discarded

Here hangs a man discarded,
  a scarecrow hoisted high,
a nonsense pointing nowhere
  to all who hurry by.

Can such a clown of sorrows
  still bring a useful word
when faith and love seem phantoms
  and every hope absurd?

Yet here is help and comfort
  for lives by comfort bound,
when drums of dazzling progress
  give strangely hollow sound:

Life, emptied of all meaning,
  drained out in bleak distress,
can share in broken silence
  my deepest emptiness;

and love that freely entered
  the pit of life's despair,
can name our hidden darkness
  and suffer with us there.

Christ, in our darkness risen,
  help all who long for light
to hold the hand of promise,
  till faith receives its sight.

Brian Wren, 1973; revised, 1994
Piece Together Praise, 1996
© 1975, 1995, Hope Publishing Company

617

Holy Spirit, Storm of Love

Holy Spirit, storm of love,
  break our self-protective walls.
    Bring us out and show us why,
      nakedly upon the cross,
    open to the wind and sky,
Jesus waits and Jesus calls.

Show us, in his tortured flesh,
  earth's Creator on display,
    broken by affairs of state,
      drinking horror, pain, and grief,
    arching in the winds of hate,
giving love and life away.

Show us how this dying love
  entered, bore, and understood
    all our deep, unconscious drives,
      each exploiting, evil thread
    woven through our nations' lives,
all our life apart from God.

Thus convicted, claimed, and called,
  freed, as Christ we freely choose,
    washed in love, reborn, renamed,
      doing justice, knowing God,
    may we witness unashamed,
confident to give good news.

News that Jesus is alive,
  as the people of the Dove,
    going out in praise and prayer,
      meet the evils of our time
    and the demons of despair
with forgiving, living love.

Brian Wren, 1985; revised, 1995
Piece Together Praise, 1996
© 1986, Hope Publishing Company

618

Deep in the Shadows of the Past

Deep in the shadows of the past,
    far out from settled lands,
some nomads traveled with their God
    across the desert sands.
The dawning hope of humankind
    by them was sensed and shown:
a promise calling them ahead,
    a future yet unknown.

While others bowed to changeless gods
    they met a mystery,
invisible, without a name:
    "I AM WHAT I WILL BE";
and by their tents, around their fires,
    in story, song, and law,
they praised, remembered, handed on
    a past that promised more.

From Exodus to Pentecost
    the promise changed and grew,
while some, remembering the past,
    recorded what they knew,
or with their letters and laments,
    their prophecy and praise,
recovered, kindled, and expressed
    new hope for changing days.

For all the writings that survived,
    for leaders long ago,
who sifted, copied, and preserved
    the Bible that we know,
give thanks, and find its story yet
    our promise, strength, and call,
the model of emerging faith,
    alive with hope for all.

Brian Wren, 1973; revised, 1994
Piece Together Praise, 1996
© 1975, 1995, Hope Publishing Company

619

In Great Calcutta Christ Is Known

In Great Calcutta Christ is known.
    Soweto thunders with his voice.
    In Salvador his friends rejoice.
He rises in the Spirit's power
    among the poorest of the earth,
    and calls the nations to rebirth.

The suffering churches sing his grace
    and pray that we may hear and live
    the gospel that they long to give.
Beset by hunger, fear, and death,
    their hopes miraculously thrive:
    they know that Jesus is alive!

And all the powers that wreck and rule
    must lose their glamour, strength, and skill
    to dazzle minds or crush the will.
The waking hopes of God's oppressed
    will not be beaten, bowed, and awed:
    They tell the world that Christ is Lord.

Where money glitters in our streets,
    applauding honor and success,
    their prophets come, in ragged dress.
In them, we hear our Savior's voice,
    like them discarded and despised,
    who calls the weak to save the wise.

They bring a promise old, yet new,
    of food and freedom for the slave,
    and joyous life beyond the grave.
"Repent, and Christ will set you free,"
    their faithful missionaries cry,
    and call us through the needle's eye.

Christ Jesus, love us through and through,
    until our wakened hearts receive
    your glorious gospel, and believe.
From barrio, bustee, and slum,
    with Asian and Hispanic voice,
    our Savior comes! Sing and rejoice!

Brian Wren, 1985
Piece Together Praise, 1996
© 1986, Hope Publishing Company
Wren notes that *barrio* and *bustee* are Spanish and Hindi
for "shanty towns."

620

Great God, Your Love Has Called Us Here

Great God, your love has called us here,
    as we, by love for love were made.
Your living likeness still we bear,
    though marred, dishonored, disobeyed.
We come, with all our heart and mind
your call to hear, your love to find.

We come with self-inflicted pains
    of broken trust and chosen wrong,
half-free, half-bound by inner chains,
    by social forces swept along,
by powers and systems close confined,
yet seeking hope for humankind.

Great God, in Christ you call our name
    and then receive us as your own,
not through some merit, right, or claim,
    but by your gracious love alone.
We strain to glimpse your mercy seat
and find you kneeling at our feet.

Then take the towel, and break the bread,
    and humble us, and call us friends.
Suffer and serve till all are fed,
    and show how grandly love intends
to work till all creation sings,
to fill all worlds, to crown all things.

Great God, in Christ you set us free
    your life to live, your joy to share.
Give us your Spirit's liberty
    to turn from guilt and dull despair
and offer all that faith can do
while love is making all things new.

Brian Wren, 1973; revised, 1982, 1989
Piece Together Praise, 1996
© 1977, 1995, Hope Publishing Company

621

O Lord, Whose Saving Name

O Lord, whose saving Name
    is life and health and rest,
to whom the children came
    and in your arms were blest,
      we seek your face;
        your love be shown,
        your presence known,
      within this place.

That love be ours to share
    with tenderness and skill,
with science, faith, and prayer,
    to work your sovereign will;
      we praise you, Lord,
        for banished pain,
        for strength again,
    for health restored.

When deepest shadows fall
    to quench life's fading spark,
be near us when we call,
    walk with us through the dark,
      our Light and Way,
        by grief and loss,
        and bitter cross,
    to endless day.

In God our hope is set,
    beneath whose rule alone
is peace from fear and fret,
    and strength beyond our own.
        His kingdom stands,
            and those this day
            for whom we pray
        are in his hands.

Join every heart to bring
    our praise to God above,
whom children's voices sing
    and whom unseen we love.
        O God of grace,
            for evermore
            your blessings pour
        upon this place.

Timothy Dudley-Smith, 1994
Great Is the Glory, 1997
© 1997, Hope Publishing Company

622
O Prince of Peace

O Prince of Peace whose promised birth
the angels sang with "Peace on earth,"
peace be to us and all beside,
    peace to us all—
peace to the world this Christmastide.

O Child who found to lay your head
no place but in a manger bed,
come where our doors stand open wide,
    peace to us all—
    peace to the world—
peace in our homes this Christmastide.

O Christ whom shepherds came to find,
their joy be ours in heart and mind;
let grief and care be laid aside,
    peace to us all—
    peace to the world—
    peace in our homes—
peace in our hearts this Christmastide.

O Savior Christ, ascended Lord,
our risen Prince of life restored,
our Love who once for sinners died,
    peace to us all—
    peace to the world—
    peace in our homes—
    peace in our hearts—
peace with our God this Christmastide.

Timothy Dudley-Smith, 1978
Lift Every Heart, 1984
© 1980, Hope Publishing Company

623
Choirs of Angels

Choirs of angels, tell abroad
all the glories of the Lord;
sound on high what God has done,
sending us his only Son.
    Christ is come on Christmas morn,
        Christ for us in flesh arrayed,
    Christ our God incarnate born
        and within a manger laid.

Shepherds, leave your flock and fold,
he of whom the prophets told,
born to bring salvation down,
comes at last to David's town.
    Christ the Lord of David's line,
        Christ the Shepherd of the sheep,
    Christ the Lamb of God divine
        in a stable lies asleep.

Watchers of the midnight skies,
follow wisdom and be wise;
take your treasures, journey far,
ride beneath the shining star.
    Christ your King has come to birth,
        Christ the Wisdom from on high;
    Christ the Light of all the earth
        sleeps to Mary's lullaby.

Christ is come, the Child adored,
Christ the Savior, Christ the Lord;
Christ who calls his servants friends,
Christ whose kingdom never ends;
    Christ the true and living Way,
        Christ in whom shall all be well.
    Christ the dawn of heaven's day,
        Christ with us, Emmanuel!

Timothy Dudley-Smith, 1996
Great Is the Glory, 1997
© 1997, Hope Publishing Company

624
Who Is There on This Easter Morning

Who is there on this Easter morning
    runs not with John to find the grave?
Nor sees how, death's dominion scorning,
    Jesus is risen, strong to save?
        Who is there on this Easter morning
          runs not with John to find the grave?

Who has not stood where Mary grieving
    to that first Easter garden came;
for very joy but half believing
    whose is the voice that calls her name?
        Who has not stood where Mary grieving
          to that first Easter garden came?

Who is there doubts that night is ended?
    Hear from on high the trumpets call!
Christ is in triumph now ascended,
    risen and reigning, Lord of all!
        Who is there doubts that night is ended?
          Hear from on high the trumpets call!

Timothy Dudley-Smith, 1980
Lift Every Heart, 1984
© 1984, Hope Publishing Company

625
Not for Tongues of Heaven's Angels

Not for tongues of heaven's angels,
    not for wisdom to discern,
not for faith that masters mountains,
    for this better gift we yearn:
        May love be ours, O Lord.

Love is humble, love is gentle,
    love is tender, true, and kind;
love is gracious, ever patient,
    generous of heart and mind:
        May love be ours, O Lord.

Never jealous, never selfish,
    love will not rejoice in wrong;
never boastful nor resentful,
    love believes and suffers long:
        May love be ours, O Lord.

In the day this world is fading
    faith and hope will play their part;
but when Christ is seen in glory
    love shall reign in every heart:
        May love be ours, O Lord.

Timothy Dudley-Smith, 1984
based on 1 Corinthians 13
Songs of Deliverance, 1988
© 1985, Hope Publishing Company

626
He Comes to Us as One Unknown

He comes to us as one unknown,
    a breath unseen, unheard;
as though within a heart of stone,
or shriveled seed in darkness sown,
    a pulse of being stirred.

He comes when souls in silence lie
    and thoughts of day depart;
half-seen upon the inward eye,
a falling star across the sky
    of night within the heart.

He comes to us in sound of seas,
    the ocean's fume and foam;
yet small and still upon the breeze,
a wind that stirs the tops of trees,
    a voice to call us home.

He comes in love as once he came
    by flesh and blood and birth;
to bear within our mortal frame
a life, a death, a saving Name,
    for every child of earth.

He comes in truth when faith is grown;
    believed, obeyed, adored:
the Christ in all the Scriptures shown,
as yet unseen, but not unknown,
    our Savior and our Lord.

Timothy Dudley-Smith, 1982
Lift Every Heart, 1984
© 1984, Hope Publishing Company
The opening line is drawn from Albert Schweitzer's
Quest for the Historical Jesus.

627
O Come to Me, the Master Said

O come to me, the Master said,
    my Father knows your need;
and I shall be, the Master said,
    your bread of life indeed.
By faith in him we live and grow
    and share the broken bread
and all his love and goodness know
    for so the Master said.

Abide in me, the Master said,
    the true and living vine;
my life shall be, the Master said,
    poured out for you as wine.
His body to the cross he gave,
    his blood he freely shed,
who came in love to seek and save,
    for so the Master said.

Believe in me, the Master said,
    for I have called you friends,
and yours shall be, the Master said,
    the life that never ends.
And so, with sin and sorrow past,
    when death itself is dead,
the Lord shall raise us up at last,
    for so the Master said.

Timothy Dudley-Smith. 1987
Songs of Deliverance, 1988
© 1988, Hope Publishing Company

628
New Songs of Celebration Render

New songs of celebration render
    to him who has great wonders done;
awed by his power his foes surrender
    and fall before the mighty One.
He has made known his great salvation
    which all his friends with joy confess;
he has revealed to every nation
    his everlasting righteousness.

Joyfully, heartily resounding,
    let every instrument and voice
peal out the praise of grace abounding,
    calling the whole world to rejoice.
Trumpets and organs, set in motion
    such sounds as make the heavens ring:
All things that live in earth and ocean,
    make music for your mighty King.

Rivers and seas and torrents roaring,
    honor the Lord with wild acclaim;
mountains and stones, look up adoring
    and find a voice to praise his name.
Righteous, commanding, ever glorious,
    praises be his that never cease:
Just is our God, whose truth victorious
    establishes the world in peace.

Erik Routley, 1972
parallel to *"Entonnons un nouveau cantique,"* by Roger Chapal, 1970,
paraphrasing Psalm 98
Cantate Domino, 1974
© 1974, Hope Publishing Company

Routley revised lines 1:3–4 to the following form, which appears in
Our Lives Be Praise, 1990:

Love sits enthroned in ageless splendor—
    come and adore the mighty One!

629
The Word of the Lord

God speaks, and all things come to be;
God speaks, and Satan's legions flee,
    scattered by love's brave splendor;
God speaks, and our forgiveness seals;
God speaks, and generous grace reveals
    in precepts wise and tender.
Though all I see must have an end,
God's statutes past all time extend
    by breadth and length unbounded.
Though we are creatures of a day,
though heaven and earth may pass away,
    God's word is deeper founded.

Grant this to me, Lord, let me live
and, living, keep your word, and give
    my life to gain its treasure.
Here but a stranger, let me trace
my path toward a resting place
    where I shall find pure pleasure.
Much kindness you have shown to me,
promise and pledge of joy to be;
    continue thus your blessing!
Wisdom that molded all my life,
guide me, in days so full of strife,
    gently my heart possessing.

Blessed are they all who hunger sore
to see your righteousness once more
    enthroned in hearts and nations.
Blessed are the pure in heart, who seek
to hear what God the Lord will speak
    in blissful contemplations.
Blessed be our God, who gives us light;
blessed be the mercy and the might
    which all the day attend us.
Blessed be the promises of grace,
blessed be the laws that still embrace,
    enlighten, and defend us.

Erik Routley, 1982
based on Psalm 119
Our Lives Be Praise, 1990
© 1983, Hope Publishing Company

630
Hands

The crippled hands reached out to cross
    the barrier sickness wove;
ten lepers cried to be made whole
to one whom they had heard could heal
and bring them back to those they love.

Distorted to a fist, the hands
    reach out where hates divide;
prise spasmed fingers open, till
over the gulfs of palsied will
new-opened hands greet and provide.

The church, divided, does not see
    its hands' deformity:
Give wholeness to their crippled prayer,
raise misshaped thoughts from their despair,
restore to us our unity.

Alan Luff, 1993
Story Song, 1993
© 1993, Stainer & Bell Ltd. and Methodist Church (UK) Division of
Education and Youth (admin. Hope Publishing Company)

631
A Hymn of the Passage of Time

Year by year, from past to future
    worship marks our upward climb,
sets the rhythm of our journey
    to eternity through time:
Though the outward things diminish
    we are held more firm by grace,
following God's heavenward calling
    and the everlasting prize.

As we seek to weave life's fabric
    on the lengthening loom of days,
may Christ guide the threads that form it,
    be the pattern it displays;
may the Father, master craftsman,
    sorrowing over each mistake,
plan for us a new perfection
    from the ugliness we make.

Though we long for the adventure
    of the mystery of bliss,
to the pilgrim's eyes the pathway
    breaks, and ends in death's abyss;
but within the dark are waiting
    hands that bear the print of nails,
which will hold us safe and bear us
    where the worship never fails.

Alan Luff, 1991
Be Happy, Saints! 1992
© 1991, Hope Publishing Company

632
True Builder of the House

True Builder of the house, give grace to us who sing
    with faithful generations that have gone before,
who having praised and prayed and worked and
        witnessed here
    rejoice in greater light upon another shore.

Here is our Jordan, where with Christ we are
    baptized;
    where we commit ourselves to Christ, who is
        the Way:
Grant us, with heart and mind and soul afire with
    love,
    to grow more like our Lord in living each new
        day.

Here is our Cana where you come as wedding guest
    to meet our present needs with water turned to
        wine:
So visit us in all life's better and life's worse
    that where the world is darkest love's clear light
        may shine.

Here is our Calvary, and we in fear have fled,
    we have denied our Lord and left him to his
        death:
Lead us to join the faithful watchers at the cross,
    then to proclaim his victory till our final breath.

Here is our Upper Room, and though we close our
    hearts
    you come and breathe on us your spirit and
        your peace:
Show us once more your nail-scarred hands and
    wounded side,
    then we can face our doubts and find our faith
        increase.

Here is Emmaus where we greet our unknown Lord
    inviting him to sit at table as our head:
Open our eyes to find the Christ who walks with us
    made known in taking wine and breaking of
        the bread.

So has our master Builder shaped his living stones
    to be his church, his royal priesthood in this
        place.
Come, Lord, today and take and mold us to your
    will,
    to give in word and work our witness to your
        grace.

Alan Luff, 1989
100 Hymns of Hope, 1992
© 1992, Hope Publishing Company

633

Grief Waits before the Tomb

Grief waits before the tomb
    and seeks the dead inside,
but earth does not have room
    to hold the one who died.
Faith turns away from death and night
and sees, beyond grief's tear-dimmed sight,
a door wide open to the light.

Christ is our open door,
    and hope is unconfined!
Like birds uncaged we soar
    towards God's love, to find
the whole creation reconciled,
and every soul through Christ revealed
as God's uniquely precious child.

The church will open doors
    to let the people in,
where wounded souls can pause,
    at rest from grief and sin;
where each will find a fruitful place
within the fellowship of grace,
and recognize God's human face.

The church will open doors
    to send God's people out,
where daring love explores
    the poles of faith and doubt;
the Holy Spirit meets us there,
whose searching and persistent prayer
will conquer evil and despair.

Let doors be opened wide,
    and let us come and go;
made one with Christ who died,
    we live with him, to show
the promise of eternal grace:
God's justice set in time and space,
each wanted child in love's embrace.

Alan Gaunt, 1992
Always from Joy, 1997
© 1996, Stainer & Bell Ltd. (admin. Hope Publishing Company)

634
Eternal God, Supreme in Tenderness

Eternal God, supreme in tenderness,
enfolding all creation in your grace;
your mercy wraps us round, and ever shall,
and in your purpose, all things shall be well.

Eternal Son, as one of us you came
to be despised, made nothing, put to shame;
and now, a mother comforting, you call,
"All shall be well, and all things shall be well."

Eternal Spirit, source of all delight,
you stream in glory through the soul's dark night;
we taste your spring of joy, for ever full,
and know within that all things shall be well.

Eternal Trinity, through grief and pain,
through all the malice by which love is slain,
through all earth's anguish and the throes of hell,
we trust to see, in you, all things made well.

Alan Gaunt, 1988
after Julian of Norwich
The Hymn Texts of Alan Gaunt, 1991
© 1991, Stainer & Bell Ltd. (admin. Hope Publishing Company)

635
Lord Christ, We Praise Your Sacrifice

Lord Christ, we praise your sacrifice,
    your life in love so freely given.
For those who took your life away
    you prayed: that they might be forgiven;
and there, in helplessness arrayed,
God's power was perfectly displayed.

Once helpless in your mother's arms,
    dependent on her mercy then;
at last, by choice, in other hands,
    you were as helpless once again;
and, at their mercy, crucified,
you claimed your victory and died.

Though helpless and rejected then,
    you're now as risen Lord acclaimed;
for ever by your sacrifice
    is God's eternal love proclaimed:
The love which, dying, brings to birth
new life and hope for all on earth.

So, living Lord, prepare us now
    your willing helplessness to share;
to give ourselves in sacrifice
    to overcome the world's despair;
in love to give our lives away
and claim your victory today.

Alan Gaunt, 1967
The Hymn Texts of Alan Gaunt, 1991
© 1991, Stainer & Bell Ltd. (admin. Hope Publishing Company)

636
The Love That Clothes Itself in Light

The Love that clothes itself in light,
    stands naked now, despised, betrayed,
receiving blows to face and head
    from hands that Love itself has made.

The Love that lifts the stars and sun,
    collapses, spent, beneath the cross;
the Love that fills the universe,
    goes on to death and total loss.

Love, helpless, comes to Calvary,
    rejected, scorned, and crucified;
Love hangs in shame, and dies alone;
    but Love abased, is glorified.

Extinguished with the sun at noon,
    Love's light transcends all history;
Love, wrapped in linen, Love entombed,
    still wraps all heaven in mystery.

Though Love is lost, Love finds us here;
    though Love is absent, Love remains;
where Love is finished, Love begins;
    where Love is dead, Love lives and reigns!

Alan Gaunt, 1989
The Hymn Texts of Alan Gaunt, 1991
© 1991, Stainer & Bell Ltd. (admin. Hope Publishing Company)

637
Break Our Hearts, Lord, in Your Mercy

Break our hearts, Lord, in your mercy:
    Come and bring us back to you,
sear us with your blazing judgment,
    purify us through and through.

Break our hearts, Lord, set them grieving,
    make us share your agony,
where, for us, Christ prayed and suffered,
    lonely in Gethsemane.

Break our hearts, Lord, crucify them
    on the cross where Jesus died,
lest our lack of love still nail him
    and our rancor pierce his side.

Break our hearts, Lord, they are aching
    from the heartache we create,
and our own sad want of mercy
    only multiplies its weight.

Break our hearts, Lord: Break and mend them,
    heal our sullen helplessness;
bind our wounded hearts together,
    in triumphant tenderness.

Alan Gaunt, 1996
Always from Joy, 1997
© 1997, Stainer & Bell Ltd. (admin. Hope Publishing Company)

638
We Do Not Know How to Pray

We do not know how to pray,
but the Spirit intercedes;
all our sighs too deep for words
    reach the heart of God.

We do not know how to pray,
but Christ Jesus intercedes;
our humanity, in him,
    moves the heart of God.

We do not know how to pray,
but the Spirit knows our needs;
all our sorrow, fear, and pain
    wound the heart of God.

We do not know how to pray,
but as long as Jesus pleads,
we shall never be cast out
    from the heart of God.

We do not know how to pray,
but Christ's Holy Spirit leads
till we find creation's peace
    in the heart of God.

Alan Gaunt, 1995
based on Romans 8:26, 33–34
Always from Joy, 1997
© 1997, Stainer & Bell Ltd. (admin. Hope Publishing Company)

639

We Pray for Peace

We pray for peace,
    but not the easy peace,
    built on complacency
    and not the truth of God.
    We pray for real peace,
the peace God's love alone can seal.

We pray for peace,
    but not the cruel peace,
    leaving God's poor bereft
    and dying in distress.
    We pray for real peace,
enriching all the human race.

We pray for peace,
    and not the evil peace,
    defending unjust laws
    and nursing prejudice,
    but for the real peace
of justice, mercy, truth, and love.

We pray for peace:
    holy communion
    with Christ our risen Lord
    and every living thing;
    God's will fulfilled on earth
and all creation reconciled.

We pray for peace,
    and for the sake of peace,
    look to the risen Christ
    who gives the grace we need,
    to serve the cause of peace
and make our own self-sacrifice.

God, give us peace:
    if you withdraw your love,
    there is no peace for us
    nor any hope of it.
    With you to lead us on,
through death or tumult, peace will come.

Alan Gaunt, 1972; revised, 1982, 1990
The Hymn Texts of Alan Gaunt, 1991
© 1991, Stainer & Bell Ltd. (admin. Hope Publishing Company)

640

Here We Find the Tent of Meeting
Welsh: Dyma babell y cyfarfod

Here we find the tent of meeting,
    here the blood that reconciles;
here is refuge for the slayer,
    here the remedy that heals;
here a space beside the Godhead
    and the sinner's nesting place,
where, for ever, God's pure justice
    greets us with a smiling face.

Sinner is my name, most shameful,
    chief of all in sinfulness;
yet such wonder! in this temple,
    finding God in quietness;
he fulfills his law completely,
    the transgressor shares his feast,
God and humans cry, "Sufficient!"
    Jesus, sacrificed, makes peace.

Boldly, I will come before him;
    his gold scepter in his hand,
points toward this favored sinner:
    Here, accepted, all can stand.
I'll press onward, shouting, "Pardon,"
    fall before my gracious Lord:
Mine the pardon, mine the cleansing,
    mine the bleaching in his blood.

O, to come like smoke in columns
    rising from this wilderness,
straight toward his throne to see him
    seated with unfrowning face;
without end, without beginning,
    witness to the One in Three,
making known the threefold glory,
    True Amen, who sets us free.

translated, Alan Gaunt, 1996
from the original by Ann Griffiths
Always from Joy, 1997
© 1997, Stainer & Bell Ltd. (admin. Hope Publishing Company)

641
O God, Your Love's Undying Flame

O God, your love's undying flame
    was seen in desert bush ablaze,
when Moses learned your secret name,
    the Lord of past and future days;
Lord, we would learn what you require,
and burn for you with living fire.

O Lord of fire, your love a flame
    that longed to set the earth ablaze:
to bring the kingdom's joy you came
    and freed us, trapped in earthbound ways;
Lord, we would share your love's desire,
and burn for you with living fire.

O Holy Spirit, tongues of flame
    that set the new-born church ablaze;
to each believer then you came,
    and lives were filled with power and praise;
O Spirit, come, our lives inspire
to burn for you with living fire.

Basil E. Bridge, 1985; revised, 1990
Rejoice and Sing, 1991
© Basil E. Bridge

642
A Faith to Share

This is the truth we hold,
    source of the joy we share,
hope that can make us bold
    trusting the name we bear;
      that "Christ has died"
      and "Christ is risen,
in Christ shall all be made alive."

This is the song of praise
    echoing down the years,
true for the present days,
    through all our doubts and fears;
      for "Christ has died"
      and "Christ is risen,
in Christ shall all be made alive."

Christ is the living Bread,
    Christ is the word to speak,
Christ is the way to tread,
    Christ is the goal to seek;
        for "Christ has died"
        and "Christ is risen,
in Christ shall all be made alive."

One in the faith we share,
    out in his name we go;
Jesus awaits us there,
    longing that all should know
        that "Christ has died"
        and "Christ is risen,
in Christ shall all be made alive."

Basil E. Bridge, 1983; revised, 1990
Rejoice and Sing, 1991
© 1991, Oxford University Press

643
Thanks Be to God, Whose Church on Earth

Thanks be to God, whose church on earth
    has stood the tests of time and place,
and everywhere proclaims new birth
    through Christ whose love reveals God's face.

Thanks be to God, whose Spirit sent
    apostles out upon his way;
from east to west the message went;
    on Greek and Roman dawned the day.

Thanks be to God, whose later voice
    from west to east sent back the word
which, through the servants of his choice,
    at last in every tongue was heard.

Thanks be to God, who now would reach
    his listeners in more global ways;
now each will send the news, and each
    receive and answer it in praise.

Thanks be to God, in whom we share
    today the mission of his Son;
may all the church that time prepare
    when, like the task, the world is one.

Caryl Micklem, 1977
Hymns and Psalms, 1983
© Ruth Micklem

644
God of Wilderness and Jungle

God of wilderness and jungle,
    bird and beast in search of prey,
how your locusts thrive on famine
    and your maggots on decay!

God of all the bitter waters
    which engulfed the psalmist's soul,
yours the chaos deep within us
    over which we've no control.

Jesus Christ accepted darkness,
    by his death transfigured hell,
yet, beyond our comprehension,
    Judas was your child as well.

When our minds can go no further,
    when you simply say, "I am,"
let us share your prophet's vision,
    wolf at peace with grazing lamb.

For there is no god beside you,
    every heartbeat is your drum,
barely noticed, yet insisting,
    kingdom, kingdom, kingdom come.

Elizabeth Cosnett, 1987
Reflecting Praise, 1993
© 1989, Stainer & Bell Ltd. (admin. Hope Publishing Company)

645

Can Man by Searching Find Out God

Can man by searching find out God,
    or formulate his ways?
Can numbers measure what he is,
    or words contain his praise?

Although his being is too bright
    for human eyes to scan,
his meaning lights our shadowed world
    through Christ, the Son of Man.

Our boastfulness is turned to shame,
    our profit counts as loss,
when earthly values stand beside
    the manger and the cross.

We there may recognize his light,
    may kindle in its rays,
find there the source of penitence,
    the starting point for praise.

There God breaks in upon our search,
    makes birth and death his own;
he speaks to us in human terms
    to make his glory known.

Elizabeth Cosnett, 1972, 1980
Rejoice in the Lord, 1985
© 1982, Stainer & Bell Ltd. (admin. Hope Publishing Company)
The author permits the change from "man" to "we"
in the opening line.

646

When Candles Are Lighted on Candlemas Day

When candles are lighted on Candlemas Day
the dark is behind us and spring's on the way.

    A glory dawns in every dark place,
    the light of Christ, the fullness of grace.

The kings have departed, the shepherds are gone,
the child and his parents are left on their own.

They go to the temple, obeying the law,
and offer two pigeons, the gift of the poor.

But Anna and Simeon recognize there
the Christ-child who came at the turn of the year.

The old who have suffered and waited so long
see hope for the world as they welcome the young.

They gaze at God's wonderful answer to prayer,
the joy of the Jews and the Gentiles' desire.

The light is increasing and spring's in the air.
Look back with thanksgiving! Look forward with
                                     awe!

They see before Mary a heart-piercing grief,
but trust is complete at the end of their life.

For Mary will follow, with tears in her eyes,
her Savior and Son to the foot of the cross.

O Spirit of God, with courage inspire
your everyday saints who face up to despair.

They pass through temptation, through failure,
                               through death.
When darkness descends they plod onward in faith.

Like Anna, like Simeon, may they have trust,
the eyes to see Jesus, and peace at the last.

The candles invite us to praise and to pray
when Christmas greets Easter on Candlemas Day.

Elizabeth Cosnett, 1992
Hymns for Everyday Saints, 2001
© 1992, Stainer & Bell Ltd. (admin. Hope Publishing Company)

647

The Kingdom of God is Justice and Joy

The kingdom of God
 is justice and joy,
for Jesus restores
 what sin would destroy;
God's power and glory
 in Jesus we know,
and here and hereafter
 the kingdom shall grow.

The kingdom of God
 is mercy and grace,
the lepers are cleansed,
 the sinners find place,
the outcast are welcomed
 God's banquet to share,
and hope is awakened
 in place of despair.

The kingdom of God
 is challenge and choice,
believe the good news,
 repent and rejoice!
His love for us sinners
 brought Christ to his cross,
our crisis of judgment
 for gain or for loss.

God's kingdom is come,
 the gift and the goal,
in Jesus begun,
 in heaven made whole;
the heirs of the kingdom
 shall answer his call,
and all things cry glory
 to God all in all.

Bryn Austin Rees, 1973
Praise for Today, 1974
© Mrs. Morfydd Rees

648

O Christ, Our Lord

O Christ, our Lord, we meet here as your people,
 and pray that we may now accept your grace:
Forgive us when we seek an earthly kingdom
 in which we hope to find an honored place.

Forgive us for our arrogant assumptions
 that we alone have found Christ's holy way;
forgive us for the cowardly evasions
 that modify your challenge to our day.

Forgive us for the mixture of our motives
 when we are confident our love is pure;
forgive us for our unforgiving judgments
 when of the Father's will we sound so sure.

Forgive us, Lord, for all our willful blindness
 to human suff'ring and to human need;
forgive us for our casual unkindness,
 the hasty word and the begrudging deed.

And in forgiving grant us of your Spirit
 the grace to lose our selves, and in the loss
to find redemption through a true devotion
 that dares reflect the passion of your cross.

Ian Alexander, ca. 1986
Rejoice and Sing, 1991
© Ian P. Alexander

649

Our Hunger Cries from Plenty, Lord

Our hunger cries from plenty, Lord:
 for bread which does not turn to stone;
for peace the world can never give;
 for truth unreached, for love unknown.

"Let all who hunger come to me!"
    Christ's bread is life, his word is true;
our lives are grounded in that love
    which is creating all things new.

Enlarge the boundaries of our love,
    O life of God, so freely given,
till all whom hunger breaks are whole
    through Christ, the broken bread of heaven.

Colin Thompson, 1985
Rejoice and Sing, 1991
© Colin P. Thompson

650
Nothing Distress You
Latin: Nada te turbe

Nothing distress you,
nothing affright you,
everything passes,
    God will abide.
Patient endeavor
accomplishes all things;
who God possesses
    needs naught beside.

Lift your mind upward,
fair are his mansions,
nothing distress you,
    cast fear away.
Follow Christ freely,
his love will light you,
nothing affright you,
    in the dark way.

See the world's glory!
Fading its splendor,
everything passes,
    all is denied.
Look ever homeward
to the eternal;
faithful in promise
    God will abide.

Love in due measure
measureless Goodness;
patient endeavor,
    run to Love's call!
Faith burning brightly
be your soul's shelter;
who hopes, believing,
    accomplishes all.

Hell may assail you,
it cannot move you;
sorrows may grieve you,
    faith may be tried.
Though you have nothing,
he is your treasure:
Who God possesses
    needs naught beside.

translated, Colin Thompson, 1986
from the original by Teresa of Ávila
Rejoice and Sing, 1991
© Colin P. Thompson

651
Reconciliation

God with humanity made one
is seen in Christ, God's only Son:
In you, Lord Christ, the Son of man,
we see God's reconciling plan.

To save a broken world you came,
and from chaotic depths reclaim
your whole creation, so we share
your reconciling work and care.

In you all humankind can see
the people God would have us be.
In you we find how God forgives;
through you, the Spirit in us lives.

Through us God calls the world again;
and constantly his love remains
with arms outstretched, to heal and bless
the refugees of emptiness.

Where race or creed or hate divide,
the church, like God, must stand beside
and stretch out reconciling hands
to join, through suffering, every land.

Then give us strength, great Lord of life,
to work until all human strife
is reconciled, and all shall praise
your endless love, your glorious ways.

David Fox, 1986; revised, 1990
Rejoice and Sing, 1991
© David Fox

652
Day Is Done

Day is done, but Love unfailing
    dwells ever here;
shadows fall, but hope, prevailing,
    calms every fear.
Loving Father, none forsaking,
take our hearts, of Love's own making,
watch our sleeping, guard our waking,
    be always near!

Dark descends, but Light unending
    shines through our night;
you are with us, ever lending
    new strength to sight;
one in love, your truth confessing,
one in hope of heaven's blessing,
may we see, in love's possessing,
    love's endless light.

Eyes will close, but you, unsleeping,
    watch by our side;
death may come: In Love's safe keeping
    still we abide.
God of love, all evil quelling,
sin forgiving, fear dispelling,
stay with us, our hearts indwelling,
    this eventide!

James Quinn, 1969
Praise for All Seasons, 1994
© 1994, Continuum International Publishing Group, Ltd.

653
Blessed Be the God of Israel

Blessed be the God of Israel,
    the ever-living Lord.
Who comes in power to save his own,
    his people Israel.

For Israel you now raise up
    salvation's tower on high
in David's house, who reigned as king
    and servant of our Lord.

Through holy prophets did he speak
    his word from days of old,
that he would save us from our foes
    and all who bear us ill.

On Sinai he gave to us
　　his covenant of love;
so with us now he keeps his word
　　in love that knows no end.

Of old he swore his solemn oath
　　to father Abraham;
from him a mighty race should spring,
　　one blessed for evermore.

He swore to set his people free
　　from fear of every foe
that we might serve him all our days
　　in goodness, love, and peace.

O tiny child, your name shall be
　　the prophet of the Lord;
the way for God you shall prepare
　　to make his coming known.

You shall proclaim to Israel
　　salvation's dawning day,
when God shall wipe away our sins
　　in his redeeming love.

The rising Sun shall shine on us
　　to bring the light of day
to all who sit in darkest night
　　and shadow of the grave.

Our footsteps God shall safely guide
　　to walk the ways of peace.
His name for evermore be blessed
　　who lives and loves and saves.

James Quinn, 1969; revised, 1985
based on Luke 1:68–79
Praise for All Seasons, 1994
© 1994, Continuum International Publishing Group, Ltd.

654
O Child of Promise, Come

O Child of promise, come!
　　O come, Emmanuel!
Come, prince of peace, to David's throne;
　　come, God with us to dwell!

The Lord's true Servant, come,
　　in whom is his delight,
on whom his holy Spirit rests,
　　the Gentiles' promised light!

O come, anointed One,
　　to show blind eyes your face!
Good tidings to the poor announce;
　　proclaim God's year of grace!

O man of sorrows, come,
　　despised and cast aside!
O bear our griefs, and by your wounds
　　redeem us from our pride!

O come, God's holy Lamb;
　　to death be meekly led!
O save the many by your blood,
　　for sin so gladly shed!

O come, Messiah King,
　　to reign in endless light
when heavenly peace at last goes forth
　　from Zion's holy height!

James Quinn, 1970
Praise for All Seasons, 1994
© 1969, Continuum International Publishing Group, Ltd.

655

Word of God, Come Down on Earth

Word of God, come down on earth,
living rain from heaven descending;
touch our hearts and bring to birth
faith and hope and love unending.
Word almighty, we revere you;
Word made flesh, we long to hear you.

Word eternal, throned on high,
Word that brought to life creation,
Word that came from heaven to die,
crucified for our salvation,
saving Word, the world restoring,
speak to us, your love outpouring.

Word that caused blind eyes to see,
speak and heal our mortal blindness;
deaf we are; our healer be;
loose our tongues to tell your kindness.
Be our Word in pity spoken,
heal the world, by our sin broken.

Word that speaks your Father's love,
one with him beyond all telling,
Word that sends us from above
God the Spirit, with us dwelling;
Word of truth, to all truth lead us;
Word of life, with one Bread feed us.

James Quinn, 1969
Praise for All Seasons, 1994
© 1969, Continuum International Publishing Group, Ltd.

656

Love Is His Word

Love is his word, love is his way.
Feasting with all, fasting alone,
living and dying, rising again.
Love, only love, is his way.

Richer than gold is the love of my Lord,
better than splendor and wealth.

Love is his way, love is his mark.
Sharing his last Passover feast.
Guest at his table, Host to the twelve,
love, only love, is his mark.

Love is his mark, love is his sign.
Bread for our strength, wine for our joy.
"This is my body, this is my blood."
Love, only love, is his sign.

Love is his sign, love is his news.
"Do this," he said, "lest you forget
all my deep sorrow, all my dear blood."
Love, only love, is his news.

Love is his news, love is his name.
We are his own, chosen and called,
family, brethren, cousins, and kin.
Love, only love, is his name.

Love is his name, love is his law.
Hear his command, all who are his:
"Love one another, I have loved you."
Love, only love, is his law.

Love is his law, love is his word:
Love of the Lord, Father and Word,
love of the Spirit, God ever one.
Love, only love, is his word.

Luke Connaughton, ca. 1970
RitualSong, 1996
© 1970, McCrimmon Publishing Co. Ltd.

657
The Holy Innocents

In Bethlehem a newborn boy
was hailed with songs of praise and joy.
Then warning came of danger near:
King Herod's troops would soon appear.

The soldiers sought the child in vain:
Not yet was he to share our pain.
But down the ages rings the cry
of those who saw their children die.

Still rage the fires of hate today,
and innocents the price must pay,
while aching hearts in every land
cry out, "We cannot understand!"

Lord Jesus, through our night of loss
shines out the wonder of your cross,
the love that cannot cease to bear
our human anguish everywhere.

May that great love our lives control
and conquer hate in every soul,
till, pledged to build and not destroy,
we share your pain and find your joy.

Rosamond E. Herklots, 1969
as revised by Herklots for *The Hymnal 1982*
The Hymnal 1982, 1985
© 1969, Oxford University Press

658
Filled with the Spirit's Power

Filled with the Spirit's power, with one accord
the infant church confessed its risen Lord.
O Holy Spirit, in the church today
no less your power of fellowship display.

Now with the mind of Christ set us on fire,
that unity may be our great desire.
Give joy and peace; give faith to hear your call,
and readiness in each to work for all.

Widen our love, good Spirit, to embrace
in your strong care all those of every race.
Like wind and fire with life among us move,
till we are known as Christ's, and Christians prove.

J. R. Peacey, 1969
Go Forth for God, 1991
© 1978, Hope Publishing Company

659
Best of All Friends

Jesus, my Lord,
    let me be near you;
by your own word
    help me to hear you.
Jesus, my Lord,
    lead me to love you,
nothing more dear,
    no one above you.

All through the day,
    sisters and brothers,
yours we will be,
    caring for others,
hearing your words,
    learning your story,
bearing your cross,
    sharing your glory.

Teach us to know
     seeing from blindness,
help us to show
     everywhere kindness.
Jesus, our Lord,
     lead us and guide us,
best of all friends,
     always beside us.

H. C. A. Gaunt
More Hymns for Today, 1980
© Oxford University Press

Therefore he who thee reveals
     hangs, O Father, on that tree
helpless; and the nails and thorns
     tell of what thy love must be.

Thou art God; no monarch thou
     throned in easy state to reign;
thou art God, whose arms of love,
     aching, spent, the world sustain.

William Hubert Vanstone, 1976
Love's Endeavour, Love's Expense, 1977
© J. W. Shore

660

A Hymn to the Creator

Morning glory, starlit sky,
     leaves in springtime, swallows' flight,
autumn gales, tremendous seas,
     sounds and scents of summer night;

soaring music, towering words,
     art's perfection, scholar's truth,
joy supreme of human love,
     memory's treasure, grace of youth;

open, Lord, are these, thy gifts,
     gifts of love to mind and sense;
hidden is love's agony,
     love's endeavor, love's expense.

Love that gives gives ever more,
     gives with zeal, with eager hands;
spares not, keeps not, all outpours,
     ventures all, its all expends.

Drained is love in making full;
     bound in setting others free;
poor in making many rich;
     weak in giving power to be.

661

How Blest the Poor Who Love the Lord

How blest the poor who love the Lord
     and hold his kingdom in their hearts;
for they perceive with inner sight
     the wealth that only God imparts!

How blest are those who hunger now—
     they shall not go unsatisfied;
because they seek for righteousness,
     their needs will always be supplied.

How blest are those who weep and mourn,
     for in their sorrow Christ appears
to share their grief and bring them hope—
     till joy shall drive away their tears.

How blest are those who, for his sake,
     know pain and insult, hate and scorn;
for he will turn the darkest night
     to great reward in heaven's dawn.

How blest are those who have refused
     to live for selfish gain alone;
though now they feel distress and pain
     they soon shall reap as they have sown.

How blest are those who seek and find
    the precious pearl of countless price,
and in God's kingdom taste the fruit
    of Jesus' perfect sacrifice!

Mollie Knight
based on Matthew 5:1–12
Baptist Praise and Worship, 1991
© 1991, Jubilate Hymns (admin. Hope Publishing Company)

662
Into a World of Dark

Into a world of dark,
    waste and disordered space,
he came, a wind that moved
    across the waters' face.

The Spirit in the wild
    breathed, and a world began.
From shapelessness came form,
    from nothingness, a plan.

Light in the darkness grew;
    land in the water stood;
and space and time became
    a beauty that was good.

Into a world of doubt,
    through doors we closed, he came,
the breath of God in power
    like wind and roaring flame.

From empty wastes of death
    on love's disordered grief
light in the darkness blazed
    and kindled new belief.

Still, with creative power,
    God's Spirit comes to give
a pattern of new life—
    our worlds begin to live.

Ann Phillips, 1972; revised, 1975, 1990
Rejoice and Sing, 1991
© 1972, 1975, 1990, The United Reformed Church

663
When the King Shall Come Again

When the King shall come again
    all his power revealing,
splendor shall announce his reign,
    life and joy and healing:
Earth no longer in decay,
    hope no more frustrated;
this is God's redemption day
    longingly awaited.

In the desert trees take root
    fresh from his creation;
plants and flowers and sweetest fruit
    join in celebration.
Rivers spring up from the earth,
    barren lands adorning:
Valleys, this is your new birth;
    mountains, greet the morning!

Strengthen feeble hands and knees;
    fainting hearts, be cheerful!
God who comes for such as these
    seeks and saves the fearful.
Deaf ears hear the silent tongues
    sing away their weeping;
blind eyes see the lifeless ones
    walking, running, leaping.

There God's highway shall be seen
   where no roaring lion,
nothing evil or unclean
   walks the road to Zion:
Ransomed people, homeward bound,
   all your praises voicing,
see your Lord with glory crowned,
   share in his rejoicing!

Christopher Idle, 1975
based on Isaiah 35
Light upon the River, 1998
© 1982, Jubilate Hymns, Ltd. (admin. Hope Publishing Company)

664
Here from All Nations

Here from all nations, all tongues and all peoples,
   countless the crowd, but their voices are one;
vast is the sight and majestic their singing:
   "God has the victory; he reigns from the throne."

These have come out of the hardest oppression,
   now they may stand in the presence of God,
serving their Lord day and night in his temple,
   ransomed and cleansed by the Lamb's precious
                                                blood.

Gone is their thirst and no more shall they hunger.
   God is their shelter, his power at their side:
Sun shall not pain them, no burning will torture;
   Jesus the Lamb is their Shepherd and Guide.

He will go with them to clear living water
   flowing from springs which his mercy supplies;
gone is their grief and their trials are over,
   God wipes away every tear from their eyes.

Blessing and glory and wisdom and power
   be to the Savior again and again;
might and thanksgiving and honor for ever
   be to our God: Hallelujah! Amen.

Christopher Idle, 1972
based on Revelation 7
Light upon the River, 1998
© 1973, Jubilate Hymns, Ltd. (admin. Hope Publishing Company)

665
Jesus, Come, for We Invite You

Jesus, come, for we invite you,
   Guest and Master, Friend and Lord;
now, as once at Cana's wedding,
   speak, and let us hear your word:
Lead us through our need or doubting,
   hope be born and joy restored.

Jesus, come! transform our pleasures,
   guide us into paths unknown;
bring your gifts, command your servants,
   let us trust in you alone:
Though your hand may work in secret,
   all shall see what you have done.

Jesus, come in new creation,
   heaven brought near by power divine;
give your unexpected glory
   changing water into wine:
Rouse the faith of your disciples—
   come, our first and greatest Sign!

Jesus, come! surprise our dullness;
   make us willing to receive
more than we can yet imagine
   all the best you have to give:
Let us find your hidden riches,
   taste your love, believe, and live!

Christopher Idle, 1979
Light upon the River, 1998
© 1982, Jubilate Hymns, Ltd. (admin. Hope Publishing Company)

666

Eternal Light, Shine in My Heart

Eternal light, shine in my heart,
    eternal hope, lift up my eyes;
eternal power, be my support,
    eternal wisdom, make me wise.

Eternal life, raise me from death,
    eternal brightness, make me see;
eternal Spirit, give me breath,
    eternal Savior, come to me:

Until by your most costly grace,
    invited by your holy word,
at last I come before your face
    to know you, my eternal God.

Christopher Idle, 1977
based on prayer by Alcuin (Ealhwine Flaccus)
Light upon the River, 1998
© 1982, Jubilate Hymns, Ltd. (admin. Hope Publishing Company)

667

O Bless the God of Israel

O bless the God of Israel
    who comes to set us free;
who visits and redeems us,
    and grants us liberty.
The prophets spoke of mercy,
    of rescue and release:
God shall fulfill the promise
    to bring our people peace.

He comes! the Son of David,
    the one whom God has given;
he comes to live among us
    and raise us up to heaven;
before him goes the herald,
    forerunner in the way,
the prophet of salvation,
    the messenger of Day.

Where once were fear and darkness
    the sun begins to rise—
the dawning of forgiveness
    upon the sinner's eyes,
to guide the feet of pilgrims
    along the paths of peace:
O bless our God and Savior,
    with songs that never cease!

Michael Perry, 1973, frequently revised
based on Luke 1:68–79
Singing to God, 1995
© 1973, Jubilate Hymns, Ltd. (admin. Hope Publishing Company)

668

Heal Me, Hands of Jesus

Heal me, hands of Jesus,
    and search out all my pain;
restore my hope, remove my fear
    and bring me peace again.

Cleanse me, blood of Jesus,
    take bitterness away;
let me forgive as one forgiven
    and bring me peace today.

Know me, mind of Jesus,
    and show me all my sin;
dispel the memories of guilt,
    and bring me peace within.

Fill me, joy of Jesus:
    Anxiety shall cease
and heaven's serenity be mine,
    for Jesus brings me peace!

Michael Perry, 1981, 1982
Singing to God, 1995
© 1982, Jubilate Hymns, Ltd. (admin. Hope Publishing Company)

669

O God beyond All Praising

O God beyond all praising,
 we worship you today
and sing the love amazing
 that songs cannot repay;
for we can only wonder
 at every gift you send,
at blessings without number
 and mercies without end:
We lift our hearts before you
 and wait upon your word,
we honor and adore you,
 our great and mighty Lord.

[The flower of earthly splendor
 in time must surely die,
its fragile bloom surrender
 to you the Lord most high;
but hidden from all nature
 the eternal seed is sown—
though small in mortal stature,
 to heaven's garden grown:
For Christ the Man from heaven
 from death has set us free,
and we through him are given
 the final victory!]

Then hear, O gracious Savior,
 accept the love we bring,
that we who know your favor
 may serve you as our king;
and whether our tomorrows
 be filled with good or ill,
we'll triumph through our sorrows
 and rise to bless you still:
to marvel at your beauty
 and glory in your ways,
and make a joyful duty
 our sacrifice of praise.

Michael Perry, stanzas 1 and 3, 1982; stanza 2, 1987
stanza 2 based on 1 Corinthians 15
Singing to God, 1995
© 1982, Jubilate Hymns, Ltd. (admin. Hope Publishing Company)
The author placed the second stanza in brackets.

670

Christ Triumphant, Ever Reigning

Christ triumphant, ever reigning,
 Savior, Master, King!
Lord of heaven, our lives sustaining,
 hear us as we sing:

  Yours the glory and the crown,
   the high renown, the eternal name.

Word incarnate, truth revealing,
 Son of Man on earth!
power and majesty concealing
 by your humble birth:

Suffering servant, scorned, ill-treated,
 victim crucified!
death is through the cross defeated,
 sinners justified:

Priestly king, enthroned for ever
 high in heaven above!
sin and death and hell shall never
 stifle hymns of love:

So, our hearts and voices raising
　　through the ages long,
ceaselessly upon you gazing,
　　this shall be our song:

671
Baptized in Water

　　Baptized in water,
　　　　sealed by the Spirit,
cleansed by the blood of Christ our King;
　　　　heirs of salvation,
　　　　　　trusting his promise—
faithfully now God's praise we sing.

　　Baptized in water,
　　　　sealed by the Spirit,
dead in the tomb with Christ our King;
　　　　one with his rising,
　　　　　　freed and forgiven,
thankfully now God's praise we sing.

　　Baptized in water,
　　　　sealed by the Spirit,
marked with the sign of Christ our King;
　　　　born of one Father,
　　　　　　we are his children—
joyfully now God's praise we sing.

672
Come to Us, Creative Spirit

Come to us, creative Spirit,
　　in our Father's house;
every natural talent foster,
　　hidden skills arouse,
that within your earthly temple
wise and simple
　　may rejoice.

Poet, painter, music-maker,
　　all your treasures bring;
craftsman, actor, graceful dancer,
　　make your offering:
Join your hands in celebration:
Let creation
　　shout and sing!

Word from God eternal springing
　　fill our minds, we pray;
and in all artistic vision
　　give integrity.
May the flame within us burning
kindle yearning
　　day by day.

In all places and forever
　　glory be expressed
to the Son, with God the Father,
　　and the Spirit blest.
In our worship and our living
keep us striving
　　towards the best.

673
Lord of Our Growing Years

Lord of our growing years,
    with us from infancy,
laughter and quick-dried tears,
    freshness and energy:

      Your grace surrounds us all our days—
      for all your gifts we bring our praise.

Lord of our strongest years,
    stretching our youthful powers,
lovers and pioneers
    when all the world seems ours:

Lord of our middle years,
    giver of steadfastness,
courage that perseveres
    when there is small success:

Lord of our older years,
    steep though the road may be,
rid us of foolish fears,
    bring us serenity:

Lord of our closing years,
    always your promise stands;
hold us, when death appears,
    safely within your hands:

David Mowbray, 1982
Hymns for Today's Church, 1982
© 1982, Jubilate Hymns, Ltd. (admin. Hope Publishing Company)

674
So Dies This Man

So dies this man, this carpenter;
    his cause, his kingdom scorned;
a dismal figure on a cross,
    deserted, scarcely mourned.

So dies this man, brother to all
    the poor and the oppressed.
"Come unto me," he said to them,
    "and I will give you rest."

So dies this man—"Father, forgive,"
    his last and loving word.
Each one who hastened him to death
    is brought in prayer to God.

So lives this man, this carpenter;
    no less a one than he
could rise to mend this broken world
    and claim our loyalty.

David Mowbray, 1988
Story Song, 1993
© 1988, Jubilate Hymns (admin. Hope Publishing Company)

675
Thank God, at Last We Can Control

Thank God, at last we can control
that iron entering the soul,
    that threat to sanity.
We dam the rising stream of pain
and help our suffering friends regain
    their peace and dignity.

Thank God for work in hospice care,
for drugs administered with prayer,
    for warmth of heart and hand.
Thank God for seeds of trust that spring
as, through unhurried listening,
    we come to understand.

We'll keep them company and stay
in touch, however steep the way,
    until our paths divide.
Then, saddened, we must let them go,
yet deep within our hearts we know
    they're met the other side.

David Mowbray, 1992
Story Song, 1993
© 1993, Stainer & Bell Ltd. and Methodist Church (UK) Division of
Education and Youth (admin. Hope Publishing Company)

676
O God, Who Gives to Humankind

O God, who gives to humankind
a searching heart and questing mind,
grant us to find your truth and laws,
and wisdom to perceive their cause.

In all our learning give us grace
to bow ourselves before your face;
as knowledge grows, Lord, keep us free
from self-destructive vanity.

Sometimes we think we understand
all workings of your mighty hand;
then through your Son help us to know
those truths which you alone can show.

Teach us to joy in things revealed,
to search with care all yet concealed,
as through Christ's light your truth we find
and worship you with heart and mind.

Edward Burns, 1969; revised, 1990
The Worshiping Church, 1990
© Edward J. Burns

677
May We, O Holy Spirit

May we, O Holy Spirit, bear your fruit—
    your joy and peace pervade each word we say;
may love become of life the very root,
    and grow more deep and strong with every day.

May patience stem the harmful word and deed,
    and kindness seek the good among the wrong;
may goodness far beyond our lips proceed,
    as manifest in action as in song.

May faithfulness endure, yet as we grow
    may gentleness lend courage to the weak;
and in our self-restraint help us to know
    that grace that made the King of Heaven meek.

Paul Wigmore, 1982
Hymns for Today's Church, 1982
© 1982, Jubilate Hymns (admin. Hope Publishing Company)

678
O Lord, Whose Human Hands Were Quick

O Lord, whose human hands were quick
to feed the hungry, heal the sick,
who love by loving deed expressed,
help me to comfort the distressed.

What is divine about my creed
if I am blind to human need?
For you have said they serve you best
who serve the helpless and oppressed.

Lord may your love translucent shine
through every loving deed of mine,
that men may see the works I do
and give the glory all to you.

Malcolm J. Bale, 1980
The Song Book of the Salvation Army, 1986
© Salvationist Publishing & Supplies Ltd.
(admin. The Copyright Company)

679
Exodus Hymn

Passover God, we remember your faithfulness,
    God of the exodus, friend of the poor;
people bowed down with the burden of powerlessness,
    sin in its ruthlessness making them slaves.

Still people shrivel, imprisoned in bitterness,
    hemmed in by fear and diminished by hate;
tormented prisoners and perishing hungry ones,
    broken humanity calls for your aid.

You summoned Moses to work for the freedom
                    march,
    you called the slaves to be people of hope;
set free from Egypt, you led them through desert
                    lands,
    loving commands gave them justice and truth.

You gave the travelers bread in the wilderness;
    strengthen us now with the bread that we share:
bread for the struggle and wine for rejoicing;
    in Christ you free us and teach us to care.

We are your people, still called to a promised land,
    called for a purpose with Christ as the way;
grant us commitment to wholeness and liberty,
    strength for the journey and grace for each day.

Christopher Ellis, 1987
Baptist Praise and Worship, 1991
© Christopher Ellis

680
Open This Book

Open this book that we may see your word
    embodied in the drama of our earth—
stories of people that your Spirit stirred,
    glimpses of hope and visions of new birth.

Open this book that we may meet the one
    who came as word-made-flesh for all to see;
show us his life, all that was said and done,
    that we might see ourselves as we could be.

Open our ears that we may hear you still;
    teach us to live as well as speak your word.
Open our eyes that we might face your will—
    the word-made-flesh in those who call you
                      "Lord."

Christopher Ellis, 1987
Baptist Praise and Worship, 1991
© Christopher Ellis

681
Early on Sunday

Early on Sunday,
Mary comes running,
says to the gardener,
    "Where is my Lord?"
Mary, stop crying:
This is no gardener.
Look at your master,
    to life restored.

Later on Sunday,
two, slowly walking,
tell their companion,
    "Jesus is dead."
Sitting at supper,
warmed by his presence,
they know their master
    as he breaks bread.

Sunday by Sunday,
as the first Easter,
Jesus comes to us,
    makes himself known.
Joy of your people,
life, resurrection,
Jesus, our master,
    we are your own.

Joyce Woolford, 1982
Baptist Praise and Worship, 1991
© Joyce Woolford

682
O Why, My God, Have You Forsaken Me

"O why, my God, have you forsaken me?"
    So cries the Son, in anguish from the cross,
and in that cry, which rings eternally,
    the Father knows the tragedy of loss.
So all the hurts the world can ever see
are known and held within the Trinity.

The Spirit grieves for fellowship denied,
    the very soul of love in sorrow bared.
That grief alone will heed the great divide,
    the paradox of isolation shared.
Thus faith and hope in fellowship abide,
with love itself for ever glorified.

So all the hopes creation has defiled
    are held within the fellowship divine,
toward the day when all is reconciled,
    and countless songs of joyful hope combine;
when he who died in God-forsaken strife
will fill the world with never-ending life!

Michael Forster, 1991
The Hymns of Michael Forster, 1998
© Kevin Mayhew Ltd.

683
It Is Complete

"It is complete!" the cry of triumph rings;
    love conquers all, enduring to the death;
in human frailty, never more divine—
    nor more alive than in this dying breath!

"It is complete!" no compromise he makes,
    for pain and death cannot his voice suppress,
nor turn his lips to harsh and spiteful words,
    and hate is overcome by gentleness.

"It is complete!" he shows the power of grace,
    reveals new realms of possibility;
calls us to share the victory of his love,
    and celebrate our true humanity.

"It is complete!" let all creation cry,
    when into plowshares all our swords we beat,
when endless streams of peace and justice flow,
    and hill to valley calls, "It is complete!"

Michael Forster, 1991
The Hymns of Michael Forster, 1998
© Kevin Mayhew Ltd.

684
Love Is the Only Law

    Love, love is the only law,
        for God and humankind:
    Love your God with all your heart,
        your strength and soul and mind;
    love your neighbor as yourself,
        of every creed and race,
turning the water of endless laws
        into the wine of grace.

Love is God's wisdom, love is God's
    strength,
    love is God's only law.
Love of such height, such depth, such
    length,
    love is God's only law.

Give dignity to the poor,
    and help the blind to see,
feed the hungry, heal the sick,
    and set the captive free.
All that God requires of you
    will then fall into place,
turning the water of endless laws
    into the wine of grace.

Let love like a river flow
    and justice like a stream,
faith become reality
    and hope your constant theme.
Then shall freedom, joy, and peace
    with righteousness embrace,
turning the water of endless laws
    into the wine of grace.

Michael Forster, 1996
The Hymns of Michael Forster, 1998
© Kevin Mayhew Ltd.

685

The Gracious Invitation

The gracious invitation stands
    for any who will come;
the Father runs with open arms
    to children heading home—
and all who trudge with weary feet
    along life's dusty road
receive at last a welcome chance
    to lose their heavy load.

No longer need we clothe our lives
    in garments soiled and torn
when Christ gives robes of righteousness
    for what was old and worn;
to those bereft of dignity
    and yearning to be whole,
forgiveness brings the healing power
    which liberates the soul.

When all that busy lives produce
    is dry futility,
we find in Christ the living source
    of full reality;
and if, within our hearts, the truth
    is what we long to hear,
the whisper of the Spirit comes
    as music to the ear.

Whoever looks for nourishment
    will find the table spread:
the finest riches heaven holds,
    foretold in wine and bread.
The banquet is for everyone,
    the greatest and the least:
For all are called as honored guests
    to come and join the feast.

Martin Leckebusch, 1996
More Than Words, 2000
© Kevin Mayhew Ltd.

686

This Grace of Sharing

Long ago you taught your people:
    "Part of what you reap is mine—
from your cattle, bring the firstborn;
    tithe the crops of field and vine."
Though beneath the law's restrictions
    we are not compelled to live,
as we reap our monthly harvest,
    make us eager, Lord, to give.

What a way of life you showed us
    through the Son you gladly gave;
never snared by earthly treasure,
    buried in a borrowed grave—
yet to all he freely offered
    riches of the deepest kind:
Let us live with his example
    firmly fixed in heart and mind.

In the lifestyle of the Spirit
    giving has a central part;
teach us, Lord, this grace of sharing
    with a cheerful, loving heart—
not a tiresome obligation,
    not a barren legal due,
but an overflow of worship:
    All we have belongs to you!

Martin Leckebusch, 1998
More Than Words, 2000
© Kevin Mayhew Ltd.

687
Dear Mother God

Dear Mother God, your wings are warm around us,
    we are enfolded in your love and care;
safe in the dark, your heartbeat's pulse surrounds us,
    you call to us, for you are always there.

You call to us, for we are in your image.
    We wait on you, the nest is cold and bare—
high overhead your wingbeats call us onward.
    Filled with your power, we ride the empty air.

Let not our freedom scorn the needs of others—
    we climb the clouds until our strong heart
                  sings—
may we enfold our sisters and our brothers,
    till all are strong, till all have eagles' wings.

Janet Wootton, 1987; revised, 1991
Reflecting Praise, 1993
© 1991, Stainer & Bell Ltd. (admin. Hope Publishing Company)

688
Creatures, Once in Safety Held

Creatures, once in safety held,
now pour out into the world.
Let the chaos waters cease!
    Plow the field and plant the vine—
    arching rainbow be the sign
of God's covenant of peace.

Promises that cannot be;
symbols filled with mystery,
giving hope in face of death.
    Out of dead wood springs the vine—
    smoking firebrand be the sign
of God's covenant of faith.

People come in awe and fear—
God will join their feasting here,
gathered on the mountaintop.
    Gourmet food and vintage wine,
    common offering be the sign
of God's covenant of hope.

Joy and sorrow meet in song—
exiles are returning home.
Let the dancers show the way,
    hear the music, taste the wine—
    living hearts will be the sign
of God's covenant of joy.

Call to mind the Upper Room,
killing cross, and empty tomb:
Christ is here in flesh and blood.
    We ourselves become the sign,
    as we share, in bread and wine,
God's great covenant renewed.

Janet Wootton, 1992
Story Song, 1993
© 1993, Stainer & Bell Ltd. and The Trustees for Methodist Church
Purposes (UK) (admin. Hope Publishing Company)

689
We Sing a Love

We sing a love that sets all people free,
that blows like wind, that burns like scorching flame,
enfolds like earth, springs up like water clear.
Come, living love, live in our hearts today.

We sing a love that seeks another's good,
that longs to serve and not to count the cost,
a love that, yielding, finds itself made new.
Come, caring love, live in our hearts today.

We sing a love, unflinching, unafraid
to be itself, despite another's wrath,
a love that stands alone and undismayed.
Come, strengthening love, live in our hearts today.

We sing a love that, wandering, will not rest
until it finds its way, its home, its source,
through joy and sadness pressing on refreshed.
Come, pilgrim love, live in our hearts today.

We sing a burning, fiery, Holy Ghost
that seeks out shades of ancient bitterness,
transfig'ring these, as Christ in every heart.
Come, joyful love, live in our hearts today.

June Boyce-Tillman, 1993
Reflecting Praise, 1993
© 1993, Stainer & Bell Ltd. and Women in Theology
(admin. Hope Publishing Company)

690
Advent Hope

The God of hope is God who comes
    to wait with us in faith,
within our darkness and our fears,
    our comforter and strength.

The God who comes is God who speaks:
    a living, human word.
Within our neighbors' joys and tears
    the voice of God is heard.

We look for God to come, and yet,
    unknown, God comes to be
till the imprisoned, trampled ones
    are in God's presence free.

We celebrate the God who is:
    Love has a human face!
God greets the humble, lifts the poor,
    and we are filled with grace.

Donald Pickard, 1983
Story Song, 1993
© 1993, Stainer & Bell Ltd. and Methodist Church (UK) Division of
Education and Youth (admin. Hope Publishing Company)

691
You Laid Aside Your Rightful Reputation

You laid aside your rightful reputation
    and gave no heed to what the world might say;
served as a slave and laid aside your garments
    to wash the feet of those who walked your way.

You touched the leper, ate with those rejected,
    received the worship of a woman's tears:
You shed the pride that keeps us from the freedom
    to love our neighbor, laying down our fears.

Help us to follow, Jesus, where you lead us
    to love, to serve, our own lives laying down;
to walk your way of humble, costly service,
    a cross its end, a ring of thorns its crown.

Draw us to you and with your love transform us:
　　the love we've seen, the love we've touched
　　　　　　　　　　　　　　　and known;
enlarge our hearts and with compassion fill us
　　to love, to serve, to follow you alone.

692
Reeling from the Realization

Reeling from the realization,
　　guilt ingrained upon her mind;
self-doubt sown within her childhood,
　　crippled by the fears that bind.

Fears that stifle conversation,
　　shrinking back from the unknown,
damaged deeply by experience,
　　longing to be loved not owned.

Exploitation is the watchword
　　of the ones who come to see:
frantic "loving," touched and tainted,
　　never valued, never free.

Then, in all of this confusion,
　　in their eyes she stands condemned,
all they see is symptomatic
　　of a life they cannot mend.

Jesus senses motivation,
　　holds a mirror to the crowd,
one by one they turn to leave her.
　　"Does no one condemn you now?"

"Woman I do not condemn you!"
　　He must know the reason why
that could penetrate her smallness,
　　that would make her fears subside.

All the filth and degradation
　　gone, her life now seems less raw:
Unconditional acceptance
　　motivates to sin no more.

693
Love Inspired the Anger

Love inspired the anger
　　that cleared a temple court,
overturned the wisdom
　　which their greed had wrought.

Love inspired the anger
　　that set the leper free
from the legal strictures
　　that brought misery.

Love inspired the anger
　　that cursed a viper's brood:
set on domination,
　　self with God confused.

Love inspires the anger
　　that curses poverty,
preaches life's enrichment
　　seeks equality.

Love inspires the anger
　　that still can set us free
from the world's conventions
　　bringing liberty.

694
When Jesus the Healer

When Jesus the healer passed through Galilee,
      Heal us, heal us today!
the deaf came to hear and the blind came to see.
      Heal us, Lord Jesus!

A paralyzed man was let down through a roof.
His sins were forgiven, his walking the proof.

The death of his daughter caused Jairus to weep.
The Lord took her hand, and he raised her from
                        sleep.

When blind Bartimaeus cried out to the Lord,
his faith made him whole and his sight was restored.

The lepers were healed and the demons cast out,
a bent woman straightened to laugh and to shout.

The twelve were commissioned and sent out by twos
to make the sick whole and to spread the good news.

There's still so much sickness and suffering today.
We gather together for healing and pray:

Peter D. Smith, 1975
The United Methodist Hymnal, 1989
© 1978, Stainer & Bell Ltd. (admin. Hope Publishing Company)

695
We Love the Jesus Stories

We love the Jesus stories
      of what was lost and found,
and how he teaches us to see
      God's kingdom all around.

He tells of hidden treasure,
      of sheep and goats and seeds,
of birds that nest in leafy trees,
      and corn and wheat and weeds.

We learn of guests and banquets,
      of talents and of debts,
of houses built on sand and rock,
      and pearls and fishing nets.

He teaches love for others,
      that God forgives our sin,
that what we do for those in need
      we do it all for him.

David M. Owen, 1986
Baptist Praise and Worship, 1991
© David M. Owen

696
Like a Tiny Seed of Mustard

Like a tiny seed of mustard,
      stored with life, invisibly,
grows and grows, each day increasing
      and becomes a mighty tree;

like the leaven in the mixture
      swells inside while hid from view,
living, rising, and transforming
      simple grain to bread anew;

like the priceless treasure, hidden
      in a field which folk pass by;
one man finds it, knows its value,
      sells his all that field to buy;

like the merchant, fine pearls seeking,
      searches, yearning for the best;
finds it, clasps it, claims and buys it,
      selling all that he possessed.

Like all these is God's great kingdom,
    growing from the smallest part;
rising, swelling, coming, dwelling,
    in each new believer's heart.

697
Walking in a Garden

Walking in a garden
    at the close of day,
Adam tried to hide him
    when he heard God say:
"Why are you so frightened,
    why are you afraid?
You have brought the winter in,
    made the flowers fade."

Walking in a garden
    where the Lord had gone,
three of the disciples,
    Peter, James, and John;
they were very weary,
    could not keep awake,
while the Lord was kneeling there,
    praying for their sake.

Walking in a garden
    at the break of day,
Mary asked the gardener
    where the body lay;
but he turned towards her,
    smiled at her and said:
"Mary, spring is here to stay,
    only death is dead."

698
The People of God

"Moses, I know you're the man,"
    the Lord said.
"You're going to work out my plan,"
    the Lord said.
"Lead all the Israelites out of slavery,
and I shall make them a wandering race
    called the people of God."

So every day,
    we're on our way,
    for we're a traveling, wandering race,
    we're the people of God.

"Don't get too set in your ways;
each step is only a phase.
I'll go before you and I shall be a sign
to guide my traveling, wandering race;
    you're the people of God."

"No matter what you may do,
I shall be faithful and true.
My love will strengthen you as you go along,
for you're my traveling, wandering race,
    you're the people of God."

"Look at the birds in the air;
they fly unhampered by care.
You will move easier if you're traveling light,
for you're a wandering, vagabond race,
    you're the people of God."

"Foxes have places to go,
but I've no home here below.
So if you want to be with me all your days,
keep up the moving and traveling on,
    you're the people of God."

699
Who Can Sound the Depths of Sorrow

Who can sound the depths of sorrow
    in the Father heart of God,
for the children we've rejected,
    for the lives so deeply scarred?
And each light that we've extinguished
    has brought darkness to our land:
        Upon our nation, upon our nation
        have mercy, Lord!

We have scorned the truth you gave us,
    we have bowed to other lords,
we have sacrificed the children
    on the altars of our gods.
O let truth again shine on us,
    let your holy fear descend:
        Upon our nation, upon our nation
        have mercy, Lord!

Who can stand before your anger;
    who can face your piercing eyes?
For you love the weak and helpless,
    and you hear the victims' cries.
Yes, you are a God of justice,
    and your judgment surely comes:
        Upon our nation, upon our nation
        have mercy, Lord!

Who will stand against the violence?
    Who will comfort those who mourn?
In an age of cruel rejection,
    who will build for love a home?
Come and shake us into action,
    come and melt our hearts of stone:
        Upon your people, upon your people,
        have mercy, Lord!

Who can sound the depths of mercy
    in the Father heart of God?
For there is a Man of Sorrows
    who for sinners shed his blood.
He can heal the wounds of nations,
    he can wash the guilty clean:
        Because of Jesus, because of Jesus,
        have mercy, Lord!

Graham Kendrick, 1988
Let's Praise, Book 1, 1988
© 1988, Make Way Music
(admin. Music Services in the Western Hemisphere)
The first four lines of stanza 3 are marked by Kendrick to be sung by
men; the first four lines of stanza 4, by women.

700
Beauty for Brokenness

Beauty for brokenness,
    hope for despair,
Lord, in the suffering,
    this is our prayer:
Bread for the children,
    justice, joy, peace,
sunrise to sunset
your kingdom increase!

Shelter for fragile lives,
    cures for their ills,
work for the craftsmen,
    trade for their skills.
Land for the dispossessed,
    rights for the weak,
voices to plead the cause
of those who can't speak.

    God of the poor,
    friend of the weak,
    give us compassion we pray;
    melt our cold hearts,
    let tears fall like rain,
    come, change our love
    from a spark to a flame.

Refuge from cruel wars,
    havens from fear,
cities for sanctuary,
    freedoms to share.
Peace to the killing fields,
    scorched earth to green;
Christ for the bitterness,
his cross for the pain.

Rest for the ravaged earth,
    oceans and streams,
plundered and poisoned,
    our future, our dreams.
Lord, end our madness,
    carelessness, greed;
make us content with
the things that we need.

Lighten our darkness,
    breathe on this flame,
until your justice burns
    brightly again;
until the nations
    learn of your ways,
seek your salvation
and bring you their praise.

Graham Kendrick, 1993
Liturgical Hymns Old and New, 1999
© 1993, Make Way Music
(admin. Music Services in the Western Hemisphere)
The author intends the refrain to be sung after stanzas 2, 4, and 5.

701
Meekness and Majesty

Meekness and majesty,
manhood and deity
in perfect harmony—
    the man who is God:
Lord of eternity
dwells in humanity,
kneels in humility
    and washes our feet.

Oh, what a mystery—
    meekness and majesty:
      Bow down and worship,
    for this is your God,
    this is your God.

Father's pure radiance,
perfect in innocence,
yet learns obedience
    to death on a cross:
suffering to give us life,
conquering through sacrifice—
and, as they crucify,
    prays, "Father, forgive."

Wisdom unsearchable,
God the invisible,
love indestructible
    in frailty appears:
Lord of infinity,
stooping so tenderly,
lifts our humanity
    to the heights of his throne.

Graham Kendrick, 1986
Baptist Praise and Worship, 1991
© 1985, ThankYou Music (admin. EMI Christian Music Publishing)

702
The Summons

Will you come and follow me
    if I but call your name?
Will you go where you don't know
    and never be the same?
Will you let my love be shown,
will you let my name be known,
will you let my life be grown
    in you and you in me?

Will you leave yourself behind
    if I but call your name?
Will you care for cruel and kind
    and never be the same?
Will you risk the hostile stare
should your life attract or scare?
Will you let me answer prayer
    in you and you in me?

Will you let the blinded see
    if I but call your name?
Will you set the prisoners free
    and never be the same?
Will you kiss the leper clean,
and do such as this unseen,
and admit to what I mean
    in you and you in me?

Will you love the "you" you hide
    if I but call your name?
Will you quell the fear inside
    and never be the same?
Will you use the faith you've found
to reshape the world around,
through my sight and touch and sound
    in you and you in me?

Lord, your summons echoes true
    when you but call my name.
Let me turn and follow you
    and never be the same.
In your company I'll go
where your love and footsteps show.
Thus I'll move and live and grow
    in you and you in me.

John Bell and Graham Maule, 1987
Heaven Shall Not Wait, 1989
© 1987, Wild Goose Resource Group, Iona Community
(admin. GIA Publications, Inc.)

703
The Hand of Heaven

We who live by sound and symbol,
    we who learn from sight and word,
find these married in the person
    of the one we call our Lord.
Taking bread to be his body,
    taking wine to be his blood,
he let thought take flesh in action,
    he let faith take root in food.

Not just once with special people,
    not just hidden deep in time,
but wherever Christ is followed,
    earthly fare becomes sublime.
Beyond wisdom to interpret,
    beyond language to record,
yet in faith and in the mystery,
    we meet Jesus Christ our Lord.

God, our Maker, send your Spirit;
    consecrate the bread we break.
Let it bring the life we long for
    and the love which we forsake.
Bind us closer to each other,
    both forgiving and forgiven;
give us grace in this and all things
    to discern the hand of heaven.

John Bell and Graham Maule, 1989; revised, 1996
HymnQuest 2000
© 1989, Wild Goose Resource Group, Iona Community
(admin. GIA Publications, Inc.)

704
These I Lay Down

Before I take the body of my Lord,
before I share his life in bread and wine,
I recognize the sorry things within–
    These I lay down.

The words of hope I often failed to give,
the prayers of kindness buried by my pride,
the signs of care I argued out of sight:
    These I lay down.

The narrowness of vision and of mind,
the need for other folk to serve my will,
and every word and silence meant to hurt:
    These I lay down.

Of those around in whom I meet my Lord,
I ask their pardon and I grant them mine
that every contradiction to Christ's peace
    might be laid down.

Lord Jesus Christ, companion at this feast,
I empty now my heart and stretch my hands,
and ask to meet you here in bread and wine
    which you lay down.

John Bell and Graham Maule, 1989
Love from Below, 1989
© 1989, Wild Goose Resource Group, Iona Community
(admin. GIA Publications, Inc.)

705
We Cannot Measure How You Heal

We cannot measure how you heal
    or answer every sufferer's prayer,
yet we believe your grace responds
    where faith and doubt unite to care.
Your hands, though bloodied on the cross,
    survive to hold and heal and warn,
to carry all through death to life
    and cradle children yet unborn.

The pain that will not go away,
    the guilt that clings from things long past,
the fear of what the future holds,
    are present as if meant to last.
But present too is love which tends
    the hurt we never hoped to find,
the private agonies inside,
    the memories that haunt the mind.

So some have come who need your help
    and some have come to make amends,
as hands which shaped and saved the world
    are present in the touch of friends.
Lord, let your Spirit meet us here
    to mend the body, mind, and soul,
to disentangle peace from pain,
    and make your broken people whole.

John Bell and Graham Maule, 1989
Love from Below, 1989
© 1989, Wild Goose Resource Group, Iona Community
(admin. GIA Publications, Inc.)

706
Enemy of Apathy

She sits like a bird, brooding on the waters.
    Hovering on the chaos of the world's first day;
she sighs and she sings, mothering creation,
    waiting to give birth to all the Word will say.

She wings over earth, resting where she wishes,
    lighting close at hand or soaring through the
                  skies;
she nests in the womb, welcoming each wonder,
    nourishing potential hidden to our eyes.

She dances in fire, startling her spectators,
    waking tongues of ecstasy where dumbness
                  reigned;
she weans and inspires all whose hearts are open,
    nor can she be captured, silenced, or restrained.

For she is the Spirit, one with God in essence,
gifted by the Savior in eternal love;
she is the key opening the scriptures,
enemy of apathy and heavenly dove.

John Bell and Graham Maule, 1988
Enemy of Apathy, 1988
© 1988, Wild Goose Resource Group, Iona Community
(admin. GIA Publications, Inc.)

707

When the Son of God Was Dying

When the Son of God was dying, long ago,
some played dice and some knelt crying, lost and low.
Cynics sneered and wagged their tongues,
mockers mimicked funeral songs:
This, while God's own Son was dying, long ago.

Crowds which once had cried, "Hosanna!" lost
their voice:
Hell had grinned to hear Barabbas was their choice;
Judas hung himself for blame;
Peter hung his head in shame,
while the crowds which cried, "Hosanna!" lost
their voice.

Horror, hurt, and pain found home in Mary's breast
watching torture's toll and hearing soldiers jest:
Where was God to hear her cry?
Why should her own Jesus die?
Grief and agony found home in Mary's breast.

Humankind repeats Golgotha every day:
God gets gagged while friends and followers turn
away.
Profit threatens peace on earth,
greed to hunger gives new birth
as the world repeats Golgotha every day.

Jesus, lay your body in this sad earth's grave;
only one who suffers can presume to save.
End hypocrisy and lies,
through our apathy arise,
bring us the salvation which our spirits crave.

John Bell and Graham Maule, 1988
Enemy of Apathy, 1988
© 1988, Wild Goose Resource Group, Iona Community
(admin. GIA Publications, Inc.)

708

As Many Stones

As many stones, their edges rough, unhewn,
may by their awkward shape lend others strength,
build up your church, Lord Christ, so that at
length
the various shapes harmoniously attune,
and we are raised, a temple to your fame,
whose worship shall give glory to your name.

For not to the likeminded did you look
to make a church constructed of one kind,
but quite unlikely folk in heart and mind
to weld in one community you took
and raised them up, a temple to your fame,
whose worship shall give glory to your name.

Then grant us, Lord, in others to delight,
not those we like, but those now called by you;
with all our awkward edges strength imbue
that we give folk shelter, warmth, and light,
that we be raised a temple to your fame
whose worship will give glory to your name.

Ian M. Fraser, 1994
Common Ground, 1998
© 1994, Stainer & Bell Ltd. (admin. Hope Publishing Company)

709
Forgiveness Is Your Gift

Forgiveness is your gift,
both cleansing and renewing,
    to catch us when we drift,
our base desires pursuing;
    and hug us back to life
    and bring us to a feast
    where all will celebrate
    the life your love released.

Your grace goes out to meet
the sinful and the doubting,
    your arms and dancing feet
speak louder than all shouting:
    O God, how great your love
    which takes us empty in,
    and, with our worth unproved,
    lets better life begin.

Ian M. Fraser, 1994
Common Ground, 1998
© 1994, Stainer & Bell Ltd. (admin. Hope Publishing Company)

710
The God Who Sings

The God who sings
a new world into being shows the way
for many voices, varied gifts to sound
    in symphony.

The God who shouts
in fury when the powerful shame the poor
will break the chains, and those who hide in fear
    he will restore.

The God who weeps
when fields lie barren and the missiles fall
throws wide his arms and offers in his love
    refuge for all.

The God who laughs
as unexpected overturns routine
releases us to risk in faith, and find
    what joy can mean.

The God who calls
in hearts of those who hear his Chosen One
forgives, transforms, empowers, renews us while
    we journey on.

Douglas Galbraith, 1997
Common Ground, 1998
© Panel on Worship, Church of Scotland

711
Sing for God's Glory

Sing for God's glory that colors the dawn of creation,
racing across the sky, trailing bright clouds of elation;
        sun of delight
        succeeds the velvet of night,
    warming the earth's exultation.

Sing for God's power that shatters the chains that
            would bind us,
searing the darkness of fear and despair that could
            blind us,
        touching our shame
        with love that will not lay blame,
    reaching out gently to find us.

Sing for God's justice disturbing each easy illusion,
tearing down tyrants and putting our pride to
            confusion;
        lifeblood of right,
        resisting evil and slight,
    offering freedom's transfusion.

Sing for God's saints who have traveled faith's
journey before us,
who in our weariness give us their hope to restore us;
in them we see
the new creation to be,
spirit of love made flesh for us.

Kathy Galloway, 1991
Common Ground, 1998
© Kathy Galloway

712

Come and Gather Round

Says Jesus, "Come and gather round.
I want to teach my friends
some truths about the love I bring,
the love that never ends.
Look to the child, here in your midst,
who has so much and more to say
of what it means to follow me,
to come and walk my way."

Christ speaks to us who, growing old,
get burdened down with care;
while caution reigns, we seldom see
God's presence everywhere.
He points to gifts that children bring—
the will to risk, the trust to dare,
through which, no matter where we are,
we'll find God always there.

When was it that we first forgot
that questions helped us grow,
or lost the openness to ask
and learn what we don't know?
Christ points to gifts that children bring,
the searching heart and lively mind
which let God's kingdom grow in those
who seek until they find.

Lord Jesus, we have gathered round
to hear you teach your friends
the truths about the love you bring,
the love which never ends.
We look to children in our midst
for they have much and more to say
and join with them to follow you,
to live and walk your way.

Leith Fisher, 1987; revised, 1997
based on Matthew 18:1–6
Common Ground, 1998
© Panel on Worship, Church of Scotland

713

We Lay Our Broken World

We lay our broken world
in sorrow at your feet,
haunted by hunger, war, and fear,
oppressed by power and hate,

where human life seems less
than profit, might, and pride:
Though to unite us all in you,
you lived and loved and died.

We bring our broken hopes
for lives of dignity;
workless and overworked you love,
and call us to be free.

We bring our broken loves,
friends parted, families torn;
then in your life and death we see
that love must be reborn.

We bring our broken selves,
confused and closed and tired;
then through your gift of healing grace
new purpose is inspired.

Come fill us, Fire of God,
our life and strength renew;
find in us love and hope and trust,
and lift us up to you.

Anna Briggs, 1984
Common Praise, 1998
© 1985, Anna Briggs

714

How the World Longs for Your Birth

How the world longs for your birth,
bearing news of human worth;
to our labor bring your mirth:
Maranatha, come, Lord, come.

How the earth awaits your seed,
parched and barren from our greed;
now to hallow it we need:
Maranatha, come, Lord, come.

How we ache to know your peace;
wars and weapons still increase;
bid our fears and hate to cease:
Maranatha, come, Lord, come.

How our minds for healing long,
broken bodies to be strong,
wounded hearts to learn your song:
Maranatha, come, Lord, come.

God, who sets your people free,
God, who comes, our flesh to be,
now we wait, your reign to see:
Maranatha, come, Lord, come.

To our darkness bring your light;
fill our longing eyes with sight.
In our lives shine ever bright:
Maranatha, come, Lord, come.

Anna Briggs, 1987
Common Praise, 1998
© 1987, Anna Briggs

715

Stay, My Child

Stay, my child, my body sharing,
girlhood's peace from me is torn;
well I know a mother's fearing,
hope miscarried, joy stillborn;
lullaby, lullaby,
God has heard a mother's cry,
lullaby.

Grow, my child, in body chosen
by the God who made the earth;
mine the answer, in confusion,
young, unready to give birth;
lullaby, lullaby,
God awaits a baby's cry,
lullaby.

Sleep, my child, for love surrounds us;
we have not been left alone.
Though disgrace and shame may hound us,
Joseph stays and shields his own;
lullaby, lullaby,
Word of God in baby's cry,
lullaby.

Wake, my child, the world is crying,
calls you, evil's power to cross;
opens you to early dying,
motherhood's most dreaded loss;
lullaby, lullaby,
pain of God in mother's cry,
lullaby.

Go, my child, God's grace protect you,
    shape your living, fill your breath;
by its power to resurrect you,
    break the grip of fear and death.
        Lullaby, lullaby,
hope for all in mother's cry,
        lullaby.

Anna Briggs, 1987
Faith Will Sing, 1993
© 1992, Hope Publishing Company

God, give us peace and, more than this,
show us the path where justice is;
and let us never be remiss
    working for peace that lasts.

Carnwadric Parish Church (Glasgow) Worship Group
aided by John Bell and Mairi Munro
Common Ground, 1998
© Carnwadric Parish Church (Glasgow) Worship Group

716

What Shall We Pray

What shall we pray for those who died,
those on whose death our lives relied?
Silenced by war but not denied,
    God give them peace.

What shall we pray for those who mourn
friendships and love, their fruit unborn?
Though years have passed, hearts still are torn;
    God give them peace.

What shall we pray for those who live
tied to the past they can't forgive,
haunted by terrors they relive?
    God give them peace.

What shall we pray for those who know
nothing of war, and cannot show
grief or regret for friend or foe?
    God give them peace.

What shall we pray for those who fear
war, in some guise, may reappear
looking attractive and sincere?
    God give them peace.

Chapter 30:
The United States, 1976–2000
(717–846)

The hymns of the British "explosion" were welcomed widely in the United States. Indeed, because US publishers produced a generation of new hymnals somewhat ahead of their English counterparts, many of the texts of Fred Pratt Green, Brian Wren, and Fred Kaan appeared in large books in the United States before receiving similar exposure in the United Kingdom. Stimulated by the accomplishments of these hymnists and encouraged by American publishers eager for new material, numerous writers in the United States began to produce new hymns. Though there was no explosion in the United States, there has been, since about 1970, sustained productivity and rich variety, displaying the diversity characteristic of American society and church life.

In the decades since 1970, American denominational and nondenominational publishing houses have issued a multitude of new hymnals. Every lineage has produced a new generation, and some have published two or more books during this span. These larger books have often been preceded—and, in many cases, followed—by supplements. Some of the smaller books were attempts to keep up with changes in repertory and the flood of new hymns. Others were aimed at particular parts of the church or aspects of its ministry.

Hymnals produced between 1960 and 1980 generally had short lives, caught as they were in a time of great change in which it was difficult to discern in what direction(s) worship and congregational song were moving. Thus, *The Book of Hymns* (United Methodist, 1966), *Hymnbook for Christian Worship* (American Baptist and Christian Church, Disciples of Christ, 1970), *The Worshipbook* (Cumberland Presbyterian Church, Presbyterian Church in the US, Presbyterian Church in the USA, 1970), *Hymns for the Living Church* (nondenominational, Hope, 1974), *The Hymnal of the United Church of Christ* (1974), and *Baptist Hymnal* (Southern Baptist, 1975) were all succeeded by new books before the end of the century.

Two books from the second half of the 1970s indicated new trends. *Hymns for the Family of God* (nondenominational, Paragon, 1976) included a significant number of choruses and songs from entertainment-oriented sources and interspersed spoken worship materials with hymns. *Lutheran Book of Worship* (Inter-Lutheran Commission on Worship, 1978) gave attention to the changing language of worship, particularly with respect to the replacement of archaic and noninclusive language through new translations, editorial alterations, and addition of new materials. Both of these books, reflecting the increased visual emphasis of the media, gave greater attention to the attractiveness of page design and the use of simple graphics.

Like its predecessor of the 1940s, *The Hymnal 1982* (Episcopal, 1985) became a standard of reference for editors in other traditions, by reflecting long and thoughtful deliberation about liturgical use and aesthetic quality, coupled with a conscious broadening of style and careful revisions to remove archaisms and promote inclusion. The release in the same year of *Rejoice in the Lord* (Reformed Church in America) might not have had such a great impact, given the small size of its sponsoring denomination, had it not been for the fact that Erik Routley had guided the editorial process. Its organization following the canonical order of the Scriptures helped to heighten awareness of the connection between the Bible and congregational song, a trend in this period. Also influential was *Westminster Praise* (1976), a small collection that Routley edited for use in the chapel at the choir college whose faculty he joined in 1975. Among the other large hymnals issued during the early and mid-1980s were *Lutheran Worship* (Missouri Synod, 1982), *The Hymnal for Worship and Celebration* (nondenominational, Word, 1986), and *Psalter Hymnal* (Christian Reformed, 1987).

The years around 1990 brought several significant collections, including *The United Methodist Hymnal* (1989), *The Presbyterian Hymnal* (Presbyterian Church, USA, 1990), *The Worshiping Church* (nondenominational, Hope, 1990), *The Baptist Hymnal* (Southern Baptist, 1991), *Hymnal: A Worship Book* (Church of the Brethren, General Conference Mennonite Church, Mennonite Church in North America, 1992), and *A New Hymnal for Colleges and Schools* (nondenominational, Yale University Press, 1992). To differing degrees, these books contain a generous number of hymns from the British "explosion," recent American writers, and the growing body of world hymnody (see chapter 32) that is being shared in English translation. These trends continued in another cluster of important books that appeared in 1995: *Chalice Hymnal* (Christian Church, Disciples of Christ), *Moravian Book of Worship*, and *The New Century Hymnal* (United Church of Christ). The latter, "boldly committed to a spirit of inclusiveness," made extensive textual revisions and commissioned many new translations to meet its objectives. Though many other books were issued to serve the wide range of denominations in the United States and the various strands of congregational life, they did not contribute significantly to the expansion of repertory characteristic of the period.

Certain growing areas can be perceived from the supplements that preceded and followed the larger collections. In 1981, two denominations issued volumes that drew from and were focused on African-American congregations: *Songs of Zion* (United Methodist) and *Lift Every Voice and Sing* (Episcopal). A second volume of the latter was published in 1993. *Lutheran Book of Worship*, as one of the earlier books of the new generation, had attracted three supplements by 1995. Two of these, *Songs of the People* (1986), a small book that contains mostly ethnic materials, and *With One Voice* (1995), came from the denominational publishing house, while the third, *Hymnal Supplement 1991*, was produced by GIA

Publications. The range of materials for Episcopal worship was expanded in *Wonder, Love, and Praise* (1997). To complement *Lutheran Worship*, the Missouri Synod published *Hymnal Supplement 98*. In 1999, the two large Lutheran bodies published a collection featuring African-American resources, *This Far by Faith*.

The increasing number of persons in the United States who speak Spanish has prompted the publication of several hymnals in that language, some of which include bilingual hymnody. These include *El Pueblo de Dios Canta* (Evangelical Lutheran, 1989), *Flor y Canto* (Roman Catholic, OCP Publications, 1989), *Mil Voces para Celebrar* (United Methodist, with participation by the Christian Church, Disciples of Christ, 1996), *¡Cantad al Señor!* (Lutheran, Missouri Synod, 1991), *Libro de Liturgia y Cantico* (Evangelical Lutheran, 1998), and *El Himnario* (Episcopal, 1998; also published as *El Himnario Presbiteriano* by the Presbyterian Church, USA, and as *Himnario Unido* by the United Church of Christ). In 1992, United Methodists issued *Voices*, a collection of Native American worship materials.

The contributions to the development of new hymnody in the United States by three publishers and one organization are notable. Hope Publishing Company has handled the North American issue of volumes by many of the leading British writers, in addition to those of Canadian Margaret Clarkson and New Zealander Shirley Erena Murray, as well as those by many hymnists in the United States. It has also produced several smaller anthologies, including *Ecumenical Praise* (1977), *Hymnal Supplement* (1984), *Hymnal Supplement II* (1987), *100 Hymns of Hope* (1992), *Supplement 96*, and *Supplement 99*. Selah Publishing Company has produced a number of single-author collections and the anthologies *Songs of Rejoicing* (1989), *New Songs of Rejoicing* (1994), and *Sing to Our God New Songs of Rejoicing* (2000). GIA Publications has made available to North American worshipers the work of both the Taizé and Iona communities, in addition to producing collections by individual writers. The Hymn Society in the United States and Canada (formerly the Hymn Society of America) has encouraged new hymns through its hymn searches and hymn-writing workshops, and has promoted their distribution by the publication of *Holding in Trust* (1992), an anthology of the best texts in which it had a hand.

The new directions in worship that emerged from the Second Vatican Council prompted the compilation of a wide variety of books to enable congregational singing in the Roman Catholic liturgy. As there is no official hymnal among American Catholics, this new arena attracted a number of publishers with differing approaches. Some found freedom and excitement in songs modeled after the folk and popular styles current at the time of the council. Others valued the legacy of the monastics and of traditional devotion, alongside the hymns of the Reformation churches. These approaches were combined in mediating ways as well.

The third edition of *Worship* (GIA, 1986) became the defining collection among American Catholics who claimed the historic hymnody of the Western church, adding to it distinctive materials for Catholic liturgy in a variety of styles. This edition succeeded and expanded earlier issues of 1971 and 1975. It was complemented by a collection of less-formal congregational song, *Gather* (1988; 2nd ed., 1994). These bodies of literature were combined in different proportions in *Gather Comprehensive* (1994), weighted toward the folk idiom, and *RitualSong* (1996), with more hymns in traditional style, as well as a significant amount of new material. To meet specific needs among Catholics, GIA also issued *Lead Me, Guide Me* (1987), a collection for African-American worshipers, and *Hymnal for the Hours* (1989).

Beginning in 1977 the *Glory and Praise* volumes (North American Liturgy Resources, subsequent issues in 1980, 1982, 1983, 1987, 1989, 1990, and 1997) provided another series of books for

Catholics whose worship featured styles influenced by popular culture. This tradition was incorporated into *JourneySongs* (OCP, 1994), which supplemented the main body of material with more traditional hymnody, following the integration of NALR with Oregon Catholic Press.

The *People's Mass Book* (World Library Publications), continuing the line begun in the *People's Hymnal* (first edition, 1955), went through several editions (1964, 1966, 1970, 1974), reaching its culmination in 1984. Another merger of publishers brought these books together with the *We Celebrate* collections (J. S. Paluch, 1976, 1980, 1982, 1986, 1990, 1994, 1997). The *Collegeville Hymnal* (Liturgical Press, 1990) was the successor to the series of *Our Parish Prays and Sings* (1958, 1965, 1966, 1967, 1971) and *Book of Sacred Song* (1977).

Though there often were dramatic differences between the new hymnals and those of the previous generation, there were also strong links in such matters as denominational, liturgical, and ethnic traditions. The connection was personified in the work of F. Bland Tucker. In his long and productive career, he contributed to the formation of hymnals for the Episcopal church in the 1940s (see 549–552) and 1980s. His translations and paraphrases offer worshipers access to biblical and historic sources. Ephesians 5:14, itself probably a fragment of a hymn from the early church, supplies the opening line of 717, which draws phrases from other portions of that letter. The presence of the Holy Spirit in Jesus' baptism and ours is the theme of 718. Tucker crafted 719 from Howard Rhys's literal translation of an Easter text by the fourth-century writer, Ephrem of Edessa, the most prolific hymnist of Syria. While reducing the length of the original, Rhys and Tucker managed to preserve the richness of New Testament allusions that characterize the original.

Another pastor-poet who was productive over a long career was Finnish-born Frank von Christierson, a Presbyterian. Several of his hymns were written in response to searches sponsored by what was at that time the Hymn Society of America. One of these,

720, invites the guidance of the Spirit in shaping prayers that direct service. Methodist pastor William Watkins Reid, Jr., contributed numerous texts to searches conducted by the Hymn Society, in which he and his father, also a hymn writer, were active. Two of his hymns written in the 1950s, "O God of every nation" and "Help us, O Lord, to learn," have appeared in a sufficient number of collections to warrant inclusion in the *Hymnal Guide*. His more recent writing is exemplified by 721, commissioned for *The United Methodist Hymnal*. Its inner stanzas use female images to express God's compassion for wayward children.

Herbert Brokering, a Lutheran minister and prolific writer, produced in 722 a modern *"Benedicite"* that shows the beginning of the shift in the worship language of American churches in the 1960s. The scenery and activity reflect its commission for the ninetieth birthday of St. Olaf College. The present version includes the final stanza that he added for *Lutheran Worship* (1981) to make a more complete theological statement. One of the earlier hymns to employ the language of the space age successfully is 723 by Catherine Cameron. It endures because the author, a Canadian-born professor of sociology, also captured the ambiguous implications of scientific advance.

Lutheran pastor and editor Jaroslav Vajda has had continued success in creative poetic forms. Like his earlier "Now" (556), 724 offers imaginative space through its use of powerful word images and lack of punctuation. The alternate words for the fourth and fifth stanzas were provided by Vajda to suit particular musical settings. Three sets of biblical triads are interwoven in 725, whereas it is a series of three gardens that provides the structure of 726. This fondness for threes is also seen in 727, which relates the parables of losing and finding from Luke 15 in intimate language and unrhymed stanzas before a more typical conclusion. The Aaronic benediction is presented as though God were speaking in 728. Vajda has also made effec-

tive translations from Slavic languages, such as the New Year's carol at 729, opening a way to Christian traditions largely unsung in English-speaking churches.

Jane Parker Huber writes with consistent concern for inclusion, mutuality of men and women in ministry, and peacemaking—aspects of the church's mission on which she has worked in the Presbyterian Church (USA). Fit to LOBE DEN HERREN, 730 articulates these themes and makes effective application of the rainbow image in stanza 4. The continuing activity of God is expressed in Trinitarian structure, but without traditional names, in 731. Multiple biblical references to peace are juxtaposed with the injustices of the world in 732 to bring into focus the need for peacemaking.

Presbyterian elder Edith Sinclair Downing came to hymn writing with a background in church music and campus ministry. Justice and compassion for those who suffer are prominent themes in her texts, which declare the character of God in sweeping terms and striking names. The depth of divine forgiveness, including compassion for those affected by substance abuse, is proclaimed in 733, with its remarkable title-phrases for the Deity. Similar appellations for God are presented in 734, which also displays her ability to use form and rhythm in a way that is both powerful and intimate. In 735, the story of the Ethiopian eunuch becomes an opportunity to see God's radical inclusiveness.

The distinguished African-American scholar and poet C. Eric Lincoln wrote 736 in response to a request by the committee preparing *The United Methodist Hymnal* for hymns with new language for God. Lincoln's images for divinity are expansive and evocative. The contrast between the human sin of exclusion and a holy and inclusive God has been muted by the substitution of the mild adjective, "fretful," for the author's original and more potent "noxious."

Jean Wiebe Janzen, born in Saskatchewan, is a Mennonite poet and teacher of writing. For *Hymnal: A Worship Book*, she wrote three superb texts based on writings of women in Christian history. Built on Mechtild of Magdeburg (1210–1297) is 737, with its intimate and shifting portrayals of "Love." The poetry of Hildegard of Bingen (1098–1179) is the background of 738, with its active images of the Spirit that offer access to all three persons of the Trinity. Maternal aspects of the Trinity are taken from Julian of Norwich (1342–ca. 1417) in 739.

English-born Bryan Jeffrey Leech, a pastor in the Evangelical Covenant Church, wrote 740 for *Hymns for the Family of God*, of which he was assistant editor. In parallel stanzas it adds the image of rain to the more familiar ones from Acts, concluding each with a personalizing refrain. Written to the opening theme from the final movement of Brahms's first symphony, 741 is a mosaic of New Testament images of the church.

Rae Whitney, also born in England, was a lay preacher in Baptist, Methodist, and Congregationalist churches before becoming an Anglican, marrying an Episcopal priest, and moving to the United States. Many of her hymns are steeped in the language of historical worship. This is readily seen in her confessional prayer for Ash Wednesday (742), with its lines from the *Book of Common Prayer*. The parables of Luke 15 are the substance of 743, with its insistent affirmation of God's activity in saving the lost (compare the different perspective and tone in Vajda's treatment at 727). Whitney's writing spans a range of styles, from the short, almost breathless, lines of 744 to the balladlike 745, with its traditional conflation of figures in the Gospels. The paradoxical relationship between incarnation and passion provides the structure of 746. Perhaps her most brilliant fusion of vocabulary, imagery, and structure is found in 747, with its roots in the writings of Ephrem the Syrian.

Jeffery Rowthorn, a native of Wales, came to the United States to accept a series of academic positions before becoming Episcopal Bishop Suffragan of Connecticut. He subsequently moved to Paris as Bishop of the American Convocation of Churches in Europe, then returned to the United States in retirement. His hymns display a fondness for parallel statements, rich with biblical content. This is seen in his paraphrase of Psalm 148 at 748, with its memorable phrase for the world that is the object of God's love: "one family with a billion names." A similar structure is seen in 749, where quotations from Jesus that set the agenda for the church's mission lead to a refrain invoking the gifts of the Spirit. Rowthorn was coeditor, with Russell Schulz-Widmar (b. 1944), of *A New Hymnal for Colleges and Schools*, which includes 750, with its parallel imperatives.

Thomas H. Troeger holds degrees in both literature and divinity and is an accomplished flutist. Cognizant of the role of music in interpreting a text, he has often collaborated with composers in writing hymns, an approach that was particularly significant in two collections done with Carol Doran (b. 1936), who was for many years Troeger's teaching colleague. Ordained first as a Presbyterian and more recently as an Episcopalian, he has distinguished himself as a preacher and teacher of preaching. He has often taken a homiletical approach in hymn writing, as in 751, which applies the insight of "Doubting" Thomas to the limits of human perception. This text shows Troeger's ability to maintain and manipulate an image or metaphor across multiple stanzas. Another text written as an adjunct to the common lectionary is 752, with its vivid connection between the man healed of demons by Jesus and our own anguish and mental illness. In his meditation on Jesus' statement of the first and greatest commandment, 753, Troeger honestly reflects the ways in which we attempt to bargain with God. A series of complementary images is used in 754, which grew from a Sunday school lesson for children based on Ephesians 2. That text's "fisted minds" displays his ability to devise an image that communicates on multiple levels.

Troeger often uses alliteration, as in his Pentecost hymn at 755. Many of his texts, such as 756, have long thoughts that extend across many lines. Each stanza of this hymn for interfaith worship is one long sentence. The conscious and effective use in his writing of a wide range of poetic devices demonstrates his belief that hymns can be intellectually and aesthetically challenging. In writing 757 on commission for *The United Methodist Hymnal*, Troeger limited himself to biblical names and images for God, using these to demonstrate that we need not diminish the mystery of God by restricting vocabulary. The range of Troeger's writing extends to such difficult issues as sexual abuse, addressed in 758, with its refrain of affirmation surrounding stanzas that acknowledge the traumas of the experience. Another type of societal concern is seen in 759, an expression of ecological responsibility for God's creation.

Before he became an Episcopal priest, Carl P. Daw, Jr., was a professor of English. His hymn writing began during his service as a consultant to the text committee for *The Hymnal 1982*. From his background in literature and theology, Daw brings a keen awareness of biblical, historical, liturgical, and literary precedents, as displayed in the notes that accompany the texts in the collections of his work. Accordingly, he has produced skillful paraphrases of biblical and liturgical texts, as well as new hymns for particular functions in worship. His version of the first song of Isaiah, 760, takes its first line from the *Book of Common Prayer*, while paying homage to Dudley-Smith's *Magnificat* (501) in the second line of stanza two. His Good Friday hymn, 761, conveys the magnitude of this event with the gravity of Watts, even as it alludes to Shakespeare and Donne. Daw has also prepared effective new versions of "*Wachet auf*" (188C) and "*Phos hilaron.*"

Written for the installation of Jeffery Rowthorn as Bishop Suffragan of Connecticut, 762 is rich historically and theologically, and is in a form reminiscent of Rowthorn's own penchant for parallel statement. This structure is employed to great effect in 763, with its stanzas about the how, where, and why of the Spirit's coming, each leading to a refrain invoking the Spirit's presence. Daw's

ability to perceive deeper meaning in biblical stories, more or less familiar, is seen in 764, with its evocative titles for Jesus, and 765, which connects the singer to Simon, the bearer of Jesus' cross.

Daw is particularly effective when contemplating the God beyond human conception, as in 766. In dealing with the ways in which this matter is entangled with gender-bound language for God, he has written texts that are challenging (767) and pastoral (768). Since 1996, Daw has been Executive Director of The Hymn Society in the United States and Canada.

A significant portion of the output of Daw and Troeger, the two most widely published hymnists from the United States, is directly related to specific passages of Scripture. Both have written with the intent to make the church's song more biblical, particularly in relation to the Christian year and the Revised Common Lectionary. This interest in reinforcing the link between hymnody and Scripture, often for homiletical purposes, is also seen in the work of several other writers, particularly Herman Stuempfle and Richard Leach.

Like Fred Pratt Green, Herman G. Stuempfle, Jr., became a hymn writer in retirement. He brings to his work a lifelong interest in words, developed in his roles as Lutheran pastor, professor of preaching, and seminary president. He often makes creative links between passages of Scripture, as in 769, which juxtaposes Psalm 107 with words from Jesus. His hymn on garden scenes in the Bible, 770, uses an intriguing turn of phrase and the poetic testimony of nature to make the essential theological points. (See other recent texts using similar patterns at 697 and 726). As an effective preacher must, Stuempfle discovers varied insights and presents in different styles. On this point, it is instructive to compare two of his hymns on the sovereignty of Jesus over nature, one direct and extroverted (771), the other more contemplative (772) with its acknowledgment of the question that arises in the minds of many hearers.

This willingness to ask aloud those questions usually whispered in church—and to respond with equally honest faith—is another mark of Stuempfle's writing. Embracing an evolutionary view of human origins, in 773 he declares, with Colossians 1:17, that all things cohere in Christ. Prompted by the writing of John Macquarrie, Stuempfle considers the possibility of life elsewhere in the universe in 774 (compare Sydney Carter's text at 522). A number of Stuempfle's texts express intimacy with God and, in so doing, show God's compassion. An example is 775, based on John 3, with insights from Kierkegaard. The maternal love of God is conveyed in 776, his treatment of Psalm 131. This same personal style is also contained in some fine devotional hymns, such as 777 and 778, both of which incorporate the experiences of those who encountered Jesus.

Richard Leach, formerly a pastor in the United Church of Christ, now a Lutheran layperson, has written numerous homiletical hymns, many interpreting lectionary passages that lacked related texts for singing. One of the more creative of these is 779, which, in relating the story of Baalam's ass, conveys an important message about the role of Spirit in the church. The more familiar story of the temptations of Jesus is connected with other events in his ministry in 780 (note that there are two versions, with one suited to Mark's particular presentation). Leach is equally effective in dealing with passages, such as the Annunciation, on which many have preceded him. His retelling at 781 conveys both the exuberance and the depth of commitment contained in Mary's response. The strong rhythm of the phrases obviates the need for end rhymes, much in the manner of James Quinn.

A similar rhythmic drive and an unexpected rhyme within the short final line of each stanza provide an intriguing shape in 782. With its form determined by the sequence of candle lighting for Advent and Christmas, this text is rich in insight and concludes with a lyrical stanza for Christmas day. An otherwise hackneyed phrase is given new meaning in 783, which forges new connections between Gospel stories within its tight structure.

United Methodist pastor John Thornburg has demonstrated an ability to present fresh perspectives. His text at 784 challenges us to see God in the ordinary and with the poor and oppressed. The last stanza captures the discouragement of those who have found little assistance in their plight. Structure, vocabulary, and imagery are joined in a striking way in 785. John A. Dalles is a Presbyterian pastor. In 786 he uses the analogy of gardening to illustrate the ways in which hope, justice, and mercy must be nurtured to produce peace. Repeated first and last lines based on Esther 4:14 form a frame for the questions of 787, which pose opportunities for ministries of caring.

Ruth C. Duck, a UCC pastor, teaches worship and has written several books about liturgy. Her concern for inclusive language in worship was evident as early as *Because We Are One People* (1974), produced by the Ecumenical Women's Center, and *Everflowing Streams* (1981), which she coedited with Michael Bausch (b. 1949). One of the texts written for the first collection, and since revised, is 788, which, in taking a different tack from Ernest Shurtleff's "Lead on, O King eternal," develops the biblical imagery more consistently. Duck's first published hymn, 789, collates an array of references from Isaiah under the theme from that book's sixtieth chapter. Many of her texts combine biblical metaphors with sensory images, as in 790. It is interesting to compare this hymn with Bland Tucker's translation from the *Didache* (552).

Though she is less likely than Troeger to focus on a single passage, Duck is skilled in linking Scripture with experience by means of lively word pictures. The series of penetrating questions in 791 presents God's compassion in such a way as to close the gap between thought and feeling, as well as that between the time of the Bible and today. The trilogy of images in 792, "as large as space, as small as cells, as deep as grace," helps worshipers in a scientific age to perceive the miraculous in creation. Duck uses a variety of gender-connected images in 793 to present the Trinity through words that include the traditional alongside the less familiar. Her interest in contemporary liturgical expression is seen in her treatments of historic hymns, such as the versions of *"Magnificat"* and *"Benedictus"* found in *The New Century Hymnal*.

Several other writers from the United Church of Christ have produced distinctive hymns that address a wide range of topics in diverse styles. This denomination has also, in *The New Century Hymnal*, been the most assertive and consistent in revising hymns to align them with its stated objectives for ministry and for language in worship. This effort included not only extensive revision, but also new translations of many historic texts, notably by Madeleine Forell Marshall. An example of her work can be seen at 199C.

Ronald S. Cole-Turner, a UCC theologian, published 794 in *Everflowing Streams*. Dosia Carlson is a UCC minister known for her work with those who are disabled. The concerns of these persons, and her own experience, are given voice in 795. A strong—and to some, disturbing—prophetic note is struck is 796, written for a Hymn Society search for texts at the time of the U.S. bicentennial. Its particular combination of historical perspective and contemporary awareness with biblical imagery and ethics is unique.

Devotional writer and UCC pastor Mary Nelson Keithan is concerned that hymns be both biblical and accessible to worshipers of all ages. Much of her work is in collaboration with tune writer John Horman (b. 1946). Her text at 797 looks for a word of peace from God in response to the turmoil of war, inner struggle, and difficult relationships. James Gertmenian appropriated the dominant image of 798 from Job 7:6 to interpret the providence of God in human life. His Lenten text, at 799, traces the inner journey through a series of images for new life. Another pastor in the UCC, James K. Manley, is known for his songs in

folk style, such as 800, a text addressed to the Holy Spirit. Its stanzas recount the actions of the Spirit, while the refrain, with which his own setting begins, is an invocation of the Spirit's presence.

Omer Westendorf was a lay leader in the development of new hymnody for Roman Catholics both before and after the Second Vatican Council. Toward that end, he founded World Library Publications and edited *The People's Hymnal* and the *People's Mass Book*, writing under several pseudonyms to disguise his large contribution to those books. As "Richard Wing" he wrote 801 for the 1976 International Eucharistic Congress in Philadelphia, drawing on the Gospel of John and 1 Corinthians 10. The dismissal hymn at 802 first appeared as the work of "J. Clifford Evers." It has appeared in numerous versions, adapted by editors to fit different understandings of the Lord's table. Both of these texts are suited to the regular participation of the faithful in the Eucharist advocated by the council. Westendorf's translation of *"Ubi caritas,"* "Where charity and love prevail," is also widely used.

Alan Hommerding, a Roman Catholic composer and editor, is, in many ways, an heir of Westendorf. The inner stanzas of 803 follow the lectionary readings through the Sundays of Lent, as the assembly makes the pilgrimage from Ash Wednesday to Easter. In his Lenten hymn at 804, John Patrick Earls, a Benedictine monk and professor of English, has provided imaginative imagery and names for the Trinity.

The most successful American Catholic writer in traditional hymnic forms is Delores Dufner, OSB. She typically writes to well-known tunes and sees her task as developing the identity of contemporary Christian community in relation to Scripture and tradition. The ancient hymns by Fortunatus, *"Vexilla regis"* and *"Pange lingua"* (with its fragment, *"Crux fidelis,"* see 156), as well as Galatians 6:14, lie behind 805. The sweep of God's creative work, which finds its fullness in Jesus, is the focus of 806, with its elegant pattern linking life, wisdom, and God in the Eternal Christ concluding each stanza.

Miriam Therese Winter became known first through her recordings in popular style with the Medical Mission Sisters and subsequently as a teacher and writer about liturgy and music. She is an articulate advocate for ecology, feminism, and justice. Her versification of the *"Magnificat,"* "My soul gives glory to my God," is widely published. At 807 is her rendering of the Song of Hannah, on which Mary's canticle is based.

David Haas is one of the leading Roman Catholic composers of music in an informal idiom for the liturgy. A well-known example of his style is 808, a setting of the Beatitudes with a joyful refrain. Haas has often been linked, in style and practice, and in shared leadership, with Marty Haugen, who has served both Catholic and Protestant congregations. Haugen's gathering song at 809 is simultaneously an inclusive invitation to participate and an invocation. Similarly energetic is 810, with a response that calls for mercy, peace, and justice in response to stanzas that build on the metaphors of Jesus for his followers. His Lenten hymn, 811, uses a structure like that of Hommerding's 803, providing stanzas for the Sundays of the season.

Liturgical scholar and priest Michael Joncas is also identified with the folk style of Catholic worship music. His most widely known piece is 812, originally a solo, with stanzas from Psalm 91 and a refrain based on Exodus 19:4. Structure, multiple names for love, and the homophones in the refrain all provide interest in 813. Daniel L. Schutte, formerly a Jesuit priest, now a layperson, is the author and composer of 814. A call to service, with connections to the story of Samuel and the call of Isaiah 6, this text is a dramatic dialogue that is intriguing, though sometimes misunderstood by worshipers.

The folk idiom has proven particularly effective for relating biblical stories in ballad style. This can be seen in the work of writers as varied as Haugen

and Stuempfle (771). Three of the better-known pieces in this style are by female writers. Suzanne Toolan, SM, is a church musician who wrote the text of 815 several years after composing the tune as a setting for another writer's text. She names women who followed Jesus, as well as the male disciples who left their work to respond to his call. Her setting of verses from the sixth chapter of John's Gospel, "I am the bread of life," is well known. Linda Wilberger Egan, a church musician who has served in several communions, wrote both text and tune of 816, a ballad about women in the Gospels. In a similar style is 817, by Jan Wesson. This retelling of Jesus' story about the Good Samaritan was written for a search for children's hymns conducted by the Hymn Society.

Jane Manton Marshall, celebrated for her work as a composer, conductor, and teacher, has also demonstrated significant gifts as a hymnist. The text at 818 affirms faith in God who is not only beyond the horizons of various facets of human experience but is also the Maker of these means of perception. A similar pattern of itemization in the final line of each stanza provides the structure of 819, an insightful ordination hymn that includes female and male models of servanthood as it balances challenge and encouragement. In an anniversary hymn for her own United Methodist congregation (820), Marshall raises a question that is real as well as rhetorical, and answers with thanks not only for the past and present, but also, as obedient faith, for the future. Another United Methodist writer and composer, Natalie Sleeth, is known primarily because of her works for children. In 821 she presents engaging and affirming images of death and life that are at once accessible to persons of all ages.

Joy F. Patterson writes both texts and tunes and has served the Presbyterian Church (USA) on several committees in the areas of worship and hymnody. The need and hope for peace in a violent world is a frequent theme in her hymns. Two of these—822, based on passages in Isaiah, and 823, drawing from John's apocalyptic writings—connect the visions of biblical figures to contemporary society. Particularly powerful is 824, which affirms God's presence in seemingly senseless suffering.

Another text that rests social ministry on a biblical foundation—in this case, the Model Prayer—is 825, by Milburn Price, a Baptist musician and educator, who is joint author (with William J. Reynolds and David Music, in various editions) of a widely used hymnology textbook. This hymn, with its message that mission is more than superficial, was written in response to a Hymn Society search. Mary Kay Beall is an American Baptist minister, writer, and editor, whose interest in the relationship between contemporary culture and worship led to a master's thesis. Her concern for children in this society prompted 826, which identifies their plight with the experiences of Jesus.

The hymn writing of United Methodist minister Daniel Charles (Dan) Damon is often light in texture, but substantial in thought. A pastor, he has empathy for persons in difficult situations. A jazz pianist, he writes in forms that leave space for imagination. A theologian, he probes beyond the surface. A singer, he often composes graceful melodies for his own texts. His fondness for short lines is nowhere more evident than in 827, which eschews the usual capitalization to represent the profound simplicity of its message. In 828 Damon names four of five physical senses, but also points to that essential means of perception for the believer, faith. That the mystery of God is the image in which we are made becomes the basis for awe, humility, and respect of others in 829.

Another pastor who writes both texts and tunes is Howard M. (Rusty) Edwards, III. He interweaves personal reflection, his Lutheran inheritance, and biblical teaching in 830, with its evocative metaphors for faith. The actions and objects of daily going and coming elicit intimate conversation with God in 831.

Gracia Grindal is a teacher and poet whose book, *Lessons in Hymnwriting*, encapsulates the expertise she has developed in guiding others. Her own work as writer and translator (see her version of "*Aus tiefer not*" at 2C) is strongly rooted in her Lutheran heritage, drawing on German and Scandinavian sources, with a particular admiration for Lina Sandell Berg (1832–1903). She has prepared many paraphrases of psalms and other Scriptures, of which the best known is 832, an unrhymed paraphrase of Luke 1:26–38. (Compare Leach's freer approach at 781). Also without rhyme is her telling of the parable of the mustard seed (833), which has an elegant balance between stanzas that are concrete and direct, and a refrain that reiterates the kingdom's mystery. The story of Jairus's daughter in 834, is one of several narrative texts in which she recounts interaction between Jesus and women. Michael Peterson's narrative of the Emmaus experience (835) was written in a class taught by Grindal at Luther Seminary. The subtly shifting final lines of the stanzas trace the changing perceptions of those who encountered Jesus after the resurrection.

Patrick Michaels is an Episcopal church musician. His Advent hymn, 836, draws from the Bible's wisdom literature in nearly every line. This text captures in hymnic form the rediscovery of the personification in Scripture of Wisdom/Sophia. The role of the biblical Word—and our own words—in bringing wholeness is given eloquent form in 837. John Core, a member of the Christian Church (Disciples of Christ), is a librarian and musician whose texts often feature shifting meanings and other forms of word play. His text at 838 imaginatively employs musical vocabulary to represent the reorientation of life brought by the Incarnation.

United Methodist musician and pastor David Robb has contributed to many Hymn Society searches. Ecology, a frequent concern in his texts, is the focus of 839, which was prompted by a study of land-use policies relating to Native Americans and draws on their vocabulary for the Creator. Robb's study of the Hebrew of 1 Kings 19:12, usually translated "a still, small voice," lies behind 840, which invites God to direct conscience and witness.

Amanda Udis-Kessler, a Unitarian Universalist sociologist and writer, is particularly invested in issues of justice and peacemaking. This concern is shown in 841, with its explication of Jubilee within a structure that is neatly balanced, both within each stanza and as a whole. This text first appeared in *Sing Justice! Do Justice!* (1998), a collection resulting from a search by the Hymn Society and Alternatives for Simple Living. The Unitarian Universalist Association issued a new hymnal, *Singing the Living Tradition,* in 1993. Mark Belletini, a UUA pastor, was chair of the editorial committee. The fresh metaphors of 842 reflect his conversation with a colleague who was dying as the result of AIDS. This text is remarkable for its tenderness as well as for the unforced parallelism in the first and last lines of each stanza.

Susan Palo Cherwien has unusual gifts for evocative language and effective structure. Both of these are evident in 843, which adds seasonal imagery to that of John 15:5 to represent an intimate and maturing relationship with Christ. Form and vocabulary communicate the cycle of life and death and life again in 844. Her psalmlike 845 makes multiple scriptural allusions in its affirmation of God's presence in times of sorrow. Presbyterian professor of religion Mary Louise Bringle burst on the hymn-writing scene by placing first in three contests in her first year as a published writer in this genre. She has demonstrated a remarkable ability to produce a polished text in a short span of time. Her winning entry in a Hymn Society search for texts related to the millennium, 846, encompasses a sweeping historical survey within a sturdy form.

717
Awake, O Sleeper, Rise from Death

Awake, O sleeper, rise from death,
    and Christ shall give you light,
so learn his love—its length and breadth,
    its fullness, depth, and height.

To us on earth he came to bring
    from sin and fear release,
to give the Spirit's unity,
    the very bond of peace.

There is one body and one hope,
    one Spirit and one call,
one Lord, one faith, and one baptism,
    one Father of us all.

Then walk in love as Christ has loved,
    who died that he might save;
with kind and gentle hearts forgive
    as God in Christ forgave.

For us Christ lived, for us he died
    and conquered in the strife.
Awake, arise, go forth in faith,
    and Christ shall give you life.

F. Bland Tucker, 1976
based on Ephesians 5:14
The Hymnal 1982, 1985
© 1980, Augsburg Publishing House

718
Christ, When for Us You Were Baptized

Christ, when for us you were baptized,
    God's Spirit on you came,
as peaceful as a dove and yet
    as urgent as a flame.

God called you his beloved Son,
    called you his servant true,
sent you his kingdom to proclaim,
    his holy will to do.

Straightway and steadfast until death
    you then obeyed his call
freely as Son of Man to serve
    and give your life for all.

Baptize us with your Spirit, Lord,
    your cross on us be signed,
that, likewise in God's service we
    may perfect freedom find.

> F. Bland Tucker, 1973; revised, 1982
> *The Hymnal 1982*, 1985
> © 1985, The Church Pension Fund

719

From God Christ's Deity Came Forth

From God Christ's deity came forth,
his manhood from humanity;
his priesthood from Melchizedek,
his royalty from David's tree:
    Praised be his Oneness.

He joined with guests at wedding feast,
yet in the wilderness did fast;
he taught within the temple's gates;
his people saw him die at last:
    Praised be his teaching.

The dissolute he did not scorn,
nor turn from those who were in sin;
he for the righteous did rejoice
but bade the fallen to come in:
    Praised be his mercy.

He did not disregard the sick;
to simple ones his word was given;
and he descended to the earth
and his work done, went up to heaven:
    Praised be his coming.

Who then, my Lord, compares to you?
The Watcher slept, the Great was small,
the Pure baptized, the Life who died,
the King abased to honor all:
    Praised be your glory.

> F. Bland Tucker, ca. 1981
> based on Howard Rhys's translation from
> Ephrem of Edessa (4th century)
> *The Hymnal 1982*, 1985
> © 1985, The Church Pension Fund

720

Eternal Spirit of the Living Christ

Eternal Spirit of the living Christ,
    I know not how to ask or what to say;
I only know my need, as deep as life,
    and only you can teach me how to pray.

Come, pray in me the prayer I need this day;
    help me to see your purpose and your will—
where I have failed, what I have done amiss;
    held in forgiving love, let me be still.

Come with the strength I lack, the vision clear
    of neighbor's need, of all humanity;
fulfillment of my life in love outpoured:
    my life in you, O Christ; your love in me.

> Frank von Christierson, 1974
> *Make a Joyful Noise*, 1987
> © 1974, The Hymn Society (admin. Hope Publishing Company)

721
O God Who Shaped Creation

O God who shaped creation
    at earth's chaotic dawn,
your word of power was spoken,
    and lo! the dark was gone!
You framed us in your image,
    you brought us into birth,
you blessed our infant footsteps
    and shared your splendored earth.

O God, with pain and anguish
    a mother sees her child
embark on dead-end pathways,
    alluring, but defiled;
so too your heart is broken
    when hate and lust increase,
when worlds you birthed and nurtured
    spurn ways that lead to peace.

Although your heart is broken
    when people scorn your ways,
you never cease your searching
    through evil's darksome maze;
and when we cease our running,
    your joys, O God, abound
like joy of searching woman
    when treasured coin is found.

O God, when trinkets tarnish
    and pleasures lose their charm,
when, wearied by our wandering,
    we seek your opened arm,
with motherlike compassion
    you share your warm embrace;
you set for us a banquet
    and heal us through your grace.

In mercy and compassion
    your goodness is revealed;
with tenderness you touch us,
    and broken hearts are healed.
You claim us as your children,
    you strip our prideful shame;
with freedom born of mercy
    we bless your holy name!

William W. Reid, Jr., 1987
The United Methodist Hymnal, 1989
© 1989, The United Methodist Publishing House
(admin. The Copyright Company)

722
Earth and All Stars

Earth and all stars!
    Loud rushing planets!
Sing to the Lord a new song!
    O victory!
    Loud shouting army!
Sing to the Lord a new song!

    He has done marvelous things.
    I too will praise him with a new song!

Hail, wind, and rain!
    Loud blowing snowstorm!
Sing to the Lord a new song!
    Flowers and trees!
    Loud rustling dry leaves!
Sing to the Lord a new song!

Trumpet and pipes!
    Loud clashing cymbals!
Sing to the Lord a new song!
    Harp, lute, and lyre!
    Loud humming cellos!
Sing to the Lord a new song!

Engines and steel!
Loud pounding hammers!
Sing to the Lord a new song!
Limestone and beams!
Loud building workers!
Sing to the Lord a new song!

Classrooms and labs!
Loud boiling test tubes!
Sing to the Lord a new song!
Athlete and band!
Loud cheering people!
Sing to the Lord a new song!

Knowledge and truth!
Loud sounding wisdom!
Sing to the Lord a new song!
Daughter and son!
Loud praying members!
Sing to the Lord a new song!

Children of God,
dying and rising,
Sing to the Lord a new song!
Heaven and earth,
hosts everlasting,
Sing to the Lord a new song!

Herbert F. Brokering, stanzas 1–6, 1964; stanza 7, 1982
Lutheran Worship, 1982
© 1969, Augsburg Publishing House

Proudly rise our modern cities,
stately buildings, row on row;
yet their windows, blank, unfeeling,
stare on canyoned streets below,
where the lonely drift unnoticed
in the city's ebb and flow,
lost to purpose and to meaning,
scarcely caring where they go.

We have ventured worlds undreamed of
since the childhood of our race;
known the ecstasy of winging
through untraveled realms of space;
probed the secrets of the atom,
yielding unimagined power,
facing us with life's destruction
or our most triumphant hour.

As each far horizon beckons,
may it challenge us anew,
children of creative purpose,
serving others, honoring you.
May our dreams prove rich with promise,
each endeavor well begun.
Great Creator, give us guidance
till our goals and yours are one.

Catherine Cameron, 1967; revised, 1975
The United Methodist Hymnal, 1989
© 1967, Hope Publishing Company

723
God, Who Stretched the Spangled Heavens

God, who stretched the spangled heavens,
infinite in time and place,
flung the suns in burning radiance
through the silent fields of space,
we, your children, in your likeness,
share inventive powers with you.
Great Creator, still creating,
show us what we yet may do.

724
God of the Sparrow

God of the sparrow
God of the whale
God of the swirling stars
How does the creature say Awe
How does the creature say Praise

God of the earthquake
God of the storm
God of the trumpet blast
    How does the creature cry Woe
    How does the creature cry Save

God of the rainbow
God of the cross
God of the empty grave
    How does the creature say Grace
    How does the creature say Thanks

God of the hungry
God of the sick
God of the prodigal
    How does the creature say Care
    How does the creature say Life

God of the neighbor
God of the foe
God of the pruning hook
    How does the creature say Love
    How does the creature say Peace

God of the ages
God near at hand
God of the loving heart
    How do your children say Joy
    How do your children say Home

Jaroslav J. Vajda, 1983
Now the Joyful Celebration, 1987
© 1983, Concordia Publishing House
Vajda provides alternate endings for lines 4:3, "wayward child," and
5:3, "olive branch."

725

Christ Goes Before

Christ goes before, and we are called to
                                    follow,
and all who follow find the Way, the Truth,
                                    the Life.

Where is that Way we near despaired of finding:
    the way that comes from God and leads to God,
    the realm where God is love and love is King,
    a whole new order for a world astray?
Who wants to live where there's no love like this?
Is this the kingdom we are ready for
        and desperate to find?

Where is that Truth we near despaired of knowing:
    the truth that comes from God and leads to God,
    the power to set us free, the power to change,
    that faces Pilate and the cross and wins?
Who wants to live where there's no peace like this?
Is this the power we are ready for
        and desperate to know?

Where is that Life we near despaired of having:
    the life that comes from God and leads to God,
    the hope of glory only Christ can give,
    that shatters death and grief with Easter joy?
Who wants to live where there's no joy like this?
Is this the glory we are ready for
        and desperate to have?

Jaroslav J. Vajda, 1987
Now the Joyful Celebration, 1987
© 1987, Concordia Publishing House

726

God, You Made This World a Garden

God, you made this world a garden,
    every harvest bearing seed.
Loving God, today as ever
    you anticipate our need;
you are ready with your answer
    long before we plead.

Take us through that other garden,
    tragic, dark Gethsemane,
where our Savior faced our future,
    set to win our amnesty:
Seed of woman, Seed of promise
      from a barren tree.

Now a universal garden,
    seeded with your living Word,
grows with peace and love and beauty,
    songs of freedom there are heard;
by your mercy, by your Spirit,
      thankful hearts are stirred.

In this corner of your garden
    planted by a faithful few,
we have thrived by their endeavor;
    as you blessed them, bless us too.
Find us, as you walk among us,
      bearing fruit for you.

Jaroslav J. Vajda, 1989
So Much to Sing About, 1991
© 1989, Concordia Publishing House

727
A Woman and a Coin

A woman and a coin—the coin is lost!
How much it means to her, what time and toil,
what part it was to play in her bright dreams!
Am I that treasured coin worth searching for?
    I'm found, and you rejoice! What love! What
        love!

A shepherd and a sheep—the sheep is lost!
Far from the flock, the one in hundred cries,
then—risking life—the shepherd's voice and staff!
Am I that treasured sheep worth dying for?
    I live, and you rejoice! What love! What love!

A parent and a child—the child is lost!
The parent feeds on memories and hope,
the prodigal on husks and one last chance.
Am I that treasured child worth waiting for?
    I'm home, and you rejoice! What love! What
        love!

Dear God, you sought us when the world was lost,
you gave your only Son at what a cost;
your Spirit welcomes home the tempest-tossed:
Now we can be all you were dreaming of.
    We're safe, and you rejoice! What love! What
        love!

Jaroslav J. Vajda, 1990
based on Luke 15
So Much to Sing About, 1991
© 1990, Concordia Publishing House

728
Go, My Children, with My Blessing

Go, my children with my blessing,
    never alone;
waking, sleeping, I am with you,
    you are my own;
    in my love's baptismal river
    I have made you mine forever,
go, my children, with my blessing,
    you are my own.

Go, my children, sins forgiven,
    at peace and pure,
here you learned how much I love you,
    what I can cure;
    here you heard my dear Son's story,
    here you touched him, saw his glory,
go, my children, sins forgiven,
    at peace and pure.

Go, my children, fed and nourished,
closer to me;
grow in love and love by serving,
joyful and free.
Here my Spirit's power filled you,
here his tender comfort stilled you;
go, my children, fed and nourished,
joyful and free.

I the Lord will bless and keep you,
and give you peace,
I the Lord will smile upon you,
and give you peace;
the Lord will be your Father,
Savior, Comforter, and Brother:
Go, my children, I will keep you,
and give you peace.

Jaroslav J. Vadja, 1983
Now the Joyful Celebration, 1987
© 1983, Concordia Publishing House

The following stanza was written for use in weddings, with the author's
suggestion that it be substituted for stanza 2 above.

In this union I have joined you,
husband and wife.
Now, my children, live together
as heirs of life:
Each the other's gladness sharing,
each the other's burdens bearing,
now, my children, live together
as heirs of life.

Jaroslav J. Vajda, 1989
So Much to Sing About, 1991
© 1990, Concordia Publishing House

729

Greet Now the Swiftly Changing Year
Czech: Rok nový zase k nám prišel

Greet now the swiftly changing year
with joy and penitence sincere.

Rejoice, rejoice, with thanks embrace
another year of grace.

Remember now the Son of God
and how he shed his infant blood.

For Jesus came to wage sin's war;
this name of names for us he bore.

His love abundant far exceeds
the volume of a whole year's needs.

With such a Lord to lead our way
in hazard or prosperity,
what need we fear in earth or space
in this new year of grace?

"All glory be to God on high,
and peace on earth!" the angels cry.

God, Father, Son, and Spirit, hear:
To all our pleas incline your ear;
upon our lives rich blessing trace
in this new year of grace.

translated, Jaroslav J. Vajda, 1968
from an anonymous 17th-century Old Czech Lutheran text
Now the Joyful Celebration, 1987
© 1969, Concordia Publishing House
In stanzas 5 and 7, the words provided take the place
of the usual refrain.

730

O God of Vision

O God of vision far greater than all human scheming,
gather us now in your presence, refreshing, redeeming.
Show us anew
life in your breathtaking view,
lovely beyond all our dreaming.

Pour out your Spirit on all now assembled before you.
May our diversity here be a means to adore you.
Women and men,
young, old, and youthful again,
make us as one, we implore you.

Grant to us insight, O God, for this time of decision.
May we dream challenging dreams of both depth
and precision.
Speak through the dark.
Dispel by lightning's bright spark
whatever clouds dim our vision.

Break the sun's rays into color, a rainbow around us.
Storm clouds, though real and near, are not enough
to confound us.
Arched in the sky,
beauty and promise are high,
giving us hope to astound us.

Grateful, we come now by Christ's invitation clear
spoken.
We seek the nourishment found in fruit crushed
and bread broken.
Christ for us all!
Come, let us answer the call,
offering our lives as the token.

Jane Parker Huber, 1982
A Singing Faith, 1987
© 1981, Jane Parker Huber (admin. Westminster/John Knox Press)

731
Creator God, Creating Still

Creator God, creating still,
by will and word and deed,
create a new humanity
to meet the present need.

Redeemer God, redeeming still,
with overflowing grace,
pour out your love on us, through us,
make this a holy place.

Sustainer God, sustaining still,
with strength for every day,
empower us now to do your will.
Correct us when we stray.

Great Trinity, for this new day
we need your presence still.
Create, redeem, sustain us now
to do your work and will.

Jane Parker Huber, 1977
A Singing Faith, 1987
© 1980, Jane Parker Huber (admin. Westminster/John Knox Press)

732
Peace to You

"Peace to you"—these words of Jesus
raise our hopes for peace on earth.
Peace!—the message sung by angels
heralding our Savior's birth.
Peace!—the resurrection greeting,
Peace!—dispelling doubt and fear.
Peace!—the world's long-cherished vision,
peace for all, both far and near.

Peace will never be discovered
while the hungry go unfed.
Peace remains a dim illusion
till each child has home and bed.
If our systems crush the spirit,
seeds of enmity are sown.
If we only think of winning,
peace and justice are unknown.

Roads to peace are often rocky,
    challenging our very soul.
"Christ, our Peace" must be our watchword;
    Christ, the pathway; Christ, the goal.
Whether inner conflict rages,
    or relationships are torn
in our nations or our households,
    love, through Christ, can be reborn.

"Peace to you!"—a call to action,
    not a sentimental phrase;
peace erasing every barrier,
    undergirding all our ways.
"Peace," Christ's resurrection greeting,
    still dispels our doubt and fright,
building unity of spirit—
    Christ, our Peace, our Hope, our Light.

Jane Parker Huber, 1994
Singing in Celebration, 1996
© 1995, Jane Parker Huber (admin. Westminster/John Knox Press)

733
The One Who Longs to Make Us Whole

The One Who Longs to Make Us Whole
    is waiting to embrace
our broken lives so we can know
    the power of healing grace.
God's love surrounds our suffering,
    and keeps us through the night.
God helps us bear our deep despair
    till we see morning light.

The One Who Saves Us from Ourselves
    is waiting to release
our hearts from chains of self-reproach,
    our failure to find peace.
When harmful habits leave us bruised,
    distraught from inner pain,
God comes to us through trusted friends,
    and helps us hope again.

The One Who Understands Our Need
    accepts us as we are;
and, like a loved one, welcomes us
    when we have wandered far.
God never says we come too late
    to be forgiven, free,
but promises we can become
    the self we're meant to be!

Edith Sinclair Downing, 1996
A Season of Clear Shining, 2000
© 1998, Selah Publishing Company, Inc.

734
Holy One Who Breathes Me

Holy One Who Breathes Me,
Love That Never Leaves Me,
    Listener to My Soul,
when my heart is broken,
you hear words unspoken;
    you would make me whole.
Love beyond my power to tell,
guiding me through every season,
    loving past all reason.

In the winter silence
you sustain my patience
    until spring breaks through.
When the flowers waken,
showing faith unshaken,
    life is born anew.
Then I, longing for your light,
glimpse eternal spring resplendent,
    gift of love transcendent.

Love That Knows No Limit,
all who trust inherit
　　your enduring grace.
Grief and pain are softened,
and our sin is pardoned
　　within your embrace.
Gratefully our hymn we raise,
for no evil can undo us
　　when your love breathes through us.

Edith Sinclair Downing, 1995
A Season of Clear Shining, 2000
© 1998, Selah Publishing Company, Inc.

And we, too, still meet angels
　　in lush or desert land,
who call on us to witness,
　　to stretch out heart and hand,
to tear down walls of privilege,
　　extend baptismal grace.
For no one is excluded
　　from our God's full embrace!

Edith Sinclair Downing, 1998
based on Acts 8:26–40
A Season of Clear Shining, 2000
© 1998, Selah Publishing Company, Inc.

735
The Angel Said to Philip

The angel said to Philip:
　　"Go now the desert way,
and find the one, bewildered,
　　who needs Good News today.
He has no hope of family,
　　cut off from culture's stream.
Tell him he is included
　　in those Christ will redeem."

The Promised One of Scripture
　　brought forth no daughter, son;
and justice was denied him,
　　though he no wrong had done.
Yet Christ began a family:
　　all those who call him Lord,
of children, men, and women,
　　bound by the Spirit's cord.

736
Let God Be God

How like a gentle spirit deep within
　　God reins our fervent passions day by day,
and gives us strength to challenge and to win
　　despite the perils of our chosen way.

Let God be God wherever life may be;
　　let every tongue bear witness to the call;
all humankind is one by God's decree;
　　let God be God, let God be God for all.

God like a mother eagle hovers near
　　on mighty wings of power manifest;
God like a gentle shepherd stills our fear,
　　and comforts us against a peaceful breast.

When in our vain pretensions we conspire
　　to shape God's image as we see our own,
hark to the voice above our base desire;
　　God is the sculptor, we the broken stone.

Through all our fretful claims of sex and race
    the universal love of God shines through,
for God is love transcending style and place
    and all the idle options we pursue.

C. Eric Lincoln, 1987
The United Methodist Hymnal, 1989
© 1989, The United Methodist Publishing House
(admin. The Copyright Company)
The author's original adjective in line 5:1 was "noxious."

737
I Cannot Dance, O Love

I cannot dance, O Love,
    unless you lead me on.
I cannot leap in gladness
    unless you lift me up.
From love to love we circle,
    beyond all knowledge grow,
for when you lead we follow,
    to new worlds you can show.

Love is the music 'round us,
    we glide as birds in air,
entwining, soul and body,
    your wings hold us with care.
Your Spirit is the harpist
    and all your children sing;
her hands the currents 'round us,
    your love the golden strings.

O blessed Love, your circling
    unites us, God and soul.
From the beginning, your arms
    embrace and make us whole.
Hold us in steps of mercy
    from which you never part,
that we may know more fully
    the dances of your heart.

Jean Wiebe Janzen, 1991
based on Mechtild of Magdeburg
Hymnal: A Worship Book, 1992
© 1991, Jean Wiebe Janzen

738
O Holy Spirit, Root of Life

O Holy Spirit, Root of life,
    Creator, cleanser of all things,
anoint our wounds, awaken us
    with lustrous movement of your wings.

Eternal Vigor, Saving One,
    you free us by your living Word,
becoming flesh to wear our pain,
    and all creation is restored.

O Holy Wisdom, Moving Force,
    encompass us with wings unfurled,
and carry us, encircling all,
    above, below, and through the world.

Jean Wiebe Janzen, 1991
based on Hildegard of Bingen
Hymnal: A Worship Book, 1992
© 1991, Jean Wiebe Janzen

739
Mothering God

Mothering God, you gave me birth
in the bright morning of this world.
Creator, Source of every breath,
you are my rain, my wind, my sun.

Mothering Christ, you took my form,
offering me your food of light,
grain of life, and grape of love,
your very body for my peace.

Mothering Spirit, nurturing one,
in arms of patience hold me close,
so that in faith I root and grow
until I flower, until I know.

Jean Wiebe Janzen, 1991
based on Julian of Norwich
Hymnal: A Worship Book, 1992
© 1991, Jean Wiebe Janzen

740

Spirit, Now Live in Me

O holy Dove of God descending,
you are the love that knows no ending,
all of our shattered dreams you're mending:
    Spirit, now live in me.

O holy Wind of God now blowing,
you are the seed that God is sowing,
you are the life that starts us growing:
    Spirit, now live in me.

O holy Rain of God now falling,
you make the Word of God enthralling,
you are that inner voice now calling:
    Spirit, now live in me.

O holy Flame of God now burning,
you are the power of Christ returning,
you are the answer to our yearning:
    Spirit, now live in me.

741

We Are God's People

We are God's people, the chosen of the Lord,
born of his Spirit, established by his Word;
    our cornerstone is Christ alone,
        and strong in him we stand:
    O let us live transparently,
and walk heart to heart and hand in hand.

We are God's loved ones, the bride of Christ our
                            Lord,
for we have known it, the love of God outpoured;
    now let us learn how to return
        the gift of love once given:
    O let us share each joy and care,
and live with a zeal that pleases heaven.

We are the body of which the Lord is Head,
called to obey him, now risen from the dead;
    he wills us be a family,
        diverse yet truly one:
    O let us give our gifts to God,
and so shall his work on earth be done.

We are a temple, the Spirit's dwelling place,
formed in great weakness, a cup to hold God's grace;
    we die alone, for on its own
        each ember loses fire:
    Yet joined in one the flame burns on
to give warmth and light, and to inspire.

742

Sunday's Palms Are Wednesday's Ashes

Sunday's palms are Wednesday's ashes
    as another Lent begins;
thus we kneel before our Maker
    in contrition for our sins.
We have marred baptismal pledges,
    in rebellion, gone astray;
now, returning, seek forgiveness;
    grant us pardon, Lord, this day!

We have failed to love our neighbors,
　　their offenses to forgive,
have not listened to their troubles
　　nor have cared just how they live;
we are jealous, proud, impatient,
　　loving (overmuch) our things;
may the yielding of our failings
　　be our Lenten offerings.

We are hasty to judge others,
　　blind to proof of human need;
and our lack of understanding
　　demonstrates our inner greed;
we have wasted earth's resources;
　　want and suffering we've ignored;
come and cleanse us, then restore us;
　　make new hearts within us, Lord!

Rae E. Whitney, 1982
With Joy Our Spirits Sing, 1995
© 1991, Selah Publishing Company, Inc.

743
It Was God Who Ran to Greet Him

It was God who ran to greet him
　　as he stumbled home in shame,
then embraced him, clothed, and fed him,
　　gave him back his family name.

It was God who swept the kitchen
　　and retrieved that precious coin;
God in woman called her neighbors,
　　"Come, and in my gladness join!"

It was God who, as a shepherd,
　　left the ninety-nine asleep
and then searched in cold and darkness
　　till he found that missing sheep.

It is God who runs to meet us,
　　conscious of our every need;
then, as we in turn help others,
　　God rejoices in each deed!

Rae E. Whitney, 1993
based on Luke 15
With Joy Our Spirits Sing, 1995
© 1993, Selah Publishing Company, Inc.

744
Music and Incense

Music and incense,
dancing and laughter,
welcome each sinner
　　now to love's feast;
Come to the party,
clothed in the finest,
freely provided
　　for every guest!

Shame and discomfort,
fear of rejection,
horror of dying,
　　panic and pain:
These will be banished
by Christ our Savior,
for he in glory
　　ever will reign.

So enter, singing,
circled by angels,
knowing Christ's kingdom
　　none can destroy;
greeted by loved ones
eagerly waiting,
come, pardoned people,
　　into his joy!

Rae E. Whitney, 1992
With Joy Our Spirits Sing, 1995
© 1994, Selah Publishing Company, Inc.

745
Myrrh-Bearing Mary

Myrrh-bearing Mary from Magdala came
seeking her Jesus, with spirit aflame;
he had commanded her sickness depart;
she now would thank him for newness of heart.

Myrrh-bearing Mary to Bethany came
seeking her Jesus who'd called her by name;
there she anointed his feet and his head
with precious oils that were meant for the dead.

Myrrh-bearing Mary to Calvary came
seeking her Jesus who hung there in shame;
and as the careless and heedless passed by,
hopeless and helpless she watched her Lord die.

Myrrh-bearing Mary to death's garden came
seeking her Jesus who'd borne the world's blame;
heartsick she stood, till she heard the Lord's voice:
"Mary!" he said, "I am risen; rejoice!"

Rae E. Whitney, 1981
With Joy Our Spirits Sing, 1995
© 1990, Selah Publishing Company, Inc.

746
Christmas Has Its Cradle

Christmas has its cradle, where a Baby cried;
did the lantern's shadow show him crucified?
Did he foresee darkly his life's willing loss?
Christmas has its cradle and Easter has its cross.

Christmas has its cradle, shepherds came to see
little Son of Mary, Lamb of God to be;
had his Father warned him, none would grant him
room
save in the Christmas cradle and in the Easter tomb?

Christmas has its cradle, wise men came to bring
myrrh and gold and incense, offerings for a King;
myrrh alone stayed with him, death's balm for this
Boy,
from the Christmas cradle and to his Easter joy.

Christmas has its cradle, where that Baby cried;
in the Easter garden, Christ lay, crucified;
when death's power was conquered, God's life
through him poured;
Christmas has its cradle and Easter has its Lord!

Rae E. Whitney, 1980
The Baptist Hymnal, 1991
© 1985, Broadman Press

747
That King, before Whose Majesty

That King, before whose majesty
the fire-bright angels tremble still,
is now a babe in Mary's arms
and subject to a mother's will.

Earth is his footstool, yet her home
is all the universe he sees;
the Lord of Lords—a little child—
explores his world on hands and knees.

How new the helplessness of God!
the action, terrifying, bold!
and how prophetic were those gifts
of myrrh and frankincense and gold!

For, when the wise men worshiped him
and offered presents from the East,
such gifts paid homage to a king
who is both sacrifice and priest.

At Christ's profound humility
both earth and heaven in wonder gaze;
this Child, the Incarnate Word of God,
is worthy of all highest praise!

Rae E. Whitney, 1986
based on lines from Ephrem of Edessa (4th century)
translated by Sebastian Brock
With Joy our Spirits Sing, 1995
© 1994, Selah Publishing Company, Inc.

748
Creating God, Your Fingers Trace

Creating God, your fingers trace
the bold designs of farthest space;
let sun and moon and stars and light
and what lies hidden praise your might.

Sustaining God, your hands uphold
earth's mysteries known or yet untold;
let water's fragile blend with air,
enabling life, proclaim your care.

Redeeming God, your arms embrace
all now despised for creed or race;
let peace, descending like a dove,
make known on earth your healing love.

Indwelling God, your gospel claims
one family with a billion names;
let every life be touched by grace
until we praise you face to face.

Jeffery W. Rowthorn, 1974
based on Psalm 148
The Hymnal 1982, 1985
© 1979, The Hymn Society (admin. Hope Publishing Company)

749
Lord, You Give the Great Commission

Lord, you give the great commission:
    "Heal the sick and preach the word."
Lest the church neglect its mission
    and the gospel go unheard,
help us witness to your purpose
    with renewed integrity;

        with the Spirit's gifts empower us
        for the work of ministry.

Lord, you call us to your service:
    "In my name baptize and teach."
That the world may trust your promise,
    life abundant meant for each,
give us all new fervor, draw us
    closer in community;

Lord, you make the common holy:
    "This my body, this my blood."
Let your priests, for earth's true glory,
    daily lift life heavenward,
asking that the world around us
    share your children's liberty;

Lord, you show us love's true measure:
    "Father, what they do, forgive."
Yet we hoard as private treasure
    all that you so freely give.
May your care and mercy lead us
    to a just society;

Lord, you bless with words assuring:
    "I am with you to the end."
Faith and hope and love restoring,
    may we serve as you intend,
and, amid the cares that claim us,
    hold in mind eternity;

Jeffery W. Rowthorn, 1978
The Hymnal 1982, 1985
© 1978, Hope Publishing Company

750
Retell What Christ's Great Love Has Done

Retell what Christ's great love has done,
how crib and cross the victory won:
God's call obeyed, temptations faced,
the good news preached, then death embraced.
Let us who share his Easter light
sing praise to God, our chief delight.

Recall the covenant of grace
in which you freely find your place:
with water washed, at table fed,
in Christ alive to self now dead.
Then with your lives, by day and night,
sing praise to God, your chief delight.

Review the tapestry of saints,
that canvas which the Spirit paints:
a prophet scorned, a teacher famed,
a host unknown and unacclaimed,
yet one and all who fought the fight
sing praise to God, their chief delight.

Rehearse the chorus of the heart,
let all earth's hopes and fears take part:
the shouts of youth, the cries of age,
the prisoners' groans, the victims' rage.
And may each voice which seeks the right
sing praise to God, its chief delight.

Rejoice at what Christ yet will do,
intent on making all things new:
the hungry filled, the peaceful blessed,
the wounded healed, each heart at rest.
Then sing, till faith gives way to sight,
in praise of God, our chief delight.

Jeffery W. Rowthorn, 1986
A New Hymnal for Colleges and Schools, 1992
© 1987, The Shadyside Presbyterian Church

751
These Things Did Thomas Count as Real

These things did Thomas count as real:
the warmth of blood, the chill of steel,
the grain of wood, the heft of stone,
the last frail twitch of flesh and bone.

The vision of his skeptic mind
was keen enough to make him blind
to any unexpected act
too large for his small world of fact.

His reasoned certainties denied
that one could live when one had died,
until his fingers read like braille
the markings of the spear and nail.

May we, O God, by grace believe
and thus the risen Christ receive,
whose raw imprinted palms reached out
and beckoned Thomas from his doubt.

Thomas H. Troeger, 1984
based on John 20:19–31
Borrowed Light, 1994
© 1994, Oxford University Press

752
Silence! Frenzied, Unclean Spirit

"Silence! frenzied, unclean spirit,"
    cried God's healing, holy One.
"Cease your ranting! Flesh can't bear it.
    Flee as night before the sun."
At Christ's voice the demon trembled,
    from its victim madly rushed,
while the crowd that was assembled
    stood in wonder, stunned and hushed.

Lord, the demons still are thriving
    in the gray cells of the mind:
tyrant voices shrill and driving,
    twisted thoughts that grip and bind,
doubts that stir the heart to panic,
    fears distorting reason's sight,
guilt that makes our loving frantic,
    reams that cloud the soul with fright.

Silence, Lord, the unclean spirit,
    in our mind and in our heart.
Speak your word that when we hear it
    all our demons shall depart.
Clear our thought and calm our feeling,
    still the fractured, warring soul.
By the power of your healing
    make us faithful, true, and whole.

Thomas H. Troeger, 1984
based on Mark 1:21–28
Borrowed Light, 1994
© 1994, Oxford University Press

753

If All You Want, Lord, Is My Heart

If all you want, Lord, is my heart,
    my heart is yours alone—
providing I may set apart
    my mind to be my own.

If all you want, Lord, is my mind,
    my mind belongs to you,
but let my heart remain inclined
    to do what it would do.

If heart and mind would both suffice,
    while I kept strength and soul,
at least I would not sacrifice
    completely my control.

But since, O God, you want them all
    to shape with your own hand,
I pray for grace to heed your call
    to live your first command.

Thomas H. Troeger, 1987
based on Matthew 22:36–40
Borrowed Light, 1994
© 1994, Oxford University Press

754

O Praise the Gracious Power

O praise the gracious power
    that tumbles walls of fear
and gathers in one house of faith
    all strangers far and near:

    We praise you Christ!
    Your cross has made us one!

O praise persistent truth
    that opens fisted minds
and eases from their anxious clutch
    the prejudice that binds:

O praise inclusive love
    encircling every race,
oblivious to gender, wealth,
    to social rank or place:

O praise the word of faith
    that claims us as God's own,
a living temple built on Christ,
    our rock and cornerstone:

O praise the tide of grace
    that laps at every shore
with visions of a world at peace
    no longer bled by war:

O praise the power, the truth,
the love, the word, the tide.
Yet more than these, O praise their source,
praise Christ the crucified:

O praise the living Christ
with faith's bright songful voice!
Announce the gospel to the world
and with these words rejoice:

Thomas H. Troeger, 1984
based on Ephesians 2:11–22
Borrowed Light, 1994
© 1994, Oxford University Press

755
Wind Who Makes All Winds that Blow

Wind who makes all winds that blow—
gusts that bend the saplings low,
gales that heave the sea in waves,
stirrings in the mind's deep caves—
aim your breath with steady power
on your church, this day, this hour.
Raise, renew the life we've lost,
Spirit God of Pentecost.

Fire who fuels all fires that burn—
suns around which planets turn,
beacons marking reefs and shoals,
shining truth to guide our souls–
come to us as once you came:
Burst in tongues of sacred flame!
Light and Power, Might and Strength,
fill your church, its breadth and length.

Holy Spirit, Wind and Flame,
move within our mortal frame.
Make our hearts an altar pyre.
Kindle them with your own fire.
Breathe and blow upon that blaze
till our lives, our deeds and ways
speak that tongue which every land
by your grace shall understand.

Thomas H. Troeger, 1983
Borrowed Light, 1994
© 1994, Oxford University Press

756
From Many Different Ancient Springs

From many different ancient springs,
O God, your rivers flow
and bear a wealth of offerings
that feed our need to know
in clearer and profounder ways
how you—unseen, divine—
meet mortal flesh through prayer and praise,
through ritual, song, and sign.

Flow on, flow on through the prayerful
heart,
flow on, O source of all our streams,
flow on and flowing on impart
the life that renews our hopes and
dreams.

We're humbled when we try to chart
each river's twisting course,
the subtle ways it shapes the heart
and bears from you its source
those meanings that elude the grasp
of all the thoughts we weave
when faithful to the scholar's task
we probe what we believe.

We gladly join with all who bring
    the fruit their streams have fed:
the varied ways we pray and sing
    and share in breaking bread,
the gift of grace that you have sown
    that opens us to see
through forms of prayer unlike our own
    prayer's rich complexity.

Far downstream, past the final bend,
    dear friends have gone from sight
whom we by prayer with thanks commend
    to that transforming light
that shone through their own lives of prayer
    and made their work and play
refractions of your love and care
    that never pass away.

Although we part, we still are bound
    by gifts that you bestow.
From depths that we have yet to sound,
    new truth and visions flow
that sweep us past the present shore
    and bear us on to greet
with great glad thanks the holy roar
    where all our rivers meet.

> Thomas H. Troeger, 1996; revised, 2000
> *Above the Moon Earth Rises*, 2002
> © 2002, Oxford University Press

757
Source and Sovereign, Rock and Cloud

Source and Sovereign, Rock and Cloud,
Fortress, Fountain, Shelter, Light,
Judge, Defender, Mercy, Might,
Life whose life all life endowed:

    May the church at prayer recall
    that no single, holy name
    but the truth that feeds them all
    is the God whom we proclaim.

Word and Wisdom, Root and Vine,
Shepherd, Savior, Servant, Lamb,
Well and Water, Bread and Wine,
Way who leads us to I AM:

Storm and Stillness, Breath and Dove,
Thunder, Tempest, Whirlwind, Fire,
Comfort, Counselor, Presence, Love,
Energies that never tire:

> Thomas H. Troeger, 1987; revised, 1997
> *Borrowed Light*, 1994
> © 1994, Oxford University Press

758
Holy and Good Is the Gift of Desire

    Holy and good is the gift of desire.
    God made our bodies for passion and fire,
    intending that love would draw from the
                flame
    lives that would shine with God's image
                and name.

God weeps for all people
    abandoned, abused.
God weeps for the women
    whose bodies are bruised.
    God weeps when the flame
    that God has infused
is turned from its purpose
    and brutally used.

God calls to the women,
    God calls to the men:
"Don't hide from the terror
    or terror will win.
    I made you for love,
    but love must begin
by facing the violence
    without and within."

God knows that our violence
    is mixed with our dust:
God's son was a victim
    of violence and lust,
    for Jesus revealed
    that women will trust
a man who in action
    is tender and just.

Thomas H. Troeger, 1988
Borrowed Light, 1994
© 1994, Oxford University Press

A death if hearts now harden,
    birth if we repent
and tend and keep the garden
    as God has always meant:
to sow without abusing
    the soil where life is grown,
to reap without our bruising
    this sunlit mossy stone.

Thomas H. Troeger, 1993
Above the Moon Earth Rises, 2002
© 2002, Oxford University Press

759

Above the Moon Earth Rises

Above the moon earth rises,
    a sunlit mossy stone,
a garden that God prizes
    where life has richly grown,
an emerald selected
    for us to guard with care,
an isle in space protected
    by one thin reef of air.

The mossy stone is grieving,
    its tears are bitter rain,
the garden is unleaving
    and all its harvests wane,
the emerald is clouded,
    its luster dims and fades,
the isle of life is shrouded
    in thick and stagnant haze.

O listen to the sighing
    of water, sky, and land,
and hear the Spirit crying
    the future is at hand.
The moss and garden thinning
    portend a death or birth,
the end or new beginning
    for all that lives on earth.

760

Surely It Is God Who Saves Me

Surely it is God who saves me;
    I shall trust and have no fear.
For the Lord defends and shields me
    and his saving help is near.
So rejoice as you draw water
    from salvation's healing spring;
in the day of your deliverance
    thank the Lord, his mercies sing.

Make God's deeds known to the peoples:
    Tell out his exalted name.
Praise the Lord, who has done great things;
    all his works God's might proclaim.
Zion, lift your voice in singing;
    for with you has come to dwell,
in your very midst the great and
    Holy One of Israel.

Carl P. Daw, Jr., 1982
based on Isaiah 12:2–6
A Year of Grace, 1990
© 1982, Hope Publishing Company

761
How Shallow Former Shadows Seem

How shallow former shadows seem
    beside this great reverse
as darkness swallows up the Light
    of all the universe:
Creation shivers at the shock,
    the temple rends its veil,
a pallid stillness stifles time,
    and nature's motions fail.

This is no midday fantasy,
    no flight of fevered brain.
With vengeance awful, grim, and real,
    chaos is come again:
The hands that formed us from the soil
    are nailed upon the cross;
the Word that gave us life and breath
    expires in utter loss.

Yet deep within this darkness lives
    a Love so fierce and free
that arcs all voids and—risk supreme!—
    embraces agony.
Its perfect testament is etched
    in iron, blood, and wood;
with awe we glimpse its true import
    and dare to call it good.

Carl P. Daw, Jr., 1989
A Year of Grace, 1990
© 1990, Hope Publishing Company

762
God the Spirit, Guide and Guardian

God the Spirit, guide and guardian,
    wind-sped flame and hovering dove,
breath of life and voice of prophets,
    sign of blessing, power of love:
Give to those who lead your people
    fresh anointing of your grace;
send them forth as bold apostles
    to your church in every place.

Christ our Savior, Sovereign, Shepherd,
    Word-made-flesh, Love crucified,
teacher, healer, suffering Servant,
    Friend of sinners, foe of pride:
In your tending may all pastors
    learn and live a Shepherd's care;
grant them courage and compassion
    shown through word and deed and prayer.

Great Creator, Life-bestower,
    Truth beyond all thought's recall,
fount of wisdom, womb of mercy,
    giving and forgiving all:
As you know our strength and weakness,
    so may those the church exalts
oversee her life steadfastly
    yet not overlook her faults.

Triune God, mysterious Being,
    undivided and diverse,
deeper than our minds can fathom,
    greater than our creeds rehearse:
Help us in our varied callings
    your full image to proclaim,
that our ministries uniting
    may give glory to your Name.

Carl P. Daw, Jr., 1987
A Year of Grace, 1990
© 1989, Hope Publishing Company

763

Like the Murmur of the Dove's Song

Like the murmur of the dove's song,
　　like the challenge of her flight
like the vigor of the wind's rush,
　　like the new flame's eager might:
　　　　Come, Holy Spirit, come.

To the members of Christ's Body,
　　to the branches of the Vine,
to the church in faith assembled,
　　to her midst as gift and sign:
　　　　Come, Holy Spirit, come.

With the healing of division,
　　with the ceaseless voice of prayer,
with the power of love and witness,
　　with the peace beyond compare:
　　　　Come, Holy Spirit, come.

Carl P. Daw, Jr., 1982
A Year of Grace, 1990
© 1982, Hope Publishing Company

764

Travelers' Child

Travelers' child laid in a manger,
　　refugee to Egypt bound,
pilgrim youth, yet not a stranger
　　when your Father's house you found:
Christ who set aside your glory
　　to reclaim our wayward race,
help us read salvation's story
　　in each passing heart and face.

Guest who vintaged wine from water,
　　wandering healer brimmed with balm,
foreigner whose hearer brought her
　　heart-thirst to your well of calm:
Savior, may we see our neighbor
　　as an emblem of your care;
in our leisure and our labor
　　give us grace to find you there.

Homeless squatter in a garden,
　　feaster in a rented room,
scapegoat for another's pardon,
　　sleeper in a borrowed tomb:
Jesus, outcast and offender
　　to those certain of God's will,
rend the veils of race and gender,
　　wealth and health, that shroud us still.

Strange wayfarer to Emmaus,
　　vague form on the distant shore,
fright to friends ("Does sense betray us?")
　　when you stood with them once more:
Risen Lord, be there to meet us
　　when life dawns eternally;
may your promised blessing greet us,
　　"In all these you welcomed me."

Carl P. Daw, Jr., 1994
New Psalms and Hymns and Spiritual Songs, 1996
© 1994, Hope Publishing Company

765

Far from Cyrene and the Libyan Coastlands

Far from Cyrene and the Libyan coastlands
Simon had ventured east across the Great Sea,
as from earth's corners faith and duty summoned
　　　　Passover pilgrims.

Jerusalem gave Simon no kind welcome:
Just as he entered, he was seized by soldiers
and forced to carry to the dreaded Skull Place
　　　　some friendless Jew's cross.

That unsought burden has become his glory;
cross-bearing Simon now is praised and honored.
So by God's wisdom much we find unwelcome
        may prove a blessing.

Crucified Savior, risen yet still wounded,
help us to take up crosses laid upon us:
daily, like Simon, sharing in your passion,
        birth pangs of new life.

Carl P. Daw, Jr., 1995
New Psalms and Hymns and Spiritual Songs, 1996
© 1996, Hope Publishing Company

766
The House of Faith Has Many Rooms

The house of faith has many rooms
        where we have never been;
there is more space within God's scope
        than we have ever seen.

We dare not limit God's domain
        to what our creeds declare,
or shrink from probing things unknown
        lest God should not be there.

The way to God is not escape,
        though truth does make us free:
The life of chosen servanthood
        is perfect liberty.

Yet still we seek at journey's end
        the last and sweetest grace:
the gift of room to turn around
        and know God face to face.

Carl P. Daw, Jr., 1989
A Year of Grace, 1990
© 1990, Hope Publishing Company

767
Wondrous God, More Named Than Known

Wondrous God, more named than known,
give us, firm and certain grown,
grace to doubt what we surmise,
lest we miss the glad surprise
when we find your truth exceeds
all the forecasts of our creeds.

Pregnant Silence, lively Calm,
Singer of creation's psalm,
great "I AM" of burning bush:
Still resist our urge to push
till you fit the names we choose,
shadows of the light we lose.

Save us from proud, empty claims
in our zeal to give you names.
Let our notions be expressed
not to limit but suggest
views that icon-like disclose
splendor more than we suppose.

God not female, God not male,
God for whom all labels fail,
Truth beyond our verbal games,
Life too vast to bound with names:
From vain wordlust set us free
to embrace your mystery.

Carl P. Daw, Jr., 1989
A Year of Grace, 1990
© 1990, Hope Publishing Company

768

O God, on Whom We Lost Our Hold

O God, on whom we lost our hold
    when all your names were changed,
we find our prayers and hymns confused,
    more awkward and estranged.
Yet there is hope in these new words,
    sweet fruit in bitter rind:
the promise of a keener faith
    than that we leave behind.

The language which we knew so well
    flowed smoothly on the tongue,
though seldom did we pause to weigh
    how things were said or sung.
But now the world is showing us
    with stunning clarity
the problems with the words we used
    to tame a mystery.

Dear God, inspire our hearts and minds
    to seek your truth anew,
and help us with each fresh insight
    to find names fit for you.
Yet never let us idolize
    the images we choose;
but as we strive, give us the grace
    to wrestle and to lose.

Carl P. Daw, Jr., 1989
A Year of Grace, 1990
© 1990, Hope Publishing Company

769

Desert Wastes Stretch On before Us

Desert wastes stretch on before us;
    throats are parched and cannot sing
praises to the God who made us,
    life's unfailing Source and Spring.
Christ, who shared our human anguish
    while the soldiers diced and cursed,
journey with us through the desert;
    join with ours your cry, "I thirst!"

Dark and dread fall all around us;
    midnight fears our hearts oppress.
What is past still haunts and holds us,
    guilt our wills cannot suppress.
Christ, who bore the cross for sinners,
    death embraced that we might live,
in the darkness, bleeding, dying,
    pray for us, "O God, forgive!"

Winds that whip the waves in fury
    sweep away security.
Life that once was peaceful, stable
    flounders in an angry sea.
Christ, who calmed the towering waters,
    made the angry winds to cease,
stay with us through storm and peril;
    speak again, "Be still, at peace!"

Desert, darkness, sudden chaos
    as through life to death we move—
nothing in the whole creation
    can your faithful care remove.
Christ, who passed through death unvanquished,
    burst the tomb where you were laid,
help us hear your Word of promise:
    "It is I; be not afraid!"

Herman G. Stuempfle, Jr., 1994
Awake Our Hearts to Praise, 2000
© 2000, GIA Publications, Inc.

770

It Was a Garden Fresh as Morn

It was a garden fresh as morn
    where Adam walked with Eve;
but sin crept through God's grove so green
    to make creation grieve.
        And silent trees bent low to hear:
            "Not yours, our will be done!"

It was a garden dark as sin
    where Jesus knelt to pray.
Within its shades disciples slept,
    and one would soon betray.
        And silent trees bent low to hear:
            "Not mine, your will be done!"

It was a garden still as death
    where Mary walked at dawn,
and, finding there an empty tomb,
    she wept that Christ was gone.
        But silent trees rejoiced to hear:
            "Fear not, for it is I!"

O garden, brighter than the sun,
    where Love was born again,
where death and sin were overcome,
    where Life renewed its reign!
        And silent trees burst out in song:
            "Creation is restored!"

Herman G. Stuempfle, Jr., 1999
Awake Our Hearts to Praise, 2000
© 2000, GIA Publications, Inc.

771

You Never Saw Old Galilee

You never saw old Galilee
    so friendly and so fair.
My mates and I sang merrily
    and never had a care,
    and never had a care.

Out where the sea runs green and cold
    and many fathoms deep,
I called my mates, "Look in the hold!
    The Master's gone asleep!
    The Master's gone asleep!"

And then the clouds grew grim and black;
    there blew an awful gale.
"Heave to, my mates, the mast will crack,
    if we don't lower the sail,
    if we don't lower the sail!"

The rain poured down, the waves leapt high,
    the winds they whipped us round
and tossed us toward the terrible sky
    and roared their terrible sound,
    and roared their terrible sound.

We roused the Master from his sleep
    and called his name in dread:
"Come save us from the awful deep
    or we're as good as dead,
    or we're as good as dead!"

Then up he stood against the gale,
    and told the storm to cease.
Tempestuous winds broke off their wail;
    waves calmed and lay at peace,
    waves calmed and lay at peace.

So, friends, although the sea be wide
    and though your boat be small,
there's naught to fear from time or tide;
    the Master's Lord of all,
    the Master's Lord of all.

Then sing, my friends, sing merrily;
    O sing both bold and brave.
The One who made the surging sea
    still rules the wind and wave,
    still rules the wind and wave.

Herman G. Stuempfle, Jr., 1989
based on Mark 4:35–41
The Word Goes Forth, 1993
© 1989, The Hymn Society (admin. Hope Publishing Company)

772

Once You Walked across the Waters

Once you walked across the waters,
    those in ancient times have said,
calmed the storm that in its fury
    filled your struggling friends with dread.
Christ, you know the honest questions
    that may fill the searching mind,
churn the heart in whose recesses
    faith and doubt lie intertwined.

Yet you walk across the centuries
    everywhere our feet have trod,
reach us over ways mysterious,
    bring to us the peace of God.
Through your Word of promise spoken,
    through the meal you fill with grace,
there, O Christ, you come among us;
    there you meet us face to face.

Time such love cannot imprison,
    by its passage never hide.
Christ, the Word before creation,
    still you walk with cosmic stride.
Stars and planets know your pathways,
    yet a child can find you near.
By the power of your compassion,
    quiet still our doubt and fear.

Come, when waters rising, raging,
    threaten our security;
when we're tossed within the tumult,
    cry for help we cannot see.
Walk, O Christ, across the ages;
    with your peace our hearts pervade.
Help us in the storm to hear you:
    "It is I; be not afraid!"

Herman G. Stuempfle, Jr., 1997
Awake Our Hearts to Praise, 2000
© 2000, GIA Publications, Inc.

773

O God, Whom Boundless Space

O God, whom boundless space
    and time cannot confine,
how can our finite minds embrace
    creation's vast design?
    In awe we search the stars;
    we probe the atom's core,
and with each step of knowledge kneel
    to praise you and adore.

When light in silence shone
    and empty oceans surged,
by your creating, guiding will
    a living cell emerged.
    Then, as the aeons passed
    and earth in orbit whirled,
you lured from life's primeval seed
    new forms to fill the world.

And we who lately came,
    creation's newest guest,
are rooted in the humble earth,
    the kin of plant and beast.
    But life's on-surging force,
    by your intent refined,
brought forth creation's highest gift—
    the searching human mind.

In Christ, your Word, we see
creation's source and goal
and catch the vision of your will—
a universe made whole.
The cosmos shall cohere,
divisions all be healed
by love that drives creation's course,
love on a cross revealed.

The flaming stars proclaim
your might and majesty,
and in each cell's mysterious depths
your ordered plan we see.
For wonders you have wrought
our thanks to you we bring,
and for creations yet to come
will praise forever sing.

Herman G. Stuempfle, Jr., 1997
Awake Our Hearts to Praise, 2000
© 2000, GIA Publications, Inc.

Is there a richer harmony
than we alone can sing,
bright hymns of joy that, joined with ours,
make all creation ring?
O God, whatever choruses
rise up from worlds unknown,
their sound will be a gift of praise
to you and you alone!

God, help us bear our human part
in cosmic harmonies
and with all life, wherever found,
fulfill your law's decrees.
Make all we are and all we do
an echo of your Word—
the song of love you sang for us
in Christ, our risen Lord.

Herman G. Stuempfle, Jr., 1993
Redeeming the Time, 1997
© 1997, GIA Publications, Inc.

774

Creator God, We Gaze in Awe

Creator God, we gaze in awe
upon the distant stars
and ask if you have given life
in other worlds than ours.
How can it be that humankind,
the child of common dust,
alone can sing in praise of you
and in your goodness trust?

You made this planet home to hold
our struggling, striving race,
so new within the universe,
but touched and formed by grace.
Among the countless galaxies
that swirl through boundless space,
have you not wakened other life
to stand before your face?

775

Alone and Filled with Fear

Alone and filled with fear,
we come to you by night,
our troubled, restless spirits drawn
to you, the Light from Light.

We dare to question you,
as though all truth we knew,
but find you are the Questioner
who knows us through and through.

You probe our deepest need,
our hidden fears address.
You lead us to the midnight hour
where we, unmasked, confess.

The Word you speak is filled
with promise and with pain:
"There is no easy road to life;
you must be born again!"

But born anew by love,
the old life left behind,
we pass from darkness into day
and life, long sought, we find.

All glory be to God
who sent to us the Son,
who will not give our spirits rest
till love's great work is done.

Herman G. Stuempfle, Jr., 1994
Redeeming the Time, 1997
© 1997, GIA Publications, Inc.

776

We Wait in Stillness, God, before You

We wait in stillness, God, before you
like sleeping child on mother's breast.
In quietness we now adore you;
our cares and fears on you we rest.

Whatever, unforeseen, befalls us,
though threat and storm may rage abroad,
your patient voice again recalls us:
"Be still, and know that I am God."

O God, serene, yet ever caring,
your peace our restlessness enfolds.
When burdens press beyond our bearing,
your gentle hand our life upholds.

Our lives, O God, we now surrender
in quiet trust, our hearts at rest.
Your love—maternal, strong, and tender—
will give your children what is best.

Herman G. Stuempfle, Jr., 1993
Redeeming the Time, 1997
© 1997, GIA Publications, Inc.

777

Would I Have Answered When You Called

Would I have answered when you called,
"Come, follow, follow me!"?
Would I at once have left behind
both work and family?
Or would the old, familiar round
have held me by its claim
and kept the spark within my heart
from bursting into flame?

Would I have followed where you led
through ancient Galilee,
on roads unknown, by ways untried,
beyond security?
Or would I soon have hurried back
where home and comfort drew,
where truth you taught would not disturb
the ordered world I knew?

Would I have matched my step with yours
when crowds cried, "Crucify!"
when on a rocky hill I saw
a cross against the sky?
Or would I too have slipped away
and left you there alone,
a dying king with crown of thorns
upon a terrible throne?

O Christ, I cannot search my heart
    through all its tangled ways,
nor can I with a certain mind
    my steadfastness appraise.
I only pray that when you call,
    "Come, follow, follow me!"
You'll give me strength beyond my own
    to follow faithfully.

Herman G. Stuempfle, Jr., 1997
Redeeming the Time, 1997
© 1997, GIA Publications, Inc.

778

Lord, Grant Us Grace to Know the Time

Lord, grant us grace to know the time
    of action or of prayer,
which hour to crowd with waiting work
    and which with you to share.

We seek your Word, as Mary sought;
    we wait in quietness,
and yet we ask for strength to serve
    with Martha's faithfulness.

Your Word alone gives needed power
    to strengthen weary hands
and helps us see in each new day
    the way of your commands.

But you have taught that love is feigned
    that fails a neighbor's need,
that faith we claim is false until
    your Word becomes our deed.

We thank you, Lord, for quiet time
    to cast on you our care
and for your Word that follows us
    when work becomes our prayer.

Herman G. Stuempfle, Jr., 1995
Redeeming the Time, 1997
© 1997, GIA Publications, Inc.

779

O for a Donkey to Carry the Church

O for a donkey to carry the church,
    a donkey strong and wise;
to see the way that lay ahead
    with open, knowing eyes.

O for a donkey who would refuse
    to go where we demand,
when God says no to ways we choose,
    despite what we had planned.

O for a donkey who would not move
    when angry voices rose;
who could not be compelled to go
    by shouted words, or blows.

O for a donkey who would speak out,
    requesting us to tell
why we would raise a hand in rage
    at one who served us well.

O for a donkey who halted till
    our eyes were opened wide
to see God's angel in the road,
    to know whom we defied!

Now praise the Spirit who carries the church,
    so strong and wise and free;
who stops, resists our rage, and speaks,
    and waits for us to see!

Richard Leach, 1996
based on Numbers 22:21–35
Memory, Take the Hand of Hope, 2000
© 1998, Selah Publishing Company, Inc.

780
Where Was the Greater Struggle

A. General version

Where was the greater struggle?—
    Where Jesus was alone
to fast and face his hunger
    among the loaves of stone—
or where five thousand gathered
    and wanted to be fed,
with words for hearts that hungered
    as well as broken bread?

Where was the greater struggle?—
    where Jesus with a glance
took in a world of kingdoms
    to reach for all at once—
or where he rose from table
    when suppertime had come,
to wash his own disciples
    and love them one by one?

Where was the greater struggle?—
    where Jesus saw thin air,
and leaping might bring angels,
    fulfilling Scripture there—
or where a cross held Jesus
    till every leap was stilled
by empire's law and order,
    and Scripture was fulfilled?

In wilderness Christ Jesus
    rehearsed for what would come,
and won a lesser struggle
    before a greater one.
Come, Spirit of the struggle,
    come, wild and holy dove,
lead us to leap for gladness,
    show us a world to love.

B. Version for Mark

Where was the greater struggle?—
    where Jesus, Spirit-blessed,
was driven by the Spirit
    into the wilderness—
or was it in his home town,
    confronted by the wise,
who said that Jesus' spirit
    came from the Lord of Flies?

Where was the greater struggle?—
    where Satan's ways were bare,
in wild and empty places
    when Jesus met them there—
or in the crowded city,
    where Satan's words and ways
were hidden like a leaven
    within its life each day?

Where was the greater struggle?—
    where Jesus' company
was animal or angel
    before his ministry—
or was the struggle greater
    where Jesus walked with friends,
and sought to teach and lead them
    and love them till the end?

In wilderness Christ Jesus
    rehearsed for what would come,
and won a lesser struggle
    before a greater one.
O Jesus, we would join you
    in wilderness and town,
that we may share your struggle
    in Lent and all year 'round.

Richard Leach, 1989, 1991
based on Mark 1:12–13 and parallels
Feel the Spirit in the Kicking, 1995
© 1992, Hope Publishing Company

781
Told of God's Favor

Told of God's favor, told of God's purpose,
Mary said, "Tell me, how can this be?"
Told of the Spirit, told of the power,
told of the promise, Mary said yes.

Yes to conceiving, yes to the body
changing and growing, yes to the flesh—
yes to the new life kicking within her,
yes to the pleasure, yes to the pain.

Yes to the waiting, yes to the labor,
yes to the hurting, yes to the birth—
yes to the baby, yes to the future,
yes to the holy, yes to the world.

Told of Christ Jesus, told of the Spirit,
can we say yes as Mary said yes?
Yes for our bodies, yes for our spirits,
yes for the future, yes for right now.

Praise to the Spirit, praise to the Most High,
sending the word that Mary was told.
Praise to Christ Jesus, who was made welcome
into our world when Mary said yes.

Richard Leach, 1990
Feel the Spirit in the Kicking, 1995
© 1994, Selah Publishing Company, Inc.

782
Hope Is a Candle

Hope is a candle, once lit by the prophets,
never consumed, though it burns through the
years;
dim in the daylight of power and privilege—
when they are gone, hope will shine on.

Peace is a candle to show us a pathway,
threatened by gusts from our rage and our greed.
Friend, feel no envy for those in the shadows—
violence and force their dead-end course.

Love is a candle whose light makes a circle,
where every face is the face of a friend.
Widen the circle by sharing and giving—
God's holy dare: Love everywhere.

Joy is a candle of mystery and laughter,
mystery of light that is born in the dark;
laughter at hearing the voice of an angel,
ever so near, casting out fear.

Christ is the light that the prophets awaited,
Christ is the lion, the lamb, and the child.
Christ is the love and the mystery and laughter—
candles, make way! Christ is the day!

Richard Leach, 1994
Feel the Spirit in the Kicking, 1995
© 1995, Selah Publishing Company, Inc.

783
An Outcast among Outcasts

An outcast among outcasts,
dismissed with double scorn,
belittled by the labels
"unclean" and "foreign born,"
came back with thanks for Jesus,
and then went on his way.
An outcast among outcasts
showed grateful faith that day.

An outcast among outcasts,
where three were crucified,
one taunted by the others,
as they hung side by side,
came back from death with power;
God had the final say.
An outcast among outcasts
shows God to us today.

For outcast among outcasts,
　　the boundaries are redrawn,
by words, "Your faith has saved you,"
　　by cross and Easter dawn.
The distant, longed-for centers
　　of power, peace, and care,
where life is free to flourish,
　　are found now everywhere.

Richard Leach, 1992
based on Luke 17:11–19, 23:39–43
Carpenter, Why Leave the Bench, 1996
© 1994, Selah Publishing Company, Inc.

784

Can God Be Seen in Other Ways

Can God be seen in other ways
　　than crowned and seated on a throne?
Is God, the source of matchless might,
　　immovable as quarried stone?

Or could it be that God is glimpsed
　　in ordinary time and space,
a sovereign not remote at all
　　but seen in every human face?

In those evicted by the world,
　　the aging man, the refugee,
the woman, youthful but abused,
　　God's image we can clearly see.

In those with crushed and splintered dreams
　　who look for little from above,
the Holy One seeks out and dwells,
　　with steadfast, hope-producing love.

John Thornburg, 1992
Covenant Hymnal, 1996
© 2003, Abingdon Press (admin. The Copyright Company)

785

God the Sculptor of the Mountains

God the sculptor of the mountains,
　　God the miller of the sand,
God the jeweler of the heavens,
　　God the potter of the land:
　　　　You are womb of all creation,
　　　　　　we are formless; shape us now.

God the nuisance to the Pharaoh,
　　God the cleaver of the sea,
God the pillar of the darkness,
　　God the beacon of the free:
　　　　You are gate of all deliverance,
　　　　　　we are sightless; lead us now.

God the unexpected infant,
　　God the calm, determined youth,
God the table-turning prophet,
　　God the resurrected Truth:
　　　　You are present every moment,
　　　　　　we are searching; meet us now.

God the dresser of the vineyard,
　　God the planter of the wheat,
God the reaper of the harvest,
　　God the source of all we eat:
　　　　You are host at every table,
　　　　　　we are hungry; feed us now.

John Thornburg, 1994; revised, 1995
Wonder, Love, and Praise, 1997
© 1993, John Thornburg

786
Come to Tend God's Garden

Come to tend God's garden,
    seeds of hope to sow,
planting fields of justice,
    watching mercy grow.
In an arid wasteland
    spread a verdant heath.
In a land of tumult
    cultivate God's peace.

As we tend God's garden,
    from its furrows rise
stems of fresh beginnings,
    stretching toward the skies.
Graciousness, our meadow,
    joyfulness, our root,
unity, our foliage,
    righteousness, our fruit.

May God's garden flourish,
    may our toil succeed.
May God bless our actions,
    every word and deed.
Serving Christ each season
    with God's diagram.
Charted by the Spirit
    for the task at hand.

John A. Dalles, 1992
Swift Currents and Still Waters, 2000
© 2000, GIA Publications, Inc.

787
God, Could It Be

God, could it be that we are called
    to bring the light of morn
into the shadow-lands of life?
    Perhaps for this we're born!

God, could it be that we are called
    to comfort those who mourn
and dry the tears of those who cry?
    Perhaps for this we're born!

God, could it be that we are called
    to mend a life that's torn
with hopeful, helpful, healing hands?
    Perhaps for this we're born!

God, could it be that we are called
    to give rest to the worn,
and guide the ones who've lost their way?
    Perhaps for this we're born!

John A. Dalles, 1996
Swift Currents and Still Waters, 2000
© 2000, GIA Publications, Inc.

788
Lead On, O Cloud of Presence

Lead on, O cloud of Presence;
    the exodus is come;
in wilderness and desert
    our tribe shall make its home.
Our bondage left behind us,
    new hopes within us grow.
We seek the land of promise
    where milk and honey flow.

Lead on, O fiery pillar;
    we follow yet with fears,
but we shall come rejoicing,
    though joy be born of tears.
We are not lost, though wandering,
    for by your light we come,
and we are still God's people.
    The journey is our home.

Lead on, O God of freedom,
　　and guide us on our way,
and help us trust the promise
　　through struggle and delay.
We pray our sons and daughters
　　may journey to that land
where justice dwells with mercy
　　and love is law's demand.

Ruth Duck, 1974; revised, 1989
Dancing in the Universe, 1992
© 1992, GIA Publications, Inc.

789
Arise, Your Light Is Come

Arise, your light is come!
　　The Spirit's call obey;
show forth the glory of your God
　　which shines on you today.

Arise, your light is come!
　　Fling wide the prison door;
proclaim the captive's liberty,
　　good tidings to the poor.

Arise, your light is come!
　　All you in sorrow born,
bind up the brokenhearted ones
　　and comfort those who mourn.

Arise, your light is come!
　　The mountains burst in song!
Rise up like eagles on the wing;
　　God's power will make us strong.

Ruth Duck, 1973
Dancing in the Universe, 1992
© 1992, GIA Publications, Inc.

790
As Grain on Scattered Hillsides

As grain on scattered hillsides,
　　when gathered, makes one bread,
God, gather all your people
　　as one in Christ our head.
We come from many places
　　and we are not the same,
yet your strong love has called us
　　to meet in Jesus' name.

A grain of wheat is fruitless
　　until in earth it lies;
then, dying to its old life,
　　it bears and multiplies.
So may we die to hatred,
　　to all our hurtful ways,
reborn to common living,
　　to love, to work, to praise.

Like yeast that brings new ferment
　　so lifeless dough may rise,
your Spirit is the leaven
　　of life that satisfies.
As salt enhances flavor,
　　enriches, and preserves,
may earth rejoice to savor
　　a church that heals and serves.

O Christ, our risen Savior;
　　O Spirit, holy dove,
come now and move among us;
　　make us a sign of love.
Come, knead and blend each texture
　　with strong and gentle hands,
that we may be one body,
　　one loaf in many lands.

Ruth Duck, 1986
Dancing in the Universe, 1992
© 1992, GIA Publications, Inc.

791
How Could a God Whose Name Is Love

How could a God whose name is love
    seek blood to pay sin's price?
Are torture, shame, and senseless death
    a holy sacrifice?
Each violent crime is tragic loss;
    how could it be God's will?
How can we glorify a cross
    when victims suffer still?

Did Jesus come as God's own child
    to share each human tear?
Did Jesus die in speaking truth
    that rulers will not hear?
If Wisdom hangs upon a tree,
    what, then, are we to do?
Must we, like Jesus, risk our lives
    for what is just and true?

In Jesus Christ we meet a God
    whose love embraces all,
who weeps when children are abused,
    who hears each sparrow fall.
When grace is ancient as the earth,
    we need not worship death.
So let us live in tender care
    for all whom Love gives breath.

Ruth Duck, 1993
Circles of Care, 1996
© 1996, The Pilgrim Press

792
Creator of All Time and Space

Creator of all time and space,
we read your image on each face.
Great Spirit of the cosmic whole,
you made us body, mind, and soul.

We thank you for the human mind,
in mystic harmony designed,
for word and image, dream and thought,
for lessons learned and answers sought.

O God of planet, moon, and sun,
we wonder, knowing all you've done,
that you befriend the human race,
and fill our lives with love and grace.

For miracles as large as space,
as small as cells, as deep as grace,
we offer you our thanks and praise,
and pledge to serve you all our days.

Ruth Duck, 1993
Circles of Care, 1996
© 1996, The Pilgrim Press

793
Womb of Life, and Source of Being

Womb of life, and source of being,
    home of every restless heart,
in your arms the worlds awakened;
    you have loved us from the start.
We, your children, gather 'round you,
    at the table you prepare.
Sharing stories, tears, and laughter,
    we are nurtured by your care.

Word in flesh, our brother Jesus,
    born to bring us second birth,
you have come to stand beside us,
    knowing weakness, knowing earth.
Priest who shares our human struggles,
    Life of Life, and Death of Death,
risen Christ, come stand among us,
    send the Spirit by your breath.

Brooding Spirit, move among us;
    be our partner, be our friend.
When our memory fails, remind us
    whose we are, what we intend.
Labor with us, aid the birthing
    of the new world yet to be,
free of servant, lord, and master,
    free for love and unity.

Mother, Brother, holy Partner;
    Father, Spirit, Only Son:
we would praise your name forever,
    one-in-three, and three-in-one.
We would share your life, your passion,
    share your word of world made new,
ever singing, ever praising,
    one with all, and one with you.

Ruth Duck, 1986; revised, 1990
Dancing in the Universe, 1992
© 1992, GIA Publications, Inc.

794
Child of Blessing, Child of Promise

Child of blessing, child of promise,
    baptized with the Spirit's sign;
with this water God has sealed you
    unto love and grace divine.

Child of love, our love's expression,
    love's creation, loved indeed!
fresh from God, refresh our spirits,
    into joy and laughter lead.

Child of joy, our dearest treasure,
    God's you are, from God you came.
Back to God we humbly give you;
    live as one who bears Christ's name.

Child of God the loving Parent,
    learn to know whose child you are.
Grow to laugh and sing and worship,
    trust and love God more than all.

Ronald S. Cole-Turner, 1981
Everflowing Streams, 1981
© 1981, Ronald S. Cole-Turner

For congregations that bless, rather than baptize, infants, the author
offers this opening stanza:

Child of blessing, child of promise,
    consecrated and assigned
to the care of God who claims you
    unto love and grace divine.

795
We Yearn, O Lord, for Wholeness

We yearn, O Lord, for wholeness
    and for your healing touch;
too long have we felt helpless;
    our burdens seemed too much.
Forgetting all pretenses,
    we make our pleadings heard.
In hope and expectation
    we wait your gracious Word.

We long to have companions
    who travel by our side,
strong friends to call and answer
    with whom we are allied;
as we lift up each other
    when struggles lay us low,
community develops;
    our faith and caring grow.

We need your living presence,
　　O Christ of Galilee,
a presence that revives us
　　and sets our spirits free.
No longer are we fearful,
　　your love pervades each place,
empower us with courage
　　to claim your healing grace.

Dosia Carlson, 1983
God's Glory, 1986
© 1986, Dosia Carlson

God in victory, God in failure,
　　steadfast through each tribal test,
save us from our shabby idols,
　　show us that your way is best;
better than the lure of power,
　　better than the lust for fame;
so in failure may we praise you,
　　and in victory bless your name.

Dosia Carlson, 1975
God's Glory, 1986
© 1975, The Hymn Society (admin. Hope Publishing Company)

796
God of Eagles, God of Sparrows

God of eagles, God of sparrows,
　　soaring spirit, earthly guide,
help our nation know true greatness
　　free from all-consuming pride.
Strengthen us for global duties
　　sharing progress that is just;
like the eagle may we venture,
　　like the sparrow may we trust.

God of valleys, God of mountains,
　　comrade in our depths and heights,
speak through all our civic leaders
　　who would nurture human rights.
May they know your daily presence
　　and affirm your ageless deeds;
through dark valleys may they follow
　　up steep mountains where love leads.

797
When Quiet Peace Is Shattered

When quiet peace is shattered
　　by dreadful noise of war,
and we are bruised and battered
　　by fighting's constant roar,

　　　　Lord, break the silence of your word
　　　　and let your healing voice be heard.
　　　　O let your healing voice be heard.

When troubles still our love-song
　　and fear beats hard within,
when anger drowns the dove's song,
　　and life's a noisy din,

When clashing wills divide us
　　and hearts refuse to mend,
when feelings scream inside us
　　and agonies won't end,

Mary Nelson Keithan, 1991
Come Away with Me, 1998
© 1997, Hinshaw Music, Inc.

798
The Weaver's Shuttle Swiftly Flies

The weaver's shuttle swiftly flies
    across the tapestry;
then patterns, textures, varied hues
    emerge for all to see.
And so our lives are woven fine
    as in that weaver's hand,
a fair design and richer still
    than we can understand.

The Weaver's shuttle swiftly flies
    across the earthly loom.
Our stories all too quickly pass
    from cradle to the tomb.
Day follows day and year on year;
    they fade as in a dream.
And none can hold the shuttle still
    or stop the flowing stream.

Who knows the patterns of our lives
    before our days are spun?
Who knows the reason why, and how,
    before it's all begun?
The One whose hand weaves all with love
    and mystery and care;
The One whose thread and warp and weft
    are flesh and earth and air!

When will we find the true design
    intended for our days?
In heaven to come, when life is done
    and nothing's left but praise?
Or shall we see in glimpses now
    the pattern God reveals,
and here embrace this earthly race
    that wounds us and that heals?

O gentle Weaver, loving God,
    we are your works of art,
and so we see eternity
    within each human heart.
In all we think and do and say,
    in all we hope and fear,
give us the eyes to recognize
    the heaven always here.

James Gertmenian, 1990
The New Century Hymnal, 1995
© 1990, James Gertmenian
The author's original verison of 5:2 was "we are your fairest art."

799
Throughout These Lenten Days and Nights

Throughout these Lenten days and nights
    we turn to walk the inward way,
where, meeting Christ, our guide and light,
    we live in hope till Easter Day.

The pilgrim Christ, the Lamb of God,
    who found in weakness greater power,
embraces us, though lost and flawed,
    and leads us to his rising hour.

We bear the silence, cross, and pain
    of human burdens, human strife,
while sisters, brothers help sustain
    our courage till the feast of life.

And though the road is hard and steep,
    the Spirit ever calls us on
through Calvary's dying, dark and deep,
    until we see the coming dawn.

So let us choose the path of One
    who wore, for us, the crown of thorn,
and slept in death that we might wake
    to life on Resurrection Morn!

Rejoice, O sons and daughters! Sing
   and shout hosannas! Raise the strain!
For Christ, whose death Good Friday brings,
   on Easter Day will live again!

James Gertmenian, 1993
The Book of Praise, 1998
© 1993, Hope Publishing Company

800
Spirit

Spirit, spirit of gentleness,
   blow through the wilderness,
     calling and free,
Spirit, spirit of restlessness,
   stir me from placidness,
     wind, wind on the sea.

You moved on the waters,
   you called to the deep;
then you coaxed up the mountains
   from the valleys of sleep,
and over the eons
   you called to each thing,
"Wake from your slumbers
   and rise on your wings."

You swept through the desert,
   you stung with the sand,
and you goaded your people
   with a law and a land,
and when they were blinded
   with their idols and lies,
then you spoke through your prophets
   to open their eyes.

You sang in a stable,
   you cried from a hill,
then you whispered in silence
   when the whole world was still,
and down in the city
   you called once again
when you blew through your people
   on the rush of the wind.

You call from tomorrow,
   you break ancient schemes,
from the bondage of sorrow
   the captives dream dreams;
our women see visions,
   our men clear their eyes.
With bold new decisions
   your people arise.

James K. Manley, 1975
Sing to God, 1984
© 1978, James K. Manley

801
Gift of Finest Wheat

You satisfy the hungry heart
   with gift of finest wheat;
come, give to us, O saving Lord,
   the bread of life to eat.

As when the shepherd calls his sheep,
   they know and heed his voice,
so when you call your family, Lord,
   we follow and rejoice.

With joyful lips we sing to you
   our praise and gratitude,
that you should count us worthy, Lord,
   to share this heavenly food.

Is not the cup we bless and share
    the blood of Christ outpoured?
Do not one cup, one loaf, declare
    our oneness in the Lord?

The mystery of your presence, Lord,
    no mortal tongue can tell:
Whom all the world cannot contain
    comes in our hearts to dwell.

You give yourself to us, O Lord;
    then selfless let us be,
to serve each other in your name
    in truth and charity.

Richard Wing (Omer Westendorf), 1975
We Celebrate with Song, 1979
© 1977, Archdiocese of Philadelphia

802
Sent Forth by God's Blessing

Sent forth by God's blessing,
    our true faith confessing,
the people of God from this dwelling take leave.
    God's sacrifice ended,
    O now be extended
the fruits of this Mass in all hearts who believe.
    The seed of Christ's teaching,
    our inner souls reaching,
shall blossom in action for God and for all.
    God's grace shall incite us,
    in love shall unite us
to further God's kingdom and answer the call.

With praise and thanksgiving
    to God who is living,
the tasks of our everyday life we embrace.
    Our faith ever sharing,
    in love ever caring,
we claim as our family all those of each race.
    One bread that has fed us,
    one light that has led us
unite us as one in the life that we share.
    Then may all the living
    with praise and thanksgiving
give honor to Christ and his name that we bear.

J. Clifford Evers (Omer Westendorf), 1964; revised, 1984
People's Mass Book, 2003
© 1964, World Library Publications

803
From Ashes to the Living Font

From ashes to the living font
    your church must journey, Lord,
baptized in grace, in grace renewed
    by your most holy word.

Through fasting, prayer, and charity
    your voice speaks deep within,
returning us to ways of truth
    and turning us from sin.

Third stanzas:
    First and Second Sunday

From desert to the mountaintop
    in Christ our way we see,
so, tempered by temptation's might
    we might transfigured be.

Third Sunday

For thirsting hearts let waters flow
    our fainting souls revive;
and at the well your waters give
    our everlasting life.

Fourth Sunday

We sit beside the road and plead,
    "Come, save us, David's son!"
Now with your vision heal our eyes,
    the world's true Light alone.

Fifth Sunday

Our graves split open, bring us back,
    your promise to proclaim;
to darkened tombs call out, "Arise!"
    and glorify your name.

From ashes to the living font,
    your church must journey still,
through cross and tomb to Easter joy,
    in Spirit-fire fulfilled.

Alan J. Hommerding, 1994
We Celebrate Worship Resource, 1994
© 1994, World Library Publications

804
As the Sun with Longer Journey

As the sun with longer journey
melts the winter's snow and ice,
with its slowly growing radiance
warms the seed beneath the earth,
may the sun of Christ's uprising
gently bring our hearts to life.

Through the days of waiting, watching
in the desert of our sin,
searching on the far horizon
for a sign of cloud or wind,
we await the healing waters
of our Savior's victory.

Praise be given to the Maker
of the seasons' yearly round:
To the Speaker through the Spoken
in their living Breath of love
as the ever-turning seasons
roll to their eternal rest.

John Patrick Earls, 1961; revised, 1989
Voices United, 1996
© 1981, 1990, Order of St. Benedict

805
Faithful Cross

Faithful cross, O tree of beauty,
    tree of Eden, tree divine!
Not a grove on earth can show us
    leaf and flower and fruit so fine.
Bearer of our Savior's body,
    tree of life, salvation's sign!

Cross of pain transformed to gladness,
    ever green and sheltering tree,
symbol once of shame and bondage,
    now the sign that we are free!
Cross of splendor, cross of glory,
    cross of love's great victory!

Christians, chant your grateful praises
    for the tree of triumph won,
proof of overflowing mercy
    and redemption in the Son.
To the cross of Christ give glory
    while the endless ages run!

Delores Dufner, 1989
Sing a New Church, 1994
© 1993, Delores Dufner (admin. OCP Publications)

806

When the Universe Was Fashioned

When the universe was fashioned—
    night and day, dry land and sea,
plants and every living creature—
    by God's word they came to be.
In that word was breath of wisdom.
    In that word was breath of life.
        In that word was breath of God.

Darkness fell, but not forever;
    love appeared, unconquered light.
Wisdom came to dwell among us—
    Child beloved, God's delight.
In that child was light of wisdom.
    In that child was light of life.
        In that child was light of God.

Human eyes have seen God's glory;
    human hands have touched God's own.
May we never cease proclaiming
    wisdom we have seen and known.
Jesus is the word of wisdom.
    Jesus is the word of life.
        Jesus is the word of God.

Delores Dufner, 1988
Sing a New Church, 1994
© 1993, Delores Dufner (admin. OCP Publications)

807

My Heart Is Overflowing

My heart is overflowing
    with gladness and with praise.
The God who guards my going
    gives meaning to my days.
Holy the Rock of Ages known in word and deed,
giving the victory, fulfilling my every need.

The living God has spoken.
    Earth answers with a song.
Weapons of war are broken,
    the weak are feeling strong.
See, we no longer hunger, crying out for bread.
Our God restores to life and raises us from the dead.

All who are poor and lowly
    will have a heavenly home.
The humble and the holy
    shall surely know shalom.
God lifts the needy from the ashes of despair,
favors the outcast and the downtrodden everywhere.

The power of compassion
    can turn the world around.
The firm in faith will fashion
    gardens from barren ground.
Echoes of joy are found resounding from the tomb.
Cheerful the childless woman: Life stirs within her
                                            womb.

The One who once created
    and now sustains the earth,
boldly anticipated
    we too would bring to birth.
Love conquers evil, setting all the captives free.
Praise God for life begetting life for eternity.

Miriam Therese Winter, 1993
based on 1 Samuel 2:1–10
Songlines, 1996
© 1993, Medical Mission Sisters

808

Blest Are They

Blest are they, the poor in spirit,
    theirs is the kingdom of God.
Blest are they, full of sorrow,
    they shall be consoled.

Rejoice and be glad!
Blessed are you, holy are you!
Rejoice and be glad!
Yours is the kingdom of God!

Blest are they, the lowly ones,
they shall inherit the earth.
Blest are they who hunger and thirst,
they shall have their fill.

Blest are they who show mercy,
mercy shall be theirs.
Blest are they, the pure of heart,
they shall see God!

Blest are they who seek peace;
they are the children of God.
Blest are they who suffer in faith,
the glory of God is theirs.

Blest are you who suffer hate,
all because of me.
Rejoice and be glad, yours is the kingdom;
shine for all to see.

David Haas, 1985
based on Matthew 5:3–11
Gather, 1988
© 1985, GIA Publications, Inc.

We are the young—our lives are a mystery,
we are the old who yearn for your face,
we have been sung throughout all of history,
called to be light to the whole human race.
Gather us in—the rich and the haughty,
gather us in—the proud and the strong;
give us a heart so meek and so lowly,
give us the courage to enter the song.

Here we will take the wine and the water,
here we will take the bread of new birth,
here you shall call your sons and your daughters,
call us anew to be salt for the earth.
Give us to drink the wine of compassion,
give us to eat the bread that is you;
nourish us well, and teach us to fashion
lives that are holy and hearts that are true.

Not in the dark of buildings confining,
not in some heaven, light-years away,
but here in this place the new light is shining,
now is the kingdom, now is the day.
Gather us in and hold us forever,
gather us in and make us your own;
gather us in—all peoples together,
fire of love in our flesh and our bone.

Marty Haugen, 1982
Gather, 1988
© 1982, GIA Publications, Inc.

809

Gather Us In

Here in this place new light is streaming,
now is the darkness vanished away,
see in this space our fears and our dreamings,
brought here to you in the light of this day.
Gather us in—the lost and forsaken,
gather us in—the blind and the lame;
call to us now, and we shall awaken,
we shall arise at the sound of our name.

810

Bring Forth the Kingdom

You are salt for the earth, O people:
salt for the kingdom of God!
Share the flavor of life, O people:
life in the kingdom of God!

Bring forth the kingdom of mercy,
bring forth the kingdom of peace;
bring forth the kingdom of justice,
bring forth the City of God!

You are a light on the hill, O people:
  Light for the City of God!
Shine so holy and bright, O people:
  Shine for the kingdom of God!

You are a seed of the Word, O people:
  Bring forth the kingdom of God!
Seeds of mercy and seeds of justice,
  grow in the kingdom of God!

We are a blest and a pilgrim people:
  bound for the kingdom of God!
Love our journey and love our homeland:
  Love is the kingdom of God!

Marty Haugen, 1986
Gather, 1988
© 1986, GIA Publications, Inc.

811
Tree of Life

Tree of Life and awesome mystery,
  in your death we are reborn;
though you die in all of history,
  still you rise with every morn.

Seed that dies to rise in glory,
  may we see ourselves in you.
If we learn to live your story,
  we may die to rise anew.

We remember truth once spoken,
  love passed on through act and word.
Every person lost and broken
  wears the body of our Lord.

Gentle Jesus, mighty Spirit,
  come inflame our hearts anew.
We may all your joy inherit
  if we bear the cross with you.

Christ, you lead and we shall follow,
  stumbling though our steps may be;
one with you in joy and sorrow,
  we the river, you the sea.

Lenten stanzas:
  General

Light of life beyond conceiving,
  mighty Spirit of our Lord,
give new strength to our believing,
  give us faith to live your word.

First Sunday

From the dawning of creation,
  you have loved us as your own;
stay with us through all temptation,
  make us turn to you alone.

Second Sunday

In our call to be a blessing,
  may we be a blessing true;
may we live and die confessing
  Christ as Lord of all we do.

Third Sunday

Living Water of salvation,
  be the fountain of each soul;
springing up in new creation,
  flow in us and make us whole.

Fourth Sunday

Give us eyes to see you clearly,
  make us children of your light;
give us hearts to live more nearly
  as your gospel shining bright.

Fifth Sunday

God of all our fear and sorrow,
    God who lives beyond our death,
hold us close through each tomorrow,
    love as near as every breath.

Marty Haugen, 1984
Gather, 1988
© 1984, GIA Publications, Inc.

812

On Eagle's Wings

You who dwell in the shelter of the Lord,
    who abide in his shadow for life,
    say to the Lord: "My refuge,
    my rock in whom I trust!"

        And he will raise you up on eagle's wings,
            bear you on the breath of dawn,
            make you to shine like the sun,
            and hold you in the palm of his hand.

The snare of the fowler will never capture you,
    and famine will bring you no fear:
    Under his wings your refuge,
    his faithfulness your shield.

You need not fear the terror of the night,
    nor the arrow that flies by day;
    though thousands fall about you,
    near you it shall not come.

For to his angels he's given a command
    to guard you in all of your ways;
    upon their hands they will bear you up,
    lest you dash your foot against a stone.

Michael Joncas, 1978
based on Psalm 91
Gather, 1988
© 1979, OCP Publications

813

O Ancient Love

O ancient love, processing through the ages;
O hidden love, revealed in human form;
O promised love, the dream of seer and sages:

        O living Love, within our hearts be born,
        O living Love, within our hearts be borne.

O homeless love, that dwells among the stranger;
O lowly love, that knows the mighty's scorn;
O hungry love, that lay within a manger:

O gentle love, caressing those in sorrow;
O tender love, that comforts those forlorn;
O hopeful love, that promises tomorrow:

O suffering love, that bears our human weakness;
O boundless love, that rises with the morn;
O mighty love, concealed in infant meekness:

Michael Joncas. 1994
Voices United, 1996
© 1994, GIA Publications, Inc.

814

Here I Am, Lord

I, the Lord of sea and sky,
I have heard my people cry.
All who dwell in dark and sin
    my hand will save.
I who made the stars of night,
I will make their darkness bright.
Who will bear my light to them?
    Whom shall I send?

Here I am, Lord.
Is it I, Lord?
I have heard you calling in the night.
I will go, Lord,
if you lead me.
I will hold your people in my heart.

I, the Lord of snow and rain,
I have borne my people's pain.
I have wept for love of them.
They turn away.
I will break their hearts of stone,
give them hearts for love alone.
I will speak my word to them.
Whom shall I send?

I, the Lord of wind and flame,
I will tend the poor and lame.
I will set a feast for them.
My hand will save.
Finest bread I will provide
till their hearts be satisfied.
I will give my life to them.
Whom shall I send?

Daniel L. Schutte, 1981
Gather, 1988
© 1981, OCP Publications

815
Two Fishermen

Two fishermen, who lived along
the Sea of Galilee,
stood by the shore to cast their nets
into an ageless sea.
Now Jesus watched them from afar,
then called them each by name;
it changed their lives, these simple men—
they'd never be the same.

Leave all things you have
and come and follow me,
and come and follow me.

And as he walked along the shore
'twas James and John he'd find,
and these two sons of Zebedee
would leave their boats behind.
Their work and all they held so dear
they left beside their nets;
their names they'd heard as Jesus called:
They came without regrets.

O Simon Peter, Andrew, James,
and John—beloved one,
you heard Christ's call to speak good news
revealed to God's own Son.
Susanna, Mary, Magdalene,
who traveled with your Lord,
you ministered to him with joy
for he is God adored.

And you, good Christians, one and all
who'd follow Jesus' way,
come, leave behind what keeps you bound
to trappings of our day,
and listen as he calls your name
to come and follow near,
for still he speaks in varied ways
to those his call will hear.

Suzanne Toolan, 1986
based on Matthew 4:18–22
The Worshiping Church, 1990
© 1986, GIA Publications, Inc.

816
The First One Ever

The first one ever, oh, ever to know
of the birth of Jesus was the Maid Mary,
was Mary the Maid of Galilee,
and blessed is she, is she who believes.
Oh, blessed is she who believes in the Lord,
oh, blessed is she who believes.
She was Mary the Maid of Galilee,
and blessed is she, is she who believes.

The first one ever, oh, ever to know
    of Messiah, Jesus, when he said, "I am he,"
was the Samaritan woman who drew from the well,
    and blessed is she, is she who perceives.
Oh, blessed is she who perceives the Lord,
    oh, blessed is she who perceives.
'Twas the Samaritan woman who drew from the well,
    and blessed is she, is she who perceives.

The first ones ever, oh, ever to know
    of the rising of Jesus, his glory to be,
were Mary, Joanna, and Magdalene,
    and blessed are they, are they who see.
Oh, blessed are they who see the Lord,
    oh, blessed are they who see.
They were Mary, Joanna, and Magdalene,
    and blessed are they, are they who see.

Linda Wilberger Egan, 1980; revised for *The Hymnal 1982*
The Hymnal 1982, 1985
© 1983, Linda Wilberger Egan

817

My Neighbor

They asked, "Who's my neighbor and whom should
                                         I love;
    for whom should I do a good deed?"
The Master related a story and said,
    "It's anyone who has a need,
    yes, anyone who has a need!"

There once was a traveler set on by thieves
    who beat him and left him to die;
a priest and a Levite each saw him in pain,
    but they turned away and walked by,
    yes, they turned away and walked by!

A certain Samaritan then came along
    to bind up his wounds and give aid;
he took him to stay at an inn until well,
    and for all the service he paid,
    yes, for all the service he paid!

I know who's my neighbor and whom I should love,
    for whom I should do a good deed;
for Christ made it clear in the story he told:
    it's anyone who has a need,
    yes, anyone who has a need!

Jan Wesson, 1981
based on Luke 10:29–37
New Hymns for Children, 1982
© 1982, The Hymn Society (admin. Hope Publishing Company)

818

Where Science Serves and Art Inspires

Where science serves and art inspires
    a struggling humankind,
there truth and beauty point to God's
    horizons of the mind.

Where joys are shared and fears which once
    lay hid in lives apart,
there love unlocks the door on God's
    horizons of the heart.

Where mind and heart together trust
    the One who makes life whole,
there faith reveals in splendor God's
    horizons of the soul.

O God, bring far horizons near,
    complete the search begun,
so what we see and dream, and what
    we do, by grace are one.

Jane M. Marshall, 1976
A New Hymnal for Colleges and Schools, 1992
© 1976, Jane M. Marshall

819
With Awe Approach the Mysteries

With awe approach the mysteries
   and wrestle with the Word
like Jacob, bruised yet strangely blest.
   Servanthood is pain.

With wisdom teach, with courage preach;
   like Deborah, lead your flock
inside the culture's danger zone.
   Servanthood is faith.

Reach out to those diseased, alone,
   to those confused, opposed;
and like a mother, heal, forgive.
   Servanthood is grace.

Fill tirelessly your call's demands,
   then rest, like Christ, apart,
refreshed by God's renewing strength.
   Servanthood is love.

Jane M. Marshall, 1996
Wonder, Love, and Praise, 1997
© 1994, Hope Publishing Company

820
What Gift Can We Bring

What gift can we bring, what present, what token?
What words can convey it, the joy of this day?
When grateful we come, remembering, rejoicing,
what song can we offer in honor and praise?

Give thanks for the past, for those who had vision,
who planted and watered so dreams could come true.
Give thanks for the now, for study, for worship,
for mission that bids us turn prayer into deed.

Give thanks for tomorrow, full of surprises,
for knowing whatever tomorrow may bring,
the Word is our promise always, forever;
we rest in God's keeping and live in God's love.

This gift we now bring, this present, this token,
these words can convey it, the joy of this day!
When grateful we come, remembering, rejoicing,
this song we now offer in honor and praise!

Jane M. Marshall, 1980, revised 1987
The United Methodist Hymnal, 1989
© 1982, Hope Publishing Company

821
Hymn of Promise

In the bulb, there is a flower;
   in the seed, an apple tree;
in cocoons, a hidden promise:
   Butterflies will soon be free!
In the cold of snow and winter
   there's a spring that waits to be,
unrevealed until its season,
   something God alone can see.

There's a song in every silence,
   seeking word and melody;
there's a dawn in every darkness,
   bringing hope to you and me.
From the past will come the future;
   what it holds, a mystery,
unrevealed until its season,
   something God alone can see.

In our end is our beginning;
 in our time, infinity.
In our doubt there is believing;
 in our life, eternity.
In our death, a resurrection;
 at the last, a victory,
unrevealed until its season,
 something God alone can see.

Natalie Sleeth, 1985
Adventures for the Soul, 1987
© 1986, Hope Publishing Company

822

Isaiah the Prophet Has Written of Old

Isaiah the prophet has written of old
 how God's new creation shall come.
Instead of the thorn tree, the fir tree shall grow;
 the wolf shall lie down with the lamb.
The mountains and hills shall burst forth into song,
 the peoples be led forth in peace,
for the earth shall be filled with the knowledge of
              God
 as the waters cover the sea.

Yet nations still prey on the meek of the world,
 and conflict turns parent from child.
Your people despoil all the sweetness of earth,
 the brier and the thorn tree grow wild.
God, bring to fruition your will for the earth,
 that no one shall hurt or destroy,
that wisdom and justice shall reign in the land
 and your people shall go forth in joy.

Joy Patterson, 1981; revised, 1993
based on Isaiah 11:6–9, 55:11–23
Come, You People of the Promise, 1994
© 1982, The Hymn Society (admin. Hope Publishing Company)

823

O Lord, You Gave Your Servant John

O Lord, you gave your servant John
 a vision of the world to come:
a radiant city filled with light,
 where you with us will make your home;
where neither grief nor pain shall dwell,
 since former things have passed away,
and where they need no sun nor moon;
 your glory lights eternal day.

Our cities, Lord, wear shrouds of pain;
 beneath our gleaming towers of wealth
the homeless crouch in rain and snow,
 the poor cry out for strength and health.
Youth's hope is dimmed by ignorance;
 unwilling, workers idled stand;
indifference walks unheeding by
 as hunger stretches out its hand.

Come, Lord, make real John's vision fair;
 come, dwell with us, make all things new;
we try in vain to save our world
 unless our help shall come from you.
Come, strengthen us to live in love;
 bid hatred, greed, injustice cease.
Your glory all the light we need,
 let all our cities shine forth peace.

Joy Patterson, 1988
Come, You People of the Promise, 1994
© 1989, Hope Publishing Company

824

When Aimless Violence Takes Those We Love

When aimless violence takes those we love,
 when random death strikes childhood's promise
               down,
when wrenching loss becomes our daily bread,
 we know, O God, you leave us not alone.

When passing years rob sight and strength and mind
    yet fail to still a strongly beating heart,
and grief becomes the fabric of our days,
    dear Lord, you do not stand from us apart.

Our faith may flicker low, and hope grow dim,
    yet you, O God, are with us in our pain;
you grieve with us and for us day by day,
    and with us, sharing sorrow, will remain.

Because your Son knew agony and loss,
    felt desolation, grief and scorn and shame,
we know you will be with us, come what may,
    your loving presence near, always the same.

Joy Patterson, 1992
Come, You People of the Promise, 1994
© 1994, Hope Publishing Company

825

O Lord, Who Came to Earth to Show

O Lord, who came to earth to show
    your way of truth and love,
who ministered to varied needs
    with grace sent from above,
equip us now likewise to go,
    and thus fulfill your word
compelling us to minister:
    Give us your love, O Lord.

Enable us to hear the cries
    of those who, in despair,
call out for someone who will hear,
    for someone who will care.
Then, hearing, let us actively
    pursue with one accord
a ministry which meets their needs:
    Give us your love, O Lord.

With superficial gestures, we
    have tried to comfort those
who struggle for fulfillment in
    the midst of all life's throes.
Invest in us a higher cause
    which, shown by Christ, our Lord,
makes us to seek their deepest needs:
    Give us your love, O Lord.

"Your kingdom come on earth," we pray
    with hearts which are resolved,
and yet, in human problems still
    we fail to be involved;
the ministries of comfort, peace,
    and hope may we afford
to all who struggle in their needs:
    Give us your love, O Lord.

Milburn Price, 1969; revised, 1991
Holding in Trust, 1992
© 1969, The Hymn Society (admin. Hope Publishing Company)

826

Lord, Bless the Child Unwanted

Lord, bless the child unwanted,
    unloved by all but you.
Bethlehem could find no room;
    you were unwanted too.

Lord, bless the child forsaken,
    alone and without care.
In Gethsemane you cried,
    alone forsaken there.

Lord, bless the child mistreated,
    whose scars we may not see.
Lamb of God, you bore the scars
    for our infirmity.

Lord, bless the hurting children
    and hear their plaintive cry.
Who knows pain as well as you,
    a Lamb who came to die?

Mary Kay Beall, 1990
Hymns for a Troubled World, 1991
© 1991, Hope Publishing Company

827
Like a Child

like a child
    love would send
        to reveal
            and to mend,
                like a child
                    and a friend,
                        Jesus comes
like a child
    we may find
        claiming heart
            soul and mind,
                like a child
                    strong and kind,
                        Jesus comes

like a child
    we will meet,
        ragged clothes
            dirty feet
                like a child
                    on the street,
                        Jesus comes
like a child
    we once knew
        coming back
            into view,
                like a child
                    born anew,
                        Jesus comes

like a child
    born to pray
        and to show
            us the way,
                like a child
                    here to stay,
                        Jesus comes
like a child
    we receive
        all that love
            can conceive,
                like a child
                    we believe
                        Jesus comes

Daniel Charles Damon, 1992
Faith Will Sing, 1993
© 1993, Hope Publishing Company

828
Not with Naked Eye

Not with naked eye,
    not with human sense:
through the eye of faith
    observe omnipotence.

God is always near,
    but is never seen:
Source of heaven and earth
    and all that lies between.

Children learn of God
    trusting what they feel;
touching, tasting, seeking,
    finding what is real.

Thomas saw the Christ
    breaking earth's routine;
blessed are those who trust
    the Holy One unseen.

Not with crafted scope,
    not with crystal lens:
vision of the Christ
    begins where seeing ends.

Daniel Charles Damon, 1989
The Sound of Welcome, 1998
© 1994, Hope Publishing Company

829
Shadow and Substance

Shadow and substance,
    wonder and mystery,
spell-binding spinner of atoms and earth;
    Soul of the cosmos,
    person and energy,
Source of our being, we sing of your worth.

We are your image,
    formed in community;
sisters and brothers of Adam and Eve.
    You gave us color,
    custom, and history;
teach us to honor what others receive.

Naming the nameless
    Spirit of unity,
scanning the heavens for signs of your care;
    God of the ages,
    give us humility;
guide us to mystical union in prayer.

Daniel Charles Damon, 1989
The Sound of Welcome, 1998
© 1994, Hope Publishing Company

830
Faith Is the Yes of the Heart

Faith is the yes of the heart
    and the playing of children.
Faith is the walk in the dark
    and the ring for the wedding.

Faith is the blush of the mind
    and the kiss of the Spirit.
Faith is the mother of love
    and the child in the making.

Faith sees the Christ in the bread
    and the Christ in the chalice.
Faith sees the rise from the dead
    and the sharing of harvest.

Faith feels the day before dawn,
    smells the rose before blooming.
Faith eats the heavenly feast,
    hears the sound of God's trumpet.

Faith is a rainbow in rain
    and a tomb that is empty.
Faith is the end from the start
    and beginnings in endings.

Rusty Edwards, 1991
The Yes of the Heart, 1993
© 1992, Hope Publishing Company

831
Key of the Morning

Key of the morning,
make way the new dawn;
unlock the future;
    open my prayers.
You are so faithful;
I will stay near you,
casting upon you
    all of my cares.

Door to the daylight,
all day I praise you,
through work and leisure;
    all is your time.
Welcome around me
gentle forgiveness,
taking your purpose,
    making it mine.

Bolt of the evening,
you are my shelter;
by your protection
    quiet my fears.
Safeguard your loved one;
keep and defend me
as you have kept me
    all through the years.

Rusty Edwards, 1994
Grateful Praise, 1998
© 1996, Hope Publishing Company

832
To a Maid Engaged to Joseph

To a maid engaged to Joseph,
    the angel Gabriel came.
"Fear not," the angel told her,
    "I come to bring good news,
good news I come to tell you,
    good news, I say, good news."

For you are highly favored
    by God the Lord of all,
who even now is with you.
    You are on earth most blest,
you are most blest, most blessed,
    God chose you, you are blest!"

But Mary was most troubled
    to hear the angel's word.
What was the angel saying?
    It troubled her to hear,
to hear the angel's message,
    it troubled her to hear.

"Fear not, for God is with you,
    and you shall bear a child.
His name shall be called Jesus,
    God's offspring from on high.
And he shall reign forever,
    forever reign on high."

"How shall this be?" said Mary,
    "I am not yet a wife."
The angel answered quickly,
    "The power of the Most High
will come upon you shortly,
    your child will be God's child."

As Mary heard the angel
    she wondered at his words.
"Behold, I am your handmaid,"
    she said unto her God.
"So be it; I am ready
    according to your Word."

Gracia Grindal, 1984
based on Luke 1:26–38
We Are One in Christ, 1996
© 1984, Hope Publishing Company

833
The Kingdom of God

The kingdom of God is like
    a grain of mustard seed.
When it is sown in the earth
    it is the smallest seed.
It is like the kingdom of God
    and a mystery.

For when it is sown, it grows
    into the largest plant,
greater than all of the herbs,
    and grows into a tree
which is like the kingdom of God
    and a mystery.

It grows so the birds can nest
    inside its crown of leaves,
deep in its shadows, away
    from evil things that prey.
It is like the kingdom of God
    and a mystery.

To what shall we liken it?
    A seed which makes a tree
larger than all of the trees
    from just the smallest seed.
It is like the kingdom of God
    and a mystery.

Gracia Grindal, 1984
based on Luke 13:18–19
We Are One in Christ, 1996
© 1987, Hope Publishing Company

834

There Was Jesus by the Water

There was Jesus by the water
    speaking to the pressing crowd,
when, behold, there came a ruler
    from the synagogue and bowed,
saying, "Come and heal my daughter,
    lay your healing hands upon her,
    heal her, Lord, that she may live."

As the Savior healed another
    news was brought that she was dead,
do not trouble Jesus further;
    Jesus heard the news and said,
"I will come and see your daughter,
    I will lay my hands upon her,
    do not fear, she yet may live."

Jesus went back with the ruler
    where they heard the mourners weep,
Jesus said unto the wailers,
    "Why this tumult, she's asleep?
I will go unto your daughter,
    and will lay my hands upon her,
    do not laugh, only believe."

Jesus touched their little daughter
    saying "Little girl, arise!"
And she rose to see her father
    and her mother's stunned surprise.
As they held their little daughter
    and they laid their hands upon her,
    trusting how he made her live.

Gracia Grindal, 1983
based on Luke 8:40–56
We Are One in Christ, 1996
© 1993, Selah Publishing Company, Inc.

835

On the Day of Resurrection

On the day of resurrection
    to Emmaus we return;
while confused, amazed, and frightened,
    Jesus comes to us, unknown.

Then this stranger asks a question,
    "What is this which troubles you?"
meets us in our pain and suffering;
    Jesus walks with us, unknown.

In our trouble, words come from him;
    burning fire within our hearts
tells to us the Scripture's meaning.
    Jesus speaks to us, unknown.

Then we near our destination.
    Then we ask the stranger in,
and he yields unto our urging,
    Jesus stays with us, unknown.

Day of sorrow is forgotten
    when the guest becomes the host.
Taking bread and blessing, breaking,
    Jesus is himself made known.

Opened eyes, renewed convictions,
    journey back to scenes of pain;
telling all that Christ is risen.
    Jesus is through us made known.

Michael Peterson, 1985
based on Luke 24:13–35
The United Methodist Hymnal, 1989
© 1987, The United Methodist Publishing House
(admin. The Copyright Company)

836
Who Comes from God

Who comes from God, as Word and Breath?
    Holy Wisdom.
Who holds the keys of life and death?
    Mighty Wisdom:
Crafter and Creator too,
eldest, she makes all things new;
Wisdom guides what God will do;
    Wisest One, Radiant One,
    welcome, great Sophia!

Who lifts her voice for all to hear?
    Joyful Wisdom.
Who shapes a thought and makes it clear?
    Truthful Wisdom:
Teacher, drawing out our best,
magnifies what we invest,
names our truth, directs our quest;
    Wisest One, Radiant One,
    welcome, great Sophia!

Whom should we seek with all our heart?
    Loving Wisdom.
Who, once revealed, will not depart?
    Faithful Wisdom:
Partner, Counselor, Comforter,
love has found none lovelier,
life is gladness lived with her;
    Wisest One, Radiant One,
    welcome, great Sophia!

Patrick Michaels, 1989
New Song, 1991
© 1989, Hope Publishing Company

837
Sometimes a Healing Word

Sometimes a healing word is comfort:
    easing the grieved or anxious heart,
giving assurance of our caring,
    treasuring each and every part.

    Come, break the silence! Let us tell
    the Word that makes us free and well.

Sometimes a healing word remembers:
    calling up days of joy or pain,
letting the past renew the present,
    till hope can mend and move again.

Sometimes a healing word is angry:
>giving a name to discontent,
shining a light on sin and grievance,
>calling a people to repent.

Sometimes a healing word takes chances:
>going where no one yet has been,
facing the dangers of the desert,
>hoping for shelter at the inn.

Sometimes a healing word will listen:
>hearing the voiceless into speech,
letting the pattern of the story
>move us to learn what it can teach.

Patrick Michaels, 1992
The Book of Praise, 1998
© 1992, Patrick Michaels

838
This Night the Music of the Spheres

This night the music of the spheres
>is somehow disarranged;
with dissonant surprise one star
untunes the sky, sets heaven ajar;
>the universe is changed.

Wise men who know the charts by heart
>and love the harmony
shall find the patterns sent askew:
how God now makes the music new
>for all humanity.

The rustic flute falls silent now,
>its tunes shall go unheard;
when night has grown this bright with grace,
such earthbound sounds must lose their place
>before the angel's word.

The shepherd's narrow world grows vast
>as glorias begin;
while God's own voice, wide as the sky,
constricts itself into a cry
>behind a crowded inn.

Tonight where sounds of earth intrude
>with voices rough and wild,
the cosmic music stops to catch,
and times its rhythms here to match
>the heartbeat of a child.

John Core, 1996
Supplement 99, 1999
© 1999, Hope Publishing Company

839
Creating God, as Guests of Yours

Creating God, as guests of yours
>on this good planet earth,
help us restore the heritage
>you gave to us at birth.

We kill the life we can't create,
>harm what we cannot heal,
create a world beyond control;
>God, shame our greedy zeal!

As stewards of your handiwork,
>Lord, teach us to employ
a disciplined dominion here
>whose deeds do not destroy.

Great Spirit of the earth and sky,
>within whose life we dwell,
reclaim the earth we thought we owned—
>and claim our lives as well!

David A. Robb, 1987
Heartsongs, 2000
© 1992, Hope Publishing Company

840
With Sounds of Gentle Stillness

With sounds of gentle stillness
    and quiet voice of calm
by which you bring your bidding
    and sing your inner psalm,
inform our thoughts and motives
    by your internal voice,
and cultivate our conscience
    at every point of choice.

Keep every sense attentive;
    within our lives instill
the heartbeat of your presence,
    to know and do your will:
Alert us to the needy,
    with hearts attuned to pain;
prepare our touch for comfort—
    our skills, for others' gain.

Forgive us when we fail you;
    reveal what we must mend;
renew your spirit in us
    that willful sin may end.
Lord, guide our thoughts and actions,
    advise us when we speak,
till private stillness strengthens
    the public walk we seek.

David A. Robb, 1989
Heartsongs, 2000
© 1994, Selah Publishing Company, Inc.

841
Proclaim the Acceptable Year of the Lord

Proclaim the acceptable year of the Lord!
    Sing tidings of glad jubilee!
Let all who have labored be granted their rest;
    let all the oppressed be set free.
Let all the indebted their debts be forgiven;
    let all who are hungry partake of earth's grain.
Proclaim the acceptable year of the Lord
    that justice and mercy may reign.

But how shall we honor the year of the Lord,
    how raise up the song of the blessed,
when debt, grain, and labor bring profit to those
    whose wealth so surpasses the rest?
Will debts be forgiven by those with the power
to offer true freedom and hope to the poor?
Oh, how shall we honor the year of the Lord
    and justice with mercy restore?

Begin by proclaiming the year of the Lord,
    then live so God's vision comes true
by feeding the hungry, releasing the slave,
    forgiving the debts you are due,
that all who have suffered may sing jubilation
and songs of great praise fill the earth, sky, and sea.
Begin by proclaiming the year of the Lord,
    then bring with your life jubilee.

Amanda Udis-Kessler, 1997
Sing Justice! Do Justice! 1998
© 1998, Selah Publishing Company, Inc.

842
O Liberating Rose

O liberating Rose,
    that glows on ragged stem,
your beauty helps all hearts
    lose power to condemn.
Your buds are tight with prophecy;
your thorns, a tougher poetry:
    You sign the whole and gift of life.

O liberating Fire
    that calls for cleansing rage
whenever hurtful lies
    distort our present age.
Your dancing dreams our liberty
to challenge each indignity:
    You sign the whole and faith of life.

O liberating Song
    whose echo now we sing,
your lyric, swelling line
    rekindles strengthening.
Your harmonies portray the time
when seeds we sow shall bloom sublime:
    You sign the whole and hope of life.

O liberating Love,
    we hear you in a sigh;
we glimpse you when we see
    a wet or weary eye;
we touch you when our hands extend
to soothe, or to embrace a friend:
    You sign the whole and source of life.

Mark L. Belletini, 1989
Singing the Living Tradition, 1993
© 1993, Unitarian Universalist Association

843
O Blessed Spring

O blessed spring, where word and sign
embrace us into Christ the Vine:
Here Christ enjoins each one to be
a branch of this life-giving tree.

Through summer heat of youthful years,
uncertain faith, rebellious tears,
sustained by Christ's infusing rain,
the boughs will shout for joy again.

When autumn cools and youth is cold,
when limbs their heavy harvest hold,
then through us, warm, the Christ will move
with gifts of beauty, wisdom, love.

As winter comes, as winters must,
we breathe our last, return to dust;
still held in Christ, our souls take wing
and trust the promise of the spring.

Christ, holy Vine, Christ, living Tree,
be praised for this blest mystery;
that Word and water thus revive
and join us to your Tree of Life.

Susan Palo Cherwien, 1993
O Blessed Spring, 1997
© 1993, Susan Palo Cherwien (admin. Augsburg Fortress)

844
Christ Is the Life

Christ is the life of all that is,
    God's pure creative Word,
whose power beyond and through all space
    the worlds to Being stirred.
Christ is the life beyond all time,
    creation's birth and breath,
whose labor brings all things to be
    and brings all things to death.

Christ is the death of all that is,
    a broad and beckoning tomb,
who welcomes us from well-worn ways
    to darkness of the womb.
Christ is the death, the sinking down
    past all desire and fear,
whose promise in the gentle dark
    bids newness to appear.

Christ is the death of all that is,
    a bright, consuming fire,
whose flames require our prior self
    as kindling for the pyre.
Christ is the death of dusty days
    of uncreative strife,
for out from fire we tread upon
    the threshold of new life.

Christ is the life of all that is,
    Beginning and the End;
creative force, most peaceful death,
    transforming burning brand.
Christ is the life, in whose wise love
    creation lives and dies
and thus forevermore shall bless
    the Source, the living Christ.

Susan Palo Cherwien, 1989
O Blessed Spring, 1997
© 1989, Susan Palo Cherwien (admin. Augsburg Fortress)

845

In Deepest Night

In deepest night, in darkest days,
when harps are hung, no songs we raise,
when silence must suffice as praise,
    yet sounding in us quietly
        there is the song of God.

When friend was lost, when love deceived,
dear Jesus wept, God was bereaved;
so with us in our grief God grieves,
    and round about us mournfully
        there are the tears of God.

When through the waters winds our path,
around us pain, around us death,
deep calls to deep, a saving breath,
    and found beside us faithfully
        There is the love of God.

Susan Palo Cherwien, 1995
O Blessed Spring, 1997
© 1995, Susan Palo Cherwien (admin. Augsburg Fortress)

846

It Started with an "Idle Tale"

It started with an "idle tale"
of women rushing from a tomb
with wondrous news to tell their friends
awaiting in an upper room.
At Pentecost, the tale burst forth
from fearful few to eager throng:
And now we join that risen church,
    baptized by fire and song!

It started with a whispered prayer,
a vigil kept on Easter eve,
a persecuted few who dared
to utter boldly: "We believe!"
Perpetua and Polycarp—
their martyrs' blood became the seed
from which arose a host of saints,
    baptized by sword and creed.

It started with a cry for change,
a sturdy vow of "Here I stand!"
Loyola, Luther, all whose zeal
spread gospel truth to distant lands.
Reformed and yet reforming still,
as pastor, prophet, priest, and pope,
laymen and women— we unite:
    baptized by faith and hope.

It started with Beatitudes . . .
Now two millennia have sped,
and still we thirst for righteousness,
as hungry children yearn for bread.
The poor, the mourning, and the meek,
not yet inheritors of earth,
we join our earnest cause to theirs:
    baptized to blessed worth.

It started with a rush of tongues
which marveling nations understood.
Today the church still hears God's call
to be a force for global good:
to tend the bruised and bleeding earth;
to pray and work that warfare cease,
and Spirit reconcile all flesh,
    baptized to love and peace.

Mary Louise Bringle, 1999
The Hymn, January 2000
© 2000, The Hymn Society (admin. Hope Publishing Company)

Chapter 31:
Canada, Australia, and New Zealand, 1976–2000 (847–904)

Hymn writing in other parts of the world where English is the primary language of worship has been rejuvenated in the last third of the twentieth century, much as in Great Britain and the United States. Hymnists in each place have, of course, reflected the distinctiveness of their geography and culture, as well as those issues that are prominent in church and society.

Four large Canadian hymnals were published in the last decade of the century: *Catholic Book of Worship III* (1994), *Voices United* (United Church of Canada, 1996), *The Book of Praise* (Presbyterian, 1998), and *Common Praise* (Anglican, 1998). Each, in ways appropriate to its context, marked the arrival of a new generation of worship resources. Note should also be made of two smaller collections from Wood Lake Books, *Songs for a Gospel People* (1987; a supplement to *The Hymn Book*, 1971), which brought much new material to the attention of Canadian worshipers and those who compiled the larger books, and *Spirit Anew* (1999).

Several hymnists who had written earlier saw their work reach a wider audience. Among these are Moir Waters, Margaret Clarkson, Walter Farquharson, Frances Davis, and Herbert O'Driscoll. Moir A. J. Waters was a United Church pastor and teacher, who served in India, where he was born, and Scotland, as well as in Canada. His text at 847, which first appeared in *The Hymn Book* (1971), appears here with revisions made for *The Hymnal 1982*. The parallel addresses that begin stanzas and the concise refrain reinforce the directness of John's proclamation.

Presbyterian teacher Margaret Clarkson has been a prolific writer of articles, textbooks, and devotional literature, in addition to texts for singing. Her hymns express a conservative, Evangelical theology in traditional poetic forms.

Based on Acts 4:23–31, 848 sweeps across time in tracing the providential presence of God. A compassionate concern for faithful witness in urban society is urgently presented in 849.

Walter Farquharson, who has also been an English teacher, is a pastor in the United Church of Canada and has served as that body's moderator. His exposition of faith in relation to the stress of family life, 850, is a hymn on the ecology of the home. Two earlier texts by him that are not included here, "For beauty of prairies" and "Give to us laughter," reflect the broader environment of the Canadian landscape. The elegant structure of 851 lists petitions and links them to the model prayer. Its author, Frances Wheeler Davis, is an Anglican teacher who has written short stories and poetry.

Born in Ireland, Anglican priest T. Herbert O'Driscoll has been dean of Christ Church Cathedral in Vancouver, warden of the College of Preachers in Washington, D.C., and rector of Christ Church, Calgary. His texts at 852 and 853 are sweeping in scope and vibrant with visual imagery. The first is an exposition of the eternal love of God declared in the refrainlike ending of each stanza; the second, a rhapsody on the metaphor of music in creation and our response of praise. In contrast to these stands 854, an introspective struggle with unanswered prayer that links our loneliness to the doubt experienced by Thomas. An earlier text by O'Driscoll may be seen at 562.

Another Anglican writer is Thomas H. Cain, who has been a professor of English literature at institutions in the United States and Canada. His baptism text at 855, written for *The Hymnal 1982*, recaptures the historic use of Lent as a period of preparation for the rite. Paul Gibson, in the same ecclesiastical tradition, has produced several paraphrases of biblical and liturgical texts. His fresh text on the annunciation in 856, with its "*Ave Maria*" refrain, was written to fit a Basque folk tune and based on a text from that region. Another hymn that makes effective use of a traditional liturgical refrain is 857, by Anglican church musician Patrick Wedd. Each of the affirmations of Christ prompts the *"Gloria"* response.

Judith Fetter wrote 858 for the anniversary of the United Church congregation of which her husband was pastor. This balladlike call to go to another culture, a summons to Sarah as well as to Abraham, anticipated by several years their acceptance of a ministry in Brazil. Another text in the style of a ballad is 859 by Anglican minister Peter Davison. In its use of "Singer" and "Song," it shows an ability to extend and connect metaphors. The ellipsis between the first two stanzas provides imaginative space at a critical point in the narrative.

David Sparks is a pastor and writer of liturgical material for the United Church. His hymn for the grieving, 860, is sensitive in its acknowledgment of the varied needs of those who have experienced loss and creative in its series of addresses to God. Lynette Miller, a minister in the United Church, has constructed in 861 a biblically rich hymn on Christian initiation and identity that begins with Galatians 3:28 and moves to other New Testament passages, particularly the sixth chapter of Romans.

United Church minister Robert M. (Rob) Johns died only three years after writing 862, with its tender portrayal of the presence of God in pain. This text is notable for its use of the womb as an image of safety, birth, and rebirth, and for its affirmation that suffering equips us for ministry. His hymn for Epiphany, 863, includes the slaughter of the Innocents within its pattern of strong contrasts. The imagery of the wounds of Jesus is used in 864 not so much for contemplation, as by the Pietists, but as a model for our compassion. The author of this text, in which the risen Christ is consistently active, is Nigel Weaver, a minister in the United Church.

Bert Polman, from the Christian Reformed tradition, has made significant contributions to hymnody as a scholar, editor, and musician. Among his several effective versifications of Scripture is 865, an expression of Christian unity based on 1 Corinthians 12. Mennonite musician and teacher

Harris Loewen has helped edit several hymnals and songbooks. One of these, *Assembly Songs* (1983), included the first publication of 866, a striking series of metaphors for God's activity in creation and consummation. Born and educated as a musician in the United States, Nancy Carle is a Presbyterian pastor in Canada. She uses inversions and engaging word pictures in 867, which exposes the extent of hunger, with each stanza prompting a prayer of commitment.

Presbyterian writer, composer, and musician Andrew Donaldson, known for his work in pop-influenced styles, has also written more traditional texts. One of these is 868, the winning entry in a search by the Presbyterian Church in Canada for a stewardship hymn on God's generosity and our response. With its invitations to share intimately in the work of God, it presents God as both giver and gift.

The most important Canadian hymn writer of the late twentieth century was Sylvia Dunstan, a prison chaplain and pastor in the United Church. Her work is powerful and varied, and one yearns for what might have been accomplished in greater maturity as a poet, had she not died in her prime. Some of her texts are homiletical gems, such as 869, which presents the temptation as a dialogue, contrasting the smooth rhyming of the Tempter with the direct and unrhymed responses of Jesus. Her hymn on the transfiguration, 870, connects the biblical account with present experience. The image of water is traced through salvation history in 871, which, according to the author, reflects the influence of Miriam Therese Winter on her writing. A cleverness in construction often adds layers of meaning to Dunstan's work. For example, there is a rich intertextual relationship in 872 between the words "holy manna," the shape note tune by that name, and the text that it commonly sets, "Brethren, we have met to worship"—all complemented by the refrain from Psalm 34. The range of her work is further displayed in a set of new texts to old Gospel Song tunes, among which is 873, a substitute for "I'll fly away." Her most skillful use of structure is in 874, perhaps the most striking series of paradoxes since George Matheson's "Make me a captive, Lord."

The Australian Hymn Book of 1977 (mentioned in chapter 27 and subsequently released in 1979 in London as *With One Voice*) has had two successors, *Sing Alleluia* (1987) and *Together in Song* (1999). All three were edited by Wesley Milgate, an English professor by vocation, in collaboration with Anglican canon Lawrence Bartlett (1933–2002). Not only did Milgate oversee the compilation of these interdenominational collections, he also wrote companions for the first two and had assembled the materials for the third at the time of his death. His Advent hymn, 875, which includes references to the postresurrection appearances and other New Testament passages, was written for a search by what was then the Hymn Society of America. An earlier text by Milgate is at 567.

Joy Merritt is an elder in the Uniting Church and a religious educator. It was in this role that she wrote 876, a text that, while true to life for children, frames each stanza with a response of gratitude appropriate for worshipers of any age.

The most significant Australian hymn writer of this era is Elizabeth J. Smith, an Anglican priest whose work is insightful, well crafted, and applicable to daily discipleship. She posits the necessity of faith lived out in 877, with its juxtaposition of such fundamental matters as life and death, hope and despair. The God who comes to us in our struggles is invoked in 878 and in 879, which affirms faith in the God who is always beyond our comprehension. In contrast to these images of darkness and introspection is 880, with its focus on the goals of Lenten spiritual disciplines. Hymn 881 is a thoughtful and practical text on evangelism, emphasizing the integrity of words and acts under the leadership of the Spirit. Smith's paean of nature, 882, is specifically Australian in its selection of scenery, flora, and fauna.

Some of the most creative hymn writing of recent decades has come from New Zealand. Much

of this has happened with the encouragement of The New Zealand Hymnbook Trust. This group, founded in 1978, includes Anglicans, Baptists, Methodists, Presbyterians, and Associated Churches of Christ. In 1982, the trust published *With One Voice* (see *The Australian Hymn Book* of 1977, above) with a *New Zealand Supplement*. Since that time, it has issued *Alleluia Aotearoa* (1993), *Carol Our Christmas* (1996), and *Faith Forever Singing* (2000).

The leading figure among New Zealand writers is Shirley Erena Murray, a Presbyterian language teacher, editor, and radio producer, whose distinctive style confronts serious issues in fresh words and varied forms. Many of her texts convey the hope that all persons will be seen as children of God and as members of one human family, while articulating the commitment needed to bring this about. She presents the richly varied *imago Dei* in 883, defeating the superficial judgments made by racism. Creative vocabulary interprets the story from Mark 3 in 884 to portray the radical inclusiveness of Jesus. Murray articulates the biblical cry for justice in numerous texts, such as 885, written for a service for Prisoners of Conscience in support of Amnesty International's "Campaign against Torture." One of her more powerful pieces is a picture of God suffering with humanity against violence in 886, with its dramatic form. She also speaks out against repression within the church in 887, which gains additional power from its deliberate match to the tune of the African-American spiritual, "Go down, Moses."

Though peace and justice are prominent themes in Murray's work, they are not the only topics she addresses with skill and ingenuity. The quiet and quieting focus of 888 develops the centering prayer shared by several spiritual traditions, a respite from the frantic pace of much contemporary culture. A similar gentleness is heard in 889, with its appeal to many relational metaphors. The experience of a New Zealand Christmas in 890 is not merely clever but offers a needed balance to the dominant Northern, Western view and is a reminder of what makes any celebration of Jesus' birth "right side up." Murray has also served as a bridge between the English-speaking tradition of New Zealand and the churches of Asia. The 2000 edition of the pan-Asian collection, *Sound the Bamboo*, includes a dozen of her paraphrases from various Asian languages, as well as several of her original texts.

Colin Gibson, a professor of English and editor for the Hymnbook Trust, writes both texts and tunes. Though he is perhaps better known for his pieces in a lighter style, his work, both textually and musically, is quite varied. Two superb texts that respond to loss show the depth of his writing. The death of his infant granddaughter prompted 891, with its honest expression of grief and undergirding hope. Built on memorable phrases from Hildegard of Bingen (1098–1179), 892 affirms God's infinite care. Somewhat in the idiom of Sydney Carter is 893, based on a drawing by Hogarth that shows a bloodthirsty mob jeering a criminal—accompanied only by a minister—on his way to the gallows. Gibson wrote this text to advocate mercy, rather than condemnation, as commentary on a church debate about the role of gay and lesbian persons. Denominational conflict also formed the background for 894, with its plea for the enlightening word that breaks and heals.

A hymn from New Zealand that appeared earlier and has circulated widely is 895 by Richard Gillard. Gillard, an amateur musician influenced by the folk music of the 1960s, was born in England and has been active in several different communions. This affirmation of mutuality in ministry has appeared, to Gillard's own tune and others, with numerous textual variants.

Ron O'Grady is a minister in the Christian Church (Disciples of Christ) who has served in several ecumenical posts. While Associate General Secretary of the Christian Council of Asia, he worked with I-to Loh in the development of Asian hymnody. Both texts included here were written for the CCA at Loh's request. In 896, O'Grady underscores the identification of Jesus with the poor. God is portrayed with both maternal and paternal images, but without stereotype, in 897.

Kathleen Mayson, a Methodist teacher and writer, and Marnie Barrell, an Anglican musician educated in theology, are among those writers who have been encouraged in their work by Shirley Murray. Mayson's 898 is an eloquent affirmation of the artistry of God and of the ways in which human artists and craftspersons may devote themselves in imitation. In her identification of Christ with the poor at 899, Barrell strikes a note similar to that of several of Murray's texts and of O'Grady's 896. Her 900 is a stirring and joyful glimpse of fulfillment, which she pictures as "the everlasting dance."

William L. (Bill) Wallace, also a Methodist, is a self-described "postdenominational Christian," who has invested much of his ministry with disadvantaged persons. A participant in the Asian Consultation on Liturgy and Music, he has explored ways in which all the senses and the imagination participate in perceiving and expressing faith. The text at 901 uses images from Asian culture to give voice to the church in that part of the world. His creative approach to names and relationships within the Trinity, 902, won first place in the 1988 "Search for New Hymns with a New Vision of the Living God," conducted by the Hymn Society of America. Two texts by Wallace make different applications of the example of Jesus in facing the challenges of life. In the more traditional 903, the responses of Jesus demonstrate how to face both grief and death. Freedom from sexism and gender stereotype is modeled by Jesus in 904.

847
Sound the Trumpet

Herald, sound the note of judgment,
    warning us of right and wrong,
turning us from sin and sadness
    till once more we sing the song.

        Sound the trumpet! Tell the message!
           Christ, the Savior King, has come!

Herald, sound the note of gladness;
    tell the news that Christ is here;
make a pathway through the desert
    for the one who brings God near.

Herald, sound the note of pardon—
    those repenting are forgiven;
God receives his wayward children,
    and to them new life is given.

Herald, sound the note of triumph;
    Christ has come to share our life,
bringing God's own love and power,
    granting victory in strife.

Moir A. J. Waters, 1968
The Hymnal 1982, 1985
© 1968, Estate of Moir A. J. Waters

848
God of Creation, All-Powerful, All-Wise

God of creation, all-powerful, all-wise,
Lord of the universe rich with surprise,
Maker, Sustainer, and Ruler of all,
we are your children—you hear when we call.

God of the ages, through time's troubled years
you are the One in whom history coheres;
nations and empires your purpose fulfill,
moving in freedom, yet working your will.

God of redemption, who wrought our rebirth,
called out your church from the ends of the earth,
still you are Savior—put darkness to flight;
overcome sin by salvation's pure light!

God of your people, your Word still stands fast—
do for us now as you've done in the past!
Yours is the kingdom—your triumph we claim,
challenging evil in Jesus' strong name.

God of our now, all our trust is in you,
Covenant-God, ever faithful and true;
Sovereign Creator, Redeemer, and Lord,
now and forever your name be adored!

Margaret Clarkson, 1987
A Singing Heart, 1987
© 1987, Hope Publishing Company

849
Our Cities Cry to You, O God

Our cities cry to you, O God,
    from out their pain and strife;
you made us for yourself alone,
    but we choose alien life.
Our goals are pleasure, gold, and power;
    injustice stalks our earth;
in vain we seek for rest, for joy,
    for sense of human worth.

Yet still you walk our streets, O Christ!
    We know your presence here
where humble Christians love and serve
    in godly grace and fear.
O Word made flesh, be seen in us!
    May all we say and do
affirm you God Incarnate still
    and turn sad hearts to you!

Your people are your hands and feet
    to serve your world today,
our lives the book our cities read
    to help them find your way.
O pour your sovereign Spirit out
    on heart and will and brain:
Inspire your church with love and power
    to ease our cities' pain!

O healing Savior, Prince of Peace,
    salvation's Source and Sum,
for you our broken cities cry—
    O come, Lord Jesus, come!
With truth your royal diadem,
    with righteousness your rod,
O come, Lord Jesus, bring to earth
    the City of our God!

Margaret Clarkson, 1981
A Singing Heart, 1987
© 1987, Van Ness Press

850

Would You Bless Our Homes and Families

Would you bless our homes and families,
    Source of life who calls us here;
in our world of stress and tension
    teach us love that conquers fear.
Help us learn to love each other
    with a love that constant stays;
teach us when we face our troubles,
    love's expressed in many ways.

When our way is undemanding,
    let us use the time that's ours
to delight in simple pleasures,
    sharing joys in gentle hours.
When our way is anxious walking
    and a heavy path we plod,
teach us trust in one another
    and in you, our gracious God.

From the homes in which we're nurtured,
    with the love that shapes us there,
teach us, God, to claim as family
    every one whose life we share.
And through all that life may offer,
    may we in your love remain;
may the love we share in families
    be alive to praise your name.

Let us reach beyond the boundaries
    of our daily thought and care
till the family you have chosen
    spills its love out everywhere.
Help us learn to love each other
    with a love that constant stays;
teach us when we face our troubles
    love's expressed in many ways.

Walter Farquharson, 1974
Songs for a Gospel People, 1987
© 1974, Walter Farquharson

851

Let There Be Light

Let there be light,
let there be understanding,
let all the nations gather,
let them be face to face;

open our lips,
open our minds to ponder,
open the door of concord
opening into grace;

perish the sword,
perish the angry judgment,
perish the bombs and hunger,
perish the fight for gain;

hallow our love,
hallow the deaths of martyrs,
hallow their holy freedom,
hallowed be thy name;

thy kingdom come,
thy spirit turn to language,
thy people speak together,
thy spirit never fade;

let there be light,
open our hearts to wonder,
perish the way of terror,
hallow the world God made.

Frances Wheeler Davis, 1968
The Hymn Book, 1971
© 1970, Frances Wheeler Davis

852
O God, beyond All Face and Form

O God, beyond all face and form,
    you willed it that creation's night
should blaze, and chaos still its storm,
    and birth a universe of light.
All things below, all things above
are formed of your eternal love.

The glory of the galaxies,
    the beauty of a baby's hand,
the thundering of restless seas,
    the glory of the forest's stand—
All things below, all things above
are formed of your eternal love.

You gave our race both form and name,
    and love for us was your intent;
then to a woman's womb love came,
    and on a cross was wholly spent.
All things below, all things above
are formed of your eternal love.

Of this great love, all loves are born,
    of self, of neighbor, and of earth.
By love shall night be turned to morn,
    and death shall never conquer birth.
All things below, all things above
are formed of God's eternal love.

Herbert O'Driscoll, 1989
Common Praise, 1998
© 1993, Herbert O'Driscoll

853
Before the Earth Had Yet Begun

Before the earth had yet begun
her journey round the burning sun,
before a seed of life had stirred,
there sounded God's creating Word.

In that bright dawning of the world,
ere ocean surged or wind unfurled,
the vaults of heaven with praises rang;
the morning stars together sang.

Thus when creation's Lord did take
the clay of earth our form to make,
God willed that to our race belong
the gifts of music, word, and song.

For us who would this God attend,
no earthly mind can comprehend
eternal glory; praise alone
is our companion by that throne.

Herbert O'Driscoll, 1986
Common Praise, 1998
© 1993, Herbert O'Driscoll

854
God, When I Stand

God, when I stand, no path before me clear,
    when every prayer seems prisoner of my pain;
come with a gentleness which calms my fear,
    Lord of my helplessness, my victory gain.

When all my prayers no answer seem to bring,
    and there is silence in my deepest soul;
when in the wilderness I find no spring,
    Lord of the desert places, keep me whole.

When the dark lord of loneliness prevails,
    and, all defeated, joy and friendship die;
come, be my joy, such love that never fails,
    pierce the self-pity of my shadowed sky.

When, as did Thomas, I presume thee dead,
    feeling and faith itself within me cold,
freshen my lips with wine, my soul with bread,
    banish my poverty with heaven's gold.

Herbert O'Driscoll, 1980
Songs for a Gospel People, 1987
© 1980, Herbert O'Driscoll

855
Eternal Lord of Love

Eternal Lord of love, behold your church
walking once more the pilgrim way of Lent,
    led by your cloud by day, by night your fire,
moved by your love and toward your presence bent:
    far off yet here–the goal of all desire.

So daily dying to the way of self,
so daily living to your way of love,
    we walk the road, Lord Jesus, that you trod,
knowing ourselves baptized into your death:
    So we are dead and live with you in God.

If dead in you, so in you we arise,
you the firstborn of all the faithful dead;
    and as through stony ground the green shoots
        break,
glorious in springtime dress of leaf and flower,
    so in the Father's glory shall we wake.

Thomas H. Cain, 1978
The Hymnal 1982, 1985
© 1982, Thomas H. Cain

856
Heavenly Message

Heavenly message, brought by an angel,
    coming to lift the hopes of the earth;
bringing to Mary, humble and lowly,
    God's invitation to give the Christ birth.

Mary, we hail you, full of God's favor,
    blessed are you, and blessed your son;
he will be called the child of the highest,
    Savior of all, the holy one.

Mary replied to Gabriel's message,
    "I am the servant, maid of the Lord.
Let it be done just as you have spoken.
    My soul rejoices in God's saving word."

In the beginning, when God had spoken,
    through God's own Word all things came to be;
now by that Word, embodied through Mary,
    God's glory blazes, that our eyes may see.

Paul Gibson, 1995
based on Luke 1:26–38
Common Praise, 1998
© Paul Gibson

857

Christ Is Atonement

Christ is atonement, the Paschal victim;
he gave his life that we might live forever.
We for redemption sing in exaltation:
"Glory to God, glory to God on high."

Christ is the great priest who sets a table,
making of bread and wine a sacred banquet.
We for this manna sing in exaltation:
"Glory to God, glory to God on high."

Christ is compassion, with us in sorrow;
he bears our burdens, shares our inmost darkness.
We for such caring sing in exaltation:
"Glory to God, glory to God on high."

Christ is our freedom, true liberation;
in freeing us he bids us live for others.
We for this challenge sing in exaltation:
"Glory to God, glory to God on high."

Patrick Wedd, 1983
Common Praise, 1998
© Patrick Wedd

858

To Abraham and Sarah

To Abraham and Sarah
	the call of God was clear:
"Go forth and I will show you
	a country rich and fair.
You need not fear the journey
	for I have pledged my word:
that you shall be my people
	and I will be your God."

From Abraham and Sarah
	arose a pilgrim race,
dependent for their journey
	on God's abundant grace;
and in their heart was written
	by God this saving word:
"that you shall be my people
	and I will be your God."

We of this generation
	on whom God's hand is laid,
can journey to the future
	secure and unafraid,
rejoicing in God's goodness
	and trusting in this word:
"that you shall be my people
	and I will be your God."

Judith Fetter, 1984
Songs for a Gospel People, 1987
© 1984, Judith Fetter

859

When Long before Time

When long before time and the worlds were begun,
when there was no earth and sky and no sun,
and all was deep silence and night reigned supreme,
and ever our Maker had only a dream . . .

. . . the silence was broken when God sang the Song,
and light pierced the darkness and rhythm began,
and with its first birth-cries creation was born,
and creaturely voices sang praise to the morn.

The sounds of the creatures were one with their
	Lord's,
their harmonies sweet and befitting the Word;
the Singer was pleased as the earth sang the Song,
the choir of the creatures reechoed it long.

Though, down through the ages, the Song
                                    disappeared—
its harmonies broken and almost unheard—
the Singer comes to us to sing it again;
our God-Is-with-Us in the world now as then.

The Light has returned as it came once before,
the Song of the Lord is our own song once more;
so let us all sing with one heart and one voice
the Song of the Singer in whom we rejoice.

To you, God the Singer, our voices we raise,
to you, Song Incarnate, we give all our praise,
to you, Holy Spirit, our life and our breath,
be glory forever, through life and through death.

Peter Davison, 1981
Songs for a Gospel People, 1987
© 1981, Peter Davison

860

Strength to the Troubled Heart

Strength to the troubled heart, we come
    with anxious and bewildered minds,
striving to reach for meaning here:
    Your peace is what we ache to find.

Joy of the thankful heart, we come;
    good memories are ours today,
of friendship given and received,
    of family care along life's way.

Friend of the lonely heart, we come;
    the void that's left is hard to fill;
strong love stays with your grieving ones,
    sure touch of grace, death's fears to still.

Sun of the rising heart, we come,
    Christ's empty tomb new courage gives,
for we are sure, embraced and safe
    within your love, our loved one lives.

David Sparks, 1994
Supplement 99, 1999
© 1997, Hope Publishing Company

861

Now There Is No Male or Female

Now there is no male or female,
    now there is no free or slave,
now there is no Jew or Gentile
    in the earth Christ died to save.
Christ has set us free for freedom:
    We no more sing slavery's creed;
old submissions cannot claim us,
    Christ has set us free indeed.

Crucified with Christ the Savior,
    baptized in his holy death,
and as Christ was raised to glory
    we have new life on this earth.
Power of water and God's naming
    turns from darkness to the light,
joins us to those who, before us,
    ran the race and fought the fight.

Death has no dominion o'er him,
    so for us death holds no power;
life's own waters now have marked us
    born to God this very hour.
From this moment and forever
    dead to sin, alive in Christ,
born of water and the Spirit,
    now in Christ we find our life.

Lynette Miller, 1985
Songs for a Gospel People, 1987
© 1985, Lynette Miller

862

In Suffering Love

In suffering love the thread of life
 is woven through our care,
for God is with us, not alone
 our pain and toil we bear.

There is a rock, a place secure
 within the storm's cold blast;
concealed within the suffering night
 God's covenant stands fast.

In love's deep womb our fears are held;
 there God's rich tears are sown
and bring to birth, in hope newborn,
 the strength to journey on.

Lord, to our hearts your joy commit,
 into our hands your pain;
so send us out to touch the world
 with blessings in your name.

In suffering love our God comes now,
 hope's vision born in gloom;
with tears and laughter shared and blessed
 the desert yet will bloom.

Robert M. Johns, 1983
Songs for a Gospel People, 1987
© 1987, Elinor Johns

863

When Heaven's Bright with Mystery

When heaven's bright with mystery
 and science searches nature's art,
when all creation yearns for peace
 and hope sinks deep in human hearts,
appear to us, O Holy Light;
lift from our eyes the shades of night.

When Herod barters power and lives
 and Rachel's weeping fills the night,
when suffering's mask marks every face,
 and Love's a refugee in flight,
reveal to us your word of grace
and make us witness to your peace.

When fragile faith, like desert wind,
 blows dry and empty, hope erased,
when withered grass and fading flower
 proclaim again our day's brief space,
breathe on the clay of our despair
and work a new creation there.

When heaven's bright with mystery
 and stars still lead an unknown way,
when love still lights a gentle path
 where courts of power can hold no sway,
there with the magi, let us kneel,
our gifts to share, God's world to heal.

Robert M. Johns, 1985
Voices United, 1991
© 1987, Carol Johns

864

The Risen Christ

The risen Christ, who walks on wounded feet
from garden tomb through darkened city street,
unlocks the door of grief, despair, and fear,
and speaks a word of peace to all who hear.

The risen Christ, who stands with wounded side,
breathes out his Spirit on them to abide
whose faith still wavers, who dare not believe,
new grace, new strength, new purpose they receive.

The risen Christ, who breaks with wounded hand
the bread for those who fail to understand,
reveals himself, despite their lingering tears,
enflames their hearts, then quickly disappears.

May we, Christ's body, walk and serve and stand
with the oppressed in this and every land,
till all are blessed and can a blessing be,
restored in Christ to true humanity.

Nigel Weaver, 1993
Voices United, 1996
© 1993, Nigel Weaver

865
We Are Members of Christ's Body

We are members of Christ's body,
    joined by faith in unity:
one in calling, joy, and suffering,
    wholesome in diversity.
We will work with gifts that differ
    towards the kingdom's destiny.

Ear and eye to one another,
    we have need of every part;
hands and feet belong together,
    guided by a loyal heart;
tendons, bones, and flesh embody
    what the Spirit's breath imparts.

When one member suffers hardship,
    we will shoulder all the pain;
when another part is honored,
    joys throughout the body reign;
for our common love is pulsing
    towards the growth of Christ's domain.

Bert Polman, 1995
based on 1 Corinthians 12:14–26
Sing! A New Creation, 2001
© 1995, Bert Polman

866
O God, Great Womb

O God, great womb of wondrous love,
    your Spirit moving on the deep
did wake a world within yourself,
    a pulsing, lighted world, from sleep.

O hearth, O heartbeat of the whole,
    your dark-light dance began the times,
the days and seasons, seconds, years,
    the ages' rhythms and the rhymes.

O fire, O firmament and sea,
    our seething ferment's energy
called forth a whirling waltz of life,
    each plant and creature and its seed.

O silent soul, O mind and strength,
    your center did conceive and bear
its male and female image-self—
    two human forms, one breath to share.

Now come with rest, O Sabbath sun,
    O sanctuary, sacred home,
we groan till all is grown complete,
    fulfilled, at peace, O great shalom.

Harris J. Loewen, 1983
Hymnal: A Worship Book, 1992
© 1983, Harris J. Loewen

867
In Jungles Deep and Deserts Dry

In jungles deep and deserts dry,
where in disease and pain they lie,
O hear the children's hungry cry:
    Lord, feed the world through me.

In deserts dry and jungles deep,
where brokenhearted parents weep
and children hungry go to sleep:
    Lord, feed the world through me.

In city street and country lane,
where fields go bare for want of rain,
and hungry eyes look up in pain:
    Lord, feed the world through me.

In country lane and city street,
where concrete welcomes weary feet,
and hunger spells a child's defeat:
    Lord, feed the world through me.

In all the world where hunger stalks,
your Holy Spirit weeps and walks.
May I, too, weep and work and walk:
    Lord, feed the world through me.

Nancy W. Carle, 1982
Worship Together, 1995
© 1995, Nancy W. Carle

868
Come, Know My Joy

"Come, know my joy," the Maker says
    and pours out works of power
that sear the sense, defy the mind,
    and fill the soul with awe,
and we with open mouth receive
    God's gifts with infant need,
and, sight unfocused, scarce perceive
    Love's presence as we feed.

The feast we join is long begun;
    God bids us welcome here
to name and use the sovereign gifts
    within our human care.
With God's own joy some seem to soar,
    a fierce and holy flame;
some gifts are thorns we scarce endure
    to touch, or face, or name.

"Come, seek my face," the Giver says,
    "with heart and soul and strength;
let fear give way to love; come, step
    upon the waves of faith."
Dear Giver, Gift, we seek your face:
    you share our thorn, our scar.
We learn your joy when by your grace
    we share the gift we are.

"Come, learn of me," the Servant says
    and multiplies a feast
of loaves and fish, of bread and wine,
    transforming every guest.
"Come," says the Host, "From west and east
    bring gifts to share—come, eat!—
none lost or wasted when God's feast
    of joy will be complete."

Andrew Donaldson, 1995
The Book of Praise, 1998
© 1995, The Presbyterian Church in Canada

869
The Temptation

From the river to the desert,
    forty days that give no rest;
fast and pray and wait and wrestle,
    face the Adversary's test;
      Prince of Peace and Prince of Darkness
      meet in lonely wilderness.

If you are the one God chooses,
    you can turn these stones to bread.
See, the children yearn and hunger,
    by your deeds the poor are fed.
        —Don't you know that it is written:
            No one lives by bread alone.

If you are the one God offers,
    leap into the angels' hands.
Show your power and your glory,
    then belief will sweep the land.
        —Don't you know that it is written:
            Do not tempt the Lord your God.

If you are the one God promised,
    you could still bow down to me.
Look at all the wealth of nations,
    I will give you all you see.
        —Don't you know that it is written:
            Worship God and God alone.

Since we are the ones you gather,
    and from sin and death have freed,
Jesus, knowing all our weakness,
    now at God's high altar plead.
        For we know that it is written
            that your grace is all we need.

Sylvia Dunstan, 1989
based on Luke 4:1–13
In Search of Hope and Grace, 1991
© 1991, GIA Publications, Inc.

870
Transfiguration

Transform us as you, transfigured,
    stood apart on Tabor's height.
Lead us up our sacred mountains,
    search us with revealing light.
Lift us from where we have fallen,
    full of questions, filled with fright.

Transform us as you, transfigured,
    once spoke with those holy ones.
We, surrounded by the witness
    of those saints whose work is done,
live in this world as your body,
    chosen daughters, chosen sons.

Transform us as you, transfigured,
    would not stay within a shrine.
Keep us from our great temptation—
    time and truth we quickly bind.
Lead us down those daily pathways
    where our love is not confined.

Sylvia Dunstan, 1989
based on Matthew 17:1–8
In Search of Hope and Grace, 1991
© 1991, GIA Publications, Inc.

871
Water

Crashing waters at creation,
    ordered by the Spirit's breath,
first to witness day's beginning
    from the brightness of night's death.

Parting water stood and trembled
    as the captives passed on through,
washing off the chains of bondage—
    channel to a life made new.

Cleansing water once at Jordan
    closed around the one foretold,
opened to reveal the glory
    ever new and ever old.

Living water, never ending,
 quench the thirst and flood the soul.
Wellspring, Source of life eternal,
 drench our dryness, make us whole.

Sylvia Dunstan, 1987
In Search of Hope and Grace, 1991
© 1991, GIA Publications, Inc.

872
All Who Hunger, Gather Gladly

All who hunger, gather gladly;
 holy manna is our bread.
Come from wilderness and wand'ring.
 Here, in truth, we will be fed.
You that yearn for days of fullness,
 all around us is our food.
Taste and see the grace eternal.
 Taste and see that God is good.

All who hunger, never strangers,
 seeker, be a welcome guest.
Come from restlessness and roaming.
 Here, in joy, we keep the feast.
We that once were lost and scattered
 in communion's love have stood.
Taste and see the grace eternal.
 Taste and see that God is good.

All who hunger, sing together;
 Jesus Christ is living bread.
Come from loneliness and longing.
 Here, in peace, we have been led.
Blest are those who from this table
 live their days in gratitude.
Taste and see the grace eternal.
 Taste and see that God is good.

Sylvia Dunstan, 1990
In Search of Hope and Grace, 1991
© 1991, GIA Publications, Inc.

873
Rejoicing

When the Lord redeems the very least,
 we will rejoice.
When the hungry gather for the feast,
 we will rejoice.

  We will rejoice with gladness.
   We will rejoice!
  All our days we'll sing to God in praise.
   We will rejoice!

When the Lord restores the sick and weak,
when the earth is given to the meek,

When the Lord lifts up the trembling hands,
when we all have strength enough to stand,

When the Lord revives the world from death,
when the word of God fills every breath,

When the Lord returns in victory,
when we live in glorious liberty,

Sylvia Dunstan
In Search of Hope and Grace, 1991
© 1991, GIA Publications, Inc.

874
Christus Paradox

You, Lord, are both Lamb and Shepherd.
 You, Lord, are both prince and slave.
You, peace-maker and sword-bringer
 of the way you took and gave.
You, the everlasting instant;
 you, whom we both scorn and crave.

Clothed in light upon the mountain,
    stripped of might upon the cross,
shining in eternal glory,
    beggared by a soldier's toss.
You, the everlasting instant;
    you who are both gift and cost.

You, who walk each day beside us,
    sit in power at God's side.
You, who preach a way that's narrow,
    have a love that reaches wide.
You, the everlasting instant;
    you, who are our pilgrim guide.

Worthy is our earthly Jesus!
    Worthy is our cosmic Christ!
Worthy your defeat and victory.
    Worthy still your peace and strife.
You, the everlasting instant;
    you, who are our death and life.

Sylvia Dunstan, 1984
In Search of Hope and Grace, 1991
© 1991, GIA Publications, Inc.

875
Your Coming, Lord, to Earth in Bethlehem

Your coming, Lord, to earth in Bethlehem
    revealed your gracious will that all might live,
by your example and your sacrifice,
    in that salvation you alone can give.

That free gift of God's grace bestowed on us
    remains a fountainhead of joy and peace;
and yet by evil tempted and enslaved
    we need to know you near, and find release.

Come to your people as of old you came
    on mountainside, at table, by the sea,
through doors closed on our fears and bleak dismay:
    And in the heart of darkness light shall be.

Walk with us, and be known in breaking bread:
    Those gathered in your name will find you here,
and sharing bread and wine in fellowship
    will know the perfect love that casts out fear.

Though often thus you come to save and bless,
    at last, we know, in glory you will come,
in cloud and fire, with angels' trumpets' sound,
    to judge, and triumph, and to claim your own.

Wesley Milgate, 1986
Sing Alleluia, 1988
© Australian Hymn Book Company

876
Thank You, Thank You, Lord

Thank you, thank you, Lord,
for everything that I can see:
    dewdrops on a spider's web,
        new leaves on a tree,
    friendly faces in the street
        smiling back at me;
thank you, thank you, Lord.

Thank you, thank you, Lord,
for everything that I can hear:
    breezes whispering in the trees,
        bird songs loud and clear,
    music on the radio,
        friends who laugh and cheer;
thank you, thank you, Lord.

Thank you, thank you, Lord,
for everything that I can do:
    running, jumping, playing sport,
        doing puzzles, too,
    reading, writing, making things,
        learning what is true;
thank you, thank you, Lord.

Thank you, thank you, Lord,
for everything that I can be:
 friend of all, and helper too,
  no one's enemy,
 someone who has learned to share,
  someone who is free;
thank you, thank you, Lord.

Joy Merritt, 1974
Sing Alleluia, 1988
© 1975, Joy Merritt

877
Faith Will Not Grow from Words Alone

Faith will not grow from words alone,
from proofs provided, Scripture known;
our faith must feel its way about,
and live with question marks and doubt.

The pattern Jesus showed, we share:
Life comes through death, hope through despair.
God is made known in brokenness,
and faith feeds on God's emptiness.

The church still tells how Jesus came
through death to glorious life again—
the strangest story! Yet, maybe,
our faith will thrive on mystery.

Faith takes the little that we know,
and calls for hope, and tells us: Go!
Love and take courage, come what may;
Christ will be with us on the way.

Elizabeth J. Smith, 1991
Songs for a Hopeful Church, 1997
© 1997, Elizabeth J. Smith

878
Gentle God, the Candle Flickers

Gentle God, the candle flickers:
 Keep it burning, shield the light.
When the flame of my hope wavers,
 guard my spirit through the night.

Gentle God, the song still echoes:
 Add your subtle harmonies.
When my love for Christ falls silent,
 sing me Easter memories.

Gentle God, the child is stirring:
 Teach it peace, and ease its pain.
When the life within me lessens,
 feed me, till it thrives again.

Gentle God, the branch is growing:
 Prune it wisely, train it well.
When my love's obedience falters,
 bind me closer to yourself.

Elizabeth J. Smith, 1988
Songs for a Hopeful Church, 1997
© 1997, Elizabeth J. Smith

879
God in the Darkness

God in the darkness, God beyond our knowing,
patient creator, seed in secret growing,
rock of the living, water ever flowing:
 Come and renew us.

God in the darkness, God in all our grieving,
friend of our tears, companion never leaving,
drawing us past the limits of believing:
 Come and renew us.

God in the darkness, God of holy dreaming,
giver of hope, and pledge of our redeeming,
Spirit of truth, our memory and meaning:
Come and renew us.

880
Love Will Be Our Lenten Calling

Love will be our Lenten calling,
love to shake and shatter sin,
waking every closed, cold spirit,
stirring new life deep within,
till the quickened heart remembers
what our Easter birth can mean.

Peace will be our Lenten living
as we turn for home again,
longing for the words of pardon,
stripping off old grief and pain,
till we stand, restored and joyful,
with the church on Easter day.

Truth will be our Lenten learning:
Hear the Crucified One call!
Shadowed by the Savior's passion,
images and idols fall,
and, in Easter's holy splendor,
God alone is all in all.

881
Holy Spirit, Go before Us

Holy Spirit, go before us,
every mind and heart prepare
for good news of life in Jesus,
for the joyful hope we share.
Gently lead the lost to safety,
gently teach them Wisdom's way,
till they come to seek you gladly,
till we find the words to say.

Holy Spirit, come and help us,
give us words to speak of Christ.
Teach us how to tell all people:
Deepest darkness can be light!
Help us tell how faithful God is,
and how Jesus sets us free;
take our words, and make them gospel
so that many may believe.

Holy Spirit, stay to show us
how to serve as Christ served us.
May our words of love be grounded
in love's actions, first and last.
Your good news is news of justice,
and the strong befriend the weak
in your service, till compassion
builds the peace the nations seek.

882
Where Wide Sky Rolls Down and Touches Red Sand

Where wide sky rolls down and touches red sand,
where sun turns to gold the grass of the land,
let spinifex, mulga, and waterhole tell
their joy in the One who made everything well.

Where rainforest calm meets reef, tide, and storm,
where green things grow lush and oceans are warm,
let every sea creature and tropical bird
exult in the light of the life-giving Word.

Where red gum and creek cross hillside and plain,
where cool tree-ferns rise to welcome the rain,
let bushland, farm, mountaintop, all of their days
delight in the Spirit who formed them for praise.

Now, people of faith, come gather around
with songs to be shared, for blessings abound!
Australians, whatever your culture or race,
come, lift up your hearts to the Giver of grace.

> Elizabeth J. Smith, 1996
> *Songs for a Hopeful Church*, 1997
> © 1997, Elizabeth J. Smith

883

O God, We Bear the Imprint of Your Face

O God, we bear the imprint of your face:
    The colors of our skin are your design,
and what we have of beauty in our race
    as man or woman, you alone define,
who stretched a living fabric on our frame
and gave to each a language and a name.

Where we are torn and pulled apart by hate
    because our race, our skin is not the same,
while we are judged unequal by the state
    and victims made because we own our name,
humanity reduced to little worth,
dishonored is your living face on earth.

O God, we share the image of your Son
    whose flesh and blood are ours, whatever skin,
in his humanity we find our own,
    and in his family our proper kin:
Christ is the brother we still crucify,
his love the language we must learn, or die.

> Shirley Erena Murray, 1981
> *In Every Corner Sing*, 1992
> © 1987, Hope Publishing Company

884

Who Is My Mother, Who Is My Brother?

Who is my mother,
    who is my brother?
all those who gather round Jesus Christ:
    Spirit-blown people,
    born from the Gospel
sit at the table, round Jesus Christ.

Differently abled,
    differently labeled
widen the circle round Jesus Christ:
    Crutches and stigmas,
    cultures' enigmas
all come together round Jesus Christ.

Love will relate us—
    color or status
can't segregate us, round Jesus Christ:
    Family failings,
    human derailings—
all are accepted, round Jesus Christ.

Bound by one vision,
met for one mission
we claim each other, round Jesus Christ:
Here is my mother,
here is my brother,
kindred in Spirit, through Jesus Christ.

Shirley Erena Murray, 1991
based on Mark 3:31–35
In Every Corner Sing, 1992
© 1992, Hope Publishing Company

885
God of Freedom, God of Justice

God of freedom, God of justice,
you whose love is strong as death,
you who saw the dark of prison,
you who knew the price of faith—
touch our world of sad oppression
with your Spirit's healing breath.

Rid the earth of torture's terror,
you whose hands were nailed to wood;
hear the cries of pain and protest,
you who shed the tears and blood—
move in us the power of pity
restless for the common good.

Make in us a captive conscience
quick to hear, to act, to plead;
make us truly sisters, brothers
of whatever race or creed—
teach us to be fully human,
open to each other's needs.

Shirley Erena Murray, 1980
In Every Corner Sing, 1992
© 1992, Hope Publishing Company

886
God Weeps

God weeps
at love withheld,
at strength misused,
at children's innocence abused,
and till we change the way we love,
God weeps.

God bleeds
at anger's fist,
at trust betrayed,
at women battered and afraid,
and till we change the way we win,
God bleeds.

God cries
at hungry mouths,
at running sores,
at creatures dying without cause,
and till we change the way we care,
God cries.

God waits
for stones to melt,
for peace to seed,
for hearts to hold each other's need,
and till we understand the Christ,
God waits.

Shirley Erena Murray, 1994
Every Day in Your Spirit, 1996
© 1996, Hope Publishing Company

887
Where God Enlightens

Where God enlightens, bless the light—
    roll the stone away,
whom God has called, let no one slight—
    roll the stone away.
      Stand up, Mary!
      You are a priest and prophet!
      Tell us the good news—
      The stone must roll away.

Where church tradition gags and binds,
    roll the stone away,
where words exclude and bias blinds,
    roll the stone away.
      Stand up, Mary,
      daughter of ancient wisdom!
      Tell of your suffering
      to roll the stone away.

Where men entomb the truth of Christ,
    roll the stone away;
where women's worth is underpriced,
    roll the stone away.
      Stand up, Mary!
      Yours is the power also!
      Cry out injustice
      and roll the stone away.

The myrrh and spices once you brought,
    (roll the stone away)
may now anoint new life, new thought,
    roll the stone away.
      Stand up, Mary!
      Come, bring your friends and brothers:
      sing resurrection—
      The stone is rolled away!

Shirley Erena Murray, 1989
Every Day in Your Spirit, 1996
© 1996, Hope Publishing Company
Compare both form and content of 390.

888
Come and Find the Quiet Center

Come and find the quiet center
    in the crowded life we lead,
find the room for hope to enter,
    find the frame where we are freed:
Clear the chaos and the clutter,
    clear our eyes that we can see
all the things that really matter,
    be at peace, and simply be.

Silence is a friend who claims us,
    cools the heat and slows the pace,
God it is who speaks and names us,
    knows our being, touches base,
making space within our thinking,
    lifting shades to show the sun,
raising courage when we're shrinking,
    finding scope for faith begun.

In the Spirit let us travel,
    open to each other's pain,
let our loves and fears unravel,
    celebrate the space we gain:
There's a place for deepest dreaming,
    there's a time for heart to care,
in the Spirit's lively scheming
    there is always room to spare!

Shirley Erena Murray, 1989
In Every Corner Sing, 1992
© 1992, Hope Publishing Company

889
Loving Spirit

Loving Spirit, loving Spirit,
    you have chosen me to be—
You have drawn me to your wonder,
    you have set your sign on me.

Like a mother you enfold me,
    hold my life within your own,
feed we with your very body,
    form me of your flesh and bone.

Like a father you protect me,
    teach me the discerning eye,
hoist me up upon your shoulder,
    let me see the world from high.

Friend and lover, in your closeness
    I am known and held and blessed:
in your promise is my comfort,
    in your presence I may rest.

Loving Spirit, loving Spirit,
    you have chosen me to be—
You have drawn me to your wonder,
    you have set your sign on me.

Shirley Erena Murray, 1986
In Every Corner Sing, 1992

890
Carol Our Christmas

Carol our Christmas, an upside-down Christmas:
    Snow is not falling and trees are not bare.
Carol the summer and welcome the Christ Child,
    warm in our sunshine and sweetness of air.

Sing of the gold and the green and the sparkle,
    water and river and lure of the beach.
Sing in the happiness of open spaces,
    sing a nativity summer can reach!

Shepherds and musterers move over hillsides,
    finding, not angels, but sheep to be shorn,
wise ones make journeys, whatever the season,
    searching for signs of the truth to be born.

Right-side-up Christmas belongs to the universe,
    made in the moment a woman gives birth:
Hope is the Jesus gift, love is the offering,
    everywhere, anywhere, here on the earth.

Shirley Erena Murray, 1986
In Every Corner Sing, 1992

891
Lord of All Love

Lord of all love, all life, and death,
giver of time and place and breath,
hear us, as now we bring our loss
into the presence of your cross.

Sing us the songs we cannot sing,
pardon the praise we cannot bring,
speak all the words we cannot say,
pray for us, Lord, we humbly pray.

That darkest mystery is here,
sorrow and pity, anger, fear;
conquer once more, dear Lord, death's sting,
faith, trust, and consolation bring.

Though precious dust return to dust,
in your good purpose we shall trust,
content to place within your care
she/he whom we love and grieve for here.

Colin Gibson, 1987
Reading the Signature, 1994

892
Nothing Is Lost on the Breath of God

Nothing is lost on the breath of God,
    nothing is lost forever;
God's breath is love, and that love will remain,
    holding the world forever.
No feather too light, no hair too fine,
    no flower too brief in its glory,
no drop in the ocean, no dust in the air,
    but is counted and told in God's story.

Nothing is lost to the eyes of God,
    nothing is lost forever.
God sees with love, and that love will remain,
    holding the world forever.
No journey too far, no distance too great,
    no valley of darkness too blinding;
no creature too humble, no child too small
    for God to be seeking and finding.

Nothing is lost to the heart of God,
    nothing is lost forever;
God's heart is love, and that love will remain,
    holding the world forever.
No impulse of love, no office of care,
    no moment of life in its fullness;
no beginning too late, no ending too soon,
    but is gathered and known in its goodness.

Colin Gibson, 1994
Songs for a Rainbow People, 1998
© 1996, Hope Publishing Company

893
The Song of the Gallows Cart

See how the crowds are gathering
    to watch the final kill;
they line the fearful roadway
    that leads to Tyburn Hill.
And who will ride the gallows cart
    beside the lonely one,
to share the jeers and bear the scorn
    until the work is done?

There's always one more sinner
    to send to Judgment Day;
there's always one more other,
    one enemy to slay.
But who will speak for mercy,
    who will plead the prisoner's part,
take on the condemnation
    and ride the gallows cart?

And once I saw Christ Jesus
    led on that way to die;
his face was pale with anguish,
    I heard his lonely cry:
"O who will tear the gibbet down,
    and who will stop this cart?
And when will love, not hatred, rule
    in every human heart?"

Colin Gibson, 1990
Reading the Signature, 1994
© 1994, Hope Publishing Company

894
Strong Word of God

Strong Word of God, spoken to all,
    in open love and simple grace,
throw down the walls of fear and scorn
    that still divide the human race.

Break down the shell of hardness, Lord,
    masking our heart's timidity;
unprison our dry souls and minds,
    unshelter us to set us free.

Body of Christ, broken for us,
    your ancient pain we still renew
on the cold crosses of our lives,
    and, loveless, know not what we do.

What other pardon shall we find?
    Where else true wholeness learn to share
than in the broken bread, the wine
    that universal love declare.

Love is the burden we decline,
    fearing the brokenness, the pain;
nerve us to walk compassion's way,
    to bear the wounds of love again.

Come, overwhelming power of God;
    let us be broken if we must,
knowing that in your steadfast love
    new life breaks forth from precious dust.

Open the tomb in which we lie
    dead to the world, ourselves, and you;
roll back the stone, end death's dark night,
    break forth in resurrection light.

Colin Gibson, 1991
Songs for a Rainbow People, 1998
© 1998, Hope Publishing Company

895
The Servant Song

Brother, sister, let me serve you,
    let me be as Christ to you;
pray that I may have the grace to
    let you be my servant too.

We are pilgrims on a journey
    and companions on the road;
we are here to help each other
    walk the mile and bear the load.

I will hold the Christ-light for you
    in the nighttime of your fear;
I will hold my hand out to you,
    speak the peace you long to hear.

I will weep when you are weeping;
    when you laugh, I'll laugh with you;
I will share your joy and sorrow
    till we've seen this journey through.

When we sing to God in heaven
    we shall find such harmony,
born of all we've known together
    of Christ's love and agony.

Brother, sister, let me serve you,
    let me be as Christ to you;
pray that I may have the grace to
    let you be my servant too.

Richard Gillard, 1974
Together in Song, 1999
© 1977, Scripture in Song (admin. Integrity Music)

896
Living in Christ with People

Jesus, the Lord, stands with the poor,
    when they are hungry, he is not fed.
When they have thirst, he will not drink,
    his too the agony when they are bled.

Jesus, the victim, loves the oppressed.
    One with the prisoner, locked in a cell,
one with the outcast, one with the slave,
    bearing the anguish of each human hell.

Jesus, the beggar, lives in the slum,
seeking compassion, hoping for grace,
suffering insults, looking for work,
all the world's agony etched on his face.

Come to us, Jesus, strengthen our wills,
bind us to fight against bondage and greed,
draw us to share with those who are weak,
living with people in every deed.

Ron O'Grady, 1981
Sound the Bamboo, 2000
© Christian Conference of Asia

897
The God of Us All

The God of us all is our Father,
he guides us when we are in danger,
he calls us to honor the stranger.

Great is the Lord,
ever adored!

The God of us all is our Mother,
she teaches us her truth and beauty,
she shows us a love beyond duty.

Our God is a Father and Mother,
surrounding us all with protection,
to give to the world new direction.

Ron O'Grady, 1980
Sound the Bamboo, 2000
© Christian Conference of Asia

898
Sometimes the Boundless Beauty

Sometimes the boundless beauty of the world
catches the throat and moists the watching eyes;
so diverse, so grand the craft of God,
so ordered and yet full of rich surprise.

Try though we will with chisel, brush, and pen,
needle and stylus, carver's cunning blade,
wheel of the potter, weaver's patient loom,
we cannot match the glory God has made.

Yet in us all the urge to beauty moves,
bidding us make, however small, our mark.
No matter that our colors pale and fade,
or that our songs are rivaled by the lark.

Hallow our efforts, all-creating God;
make them more real, these shadows of your art;
worthy your grace, and seal of provenance,
sprung from the mind and nurtured in the heart.

Kathleen M. Mayson, 1988
Songs for a Rainbow People, 1998
© 1998, Kathleen M. Mayson

899
We Stand with Christ

We do not hope to ease our minds
by simple answers, shifted blame,
while Christ is homeless, hungry, poor,
and we are rich who bear his name.
As long as justice is a dream
and human dignity denied,
we stand with Christ; disturb us still
till every need is satisfied.

We cannot ask to live at peace
in comfort and security
while Christ is tried in Pilate's hall
and drags his cross to Calvary.
As long as hatred stifles truth
and freedom is betrayed by fear,
we stand with Christ; give us no peace
till his peace reigns in triumph here.

We will not pray to be preserved
    from any depths of agony
while Christ's despairing cry rings out:
    God, why have you abandoned me?
As long as we have hope to share
    of life renewed beyond the pain,
we stand with Christ all through the night
    till Easter morning dawns again.

Marnie Barrell, 1989
Alleluia Aotearoa, 1993
© Marnie Barrell

900
Great and Deep the Spirit's Purpose

Great and deep the Spirit's purpose,
    hidden now in mystery;
nature bursts with joyful promise,
    ripe with what is yet to be.
In a wealth of rich invention,
    still the work of art unfolds:
Barely have we seen, and faintly,
    what God's great salvation holds.

Great and deep the Spirit's purpose,
    making Jesus seen and heard.
Every age of God's creation
    grasps new meaning from the Word.
Show us, Holy Spirit, show us
    your new work begun today:
Eyes and ears and hearts are open,
    teach us what to do and say.

Great and deep the Spirit's purpose:
    all God's children brought to birth,
freed from hunger, fear, and evil
    every corner of the earth;
and a million million voices
    speak with joy the Savior's name;
every face reflects his image,
    never any two the same.

Great and deep the Spirit's purpose,
    nothing shall be left to chance.
All that lives will be united
    in the everlasting dance.
All fulfilled and all perfected,
    each uniquely loved and known,
Christ in glory unimagined
    once for all receives his own.

Marnie Barrell, 1988
Alleluia Aotearoa, 1993
© Marnie Barrell

901
Sound a Mystic Bamboo Song

Sound a mystic bamboo song;
    raise a chanting lyric voice;
beat the drum and play the flute;
    let the Asian church rejoice.

See the Christ in tribal cloth
    living in a squatter's shed;
bending as she plants the rice,
    sleeping on a pavement bed.

Free the Christ within the poor;
    break the chains of wealth and power;
let the age of sharing dawn;
    sing the promised gospel hour.

May your lively spirit, God,
    blow throughout this ravished earth;
giving cultures, creatures, plants
    wholeness, stillness, growth, and worth.

William L. (Bill) Wallace, 1992
"The Hymn Society Annual Conference Program Book," 1999
© 2001, Selah Publishing Company, Inc.

902
O Threefold God of Tender Unity

O threefold God of tender unity,
life's great unknown that binds and sets us free;
felt in our loving, greater than our thought,
you are the mystery found, the mystery sought.

O blaze of radiance, source of light that blinds,
the fiery splendor of prophetic minds,
you live in mystery, yet within us dwell;
life springs from you as from a living well.

Most loving Parent, Child of joys and pains,
creative Spirit, life force that sustains,
in bone and flesh, in blood we touch your hand,
your face we see in water, air, and land.

In every making, each creative dream
and in the flowing of life's healing stream—
when love is born or people reconciled,
we share your life, O Parent, Spirit, Child.

O threefold God of tender unity,
life's great unknown that binds and sets us free;
felt in our loving, greater than our thought,
you are the mystery found, the mystery sought.

William L. (Bill) Wallace, 1988
Singing the Circle, Book 2, 1990
© 2001, Selah Publishing Company, Inc.

903
Why Has God Forsaken Me

"Why has God forsaken me?"
    cried our Savior from the cross
as he shared the loneliness
    of our deepest grief and loss.

At the tomb of Lazarus
    Jesus wept with open grief:
Grant us, God, the tears which heal
    all our pain and unbelief.

Jesus, as his life expired,
    placed himself within God's care:
At our dying, Christ, may we
    trust the love which conquers fear.

Mystery shrouds our life and death
    but we need not be afraid,
for the mystery's heart is Love,
    God's great love which Christ displayed.

William L. (Bill) Wallace, 1979; revised, 1990
Singing the Circle, Book 2, 1990
© 2001, Selah Publishing Co., Inc.

904
Although a Man, Yes, Mary's Son

Although a man, yes, Mary's son,
    your life affirmed the womanly:
You claimed your sisters, dearest Christ,
    as equals in your company.

You free us all to laugh and cry,
    to know when others need our touch,
to nurture earth, her children too,
    through God who mothers us so much.

Entrenched control of wealth and power
    remains within the rule of men—
let us who share the flesh of Christ
    share power and be newborn again.

God help us each to be at ease
    with both our strength and tenderness,
that male and female in our heart
    may be as one in graciousness.

William L. (Bill) Wallace, 1986
Sound the Bamboo, 1990
© 2001, Selah Publishing Company, Inc.

Chapter 32:
World Hymnody, 1976–2000
(905–980)

With considerable foresight, Routley observed at the end of chapter 28 that his survey of "modern foreign sources" was "only the prologue to a development in hymnody which is already energetic and will become decisive." The intervening decades have borne out his prophecy, in ways perhaps exceeding even his remarkable vision. Much of what is being shared is less "foreign," if not entirely familiar, thanks to the committed work of numerous persons, many of whom figure in this narrative; the good will of many more; and, one senses with some confidence, the guidance of the Holy Spirit.

One of the challenges in discussing this literature is finding a label that comprehends and characterizes its immensity and diversity. Each piece in some way reflects the cultural and religious setting from which it comes, yet its sharing is deliberately international and ecumenical. This is part of its promise: that in a world seemingly bent on Babel, we may catch a glimpse of Pentecost. That is the declaration of Psalm 67 and of the text at 970. The world views, theologies, and aesthetic presuppositions of these pieces differ from one another and, certainly, from the singing traditions—varied as they are—of most English-speaking churches. For this very reason, they offer valuable new perspectives to the Western church. That is the promise articulated by Brian Wren in the text at 619.

Given the readership of this volume, and the tradition from which it emerges, the texts included are limited to those available for singing in English. The substantial differences between some of the original languages and English—in poetic form as well as in imagery—mean that what appears in translation is often a paraphrase. Yet, in the best of these, it is striking how powerfully an idea, an insight, or a metaphor communicates. These materials would not be accessible to English-speaking worshipers without the skills of translators and versifiers. Prominent among these are the Dutch-English hymnist, Fred Kaan; James Minchin, an Australian Anglican priest; and George Lockwood, a United Methodist pastor from the United States.

Many songs from "global" sources are brief and depend on repetition, often with variation or improvisation, for their effectiveness. They are not included here, though some are mentioned, for to present these short texts in cold print would not in any fair way represent their meaning or power. It must be acknowledged that it is in the experience of these songs in particular that one can with one's whole being feel the spiritual vitality of Christian worship shaped by those cultures. The inclusion of some of these traditional repetitive songs in recent hymnals for English-speaking congregations indicates growing openness to both their styles and their witness.

The sharing of hymns across linguistic barriers has been greatly facilitated by the publication of several collections designed specifically for this purpose. Many of these have been developed through the World Council of Churches or affiliated organizations. Worship at meetings of the WCC has done much to encourage the valuing of differing styles of congregational song. Particularly important was the 1983 meeting in Vancouver, in which Dieter Trautwein brought together I-to Loh, Patrick Matsikenyiri, and Pablo Sosa. These gifted scholars and worship leaders have done much to promote the sharing of materials, expertise, and experience. The 1999 meeting of the Hymn Society in the United States and Canada, also in Vancouver, brought together these same four figures as a sign that such mutuality is an enduring phenomenon.

Among the collections of this literature that are broadest in scope are *International Songbook* (1990) by the World Mennonite Council; *Many and Great* (1990) and *Sent by the Lord* (1991), both from the Iona community; *World Praise* (1993); *Aleluya: Let the Whole World Sing* (1994), from the

Lausanne II Congress; *Thuma Mina* (1995), from the WCC; *Global Songs—Local Voices* (1995); *Global Praise 1* (1996); *Global Songs 2* (1997); and *Halle, Halle* (1999). The last, a small volume edited by the American church music scholar Michael Hawn and designed for children's choirs, contains information about cultural context, liturgical use, and performance practice. It is a superb resource for introducing English-speaking congregations to a representative sampling of this literature. While some items from these cultures had been included in earlier denominational books, the first to have them in significant numbers is *The United Methodist Hymnal*. This lead has been followed by *The Presbyterian Hymnal, Hymnal: A Worship Book, The New Century Hymnal*, and *Chalice Hymnal*.

The German minister Dieter Trautwein has helped lead numerous international and ecumenical projects in worship, particularly in congregational song, including the 1974 edition of *Cantate Domino* and *Thuma Mina*. The concern that he and the World Council share for unity in the church is reflected in 905, with its affirmation of the blessing of God in community. Trautwein has been a promoter of new music in German congregations and a productive contributor. An earlier text of his is at 574.

Another German advocate of new idioms in worship is Eckart Bücken, who has extensive experience in work with youth. The straightforward statements of 906 are a reminder that God's gifts are for our stewardship in caring for God's world. The text at 907 is an affirmation by Gerhard Schnath and Rudolf Otto Wiemar that there will be a future of redemption, community, and renewal. Schnath was an Evangelical pastor in Westphalia; Wiemer, a teacher and writer in his native Thuringia, as well as in Bohemia and Lower Saxony. Methodist minister Hartmut Handt has served congregations in the United States and in Germany and has written about church music and worship. His parallel statements in 908 echo John Wesley's teaching that faith which overcomes must be active and visible.

The hymnist whose works have circulated most widely from the Netherlands is Huub Oosterhuis, a Jesuit priest and a leader in revitalizing Catholic worship following the Second Vatican Council. His text about the church at 909 identifies it as ordinary people transformed by the presence of Christ in bringing justice and peace to the world. The revelation of God's glory, incorporating themes of the Epiphany, is the substance of his hymn for Christmas Eve, 910. For another text by Oosterhuis, see 575.

The Norwegian Lutheran writer Svein Ellingsen is known not only as a hymnist, but also as a painter and teacher. Such is his stature that he has been granted a government stipend to support his work. His description of the insistent call of God in hymn 911 shows the tenderness and immediacy that exist side by side in many of his texts. With its many stanzas linked by their last lines, 912 perceives God's present reign in light of that which is to come. The evening hymn at 913 moves from unease and regret through forgiveness to peace. These three texts are included in *Praises Resound* (1991), a bilingual collection of his hymns, with English translations by Hedwig T. Durnbaugh.

The prolific Swedish hymnwriter Anders Frostenson treats human freedom and sin within the breadth of God's love in 914. One of Frostenson's earlier texts is found at 577. The dominant phrase of 915 reiterates the theme of a 1991 conference on justice, peace, and the integrity of creation convened by the Swedish Christian Council. Its author, Per Harling, a liturgist for the Church of Sweden, writes in English as well as Swedish. New and familiar images for the Trinity are intertwined in 916 by Tomas Boström, a Methodist minister who writes both texts and tunes.

Four texts from Spain reflect the vitality of an idiom related to folk song that has spread widely since the Second Vatican Council. Numerous recordings helped the musician and priest Cesáreo Gabaraín to become one of the leading figures in this movement. His communion hymn, 917, traces the wheat and grapes from the field to the table and into the nurture of Christian community and service, using an analogy at least as ancient as the *Didache* (see 552, as well as 790). The call of Christ to discipleship is recounted and personalized in 918. Other popular texts by Gabaraín include "Walk on, O people of God" (*"Camina, pueblo de Dios"*) and "You are the seed" (*"Sois la semilla"*). Another pioneer in this style is Alberto Taulé, also a priest and music producer, as well as a writer. His Advent hymn, 919, with its picture of earth's longing for the coming of Christ, was written in the language of Catalonia, the region bordering France. Based on the parable of Matthew 25, 920 presents the generosity of the poor as witness. Almost nothing is known of its authors, J. A. Olivar and Miguel Manzano.

The songs of the ecumenical community at Taizé, a village in France, form a body of song that makes a distinctive contribution to world hymnody. They have become a common ground for worship in many settings because of their lack of identification with a particular culture or tradition. The music of Taizé shares certain traits with the congregational song of many traditional cultures, in that the texts—whether in Latin or various vernacular language—are simple and the settings are brief and intended for repetition. The spread of these songs through English-speaking churches is evidenced by the appearance of several in the *Hymnal Guide*.

Most indigenous African hymns have brief texts, often performed in a call-and-response pattern, using much repetition and some word substitution, along with improvisation. Their effectiveness in worship is owed to participation that involves not only the whole person, in dancing and playing instruments or clapping, but also the whole worshiping community. Among the pieces found in hymnals for English-speaking congregations that represent this literature are three songs from South Africa: *"Amen, siyakudu-*

misa" (Xhosa, by Stephen C. Molefe, ca. 1917–1987; "Amen, we praise your name, O God"), *"Thuma mina"* (Xhosa, traditional; "Send me, Lord"), and *"Siyahamba"* (Zulu/Xhosa, traditional; "We are walking in the light of God"). Multistanza texts seem to be primarily the work of nonnatives, such as Howard Olson and Tom Colvin, both of whom have expressed the hope that their work will be succeeded by that of African writers. In African worship, the community is often the author-composer of a hymn. Such is the case with 921, a text about Christian community, by the Nairobi Mennonite Church Choir.

One of the leaders in making African hymnody accessible to a wider audience is the American Lutheran teacher and Bible translator Howard Olson. Olson spent more than four decades in Tanzania, collecting and translating indigenous materials, interpreting these to non-African worshipers, encouraging new writing, and producing texts himself. Hymn 922 is his translation of an anonymous Swahili text about the presence of grace in our lives through the Spirit. Joas Kijugo, a Tanzanian Lutheran musician and teacher, wrote the Swahili original of 923, with its call-and-response pattern. Similar in content to a Gospel Song, but in the idiom of the Kinga people of Southern Tanzania, is 924, by Ndilivako Ndwela. Olson engaged American hymnist Thomas Troeger to convey in English the structure of Andrew Kyomo's 925, with its far-reaching joy. Kyomo is a Moravian teacher at Bishop Kisanji University in Tanzania. Olson's own work in dialogue with Christians in Tanzania is shown in 926, based loosely on a text by one of his students, Enock Kalembo. This text on stewardship alludes to both the Sermon on the Mount and the parable of the rich fool and contains a penetrating restatement of "you can't take it with you": "shrouds have no pockets." It was Olson who first published the original of 927 by Wilson Niwagila. The author of this invocation of the Holy Spirit was one of the successors to Olson as principal of

Lutheran Theological College, now Makumira University College.

Tom Colvin was a Scottish Presbyterian (later, United Reformed) minister and a member of the Iona community who spent much of his career in Malawi and Ghana. He connected African cultures and traditional Western hymnody by writing multistanza texts to indigenous tunes, with content that reflects the interaction between the Gospel and the settings where he served. His best-known hymn is 928, written for the church in Ghana to teach servanthood after the model of Jesus. A text about the "Spirit-friend" (929) is set to a tune from the Gonja people of northern Ghana that was collected by the first Christian minister from that group. A dance from Malawi is used for the call-and-response naming song at 930 that teaches the theology of the incarnation. Other ways in which Colvin has related his hymns to indigenous culture are by building on the work of African writers and incorporating familiar language for God. Both of these approaches are seen in 931, which is based on a text by Charles Chunula (d. 1910) and identifies God with a name used in Malawi. This hymn speaks powerfully to the Western church of the certainty of God's presence celebrated in the midst of oppression. A bold and direct hymn on repentance, 932, was fashioned by John Bell of the Iona community from a text by the Ugandan Anglican minister Cranmer Mugisha.

Patrick Matsikenyiri (b. 1937), a teacher and musician in the United Methodist Church in Zimbabwe, has been instrumental in the sharing of African hymns through his work with various pan-African groups, with Methodists in many countries, and with the World Council of Churches. With S T Kimbrough, Jr., and Carlton R. Young (b. 1926), he compiled *Africa Praise Songbook* (1998), which contains congregational songs in their original languages and in English translation.

The rich and varied hymns of the churches of Asia have been shared across that region and throughout the world, thanks in large measure to the tireless efforts of I-to Loh, a Presbyterian musicologist, teacher, and composer from Taiwan. He has edited significant collections that have made these materials broadly available, including *New Songs of Asian Cities* (1972) and *Sound the Bamboo* (1990, trial edition; 2000) for the Christian Conference of Asia. His collaborators in the massive work of the more recent project were Francisco Feliciano of the Philippines and James Minchin of Australia. Loh also edited *Hymns from the Four Winds* (1983), an anthology of Asian hymns published by the United Methodist Church in the United States. Many of the texts from Asia that follow have come into English usage through these collections. Unfortunately, little information is available about many of the authors.

Sound the Bamboo succeeds the *E. A. C. C. Hymnal* (1963) and gives more attention to the textual and musical styles of Asian churches. The earlier book was the work of Daniel Thambyrajah Niles, a native of Ceylon (now Sri Lanka) and a Methodist minister who gathered, translated, and wrote hymns (see 582, 588, 955). Niles was prominent in international ecumenical ministries and was cofounder of the East Asian Christian Conference, the forerunner of the CCA.

Three examples come from the Indian subcontinent. A prayer to the Holy Spirit to call forth worship and singing, 933, with its "hallelujah" refrain, was written in the Tamil language by noted scholar T. Dayanandan Francis. The countermaterialistic text of 934 is by Dibya Khaling of Nepal. Walter Marasinghe, of Sri Lanka, wrote the picturesque text about the God of creation, 935, while in the Philippines in 1980 for a workshop on music and liturgy.

Songsan Prasopsin, who writes in Thai, is the author of the morning prayer for faithful discipleship at 936. The first Vietnamese hymn to be included in a hymnal in the United States is 937 by Dao Kim, about whom nothing is known. This text incorporates numerous phrases from the Psalms.

The pioneering hymns of Timothy Tingfang Lew, who came to the United States late in his life, were mentioned in chapter 28 (585, 586). Another of his texts, "O Christ, the great foundation," though written in 1933, did not appear in the translation by Mildred A. Wiant (1898–2001) until 1966 and was not widely published until a decade later. It has since been included in a number of books in England and the United States in a version from the Jubilate Hymns group. A more recent Chinese hymn by Weifan Wang, 938, appropriates images from the Song of Solomon.

The greatest contribution of Taiwan to world hymnody lies in the work of I-to Loh. Through the Asian Institute for Liturgy and Music, the Christian Council of Asia, and the World Council of Churches, he has encouraged the development of congregational song that embodies the distinctive voice of each culture. See, for example, his translation at 951. Loh also compiled *Ban-bîn Siong-chàn* (1995), a collection for churches in Taiwan that presents hymns from many cultures.

Two older Taiwanese texts have come into English use in recent years. Number 939 is a traditional creation hymn translated by Boris and Clare Anderson, English missionaries from the United Reformed Church, and set to a folk tune, often in Loh's harmonization. The biblical image of the burning bush is linked to the persecuted church in 940 by Chun-ming Kao, who was imprisoned for his faith.

The vitality of the rapidly growing church in Korea is expressed in song. A glimpse of this hymnody was offered by ten translations of Korean hymns in *The Korean-English Hymnal* (1978). The hymn of reconciliation and unity at 941 was written by Hyun Sul Hong, president of Methodist Theological Seminary in Seoul. Educated in the United States, as was Hong, Helen Kim, a Methodist, served as president of Ewha College and represented her nation at numerous international religious and charitable conferences. Her text at 942 asks Jesus to calm the tempestuous individual

life as he did the sea in Mark 4. A third Methodist writer is Ho Un Lee, from the Northern part of the divided peninsula, who based 943 on 2 Corinthians 5:17. Ok In Lim, a professor of literature, wrote the harvest hymn at 944 that, in praising the providence of God and the hope for the growth of faith, includes both natural beauty and the human role in planting, tending, and harvesting. The dignity of labor and the identification of Christ with the laborer permeate 945 by Byung Soo Oh.

The most widely published of recent Japanese hymns is 946, by Tokuo Yamaguchi, a United Church of Christ (formerly Methodist) pastor. Written for an international Christian Education Convention in Tokyo in 1958, this text takes its shape from John 14:6, the theme of the conference. The balladlike 947, by Nobuo Befu, recounts incidents in which Jesus spoke words of peace. The daily routine of the field worker prompts a cycle of grateful prayer in 948 by Masuko Endo. Yasushige Imakoma, a pastor in the United Church, uses nature imagery in parallel structure to frame 949, an invocation of God's presence. These two texts were translated into English by Nobuaki Hanaoka, who, though born in Japan, has been pastor of Baptist and United Methodist congregations in the United States. He has also produced original hymns, including 950, a song of thanksgiving and praise in parallel stanzas, which was written in English. From the Okinawan writer Seiei Yokota comes 951, which employs nature in proclaiming and praising the work of Christ.

In the Philippines, new hymns are being written in native languages and in English. Francisco Feliciano, director of the Asian Institute for Liturgy and Music, is not only a teacher, compiler, and editor, but also an important writer. His contemplative 952, written in English while he was a student in Germany, shows, especially in Feliciano's own musical setting, the influence of Buddhist philosophy. Two hymns by Melchizedek Solis present Christian responses to life in an unjust society: 953 hears God's voice above the struggle and bears witness to the One who liberates the oppressor as well as the oppressed, while 954 similarly looks beyond hate, placing hope in the Holy Spirit's leadership of the next generation. In ministries in the Philippines, Thailand, and the United States, Solis has been active as a conciliator in the quest for human rights.

Elena G. Maquiso was a religious educator and a compiler of hymns for children. Though proficient in English from doctoral study in the United States, she wrote several texts in Cebuano, a Philippine language. Her gentle but earnest prayer to the Trinity, 955, comes to us in the translation by D. T. Niles. Similar in tone is 956, a reflective evening hymn that acknowledges both natural and human surroundings. Biblical stories of God's power to set free (Luke 9, Acts 9, and John 5) form the basis of Ramon Oliano's 957. The rhyme pattern of the original Ikalahan is preserved in the translation.

The last two Asian examples come from Indonesia. The comforting words of Jesus are paraphrased by Rudolf R. Pantou in 958. The evening hymn by Fridolin Ukur, 959, is vivid and sweeping in its scope, encompassing both scenes of nature and the suffering of impoverished children.

Some of the hymns from Latin America that have found wide usefulness in English translation are by unknown authors. Even the country of origin is uncertain for two of these, 960, with its recollections of David, and the hymn of praise known by its Spanish incipit, *"Alabaré a mi Señor,"* which exists in a variety of English versions. The anonymous Puerto Rican hymn at 961 traces the story of the magi and incorporates the song of the angels in its refrain. José Maria Santini's 962 includes both natural scenes and intriguing contrasts in the story of the nativity.

With its message that Jesus is powerful, yet cares for us, the Gospel Song at 963 has long been a favorite among Spanish-speaking worshipers and has found its way in English into many translations. Its author, Vicente Mendoza, was a Methodist evangelist, pastor, and teacher in Mexico, who

wrote or translated more than 300 hymns. The excitement of the triumphal entry is conveyed by 964, which adds an eschatological dimension in its final stanza. This is by Rubén Ruíz (Avila), a musician whose own tune complements the text.

The works of two editors and hymnists born in Mexico who have come to the United States illustrate the diminishing significance of national borders in defining ethnic and linguistic patterns of worship. These are Roberto Escamilla, who directed the project that produced *Celebremos* (1979) and *Celebremos II* (1983), and Carlos Rosas, editor of *Alabanza y Gloria* (1992). Escamilla, a distinguished teacher who has served in several roles with the United Methodist Church, wrote stanzas 2 through 4 of 965, adding to an anonymous folk hymn based on Romans 14:7–8. Rosas, a prolific Roman Catholic musician who has lived in Texas for many years, refers to Psalm 19 and Genesis 1 in 966, with its psalmlike "alleluia" refrain. Building on the image of God in humanity, 967 traces the roots of injustice and urges compassion for the poor.

The next two hymns come from the island nations of the Caribbean. Hugh B. Sherlock was a Methodist minister in Jamaica and the author of the national anthem chosen when that country achieved independence in 1962. He wrote 968 for a denominational emphasis on renewal. Because it was written at a time when the tone of the King James Version was still dominant, its appearance has usually been in one of several revised versions, including one substantially altered by Michael Saward. This text links the global reach of Matthew 28:19–20 with the author's own ministry among the poor. A popular Carribean song is "Halle, halle," a folk tune to which oral tradition has improvised many different texts. The stanzas at 969 are based on the "I am" sayings from the gospel of John and Toplady's "Rock of ages" (80) and were put in written form by George Mulrain, a Methodist from Trinidad and Tobago who teaches theology in Jamaica.

The joining of different peoples and different places in praise of God is a prominent theme in both Protestant and Catholic hymns that are being shared across cultural and linguistic barriers. The unity of all peoples in God's love is declared by 970. Its author, the Methodist church historian Justo L. González, was born in Cuba and has been a theological educator and writer in Puerto Rico and the United States. The same concept is celebrated in 971 by Rafael Zamora, a Roman Catholic priest from Costa Rica, who wrote this text for the worship of an international liturgy workshop held in Rio de Janeiro in 1993.

The most visible advocate for the development of congregational song in indigenous idioms of South and Central America is Pablo Sosa, a Methodist pastor, liturgist, and musician from Argentina. Sosa has promoted the sharing of this literature through his energetic leadership in the World Council of Churches and other international groups and by his involvement in compiling several collections, including the multiple volumes of *Cancionero Abierto* (first volume, 1974). Though he has been more productive as a composer, arranger, and translator than as an author, it is fitting that his best-known text, 972, is a hymn of unity, based on Psalm 133. This is set to his own tune, which is in the style of an Argentinean dance, the *charmarita*.

Argentinean poet Nicolás Martínez, a pastor in the Christian Church (Disciples of Christ), was involved, with Sosa, in preparing the interdenominational collection *Cántico Nuevo* (1962). His paraphrase of 1 Corinthians 15:12–23, at 973, written for that anthology, where it was paired with Sosa's tune, CENTRAL, was one of the first substantial pieces of contemporary hymn writing in Latin America. It was translated by Fred Kaan for *Cantate Domino* (1974).

Federico J. Pagura, a native of Argentina, has been the Methodist bishop of Costa Rica and Panama, and of Argentina. He has also been a leader in promoting music for worship in folk and popular styles and in translating hymns from other parts of the world into Spanish. His own hymns carry prophetic force. Of three *"porque"* (because) texts written in the 1970s, 974 has found the widest circulation. Recalling the identify of Christ with the poor, it celebrates the hope of freedom and has often been sung as a song of solidarity. Pagura is also the author of 975, which appears in *Cantate Domino* (1974) translated in a paraphrase by Fred Pratt Green.

Mortimer Arias, a noted evangelist and author, was executive pastor of the Methodist Church in his native Uruguay and bishop of Bolivia. He has also taught at schools in United States and served as president of a seminary in Costa Rica. His awareness of the presence of God in daily life is vividly expressed in 976.

Methodist theologian and teacher Jaci Maraschin is a prolific composer and compiler of church music in Brazil. His text at 977 is a prayer for deliverance from oppression to service. Simei Monteiro, also a Methodist, is a professor of music and worship, currently serving on the staff of the World Council of Churches. She wrote 978 out of her concern for the children who live on the street in Brazilian cities, further contextualizing the incarnation by her own tune in the style of a *samba*. The ancient cry of *"Veni, creator Spiritus"* is brought to the needs and the apathy of modern culture in 979. The welcome and, indeed, the necessity of Christian community are celebrated in 980, which must, of course, be danced as well as sung. The message of this text was modeled in its composition, which was not by an individual, but by the group of persons identified as its authors. The leader of this collaborative effort, Ernesto Cardoso, was a Methodist pastor and musician who worked with the WCC in creation and compilation of resources for worship.

905

Bless, and Keep Us, God, in Your Love United
German: Komm, Herr, segne uns

Bless, and keep us, God, in your love united,
from your family never separated.
You make all things new as we follow after;
whether tears or laughter, we belong to you.

Blessing shrivels up when your children hoard it;
move us then to share, for we can afford it:
Blessing only grows in the act of sharing,
in a life of caring; love that heals and grows.

Fill your world with peace, such as you intended.
Teach us to prize the earth, love, replenish, tend it.
God, uplift, fulfill all who sow in sadness,
let them reap with gladness, by your kingdom
thrilled.

You renew our life, changing tears to laughter;
we belong to you, so we follow after.
Bless and keep us, God, in your love united,
never separated from your living Word.

Dieter Trautwein, 1979
translated, Fred Kaan, 1980
The Only Earth We Know, 1999
© 1985, Hope Publishing Company

906

God Gave Us Breath
German: Gott gab uns Atem

God gave us breath, life in us to waken,
he gave us eyes to see face to face.
God gave to us the earth, with all within it,
that we keep faith in time and space.

God gave us ears so that we might listen,
words he has given to understand.
Never will God destroy his creation.
He made it good—a precious land.

God gave us hands to reach out and take care.
He gave us feet to stand up for right.
God himself will with us change the world's face.
We enter life in God's new light.

Eckart Bücken, 1982
translated, Sybille Fritsch-Oppermann, 1994
Thuma Mina, 1995
© Strube Publishing

907

The Time Will Come
German: Es kommt die Zeit

The day will come
when human dreams will reach fulfillment,
when this whole creation is to be redeemed
through justice, peace, and joy.

Then shall the people with God walk
hand in hand;
then shall the people with God walk
hand in hand.

The day will come
when nations will embrace each other,
when all shall be free and yet together bound,
safe in one earthly home.

The day will come
when earth will be renewed and flourish
through people who care for the Creator's gifts
of water, air, and fire.

Gerhard Schnath and Rudolf Otto Wiemer, 1975
translated, Fred Kaan, 1995
Thuma Mina, 1995
© 1995, Hope Publishing Company

908
Trusting in Jesus
German: Glauben heißt: Christus

Trusting in Jesus means bearing him witness;
also, confessing by thinking and doing.
Teach us to trust, Lord.

Trusting means loving when others are hating,
caring for life and embrace of your neighbor.
Teach us to love, Lord.

Trusting means hoping for those who have lost hope,
daring a dream in their hearts for tomorrow.
Teach us to hope, Lord.

Trusting means comfort for those who are burdened,
bonding of hearts in all sorrow and mourning.
Teach us to comfort.

Trusting means action when others do nothing,
being a neighbor in love with rejoicing.
Teach us to act, Lord.

Hartmut Handt, 1978
translated, S T Kimbrough, Jr., 1995
Global Praise 1, 1996
© 1996, General Board of Global Ministries, GBGMusik

909
What Is This Place
Dutch: Zomaar een dak boven wat hoofden

What is this place, where we are meeting?
Only a house, the earth its floor,
walls and a roof, sheltering people,
windows for light, an open door.
Yet it becomes a body that lives
when we are gathered here,
and know our God is near.

Words from afar, stars that are falling,
sparks that are sown in us like seed,
names for our God, dreams, signs, and wonders
sent from the past are all we need.
We in this place remember and speak
again what we have heard:
God's free redeeming word.

And we accept bread at his table,
broken and shared, a living sign.
Here in this world, dying and living,
we are each other's bread and wine.
This is the place where we can receive
what we need to increase:
our justice and God's peace.

Huub Oosterhuis, 1968
translated, N. David Smith, 1972
JourneySongs, 1994
© 1984, TEAM Productions (admin. OCP Publications)

910
In Deepest Night
Dutch: Komt ons in deipe nacht ter ore

In deepest night we hear the story:
The morning star has risen plain;
for us an infant has been born,
"the Lord-shall-save-us" is his name.
Open your hearts, believe your senses,
and trust in what you plainly see:
how God's own word from highest heaven
is wrought in us so humanly.

To us no other sign is given,
no other light comes breaking through:
This man alone is our companion,
a God who is our brother, too.
Sing for your God who has unfolded
in Jesus his great love for all.
The world becomes a new creation,
all flesh receives his saving call.

The way the sun comes up in glory,
    a bridegroom shedding light and fire,
so comes the king of peace to join us,
    and, once for all, has come his hour.
And joining everyone together,
    his love doled out as nourishment,
he gives his body to our keeping
    that we may live his covenant.

Huub Oosterhuis, 1967
translated, N. David Smith, 1968
JourneySongs, 1994
© 1985, TEAM Productions (admin. OCP Publications)

911

There Is a Voice That Never Ceases Seeking
Norwegian: Det er en røst som uopphørlig søker

There is a voice that never ceases seeking
    to bring our anguished heart within its call,
and from an unseen world a hand is offered
    to raise us up from our defeat and fall.

Through grace God offers life within his kingdom
    where all is pardoned, canceled, and repealed.
We may believe: There is no past to haunt us,
    this moment holds the gift of life, concealed.

It is the choice we make today that matters!
    God never asks us where our feet have trod.
His question comes to us today, this moment:
    Where do you stand—right now—before your
                                 God?

Oh, what great freedom, Lord, is waiting for us
    when we are captured by your hand, your word!
Let our own hopes and selfish dreams be broken
    and grant us life, a future with you, Lord!

Svein Ellingsen, 1977
translated, Hedwig T. Durnbaugh, 1986; revised, 1990
Praises Resound, 1991
© 1991, Hedwig T. Durnbaugh

912

Lord, the Coming of Your Hour
Norwegian: Herre, når din time kommer

Lord, the coming of your hour
will reveal to us your kingdom
and in clarity will show us
all creation, freed, perfected!
    We shall see you as you are!

Then your kingdom, no more hidden,
rises up in songs of praises!
Earth is freed of pain and sorrow,
death has lost its power forever!
    We shall see you as you are!

While in waiting for your hour
we shall know your kingdom's presence,
like the hidden streams of water,
like the wind through treetops moving,
    till we see you as you are!

At the font you were beside us;
you are present in communion.
Through these gifts we taste the promise
of your kingdom's festal banquet
    when we see you as you are!

Grant us grace that while in waiting
we may live as faithful servants.
Grant us willingness to suffer
through your Spirit working in us,
    who can see you as you are!

Here on earth where all is broken
we can hear your word and promise.
Here, where death still holds the power
hope is given by your Spirit:
    We shall see you as you are!

When the day of Christ is dawning,
out of death your voice will call us.
No more darkness to enshroud us!
For all time your goodness governs!
     We shall see you as you are!

Lord, reveal to us your kingdom!
Yours the power! Yours the glory!
Yours the judgment! Yours the mercy!
Hallelujah! It is finished!
     We shall see you as you are!

Svein Ellingsen, 1976
translated, Hedwig T. Durnbaugh, 1991
Praises Resound, 1991
© 1991, Hedwig T. Durnbaugh

913

In the Stillness of the Evening
Norwegian: I de sene timers stillhet

In the stillness of the evening
inner restlessness befalls me
     which I cannot overpower.
In the midst of joy and gladness
at the day's abundant blessings,
     silent pain is ever near me.

My defeats loom large before me,
and I know the day now passing
     has been crushed to many pieces.
But as day draws to its closing
I surrender all my unrest
     to the One who is beside me.

God is greater than our conscience!
He who knows that I am helpless,
     from the weight of guilt will free me.
All my troubled thoughts are quiet
for I am, in all my weakness,
     still beloved and accepted.

Jesus Christ's own word and promise
comes to me, a gift of mercy:
     "All your sins are now forgiven!"
Thus the pieces lying broken
shall this very day be lifted
     into love's eternal wholeness.

If new days to me are given,
every hour with grace abounding
     will give hope of new beginnings.
Peace of mind protects my slumber.
Courage is restored for living.
     I can meet the new tomorrow!

Svein Ellingsen, 1971
translated, Hedwig T. Durnbaugh, 1985; revised, 1990
Praises Resound, 1991
© 1991, Hedwig T. Durnbaugh

914

The Love of God
Swedish: Guds kärlek

Your love, O God, is broad like beach and meadow,
     wide as the wind, and an eternal home.
You leave us free to seek you or reject you,
     you give us room to answer "Yes" or "No."

          Your love, O God, is broad like beach
                                   and meadow,
               wide as the wind, and an eternal home.

We long for freedom where our truest being
     is given hope and courage to unfold.
We seek in freedom space and scope for dreaming,
     and look for ground where trees and plants can
                                             grow.

But there are walls that keep us all divided;
     we fence each other in with hate and war.
Fear is the bricks-and-mortar of our prison,
     our pride of self the prison coat we wear.

O judge us, God, and in your judgment free us,
and set our feet in freedom's open space;
take us as far as your compassion wanders
among the children of the human race.

Anders Frostenson, 1968
translated, Fred Kaan, 1972; revised, 1989
The Only Earth We Know, 1999
© 1974, 1989, Hope Publishing Company

915

For Sake of Life
Swedish: För livets skull

For sake of life the face of truth will brighten.
For sake of life the seeds of hope will root.
For sake of life the way of peace will lighten
for those who dare to walk—for sake of life.

For sake of life the fields are being seeded.
For sake of life there's still growth in the earth.
For sake of life we'll share with all that need it
the bread from common soil—for sake of life.

For sake of life a righteous wrath needs power.
For sake of life let streams of justice roll.
For sake of life the springs of joy with mother
the newborn child of hope—for sake of life.

For sake of life our God became an infant.
For sake of life he lived and died for all.
For sake of life the time of God is constant.
The kingdom is at hand—for sake of life.

Per Harling, 1991
translated, Per Harling, 1993
Global Praise 1, 1996
© 1991, 1993, 1996, General Board of Global Ministries, GBGMusik

916

I Believe in a God
Swedish: Jag tror på en Gud

I believe in a God, one only,
an artist who's painting life.
With words and with colors
all life is formed by eternal light.

I believe in a God, one only,
a godchild of humankind.
With love and with truth
he opens eternity in my mind.

I believe in a God, one only,
one Spirit, a mystery,
that's breathing with me
for now on and into eternity.

Tomas Boström, 1992
translated, Per Harling, 1995
Global Praise 1, 1996
© Per Harling

917

Sheaves of Summer
Spanish: Una espiga

Sheaves of summer turned golden by the sun,
grapes in bunches cut down when ripe and red,
are converted into the bread and wine of God's love
in the body and blood of our dear Lord.

We are sharing the same communion meal,
we are wheat by the same great Sower sown;
like a millstone life grinds us down with sorrow and
pain,
but God makes us new people bound by love.

Like the grains which become one same whole
loaf,
like the notes that are woven into song,
like the droplets of water that are blended in the sea,
we, as Christians, one body shall become.

At God's table together we shall sit.
As God's children, Christ's body we will share.
One same hope we will sing together as we walk
along.
Brothers, sisters, in life, in love, we'll be.

Cesáreo Gabaraín, 1973
translated, George Lockwood, 1987
The United Methodist Hymnal, 1989
© 1989, The United Methodist Publishing House
(admin. The Copyright Company)

918
Fishers of Men
Spanish: Pescador de hombres

Lord, you have come to the lakeshore
looking neither for wealthy nor wise ones;
you only asked me to follow humbly.

O Lord, with your eyes you have searched
me,
and while smiling have spoken my name;
now my boat's left on the shoreline behind
me;
by your side I will seek other seas.

You know so well my possessions;
my boat carries no gold and no weapons;
you will find there my nets and labor.

You need my hands, full of caring
through my labors to give others rest,
and constant love that keeps on loving.

You, who have fished other oceans,
ever longed for by souls who are waiting,
my loving friend, as thus you call me.

Cesáreo Gabaraín, ca. 1979
translated, Gertrude C. Suppe, George Lockwood,
and Raquel Gutiérrez-Achon, 1987
The United Methodist Hymnal, 1989
© 1989, The United Methodist Publishing House
(admin. The Copyright Company)

919
All Earth Is Waiting to See the Promised One
Catalan: Toda la tierra espera al Salvador

All earth is waiting to see the Promised One,
and the open furrows, the sowing of the Lord.
All the world, bound and struggling, seeks true
liberty;
it cries out for justice and searches for the truth.

Thus says the prophet to those of Israel,
"A virgin mother will bear Emmanuel,"
for his name is "God with us," our brother shall be,
with him hope will blossom once more within our
hearts.

Mountains and valleys will have to be made
plain;
open new highways, new highways for the Lord.
He is now coming closer, so come all and see,
and open the doorways as wide as wide can be.

In lowly stable the Promised One appeared,
yet, feel his presence throughout the earth today,
for he lives in all Christians and is with us now;
again, with his coming he brings us liberty.

Alberto Taulé, 1972
translated, Gertrude C. Suppe, 1987
The United Methodist Hymnal, 1989
© 1989, The United Methodist Publishing House
(admin. The Copyright Company)

920

God Still Goes That Road with Us
Spanish: Va Dios mismo en nuestro caminar

When the poor ones who have nothing share with
strangers,
when the thirsty, water give unto us all,
when the crippled in their weakness strengthen
others,

then we know that God still goes that
road with us;
then we know that God still goes that
road with us.

When at last all those who suffer find their comfort,
when they hope, though even hope seems
hopelessness,
when we love, though hate at times seems all
around us,

When our joy fills up our cup to overflowing,
when our lips can speak no words other than
true,
when we know that love for simple things is better,

When our homes are filled with goodness in
abundance,
when we learn how to make peace instead of war,
when each stranger that we meet is called a neighbor,

J. A. Olivar and Miguel Manzano, 1971
translated, George Lockwood, 1975; revised, 1980
The United Methodist Hymnal, 1989
© 1980, The United Methodist Publishing House
(admin. The Copyright Company)

921

We Are Members of the Church of Christ
Swahili: Umekuwa mwangaza kweli

We are members of the church of Christ.
In this body each one for the other cares:
You my light, and I your guide will be,
as we build the faith community.

You will help me stand upon the rock,
I will comfort you in times of grief and pain.
We will help each other to be firm,
and together build the church of Christ.

And to you, Almighty Lord and God,
we draw near, believing in your holy word.
Guide and keep us in your path we pray,
in the ways of peace and joy each day.

Fill us, Lord, with goodness from above,
that to all the nations we may show your love;
that all peoples know your power and grace,
your salvation and abundant peace.

Teach us, Lord, your truth that changes not,
be our shield, our strong defense along the way.
As your children, keep us in your care,
may your eyes watch o'er us everywhere.

Give us light that we may understand.
Help us, Lord, to be the salt of all the earth.
Help us in the fellowship of faith,
bear the torch of your eternal truth.

Kennedy Bobo and the Nairobi Mennonite Church Choir, 1988
translated, Esther C. Bergen, 1990
International Songbook, 1990
© 1990, Mennonite World Conference

922

We Have from the Lord Received Grace
Swahili: Tumepokea neema; tuimbe sote kwa shangwe

We have from the Lord received grace.
  Extol his mercies forever.
His Spirit he sent to our race,
  from whom no one us can sever.

    O Christians, ours is joy indeed,
      for it is truly unending,
    and power in both word and deed
      our Savior to us extending.

O Spirit of truth and of light,
  dispel deceit and all darkness.
Make truer and clearer our sight
  to recognize sin's dread starkness.

Come Spirit, abide in our hearts;
  transform our weakness to power,
that to others we may impart
  word of your grace every hour.

The promise which Christ gave mankind
  has been fulfilled to perfection.
He sent us his Spirit in whom we have
  sure hope and protection.

God Almighty, Father and Son,
  and Holy Spirit all-knowing,
distinct, yet united as One,
  accept the praise we're bestowing.

anonymous
translated, Howard S. Olson, 1965
Lead Us, Lord, 1977
© 1977, Augsburg Publishing House

923

Who Is He? Christ the Savior
Swahili: Ni nani? Ni mwokozi wa dunia

Who is he?
    Christ the Savior, none more holy.
Amazing!
      He a King, yet lived so lowly.

      Hosanna,
        there in heaven abounding,
      hosanna,
        here on earth, too, resounding.

No chariot,
      for our Jesus, Prince all glorious.
A donkey
        was provided, how inglorious.

Rejoicing,
      lift your voices in thanksgiving.
Inviting
      Christ to come, in your heart living.

Christ calls us,
      all's in vain for which we've striven.
Empowered
      through his grace we rise forgiven.

Joas Kijugo
translated, Howard S. Olson, 1987
Set Free, 1993
© 1993, Augsburg Publishing House

924

The Way Is Jesus
Swahili: Kule mbinguni nataka kwenda

To go to heaven my heart is longing.
How shall I get there without prolonging?

    The way is Jesus. He changes never.
    The Savior wants you with him forever.

The peace of heaven all else excelling;
the place celestial where God is dwelling.

The Father loves us as no one other.
He sent us Jesus to be our brother.

Why delay longer? This is the best day
to choose to follow Jesus, the true way.

Ndilivako Ndwela, ca. 1965
translated, Howard S. Olson, 1965
Lead Us, Lord, 1977
© 1977, Augsburg Publishing House

925

Come Singing, Come Singing
Swahili: Sifuni, sifuni upendo wake Mungu

Come singing, come singing:
    God is love no limit bounds.
Set ringing, set ringing
    all the world with joyful sounds.
Blend your adoration
    with your neighbor's caroling.
All in God's creation
    have a song of praise to sing.

    What the ancient prophets dreamed,
        now at last, appears:
    God has come to cut a path through our
        thickest fears.
    Joy is rising from a world that's lost, sad
        and torn:
    Joy because God's Son the Savior Christ is
        born.

Come bringing, come bringing
    songs of thanks that love abounds.
Love's springing, love's springing,
    blooming in unlikely grounds.
Every race and nation:
    Sing with joy for all God's done.
For your liberation
    from the tangles you have spun.

Keep singing, keep singing
    songs of peace the angels sing.
Keep clinging, keep clinging
    to the hope their anthems bring:
Peace shall be the blessing
    when our daily deeds are one.
With the heart's confessing
    and the will of God is done.

Hearts winging, hearts winging
    at the news that Christ has come,
hope springing, hope springing:
    Save us, save us, David's son!
Join the magi bringing
    gifts more golden than the sun.
Join creation singing,
    praising God's anointed one.

Andrew Kyomo, 1963
translated, Howard S. Olson, 1965
paraphrased, Thomas H. Troeger, 1988
Set Free, 1993
© 1994, Oxford University Press

926
God Made Us Stewards

God made us stewards of all earth's bounty.
        Using possessions as a trust,
we just give God back what we've been given.

        Lay not up riches where moth and rust
                                            consume.
        Make God your treasure,
            serving God be your greatest pleasure.

Life has more meaning than mere obtaining.
        Things are but things and will not last.
Only what is done for Christ remains sure.

There was a farmer who prospered greatly.
        Eating and drinking were his joy.
Bulging barns he traded for his own soul.

Death plays no favorites. Shrouds have no pockets.
     You cannot take it to the grave.
Use it or the blessing will evade you.

Moths pay no interest. Rust has no luster.
     Thieves only plunder what you hoard.
Share all God has given or you lose it.

Howard S. Olson, 1965
Set Free, 1993
© Lutheran Theological College

927
Come among Us, Loving Spirit
Swahili: Njoo kwetu, Roho mwema

Come among us, loving Spirit,
     touch us and make us whole.
Show us glimpses of the kingdom,
     use us to spread its rule.

     Loving Spirit, fill us with your life.
     Loving Spirit, fill us with your life.

Loving Spirit, come and kindle
     faith in our Lord, God's son.
Make your people in their worship
     and in their action one.

Spirit, bless us with awareness
     that you are down-to-earth.
Give us courage, bring among us
     love like a child to birth.

Loving Spirit, let your wisdom
     guide what we think and do.
Make us willing and responsive
     as you make all things new.

From the grip of fear and conflict,
     Spirit, your world release.
Help your people to discover
     things that will make for peace.

Wilson Niwagila, 1966
translated, Fred Kaan, 1990
Thuma Mina, 1995
© United Evangelical Mission

928
Yesu, Yesu

Yesu, Yesu, fill us with your love,
     show us how to serve the neighbors we
          have from you.

     Kneels at the feet of his friends,
     silently washes their feet,
Master who acts as a slave to them.

     Neighbors are wealthy and poor,
     varied in color and race,
neighbors are near us and far away.

     These are the ones we should serve,
     these are the ones we should love,
all these are neighbors to us and you.

     Loving puts us on our knees,
     silently washing their feet,
this is the way we should live with you.

Tom Colvin, 1968; revised, 1997
Come, Let Us Walk This Road Together, 1997
© 1969, Hope Publishing Company

929
God Sends Us His Spirit

God sends us the Spirit to befriend and help us,
     re-create and guide us, Spirit-friend.
Spirit who enlivens, sanctifies, enlightens,
     sets us free, is now our Spirit-friend.

Spirit of our Maker, Spirit-friend,
Spirit of our Savior, Spirit-friend,
Spirit of God's people, Spirit-friend.

Darkened roads are clearer, heavy burdens lighter,
when we're walking with our Spirit-friend.
Now we need not fear the powers of the darkness,
none can overcome our Spirit-friend.

Now we are God's people, bonded by your presence,
agents of your purpose, Spirit-friend.
Lead us forward ever, slipping backward never,
to your remade world, our Spirit-friend.

Tom Colvin, 1976; revised, 1997
Come, Let Us Walk This Road Together, 1997
© 1976, 1997, Hope Publishing Company

930
That Boy-Child of Mary

That boy-child of Mary was born in a stable,
a manger his cradle in Bethlehem.

What shall we call him, child of the manger?
What name is given in Bethlehem?

His name is Jesus, God ever with us,
God given for us in Bethlehem.

How can he save us, how can he help us,
born here among us in Bethlehem?

Gift of the Father, to human mother,
makes him our brother of Bethlehem.

One with the Father, he is our Savior,
heaven-sent helper of Bethlehem.

Gladly we praise him, love and adore him
give ourselves to him of Bethlehem.

Tom Colvin, 1969
The United Methodist Hymnal, 1989
© 1969, Hope Publishing Company

931
Chiuta Is Our Sure Defense

Chiuta is our sure defense,
in whom it's safe to put our trust each day.
See how the wicked cheat the poor
and plot to kill those standing in their way.

Chiuta is our strength and shelter,
our certain help in time of fear.
Though storms may rage and earth be
shaken,
we stay protected in God's care.

Chiuta laughs at wicked folk
whose pride will burst and selfish plotting cease.
The humble will possess the land
and will enjoy prosperity and peace.

So do not fear, be patient still;
our God will act, God's way will be made clear.
Trust that our God will help us soon;
Chiuta's love will drive out all our fear.

Tom Colvin
based on Charles Chinula, ca. 1900
Come, Let Us Walk This Road Together, 1997
© 1997, Hope Publishing Company
Chiuta is the Tumbala name for the chief deity.

932
Come and Let Us Worship God

Come and let us worship God,
turn to serve the living Lord,
move from where we are misled,
do as ancient prophets said.

O our ever-loving God,
we, the creatures of your word,
come to make our home in you,
knowing that your word is true.

Though society goes astray,
keen to find an easier way,
let our eyes be on God's care
evident and everywhere.

Let us hear our Maker's voice
and let Christ inform each choice.
Sister women, brother men,
let us turn to God again.

Cranmer Mugisha
translated and paraphrased, John Bell, 1997
One Is the Body, 2001
© 1999, Wild Goose Resource Group, Iona Community
(admin. GIA Publications, Inc.)

933

Thousands and Thousands of Songs
Tamil: Aayiram, aayiram padelgellei

Thousands and thousands of songs full of praise,
    Spirit of holiness, draw from our hearts;
may each one add to the glory of Christ,
    so form a sweet honeycomb rich in art.

    Hallelujah, hallelujah!
    Sing hallelujah for the day.
    Sorrow's night gone, sorrow's night gone,
    joy arrives announced by the dawn.

Now for the sake of this age and its hopes,
    Spirit of holiness, teach us your ways,
coax our best music and words into flame,
    light myriad candles of worship and praise.

All times of year, every season and mood,
    Spirit of holiness, capture for love;
search out the longings of all humankind,
    join them to Christ's songs of Zion above.

T. Dayanandan Francis
translated, James Minchin
Sound the Bamboo, 2000
© Christian Conference of Asia

934

Friends, Listen Humbly
Nepali: Lau suna sathi satya ko bani

Friends, listen humbly,
God's Word is truly
spoken by Jesus' cross:
From his dear body,
sacrificed freely,
life-giving water flows.
Ponder most surely
this saving mystery:
God's love in Christ has come;
serving the friendless,
he pardoned sinners,
his blood our healing won.

Empty and short-lived
are the enticements
money and science boast.
Nor can religion,
doctrine or ritual
satisfy restless hearts.
You will discover
there's but one Savior,
head crowned with thorns, God's Son:
Serving the friendless,
he pardoned sinners,
his blood our healing won.

Countless the gurus,
countless the idols,
humans too blindly trust.
There is but one Lord
we may rely on,
whatever course we run.
Turn to Christ Jesus,
he's gone before you,
opening the way, truth, life.
Make him your captain,
each day's companion,
holding you firm in strife.

Dibya Khaling, 1989
translated, Loknath Manaen, 1989; paraphrased, James Minchin, 1989
Sound the Bamboo, 2000
© Christian Conference of Asia

935
Grandeur of God

Full of wondrous beauty are God's artful ways;
listen, my friends,
Spirit descend,
give us the joy to proclaim God's praise.
Majesty belongs to one name always.

Mountains raise their spires to the vault of the sky,
rivers flow down
rifts in the ground;
here forests thrive as their trees grow high;
there the desert spreads, sand all parched and dry.

Fiercest are the beasts who must kill for their food—
lions' warning growl,
wolves' cruel howl;
playful the deer and cub elephants' mood;
God alone can call all creation good.

Sun by day gives warmth, brings each new bud into
flower;
moon's lustrous light
rescues the night;
who but the Lord can ordain, empower
worlds both great and small, each to have its
hour?

I can frame no words which will match the angel's
psalms;
heaven and earth
tell of God's worth.
All we can do is to rest in God's arms
captured by one name, Love, and its sweet
charms.

E. Walter Marasinghe, 1980
paraphrased, James Minchin, 1980
Sound the Bamboo, 2000
© Christian Conference of Asia

936
Day of Joy, Let Us Be Glad
Thai: Saen suksan wan prachum nii

Day of joy, let us be glad,
God has given us today for joy.
Do not be troubled by misfortune's threat,
the Lord will pour blessings on your head.
Let your soul rejoice,
let your soul be filled with hope on this blessed day.

Bless this day, fill it with love,
help us lead a life of charity.
Give us eternal grace and fortitude
to overcome sins that shackle us.
May we win the fight
of the good and evil thoughts raging in our hearts.

Jesus Christ, we give you thanks,
may this day be spent in praising you.
How precious is the blood you shed for us;
we glorify you for saving us.
You are all in all,
be the center of our lives now and evermore.

Songsan Prasopsin
translated, Boonmee Julkiree
paraphrased, Rolando S. Tinio and James Minchin, 1989
Sound the Bamboo, 2000
© Christian Conference of Asia

937

My prayer rises to heaven
Vietnamese: Ca khuc tram huong

My prayer rises to heaven, to the mystery of
God's power,
as the smoke ascends when the precious
incense burns.
Have mercy on us, Lord, and grant us
your grace.
My voice glorifies the Lord God of majesty,
as the night bird sings at the dawning
of day.
This my offering to God, the Lord of
all.

As the thirsty earth looks to heaven for life-giving
rain to save flower and tree,
so I raise my hands high in prayer: Defend me from
people who try to harm me.

O Lord God, how I wish that I could live with you
for the rest of my life;
dwelling in your house I would feel assured that my
prayers would be always in your sight.

O Lord God, you are love and justice and truth; all
your judgments are just.
O Lord God, you are truth beyond compare. Lord,
in you do I trust.

Dao Kim
translated, anonymous
The United Methodist Hymnal, 1989
© Nguyen D. Viet-Chau,
Dan Chua Catholic Magazine and Publications

938

Winter Has Passed, the Rain is O'er
Mandarin: Dong-tian yi wang, yu-shui yi zhi

Winter has passed, the rain is o'er,
earth is abloom, songs fill the air.
Linger no more, why must you wait?
"Rise up my love, come follow me."

Jesus, my Lord, my love, my all,
body and soul forever yours,
in dale so dark I long for you,
abide with me in spring anew.

O Lord, your face I long to see,
your still small voice, reveal to me.
Your tender care, your joy so dear,
"O precious dove, with me be near."

O my beloved I'll follow you,
far from the rocks, the hills, and sea.
Midst all the song and blossoms new,
in your firm steps, I'll follow you.

Weifan Wang, stanzas 1957, refrain 1982
based on Song of Solomon 2:10–14
translated, Ewing W. Carroll, Jr., 1989
Sound the Bamboo, 2000
© Christian Conference of Asia

939

God Created Heaven and Earth

Taiwanese (Hokkien): Chin Chú Siōng-tè chō thiⁿ-tōe

God created heaven and earth,
all things perfect brought to birth;
God's great power made dark and light,
earth revolving day and night.

Let us praise God's mercy great,
all our needs that love await;
God, who fashions all that lives,
to each one a blessing gives.

God is One, will ever be:
Idols are mere vanity;
handmade gods of wood and clay
cannot help us when we pray.

But God's grace beyond compare
saves us all from death's despair;
so earth's creatures small and great
give thanks for that blessed state.

anonymous (traditional), Taiwanese
translated, Boris Anderson and Clare Anderson, 1961; revised, 1981
Hymns from the Four Winds, 1983
© 1983, Boris and Clare Anderson

940

Watch the Bush of Thorns

Taiwanese (Hokkien): Chhì-phè hōˑhé sio

Watch the bush of thorns
being licked by fierce flame—
the bush is not consumed,
but still stays the same.

When fire and heat subside,
seed growth soon resumes;
the spring wakes what had died,
and brings forth new blooms.

Watch the burning bush,
by God's will kept whole:
When Christians face hard trial,
love's power nerves their soul.

Watch the suffering thorns,
though burning still alive—
if persecution strikes,
then Christ's church revives!

Courage fills our hearts
as Jesus Christ's friends!
With him in test of fire,
our faith finds true strength.

Chun-ming Kao
translated, James Minchin
Sound the Bamboo, 2000
© Christian Conference of Asia

941

God Made All People of the World

Korean: Een nyoo nun hah nah dae gae

God made all people of the world
into one big family.
Brothers and sisters all are we,
helping, working side by side,
one in God, building one world,
one in God, building one world.

Our hearts are full of sin and pride;
fear destroys our unity.
Hatred and prejudice arise;
walls divide our family;
strangers now, broken our world,
strangers now, broken our world.

Jesus has shown us how to love,
    reconciling humankind.
We live believing in his name,
    finding confidence and love,
born in Christ to a new world,
born in Christ to a new world.

Heirs both of glory and of shame,
    we are people of this land.
Yet we are hoping in the Lord,
    strong in faith and one in love,
bringing light into the world,
bringing light into the world.

Hyun Sul Hong, 1967
translated, David Kim and Chang Hee Son
Chalice Hymnal, 1995
© Korean-English Hymnbook Publication Commission

942

Lonely the Boat
Korean: Kamkamhan bam sanaun

Lonely the boat, sailing at sea,
    tossed on a cold, stormy night;
cruel the sea which seemed so wide,
    with waves so high.
This single ship sailed the deep sea,
    straight into the gale;
O Lord, great is the peril,
    dangers to all assail.

Strong winds arose in all their rage,
    tossing the tiny lone boat;
waves billowing high, tossing the boat,
    lost and afloat.
The sailor stood all alone,
    wondering what to do.
O Lord, so helpless was he,
    wondering what to do.

Trembling with fear, deep in despair,
    looking for help all around,
the sailor saw light from above.
    "Help can be found;
my God is here in my small boat,
    standing by my side;
Oh, I trust in the Savior,
    now in my life abide.

"Pleading for your mercy, O Lord,
    even a sinner like me;
command, O Lord, calm to the sea,
    as in Galilee!
Please save my life from all danger,
    grant a peaceful life;
O please be merciful, Lord,
    in times of calm and strife.

"Storms in our lives, cruel and cold,
    surely will arise again,
threatening lives, threatening us
    on life's wild sea.
Powerful and great, God's hand is there,
    firmly in control.
O Lord, calm peace comes from you,
    peace comes to my lone soul."

Helen Walrahm Kim, 1921
translated, Hae Jong Kim, 1980
paraphrased, Linda Sugano and Doug Sugano, 1981
altered, Hope Omachi-Kawashima, 1987
The United Methodist Hymnal, 1989
© 1967, 1989, The United Methodist Publishing House
(admin. The Copyright Company)

943

Now a New Life I Live
Korean: Nah ee jaeh joo neem ae say

Now a new life I live that Jesus gave to me.
Everything now is new, old things have passed away.
This new life that's in me like the living water flows.
Like rays of bright sunshine, his love within me glows.

We taste eternal life; we're living in the Lord.
Now and forever we'll be living in the Lord.

Hidden in Jesus Christ life have we found anew.
Things I enjoyed before no longer do I love.
Blessings and heavenly peace now surely are my own.
Singing praise, breathing prayer, I shall live with
my Lord.

Mountains and flowing streams, nature is now all
new.
Sinners and enemies have all become my friends.
Those who have gained new life now taste eternal
life.
Here the new heaven begins in my heart with the
Lord.

The way we follow him is far and narrow, too.
Praising him joyfully, I'll follow still the Lord.
I have eternal life with him who is the Life.
Day by day serving him, I shall live with the Lord.

Ho Un Lee, 1967
translated, Hae Jong Kim, 1980
Hymns from the Four Winds, 1983
© 1983, Hae Jong Kim

944

Mountains Are All Aglow
Korean: Sanmada buritanda

Mountains are all aglow with autumn colors so
bright;
rivers are filled with water, giving life to our days.
Golden fields wave their praise to God's bountiful
harvest;
gratefully, skyward arising, hear our joyous songs
of praise!

Reaching far as earthly eyes can see,
reaching far as humble hands can toil,
every harvest is from our Lord;
every blessing is from our God.
Praise for the harvest, thanks to God.
Praise for the harvest, give praise to God.

Every land so abundantly rich the harvest bears;
every orchard is filled with luscious, ripened
new fruit.
Sun and rain by the Lord's design shall come at
proper time.
Working hard, God has given us reasons for
deep gratitude.

Early spring is the time to sow all God's rich seeds
of life.
Working hard, tilling God's earth; making
preparation.
Looking forward to rewards of harvest so plentiful;
promised blessings will soon be ours in each
revelation.

Praise the Lord as we're planting God's word deep
in each heart.
God has sent sunshine and the rain so the
seedlings may grow.
Desert lands which seem barren, flowers still might
bloom;
trusting in God's promises, our thanks to God
we will show!

Ok In Lim, 1967
translated, Hae Jong Kim, 1988
paraphrased, Hope Omachi-Kawashima, 1988
The United Methodist Hymnal, 1989
© 1989, The United Methodist Publishing House
(admin. The Copyright Company)

945
Jesus Christ, Workers' Lord
Korean: Uriŭn bujirŏnhan

Jesus Christ, workers' Lord, we are servants to
you.
This wondrous world, all of the earth, all creation
is yours.
We would work, helping to bloom lovely
flowers so rare.
Labor and toil, joined with your gifts, bring fresh
fruits of love.

Workers we, giving our lives in full service to
you.
With freedom blessed, under your rule, citizens all
are we.
On the fields sowing the grain, harvest soon
we'll reap:
in factories, making the tools, tools assisting our
need.

Royal are we, working to serve Jesus, Savior
and King.
One family living in peace, partners sharing the
earth.
Tools in hand we have reaped rich harvest of
grains.
By grace of God, we will receive gifts enough for us
all.

This lost world, in God's name, we would
reclaim in love.
New life is brought, marvelous gift, all inherit the
earth.
Now may we from the dust fertile land restore,
that there shall come God's paradise, life from death
shall arise!

Byung Soo Oh, 1980
translated, T. Tom Lee, 1980
paraphrased, Elise Shoemaker, 1981
Hymns from the Four Winds, 1983
© 1983, Abingdon Press (admin. The Copyright Company)

946
Here, O Lord, Your Servants Gather
Japanese: Sekai no tomo to te o tsunagi

Here, O Lord, your servants gather,
hand we link with hand;
looking toward our Savior's cross,
joined in love we stand.
As we seek the realm of God,
we unite to pray:
Jesus Savior, guide our steps,
for you are the Way.

Many are the tongues we speak,
scattered are the lands,
yet our hearts are one in God,
one in love's demands.
E'en in darkness hope appears,
calling age and youth:
Jesus, teacher, dwell with us,
for you are the Truth.

Nature's secrets open wide,
changes never cease.
Where, oh, where can weary souls
find the source of peace?
Unto all those sore distressed,
torn by endless strife:
Jesus, healer, bring your balm,
for you are the Life.

Grant, O God, an age renewed,
    filled with deathless love;
help us as we work and pray,
    send us from above
truth and courage, faith and power,
    needed in our strife:
Jesus, Master, be our Way,
    be our Truth, our Life.

Tokuo Yamaguchi, 1958
translated, Everett M. Stowe, 1958
altered in *Cantate Domino*, 1972
The United Methodist Hymnal, 1989
© 1958, United Methodist Publishing House
(admin. The Copyright Company)
This is the more widely published translation. The *E. A. C. C. Hymnal*,
1963, contains another, beginning "All throughout the world,"
by an unidentified translator.
Sound the Bamboo, 2000, has "meet" for "gather" in the first line,
matching the syllable count of the original and of the other stanzas.

947

In Old Galilee, When Sweet Breezes Blew
Japanese: Gariraya no kaze kaoru oka de

In old Galilee, when sweet breezes blew o'er the lake
    where he spoke to crowds when they came to
        hear
            those words of grace that gave them promise;
            O speak to me now, and let me hear
                those words of grace.

On that stormy day, when waves billowed high on
        the lake,
    his disciples feared till he spoke to them
            those words of power that gave them
                courage;
            O speak to me now, and let me hear
                those words of power.

On that cross he hung, to die for the sins of the
        world,
    from Golgotha's shame he called out in pain
        those saving words of hope to sinners;
        O speak to me now, and let me hear
            those saving words.

On that eventide two friends for Emmaus were
        bound,
    recognized him not till he spoke again
        those words of life to his disciples;
        O speak to me now, and let me hear
            those words of life.

Nobuo Befu, 1973
translated, George Gish, Jr., 1989
Sound the Bamboo, 2000
© Christian Conference of Asia

948

In the Dawn of the Morn
Japanese: No ni idete

In the dawn of the morn,
with the dews fresh and clear,
    I start the new day:
With the sickle held in hand,
    I stand on the grass.
'Tis the prayer I pray to you,
    "Grateful for your day."

In the ray of the sun,
on the dike in the field,
    I lay down my plow;
with my hands together clasped,
    I kneel on the earth.
'Tis the prayer I pray to you,
    "Grateful for your earth."

In the dim light of eve,
with the feet washed and cleansed,
 I sit on the floor;
with the loving family,
 humble meal we share.
'Tis the prayer I pray to you,
 "Grateful for your love."

Masuko Endo, 1965
translated, Nobuaki Hanaoka, 1980
Hymns from the Four Winds, 1983
© 1983, Nobuaki Hanaoka

949
Send Your Word
Japanese: Mikotoba o kudasai

Send your Word, O Lord, like the rain,
 falling down upon the earth.
  Send your Word.
  We seek your endless grace,
with souls that hunger and thirst,
  sorrow and agonize.
We would all be lost in dark
 without your guiding light.

Send your Word, O Lord, like the wind,
 blowing down upon the earth.
  Send your Word.
  We seek your wondrous power,
pureness that rejects all sins,
  though they persist and cling.
Bring us to complete victory;
  set us all free indeed.

Send your Word, O Lord, like the dew,
 coming gently upon the hills.
  Send your Word.
  We seek your endless love,
for life that suffers in strife,
  with adversities and hurts,
send your healing power of love;
 we long for your new world.

Yasushige Imakoma, 1965
translated, Nobuaki Hanaoka, 1980
Hymns from the Four Winds, 1983
© 1983, The United Methodist Publishing House
(admin. The Copyright Company)

950
Praise the Lord

 Praise the Lord, praise the Lord,
for the greenness of the trees,
for the beauty of the flowers,
for the blueness of the sky,
for the greatness of the sea;
 praise the Lord, praise the Lord,
  now and forever.

 Thanks to God, thanks to God,
for the gift of friends in Christ,
for the church, our house of faith,
for the gift of wondrous love,
for the gift of endless grace;
 thanks to God, thanks to God,
  now and forever.

Glory to God, glory to God,
for the grace of Christ, the Son,
for the love of parent God,
for the comfort and the strength
of the Spirit, Holy God;
glory to God, glory to God,
now and forever.

Nobuaki Hanaoka, 1980
Hymns from the Four Winds, 1983
© 1983, Nobuaki Hanaoka

951
Come, Smell the Scent of Sweet Wild Flowers
Okinawan: Uga di uga mi busha

Come, smell the scent of sweet wild flowers,
come, sing with the stars up high;
proclaim the praise of Christ Jesus:
God's Son who makes all new.

We who are sinners feel shame-faced,
but we're called as Christ's chosen,
Oh, what a joy! This good news tells:
Our God has sinners healed.

In Christ reborn as his kindred
we love singing God's glory,
all evil flees before Jesus,
our God o'ercomes all foes.

With open arms on cross outstretched,
all earth touched by Christ's body,
saved by his grace, we trust such love,
we share this hope with all.

In dead of night our boat's sailing,
the Big Dipper guides homeward.
Seek when it's dark, the cross shining,
our Savior guides us home.

Let us give praise to you, Master,
in your footsteps following.
May all we say or do daily
give glory to your name.

Seiei Yokota, 1989
translated, I-to Loh, 1989
paraphrased, Ronald Hines and James Minchin, 1989
Sound the Bamboo, 2000
© Christian Conference of Asia

952
Still, I Search for My God

Still,
I search for my God
in silence,
I marvel at the universe,
the world it contains,
its beauty,
its harmony!
Creator of such perfection,
who else could it be?

Come,
listen to the trees,
the green fields,
the rivers and the morning breeze,
the birds of the air—
all singing
their Maker's praise!
Creator of countless wonders,
who else could it be?

Yes,
I am filled with joy
and breathe in
the presence of the Lord, my God,
your praise I will sing,
your power
declare in chant,
and when I am moved to worship,
peace reigns in my heart.

Francisco F. Feliciano, 1977; revised, ca. 2000
Sound the Bamboo, 2000
© Christian Conference of Asia

953
Beyond Loud Protestations

Beyond loud protestations,
    above the clash of castes,
o'er violent demonstrations
    against abuse and lusts,
your reconciliation
    draws rival hearts around,
breaking bread and celebration
    with enemies, love bound.

We heed the hungry crying
    in pain from furious wants;
the rich are damned to grieving,
    prisoners to death's own taunts.
With songs of liberation,
    released from chains of greed,
with you from death's damnation,
    we march as sinners freed.

We pray you'll give the Life Source,
    our shield against the foe
as pilgrims on the peace course
    the way of Christ we know,
like him our goals are bridges
    o'er chasms gouged by wars,
we scale Golgotha's ridges,
    bear cross and shame and scars.

Melchizedek M. Solis, 1981
Hymns from the Four Winds, 1983
© 1983, Melchizedek M. Solis and Mutya Lopez Solis

954
Valley Psalm to the Holy Spirit

Come, Holy Spirit, come, show us our way
through nightmare alleys of our history.
    Entrust our children with builder's vision.
    Empower them to soar above hate barriers,
        for they shall lead us all together
        to shape your new city in our time.

Come, Holy Spirit, come, link arms and hearts;
unite us in our stand for truth and justice.
    Entrust our children with builder's vision.
    Empower them to soar above hate barriers,
        for they shall lead us all together
        to break evil dens and prison cells.

Inspire our rising youth to dream bold dreams
upon wrath's rubble and restore community.
    Entrust our children with builder's vision.
    Empower them to soar above hate barriers,
        for they shall lead us all together
        to share Christ's true love for making peace.

Melchizedek M. Solis, 1979
Hymns from the Four Winds, 1983
© 1983, Melchizedek M. Solis and Mutya Lopez Solis

955
Father in Heaven
Cebuano:

Father in heaven,
grant to thy children
mercy and blessing,
songs never ceasing,
love to unite us,
grace to redeem us,
O God in heaven,
    dear Lord, our God.

Jesus, Redeemer,
may we remember
thy gracious passion,
thy resurrection.
Worship we bring thee,
praise we shall sing thee,
Jesus, Redeemer,
    Jesus, our Lord.

Spirit descending,
whose is the blessing,
strength for the weary,
help for the needy;
sealed in our sonship
thine be our worship,
Spirit descending,
    Spirit adored.

Elena G. Masquiso, 1961
translated, D. T. Niles, 1964
E. A. C. C. Hymnal, 1964
The United Methodist Hymnal, 1989,
changed the opening line to "O God in heaven,"
and altered "sonship" to "kinship" in line 3:5.
© Christian Conference of Asia

956
Now the Day Is Ending
Cebuano: Salup na ang adlaw

Now the day is ending,
darkness is descending,
now the birds returning,
seek their nest's protection.
All our work is finished
    time of rest has come.
Now for your care this day,
    Lord, we give you thanks.

In our work and living,
in this day now ending,
your name have we hallowed,
your will have we followed?
If today we failed you,
    Lord, forgive, we pray.
Bless with peace our sleeping;
    be our guard and stay.

If by being careless,
we have hurt our neighbors,
Lord, we ask for mercy,
pardon our offenses.
Grant to us, O dear Lord,
    reconciling love,
that at one we may be
    as we take our rest.

If we failed to help the
one who needed comfort,
or cruel words have spoken,
words that hurt and wounded.
Grant us, Lord, your pardon.
    May we not forget,
what you have commanded,
    to love one and all.

Thanks to you, Lord blessed,
for the day that's ended.
Cover our shortcomings
with your love forgiving
and with rest refresh us;
    grant a night of peace.
May we rise tomorrow,
    strengthened and renewed.

Elena G. Maquiso, 1970
translated, Cirilo Rigos and Ellsworth Chandlee, 1981
Hymns from the Four Winds, 1983
© 1983, Cirilo Rigos

957

You Have Made Us from Above
Ikalahan: Amamin wad nangkayang

You have made us from above;
look on us with kindly love;
Lord, we ask you, set us free,
wash us clean, yes, set us free;
draw from us what we can be.

To Damascus blessed Paul
set out once as bigot Saul,
would not let your people be,
till you challenged him to see,
Jesus, not the law, sets free.

Down from Nazareth Jesus came,
ministered in true love's name,
fed the crowd of Galilee,
taught them your reality,
drew from them what they could be.

Bring to mind Bethesda's pool—
sick were healed in waters cool.
Still today, we ask you, be
balm for our infirmity;
draw from us what we can be.

Ramon Oliano
translated, Delbert Rice
paraphrased, James Minchin
Sound the Bamboo, 2000
© Christian Conference of Asia

958

Soft the Master's Love Song, and Beautiful to Hear
Indonesian: Lirih terdengar lagu kasih yang merdu

Soft the Master's love song, and beautiful to hear:
"Come to me, you poor, all who stumble in distress;
relief from toil I offer, come to me for rest."

"If you're burdened down, let me bear the strain for
                                                    you.
You must not despair: Through my Easter, death
                                                has died;
so journey on with courage, I am by your side."

Jesus, you are strong; I am weak, a foolish child;
I will turn to you, boast in you alone, my friend.
Your words give life to live by, love that has no end.

Rudolf R. Pantou
translated, James Minchin
Sound the Bamboo, 2000
© Christian Conference of Asia

959

The Sky Ablaze in Color
Indonesian: Senja mèrah darah

The sky ablaze in color, evening now falls deep,
the birds returning to their nests above to sleep,
weary people after work moving slowly home,
rickshaw drivers sighing, feel pain deep in their bones.

    So my prayer restless spreads its wings,
    flees to God, who compassion brings.

The night with darkness thick, no light of sun to see,
the moon her cares is hiding in the trembling trees.
Hungry children are afraid, naked, filled with fears,
tiny bodies covered just with their mother's tears.

Rains lash out at the earth and lightnings striking
bold,
the winds blow loud and mighty through the night
grown old,
children shiver in the cold damp, their clothing torn,
and they have no beds, no blankets to keep warm.

Fridolin Ukur
translated, Jeffrey T. Myers and Dieter Trautwein, 1995
Thuma Mina, 1995
© Strube Publishing

960

If the Spirit of the Lord Moves
Spanish: Si el Espíritu de Dios

If the Spirit of the Lord moves in my soul,
like David, the shepherd, I sing.

If the Spirit of the Lord moves in my soul,
like David, the sinner, I pray.

If the Spirit of the Lord moves in my soul,
like David, the victor, I dance.

If the Spirit of the Lord moves in my soul,
like David, the poet, I praise.

anonymous
translated, editors of *International Songbook*, 1978
International Songbook, 1990
© 1978, 1990, Mennonite World Conference

961

From a Distant Home
Spanish: De tierra lejana venimos

From a distant home the Savior we come seeking,
using as our guide the star so brightly beaming.

Lovely eastern star that tells us of God's
morning,
heaven's wondrous light, O never cease thy
shining!
Glory in the highest to the Son of Heaven,
and upon the earth be peace and love
to all.

Glowing gold I bring the newborn babe so holy,
token of his power to reign above in glory.

Frankincense I bring the child of God's own choosing,
token of our prayers to heaven ever rising.

Bitter myrrh have I to give the infant Jesus,
token of the pain that he will bear to save us.

anonymous (traditional), Puerto Rico
translated, George K. Evans, 1963
The United Methodist Hymnal, 1989
© 1963, 1980, Walton Music

962

The Nighttime of the Poor
Spanish: La noche de los pobres

Born is now a baby,
brushwood is his awning,
eyes as blue as dawning light;
willows bend to whisper
lullabies around him,
and the moon is round and full.

In the nighttime of the poor ones,
in the nighttime of God's love,
it's the pauper that's the King;
it's the starving that's the Bread;
it's the cold child that's the Sun.
Sleep, baby Jesus; above you there watch
four silent stars in the bright Southern
Cross.

Soft his mother's kisses
while the child is sleeping,
warm and close the breathing ox.
Colorful the shepherds
drawn by love have hurried
to bring greetings honeyed sweet.

José Maria Santini
translated, Ivor H. Jones
"The Hymn Society Annual Conference Program Book," 1999
© Ivor H. Jones

963

O Jesus, My King and My Sovereign
Spanish: Jesús es mi Rey sobeano

O Jesus, my King and my Sovereign,
my joy is to sing him my praise.
He's king, yet he treats me like family,
he's king, yet he shares all his love.
He left all his glory in heaven
to come lift my life from the ashes.

I'm happy today,
life's joy came to stay through him.

O Jesus, my friend and my yearning,
in darkness and light always near;
he walks at my side, patient, humble,
and gives me his comfort and cheer.
That's why I will faithfully follow,
because he's my King and companion.

O Lord, tell me what could I give you
for all your great goodness to me?
Could this be enough: serve and love you,
committing my whole life to thee?
If so, then accept my devotion,
to you only now I surrender.

Vicente Mendoza, 1921
translated, Esther Frances, 1982
altered, George Lockwood, 1988
The United Methodist Hymnal, 1989
© 1982, The United Methodist Publishing House
(admin. The Copyright Company)

964

Cloaks and Palms
Spanish: Mantos y palmas

Filled with excitement, all the happy throng
spread cloaks and branches on the city streets.
There in the distance they begin to see,
riding on a donkey, comes the Son of God.

From every corner a thousand voices sing
praises to him who comes in the name of
God.
With one great shout of acclamation loud
triumphant song breaks forth:
"Hosanna, hosanna to the King!
Hosanna, hosanna to the King!"

As in that entrance to Jerusalem,
we sing hosannas to the Christ, our King,
to the living Savior who still calls today,
asking us to follow him with love and faith.

As in that entrance to Jerusalem,
we'll join together singing to our Lord.
When Christ returns in glory from on high,
he'll take us then to our eternal home.

Rubén Ruíz (Avila), 1972
translated, stanzas 1 and 2, Gertrude C. Suppe, 1979; revised, 1987
translated, stanza 3, C. Michael Hawn, 1999
Halle, Halle, 1999
stanzas 1 and 2, © 1979, The United Methodist Publishing House
(admin. The Copyright Company)
stanza 3, © 1999, Choristers Guild

965

When We Are Living
Spanish: Pues si vivimos

When we are living, it is in Christ Jesus,
and when we're dying, it is in the Lord.
Both in our living and in our dying,

we belong to God;
we belong to God.

Through all our living, we our fruits must give.
Good works of service are for offering,
when we are giving, or when receiving,

'Mid times of sorrow and in times of pain,
when sensing beauty or in love's embrace,
whether we suffer, or sing rejoicing,

Across this wide world, we shall always find
those who are crying with no peace of mind,
but when we help them, or when we feed them,

stanza 1, anonymous
translated, Elise S. Eslinger, 1983
stanzas 2–4, Roberto Escamilla, 1983
translated, George Lockwood, 1987
The United Methodist Hymnal, 1989
© 1989, The United Methodist Publishing House
(admin. The Copyright Company)

966
O Sing unto the Lord
Spanish: Cantemos al Señor

O sing unto the Lord
a hymn of celebration;
O sing a song of love,
every day a new creation;
God made the sky and sea,
the sun and stars of heaven
and saw that they were good;
all creation sings in splendor:

Alleluia! Alleluia!
O sing unto the Lord. Alleluia!

O sing unto the Lord
a hymn of joy and praising;
a song that shares our love,
our faith and hopeful waiting.
Creation shouts to all
that God is grand and glorious;
and so we sing our song
to the God of grace and beauty:

Carlos Rosas, 1976
translated, C. Michael Hawn, 1999
Halle, Halle, 1999
© 1999, Choristers Guild

967
In the Beginning
Spanish: En el principio

In the beginning God created humanity
with loving kindness, and with mercy from above.
We, in God's goodness, were made in the image of
God.

God, shed your light,
let us see your greatness in humankind.
God, shed your light,
let us see your image in all humankind.

Then our desiring and our greed for so many things,
and all our striving to gain power and control
brought forth injustice, with oppression and its pain.

Now there are many working hard from day to day,
the poor and needy, at the mercy of the rich.
O God, have mercy, take away their sorrow and pain.

Carlos Rosas, 1991
translated, Luis Ferrer, 1994
Chalice Hymnal, 1995
© 1995, Chalice Press

968
A Song of Renewal

Lord, your church on earth is seeking
    your renewal from above.
Teach us all the art of speaking
    with the accent of your love.
We would heed your great commission:
    Go you into every place,
preach, baptize, fulfill my mission,
    serve with love and share my grace.

Freedom give to those in bondage,
    lift the burdens caused by sin;
give new hope, new strength and courage,
    grant release from fears within.
Light for darkness, joy for sorrow;
    love for hatred, peace for strife:
These and countless blessings follow
    as the Spirit gives new life.

In the slums of every city
    where the bruised and lonely dwell,
we shall show the Savior's pity;
    we shall of his mercy tell.
In all lands and with all races
    we shall serve and seek to bring
all mankind to render praises
    Christ, to thee, redeemer, king.

Hugh B. Sherlock, 1965
as revised in Sing a New Song, No. 3, 1981
© Hugh B. Sherlock

969
Halle, Halle

    Halle, halle, hallelujah.
    Halle, halle, hallelujah.
    Halle, halle, hallelujah.
    Hallelujah, hallelujah.

I AM, the Rock of Ages cleft for me;
I AM, the let me hide myself in thee;
I AM, the Rock of Ages cleft for me;
    Hallelujah, hallelujah.

I AM, the nothing in my hands I bring;
I AM, the simply to thy cross I cling;
I AM, the nothing in my hands I bring;
    Hallelujah, hallelujah.

I AM the Bread of Life, feed on me;
I AM the One True Vine, grow in me;
I AM the Bread of Life, feed on me;
    Hallelujah, hallelujah.

I AM the Resurrection, live in me;
I AM the Way, the Truth, follow me;
I AM the Resurrection, live in me;
    Hallelujah, hallelujah.

George Mulrain
based on oral tradition
Global Praise 1, 1996
© 1996, General Board of Global Ministries, GBGMusik

970
From All Four of Earth's Faraway Corners
Spanish: De los cuatro rincones del mundo

From all four of earth's faraway corners,
flows together the blood of all races
in this people who sing of their trials,
    in this people who cry of their faith;
hardy blood that was brought by the Spanish,
noble blood of the suffering Indian,
blood of slaves who stood heavy oppression,
    all the blood that was bought on the cross.

From all four of earth's faraway corners,
from the flowering meadows of Cuba,
from African coast and all Asia
    from Borinquen, Quisqueya, Aztlán,
God in secret has long been designing
to this moment so blessed to bring us,
bind us all to the same destination
    and a kingdom create of us all.

In all four of earth's faraway corners
sin is building embittering barriers;
but our faith has no fear of such borders,
    we know justice and peace will prevail.
To all four of earth's faraway corners
we're a people who point to tomorrow,
when the world, living sovereign and peaceful,
    is united in bonds of God's love.

Justo L. González, 1987
translated, George Lockwood, 1992
Mil Voces para Celebrar, 1996
© 1996, Abingdon Press (admin. The Copyright Company)

971
Thanks, Always Thanks
Spanish: Gracias, muchas gracias

Thanks, always thanks,
always thanks to you, my Lord.
Thanks, always thanks,
always thanks to you, my Lord.

With all our laughter and all of our song,
    with all our struggle and sorrow,
ourselves we offer; to you we belong.
    Your word brings hope for the morrow.
Longing for life which comes only from you,
    we wait the strength for tomorrow.
Taking what we give, you make something new
for all people, all our sisters and friends.

Forest and river, tall mountain and sea,
    city with noisy throngs teeming,
land bearing fruit for a bright jubilee,
    dancing and drawing and dreaming;
all that we are is surrendered to you,
    carried in your hands, redeeming,
changing what we give to make something new
for all people, all our brothers and friends.

Rafael Zamora, 1993
translated, Terry MacArthur, 1993
Thuma Mina, 1995
© World Council of Churches

972
Behold, How Pleasant
Spanish: Miren qué bueno

Behold, how pleasant, how good it is!
Behold, how pleasant, how good it is!

How pleasant and harmonious when God's people
    are together:
fragrant as precious oil when running fresh on
    Aaron's head.

How pleasant and harmonious when God's people
    are together:
fresh like the morning dew that falls on Zion's holy
    hill.

How pleasant and harmonious when God's people
    are together:
There is where God bestows the blessing—life for
    evermore.

Pablo Sosa, 1970
based on Psalm 133
translated, Pablo Sosa, 1986
Songs for a Gospel People, 1987
© Pablo Sosa, Instituto Superior Evangelico de Estudios Teologicos

973

Christ Is Risen
Spanish: Cristo vive

Christ is risen, Christ is living,
    dry your tears, be unafraid!
Death and darkness could not hold him,
    nor the tomb in which he laid.
Do not look among the dead for
    one who lives for evermore;
tell the world that Christ is risen,
    make it known he goes before.

If the Lord had never risen,
    we'd have nothing to believe.
But his promise can be trusted:
    "You will live, because I live."
As we share the death of Adam,
    so in Christ we live again.
Death has lost its sting and terror;
    Christ the Lord has come to reign.

Death has lost its old dominion,
    let the world rejoice and shout!
Christ, the firstborn of the living,
    gives us life and leads us out.
Let us thank our God who causes
    hope to spring up from the ground.
Christ is risen, Christ is giving
    life eternal, life profound.

Nicolás Martínez, 1960
based on 1 Corinthians 15:12–23
translated, Fred Kaan, 1972
Cantate Domino, 1974
© 1974, Hope Publishing Company

974

We Have Hope
Spanish: Tenemos esperanza

Because Christ came to enter in our journey,
because he broke the silence of our sorrow,
because he filled the whole world with his glory,
and came to light the darkness of our morrow;
because he came a stranger poor and lowly,
because he lived, proclaiming love and healing,
because he opened hearts of hungry people,
and brought new life to all who would receive it:

    In hope we are forever celebrating,
    with courage in our struggle we are waiting,
    in trust and reassurance we are claiming:
    This is our song of freedom for all people.
    In hope we are forever celebrating,
    with courage in our struggle we are waiting,
    in trust and reassurance we are claiming:
        This is our song.

Because he dealt with all the angry merchants
and he declared the evil of their doings,
because he lifted every child and woman
and put aside the proud and hateful people,
because he bore a cross for all our sorrow
and knew our every weakness and temptation,
because he took the pain of condemnation
and then he died for every kind of person:

Because his triumph came one early morning
and he defeated death and fear and sorrow,
because he moved triumphant to the future
to bring a kingdom saving all tomorrow,
because he lights the path of all the children
and with his fire he brings to life new meaning,
because his light is fountain for our witness,
we know he'll lead us all into his kingdom.

Federico J. Pagura, ca. 1970
translated, George Lockwood
Celebremos, Segunda Parte, 1983
© 1979, 2002, General Board of Global Ministries, GBGMusik

975
Blest Be the King
Spanish: Benedito el Rey

Blest be the King whose coming is in the name of
    God!
For him let doors be opened, no hearts against him
    barred!
Not robed in royal splendor, in power and pomp
    comes he,
but clad as are the poorest—such his humility!

Blest be the King whose coming is in the name of
    God!
By those who truly listen his voice is truly heard.
Pity the proud and haughty, who have not learned
    to heed
the Christ who is the Promise and has our ransom
    paid.

Blest be the King whose coming is in the name of
    God!
He only to the humble reveals the face of God.
All power is his, all glory! All things are in his hand,
all ages and all peoples, till time itself shall end!

Blest be the King whose coming is in the name of
    God!
He offers to the burdened the rest and grace they
    need.
Gentle is he and humble! And light his yoke shall be,
for he would have us bear it so he can make us free.

Federico J. Pagura, 1960
paraphrased, Fred Pratt Green, 1973
The Hymns and Ballads of Fred Pratt Green, 1982
© 1974, Hope Publishing Company

976
Mingled in All Our Living
Spanish: En medio de la vida

Mingled in all our living
    your presence, Lord, I feel,
closer than my own sighing,
    your love sustaining me.
You cause the pulse of blood, Lord,
    to flow in every vein,
my heart responds in gladness,
    life's rhythm beats within.

    O Lord of earth and heaven,
      I give my life to you,
    loving you in my neighbor,
      praising you in the world.

You stand beside the worker
    in factory and farm;
daily incessant clamor
    sounding a hymn of life.
In every hammer's pounding,
    typewriter's clacking key,
we hear a tune of praising,
    creation's melody.

You're in the sound of laughter
    and in the flow of tears,
sharing with all your people
    the fight for human good.
You came in Christ incarnate
    that life might be redeemed,
pledging us to your kingdom,
    helping the world to change.

Mortimer Arias, ca. 1973
translated, Len Lythgoe, 1983
"The Hymn Society Annual Conference Program Book," 1999
© Len Lythgoe

977
Come to Be Our Hope, Lord Jesus
Portuguese: Vem, Jesus nossa esperança

Come to be our hope, Lord Jesus,
    come to set our people free;
from oppression come, release us,
    turn defeat to victory!
Come, release from every prison
    those who suffer in our land:
In your love we find the reason
    still to live and understand.

Come to build your new creation
    through the road of servanthood;
give new life to every nation,
    changing evil into good.
Come and open our tomorrow
    for a kingdom now so near;
take away all human sorrow—
    Give us hope in place of fear.

Jaci Maraschin, 1978
translated, Jaci Maraschin, 1989
World Praise, 1993
© 1989, Lutheran World Federation

978
A Child
Portuguese: Um menino

Look in the face of children everywhere
and see a child of God, a gift of love.
Find in the face of every newborn child
the Son of God, the Savior of the world.

He's the Word who has come to all people,
    lives among us in grace and in truth.
He's the Light that illumines our history;
    in his face shines the glory of God!

The invisible God is now with us,
    who created from nothing all life.
He's the child who was born to bring justice
    and renew us with hope and with peace.

He is tiny, an infant so fragile,
    yet he fills the whole world with his love.
He is human, a child born so humble,
    yet he brings us the fullness of life.

Simei Monteiro, 1987
translated, C. Michael Hawn, 1998
Halle, Halle, 1999
© 1987, Simei Monteiro

979
Come, O Come Creating Spirit
Portuguese: Vem, Santo Espíritu

Come, O come, creating Spirit,
    you can change our way of thought;
to the written word give meaning,
    wider vision you have brought.
Touch our earth, dried out with sorrow,
    touch our world of arid death.
On the dry bones of this valley
    blow your loving, living breath.

Come, O Spirit of compassion,
    crying out, you intercede,
echoing our lamentation;
    cheer the voice in which we plead.
Be the flame that feeds our courage,
    be the fire that fills our veins,
from our apathy's inaction
    come and free us from these chains.

Come, O come, you gift of heaven
    and convince us of our sin;
halt the weapons of destruction
    and our madness, deep within.
Change our foolish ways of working
    into plans for life and scope,
come and flood our world with wisdom,
    come and flood our age with hope!

Simei Monteiro, ca. 1984
translated, Shirley Erena Murray, 1999
"The Hymn Society Annual Conference Program Book," 1999
© 1999, Hope Publishing Company

980
New Moment
Portuguese: Momento novo

God calls his people now to a new life,
    walking along together hand in hand.
The time is ripe for changing, the moment is now.
Let's walk together: No one can go alone!

    So, come and join!
    Get in a circle with all the people;
    your hands and hearts are important.

We must not think that things are always easy,
    while wicked people cause suffering and death,
and many others don't seem to care at all.
Let's walk together: No one can go alone!

The power today that makes new life burst forth
    is now in us through the gift of grace.
It's God who calls us to work together for justice.
Let's walk together: No one can go alone!

Ernesto Barros Cardoso, Paulo Roberto Salles Garcia,
Déa Cristiane Kerr Affini, Eder Soares de Almeida,
Tércio Bretanha Junker, Darlene Barbosa Schutzer, 1983
translated, Sonya Ingwersen, 1988
Thuma Mina, 1995
© World Council of Churches

Epilogue (981–982)

In concluding the first edition of *Panorama*, Routley wrote:

> None the less, the circle must for the moment be closed, not with a wall but with an easily opened gate. Isaac Watts shall have the last word. Nobody who writes or sings hymns in any language or climate will be able to afford to ignore what Watts says in his last couplet.

981

A Song of Praise to the Blessed Trinity

I give immortal praise
    to God the Father's love,
for all my comforts here
    and better hopes above:
        He sent his own
            eternal Son
        to die for sins
            that man had done.

To God the Son belongs
    immortal glory too,
who bought us with his blood
    from everlasting woe:
        And now he lives,
            and now he reigns,
        and sees the fruit
            of all his pains.

To God the Spirit's name
    immortal worship give,
whose new-creating power
    makes the dead sinner live:
        His work completes
            the grand design,
        and fills the soul
            with joy divine.

Almighty God! to thee
    be endless honors done,
the undivided Three,
    and the mysterious One:
        Where reason fails
            with all her powers,
        there faith prevails
            and love adores.

Isaac Watts
Hymns and Spiritual Songs, 1707, III, 38
In the first edition of this book, Routley presented the text in the first person plural, "We give immortal praise."

As this new edition shows, many have joined the procession through this gate, and the church continues to bear "witness to the truth in every tongue." Therefore, it seems fitting that the last word offered here should be from Routley himself. Borrowing from his beloved Watts the felicitous phrase "duty and delight" (which became the title of a memorial *Festschrift*), he presented a poetic expression of his theology of congregational song.

982

In Praise of God Meet Duty and Delight

In praise of God meet duty and delight,
    angels and creatures, men and spirits blessed;
in praise is earth transfigured by the sound
    and sight of heaven's everlasting feast.

In praise the artist and the craftsman meet,
    inspired, obedient, patient, practical;
in praise join instrument and voice and sound
    to make one music for the Lord of all.

The desert is refreshed by songs of praise,
    relaxed the frown of pride, the stress of grief;
in praise forgotten all our human spite;
    in praise the burdened heart finds sure relief.

No skill of ours, no music made on earth,
    no mortal song could scale the height of heaven;
yet stands the cross, through grace ineffable
    an instrument of praise to sinners given.

So, confident and festive, let us sing
    of wisdom, power, and mercy there made known;
the song of Moses and the Lamb be ours,
    through Christ raised up to life in God alone.

Erik Routley, 1976
Our Lives Be Praise, 1990
© 1977, Hope Publishing Company

The phrase, "duty and delight" is drawn from Watts's paraphrase of
Psalm 147, which begins:

Praise ye the Lord; 'tis good to raise
our hearts and voices in his praise;
his nature and his works invite
to make this duty our delight.

Soli Deo gloria!

List of Copyright Holders

821 Words © 1986 Hope Publishing Company, Carol Stream, IL 60188. All rights reserved. Used by permission.

822 Words © 1982 The Hymn Society (admin. Hope Publishing Company, Carol Stream, IL 60188). All rights reserved. Used by permission.

823 Words © 1989 Hope Publishing Company, Carol Stream, IL 60188. All rights reserved. Used by permission.

824 Words © 1994 Hope Publishing Company, Carol Stream, IL 60188. All rights reserved. Used by permission.

825 Words © 1969 The Hymn Society (admin. Hope Publishing Company, Carol Stream, IL 60188). All rights reserved. Used by permission.

826 Words © 1991 Hope Publishing Company, Carol Stream, IL 60188. All rights reserved. Used by permission.

827 Words © 1993 Hope Publishing Company, Carol Stream, IL 60188. All rights reserved. Used by permission.

828 Words © 1994 Hope Publishing Company, Carol Stream, IL 60188. All rights reserved. Used by permission.

829 Words © 1994 Hope Publishing Company, Carol Stream, IL 60188. All rights reserved. Used by permission.

830 Words © 1992 Hope Publishing Company, Carol Stream, IL 60188. All rights reserved. Used by permission.

831 Words © 1996 Hope Publishing Company, Carol Stream, IL 60188. All rights reserved. Used by permission.

832 Words © 1984 Hope Publishing Company, Carol Stream, IL 60188. All rights reserved. Used by permission.

833 Words © 1987 Hope Publishing Company, Carol Stream, IL 60188). All rights reserved. Used by permission.

834 Text © 1993 Selah Publishing Co., Inc. www.selahpub.com All rights reserved. Used by permission.

835 © 1987 The United Methodist Publishing House (Administered by The Copyright Company c/o The Copyright Company, Nashville, TN) All Rights Reserved. International Copyright Secured. Used By Permission.

836 Words © 1989 Hope Publishing Company, Carol Stream, IL 60188. All rights reserved. Used by permission.

837 © 1992 Patrick Michaels

838 Words © 1999 Hope Publishing Company, Carol Stream, IL 60188. All rights reserved. Used by permission.

839 Words © 1992 Hope Publishing Company, Carol Stream, IL 60188. All rights reserved. Used by permission.

840 Text © 1994 Selah Publishing Co., Inc. www.selahpub.com All rights reserved. Used by permission.

841 Text © 1998 Selah Publishing Co., Inc. www.selahpub.com All rights reserved. Used by permission.

842 From "O Liberating Rose" by Mark L. Belletini in *Singing the Living Tradition*. Boston: © Unitarian Universalist Association, 1993. Reprinted by permission of the Unitarian Universalist Association.

843 Text © 1993 Susan Palo Cherwien. Used by permission of Augsburg Fortress.

844 Text © 1989 Susan Palo Cherwien. Used by permission of Augsburg Fortress.

845 Text © 1995 Susan Palo Cherwien. Used by permission of Augsburg Fortress.

846 Words © 2000 The Hymn Society (admin. Hope Publishing Company, Carol Stream, IL 60188). All rights reserved. Used by permission.

847 © 1968 Estate of Moir A. J. Waters

848 Words © 1987 Hope Publishing Company, Carol Stream, IL 60188. All rights reserved. Used by permission.

849 ©1987 Margaret Clarkson

850 © 1974 Walter Farquharson

851 © 1970 Frances Wheeler Davis

852 © 1993 Herbert O'Driscoll

853 © 1993 Herbert O'Driscoll

854 © 1980 Herbert O'Driscoll

855 © 1982 Thomas H. Cain

856 © Paul Gibson

857 © Patrick Wedd

858 © 1984 Judith Fetter

859 © 1981 Peter Davison

860 Words © 1997 Hope Publishing Company, Carol Stream, IL 60188. All rights reserved. Used by permission.

861 © 1985 Lynette Miller

862 © 1987 Elinor Johns

863 © 1987 Carol Johns

864 © 1993 Nigel Weaver

865 © 1995 Bert Polman

866 © 1983 Harris J. Loewen

867 © 1995 Nancy W. Carle

868 © 1995 The Presbyterian Church in Canada

869 © 1991 GIA Publications, Inc.

870 © 1991 GIA Publications, Inc.

871 © 1991 GIA Publications, Inc.

872 © 1991 GIA Publications, Inc.

873 © 1991 GIA Publications, Inc.

874 © 1991 GIA Publications, Inc.

875 © Australian Hymn Book Company

876 © 1975 Joy Merritt

877 © 1997 Elizabeth J. Smith

878 © 1997 Elizabeth J. Smith

879 © 1997 Elizabeth J. Smith

880 © 1997 Elizabeth J. Smith

881 © 1997 Elizabeth J. Smith

882 © 1997 Elizabeth J. Smith

883 Words © 1987 Hope Publishing Company, Carol Stream, IL 60188. All rights reserved. Used by permission.

884 Words © 1992 Hope Publishing Company, Carol Stream, IL 60188. All rights reserved. Used by permission.

885 Words © 1992 Hope Publishing Company, Carol Stream, IL 60188. All rights reserved. Used by permission.

886 Words © 1996 Hope Publishing Company, Carol Stream, IL 60188. All rights reserved. Used by permission.

887 Words © 1996 Hope Publishing Company, Carol Stream, IL 60188. All rights reserved. Used by permission.

888 Words © 1992 Hope Publishing Company, Carol Stream, IL 60188. All rights reserved. Used by permission.

889 Words © 1987 The Hymn Society (admin. Hope Publishing Company, Carol Stream, IL 60188). All rights reserved. Used by permission

890 Words © 1992 Hope Publishing Company, Carol Stream, IL 60188. All rights reserved. Used by permission.

891 Words © 1994 Hope Publishing Company, Carol Stream, IL 60188. All rights reserved. Used by permission.

892 Words © 1996 Hope Publishing Company, Carol Stream, IL 60188. All rights reserved. Used by permission.

893 Words © 1994 Hope Publishing Company, Carol Stream, IL 60188. All rights reserved. Used by permission.

894 Words © 1998 Hope Publishing Company, Carol Stream, IL 60188. All rights reserved. Used by permission.

895 © 1977 Scripture in Song (c/o Integrity Music). All rights reserved. International copyright secured. Used by permission.

896 © Christian Conference of Asia

897 © Christian Conference of Asia

898 © 1998 Kathleen M. Mayson

899 © Marnie Barrell

900 © Marnie Barrell

901 Text © 2001 Selah Publishing Co., Inc. www.selahpub.com All rights reserved. Used by permission.

902 Text © 2001 Selah Publishing Co., Inc. www.selahpub.com All rights reserved. Used by permission.

903 Text © 2001 Selah Publishing Co., Inc. www.selahpub.com All rights reserved. Used by permission.

904 Text © 2001 Selah Publishing Co., Inc. www.selahpub.com All rights reserved. Used by permission.

905 Words © 1985 Hope Publishing Company, Carol Stream, IL 60188. All rights reserved. Used by permission.

906 © Strube Publishing, Munich-Berlin, Germany

907 © 1995 Hope Publishing Company, Carol Stream, IL 60188. All rights reserved. Used by permission.

908 German words and English trans. © 1996 General Board of Global Ministries, GBGMusik, 475 Riverside Drive, New York, NY 10115. All rights reserved. Used by permission.

909 Text © 1967, Gooi En Sticht, Bv., Baarn, The Netherlands. All rights reserved. Exclusive Agent for English-language countries: OCP Publications, 5536 NE Hassalo, Portland, OR 97213. All rights reserved. Used with permission.

Index of Authors and Translators

a = altered

p = paraphrased

t = translated

* = wrote original text or translation, which is not in this book

---

Index of First Lines of Hymns

The numbers to the left indicate the text number, rather than the page number, in this volume of each item. The numbers to the right provide cross-references for those items that also appear in the 2005 edition of Routley's *An English-Speaking Hymnal Guide*, edited and expanded by Peter Cutts.

D

E

I

M